HISTORY OF
THE SECOND WORLD WAR
UNITED KINGDOM MILITARY SERIES

Edited by J. R. M. BUTLER

A

The authors of the Military Histories have been given full access to official documents. They and the editor are alone responsible for the statements made and the views expressed.

The fast convoy KMF.1 on passage with the assault forces for
North Africa, November 1942

Off Algiers on the morning after the assault, November 1942

(*See pp. 315-325*)

THE WAR AT SEA
1939–1945

BY

CAPTAIN S. W. ROSKILL, D.S.C., R.N.

VOLUME II
THE PERIOD OF BALANCE

This edition of The War at Sea: Volume Two
first published in 2004
by The Naval & Military Press Ltd

Published by
The Naval & Military Press Ltd
Unit 10 Ridgewood Industrial Park,
Uckfield, East Sussex,
TN22 5QE England
Tel: +44 (0) 1825 749494
Fax: +44 (0) 1825 765701
www.naval–military-press.com

The War at Sea: Volume Two first published in 1956.

*In reprinting in facsimile from the original, any imperfections are inevitably reproduced
and the quality may fall short of modern type and cartographic standards.*

CONTENTS

APPENDICES

LIST OF MAPS

LIST OF TABLES

LIST OF ILLUSTRATIONS

AUTHOR'S PREFACE

THE sources used for this second volume of 'The War at Sea' are, in general, similar to those described in my preface to the first volume; but, as is to be expected, certain new problems have arisen. As the acute strains and difficulties of the Defensive Phase, with its inevitable but tragic toll of Allied maritime losses receded, the opportunity to keep and to preserve better records improved in the British services. Conversely, as the tide of the enemy's offensive and success began to ebb, his written records showed some deterioration, and his losses produced gaps in them. To fill the gaps in the German records has proved no easy task, and I have relied more than ever on Commander M. G. Saunders, R.N., and the Admiralty's Foreign Documents Section to meet my needs in that respect. He and his assistants have shown uncanny skill in tracing what happened when the original sources, such as the logs of enemy ships, were lost when those ships were sunk. I find it hard to express the sum of my gratitude for the thorough and painstaking work of this nature undertaken on my behalf.

When the first draft of this second volume was less than half finished I was lucky enough to obtain the help of Commander Geoffrey Hare, R.N. His enthusiasm for the work and his thoroughness in checking the many obscure points which inevitably arise have taken an immense burden off me; and without his assistance the preparation of this volume would never have progressed so fast or so smoothly.

I also owe a great debt to my colleagues who are engaged on the campaign volumes of this series, Captains G. R. G. Allen, F. C. Flynn and C. T. Addis, Royal Navy, who have generously allowed me to exploit their own research in the fields with which they are particularly concerned, and to use it for my own purposes. They have also read and criticised the chapters dealing with the maritime war in their own theatres. Without their help it would have been impossible for one writer to cover an ever-widening field of battle.

It has not been easy to decide how much space should be given to operations which were wholly or mainly undertaken by the United States Navy. That service's tremendous accomplishments are being fully and graphically described in Professor S. E. Morison's many volumes of the 'History of United States Naval Operations', and it would plainly have been redundant for me to duplicate what he has written. I have not found it possible to work to any precise rules regarding the inclusion, condensation or omission of American-fought battles. I have indeed not tried to formulate such rules, but have instead tried to work to what seemed to me sensible, if arbitrary, principles. Thus, if the fate of important British territories was concerned, or if the British Empire's maritime forces, even though under American command, were present in appreciable strength, I have felt it to be justifiable to record the doings of the latter at some length. But if, as in the North and Central Pacific theatres the strategy was American-born and the forces came almost wholly from the same country's services, I have dealt with events briefly, even cursorily. It thus happens that more space is devoted to the Battle of the Java Sea than to the campaign in the Aleutians, or to the great battles of Coral Sea and Midway. The summary manner in which the latter are here treated does not, of course, indicate any desire to belittle the importance of those battles, nor to conceal admiration for the manner in which they were fought. Although after the early months of 1942 the Pacific War receives relatively little space in this volume, it is intended to deal more fully with events in that vast theatre after the British Pacific Fleet arrived there; but that does not occur until my final volume. I must, however, acknowledge my debt to Professor Morison, not only for the value that his books have been to me, but for his kindness in answering many questions concerning operations in which his country's ships as well as British ones were involved. The U.S. Navy Department's Office of Naval History under Rear-Admiral J. B. Heffernan, U.S.N., has also given me generous help in comparing British records with its own.

It was to be expected that criticisms of my first volume would reach me after publication, but I have been encouraged by the fact that they have been generous rather than severe. It has been very noticeable that critics have regarded my sins as being more those of omission than of commission, particularly with regard to events in which they themselves took part. They may perhaps not fully realise the extent to which compression has to be applied to keep these volumes within their appointed compass; nor that my charter is not to tell the story of naval operations in full detail (as was that of Sir Julian Corbett and his successors after the 1914–18 war), but to describe the War at Sea *as a whole*, and from a two-service angle.

In the period covered by this book maritime operations fall naturally into three approximately equal phases, namely from the 1st of January to the 31st of July 1942, from the 1st of August 1942 to the end of that year, and from the 1st of January to the 31st of May 1943. To help the reader to relate what is here described to other important events, not directly connected with the war at sea, I have inserted at the beginning of each of the three phases a chronological summary of such events.

Once again I must acknowledge my debt to the many officers of all services who have read my drafts and given me their experienced advice. My first volume seems to have penetrated to distant lands, from some of which I have received most interesting letters containing recollections which have been of use to me in this second volume. The generosity of these correspondents has touched me, showing as it does the warmth of the affection felt towards the Royal Navy by those who served in it, sometimes only temporarily, during the war.

I wish particularly to thank Mrs L. Rosewarne for her permission to reveal, in the heading to Chapter XV, the name of the writer of the famous and very moving 'Airman's letter to his Mother', and Mrs B. G. Scurfield for her permission to quote from her husband's equally fine letter in Chapter XIII. I am once again indebted to the Director, Mr F. G. G. Carr, and the Trustees of the National Maritime Museum for permission to reproduce certain of the works of British War Artists, the originals of which are the property of the Museum, and to Mr A. J. Charge of the Imperial War Musuem for assistance in selecting illustrations. Captain H. J. Reinicke, formerly of the German Navy, has allowed me to reproduce certain photographs in his possession.

Lieutenant-Commander P. K. Kemp, R.N., the Admiralty archivist, has been most helpful to me in finding references and checking quotations, and Mr Christopher Lloyd, Assistant Professor of History in the Royal Naval College, Greenwich, has been kind enough to verify various historical points. For the whole of the Royal Air Force's part in the maritime war I owe more than I can express to Captain D. V. Peyton-Ward, R.N., of the Air Historical Branch. That branch and the Admiralty's Historical Section under Rear-Admiral R. M. Bellairs have again given me quite invaluable help. Mr G. H. Hurford of the Admiralty has once again helped with the laborious but essential work of indexing the book. Finally, I cannot close this foreword without repeating that without the untiring advice of Professor J. R. M. Butler, the editor of this whole series, this volume, like the first, could never have reached the public.

S. W. Roskill.

Cabinet Office,
   August 1956.

'The [British] Navy . . . remained vigorous; the possessor of actual, and yet more of reserved strength in the genius and pursuits of the people—in a continuous tradition, which struck its roots far back in a great past—and above all in a body of officers, veterans of . . . earlier wars, . . . steeped to the core in those professional habits and feelings which . . . transmit themselves quickly to the juniors'.

A. T. Mahan. *The Influence of Sea Power on the French Revolution and Empire*, Vol. I, p. 69.

CHRONOLOGICAL SUMMARY

OF PRINCIPAL EVENTS

JANUARY 1942–JULY 1942

B

1942	Atlantic	Arctic	Mediterranean	Indian Ocean	Pacific	Europe
January	Start of U-boat campaign in American and Canadian waters resulting in heavy shipping losses	1-11 PQ.7B 8-17 PQ.8	21 Start of enemy counter-offensive in North Africa	Japanese over-run Malaya	2 Fall of Manila 15 ABDA area established	
February	Heavy shipping losses in the Caribbean and off the North American coast	1-10 PQ.9-PQ.10 6-23 PQ.11	12-15 Malta convoy operations from Egypt		Japanese over-run Netherlands East Indies 15 Fall of Singapore 24 ABDA area dissolved 27 Battle of Java Sea	12 *Scharnhorst* and *Gneisenau* escape up-Channel
March	Continued heavy shipping losses off the American coast	1-12 PQ.12. Sortie by *Tirpitz* against this Convoy 20-31 PQ.13	20-23 Malta convoy operations leading to the Second Battle of Sirte	8 Fall of Rangoon 23 Japanese occupy Andaman Islands	8 Japanese land in New Guinea 9 Surrender in Java 19 Heavy Japanese air raid on Darwin	28 Raid on St. Nazaire
April	Continued heavy shipping losses off the American coast	8-19 PQ.14	Period of sustained enemy air attacks on Malta.	5 Japanese naval air raid on Colombo	4 Reorganisation of command areas in the Pacific	

Month						
May	Heavy shipping losses in the Caribbean and Gulf of Mexico	26 April–5 May PQ.15 21–30 PQ.16	47 Fighter aircraft flown to Malta from aircraft carriers 5 Tenth submarine Flotilla leaves Malta Continued heavy enemy air attacks on Malta 77 Fighter aircraft flown in from aircraft carriers	9 Japanese naval air raid on Trincomalee. Eastern fleet withdraws to East Africa. Japanese striking force returns to the Pacific 4 British landings in Madagascar 15 Japanese reach Indian frontier	18 American air raid on Tokyo 7 Battle of the Coral Sea	
June	Continued heavy shipping losses in the Caribbean and Gulf of Mexico. Bay of Biscay offensive intensified with searchlight-fitted aircraft	27 June–11 July PQ.17	12–16 Malta convoy operations 'Harpoon' and 'Vigorous' 21 Fall of Tobruk		4 Battle of Midway 7 Japanese landings in the Aleutians	
July	Shipping losses in the West Atlantic much less severe as result of introduction of full convoy system	5–10 Severe losses in PQ.17	1 Enemy reaches El Alamein. Axis advance checked 22 Tenth submarine Flotilla returns to Malta	Japanese submarine attacks off the east coast of South Africa		27 Fall of Rostov

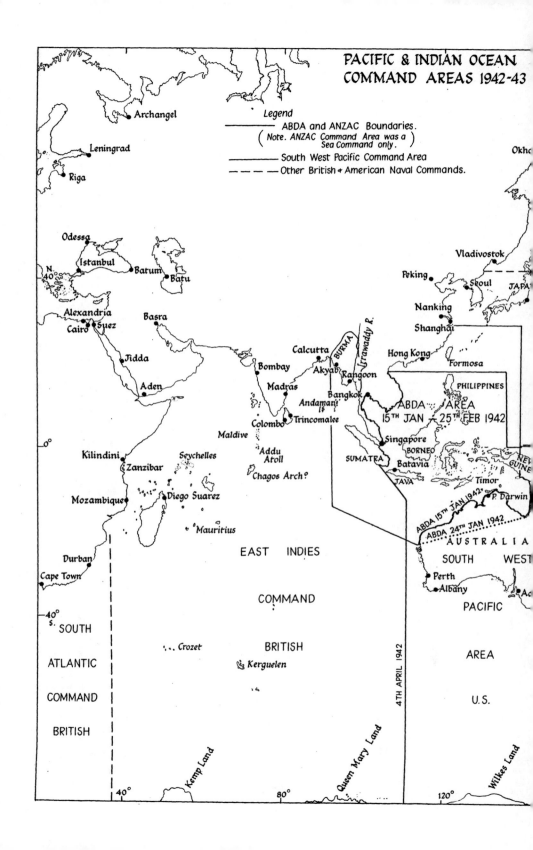

PACIFIC & INDIAN OCEAN
COMMAND AREAS 1942-43

Archangel

Leningrad

Riga

Okho

Legend
———— ABDA and ANZAC Boundaries.
(*Note. ANZAC Command Area was a*)
           Sea Command only.
———— South West Pacific Command Area
– – – – Other British & American Naval Commands.

Odessa
Istanbul   Batum
N. 40°   Batu

Vladivostok

Peking

Seoul   JAPA

Alexandria   Basra
Cairo Suez

Nanking

Shanghai

Jidda

Calcutta

Hong Kong

Formosa

Aden

Bombay

Akyab Rangoon

PHILIPPINES

Madras

Bangkok

Andaman Is

ABDA AREA
15TH JAN – 25TH FEB 1942

Colombo Trincomalee

Maldive

Singapore   BORNEO

Kilindini

Seychelles

Addu
Atoll

SUMATRA   Batavia

NEW
GUINE

Zanzibar

Chagos Arch?

JAVA

Timor

Mozambique

Diego Suarez

P. Darwin

Mauritius

ABDA 15TH JAN 1942

ABDA 24TH JAN 1942

AUSTRALIA

Durban

EAST   INDIES

SOUTH   WEST

Cape Town

Perth
Albany

Ad

COMMAND

PACIFIC

40°
S. SOUTH

Crozet

BRITISH

AREA

ATLANTIC

Kerguelen

U.S.

COMMAND

4TH APRIL 1942

BRITISH

Kemp Land

Queen Mary Land

Wilkes Land

40°   80°   120°

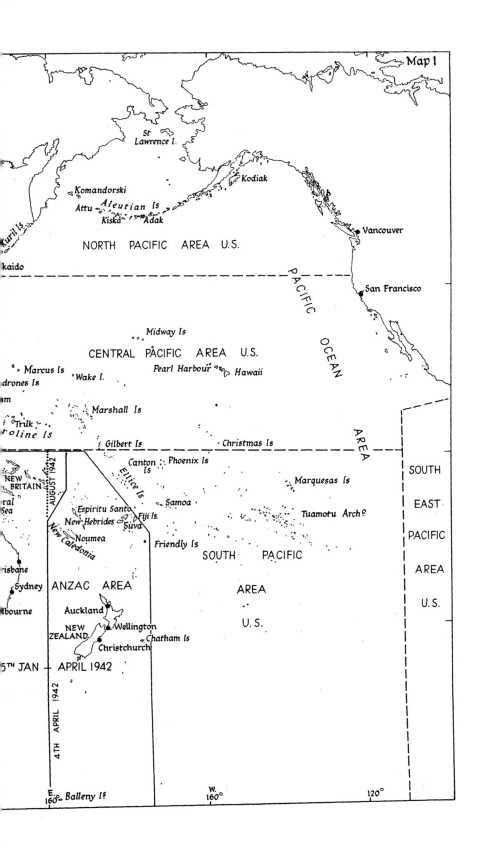

Map 1

St
Lawrence I.

Kodiak

Komandorski

Attu *Aleutian Is*

Kiska Adak

Kuril Is

NORTH   PACIFIC   AREA   U.S.

Vancouver

kaido

PACIFIC

San Francisco

Midway Is

CENTRAL   PACIFIC   AREA   U.S.

OCEAN

Marcus Is

Pearl Harbour   Hawaii

Wake I.

drones Is

im

Marshall Is

Truk

roline Is

AREA

Gilbert Is   • Christmas Is

AUGUST 1942

NEW
BRITAIN

Canton :: Phoenix Is
Is

SOUTH

Ellice Is

Marquesas Is

EAST

ral
Sea

Espiritu Santo

New Hebrides   Fiji Is.
Suva

Samoa

Tuamotu Arch?

PACIFIC

New Caledonia

Noumea

Friendly Is

SOUTH   PACIFIC

AREA

risbane

Sydney

ANZAC   AREA

AREA

U.S.

bourne

Auckland

U.S.

NEW
ZEALAND

Wellington

Chatham Is

Christchurch

5TH JAN — APRIL 1942

4TH APRIL 1942

E.
160° Balleny Is

W.
160°

120°

CHAPTER I

THE PACIFIC AND INDIAN OCEANS
1st January–31st July, 1942

> 'When I reflect how I have longed and
> prayed for the entry of the United States
> into the war, I find it difficult to realise
> how gravely our British affairs have deteri-
> orated . . . since December 7th'.
> W. S. Churchill to F. D. Roosevelt,
> 5th March 1942.[1]

THE Prime Minister's uncomplaining but ominous words stated no more than the bare truth. After two-and-a-half years of war, throughout which her maritime services had been strained as never before, Britain and the loyal Dominions found themselves, in the first six months of 1942, required to face a crisis compared to which all the currents of success and failure experienced since 1940 appeared comparatively trivial. Mr Churchill certainly realised, and British fighting men instinctively felt, that we had only to survive those critical months, gaining time for the vast strength and lately-aroused resolution of our new Ally to be deployed, to see the storm clouds of defeat finally dispersed. Yet as each month passed, even the most resolute may at times have wondered whether we could survive—whether American help was this time going to come too late.

The first volume of this history ended on a note of crushing, far-spread disaster for Britain. If the reader should expect this second volume to open in happier vein, he must be immediately disillusioned. The balance had to tilt yet further, much further against us before it could be brought central; and as it was the sweeping tide of Japanese success which chiefly caused that adverse movement, it is to the eastern theatre of war that we must first turn.[2]

If ever students should, in the years to come, seek an example of the consequences of loss of maritime control over waters adjacent to countries in which world powers held great interests, they will surely need to look no further than the events in the Pacific and Indian Oceans during the early months of 1942. The process had begun in

---

[1] *The Second World War*, Vol. IV, p. 169.

[2] For a full account of the British Services' part in the fighting in the eastern theatres of the war the reader is referred to the volumes of this series entitled *The War against Japan* by S. W. Kirby. (Vols. I & II in preparation.)

December 1941 when a great part of the American Pacific Fleet was destroyed in Pearl Harbour, and the embryo British Eastern Fleet was extinguished in the South China Sea. In the succeeding weeks disaster followed hard on disaster, and disintegration spread rapidly over the whole theatre of British and Dutch responsibility. Neither Britain nor America possessed forces which could be sent out in sufficient strength, and with sufficient speed, to check the flood of Japanese success; nor, once Singapore was imperilled, was there a well-found and properly defended base from which such forces could have worked had they been available. The process of dissolution was, perhaps, accelerated by the lack of an integrated Allied command organisation, through the tendency of each of the countries concerned to place its own interests first, and their understandable desire to use what forces they possessed to defend their own territories, rather than to throw them all into one common pool for the protection of the whole theatre. Not until some weeks after Japan had struck was the first attempt made to create a unified command. At the Washington 'Arcadia' conference, held in late December 1941, A.B.D.A. (American-British-Dutch-Australian) and A.N.Z.A.C. command areas were agreed.[1] On the 3rd of January 1942 General Wavell accepted command of the former, and a week later he set up his headquarters at Bandoeng in western Java. Rarely can a Commander-in-Chief have assumed great responsibilities in less auspicious circumstances. The Philippines had, except for the Manila Bay defences, already fallen; a large part of Malaya had been overrun; the enemy had landed in Borneo and the Celebes, and the threat to Java was plain. The naval command of the A.B.D.A. area was vested in Admiral T. C. Hart, U.S.N., the former commander of the American Asiatic Fleet. His deputy was Rear-Admiral A. F. E. Palliser, who had originally gone out to serve as Chief of Staff to Admiral Phillips in the *Prince of Wales*. The principal naval forces nominally serving under Admiral Hart are shown below.

Table 1. A.B.D.A. Command Naval Forces, January 1942

	American	British[2]	Dutch
Cruisers . .	*Houston* (8″) *Marblehead* (6″) *Boise* (6″)	*Danae* (Old 6″) *Durban* (Old 6″) *Dragon* (Old 6″)	*Java* (5·9″) *Tromp* (5·9″) *De Ruyter* (5·9″)
Destroyers . .	12	6	7
Sloops . .	—	2	—
Submarines .	25	—	16[3]
Seaplane tenders	3 (Attendant on 25 Catalinas)	—	—

[1] See Map 1 (opp. p. 5).

[2] The composition of the British forces changed constantly. The cruisers *Exeter, Hobart* (R.A.N.) and *Perth* (R.A.N.) and two submarines joined the command later.

[3] One Dutch submarine was non-operational.

The British naval forces in the A.B.D.A. area were known as the 'China Force' and were under the immediate command of Commodore J. A. Collins, R.A.N. But they were to be regarded as a detachment from the Eastern Fleet of Admiral Sir Geoffrey Layton, who had transferred his headquarters firstly from Singapore to Batavia and then, after the A.B.D.A. command had been formed, to Colombo. These complicated command arrangements were not improved by the decision that Allied forces in the A.B.D.A. area would normally work under their own national commanders, whose activities Admiral Hart was expected to be able to co-ordinate.[1]

To turn now to the A.N.Z.A.C. area, the command of its naval forces was given to Vice-Admiral H. F. Leary, U.S.N., but their strategic direction was in the hands of the American Commander-in-Chief, Pacific Fleet, at Pearl Harbour. The Anzac Squadron, whose principal warships were the Australian cruisers *Australia*, *Canberra* and the much older *Adelaide*, the New Zealand cruisers *Achilles* and *Leander* and the American cruiser *Chicago*, was commanded by Rear-Admiral J. G. Crace.

So much for the scattered naval forces available early in 1942 to oppose the powerful southward thrusts which the Japanese were then developing. The western thrust was aimed at Singapore and Sumatra; the central one was coming down the eastern coast of Borneo towards Java, while the eastern one was seizing Allied bases in the Celebes, Amboina and the islands to the east of Java.[2] A fourth thrust soon became apparent still further to the east, and was aimed at New Guinea, the Bismarck Archipelago and the Solomon Islands. The method employed by the Japanese was to drive down each of their lines of advance, striking first at the air bases with shore-based or carrier-borne aircraft as might be appropriate, and then following up with sea-borne landings. Once each base had been secured they prepared for the next southward leap. The assaults were conducted with relentless efficiency and precision, though the opposition which Allied garrisons could offer was admittedly very weak. We will briefly follow the events in each command area in turn.

The main task of the surface forces of the A.B.D.A. command was initially to convey supplies and reinforcements to Singapore. The Japanese advance down the Malay peninsula soon closed the Malacca Straits to our convoys, which thereafter had to be routed south of Sumatra and approach Singapore through the Sunda Straits.[3] Between the 1st of January and the 8th of February, when it was

---

[1] The national commanders were: British, Commodore J. A. Collins, R.A.N.; American, Admiral T. C. Hart, U.S.N. (also Naval Commander A.B.D.A. area); Dutch, Vice-Admiral C. E. L. Helfrich, R.Neth.Navy.

[2] See Map 2 (opp. p. 9).

[3] See Map 2.

decided that it was useless to throw in more reinforcements, the British and Dutch warships escorted in seven convoys comprising forty-four ships, many of them large troop transports. In all 45,000 fighting men of all services, besides large quantities of stores and equipment, were safely taken to Singapore during those five weeks. Considering the scale of sea and air attack to which our convoys were constantly exposed, the achievement was remarkable. Only in the last one, when the liner *Empress of Asia* (16,909 tons) was bombed and set on fire, was a ship lost. It was when escorting one of these convoys that the destroyer *Jupiter* scored a success by sinking a large Japanese submarine off the Sunda Straits.

Not only were military reinforcements poured into Singapore, but the desperate need for more aircraft, and especially for fighters, had to be met. The convoy which arrived on the 8th of January carried fifty-one crated Hurricanes, which were at once erected and flung into battle. Next the fleet carrier *Indomitable* came round the Cape to Port Sudan, embarked fifty more there and at once sailed east. They were flown off to Batavia on the 27th and 28th from a position south of Java; and most of them went straight on to Singapore. Early in February the aircraft transport *Athene* delivered to Batavia forty more Hurricanes, which she had embarked at Takoradi on the Gold Coast. It is not the smallest of the many tragedies which scar this terrible period that all these successful sea-borne reinforcement operations were of no avail.

The Navy's success in escorting in the troops, equipment and air-craft was not its only service and, unfortunately, was not by itself enough. The Army's seaward flanks were completely exposed, and they appealed to the Navy to interfere with the Japanese landings which were being made behind our lines on the west coast of Malaya. To give this support was, of course, a traditional function of the Navy. But on this occasion we simply did not possess the forces to carry it out effectively; and because air cover was lacking, such little ships and craft as could be spared could only work by night. Though they failed to bring the Army any substantial relief, they did successfully evacuate 2,700 cut-off troops at the end of January. There can be little doubt that the failure to control the coastal waters on the Army's flanks contributed to the collapse on land.

By the end of January Singapore was under constant and heavy air bombardment, and the naval base could not continue to function. Preparations were made to destroy the immense quantities of stores, and to deny the enemy use of its facilities; but when the island fell much was actually left intact. Warships which had been refitting were towed away, but the big floating dock could not be removed and had to be scuttled. This great base, the only one on which we had expended any considerable money between the wars, was then

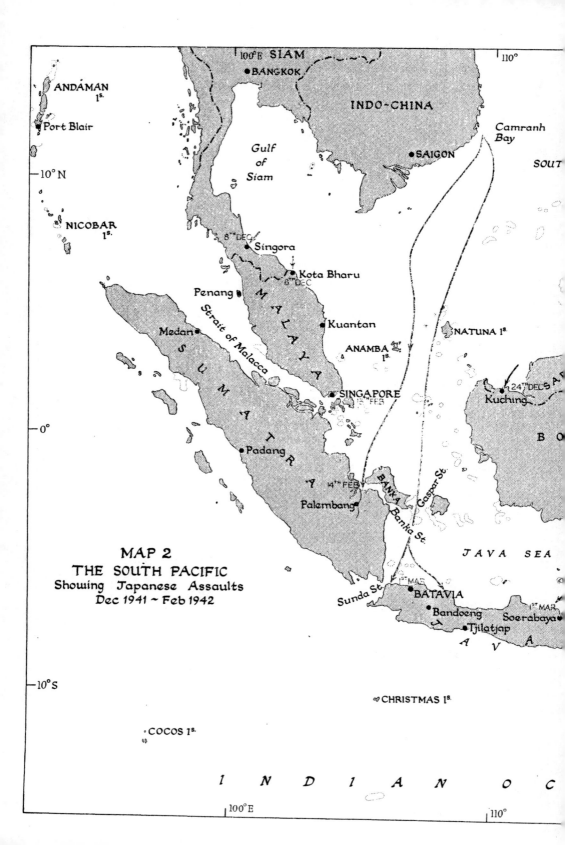

ANDAMAN IS.

Port Blair

SIAM
100°E
BANGKOK

INDO-CHINA

Gulf
of
Siam

SAIGON

Camranh
Bay

110°

SOUT

10°N

NICOBAR
IS.

8TH DEC
Singora
Kota Bharu
8TH DEC

Penang

Kuantan

MALAYA

Strait of Malacca

ANAMBA
IS.

NATUNA IS.

Medan

SUMATRA

SINGAPORE
15TH FEB

24TH DEC
Kuching

BOR

0°

Padang

BANKA
Palembang
Banka St.
Gaspar St.

14TH FEB

JAVA SEA

MAP 2
THE SOUTH PACIFIC
Showing Japanese Assaults
Dec 1941 ~ Feb 1942

Sunda St.

1ST MAR
BATAVIA
Bandoeng
Tjilatjap

Soerabaya
1ST MAR

JAVA

10°S

CHRISTMAS IS.

COCOS IS.

INDIAN OC

100°E

110°

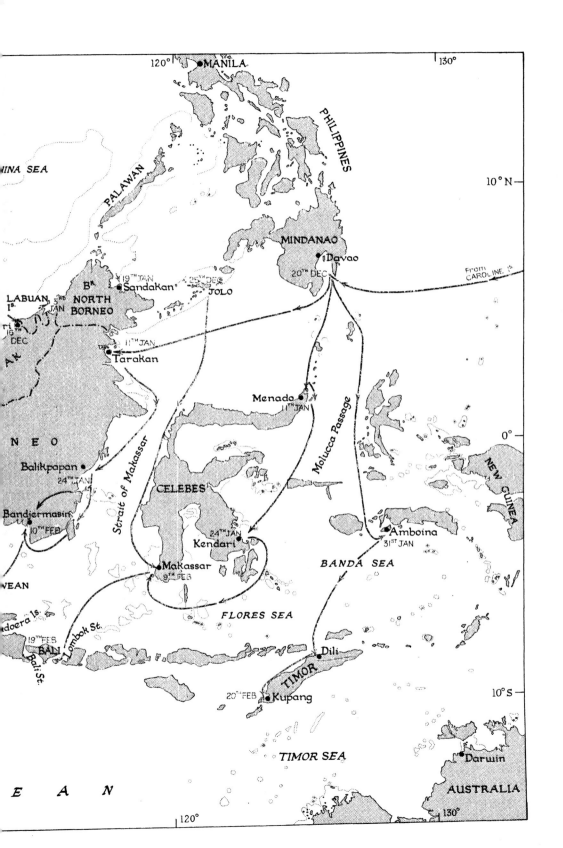

CHINA SEA

MANILA

120°

130°

PHILIPPINES

10° N

PALAWAN

MINDANAO

Davao

From
CAROLINE IS.

19ᵀᴴ JAN

25ᵀᴴ DEC

20ᵀᴴ DEC

LABUAN
1ˢᵗ
JAN

Bⁿ
NORTH
BORNEO

Sandakan

JOLO

Sᵗri
16ᵀᴴ
DEC

3ᴿᴰ
JAN

Menado

11ᵀᴴ JAN

A K

11ᵀᴴ JAN

Tarakan

Molucca Passage

0°

N E O

Balikpapan

CELEBES

NEW GUINEA

24ᵀᴴ JAN

Amboina

Bandjermasin

Strait of Makassar

Kendari

31ˢᵗ JAN

10ᵀᴴ FEB

24ᵀᴴ JAN

BANDA SEA

WEAN

Makassar

9ᵀᴴ FEB

FLORES SEA

Madoera Is.

19ᵀᴴ FEB

Lombok St.

BALI

Dili

Bali St.

TIMOR

10° S

20ᵀᴴ FEB

Kupang

TIMOR SEA

Darwin

E   A   N

120°

AUSTRALIA

130°

closed. From the 3rd of February onwards shipping was heavily bombed in the approaches to Singapore and in the harbours. By the 9th the Japanese had gained a foothold on the island, and the inward flow of British reinforcements was stopped. Three days later all possible ships were cleared from the harbours, taking with them many persons who were not required for the defence of the fortress. These were the last ships to reach safety.

Thus was the stage set for the final tragedy. On the 15th of February Singapore surrendered. For the previous days and nights a stream of small craft poured across the Straits towards Sumatra, carrying unauthorised as well as authorised refugees. By then Japanese surface ships were working close off-shore; and they played havoc among these vessels almost with impunity. Some refugees reached the adjacent, and temporarily friendly islands only to die of starvation or disease; many of their craft were sunk; some had their occupants captured; few survived. An Army in retreat on land always brings cruel ordeals to its men and to the civilian population of the countries through which it passes; but fighting forces which, after a series of crushing defeats on land, find themselves cut off from retreat by sea, embarrassed by a large civilian population of many races, and in some units stricken by collapse of morale, are even more terrible to behold. Rarely in history can the consequences of defeat have been more bitterly reaped than at Singapore in February 1942. In the final days there were deeds of heroism and self-sacrifice; but there were discreditable episodes as well. There is no need to dwell on the latter, but that they occurred should not be forgotten; of the former one shining example will be mentioned.

The *Li Wo* was a small auxiliary patrol vessel commanded by Lieutenant T. S. Wilkinson, R.N.R. Her armament was one old 4-inch gun. On the 14th of February, to the south of Singapore, she encountered the advance guard of a Japanese invasion force bound for Sumatra, and at once turned towards the immensely superior enemy to engage. For a time she was, almost miraculously, unharmed; but there could only be one end, and when he realised that it was approaching, Lieutenant Wilkinson rammed a transport which he had already hit and set on fire. Then the Japanese guns found their mark, and the disabled little ship was blown out of the water. Of the crew and the many passengers embarked in the *Li Wo*, only ten survived. When the story of her last fight became known after the war, Lieutenant Wilkinson was awarded a posthumous Victoria Cross.

Before Singapore had fallen an enemy invasion force, coming south from Camranh Bay in Indo-China, was sighted off the Anamba Islands.[1] At A.B.D.A. headquarters it was estimated that it was

---

probably bound for southern Sumatra. Orders were therefore given to assemble at Batavia as powerful a striking force as could be collected. It consisted in all of the cruisers *De Ruyter*, *Java*, *Tromp*, *Exeter* and *Hobart*, four Dutch and six American destroyers. Rear-Admiral K. W. F. M. Doorman of the Royal Netherlands Navy was in command, with his flag in the *De Ruyter*. It was the 14th of February before he had assembled his scattered ships, and by then the Japanese expedition was approaching the Banka Straits, to make its landings at Palembang in south-east Sumatra.

Admiral Doorman sailed north on the evening of the 14th; next morning he was sighted from the air, and the Japanese turned away their main convoy, while the covering forces prepared to deal with the Allied squadron. Heavy air attacks from the carrier *Ryujo's* planes and shore-based aircraft followed. Though no Allied ship was hit, two American destroyers were damaged by near misses and had to withdraw. In such circumstances, Doorman considered it useless to persevere, and retired southwards. His decision certainly caused surprise at Allied Headquarters, and indeed now appears to have been a critical one; for it left the route for the invasion of Sumatra wide open to the Japanese. On the 16th they landed at Palembang, and thus they isolated Java, the key Allied position, from the west. Simultaneously the enemy's plans to assault Java from the north and east were taking shape. This was the function of the centre and eastern spearheads of the Japanese southward drives already mentioned. The former, coming down the Makassar Straits, did not have matters all its own way. It was attacked off Balikpapan in Borneo firstly by Dutch submarines and then by an American striking force of four destroyers, which found the enemy transports in the exposed anchorage in the early hours of the 24th of January and attacked for about an hour with guns and torpedoes.[1] They sank four transports, one cargo ship and a patrol vessel without damage to themselves; but the success had no effect on the enemy's southward progress. The Japanese soon secured the bases in Borneo, and thus approached one stage nearer their objective of Soerabaya, the main Allied base in eastern Java. Next, further to the east, they assaulted the important island of Amboina in overwhelming strength on the last day of January; by the capture of its naval and air bases one more Allied outpost guarding the chain of islands running to the east of Java fell into enemy hands.

By this time Admiral Hart had formed a combined American and Dutch striking force, under Admiral Doorman's command, to oppose the threat to eastern Java. The problem of how best to use it was difficult, for not only were the distances from Soerabaya to the waters

---

[1] See S. E. Morison. *The History of United States Naval Operations*, Vol. III, pp. 285–291, for an account of the Battle off Balikpapan.

so far reached by the enemy invasion fleets very great, but the striking force could never be given air cover at such distances from Java. The best hope seemed to lie in making night attacks, followed by immediate withdrawal.

On the 1st of February Allied reconnaissance aircraft reported a force of some twenty transports and numerous warships off Balikpapan, and it was guessed that a new lunge was intended against Makassar or southern Borneo. Admiral Doorman's squadron assembled at Soerabaya, and sailed for the Makassar Straits early on the 4th. Japanese aircraft quickly found it, and the American cruisers *Marblehead* and *Houston* were both badly damaged. Doorman then retired through the Lombok Strait to Tjilatjap on the south coast of Java. The *Marblehead* reached port, and eventually got back to America after a circuitous journey by Ceylon and the Cape of Good Hope. The *Houston*, though she had one turret out of action, stayed with the diminishing Allied fleet. But the enemy's intention to occupy Makassar and the south of Borneo was carried out unhindered, and he had moved another stage towards isolating Java from the east.[1]

The fall of Amboina brought imminent danger to the island of Timor, an essential link on the air route from Australia to Java. The air base in the Dutch part of the island was already being constantly bombed, so General Wavell decided that the anti-aircraft defences must, for all the slenderness of his resources, be strengthened. On the 15th a battery from Java arrived, and that same night a convoy with reinforcements sailed for Timor from Port Darwin, escorted by the *Houston* and four smaller ships. It, too, was at once sighted and attacked from the air, but no losses were suffered. When it was learnt at A.B.D.A. Headquarters that the assault on Timor was imminent, and that strong Japanese forces were in the vicinity, the convoy was ordered to return to Darwin. The enemy attacked the islands of Bali, just east of Java, and of Timor, on the 19th and 20th of February. He seized the bases on Timor on the 20th, but the Dutch and Australian garrison continued to resist stubbornly in the hinterland until January 1943. They received occasional supplies during their long resistance, and the survivors were finally evacuated by sea.

Admiral Doorman, whose forces had been scattered as a result of earlier sorties, sailed from Tjilatjap on the 18th to try to attack the Bali expedition. Lacking time to concentrate all his ships he decided to attack in two waves. But the enemy landing had already taken place when Doorman's first flight of two cruisers and three destroyers arrived off Bali, and they found few targets. Two Japanese destroyers were damaged, and one Dutch destroyer sunk in the ensuing engagement. When the second flight, consisting of the *Tromp* and four

---

[1] See Map 2 (opp. p. 9).

American destroyers came in three hours later, another inconclusive action took place with enemy destroyers. In it the *Tromp* was badly damaged. She was sent to Australia for repairs. The attempt to frustrate the assault on Bali thus wholly failed, in spite of the Allied forces having, for once, been in superior strength; and more losses had been suffered for no appreciable gain. On the 20th of February the enemy occupied the island, and at once brought the airfield into use. Java was now entirely cut off from the east as well as from the west.

Meanwhile the Japanese had turned their attention to Port Darwin, the only Allied advance base on the Australian continent. A very powerful force of four carriers, two battleships and three cruisers under Admiral Nagumo's command entered the Banda Sea undetected and, on the 19th, launched some 150 strike aircraft with a powerful fighter escort at the base. A Japanese shore-based air flotilla from the Celebes also took part in the raid. At Port Darwin there were almost no anti-aircraft or fighter defences, and the harbour was crowded with shipping, including the convoy recently returned from Timor. Surprise was complete, and great damage was done to the port and to the shipping in it. Twelve ships were sunk, and Darwin was put out of action as a base for several months. The last reinforcement link to Java was thus broken.

General Wavell now realised that the culminating blow after all these preliminary enemy assaults and landings, namely the invasion of Java itself, was about to fall; and he was forced to admit that the island could not hold out for long. The security of Australia and of Burma were, he considered, more vital to the Allied cause, and he told the Chiefs of Staff that their defence should not be weakened to reinforce Java. On the 21st the Chiefs of Staff ordered the island to be defended to the last, but agreed that no more land reinforcements would be sent there. General Wavell was also told that A.B.D.A. Headquarters were to leave, and on the 25th his command was dissolved. The Dutch Commanders took over the surviving Allied sea, land and air forces, and General Wavell returned to India. Thus ended the first attempt to work an inter-allied command. It had been formed in a hurry to meet a situation which was moving from crisis to crisis; it was dissolved at a moment when it was obvious that the successive defeats which we had suffered could only end in complete collapse.

The surviving naval forces were all now placed under Admiral Helfrich, Royal Netherlands Navy, with Rear-Admiral Palliser in command of the British ships. There were in all eight cruisers and twelve destroyers left in Java; but all had been steaming and fighting under conditions of great strain and hazard for the past three months, and many had been damaged. Yet they were now required to defend

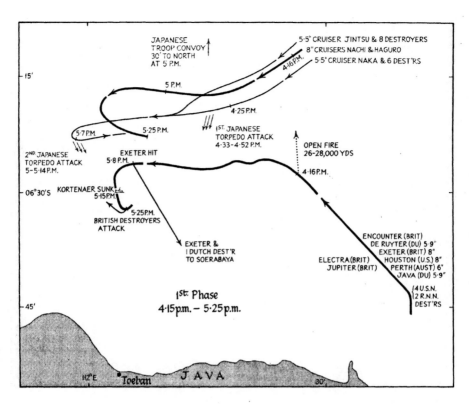

JAPANESE
TROOP CONVOY
30' TO NORTH
AT 5 P.M.

5·5" CRUISER JINTSU & 8 DESTROYERS
8" CRUISERS NACHI & HAGURO
5·5" CRUISER NAKA & 6 DEST'RS

4·16 P.M.

5 P.M.

4·25 P.M.

5·7 P.M.

5·25 P.M.

1ST JAPANESE
TORPEDO ATTACK
4·33-4·52 P.M.

OPEN FIRE
26-28,000 YDS

2ND JAPANESE
TORPEDO ATTACK
5-5·14 P.M.

EXETER HIT
5·8 P.M.

4·16 P.M.

KORTENAER SUNK
5·15 P.M.

5·25 P.M.
BRITISH DESTROYERS
ATTACK

EXETER &
I DUTCH DEST'R
TO SOERABAYA

ENCOUNTER (BRIT)
DE RUYTER (DU) 5·9"
EXETER (BRIT) 8"
HOUSTON (U.S.) 8"
PERTH (AUST) 6"
JAVA (DU) 5·9"

ELECTRA (BRIT)
JUPITER (BRIT)

/4 U.S.N.
2 R.N.N.
DEST'RS

1st Phase
4·15 p.m. – 5·25 p.m.

J A V A

112° E   • Toeban   30'

15'

06°30'S

45'

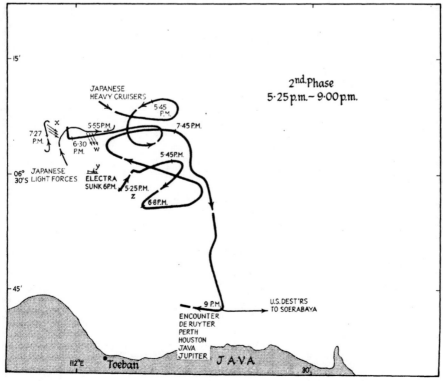

2nd Phase
5·25 p.m. – 9·00 p.m.

JAPANESE
HEAVY CRUISERS

5·45
P.M.

5·55 P.M.

7·45 P.M.

x

7·27
P.M.

6·30
P.M.

w

5·45 P.M.

JAPANESE
LIGHT FORCES

y

ELECTRA
SUNK 6 P.M.

5·25 P.M.

z

6·8 P.M.

9 P.M.

U.S. DEST'RS
TO SOERABAYA

ENCOUNTER
DE RUYTER
PERTH
HOUSTON
JAVA
JUPITER

J A V A

112° E   • Toeban   30'

15'

06°
30'S

45'

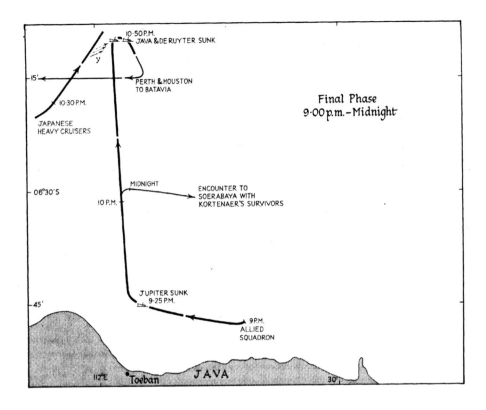

Map 3

The Battle of the Java Sea
27th. Feb. 1942

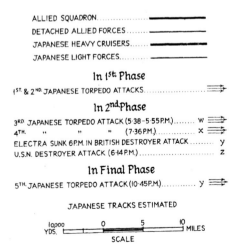

ALLIED SQUADRON...................
DETACHED ALLIED FORCES........
JAPANESE HEAVY CRUISERS.......
JAPANESE LIGHT FORCES..........

In 1st Phase
1ST. & 2ND. JAPANESE TORPEDO ATTACKS....................

In 2nd Phase
3RD. JAPANESE TORPEDO ATTACK (5·38–5·55 P.M.)........ W
4TH.   "   "   "   (7·36 P.M.)............... X
ELECTRA SUNK 6 P.M. IN BRITISH DESTROYER ATTACK .... Y
U.S.N. DESTROYER ATTACK (6·14 P.M.)............................ Z

In Final Phase
5TH. JAPANESE TORPEDO ATTACK (10·45 P.M.)............. Y

JAPANESE TRACKS ESTIMATED

10,000 YDS.   0   5   10 MILES
SCALE

an island some 550 miles long against attack from either east or west, or from both directions simultaneously. To meet the double threat Helfrich decided to divide his ships into an eastern force, consisting of the American and Dutch ships based on Soerabaya, and a western force of British and Australian ships based on Batavia. On the 25th he considered that the threat from the east would develop first, and ordered the eastern force to be strengthened at the expense of the western. The *Exeter*, *Perth* and the destroyers *Jupiter*, *Electra* and *Encounter* all came at once to Soerabaya. On the two following nights the rest of the western force searched unavailingly for an enemy convoy reported to be approaching that end of Java, but sighted nothing. The *Hobart* (R.A.N.), *Danae* and *Dragon* and two destroyers ultimately reached Ceylon safely.

Admiral Doorman now had at Soerabaya quite a powerful 'Combined Striking Force'. Two 8-inch cruisers (*Exeter* and *Houston*), three 6-inch cruisers (*De Ruyter*, *Java* and *Perth*) and ten destroyers were under his command; but he was gravely deficient in air co-operation and cover, and his ships had never before worked at sea as an integrated force, nor had the chance to develop a common tactical doctrine. Communications were also unsatisfactory, while many of the ships were old and had already been driven too hard; lastly, their men were approaching exhaustion. It was not a force which could be expected to fight a triumphant and superior enemy successfully. Yet the attempt had to be made.

On the afternoon of the 26th, the very day that the Allied squadron had assembled, a large invasion force was reported some 190 miles north-east of Soerabaya. Admiral Helfrich at once ordered Doorman's striking force to sea to attack it, and he sailed at 6.30 p.m. that evening. After considering the various alternatives Doorman decided to cover the most likely landing places by patrolling off the north coast of Java. Having only occasional air reconnaissance to help him he was operating more or less blindfold. No enemy forces having been sighted by the afternoon of the 27th, Doorman set course for Soerabaya to refuel his destroyers. Just as he was entering harbour, up-to-date reports of two enemy convoys, the nearer one only eighty miles away, were received, and the Admiral at once reversed his course. This was in fact the eastern Japanese invasion force under Rear-Admiral Nishimura. It was covered and escorted by two 8-inch and two 5·5-inch cruisers and fourteen destroyers. On paper the opposing forces were evenly matched, but greater advantages than mere gun power lay with the enemy, for he had good air reconnaissance and co-operation, and his ships were an integrated and highly trained force. Admiral Doorman asked for air support for his fleet, but Allied headquarters ordered the only striking force available (nine old torpedo-bombers of No. 36 Squadron of the R.A.F., escorted by eight

Buffalo fighters) to attack the Japanese transports, which had turned away from Java as soon as a naval action appeared imminent.

At about 4.0 p.m. the *Electra* (Commander C. W. May), which was five miles ahead of the Allied cruisers, sighted smoke to the north and made an enemy report. Very soon the opposing cruisers were in sight of each other, and fire was opened by the heavy ships at long range. The smaller ships were out-ranged, and could take no part. It seems likely that Admiral Doorman decided to keep his cruisers concentrated and to fight in single line ahead because his ships had done no training together, and difficulties in communications made more complicated manoeuvres too risky to attempt. The enemy held the advantage in speed, and had Doorman continued on his initial course it is certain that he would quickly have found himself at a grave tactical disadvantage. In technical language the Japanese would have 'crossed his T'. It was probably to prevent this happening that, soon after opening fire, the Dutch Admiral altered 20 degrees to port; but to the great disappointment of Captain H. M. L. Waller, R.A.N., of the *Perth*, and probably of the Dutch cruiser captains as well, their ships were still out-ranged and unable to join in the battle.[1] Only one shell hit, on the *De Ruyter*, was suffered by the Allied squadron in this phase. Next the Japanese destroyer flotilla attacked with torpedoes, but fired at long range and wholly without success. It may have been the torpedo threat which made the Admiral turn yet more to port at 4.29. For half-an-hour sporadic fighting continued, with the smaller Allied cruisers still out-ranged. Soon after 5.0 p.m. another enemy torpedo attack developed from fine on the starboard bow of Doorman's squadron, and at almost the same moment the *Exeter* (Captain O. L. Gordon) was hit in the boiler room by an 8-inch shell. Her speed was drastically reduced and she hauled out of the line. The *Houston* turned as well to avoid the *Exeter*, and the *Perth* and *Java*, thinking an alteration must have been signalled, followed them round. The *De Ruyter* for a time held on. Thus complete confusion was caused in the Allied line by one hit on one ship, and at a critical moment. Luckily only one enemy torpedo found its mark. The Dutch destroyer *Kortenaer* was hit and sank immediately.

While the destroyers screened the crippled *Exeter* with smoke, Doorman reformed his line and led the other cruisers between her and the enemy. At the same time he ordered the three British destroyers to counter-attack. Widely separated as they were they could only act independently, and in the next phase of confused fighting in and out of the smoke the *Electra* was stopped and then sunk, after having fought her guns to the end. An American sub-

---

[1] See Map 3, 1st Phase (opp. p. 13).

marine picked up fifty-four survivors nine hours later, but Commander May was not among them. The *Exeter* had meanwhile been ordered back to Soerabaya with one Dutch destroyer as escort, while the other ships continued to fire at enemies intermittently sighted through the smoke between 5.25 and 5.55 p.m. During this period a third Japanese torpedo attack was made; but this time no hits were scored.[1]

At about 6 p.m. Doorman ordered the American destroyers to attack, but quickly cancelled the order and instead told them to cover his retirement with smoke. The American ships considered that the best way to accomplish the Admiral's purpose was to attack; they therefore drove through the smoke screen they had just laid to seek the enemy heavy cruisers. They fired their torpedoes, though at too great range to have any chance of success, and then withdrew.

But the long day's fighting was by no means yet ended. By 6.15 darkness was falling and the opposing warships had lost touch with each other. Doorman now led his surviving ships north, presumably to try and work round towards the enemy convoy. But he was unaware of its true position, and as the Japanese Admiral had in fact kept it well clear of the field of battle, the Allied squadron never had any chance of finding it. Moreover, cruiser and destroyer reinforcements had now joined Nishimura's force.

Just before 7.30 contact was regained and the battle's night phase began with Japanese aircraft dropping flares to light up the Allied ships and betray their every movement. Doorman's predicament was now graver than ever, for his reduced force had no hope of concealing itself. At 7.45 he turned south for the coast of Java, and when he was close off shore at 9 p.m. he steered west along the coast.[2] The four American destroyers now had to return to port for fuel. At 9.25 the destroyer *Jupiter* suddenly blew up. It is possible that she struck a stray mine, for the Dutch had that day laid a defensive field in the vicinity.[3] Some of her crew reached shore, while others, including her Captain (Lieutenant-Commander N. V. J. T. Thew) were picked up later by the Japanese and made prisoner.

Soon after suffering this new blow Doorman turned north again. He now had only four cruisers and one destroyer, the *Encounter* (Lieutenant-Commander E. V. St. J. Morgan) with him. Then the squadron fortuitously found the survivors of the earlier sunk *Kortenaer*. The *Encounter* picked up over 100, and at about midnight she returned to Soerabaya to land them. At about 10.30 p.m. the

---

[1] See Map 3 (opp. p. 13), 2nd Phase.

[2] See Map 3, Final Phase.

[3] Rumours that the *Jupiter* might have been sunk by the American submarine S.38, which was in the vicinity at the time, have no foundation. Her patrol report makes it quite clear that she fired no torpedoes on that day. (Patrol report seen by author in U.S. Navy Department).

Allied squadron sighted enemy cruisers to port, and fire was at once opened. The *De Ruyter* was soon hit and turned away to starboard. While the others were following her round, first the *Java* and then the *De Ruyter* blew up. The Japanese cruisers had fired torpedoes, and this time they were only too successful. Captain Waller of the *Perth* now decided to break off the action, and with the *Houston*, which was damaged and almost out of ammunition, following him, he set course west for Batavia. They arrived there at 2 p.m. on the 28th of February. The *Exeter*, also damaged, the *Encounter*, one Dutch and five American destroyers were by that time back in Soerabaya. Admiral Doorman was lost with his ship; and the Combined Striking Force had ceased to exist.

Though it is possible that more skilful tactical handling could have inflicted losses on the enemy and made his object more difficult of accomplishment, the final outcome of the Battle of the Java Sea could hardly have been other than it was; for the enemy had great strength available to reinforce his spearhead, and held the advantage in the air. With the extinction of the Combined Striking Force the last glimmer of hope that control of the waters off Java could be disputed had gone. It now became a question of trying to extricate the surviving ships from the trap which had closed on them. The *Perth* and *Houston* were ordered by Helfrich to leave Batavia that night, and pass through the Sunda Strait to Tjilatjap. It was hoped that the way of escape was not yet barred. The two cruisers sailed at 9 p.m. Two hours later they ran right into the Japanese invasion fleet at the entrance to the Sunda Strait. There they fought the last of their many actions, and were sunk after doing much damage to the enemy transports. Their end was a glorious one, for they fought till not a round was left in their magazines. Of the 682 officers and men in the *Perth's* company only 229 returned home after the war. Captain Waller and Captain A. H. Rooks, U.S.N., of the *Houston*, were both lost with their ships. The young Australian Navy has every reason to remember with pride the story of the *Perth's* last battles.[1] Meanwhile the final act was also being played out in the east of Java. Four of the five American destroyers got away from Soerabaya, and escaped by the narrow Bali Strait unscathed. They reached Australia on the 4th of March. The *Exeter* could not use the shallow eastern channel out of Soerabaya. She, the *Encounter* and the last American destroyer, the *Pope*, were ordered to sail north for some distance, and then turn west for the Sunda Strait. Admiral Palliser believed that to route them far from the coast gave them their best chance of escape; but it was a forlorn hope, especially as the *Exeter's* speed was initially only sixteen knots. The alternative of passing north of

---

[1] A graphic record of the *Perth's* last fight, compiled from survivors after the war, is to be found in *Proud Echo* by Ronald McKie (Angus and Robertson, Sydney, 1953).

Madoera Island, and then south by the Bali or Lombok Strait was considered by the naval command, but was rejected because enemy aircraft were known to be working from Bali.[1] None the less it now seems that such a course involved the lesser risks.

The three ships sailed at dusk on the 28th of February, and the splendid repair work of the *Exeter's* engine room staff soon enabled her to work up to twenty-three knots. At dawn next day the sea and skies were clear, and hopes rose correspondingly; but not for long. At 7.30 a.m. warships were sighted ahead. Evasion was tried, but by 9.40 four enemy cruisers and a number of destroyers were closing in. Escape was no longer possible. For some time the unequal battle was fought without disaster, for the destroyers skilfully shielded the cruiser with their smoke. But at 11.20 the *Exeter* was badly hit, caught fire and eventually came to a standstill. She was then repeatedly struck, and finally sank at about 11.40. The destroyers did not survive her for long. The *Encounter* was sunk by shell fire and the *Pope* by dive-bombers, which the enemy had called to the scene. Over 800 survivors from the two British ships, including Captain Gordon and Lieutenant-Commander Morgan, were picked up and made prisoners-of-war. After their release in 1945 they and the senior surviving officers of other lost ships rendered their long-delayed reports on these battles to the Admiralty. One cannot but marvel at the clearness and accuracy of these accounts, written as they were three-and-a-half years after the events which they described, and from such tenuous records as the officers had managed to secrete from the persistent searches of their captors. In all the annals of sea fights there can exist few more moving documents. Although for days, if not weeks, previously all those ships' companies must have known, with ever-increasing certainty, that there could be only one end, there is not the slightest sign that any man wavered.

Captain Gordon and his Chief Engineer, Commander (E) A. H. Drake, told with the utmost restraint how their ship—that same *Exeter* which had fought the *Graf Spee* off the River Plate in December 1939[2]—went out three years later, on the other side of the world, again to give battle to an overwhelmingly superior enemy; how, after hours of stubborn fighting she received injuries which almost incapacitated the ship; and how she was none the less repaired sufficiently to go to sea again next day and continue the battle.

Lieutenant-Commander Morgan, and the other officers of the *Encounter* who survived, wrote a parallel account of the loss of their ship. In it Morgan described how, right at the end, he went round the ship and 'found the mess decks clear, the engine-room flooded and at least one boiler room on fire. Having satisfied myself that

---

[1] See Map 2 (opp. p. 9).
[2] See Vol. I, pp. 118–21.

C

there was nothing further to be done, and that the ship was sinking, I told the remainder [of the crew] to abandon ship. When they had all done so I left the ship myself . . . I was still hopeful of being recovered by our own ships. The next day at about 10.00 a.m. [twenty-two hours after the ships had sunk] a Japanese destroyer re-appeared, and it was apparent to me that we were unlikely to have any forces in the vicinity. I therefore advised those who were with me in the water that their only hope of rescue was at hand. Having seen the remainder of the party recovered, I swam to the destroyer and surrendered myself'.

One more incident in this tragic series must be preserved. It was mentioned previously how, in the very early hours of the day after she was sunk, an American submarine found some survivors from the *Electra*. In his report the Captain of the submarine told how 'during rescue operations [in the dark] some difficulty was experienced in locating one man, who was swimming in a life-jacket. He, realising that there remained one more life-raft load to be picked up, sang out "Leave me. I can't make it. Get the rest". Needless to say, we got him as well as the life-raft load. His name was Benjamin Roberts, Able Seaman. His action made a tremendous impression on the officers and men of this ship'.

Thus fell the final curtain on the long-drawn agony of the Allied ships involved in the attempt to defend Java.

Meanwhile, the enemy had sent powerful forces to the south of Java to cut off the escape of ships from Tjilatjap.[1] The destroyer *Stronghold*, the sloop *Yarra* (R.A.N.), two American destroyers and many valuable auxiliary vessels were lost; but four corvettes and two minesweepers, one of them carrying Commodore Collins, succeeded in reaching Australia. Admiral Helfrich resigned his Allied command on the 1st of March, when there were in fact no Allied ships left for him to command. He finally reached Colombo by air, while Admiral Palliser flew to Australia. On the same day that Helfrich resigned, the enemy landed at both ends of Java, and a week later the Allied land forces surrendered. By the end of the month the Japanese were in complete control of that immensely wealthy island, and had achieved the major part of the first phase of their vast scheme of conquest. The cost to the Japanese Navy had been almost trivial, but to the Allies it had been very much the reverse. Quite apart from the great losses of men and equipment suffered on land, and the far-reaching economic consequences of the surrender of such valuable territories, the Allied navies had in all lost two capital ships, five cruisers, one seaplane carrier and seventeen destroyers in the attempt to defend south-east Asia. Rarely can

---

[1] See Map 2 (opp. p. 9).

so much have been won for so small a cost as was accomplished by Japan between December 1941 and March 1942.

The main Japanese fleet was all this time commanded by Admiral Yamamoto, but it had taken no part in the operations so far discussed.[1] It had been the Striking Force of Admiral Nagumo, primarily composed of the fleet carriers, which had attacked Pearl Harbour in the previous December; and that same force had made the deadly attack on Port Darwin on the 19th of February.[2] The operations against Malaya and the East Indies had been entrusted to the Southern Force commanded by Vice-Admiral Kondo. His zone of command had been divided into a western sector (the South China Sea, Malaya and Sumatra) under Vice-Admiral Ozawa, and an eastern sector (the Philippines, Straits of Makassar and the Java Sea) under Vice-Admiral Takahashi.[3] For the invasion of Java, Ozawa and Takahashi had joined forces, to make the simultaneous western and eastern landings respectively. Admiral Kondo's heavy ships had lain in the background to give support if it had been needed, and Nagumo's striking force had joined him in late February and early March to deal the heavy blow at Darwin already mentioned, and had also swept the sea south of Java during the final stages of the campaigns. In spite of the weakness of the opposition offered to them, the way in which all these operations had been conducted left no room for doubt regarding the skill, power and efficiency of the Japanese Navy.

But the first phase of Japan's plans for aggrandisement went further than the seizure of the Philippines, Malaya and the Dutch East Indies. The Bismarck Archipelago was to be their new bastion in the east[4], and Burma was to be occupied in the west. The latter had been included in General Wavell's A.B.D.A. Command, but in Allied circles it had been widely held that Japan could not launch a full scale invasion there at the same time as she was driving southwards. By the end of January it was plain that this belief was wide of the mark, since a heavy attack was then being launched against Burma from Siam. It culminated in the fall of Rangoon on the 8th of March, one day before Java surrendered. There was little that Admiral Layton's tenuous Eastern Fleet could do to help the hardpressed Army in Burma; for he wholly lacked the large numbers of light craft needed to control its long and shallow coastal waters; and even had he possessed them the lack of air cover would have prevented them working there effectively. The naval forces in the theatre consisted of the few motor-launches and auxiliary craft of

---

[1] Appendix L. gives the composition and disposition of the Japanese Navy on 7th December 1941.

[2] See p. 12

[3] See Map 2 (opp. p. 9).

[4] See Map 5 (opp. p. 33).

the Burma R.N.V.R., which had only come into existence in June 1940. Early in February 1942, when it was obvious that serious trouble was blowing up on the coast of Burma, Rear-Admiral Cosmo Graham, who had been doing excellent work as Senior Naval Officer, Persian Gulf, since the start of the war, was appointed Commodore, Burma Coast. He arrived on the 15th, four days before the removal of civilians from Rangoon started. There was little he could do except to organise the evacuation, and prepare for the inevitable demolitions. It is estimated that over 100,000 persons escaped from Rangoon to Calcutta by sea. Our maritime control was at least sufficient to make this possible. A party of about 100 Royal Marines was sent to Burma from Colombo, and they fought in support of the Army in traditionally amphibious manner from motor-launches working on the river. But they were too few to dispute control of the great Irrawaddy waterway effectively, and about half of them were lost.

At a conference held by the Governor on the 27th of February it was decided to go ahead with the military evacuation of Rangoon, and to prepare to destroy its important facilities. General Wavell reached Delhi from Java that very day, and almost his first act was to suspend the orders for withdrawal and demolition. He has stated that 'on balance . . . we gained by the delay'[1], but to the men on the spot the reversal of orders inevitably caused confusion and difficulties. An Indian brigade was rushed in to try to stiffen the defences, but such eleventh-hour measures could not affect the issue. Graham and the demolition parties did not leave until the 8th of March, by which time they had done all that they could. Looting, treachery, arson and desertion were then rife throughout this great port and city. The Governor described the final apocalyptic scene in these words: 'All along the normally thronged foreshore not a sign of human life was to be seen . . . it was almost dark, and the flames topped by columns of dense black smoke rising thousands of feet into the air from the oil refineries presented an awe-inspiring sight. As night fell the whole sky was lurid with the glare of that inferno'. Two days after the final evacuation Graham summed up the tragedy in a letter to his wife. 'This melancholy experience—of sinking one's own vessels and blowing up a refinery . . . can be blamed on no one person. The indictment is against the whole nation for generations of neglect and comfortable living. We have had the butter'.[2]

Before the fall of Rangoon some partially completed motor-mine-sweepers were towed away to India, while others which could not be

---

[1] Despatch by General Sir Archibald P. Wavell. Supplement to the London Gazette of the 5th of March 1948, para. 21.

[2] Letter of 8th March 1942, printed in *A Space for Delight*. The letters of Rear-Admiral Cosmo Graham to his wife. (H. F. and G. Witherby Ltd. 1954), p. 192.

shifted were destroyed. Graham and the surviving small craft of the Burma Navy then went to Akyab. There they were reinforced by two sloops and some smaller vessels from India. But the tide of dissolution could not be stemmed for long, and on the 4th of May Akyab also was abandoned.

While the campaign in Burma thus moved to its tragic but inevitable conclusion, far away to the south-east the Japanese had occupied the important bases of Rabaul and Kavieng in the Bismarck Archipelago, and others in New Guinea.[1] Here were stationed the naval and air forces which were intended to command the north-eastern approaches to Australia.

Thus, in a matter of four months, was the first phase of Japan's vast ambitions accomplished, and with an ease which had surprised even her own rulers. But the ambitions of the conqueror were by no means satiated, and the very ease with which they had gained so much tempted them to try for more. Thereby Japan sowed the seeds of her own downfall. Instead of consolidating the gains so far made, her rulers decided at once to extend the perimeter of their conquests to include the Solomon Islands, the New Hebrides, the Fiji Islands and Samoa.[2] In the central Pacific Japanese eyes were now on Midway Island, which commanded the approaches to Hawaii, and in the far north on the Aleutians, which commanded the shortest invasion route from America to Japan. All this rapacity showed, however, as great an overestimate of Japan's own strength as it revealed ignorance of America's determination, power of recovery and industrial capacity. It would have been hard enough to protect all that Japan had won; to disperse her strength still wider was to prove fatal.

To turn now to Allied plans, the collapse of the A.B.D.A. Command plainly demanded a complete recasting of the command organisation. Towards the end of March a new division of strategic responsibility was agreed between Britain and America. The United States assumed responsibility for the whole, vast Pacific theatre, including Australia and New Zealand; while Britain's foreign commitments became the Middle East theatre and the Indian Ocean, including Malaya and Sumatra.[3] We will follow the course of events in the Indian Ocean first, and return later to the Pacific.

Readers of our first volume will remember that the Admiralty's strategy to counter the increasingly aggressive attitude of Japan had been to build up a substantial fleet in Ceylon, whence the vital routes across the Indian Ocean could be guarded.[4] It had originally been

---

[1] See Map 5 (opp. p. 33).
[2] See Map 1 (opp. p. 5).
[3] See Map 1.
[4] See Vol. I, pp. 554–557.

hoped to complete this plan by March 1942, so that the fleet would be able to move to Singapore as and when the situation further east demanded it. But it was not to be. The suddenness of Japan's on-slaught, and the ruthless efficiency with which her carefully laid plans were implemented, rendered any such gradual development of British strategy impossible; and the first reinforcements sent east had met with immediate disaster. By the beginning of 1942 the need to build up a new fleet in the Indian Ocean, where the threat to our maritime control was all too plain, was greater than ever; but it was desperately hard to find ships for such a purpose while the Royal Navy's heavy commitments in the Arctic, the Atlantic and the Mediterranean remained unabated. As early as the 8th of March the First Sea Lord sent the Prime Minister a prescient warning that Ceylon was now threatened, and 'a similar state to Malaya [was] likely to arise'. Its loss would, in Admiral Pound's view, 'undermine our whole strategic position in the Middle as well as the Far East'. The new Commander-in-Chief, Eastern Fleet, Admiral Sir James Somerville[1], would be told to use the battleships *Ramillies* and *Royal Sovereign* to protect Ceylon, keeping them at Colombo. Other rein-forcements were being sent to him as quickly as possible. In the light of after events it certainly seems that the Naval Staff failed to realise the true nature of the threat to Ceylon, when they expressed a belief that it could be protected by a couple of old battleships. When this idea reached Admiral Somerville his reaction was to ask the First Sea Lord 'how is it considered that two R-class [battleships] under fighter cover can repel a landing? It seems to me that unless we have a balanced force we may get a repetition of *Prince of Wales* and *Repulse*'. On the question of co-operation with the United States Admiral Pound told the Prime Minister that he considered the 'idea of combining with the American battle fleet attractive but impractic-able. We cannot', he continued, 'join the Americans in the Pacific, nor they [join] us in the Indian Ocean without uncovering our vital areas. Each must retain and strengthen its battle fleet where it is'.

While on his way out to his new command Admiral Somerville sent the First Sea Lord a letter in which he analysed his prospects. The loss of Ceylon was obviously the greatest danger, and if the Japanese launched an attack on the island with their whole naval strength he could do little against them. If, on the other hand, an attack was made on a smaller scale, he considered that 'the best counter is to keep an Eastern Fleet in being, and to avoid losses by attrition'. This purpose could be accomplished 'by keeping the fleet at sea as much as possible, and [by making] feints to the east of Ceylon from time to time'. Somerville also gave warning that if the

---

[1] Recently in command of Force H., working from Gibraltar. See Vol. I, p. 242.

Japanese captured Ceylon 'it will be extremely difficult, but not necessarily impossible, to maintain our communications to the Middle East. But if the Japanese capture Ceylon *and* destroy the greater part of the Eastern Fleet, then . . . the situation becomes really desperate'.

In spite of the acute difficulties of these anxious days the Admiralty had by the end of March scraped together a force which on paper looked substantial. Admiral Somerville arrived at Colombo on the 26th of that month, and he then took over command of the Eastern Fleet from Admiral Layton. His fleet consisted of the two large carriers *Indomitable* and *Formidable*, the small carrier *Hermes*, the battleships *Warspite* (recently returned from repairing battle damage received off Crete in America[1]), *Resolution, Ramillies, Royal Sovereign* and *Revenge*, two heavy and five light cruisers (including the Dutch *Heemskerck*), sixteen destroyers and seven submarines. It was fully realised that in this vast theatre maritime air power would be of critical importance, and the Admiralty had done its best to meet the need by giving to Somerville a large proportion of our surviving carriers. None the less his air element was not nearly strong enough to deal with the main Japanese striking forces, whose power and efficiency had been demonstrated all too convincingly. His three carriers had between them only some fifty-seven strike aircraft and three dozen fighters. Furthermore, there were insufficient shore-based long-range reconnaissance aircraft, and almost no shore-based air striking forces. If Admiral Nagumo's carrier force came into the Indian Ocean it would heavily outnumber Somerville's air strength. Nor was that the end of his deficiencies. The R-class battleships were old, slow and ill-protected, and might well prove more of a liability than an asset; many of the cruisers were also old and unmodernised, and some of the destroyers were in urgent need of refitting. Lastly, the state of his main bases at Colombo, Trincomalee and Addu Atoll was such as might well cause any Commander-in-Chief concern[2]; and his fleet was far from being adequately trained to undertake co-ordinated and intricate operations.

Admiral Layton was one of the officers who came out of the successive disasters of Malaya and the East Indies with his reputation for forcefulness and resolute determination enhanced. When he reached Ceylon from Batavia in mid-January he found much to cause him misgivings. There was, he considered, the same atmosphere of inertia and complacent optimism which had contributed to the *débâcle* in Malaya. And he signalled to London that the greatest need was for a single all-powerful central authority. To his

---

[1] See Vol. I, p. 442.

[2] See Map 4 (opp. p. 25).

surprise the British Government's reply was to appoint him as Commander-in-Chief, Ceylon, with wide powers over all the service and civilian authorities in the island, including the Governor. With characteristic energy he set about tearing down the barriers of narrow departmentalism, and welding all the numerous elements needed to give of their best in the defence of Ceylon into a closely-knit team. It is now clear that he was given these great responsibilities just in time; the fact that Ceylon was successfully defended and came to serve satisfactorily as the central hub of our maritime power in those waters owed much to Admiral Layton's determination.

Admirals Layton and Somerville were both strong personalities, and although there were occasional differences of opinion, notably over whether the Commander-in-Chief, Ceylon, exercised any measure of control over the Eastern Fleet, these were easily resolved. Between them they formed a powerful team to work for the ultimate restoration of British maritime power in the East. Somerville warmly welcomed Layton's new appointment, and remarked of his colleague's work that he 'takes complete charge of Ceylon and stands no nonsense from anyone . . . He pulls all the Ministers' legs . . . and they work for him all the harder'. With General Wavell the Navy's relations were excellent, and that great soldier quickly grasped the diversity and magnitude of the problems with which the sister service was faced. As Somerville expressed it when the three of them were in conference, the Eastern Fleet not only shared in the defence of India and Ceylon, but was responsible for the security of the sea routes 'from the Cape eastwards to Australia and northwards to Aden and the Persian Gulf'. It was moreover 'an important force to be used in the ultimate operations of ejecting the enemy from Malaya and the Dutch East Indies'. But in April 1942, such plans were almost visionary, for the first need was to defend what we still held.

Admiral Layton's expectation that Ceylon would not for long remain immune from attack was quickly proved correct. After occupying the Andaman Islands and northern Sumatra the Japanese fleet prepared to strike. Their purpose was to demonstrate their invincibility to the Indian continent at a time when Anglo-Indian relations were far from easy, to knock out the Eastern Fleet and to prevent its interference with the Burma operations. In the middle of March Admiral Kondo issued orders for a two-pronged drive into the Indian Ocean. The main blow was to be struck against Ceylon by Nagumo's well-tried and so far consistently successful striking force of five carriers with some 300 aircraft on board, four battleships, three cruisers and eight destroyers. His colleague Ozawa was meanwhile to sweep our shipping from the Bay of Bengal with one light carrier, six cruisers and eight destroyers. It was a bold plan, and

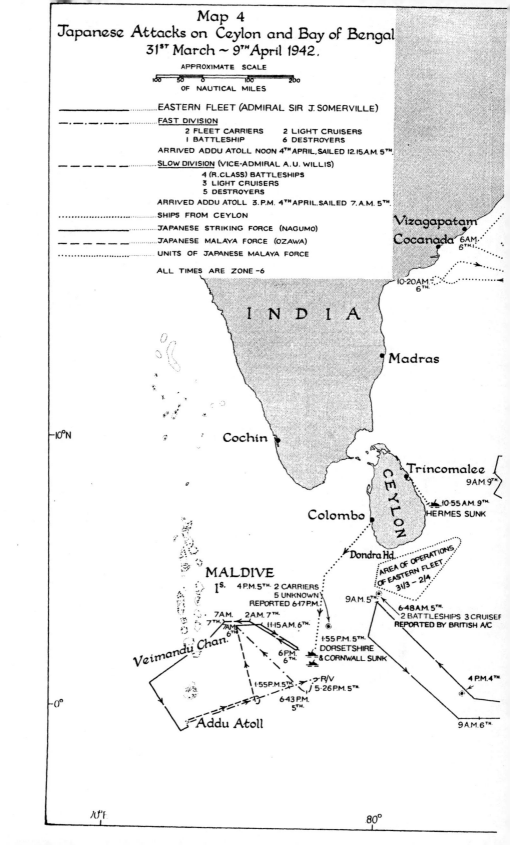

Map 4
Japanese Attacks on Ceylon and Bay of Bengal
31ˢᵀ March ~ 9ᵀᴴ April 1942.

APPROXIMATE SCALE

100   50   0   100   200

OF NAUTICAL MILES

——————— ········ EASTERN FLEET (ADMIRAL SIR J. SOMERVILLE)

—·—·—·—·— ········ FAST DIVISION
   2 FLEET CARRIERS   2 LIGHT CRUISERS
   1 BATTLESHIP   6 DESTROYERS
   ARRIVED ADDU ATOLL NOON 4ᵀᴴ APRIL, SAILED 12.15 A.M. 5ᵀᴴ.

—— —— —— ········ SLOW DIVISION (VICE-ADMIRAL A.U. WILLIS)
   4 (R. CLASS) BATTLESHIPS
   3 LIGHT CRUISERS
   5 DESTROYERS
   ARRIVED ADDU ATOLL 3 P.M. 4ᵀᴴ APRIL, SAILED 7 A.M. 5ᵀᴴ.

·············· SHIPS FROM CEYLON

——————— JAPANESE STRIKING FORCE (NAGUMO)

—— —— —— JAPANESE MALAYA FORCE (OZAWA)

·············· UNITS OF JAPANESE MALAYA FORCE

ALL TIMES ARE ZONE −6

I N D I A

Vizagapatam
Cocanada   6 A.M.
             6ᵀᴴ.

10-20 A.M.
6ᵀᴴ.

Madras

—10°N

Cochin

Trincomalee
9 A.M. 9ᵀᴴ.

C E Y L O N

10-55 A.M. 9ᵀᴴ.
HERMES SUNK

Colombo

Dondra Hd.

AREA OF OPERATIONS
OF EASTERN FLEET
31/3 − 2/4

MALDIVE
Iˢ.   4 P.M. 5ᵀᴴ. 2 CARRIERS
       5 UNKNOWN
       REPORTED 6·17 P.M.

9 A.M. 5ᵀᴴ.

6·48 A.M. 5ᵀᴴ.
2 BATTLESHIPS 3 CRUISER
REPORTED BY BRITISH A/C

7 A.M.   2 A.M. 7ᵀᴴ.
7ᵀᴴ.
7 A.M.   11·15 A.M. 6ᵀᴴ.
6ᵀᴴ.

Veimandu Chan.

6 P.M.
6ᵀᴴ.

1·55 P.M. 5ᵀᴴ.
DORSETSHIRE
& CORNWALL SUNK

4 P.M. 4ᵀᴴ

1·55 P.M. 5ᵀᴴ.   R/V
               5·26 P.M. 5ᵀᴴ.

6·43 P.M.
5ᵀᴴ.

—0°

Addu Atoll

9 A.M. 6ᵀᴴ.

70°E

80°

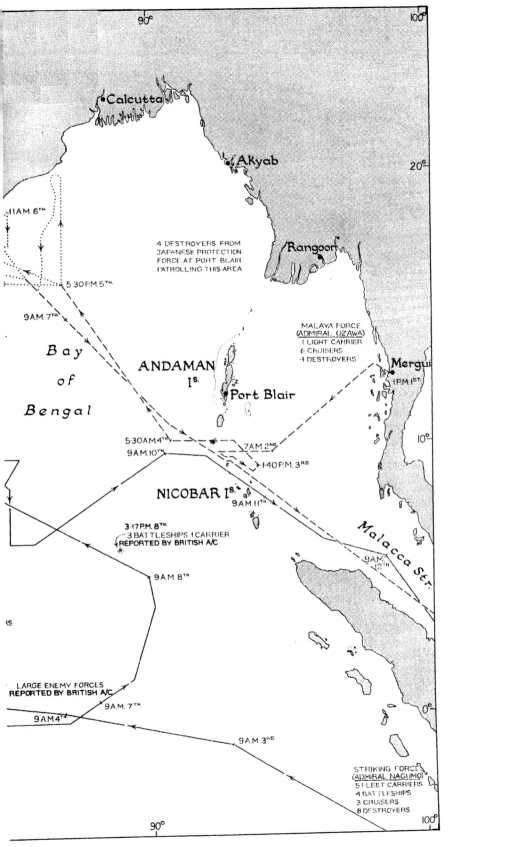

90°

100°

●Calcutta

Akyab

20°

11AM 6TH

4 DESTROYERS FROM
JAPANESE PROTECTION
FORCE AT PORT BLAIR
PATROLLING THIS AREA

Rangoon

5·30 P.M. 5TH

9AM 7TH

Bay

of

Bengal

ANDAMAN
IS.

Port Blair

MALAYA FORCE
(ADMIRAL OZAWA)
1 LIGHT CARRIER
6 CRUISERS
4 DESTROYERS

Mergui

1 P.M. 1ST

10°

5·30 A.M. 4TH
9 A.M. 10TH

7 A.M. 2ND

1·40 P.M. 3RD

NICOBAR IS.

9 A.M. 11TH

3·17 P.M. 8TH
3 BATTLESHIPS 1 CARRIER
REPORTED BY BRITISH A/C

9 A.M 8TH

Malacca Str.

9 A.M
12TH

IS

LARGE ENEMY FORCES
REPORTED BY BRITISH A/C

9 A.M. 7TH

0°

9 A.M. 4TH

9 A.M. 3RD

STRIKING FORCE
(ADMIRAL NAGUMO)
5 FLEET CARRIERS
4 BATTLESHIPS
3 CRUISERS
8 DESTROYERS

90°

100°

Somerville had nothing like the power necessary to counter it. He had in fact only just taken over his new command when intelligence regarding Japanese intentions reached him.

Admirals Somerville and Layton well knew that in their present condition the bases at Colombo and Trincomalee could not serve the fleet satisfactorily, and that, with the Japanese so close, its ships must be in constant danger while using them. It had, therefore, been decided to work from a secret base at Addu Atoll, the southernmost of the Maldive Islands, 600 miles south-west of Ceylon.[1] There the fleet would be comparatively safe from surprise attack, and could train and exercise invisible to prying enemy eyes. But the atoll, though already in use as an anchorage and fuelling base, wholly lacked anti-submarine and anti-aircraft defences. We now know that the Japanese never learnt of the development of Addu Atoll as a base.

Intelligence indicated that the attack on Colombo and Trincomalee was to be expected on or about the 1st of April; Somerville expected it to be made at dawn from the south-east. He therefore concentrated his ships south of Ceylon on the last day of March, in a position from which his carriers could launch a night attack. He was determined at all costs to avoid being attacked by the enemy's carrier aircraft and, because of his inferior strength, to decline fleet action. He knew that whatever the weakness of his present fleet might be, it was the last that Britain could send into the Indian Ocean. The country simply could not afford that it should be hazarded. The time to take risks would, he hoped, come later. For the present he could only cling to the essentials, of which the greatest must be to preserve his fleet. The success of his plan depended greatly on early and accurate warning of enemy movements. Accordingly the six Catalinas, which were all that No. 205 Squadron of the R.A.F. had available in Ceylon, were ordered to fly patrols to a depth of 420 miles to the south-east. During daylight the fleet was kept outside the waters which enemy reconnaissance aircraft were likely to search. Somerville not only had a very difficult strategic problem to solve, but was beset by tactical troubles, the chief of which stemmed from the slowness of the R-class battleships. He decided to divide his fleet into a fast division (*Indomitable, Formidable, Warspite*, and the cruisers *Cornwall, Emerald* and *Enterprise*), and a slow division consisting of the R-class battleships and the remaining cruisers. His destroyers were shared about equally between the two divisions.

On the 31st of March fresh intelligence appeared to confirm Somerville's expectation that the attack would be made very soon; but the air patrols had so far sighted nothing. Next day his fleet was

---

[1] See Map 4.

cruising to the south of Ceylon, and the *Dorsetshire*, which had abruptly stopped a refit in Colombo, joined the flag. On the 1st and 2nd of April Somerville swept east by night and west by day, still awaiting reports from the reconnaissance aircraft. But nothing came in.

Late on the evening of the 2nd Somerville reviewed the situation. As no more reports of enemy intentions had reached him from Ceylon, he came to the conclusion that either we had been mistaken in expecting carrier-borne air attack, or that the Japanese had become aware of his concentration and had, therefore, postponed their plan. Some of his ships needed refuelling, and others were running short of water. He decided that the apparent lull gave him his best chance to replenish his fleet, and therefore returned to Addu Atoll. The *Dorsetshire* was ordered to continue her refit at Colombo, and the *Cornwall* was sent to provide onward escort for an Australian troop convoy due to arrive there on the 8th; the *Hermes* and one destroyer were sent to Trincomalee to prepare for the assault on Madagascar, to which the carrier had been allocated.[1] Just after the main body of the fleet reached Addu Atoll on the afternoon of the 4th of April, a Catalina reported strong enemy surface forces 360 miles south-east of Ceylon and steering towards it.[2] The long-awaited sighting report came at an unlucky moment. The fast division was in the middle of refuelling, and the slow division could not be ready for sea till next day.

Somerville decided that his best plan was to sail the fast division as soon as possible, leaving the slower ships to follow. He could not now intercept before the expected attack was launched, but he hoped to get in a night torpedo-bomber attack on the retiring enemy. Meanwhile in Ceylon Admiral Layton had brought the defences to the alert, and had cleared the harbours of all ships which could be got to sea. He knew that, with Somerville's fleet 600 miles away, the island's defences must stand entirely on their own legs. The two heavy cruisers, which had just reached Colombo, were sent south to meet the fast division, while the *Hermes* was ordered to sail from Trincomalee and keep clear to the north-east. At dawn on the 5th of April, which was Easter Sunday, air reports placed the enemy only 120 miles away. At 8 a.m. the attack on Colombo, by ninety-one bombers and three dozen fighters, started. The fighter defences of the island comprised three squadrons of Hurricanes, of which two were at Colombo and one at Trincomalee. There were also two squadrons of naval Fulmars ashore. Forty-two fighters took off to meet the enemy, and in the fierce air fighting which followed seven attackers

---

[1] See pp. 186–192.
[2] See Map 4 (opp. p. 25).

were destroyed for the loss of nineteen of our own aircraft. Unhappily six naval Swordfish, sent from Trincomalee as a torpedo striking force, arrived at the height of the fighting, and were all shot down. Shipping in the harbour and the port's equipment suffered relatively little, thanks to Admiral Layton's precautions. The attack had nothing like the deadly effect of the earlier one on Port Darwin, and Colombo was not put out of action.

The *Dorsetshire* and *Cornwall* had sailed late on the 4th to rendez-vous with Admiral Somerville.[1] Next morning enemy reconnaissance aircraft were sighted and reported by Captain A. W. S. Agar, V.C., of the *Dorsetshire*. Early in the afternoon a heavy attack by more than fifty bombers developed. Both ships quickly received many hits, and they sank in a few minutes. Once again Nagumo's carrier aircraft had shown how deadly they were against ships which lacked fighter cover. Survivors from the two ships collected around the few boats, rafts and wreckage. Late next afternoon, the 6th, the *Enterprise* and two destroyers detached by Admiral Somerville picked up 1,122 officers and men; but two valuable ships and 424 lives were lost.

To return now to the main fleet, the reports which came in on the 5th left Somerville in a good deal of doubt regarding the enemy's whereabouts. The slow division was still far astern, so the Admiral could not look to it for support. In the evening it seemed that the enemy might be making for Addu Atoll, so Somerville turned south. Then a more reliable report caused him to alter to the north-west.[2] Searches were flown all that night; but nothing was sighted. Early on the 6th the slow and fast divisions met, but by that time the enemy had vanished. Somerville was still plagued by the possibility that Nagumo might be near Addu Atoll, either to attack it or to await the fleet's return to its vicinity. When Admiral Layton signalled that he estimated that a strong enemy force was between that base and Ceylon, Somerville decided that he must keep clear. Flying constant air searches he finally approached the atoll from the west, entered the harbour at 11 a.m. on the 8th and refuelled.

In fact Nagumo had withdrawn to the east after attacking Colombo, to prepare for a raid on Trincomalee. From the 6th to the 8th his reconnaissance aircraft did their utmost to find Somerville's fleet, but they sought him to the south-east of Ceylon, what time he was far to the west. We may be thankful that they never found him. On the afternoon of the 8th a Catalina reported a large force 400 miles east of Ceylon, steering once more towards the island. That night the harbour of Trincomalee was cleared of shipping. The *Hermes*, the destroyer *Vampire* and several merchantmen and fleet

---

[1] See Map 4 (opp. p. 25).
[2] See Map 4.

auxiliaries were sent south and told to hug the coast. Early on the 9th the approach of enemy aircraft was detected. Their strength was about the same as at Colombo, but here only twenty-two fighters rose to meet them. A good deal of damage was done to shore installations. Nine R.A.F. Blenheims of No. 11 Squadron—all we had to strike back with—took off to find the enemy; but they got no hits, and five of their number were lost.

The ships sent out from Trincomalee were about sixty-five miles from the base when the attack took place. At 9 a.m. on the 9th they reversed course to enter harbour. By ill luck they were then reported by a Japanese reconnaissance aircraft, and at about 10.30 a.m. they were attacked by crushing strength. The shore-based fighters could not reach them in time, and forty bomb hits in ten minutes sank the *Hermes*. The *Vampire* soon shared her fate, as did the corvette *Hollyhock* and two tankers. Happily, over 600 survivors were rescued by a nearby hospital ship.

At the time we believed that the defending fighters had inflicted heavy losses on the Japanese carrier planes, especially over Colombo; but it is now plain that the claims were greatly exaggerated. According to Japanese records the whole operation only cost them seventeen aircraft.

Meanwhile the smaller of the two Japanese task forces, that of Admiral Ozawa, had been running riot in the Bay of Bengal, where our coastwise shipping was being sailed in small unescorted groups.[1] In the short space of five days, between the 4th and 9th of April, twenty-three merchantmen of 112,312 tons were sunk. At about the same time Japanese U-boats started to work off the west coast of India, and in the first ten days of the same month they accounted for five more ships of 32,404 tons. Our trade and military traffic on both sides of the Indian sub-continent were completely disrupted.

In the early hours of the 7th, two days before the attack on Trincomalee and the sinking of the *Hermes*, the Admiralty signalled to Somerville that their hope that the presence of his fleet and American pressure would together discourage the Japanese from sending powerful forces into the Indian Ocean had evidently proved vain. If the enemy cared to concentrate the forces which were scouring those waters, Somerville's fleet was, they realised, inferior in all respects. In such circumstances the R-class battleships might be 'more of a liability than an asset', and the Commander-in-Chief was given discretion to withdraw them to Africa. With regard to the rest of his fleet the Admiralty considered that it must not use Colombo for the present. This was very different from the hopes expressed five weeks earlier by the Admiralty regarding the defence of Ceylon.[2]

---

[1] See Map 4 (opp. p. 25).
[2] See p. 22.

On the 8th Somerville replied agreeing to the Admiralty's proposals, and at the same time underlined the grim truth about his situation. He was in no doubt of the probable consequences of continuing to operate near Ceylon. Our shore-based and carrier-borne air strength was quite inadequate to deal with such numbers as Nagumo was able to throw in. The battle fleet could not at present be protected in those waters, and in such circumstances was only a liability. In the Ceylon bases his ships could find little security against air attacks; in Addu Atoll none at all. Accordingly he was sending his slow division to Kilindini in East Africa to guard the WS. convoy route, but would keep the fast division in Indian waters, to be ready to deal with any attempt by the enemy to command those waters with light forces only. But he would stay clear of Ceylon. On the 10th, Somerville returned to the same theme, and urged his need for more carrier strength and for the slow battleships to be replaced by modern units of long endurance. The *Malaya*, which had been offered by the Admiralty, was rejected by the Commander-in-Chief because of her short endurance. The *Nelson* and *Rodney*, due to leave the Clyde in late May and early June and to reach Kilindini on the 7th of July, would be better.[1] Until modern reinforcements reached him Somerville could only 'create diversions and false scents, since I am now the poor fox'. His needs were not disputed at home; but to meet them at once was a totally different matter.

In London the crisis which had suddenly, though not unexpectedly, blown up in the Indian Ocean aroused the gravest anxieties. On the 7th of April, Mr. Churchill told President Roosevelt that it seemed that the Japanese might be contemplating the invasion of Ceylon, and asked whether the Pacific Fleet could take such action as would compel the Japanese striking forces to return to the Pacific.[2] Eight days later he returned to the same ominous theme with an outline of the strategic consequences of Japanese control over the Indian Ocean. 'With so much of the weight of Japan thrown upon us we have', wrote Mr. Churchill, 'more than we can bear'.[3] He asked whether the American Pacific Fleet could at once move back to Pearl Harbour, whether United States naval reinforcements could be sent direct to Somerville or, alternatively, whether they could come to Scapa to enable us to release powerful modern ships to the Indian Ocean. In the Prime Minister's view, we needed eight or nine weeks' respite, at the end of which we should have ample forces (including the *Illustrious*, *Valiant*, *Nelson* and *Rodney*) available to reinforce the Eastern Fleet. On the 17th the President replied declin-

---

[1] This movement was not actually carried out.
[2] W. S. Churchill. *The Second World War*, Vol. IV, pp. 159–160. (Henceforth referred to as 'Churchill, Vol. I, II, etc.).
[3] Churchill, Vol. IV, p. 162.

ing to send American warships into the Indian Ocean, but he offered temporarily to replace some of the Home Fleet's battleships if they were sent east. He also said that measures were in hand in the Pacific which 'we hope you will find effective when they can be made known to you shortly'. The President may have been referring to the carrier-borne air raid on Tokyo[1] or to the despatch of the task force which was soon to fight the Battle of the Coral Sea.[2]

To General Wavell in India the situation naturally appeared critical, and he complained to the Chiefs of Staff that he had been misled regarding the ability of the Navy to exercise such control of the Indian Ocean as would make the invasion of Ceylon or southern India impossible. While on passage in the *Warspite* from Bombay to Colombo to confer with Admiral Layton, he received Mr Churchill's reply. It was as ever undaunted. The Eastern Fleet would, said the Prime Minister, be built up to such strength as would force the enemy, if they proposed to invade Ceylon or India, 'to make a larger detachment from their main fleet than they would wish . . . but if in the meantime Ceylon, [and] particularly Colombo, is lost all this gathering of a naval force will be futile'.[3] In other words, the Commanders-in-Chief must hold on to the bare strategic essentials with hope and faith equal to the Prime Minister's, and must share his belief that a happier day would soon dawn.

But the Japanese actually had no further designs for conquest in the Indian Ocean. Nagumo's carriers returned to Japan after the raid on Trincomalee, to prepare for operations in the central Pacific in May and June. Their recall remained, however, shrouded from British eyes for some time, and a paradoxical situation thus arose; for while the Eastern Fleet had mostly withdrawn to East Africa, the enemy whom Somerville chiefly feared had withdrawn beyond the Malacca Straits. Within a few days of the attacks on Ceylon four thousand miles of ocean separated the main forces of the two contestants for control of the Indian Ocean. Nor did the Japanese fleet ever again enter those waters in force. Our shipping was thereafter molested only by submarines and surface raiders, as will be told in a later chapter.[4] As to conditions at Colombo and Trincomalee, although the air attacks caused a big exodus and a decline of morale, there was a rapid recovery. By the middle of May Admiral Layton was able to tell the First Sea Lord that 'the people have got their chins up and are pulling well together', that the tone of the local Press was confident, and that the working of Colombo harbour, which had been about one-third of its full capacity in February and

---

[1] See p. 34.
[2] See p. 35–36.
[3] Churchill, Vol. IV, p. 163.
[4] See pp. 184–185.

had dropped to nothing after the air attacks, was now greatly improved and rising daily. Though no one realised it at the time, the crisis had passed.

It is difficult to resist the temptation to speculate on the course which events might have taken during those critical days in the Indian Ocean. In the first place it must be remembered that the treacherous Japanese onslaught on Britain and the United States, though not wholly unexpected, caught both us and the Americans by surprise when it came; and that we both suffered severe losses in the first few days of combat with this new enemy. Nor can it be doubted that the efficiency of the Japanese Navy, and especially of its air arm, was greatly underrated in some British circles. But our inability to protect our interests in the east, and to control sea routes over which British trade had flowed unhindered for nearly two centuries, stemmed from deeper causes than these. Never since the end of the First World War had the Royal Navy possessed the strength to fight a major enemy in the Far East as well as in the Atlantic, the Arctic and the Mediterranean. We had already, when France dropped out and Italy came in, taken on far more than had been believed possible when the 1939 War Plans were framed[1]—and had done so with triumphant success, though at the cost of very severe losses. No maritime nation can wage a world-wide struggle almost alone for nearly two-and-a-half years without suffering losses; but one has only to glance at the tragically lengthy toll of British warships sunk between 1939 and 1942 to realise that the price paid for keeping the seas open during those long years had deprived us of the fleet which could have fought Japan on something like equal terms. Thus, when the need to build up an Eastern Fleet arose, it had to be done hurriedly, and could only be done with what ships could be scraped together from other sources. The first attempt ended in utter disaster, and the second very nearly ended in a greater one. Admiral Somerville ran all and more of the risks which he could justifiably take by moving to the south of Ceylon to try to protect that indispensable island from the sea; and one may feel that the goddess of fortune aided his escape. His action in restarting normal movements within his command before the attack on Colombo had taken place now seems to have been premature, and it certainly led to the loss of the *Dorsetshire* and *Cornwall*. When the report on these events reached London Mr Churchill remarked that in his opinion Admiral Somerville had imprudently dispersed his forces. The First Sea Lord declared that this could not 'be allowed to go unchallenged' and the First Lord sent to the Prime Minister a reasoned explanation of all the circumstances surrounding the Admiral's actions. But, even had Admiral Somerville kept those ships with his main fleet, he still

---

[1] See Vol. I, Chapter IV.

could not possibly have challenged Nagumo successfully, though the ships would in that case presumably have been preserved along with the rest. What Somerville chiefly lacked was, of course, adequate carrier-borne air strength; but the shore-based air reconnaissance and striking power were also far too weak, and his bases were inadequately defended against attack on such a scale. Given two or three more fleet carriers in substitution for the old and cumbersome R-class battleships, a dozen more long-range reconnaissance aircraft and a few squadrons of shore-based torpedo-bombers, he could have challenged Nagumo with confidence. The margin of his needs over his resources does not now seem very large; but to achieve success the needs had to be filled with modern ships and aircraft, not with the resurrected survivals of an earlier struggle. To Britain the sweeping of our shipping from the Bay of Bengal, and the unopposed incursion of a major force into waters over which we had so long held undisputed control, had presented almost as serious a menace as the forays of German warships into the Atlantic. A lifeline can, after all, be cut at either end or in the middle. But because this threat was far away from our own shores the need to prepare against it in peace time, and the provision of the necessary ships and money to do so, may have appeared less urgent than the numerous calls nearer home. Even today the full gravity of the events of April 1942 seems to have come home to us far less vividly than similar events in the Atlantic. The chief lessons are, of course, that a maritime power which is utterly dependent on sea communications must possess adequately equipped and defended bases at all the many overseas strategic centres from which she may at any time have to operate her defensive forces; and secondly that she will always need a strategic reserve of ships and aircraft capable of being quickly switched to the threatened centres. In the event we were saved from disaster in the Indian Ocean, though more by good fortune than by our own exertions. For when matters looked most grim for us the Japanese diverted their forces to the central Pacific. The advantage which they had gained in the Indian Ocean was thus never pressed home, and the transfer of their main strength to the east led, two months later, to the decisive battle of Midway, in which Nagumo's carrier striking force was destroyed.

At the end of May the Admiralty was planning for the Eastern Fleet to return to Ceylon late in July. That movement must, of course, be the first step towards re-establishing our control over the Indian Ocean. Colombo would, so they hoped, then be able to take six or seven big ships (battleships or carriers) simultaneously; but another nine months would be needed before Trincomalee could be made ready to receive a major fleet and also adequate shore-based air forces. Addu Atoll could not, in the Admiralty's view, be made

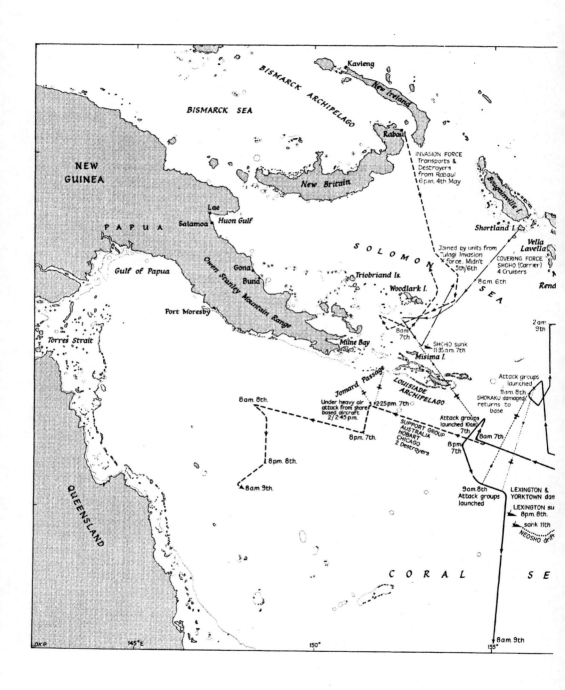

Kavieng

BISMARCK ARCHIPELAGO

New Ireland

BISMARCK SEA

Rabaul

INVASION FORCE
Transports &
Destroyers
from Rabaul
6 p.m. 4th May

Bougainville I.

NEW GUINEA

New Britain

Shortland I.

Vella Lavella

P A P U A

Lae
Salamoa
Huon Gulf

Owen Stanley Mountain Range

SOLOMON SEA

Joined by units from
Tulagi Invasion
force. Midn't
5th/6th

COVERING FORCE
SHOHO (Carrier)
4 Cruisers

8 a.m. 6th

Rend

Gulf of Papua

Gona
Buna

Triobriand Is.

Woodlark I.

Port Moresby

Torres Strait

Milne Bay

8am 7th

SHOHO sunk
11:35 a.m. 7th

2 am 9th

Misima I.

Attack groups
launched
11am 8th
SHOKAKU damaged
returns to base

Jomard Passage

LOUISIADE ARCHIPELAGO

8am. 8th.

Under heavy air
attack from shore
based aircraft
2/2:45 p.m.

2:25 pm. 7th

Attack groups
launched 10am
7th

8am 7th

8pm. 7th.

8pm 7th

SUPPORT GROUP
AUSTRALIA
HOBART
CHICAGO
2 Destroyers

8pm. 8th.

9am 8th
Attack groups
launched

LEXINGTON &
YORKTOWN dam

8am 9th.

LEXINGTON su
8pm. 8th.

sank 11th

NEOSHO drif

QUEENSLAND

C O R A L   S E

8am 9th

DKP

145°E

150°

155°

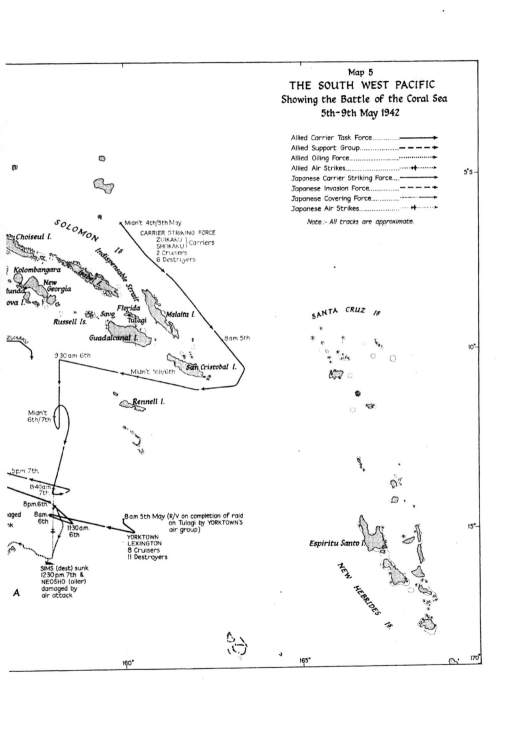

Map 5
THE SOUTH WEST PACIFIC
Showing the Battle of the Coral Sea
5th–9th May 1942

Allied Carrier Task Force.............——————▶
Allied Support Group.................– – – – –▶
Allied Oiling Force.........................··············▶
Allied Air Strikes..............................╫——▶
Japanese Carrier Striking Force....——————
Japanese Invasion Force.............– – – – –▶
Japanese Covering Force.............·—·—·—·—▶
Japanese Air Strikes...................╫·······▶

Note:- All tracks are approximate.

5°S

Midn't 4th/5th May
CARRIER STRIKING FORCE
ZUIKAKU } Carriers
SHOKAKU }
2 Cruisers
6 Destroyers

SOLOMON Is
Choiseul I.
Kolombangara
New
Georgia
Indispensable Strait
fundd
ova I.
Russell Is.
Savo
Florida
Tulagi
Malaita I.
Guadalcanal I.
San Cristobal I.
8am 5th

SANTA CRUZ Is

10°

ZUIKAKU

9.30am 6th

Midn't 5th/6th

Rennell I.

Midn't
6th/7th

5p.m. 7th.
8.40am.
7th.

8pm.6th.
aged
8am.
hk
6th

8am 5th May (R/V on completion of raid
on Tulagi by YORKTOWN'S
air group)

1130a.m.
6th

YORKTOWN
LEXINGTON
8 Cruisers
11 Destroyers

Espiritu Santo I.

15°

SIMS (dest) sunk
1230 p.m. 7th &
NEOSHO (oiler)
damaged by
air attack

A

NEW HEBRIDES Is

160°   165°   170°

into a really satisfactory base in under one-and-a-half to two years, but work was proceeding there. A large programme of works of a greater or smaller nature was also to be undertaken at Kilindini, Diego Suarez in Madagascar, Seychelles and Mauritius,[1] all of which had been very deficient in, if not wholly without base facilities when Japan entered the war. Admiral Somerville, in his reply to these proposals, expressed the view that Kilindini (Mombasa) should be made the principal base, for neither Colombo nor Trincomalee could wholly fill the function. Kilindini, on the other hand, was excellently placed for the defence of the Middle East supply route, and all the paraphernalia of a big fleet's shore organisation could be satisfactorily established there. Seychelles, Mauritius and Diego Garcia (in the Chagos Archipelago) all needed protection to enable them to be used as fuelling bases, and the Commander-in-Chief considered the first of these three by far the most important. Diego Suarez in Madagascar, where there was a dock, would be valuable to relieve the congestion at Durban and Colombo.[2] But the outstanding need of his fleet was for 'action of some sort', and he was hoping to make carrier air attacks on Port Blair in the Andaman Islands or on Sabang in Sumatra as soon as he had enough strength, and had trained his fleet to the necessary pitch.

It was indeed inevitable that the establishment of well-found bases at such a distance from home should prove one of the most intractable of the many problems which faced the Admiralty; and it now seems all too clear that our acute difficulties in the Indian Ocean during the first half of 1942 stemmed largely from failure to provide proper bases in peace time.

We must now turn to the American strategic zone and retrace our steps a few weeks to follow the events which had taken place there since the fall of the Dutch East Indies. The main purpose of American strategy was now to prevent the Japanese capturing the chain of island bases running from Samoa in the east, through the Fiji Islands, the New Hebrides and New Caledonia to New Guinea in the west, and so bestriding the vital reinforcement route to Australia and New Zealand.[3] Early in 1942 urgent steps had been taken to reinforce the garrisons in some of these islands, and to establish protected fuelling bases in them. At that time they possessed almost nothing to enable them to fulfil their new function, except the natural qualities of their extensive and well-sheltered harbours. The Australians reinforced Port Moresby in New Guinea; New Zealand

---

[1] See Map 1 (opp. p. 5). Diego Suarez was captured on 7th May 1942. See p. 191.
[2] See Map 1.
[3] See Map 1.

D

did the same for Suva in Fiji; and the Americans, besides shipping troops, stores and aircraft to Australia, developed bases in the Friendly Islands, Christmas Island, Canton Island, and at Nouméa in New Caledonia.[1] The last named, which possessed a magnificent harbour, was a French colony which had joined de Gaulle's cause. It was to become the first major advanced base of the forces assembling to stop further Japanese penetration southwards. But, for all the fiery energy and technical skill devoted by the Americans to creating these bases out of almost nothing, the great distances over which all the equipment had to be hauled made it an inevitably slow process; and meanwhile Allied strategy had to remain defensive.

Whilst we are dealing with the essential, if slow, process of creating the necessary advanced bases in this vast theatre it should be mentioned that late in May the American naval and military commanders ordered the occupation of Espiritu Santo in the northern New Hebrides. This harbour was some 300 miles nearer than Nouméa to the waters around the Solomon Islands, in which it was realised that the Japanese challenge would have to be seriously met. The first forces were taken to Espiritu Santo by the New Zealand cruiser *Leander*, and were flung ashore on what was at the time a peaceful coconut-clad tropical island occupied by a few French planters. It was difficult to realise that within a few months the Americans would have transformed it into one of the busiest maritime bases in the world. It played a very important part in the later heavy fighting for control of the Solomon Islands.[2]

Although in April 1942 the Allies could not yet afford to risk a major counter-attack, task forces had been formed around the four American fleet carriers, and they operated against the enemy from Wake and Marcus Islands in the north to Rabaul in New Britain in the south. No spectacular results were achieved, nor were they expected; but valuable experience was gained. This defensive phase included the well-known raid on Tokyo and other Japanese cities by sixteen United States Army bombers under Lieutenant-Colonel J. H. Doolittle. They were launched from the *Hornet* 680 miles from their target on the 18th of April, but could in no event have landed on to the carrier again. They were therefore ordered to fly to friendly airfields in China. Only four of the sixteen bombers got down successfully, but the majority of the aircrews who took part in this daring venture survived.[3] The raid had the effect of making the Japanese hasten their plans to capture Midway Island.

That same month of April saw a reorganization in the Pacific.

---

[1] See Map 1 (opp. p. 5).
[2] See Chapter IX.
[3] For an account of this raid see S. E. Morison, *The History of United States Naval Operations*, Vol. III, pp. 389–398. (Henceforth referred to as 'Morison, Vol. I, II' etc.)

General D. MacArthur was appointed Supreme Allied Commander, South-West Pacific, which included Australia, and Admiral C. W. Nimitz, U.S.N. became Commander-in-Chief of the vast Pacific theatre stretching from the Aleutians to New Zealand.[1] Admiral Nimitz's responsibility was sub-divided into North, Central, and South Pacific, and Admiral R. L. Ghormley, U.S.N., was appointed to command the last named, covering the waters with which we here are particularly concerned.[2] The naval forces under General MacArthur were commanded by Vice-Admiral H. F. Leary, U.S.N., and included the Australian Navy's warships which had originally formed part of the Anzac Force.[3] The New Zealand warships now came under Admiral Ghormley. Hardly had this redistribution of responsibilities become effective when measures had to be taken to deal with the next Japanese move, aimed at the capture of Port Moresby in south-east New Guinea. On the 20th of April a strong enemy expedition escorted by cruisers and destroyers sailed from Truk in the Caroline Islands for Rabaul, whence it steamed southwards towards the Coral Sea. From it a small force was detached to occupy Tulagi in the Solomons, which was accomplished on the 3rd of May. The importance of Tulagi lay in its command of the excellent anchorage in adjacent Purvis Bay, and of the narrow waters between it and the island of Guadacanal.[4]

The invasion force for Moresby was powerfully covered by the light fleet carrier *Shoho* and four heavy cruisers, while a striking force of two large carriers (*Zuikaku* and *Shokaku*), two heavy cruisers and six destroyers prepared to enter the Coral Sea from the east.[5] The Japanese hoped to surprise the Allied forces sent to deal with the invasion fleet by attacking them from the rear with the striking force. By the 17th of April intelligence had indicated what was in the wind, and Admiral Nimitz sent down two powerful task forces formed around the fleet carriers *Lexington* and *Yorktown*, and a third force composed of cruisers. In addition the available Australian ships (*Australia* and *Hobart*) under Rear-Admiral J. G. Crace, and American ships from Admiral Leary's command, were put under Rear-Admiral F. J. Fletcher, U.S.N., who was in charge of the actual operations. It was not the last occasion when timely and accurate intelligence enabled Allied forces to be moved over big distances to a critical point. Indeed, all the great battles in the Pacific, from the Aleutians to the Coral Sea, demonstrate the tremendous advantage

---

[1] See Map 1 (opp. p. 5).

[2] Admiral Ghormley had been in London since July 1940 as head of the strong U.S. Naval Mission then sent over. See Vol. I, Appendix P.

[3] See p. 7.

[4] See Map 22 (p. 220).

[5] See Map 5 (opp. p. 33).

which the intelligence services can place in the hands of a nation's combat forces.

During the 4th and 5th of May the opposing fleets were still unaware of each other's strength and whereabouts, but early on the 6th the invasion force bound for Moresby was sighted by a reconnaissance aircraft off the eastern tip of New Guinea. On the morning of the 7th the American carrier aircraft found and sank the *Shoho*. Admiral Crace's force was heavily attacked by shore-based aircraft, but suffered no damage.

Throughout the 7th each side's search aircraft tried to locate the other's main forces. The Japanese succeeded, but the subsequent striking force failed to find Admiral Fletcher's ships in the prevailing low visibility, and returned to the carriers having accomplished nothing except the destruction of a detached fleet oiler and her destroyer escort. Early next morning the crisis came with simultaneous sighting by both sides of the other's fleet carriers. Striking forces were at once launched. The *Shokaku* was severely damaged; but both American carriers were hit. At first the *Lexington*'s damage did not seem serious, but later a violent explosion occurred, uncontrollable fires broke out, and she had to be abandoned and sunk. But the Japanese force had also suffered heavily, especially in aircraft, and their commander decided to withdraw.[1]

In a tactical sense the Battle of the Coral Sea was a drawn fight, but in terms of strategy it was an Allied victory; for the enemy failed to gain control of the Coral Sea, or to seize the important base of Port Moresby. Not only did the battle mark the opening of a new era in maritime tactics, for not a single surface ship of either side sighted the enemy, but it was also to prove the turning point in the struggle in the south Pacific. But this was, of course, not at once apparent, and the loss of the *Lexington* at a time when superiority in carrier strength lay with the enemy caused a good deal of anxiety. The *Hornet* and *Enterprise* were sent south in case the challenge was renewed, but when intelligence of Japanese intentions in the central Pacific came to hand they were recalled. In the enemy's camp the Coral Sea battle was not regarded as a serious setback, and they went ahead with their plans to attack Midway Island and the Aleutians. They hoped to seize Midway which 'acts as a sentry for Hawaii', to provoke action with the main American fleet, and to destroy it piecemeal and finally. The Aleutian operations aimed at the occupation of Attu, Kiska and Adak[2], but were chiefly intended to draw the Americans north and so aid the achievement of the main object of fighting a fleet action off Midway.

[1] For a full account of the Battle of the Coral Sea, see Morison, Vol. IV, pp. 21–64, and S. W. Kirby, *The War against Japan*, Vol. II. (In preparation.)

[2] See Map 1 (opp. p. 5).

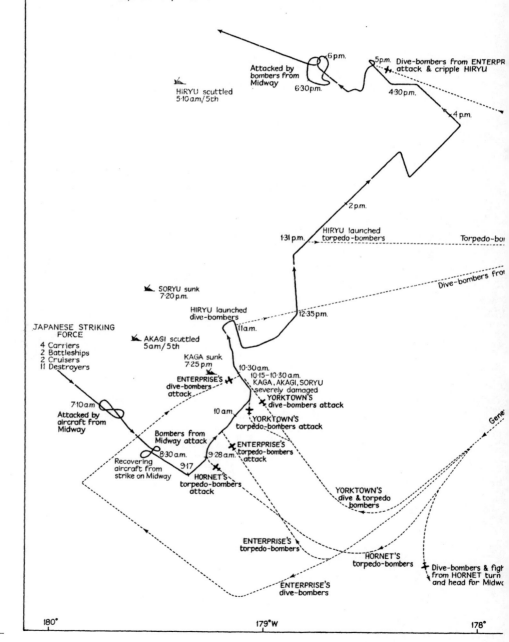

Map 6

THE BATTLE OF MIDWAY
4th June 1942

TASK FORCE 16 (ENTERPRISE, HORNET) .... ⟶
TASK FORCE 17 (YORKTOWN) .... ⟶ (dashed)
Tracks of Allied carrier air strikes .... ⟶ (dot-dash)
JAPANESE STRIKING FORCE .... ⟶
Tracks of Japanese carrier air strikes .... ⟶ (dot-dash)

Note:- All tracks are approximate, as are positions
in which Japanese ships were sunk

6 p.m.

5 p.m. Dive-bombers from ENTERPR
attack & cripple HIRYU

Attacked by
bombers from
Midway

6·30 p.m.

4·30 p.m.

HIRYU scuttled
5·10 a.m./5th

4 p.m.

2 p.m.

HIRYU launched
torpedo-bombers

Torpedo-bo

1·31 p.m.

Dive-bombers fro

SORYU sunk
7·20 p.m.

HIRYU launched
dive-bombers

12·35 p.m.

11 a.m.

JAPANESE STRIKING
FORCE

4 Carriers
2 Battleships
2 Cruisers
11 Destroyers

AKAGI scuttled
5 a.m./5th

KAGA sunk
7·25 p.m

10·30 a.m.

10·15-10·30 a.m.
KAGA, AKAGI, SORYU
severely damaged

ENTERPRISE'S
dive-bombers
attack

YORKTOWN'S
dive-bombers attack

7·10 a.m.

10 a.m.

YORKTOWN'S
torpedo-bombers attack

Attacked by
aircraft from
Midway

Bombers from
Midway attack

ENTERPRISE'S
torpedo-bombers
attack

Recovering
aircraft from
strike on Midway

8·30 a.m.

9·28 a.m.

9·17

HORNET'S
torpedo-bombers
attack

YORKTOWN'S
dive & torpedo
bombers

Gene

ENTERPRISE'S
torpedo-bombers

HORNET'S
torpedo-bombers

Dive-bombers & figh
from HORNET turn
and head for Midw

ENTERPRISE'S
dive-bombers

180°   179°W   178°

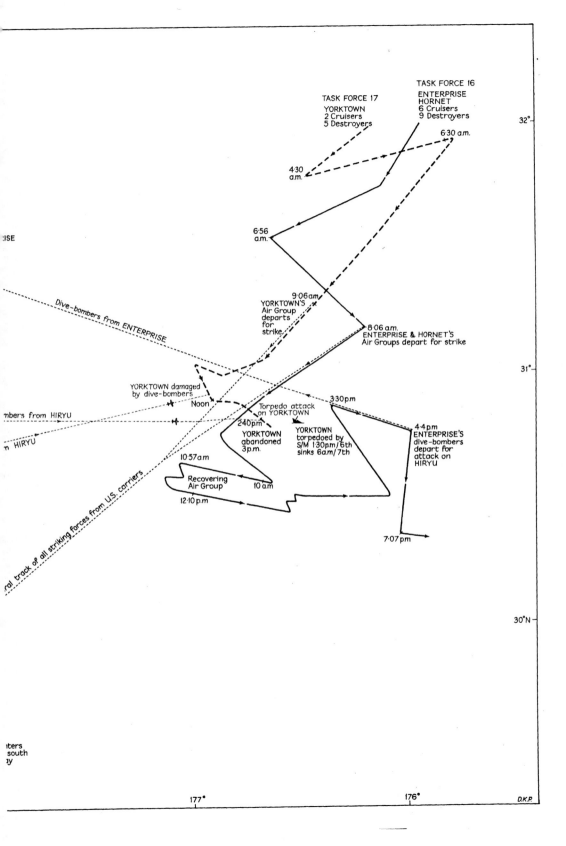

TASK FORCE 17
YORKTOWN
2 Cruisers
5 Destroyers

TASK FORCE 16
ENTERPRISE
HORNET
6 Cruisers
9 Destroyers

6·30 a.m.

32°

4·30
a.m.

6·56
a.m.

RISE

Dive-bombers from ENTERPRISE

9·06 a.m.
YORKTOWN'S
Air Group
departs
for
strike

8·06 a.m.
ENTERPRISE & HORNET'S
Air Groups depart for strike

31°

YORKTOWN damaged
by dive-bombers
Noon

3·30 p.m.

Torpedo attack
on YORKTOWN

mbers from HIRYU

2·40 p.m.
YORKTOWN
abandoned
3 p.m.

YORKTOWN
torpedoed by
S/M 1·30 p.m/6th
sinks 6 a.m/7th

4·4 p.m
ENTERPRISE'S
dive-bombers
depart for
attack on
HIRYU

n HIRYU

10·57 a.m.

Recovering
Air Group

10 a.m

7·07 pm

12·10 p.m.

ral track of all striking forces from U.S. carriers

30°N

ters
south
y

177°

176°

D.K.P.

By the middle of May the Americans had good evidence that a movement to the east, and in great strength, was intended by the Japanese Navy. In aircraft carriers the U.S. Navy's position was by no means happy. The *Lexington* had recently been sunk, the *Wasp* was on her way back to America after completing her invaluable reinforcements of Malta[1], and the *Saratoga*, having just completed repairs, was not yet ready for battle. The *Yorktown* had been damaged at Coral Sea, but was rapidly made fit for service at Pearl Harbour. She, the *Enterprise* and the *Hornet* were all that could be mustered to meet the threat from four (or possibly six) Japanese carriers. The aircraft complement of the three American ships totalled 233. We now know that 272 aircraft were embarked in Nagumo's striking force. It was natural for the U.S. Navy Department to seek means of mitigating its inferiority in carrier air strength. It is clear from the Admiralty's records that neither the nature nor the quality of the American Navy's intelligence regarding Japanese movements and intentions reached London until the 19th or 20th May. On the former date Admiral E. J. King, the American Chief of Naval Operations, signalled an 'appreciation' to Admiral Pound and asked either for a British aircraft carrier to be moved from the Indian Ocean to the south-west Pacific, or for air attacks to be made on Rangoon and the Andaman Islands, or for action to be taken to interrupt Japanese communications between Singapore and Rangoon. Not until late on the 22nd when, at the First Sea Lord's suggestion, Admiral Little, the head of the British Admiralty Delegation in Washington, had an interview with Admiral King, did the Admiralty become aware that an attack on Midway Island and the Aleutians appeared from intelligence to be a really strong probability. Though it is true that the Admiralty was unable at that time to meet the American request for the transfer of a British carrier to the Pacific, it is important that the problem which faced the British authorities should be viewed in the light of their other world-wide commitments.[2] The Eastern Fleet had recently completed the Madagascar operations, of which more will be said in a later chapter,[3] and two of its carriers were undergoing repairs at Kilindini. Furthermore, a large proportion of its strength was about to pass into the Mediterranean to assist in the June convoy to Malta.[4] None the less the Admiralty asked Admiral Somerville whether he could move a powerful force to Colombo, and possibly attack Sumatra or the Andaman Islands. Somerville considered that the best he could do with the ships left to him was to make a diversionary movement

---

[1] See pp. 57–59 and 60–61.
[2] Cf. Morison, Vol. IV, p. 81 footnote.
[3] See pp. 186–192.
[4] Operation 'Vigorous'. See pp. 67–71.

towards Ceylon. He would sail for that purpose on the 27th–28th May. It is hard to see what other help we could have given to our American Allies at their time of anxiety. Lest it still be felt that British carriers could have quickly reinforced the U.S. Pacific Fleet, it should be pointed out that they could hardly have covered the 11,000 miles from Kilindini to Pearl Harbour by the south of Australia in time to take part in the Battle of Midway. If any misunderstanding arose on this occasion, it seems that it was brought about partly by American slowness in giving the Admiralty the full intelligence of which they were possessed by the middle of May.

As the month of May drew to a close Admiral Nimitz completed his preparations.[1] Strong air reconnaissance and submarine patrols were established, and his striking power was built around Rear-Admiral F. J. Fletcher's Carrier Striking Force. The enemy's orders were issued on the 5th of May, and said that 'the Commander-in-Chief Combined Fleet will . . . invade and occupy strategic points in the western Aleutians and Midway Island'. The Japanese fleet, which was superior in all classes, started to move out from its bases between the 24th and 27th. Nagumo was again in command of the fleet carriers *Akagi*, *Kaga*, *Hiryu* and *Soryu*, but he was this time supported by Yamamoto's full strength of seven battleships, a light fleet carrier and a host of smaller ships. The Midway Occupation Force under Admiral Kondo covered and escorted the transports, while a smaller fleet, which included two light carriers, looked after the assault forces destined simultaneously to attack the western Aleutians. Admiral Nimitz had already decided not to allow his slender forces to be drawn off to counter this northern threat.

The great enemy Armada bound for Midway had the good fortune to be shielded by low visibility until the 3rd of June. Rear-Admiral Fletcher with the *Yorktown* and Rear-Admiral R. A. Spruance with the *Enterprise* and *Hornet* sailed from Pearl Harbour before the end of May, fuelled at sea and concentrated north-east of Midway Island on the 2nd of June.[2] The first sighting report came in next morning, actually on the enemy transport group. Attacks by American land-based aircraft followed, but they only damaged one ship. Fletcher, who expected the enemy carriers to attack Midway early on the 4th wisely held off during these first contacts.

At 5.34 a.m. on the 4th Nagumo's ships were sighted and reported about 200 miles south-west of the American carriers. The first enemy striking force bound for Midway had been flown off an hour earlier,

---

[1] For the following brief account of the Battle of Midway I am deeply indebted to the full and brilliantly told story in Volume IV of Professor S. E. Morison's *History of United States Naval Operations*. I have thought it best also to follow his system of using West Longitude date and Zone plus 12 time to relate the movements of the forces of both sides in a battle which, as he says, 'was fought across the International Date Line'.

[2] See Map 6 (opp. p. 37).

and the hundred-odd Japanese planes hit the small island base hard. But on this occasion to get in the first blow was not to prove an advantage; for Nagumo had committed half his striking power before he knew that American carriers were in the vicinity, and looking for him. At first Nagumo fared fortunately; for the land-based bombers and torpedo-bombers sent out from Midway did him no damage, and themselves suffered heavy losses. Then, at 7.15, he made the fatal mistake of ordering the ninety-three aircraft which he had kept in hand to deal with enemy warships to change their torpedoes for bombs, and prepare to make a second attack on the island base. Thirteen minutes later a Japanese cruiser's aircraft reported enemy surface ships, but made no mention of carriers. This made the Japanese Admiral hesitate, but it was 7.45 before he changed his mind and ordered his second striking force to prepare to attack the ship targets. Inevitably great confusion resulted on board the Japanese carriers. The first wave was about to return from Midway, and would soon have to land on to refuel and rearm, what time the second wave was trying to arm with bombs instead of torpedoes or, if it had already done so, to change back again to torpedoes.

Admiral Spruance, who aimed to catch the enemy while refuelling his planes, did not start to fly off his strike aircraft until just after 7 a.m. From the *Enterprise* and *Hornet* sixty-seven dive-bombers and twenty-nine torpedo-bombers, escorted by two score fighters, were despatched. Admiral Fletcher delayed his launch from the *Yorktown* for more than an hour, in case more enemy carriers were sighted. Meanwhile Nagumo continued to steam towards Midway, flew on most of his first striking force and then, at 9.17, turned north-east towards the American ships. He was caught exactly as Spruance had hoped—with all his strike aircraft on board to refuel and rearm. But his alteration of course to the north-east brought him one stroke of luck, for it caused the entire group of thirty-five dive-bombers from the *Hornet* to miss him; and that not only temporarily saved his ships, but left the American torpedo-bombers to attack alone. They went in most gallantly, suffered terrible losses, but obtained no hits. Out of forty-one torpedo aircraft from the three carriers only six returned. Happily the dive-bombers from the *Enterprise* and *Yorktown* soon came on the scene, and immediately transformed the battle. They attacked at about 10.30 while the Japanese ships were turning in all directions to avoid torpedoes. The *Enterprise's* group of thirty-seven aircraft did lethal damage to the *Akagi* (Nagumo's flagship) and the *Kaga*. At almost the same time the *Yorktown's* group struck the *Soryu*, and with just as deadly effect. By noon the three Japanese carriers were sinking; but American aircraft losses had been heavy, and one Japanese carrier, the *Hiryu*, was still afloat with an intact air group on board.

The *Hiryu* launched her full strength in two flights at about 11 a.m. and 1.30 p.m. to attack the *Yorktown*, which the enemy believed to be the only American carrier present. Admiral Yamamoto had meanwhile called down the two light carriers from the Aleutians expedition to join him. He hoped to engage in a general fleet action next morning. In spite of good work by her protecting fighters the *Yorktown* received three bomb hits, which started bad fires. Admiral Fletcher, like Nagumo a little earlier, had to shift his flag to a cruiser. Just when the damage was being got under control the second wave from the *Hiryu* came in, and two of their torpedoes crippled the *Yorktown*. The ship was abandoned, as it turned out prematurely; for she remained afloat, was boarded again next day, righted and got in tow, only to be torpedoed by a Japanese submarine on the 6th. She finally sank on the 7th. The Americans had to learn the hard way from the loss of this fine ship what we had learnt from a similar experience with the *Ark Royal*, namely that a list appears more dangerous than it is, that counter-flooding must be employed as soon as possible, and that a damaged ship should never be wholly abandoned.[1] But it was a heavy blow, coming at such a time.

Before the *Yorktown* was first hit search aircraft were looking for the surviving Japanese carrier. At 2.45 p.m. she was sighted, and the *Enterprise* again launched her redoubtable dive-bombers. At 5 p.m. they found the *Hiryu*, and dealt with her as effectively as with the earlier three. She sank next morning, and that was the end of Nagumo's famous and feared striking force, and of its 272 aircraft. Pearl Harbour, the ships lost off Kuantan, and those sunk at Port Darwin and off Ceylon had been amply avenged.

For some hours after this Yamamoto refused to bow to the inevitable. Not till the early hours of the 5th did he order a general retirement. Spruance had done brilliantly, and one cannot but accept the American historian's view that he was wise not to commit his two surviving carriers and their depleted aircrews to a headlong pursuit.[2] Had he continued westwards instead of withdrawing east with the *Enterprise* and *Hornet*, he might well have run right into the powerful surface forces which were seeking action with him during the night of the 4th–5th.

One more success sealed this splendid victory. A powerful Japanese squadron of four heavy cruisers had been ordered to bombard Midway in the early hours of the 5th. On sighting an American submarine an emergency turn was ordered, and in executing it the *Mogami* rammed the *Mikuma*. Both were damaged, and the former caught fire. A searching Catalina soon found the cripples. Shore-based aircraft from Midway attacked first, but it was once again the

[1] See Vol. I, pp. 533–534.
[2] See Morison, Vol. IV, pp. 140–143.

dive-bombers of the *Enterprise* and *Hornet* which did the execution. At 8 a.m. on the 6th both enemies were hit, and although the · *Mogami* survived and managed to struggle into Truk, her sister ship was sunk. It was these two ships which had sunk the *Houston* and *Perth* off the Java coast the previous February.[1]

Meanwhile Yamamoto had concentrated his great fleet, including the ships which had been covering the Aleutians expedition. Although he had ordered a general retirement in the early hours of the 5th, and had abandoned the assault on Midway, he still hoped to bring about a fleet action, or to draw Spruance within range of shore-based bombers from Wake Island. On the 6th, as soon as he heard of the carriers' attack on the *Mogami* and *Mikuma*, he sent a powerful cruiser force to find and attack the *Enterprise* and *Hornet*. That afternoon he turned his main body south, still hoping to intercept the American ships. But Spruance had no intention of being drawn into such a trap. Early on the 7th Yamamoto turned west for his fuelling rendezvous. Next day his offensive hopes were finally abandoned, and he returned whence he had come. His entire plan had been wrecked by 'four score American naval airmen', and that in spite of the great Japanese superiority in ships and gunpower.

In terms of naval tactics the victory of Midway was revolutionary. Many actions in which British aircraft carriers had fought earlier in the war, such as Taranto, Matapan and the pursuit of the *Bismarck*, had pointed the way to where the striking power now chiefly lay[2]; and Coral Sea had emphasised the lessons.[3] But it was in this great battle that the decisiveness of carrier-borne air weapons was finally and decisively proved. Virtually all the damage done on both sides was accomplished by them. The shore-based aircraft, though numerous and most gallantly flown, accomplished practically nothing, and their losses were heavy. Only the sinking of the *Yorktown* marred the completeness of the victory.

In terms of strategy the consequences were far reaching. The dominance of the Japanese navy in the Pacific had lasted for a few days short of six months. At Midway it was destroyed in a few hours. Never again could they build up a carrier force so powerful and so highly trained as Admiral Nagumo's, and henceforth they were steadily forced back on the defensive. On the other hand, American strength and skill were growing at a rate which, at the beginning of the year, had seemed fantastically impossible; and the power of the new task forces was soon to make itself felt throughout the length and breadth of the whole Pacific theatre. The strategic situation had been transformed overnight; and it in no way belittles the accom-

---

[1] See p. 16.
[2] See Vol. I, pp. 300–301, 427–431 and 394–418 respectively.
[3] See p. 36.

plishments of the ships which entered the fight later to remind
posterity that the checking of Japanese ambitions in the Coral Sea
and their decisive defeat at Midway were almost wholly accomplished by the four pre-war American carriers *Lexington, Yorktown,
Enterprise* and *Hornet.* Rarely can such rich benefits have been derived
from so few ships.

The Japanese plans were, of course, radically altered as a result of
this defeat, though the change was not at once accepted. In the
north they had seized the Aleutian Islands of Attu and Kiska;[1] in
the south they held a foothold in the strategically important Solomon
Islands, and still aimed to capture Samoa, Fiji and New Caledonia.
They knew that forces were being built up for an Allied counter-
offensive in these latter waters. Orders to launch attacks against the
Allied island bases had been given on the 18th of May, but after the
Battle of Midway they were postponed for two months. Then, on the
11th of July, the orders were cancelled, and a new directive naming
Port Moresby again as the main object was issued. This time it was
to be attacked overland from the bases which the enemy had seized
in northern New Guinea. The campaign opened on the 21st of July,
just when the Americans were preparing to launch their counter-
blow against the Solomon Islands. The fierce land and sea fighting
which developed from these rival offensives will form an important
part of a later chapter.

---

[1] See Map 1 (opp. p. 5).

CHAPTER II

THE AFRICAN CAMPAIGNS
1st January–31st July, 1942

'I am in desperation about Malta—we shall
lose it, I am afraid, past redemption.'
Nelson to Lieutenant-General Sir
James Erskine, 26th October 1799.

THE year 1941 had ended with the fortunes of the Mediterranean Fleet at a very low ebb.[1] The heavy losses suffered
in the closing months, diversions to the Far East, and the
strengthening of the German Air Force had forced us back on the
defensive once again; and the events of the first six months of 1942,
after another false dawn on land, produced the greatest period of
trial since Greece and Crete, and the greatest threat to our hold on
the whole Middle East position.

Admiral Pound had no illusions regarding the dangers we were
facing in the Mediterranean. At the end of 1941 he wrote to Admiral
Cunningham that 'There is nothing I should like better than to send
you a present of twenty or thirty destroyers and a dozen cruisers
. . . You know, however, how terribly hard-pressed we are in every
direction, and this will account for the smallness of our presents'.
Early in the New Year he warned all the naval Commanders-in-
Chief that 'the withdrawal of [the heavy ships] of the fleet from the
Mediterranean meant that the control of those waters depended on
our smaller warships supported by aircraft. The support of the Royal
Air Force was essential if Malta was to be held. The fall of Malta
would have incalculable results'. The period covered by this chapter
thus became a protracted and critical struggle to control the Mediterranean sea routes sufficiently to prevent the fall of Malta, and to
frustrate the enemy's purpose of building up his African army to
decisive strength.

At the beginning of January the Army of the Nile was still on the
offensive. Bardia fell on the 2nd and very soon afterwards the
Inshore Squadron (now commanded by Captain A. L. Poland)
prepared to escort stores and military equipment to Benghazi, which
we had captured for the second time on Christmas Eve 1941.[2] Very

---

[1] See Vol. I, pp. 538–540.
[2] See I. S. O. Playfair. *The Mediterranean and Middle East*, Vol. III, (in preparation) for a full account of these campaigns.

43

heavy commitments were falling on the fleet not only to supply the
army's needs through Tobruk, Derna and Benghazi, but to safeguard the heavy traffic between Port Said and Alexandria, the flow
of oil from Haifa to the main bases, and also the essential convoys to
Cyprus and ports on the Levant coast. Admiral Cunningham's
resources in asdic-fitted flotilla vessels totalled only about sixty,
including his few and precious fleet destroyers, and he warned the
Admiralty that he could 'by no means guarantee the security of the
Army's supply to Tripoli should we reach there'. Such circumstances
were not, however, to arise for many months to come, because the
enemy was so successful in passing supplies to Africa under cover of
his greatly superior naval and air strength that Rommel was soon
able to resume the offensive. In January two Italian 'battleship
convoys' got through to Tripoli, the first completely unscathed and
the second for the loss of one large ship sunk by air attack. Our
surface forces in Malta were far too weak to accept action with such
powerful enemy escorts, and although our submarines and aircraft
(both Fleet Air Arm and Royal Air Force), working from Malta and
from Cyrenaica, did all that they could, their numbers were inadequate to inflict decisive losses. Furthermore, we had to devote
much of our available effort to the ever-acute problem of keeping
Malta supplied. On the 8th of January the fast supply ship *Glengyle*
was safely taken there, and the *Breconshire* was brought out. The
double movement was covered and escorted by Rear-Admiral
P. Vian in the light cruiser *Naiad*, with the *Euryalus*, *Dido* and some
half-dozen destroyers. These new light cruisers, though of only
5,450 tons displacement, had good dual-purpose main armaments.
They had perforce to be used as the main escorts, the 'battle force'
on which the smaller vessels could depend for support in need, and
they did remarkable service in that capacity.[1] But it was in reality
something of a bluff, forced on us by the simple fact that these were
the most powerful ships on the station; and the enemy could, had he
accepted the many challenges offered, have called the bluff by
forcing close action. It was, without doubt, the determined and
spirited leadership of the 15th Cruiser Squadron's Commander
which prevented that ever happening.

In the middle of January another convoy, of four merchant ships,
sailed from the east for Malta. The anti-aircraft cruiser *Carlisle* and
two divisions of destroyers left with the merchantmen, and Admiral
Vian with his three light cruisers and six more destroyers left a day
later to overtake the convoy and reinforce the escorts. The *Penelope*
(Captain A. D. Nicholl) and five destroyers (Force K) meanwhile
sailed from Malta to meet the main body. By the 18th all forces were

---

[1] See Vol. I, p. 9, footnote 1.

united. One of the four merchantmen (the *Thermopylae*) developed defects, and was detached to Benghazi. She was later badly damaged by bombing and had to be sunk. The other three ships arrived in Malta safely. Air attacks on the main convoy were successfully countered by fighters of No. 201 Naval Co-operation Group, sent out from the airfields in Cyrenaica, by the escorts' gunfire and by Malta-based Hurricanes, as soon as the convoy came within their range. Unhappily, the loss of the advanced airfields was soon to deprive our surface ships of such effective cover, and operations in the central basin then at once became far more difficult and, finally, impossible. The only warship lost on this occasion was the destroyer *Gurkha*, which was torpedoed by U.133 on the 17th.[1] The Dutch ship *Isaac Sweers* gallantly towed her clear of burning oil fuel, and nearly all the crew were rescued. As soon as it was known that the Italian fleet had no intention of threatening his charges, Admiral Vian turned east again. On the 20th his forces were back in Alexandria. At Malta Admiral Sir Wilbraham Ford remained just long enough to see this convoy arrive. He had been there for almost exactly five years, and had contributed a great deal to remedying the early deficiencies in the defences of the island base, even though most of his bricks had to be made with little or no straw. His departure was widely regretted among the British services and the Maltese. Vice-Admiral Sir Ralph Leatham, who had formerly been Commander-in-Chief, East Indies, took over in Malta on the 19th of January.

Very soon after the convoy had arrived another operation was started to pass the *Breconshire* once more into Malta, and to bring out two empty ships of the last convoy. The escort and covering arrangements were similar to those which had recently proved so successful; all forces met east of the island on the 26th, the Malta and Alexandria escorts then exchanged their merchant ship charges, and all completed their journeys safely. That, however, was to be the last comparatively easy movement to and from the beleaguered island; for the land situation was meanwhile developing very unfavourably for us. On the 21st of January Rommel began his counter-offensive from El Agheila, and two days later Admiral Cunningham's War Diary noted that 'it began to appear dangerous'. Unloading of store ships at Benghazi had just begun to go smoothly, when preparations were once more made to abandon that very valuable advanced base. Two nights later naval vessels, lighters, tugs and all the paraphernalia needed to work the port, so recently and hopefully carried

---

[1] The last ship called *Gurkha*, one of the pre-war *Tribal*-class, was sunk off Norway on 9th April 1940 (see Vol. I, p. 171). This *Gurkha* was one of the *Laforey*-class and was originally to have been named *Larne*. After the loss of the first *Gurkha* she was renamed, as a naval compliment to the great fighting qualities of the Gurkha regiments.

there, started off to the east once again, sailing in three convoys and escorted by the hardworked Inshore Squadron's little ships.

To Admiral Cunningham the Axis successes on land were a heavy blow, and a note of deep anxiety can be detected in the letters he sent home at this time. Early in February he wrote to the First Sea Lord as follows: 'I am, as I am sure you are, bitterly disappointed at the turn the Libyan campaign has taken . . . I know it is not due to any naval shortcomings. We had just landed over 2,500 tons of petrol and over 3,000 tons of other stores at Benghazi, and had doubled the amount we had guaranteed to land daily at Tobruk . . . I have pressed on the Commander-in-Chief, Middle East Forces, the necessity of holding a line as far forward as possible . . · I am alarmed about Malta's supplies . . . If we could hold as far forward as Derna I believe we could supply [the island] from here . . . but we are already behind that line'. His apprehensions were soon to be proved only too well grounded.

There can be no period of the war in any theatre which illustrates more clearly the fundamental interdependence of the three services than this in the eastern Mediterranean—though similar examples were constantly being reproduced in all the other theatres. If the Army was driven back on land and the advanced airfields were lost, the Royal Air Force could no longer cover our Malta convoys, nor could our air striking forces attack the enemy's traffic to Tripoli. If Malta could not be supplied, the naval and air forces based there were bound gradually to become ineffective. If that happened the enemy's supply route was made much safer; and he could therefore reinforce the Afrika Korps quicker than we could build up the Army of the Nile. This in turn would make our condition on land more precarious. The circle was a complete one. The Navy depended on air cover, the R.A.F. on the soldiers holding the advanced airfields, and the Army on the other two services stopping the enemy convoys. And the circle of interdependence was now to be most grievously breached. In January, although it was true that, in the Commander-in-Chief's words, 'the magnificent efforts of our submarines, Fleet Air Arm and Royal Air Force aircraft' had been an outstanding feature, their successes had been inadequate to prevent the tide turning on land. Our submarines sank eight ships of 22,131 tons during the month, and aircraft added two more totalling 18,839 tons.[1] One of the latter was the valuable troop transport *Victoria* (13,098 tons) which was sunk by the combined efforts of the R.A.F. and of naval torpedo-bombers from Malta on the 23rd of January. But in spite of these successes 60,000 tons of Axis supplies were safely unloaded in North African ports. Moreover, although six more submarines

---

[1] See Table 3 (p. 76).

arrived on the station, such reinforcements were offset by the diversion of ships to the Eastern Fleet, which was occurring all the time. In particular the new fleet carrier *Indomitable* was being used to carry urgently needed fighters from Egypt to the Far East[1], and a destroyer escort had to be provided for her. Preparations were also in hand to move large numbers of troops, including an armoured division, to Malaya; and Admiral Cunningham had to take emergency steps to convert twenty fast cargo ships to carry the troops. In the event the deterioration of our position in North Africa prevented the large-scale reinforcement of Malaya at the expense of the Army of the Nile; but the need was long in the foreground of the Commanders-in-Chiefs' many problems.

As the German armies overran the Russian Black Sea ports it was natural that our Ally should try to save as much as possible of his shipping, which appeared likely to be trapped inside the Black Sea. After discussions in Ankara it was agreed that a number of ships, mostly tankers, should break out through the Bosphorus and the Dardanelles, and try to reach British ports. An icebreaker and three tankers made their attempts individually on various dates between December 1941 and February 1942. British 'conducting officers' were put on board in the Bosphorus, but the ships' crews were mostly Russian. The enemy, as he was bound to do, learnt what was in the wind, and managed to sink one tanker south of the Dardanelles; but the others ultimately arrived in Cyprus safely, though not without some narrow escapes.[2] The Russian authorities were warmly grateful for our help and co-operation in undertaking this daring and original venture.

Early in February Admiral Cunningham prepared to send another convoy to Malta from the east. The island base was now being more heavily attacked from the air, but the bombing had not yet produced a critical situation. On the 12th the convoy sailed from Alexandria in two sections. The merchantmen were the *Clan Chattan, Clan Campbell* and *Rowallan Castle*, and the escorts for the first part of the journey were again the *Carlisle* and eight destroyers. It will be remarked how often the fast merchant ships of good lifting and carrying capacity, such as of the 'Clan', 'Glen', 'City' and 'Blue Star' Lines appear in operations of this nature. They were still for the most part manned by their Merchant Navy crews, and were of inestimable value; but we never had enough of them.

Admiral Vian sailed some hours after the main convoy with the 15th Cruiser Squadron (two ships), and eight destroyers. On the 13th of February four empty ships, one of them the *Breconshire*,

---

[1] See p. 8.
[2] See *No Stars to Guide* by A. Seligman (Hodder and Stoughton, 1947) for an account of the way these Russian ships escaped.

sailed east from Malta, escorted by the *Penelope* and six Malta-based destroyers. Admiral Vian met the west-bound convoy early on the 14th, but the *Clan Campbell* had already been damaged by bombing and was sent to Tobruk. Next the *Clan Chattan* was hit, caught fire and had to be sunk. The Malta and Alexandria forces joined each other that afternoon, but the last ship of the loaded convoy, the *Rowallan Castle*, was near-missed and disabled. Efforts were made to tow her, but when it was plain that she could not reach Malta before dark, Admiral Cunningham ordered her to be sunk. It thus happened that Malta received no supplies at all from this substantial effort; and we had lost two fine merchantmen. It had been an ominous experience, and the consolation of the empty ships' safe passage to the east was a small one.

Concurrently with this unsuccessful attempt to revictual Malta the enemy was planning another 'battleship convoy' to Tripoli. By the 16th of February we had plain indications of what was in train, so four submarines were sent to patrol off the probable departure ports and five off Tripoli. On the 22nd reconnaissance aircraft located powerful enemy surface forces and two convoys of merchantmen in the central Ionian Sea, steaming towards Tripoli. Our submarines on patrol off the latter port were increased to eight, and the torpedo-bomber striking forces from Malta and the western desert set out to attack. But the convoys' route passed at the extreme range of our strike aircraft, and none of them managed to attack. Bad weather, which prevented the use of high speed, kept the Malta-based surface ships in harbour, and only one submarine got in an attack at long range; it, too, was unsuccessful. By the 24th we knew that the enemy convoys had arrived safely.

Towards the end of the month the anxieties caused by the disintegration of the Allied position in the Far East, and our precarious hold on the vital sea communications in the Indian Ocean, again impinged on our Mediterranean strategy. Six more destroyers were detached to the Eastern Fleet, and as a result Admiral Cunningham reorganised his meagre remaining strength into three flotillas. They were the 14th Flotilla led by the *Jervis*, the 22nd led by the *Sikh* (each of which consisted of eight fleet destroyers), and the 5th Flotilla, composed of about eight *Hunt*-class ships. On the 25th the *Indomitable*, flagship of Rear-Admiral D. W. Boyd, commanding the Eastern Fleet aircraft carriers, arrived at Port Sudan to pick up more fighter aircraft for the Far East, while the seaplane carrier *Engadine* carried out a similar service with cased naval fighters. The hurried attempt to reinforce our fighter strength against the sweeping tide of the Japanese advances was made too late to affect the situation[1], and

---

[1] See p. 8.

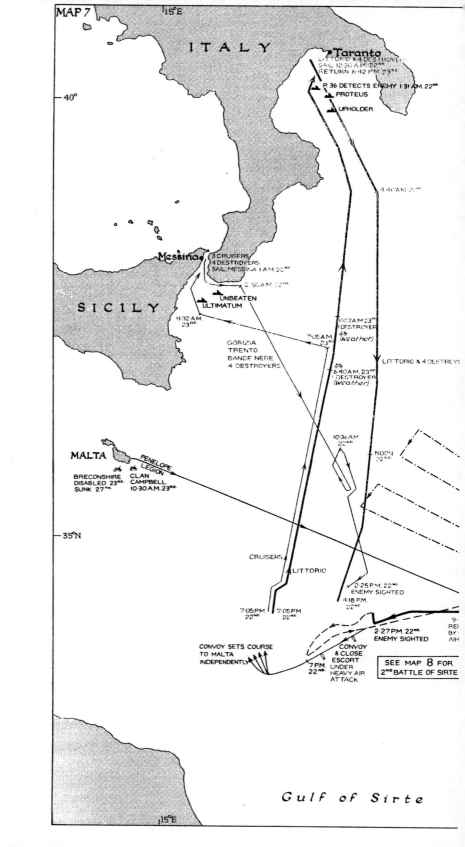

MAP 7

15°E

ITALY

— 40°

Taranto

LITTORIO & 4 DESTROYERS
SAIL 12:30 A.M. 22ND
RETURN 6:42 P.M. 23RD

P.36 DETECTS ENEMY 1:31 A.M. 22ND
PROTEUS
UPHOLDER

4:40 A.M. 23RD

Messina

3 CRUISERS
4 DESTROYERS
SAIL MESSINA 1 A.M. 22ND

2:50 A.M. 22ND

SICILY

UNBEATEN
ULTIMATUM

11:32 A.M.
23RD

7:05 A.M.
23RD

10:07 A.M. 23RD
1 DESTROYER
(Weather)

GORIZIA
TRENTO
BANDE NERE
4 DESTROYERS

6:40 A.M. 23RD
1 DESTROYER
(Weather)

LITTORIO & 4 DESTROYERS

10:36 A.M.
22ND

NOON
22ND

MALTA

PENELOPE
LEGION

BRECONSHIRE   CLAN
DISABLED 23RD   CAMPBELL
SUNK 27TH.   10:30 A.M. 23RD.

— 35°N

CRUISERS

LITTORIO

2:25 P.M. 22ND
ENEMY SIGHTED

4:18 P.M.
22ND

7:05 P.M.   7:05 P.M.
22ND   22ND

2:27 P.M. 22ND
ENEMY SIGHTED

9-
RE
BY
AIR

CONVOY SETS COURSE
TO MALTA
INDEPENDENTLY

7 P.M.
22ND

CONVOY
& CLOSE
ESCORT
UNDER
HEAVY AIR
ATTACK

SEE MAP 8 FOR
2ND BATTLE OF SIRTE

Gulf of Sirte

15°E

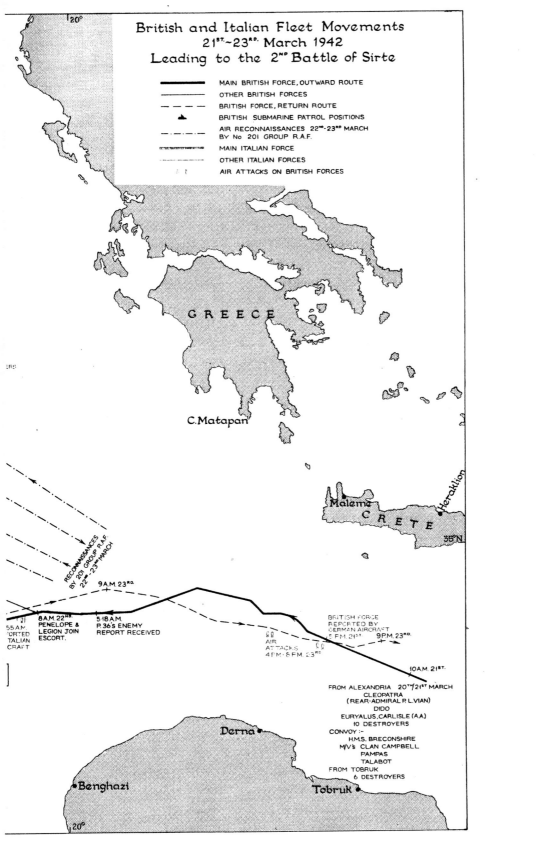

British and Italian Fleet Movements
21ST~23RD March 1942
Leading to the 2ND Battle of Sirte

━━━━━━━━	MAIN BRITISH FORCE, OUTWARD ROUTE
────────	OTHER BRITISH FORCES
─ ─ ─ ─ ─	BRITISH FORCE, RETURN ROUTE
◂	BRITISH SUBMARINE PATROL POSITIONS
─·─·─·─	AIR RECONNAISSANCES 22ND-23RD MARCH BY No 201 GROUP R.A.F.
▭▭▭▭▭	MAIN ITALIAN FORCE
··········	OTHER ITALIAN FORCES
≀≀ ≀	AIR ATTACKS ON BRITISH FORCES

20°

GREECE

C.Matapan

ERS

RECONNAISSANCES BY 201 GROUP R.A.F. 22ND-23RD MARCH

Maleme

CRETE

Heraklion

36°N

9 A.M. 23RD.

55 A.M.
PORTED
TALIAN
CRAFT

8 A.M. 22ND.
PENELOPE &
LEGION JOIN
ESCORT.

5·18 A.M.
P.36's ENEMY
REPORT RECEIVED

AIR
ATTACKS
4 P.M.-5 P.M. 23RD.

BRITISH FORCE
REPORTED BY
GERMAN AIRCRAFT
5 P.M. 21ST.   9 P.M. 23RD.

10 A.M. 21ST.

FROM ALEXANDRIA 20TH/21ST MARCH
CLEOPATRA
(REAR-ADMIRAL P. L. VIAN)
DIDO
EURYALUS, CARLISLE (A.A.)
10 DESTROYERS
CONVOY :-
H.M.S. BRECONSHIRE
M/V's CLAN CAMPBELL
PAMPAS
TALABOT
FROM TOBRUK
6 DESTROYERS

Derna

Benghazi

Tobruk

20°

the use once again of a fleet carrier on aircraft ferry trips inevitably deprived the operational fleets of the vital element of carrier-borne air power. It is easy to imagine how Sir Andrew Cunningham would have reacted to the Italians' 'battleship convoys' had the *Indomitable* and adequate heavy ship strength been available to him; and had those convoys been stopped Rommel's advance into Egypt could hardly have been carried out.

Yet another diversion of strength from the Mediterranean took place in the middle of February. When the *Scharnhorst* and *Gneisenau* began to show signs of activity in Brest[1], the Admiralty became anxious about a break-out into the Atlantic and, in particular, for the safety of the big troop convoy WS.16 which consisted of twenty important ships, and was due to sail on the 16th. Force H, now commanded by Rear-Admiral E. N. Syfret, who had relieved Admiral Somerville in January on the latter's appointment to command the Eastern Fleet, was therefore recalled to the Clyde. Its ships did not return to their normal station until the 24th, by which time the enemy's Brest squadron had made the passage up-Channel to Germany. On the 27th Admiral Syfret sailed from Gibraltar to the east with his full strength to fly air reinforcements to Malta, but defects in the aircrafts' fuel tanks frustrated the attempt. It was repeated by the *Malaya, Eagle, Argus, Hermione* and destroyers on the 6th of March; seven Blenheims from Gibraltar and fifteen Spitfires from the carriers reached Malta safely on the 7th. These were the first Spitfires to join in the defence of the island.

Though we had not succeeded in interfering with the enemy's main convoys to North Africa, in February the Mediterranean submarines again took a satisfactory toll of Axis shipping (seven ships of 31,220 tons); but the *Tempest* was sunk by an Italian torpedo-boat and P.38 by a mine.[2] The *Thrasher* attacked a ship off Suda Bay on the 16th and in return was heavily engaged by enemy aircraft and anti-submarine forces. When she surfaced after dark two unexploded bombs were found inside her hull casing. They were safely removed at imminent risk to themselves by Lieutenant P. S. W. Roberts and Petty Officer T. W. Gould. Apart from the danger of the bombs exploding, the two volunteers had no possibility of escape

---

[1] See pp. 150–161.

[2] New submarines of the various War Programmes had only been given numbers by the Admiralty. The Prime Minister took exception to this practice, urged the Admiralty to find names for them all, and himself offered suggestions (see his minutes to First Sea Lord and First Lord of 19th and 27th December 1942 respectively, reproduced in *The Second World War*, Vol. IV, pp. 815 and 818). The naming of the numbered submarines took place at various dates, but a few, of which P.38 was one, were lost before they received their names. In these volumes, where a submarine received a name, she is always referred to by it, even though she may not have been named at the date of her first appearance in the narrative.

E

if the submarine had suddenly dived. Both were awarded the Victoria Cross.

Bombing raids on Malta were now increasing in weight, but had not yet seriously interfered with the submarine, surface ship and air offensives conducted from the fortress base. But such interference soon began, and as a foretaste of things to come the submarine base was heavily attacked early in March, and three of the 10th Flotilla's boats were damaged.

By the 9th of March the enemy was known again to be active in sending supply ships to Africa. Two convoys, one outward and one homeward bound, were sighted 200 miles east of Tripoli. The Malta air striking force could not reach them. Eight R.A.F. Beauforts of No. 39 Squadron from the Western Desert attacked, but did not achieve any success. In the early hours of the 10th Admiral Vian sailed from Alexandria to intercept the enemy with his three light cruisers and nine destroyers. The chance was seized to bring out from Malta the *Cleopatra* and the damaged destroyer *Kingston*. They were heavily attacked on the way, but got through safely. Again No. 201 Group's Beaufighters gave excellent protection to the ships, but late on the evening of the 11th the cruiser flagship, the *Naiad*, was torpedoed and sunk by U.565 about fifty miles off the north African shore between Mersa Matruh and Sollum. The Admiral and the great majority of her crew were picked up by the destroyers, the flag was transferred to the *Dido* and on the 12th Vian's depleted force was back in Alexandria. Admiral Cunningham felt this deeply. 'Such a loss, that little *Naiad*', he wrote to the First Sea Lord. 'A highly efficient weapon, and a ship's company with a grand spirit'.

German as well as Italian submarines were at the time very active both against the inshore shipping route used to carry the Army's supplies to Cyrenaican ports, and against our convoys which ran from the Canal up the Levant coast to Haifa and Beirut. It was always difficult to find enough escorts for this traffic, and the balance of success still lay with the U-boats. None the less two Germans (U.577 and U.374) and two Italians (the *Ammiraglio Saint Bon* and the *Medusa*) were sunk in January, and three more Italians (the *Ammiraglio Millo*, *Guglielmotti* and *Tricheco*) and one German U-boat were destroyed in March. What was especially remarkable was that six of these eight successes fell to our own submarines. The *Unbeaten* (Lieutenant-Commander E. A. Woodward) and the *Upholder* (Lieutenant-Commander M. D. Wanklyn) each sank two enemies, and the *Thorn* and *Ultimatum* accounted for the other two. In March our submarines sank a further six ships (17,298 tons), and the *Torbay* penetrated most daringly into Corfu harbour in search of enemy shipping. For this, the climax of many highly adventurous patrols, her Captain, Commander A. C. C. Miers, received the Victoria

Cross. The Royal Air Force added four enemy ships (13,192 tons) to the score for the month when, on 2nd–3rd of March, No. 37 Squadron's Wellingtons made a highly successful raid on Palermo Harbour.

At the beginning of this phase, out of a total operational strength of ninety-one German U-boats, twenty-one were working inside the Mediterranean.[1] As the two sunk in January were replaced by new arrivals, their total remained fairly constant for the first three months of the year. Between March and June, however, we sank five of their number[2], and as no more reinforcements arrived until the autumn their strength had declined to sixteen at the end of July. It will be told later how they caused us substantial losses.

Two days after Admiral Vian had returned to Alexandria in a different flagship from that in which he had left, his squadron was off to sea again—this time to bombard enemy installations on the island of Rhodes in the early hours of the 15th of March. Next day they were back in Alexandria, though not for long, because a new attempt to supply Malta from the east was in train. On the 20th the hard-worked naval supply ship *Breconshire* (Captain C. A. G. Hutchison) and the merchantmen *Clan Campbell*, *Pampas* and *Talabot* sailed in convoy, escorted by the *Carlisle* and six destroyers. Admiral Vian with the *Cleopatra*, *Dido* and *Euryalus* and four more destroyers left soon afterwards to overtake the convoy, while six *Hunt*-class destroyers of the 5th Flotilla joined up later from Tobruk.[3] The Army meanwhile staged a threat to the enemy's shore airfields in order to divert his attention from the convoy. By daylight on the 21st all the naval forces were in company. Early next day they were joined by the *Penelope* and *Legion* from Malta. As our forces had already been reported by enemy aircraft, and the submarine P.36 had signalled that heavy units had left Taranto at about 1.30 a.m., Admiral Vian knew that a major surface encounter was likely to take place during the afternoon of the 22nd. Actually the battleship *Littorio* (nine 15-inch guns) and six destroyers (two of which soon turned back) had sailed from Taranto, and the cruisers *Gorizia* and *Trento* (8-inch) and *Giovanni Delle Bande Nere* (6-inch) and four more destroyers had left Messina in the early hours of that morning to intercept our convoy.

Come what might, Admiral Vian was determined that the convoy should go on to Malta. He had already decided what his tactics would be in the event of an encounter such as now appeared imminent, and his squadron had rehearsed the manoeuvres before sailing. This foresight was magnificently rewarded by the unhesitating way

---

[1] See Vol. I, pp. 473–5 regarding the arrival of German U-boats in the Mediterranean.
[2] See Appendix J.
[3] See Map 7 (opp. p. 49).

in which the cruisers and destroyers carried out the Admiral's intentions, as soon as a prearranged signal to 'carry out diversionary tactics, using smoke to cover the escape of the convoy' was made. The Admiral's orders had been sent by air to the *Penelope* in Malta, but she had not received them by the time she sailed. Captain Nicholl thus found himself fighting in a long series of fast-moving, intricate actions without having received one word of written or spoken instructions from his Admiral. Yet so decisive was Vian's leadership that the *Penelope's* Captain was never in any doubt regarding what was required of him.

At 12.30 p.m. the Admiral ordered the necessary preparatory moves. His forces were organised in six divisions.[1] On the approach of the enemy the first five were to stand out from the convoy, and concentrate in their several divisions as a striking force. The sixth would prepare to lay smoke across the wake of the convoy, while the remaining five *Hunt*-class destroyers re-formed as its close escort. The *Euryalus* was the first ship to sight the enemy, at 2.27 p.m. The Admiral at once made the pre-arranged signal, and the striking forces began to move out to the north towards the Italian squadron of two 8-inch and one 6-inch cruiser and four destroyers. The wind was blowing strongly (twenty-five knots) from the south-east, and the sea was rough. The strength and direction of the wind were ideal to shroud the convoy with the smoke screen now laid by all the warships except the convoy's close escort.[2] The convoy meanwhile turned to the south-west, and was soon engaged in a heavy air battle of its own.

As soon as he recognized the enemy to be cruisers and not, as he had first thought, battleships, Admiral Vian led off with the *Cleopatra* and *Euryalus* to attack them. The enemy, however, turned right away, and in the long-range gun duel which followed no damage was done to either side. At 3.35 p.m. Vian told his Commander-in-Chief that the enemy had been driven off, and an hour later he himself had nearly overtaken the convoy. So ended the first phase of the battle. The convoy had meanwhile been splendidly defended by the little *Hunts'* 4-inch guns, and the air attacks had done no damage.

No sooner had the Admiral again taken the convoy under his personal protection than an even graver threat developed. The Italian battleship *Littorio* and also the three enemy cruisers were sighted to the north-east. The *Littorio's* force and the cruisers joined

---

[1] Division 1 *Jervis, Kipling, Kelvin, Kingston.*
     ,,   2 *Dido, Penelope, Legion.*
     ,,   3 *Zulu, Hasty.*
     ,,   4 *Cleopatra* (flagship), *Euryalus.*
     ,,   5 *Sikh, Lively, Hero, Havock.*
     ,,   6 *Carlisle, Avon Vale* (smoke layers).
[2] See Map 8 (opp. p. 53).

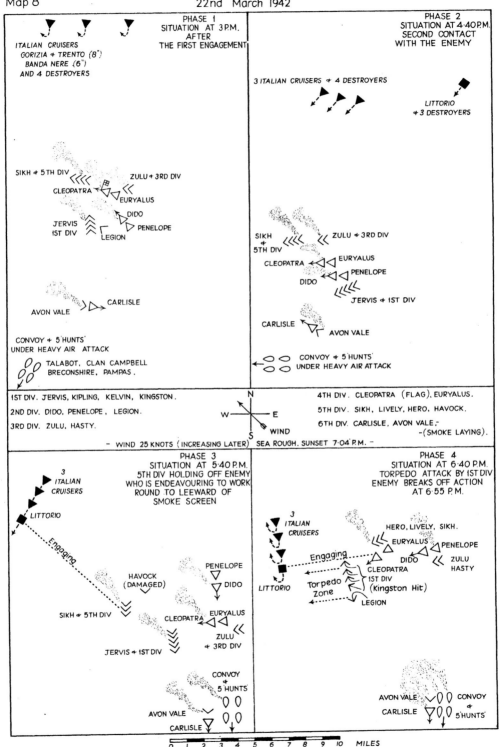

Map 8

SECOND BATTLE OF SIRTE
22nd March 1942

PHASE 1
SITUATION AT 3 P.M.
AFTER
THE FIRST ENGAGEMENT

ITALIAN CRUISERS
GORIZIA & TRENTO (8")
BANDA NERE (6")
AND 4 DESTROYERS

SIKH & 5TH DIV
ZULU & 3RD DIV
CLEOPATRA
EURYALUS
DIDO
JERVIS
1ST DIV
PENELOPE
LEGION

AVON VALE
CARLISLE

CONVOY & 5 'HUNTS'
UNDER HEAVY AIR ATTACK
TALABOT, CLAN CAMPBELL
BRECONSHIRE, PAMPAS.

PHASE 2
SITUATION AT 4·40 P.M.
SECOND CONTACT
WITH THE ENEMY

3 ITALIAN CRUISERS & 4 DESTROYERS

LITTORIO
& 3 DESTROYERS

SIKH
&
5TH DIV
ZULU & 3RD DIV
EURYALUS
CLEOPATRA
PENELOPE
DIDO
JERVIS & 1ST DIV

CARLISLE
AVON VALE

CONVOY & 5 'HUNTS'
UNDER HEAVY AIR ATTACK

1ST DIV. JERVIS, KIPLING, KELVIN, KINGSTON.

2ND DIV. DIDO, PENELOPE, LEGION.

3RD DIV. ZULU, HASTY.

N
W — E
S
WIND

— WIND 25 KNOTS (INCREASING LATER) SEA ROUGH. SUNSET 7·04 P.M. —

4TH DIV. CLEOPATRA (FLAG), EURYALUS.

5TH DIV. SIKH, LIVELY, HERO, HAVOCK.

6TH DIV. CARLISLE, AVON VALE, -
-(SMOKE LAYING).

PHASE 3
SITUATION AT 5·40 P.M.
5TH DIV HOLDING OFF ENEMY
WHO IS ENDEAVOURING TO WORK
ROUND TO LEEWARD OF
SMOKE SCREEN

3
ITALIAN
CRUISERS

LITTORIO

Engaging

HAVOCK
(DAMAGED)
PENELOPE
DIDO

SIKH & 5TH DIV
CLEOPATRA
EURYALUS
ZULU
& 3RD DIV
JERVIS & 1ST DIV

CONVOY
&
5 'HUNTS'

AVON VALE
CARLISLE

PHASE 4
SITUATION AT 6·40 P.M.
TORPEDO ATTACK BY 1ST DIV
ENEMY BREAKS OFF ACTION
AT 6·55 P.M.

3
ITALIAN
CRUISERS
HERO, LIVELY, SIKH.
EURYALUS
PENELOPE
Engaging
DIDO
ZULU
CLEOPATRA
HASTY
LITTORIO
Torpedo
Zone
1ST DIV
(Kingston Hit)
LEGION

AVON VALE
CARLISLE
CONVOY
&
5 'HUNTS'

0 1 2 3 4 5 6 7 8 9 10 MILES
Scale Approx Only

company at about 4.40 p.m., just when the British striking forces started to repeat their tactics of standing towards the enemy and laying smoke.[1] From now until 7 p.m. there took place a series of actions, with the British ships plunging in and out of 'the enormous area of smoke', and the enemy trying to work round to the west of the zone of obscurity which we had created, and so close the convoy. As the smoke was drifting fast to leeward, and the Italians refused to enter it for fear of the destroyers' torpedoes, for a time they were kept well away from their quarry. None the less, and in spite of the convoy having turned to a south-westerly course, the enemy's greatly superior speed was bound ultimately to bring him within striking range—if he held on long enough. Hence the vital need for our light forces to threaten him, and to force him to turn away.

It was probably the first time since the days of sail when to hold the 'weather gauge' was decisively important. Vian expected the enemy to try and wrest it from him by working to the east of the smoke, and at 5.30 he steered in that direction to head him off. This nearly gave the Italians their chance, for their main force was sighted ten minutes later at only eight miles' range by the 5th division of destroyers—the *Sikh* (Captain St. J. A. Micklethwait), *Lively* and *Hero*. The fourth ship, the *Havock*, had just been hit by a 15-inch shell and sent to join the convoy. The three destroyers engaged with guns and torpedoes, and tried to extend the smoke screen further west to shield the now seriously threatened merchantmen. With seas sweeping over them, rolling and pitching violently, blinded by smoke and spray, and under heavy fire they struggled south, fighting their guns under most difficult conditions. By 6 p.m. the enemy was none the less drawing slowly ahead; but what Micklethwait described with characteristic understatement as the 'somewhat unequal contest' still continued.[2]

Meanwhile, the British cruisers had turned back to the west. At almost exactly 6 p.m., just at the critical time, the *Cleopatra* suddenly came clear of the smoke, and she and the *Euryalus* engaged the *Littorio* at about 13,000 yards. The British flagship fired torpedoes, and the enemy turned away. A respite, though quickly to be proved only a temporary one, had been gained. With the range down to only 6,000 yards Captain Micklethwait's destroyers hauled round to the north to lay a new smoke screen. They had played their part most successfully, and had saved a situation which at one time looked desperate. As soon as he knew that these enemies had borne away from the direction of the convoy, Admiral Vian steered east once again to prevent the Italian cruisers, for whom he could not at the time account, from working round to windward of the smoke.

---

[1] See Map 8. Phase 2.
[2] See Map 8. Phase 3.

He held to an easterly course till 6.17 p.m. When he could see that there were no enemies in that direction, he at once turned back again to relieve the pressure on the destroyers.

It was now the turn of the 1st division of destroyers (*Jervis, Kipling, Kelvin* and *Kingston* under Captain A. L. Poland). They had received Micklethwait's report of the nearness of the enemy, and at 6.08 they steered to close him. At 6.34 the *Littorio* was sighted 12,000 yards away. In line abreast, at twenty-eight knots, their forward guns firing and they themselves under heavy but erratic fire, Captain Poland's ships moved in to attack with torpedoes.[1] At 6.41, when the range was only three miles, they turned and fired twenty-five torpedoes. The *Kingston* received a 15-inch-shell hit at the time and was crippled; but she got her torpedoes away. None of the torpedoes hit, but their threat caused the Italian Admiral again to turn away. Admiral Vian's cruisers came back in time to support Poland's destroyers with their guns as the torpedo attack was being made. Between 6.30 and 6.40 p.m. the little cruisers fought another gun action with the giant *Littorio* and the Italian cruisers. It ended soon after the 1st division's attack was completed. Finally, Micklethwait's three surviving ships came into action once more. At 6.55 they also turned to fire torpedoes, but smoke obscured the target at the critical moment and only the *Lively* got hers off. She, like the *Kingston*, received damage from a 15-inch shell as she turned to fire. Again none of the torpedoes hit, but the enemy was now resolutely retiring to the north-west, and the battle was over. True, our ships had expended a great deal of ammunition without causing appreciable injury to the far more heavily protected Italian ships; but they had defeated their purpose of attacking the convoy. It was indeed a classic example of the ability of a weaker force, handled with skill and determination, to parry the intentions of a far stronger enemy; and, apart from the deeds of his destroyer, the *Cossack*[2], Admiral Vian's name will always be associated with the First and Second Battles of Sirte, fought on the 17th of December 1941 and the 22nd of March 1942.[3] The tactics which he employed were, it is interesting to remember, similar to those which Kempenfeldt had proposed over 160 years previously to the great First Lord Sir Charles Middleton (later Lord Barham).[4]

---

[1] See Map 8 (opp. p. 53), Phase 4.
[2] See Vol. I, pp. 151–153 and 414.
[3] See Vol. I, p. 535, regarding the First Battle of Sirte.
[4] 'Much . . . depends upon this fleet; 'tis an inferior against a superior fleet; therefore the greatest skill and address is requisite to counteract the designs of the enemy, to watch and seize the favourable opportunity for action . . . to hover near the enemy, keep him at bay, and prevent his attempting to execute anything but at risk and hazard to command their attention and oblige them to think of nothing but being on their guard against your attack'. Kempenfeldt to Middleton, July 1779. (The Barham Papers, Navy Records Society, Vol. I, p. 292.)

At dusk, and in face of a rising gale, Admiral Vian turned east
with those of his ships which were fit to make the passage back to
Alexandria. The damaged *Havock* and *Kingston* could not do so, and
had to struggle on to Malta. At about 7 p.m. Captain Hutchison of
the *Breconshire* dispersed the convoy on slightly diverging courses for
Malta. Each ship had a few destroyers as escort. Unfortunately the
delays caused by the recent battle prevented the convoy making
harbour early on the 23rd, and this gave the German bombers
another chance. They renewed their attacks at daylight, and the
escorts were handicapped by being desperately short of ammunition.
None the less the *Pampas* and *Talabot* entered the Grand Harbour at
about 9.30 a.m. 'to the cheers of the populace'. The *Breconshire* was
not so lucky. She was hit and disabled only eight miles from her
destination. The *Penelope* tried to tow her, but in the prevailing heavy
sea it proved impossible. She was finally taken to Marsaxlokk harbour, on the south side of Malta, on the 25th; but two days later she
was there sunk by more bombing attacks. Some of her cargo of fuel
was later salved, but her hull remained until after the war on the
rocks of the island which she had so often fought to supply. Lastly,
the *Clan Campbell* was hit at 10.20 on the 23rd, twenty miles from
Malta, and sank quickly. The welcoming cheers of the Maltese for
the arrival of the *Pampas* and *Talabot* were, unhappily, soon proved
premature. For in the savage air attacks which the Luftwaffe again
turned on to the island fortress they were both hit. Only about a
fifth of the 26,000 tons of cargo loaded in the convoy for Malta was
safely landed. It was plain that the crisis of supply had not, for all
the gallantry of the effort, been surmounted; and that the time of
greatest trial for the Maltese, and for the soldiers, sailors and airmen
defending their island, was close at hand.

Admiral Vian's force received a heart-warming welcome from all
the ships in the port when they reached Alexandria on the 24th. The
Commander-in-Chief signalled 'Well done 15th Cruiser Squadron
and destroyers,' and the Prime Minister sent his congratulations.
But however well deserved were the reception and the messages, the
cruel facts were that the object of the operation had not been fully
accomplished, and that the Mediterranean Fleet had again been
grievously weakened, especially in destroyers. Nine fleet destroyers
at Alexandria and four more at Malta, as well as one *Hunt*-class ship,
were all damaged in greater or less degree. On the 24th the *Southwold*
was mined and sunk off the Grand Harbour while helping to shield
the *Breconshire*. Two days later the *Legion* and the submarine P.39
were sunk in Malta, and as if that was not enough the *Jaguar* and a
Royal Fleet Auxiliary oiler were torpedoed and sunk by a U-boat
off the African coast. By way of recompense, on the 1st of April the
submarine *Urge* (Lieutenant-Commander E. P. Tomkinson) sank

the Italian cruiser *Giovanni delle Bande Nere* north of Sicily. Admiral Cunningham told the London authorities the bare truth when, on the 28th of this very difficult month, he signalled that to run another convoy to Malta he must have more destroyers, and that there must be greater fighter strength at the receiving end; some means, he said, had also to be found to divert the attention of the enemy air and surface forces from the next convoy.

But it was actually Admiral Cunningham's successor who had to deal with these acute problems; for on the 1st of April Admiral Pridham-Wippell hoisted his flag in the *Valiant* in temporary succession to his former Commander-in-Chief, whose next appointment was to Washington as head of the British naval mission and as Admiral Pound's representative on the Combined Chiefs of Staff Committee. But Admiral Cunningham's departure made a break in the Mediterranean Fleet's life which could never be healed. Though he returned to the same command later in the year, and then saw the tide turn to victory in the theatre with which his name will always be associated, it is for the first, long period of his command from the 1st of June 1939 to the 1st of April 1942 that he will mainly be remembered. For he then led his famous fleet both in great victories like Taranto and Matapan and through grave trials like Greece and Crete. Through all those many months it was his ardent, determined spirit, his relentless seeking for a chance to strike offensive blows, which fired and inspired the officers and men of his fleet, and which won their unstinted admiration and affection. Only rarely, but always when he is most needed, does Britain find a leader of Cunningham's great qualities; and all who served under him in the Mediterranean will remember him, and will pass on to generations still to come how 'A.B.C.' led them, demanded all from them—and received all that they could give in return. Perhaps an anecdote, told to the author of this history by one of the Admiral's staff officers, epitomises Admiral Cunningham's strength of character and indomitable determination better than many pages recounting all his battles. At the time of Crete, when the fleet was suffering heavy losses every day, the staff officer said to his Commander-in-Chief that the Navy could not go on fighting the Luftwaffe single-handed.[1] It was, he considered, merely butting one's head against a brick wall. To that opinion the Admiral replied: 'What you have forgotten, you miserable undertaker, is that you may be loosening a brick'. Yet all who knew their Commander realised how deeply he felt then, and at all times of tragedy, the loss of so many of his fine ships and of their irreplaceable officers and men. 'I look forward to the day', he said in his farewell message, 'when the Mediterranean Fleet will sweep

---

[1] See Vol. I, pp. 440–449.

The Second Battle of Sirte, 22nd March 1942.
H.M.S. *Cleopatra* laying smoke screens. (See pp. 52–54) Taken from H.M.S. *Euryalus*.

The Second Battle of Sirte. 22nd March 1942.
H.M.S. *Kipling* in action.

Malta Convoy, March 1942. The merchant ship *Pampas*, one of the only two ships to reach Malta after the Second Battle of Sirte, severely damaged in harbour.

Grand Harbour, Malta, February 1942. Wreck of H.M.S. *Maori*, damaged by bombing, in the foreground.

The light cruiser *Penelope* ('H.M.S. *Pepperpot*') after her escape from Malta, 8th April 1942 (see p. 58).

Convoy to Malta, Operation 'Vigorous', June 1942, showing 15th Cruiser Squadron and merchantmen. (See pp. 67–71).

Convoy to Malta, Operation 'Vigorous', June 1942. Ships of the 15th Cruiser Squadron with the dummy battleship *Centurion* in the background. (See p. 68).

the sea clear and re-establish our age-old control of this waterway so vital to the British Empire'. Happily, he was to be there again when that day arrived, for in August it was decided that he should be Naval Commander-in-Chief for the invasion of North Africa, and in October he returned to London to give his whole attention to the planning and launching of the first Allied offensive.

And so we come to the month of April 1942, and to the supreme trial of Malta. The savage raids, which had started with the arrival of the last convoy at the end of March, now took place almost daily. On the 1st, two more of the 10th Flotilla's submarines were sunk, and several others were damaged. The German bombers concentrated mainly on Captain Nicholl's *Penelope* and on the destroyer *Lance*, which were in dock, and on the island's airfields. The dockyard staff under Admiral Leatham was doing its utmost to make every possible ship fit to sail, but in four heavy raids made on the 5th the *Lance* was sunk in dock, the *Kingston* was hit, and the *Gallant*, which had been crippled in January 1941 and had been in Malta ever since, received such further damage that she had to be beached. Enormous destruction was done in the dockyard, and on the airfields no less than 126 aircraft were destroyed or damaged in April. Twenty more were lost in air combats, and the total losses suffered by the Malta-based R.A.F. amounted to the virtual extinction of the island's air strength.

The Admiralty now proposed that the 10th Submarine Flotilla should be transferred to Alexandria, but Admirals Cunningham and Leatham and the flotilla's own Commanding Officer (Captain G. W. G. Simpson) all wished to hold on at Malta, even though the submarines had now to submerge by day to avoid damage in the incessant air raids. None the less the transfer of the flotilla to Alexandria had to be made before the end of the month. The reasons were that the failure to preserve the Spitfires flown in during the *Wasp's* first ferry trip (to be recounted shortly) had convinced the flotilla's commander that enemy minelaying, by aircraft as well as surface vessels, would continue; and secondly that heavy losses to our minesweepers had prevented the approach channels being swept clear of mines. When Captain Simpson reviewed the many trials of the flotilla which he had commanded for the previous two years, and which had lost no less than half its officers and men during that period, he left on record his opinion that the pre-war failure to build submarine shelters in the easily-quarried rock of the Malta cliffs was one of our most expensive negligences.

In 1936 the submarine service had proposed that this should be done, and the Commander-in-Chief, Mediterranean, (Admiral Sir Dudley

Pound) supported the suggestion. The Governor of Malta forwarded the proposal as first priority in a list of 'items which are desirable if sound strategy is to be observed in the problem of holding Malta'; but it was rejected under a Cabinet decision of July 1937 which debarred any strengthening of Mediterranean and Red Sea bases 'involving formidable expenditure'. It may be remarked that the estimated cost of the shelters was £300,000, which was about the same as the cost of one submarine.

The *Havock* was the first of the damaged ships to leave Malta for Gibraltar. By a sad error of judgment, understandable after so long a strain, she ran aground on the Tunisian coast on the 6th and had to be destroyed. Her crew and the many passengers she was carrying were interned by the French; but it was a tragic end to another fleet destroyer and, moreover, one whose fighting record extended from the 1st Battle of Narvik and the operations off the Dutch coast in 1940 to the action off Cape Spada and the battles of Cape Matapan, Crete and second Sirte in the Mediterranean.[1]

Desperate efforts were made to get the *Penelope* undocked and away. On the 7th, 300 enemy aircraft attacked, but did not hit her; next morning she was damaged by a near-miss. The manner in which the many holes in her hull had been temporarily plugged caused her company to nickname their ship 'H.M.S. Pepperpot'. Yet on the 8th she was undocked, just before a bomb fell right in the middle of her berth. By the evening she had to replenish with anti-aircraft ammunition, of which she had fired huge quantities; and she shifted alongside a wharf to do so. Her Captain was wounded at that time, but insisted on staying with his ship, whose 'spirit and gunnery' were described by Admiral Leatham as 'an inspiration'. At 9.55 p.m. on the 8th, after 'a desperate but stirring final day at Malta', she sailed. Though attacked many times on her westward passage she reached Gibraltar safely on the 10th—but with her magazines once more almost empty.

Still the attacks on Malta continued with sustained fury. The *Kingston* was sunk in dock, the *Pampas* was hit again, and loss of sweepers was rapidly producing a new crisis, with the harbour entrances closed by mines. By the 12th Malta dockyard was, except for the underground workshops, virtually out of action. The enemy seized the opportunity to run two more convoys to Africa; and this time dared to route them quite close to the east of Malta. They were located by Beauforts from Egypt, but the loss of five out of eight of the attacking aircraft almost extinguished our air striking power from that direction. On the 18th of April, when heavy air attacks were resumed after a brief lull, there was more bad news. The Chiefs

---

[1] See Vol. I, pp. 173–175, 299 and 430, and pp. 51–54 of this volume.

of Staff had decided that 'in view of the general naval situation' to run a convoy from Gibraltar to Malta in May would be impossible. It cannot be doubted that the anxieties caused by the heavy shipping losses then being suffered in the western Atlantic[1], the arrival of powerful German surface forces, including the *Tirpitz*, in Norway to threaten our Arctic convoys[2], and the Japanese carrier raid into the Indian Ocean, which caused us yet more naval and merchant shipping losses[3], all contributed to the decision. But although Malta would have to tighten its belt still further, the Chiefs of Staff and War Cabinet were very far from abandoning the island to its fate. Mr Churchill has told how he obtained from President Roosevelt the services of the U.S.S. *Wasp* (Captain J. W. Reeves Jr., U.S.N.), which was already in British waters, to fly in Spitfire reinforcements.[4] She embarked the fighters at Glasgow on the 13th of April and sailed on the following day, escorted by the *Renown* (Commodore C. S. Daniel), *Charybdis*, *Cairo* and American as well as British destroyers. The force passed through the Straits of Gibraltar in the very early hours of the 19th to avoid recognition from the shore, and on the 20th forty-seven Spitfires were flown off. All but one reached Malta safely, and a week later the *Wasp* was back in Scapa Flow.[5]

Heavy attacks were at once turned on to the island's airfields, and many of the fighter reinforcements fought their first battles over Malta that same day. They suffered severely, both in the air and on the ground, and within a few days it was plain that the Luftwaffe had drawn the *Wasp's* sting, and that more reinforcements and better arrangements to receive them were essential if Malta was to be saved. None the less this gesture by our Ally, made at a critical time for her own forces in the Pacific, was the brightest feature in a dark month for the Mediterranean. Though our submarines continued their unremitting offensive against the enemy supply ships, and the *Urge*, *Thrasher*, *Turbulent* and *Torbay* did particularly well, no less than four of their number were sunk in April; and included in the casualties was the famous *Upholder* of Lieutenant-Commander M. D. Wanklyn, V.C., whose loss was felt throughout the whole Mediterranean Fleet. It is probable that she was sunk by an Italian torpedo-boat when trying to attack a convoy off Tripoli on the 14th of April.

It has already been mentioned that our torpedo-bomber striking forces, working from Egypt as well as from Malta, had been almost extinguished by the end of the month. It was plain that if the enemy

---

[1] See pp. 95–101.

[2] See p. 116.

[3] See pp. 27—28.

[4] See Churchill, Vol. IV, pp. 268–269.

[5] See Morison, Vol. I, pp. 194–196.

was not to drive us out of Egypt our submarines and torpedo-carrying aircraft must be reinforced at once. The strategic significance of the neutralisation of Malta is well emphasised by the fact that in April Axis supplies reached North Africa practically unimpeded, and this enabled Rommel to open his new offensive on the 26th of May. The Eighth Army was soon driven out of Cyrenaica, and by the end of June the Afrika Korps was within sixty miles of Alexandria. Luckily the Germans transferred a large proportion of the Luftwaffe's strength to other theatres towards the end of April, leaving the Italian Air Force to continue the offensive against the island base. This, combined with the timely arrival of more Spitfire reinforcements (to be recounted shortly) enabled the R.A.F. to recover air supremacy over the island.

Though morale remained wonderfully high in Malta, and the whole free world joined in the congratulations showered upon the islanders when H.M. the King, on the 16th of April made them the unique award of the George Cross[1], it was plain that the emergency measures, such as running essential stores in by submarine or single fast warships, could not be enough. The island could survive without a convoy in May; but in June one would have to go through. On the 22nd of April the matter was discussed by the Defence Committee. The Prime Minister was firmly determined that the May convoy to Russia (PQ.16) should be run[2]; nor was he prepared to abandon the assault on Madagascar, which was soon to be launched. Later chapters will tell how both these commitments were successfully met.[3] By the end of June the Eastern Fleet might possess four capital ships, besides those of the R-class, and three modern carriers. To bring a substantial proportion of Admiral Somerville's strength through the Suez Canal and use it to succour Malta might lead to 'paying forfeits' in the Indian Ocean, but Mr Churchill was prepared to accept the risk; for, as he soon told General Auchinleck, 'we are determined that Malta should not be allowed to fall'.[4] The Prime Minister's outline plan was approved by the Defence Committee, and although it was not actually carried out it is none the less important historically, because it shows the lengths to which the British Government was prepared to go to save Malta.

The heavy losses suffered by the recent Spitfire reinforcements made it essential for the April operation to be repeated as quickly as possible. President Roosevelt made the *Wasp* available once more,

---

[1] The closest parallel to the award of the George Cross to Malta is that of the Distinguished Service Cross to the city of Dunkirk in the 1914–18 War.

[2] See pp. 130–132.

[3] See Chapters V and VII.

[4] Churchill, Vol. IV, p. 275.

and she brought out her second instalment of fighters from Britain. On the night of the 7th–8th of May she was joined off Gibraltar by the *Eagle*, with her quota of seventeen Spitfires, and by Commodore Daniel's force. On the 9th the fighters took off from the carriers, and all but three of the sixty-four reached Malta. Greatly improved arrangements had been made to receive, refuel and rearm them quickly. The new arrivals were thus ready when the enemy bombers attacked, and in the fierce air fighting which followed they inflicted heavy losses on the Luftwaffe. It was the turning point in the Battle for Malta. The fast minelayer *Welshman* sailed east with the carriers, and went right through with a special cargo of stores and ammunition. 'We are quite likely to lose this ship', wrote the First Sea Lord to Mr Churchill, 'but in view of the urgency . . . there appears to be no alternative'. In fact she not only reached Malta intact, but disembarked her cargo and sailed on the return journey all within seven hours. Nor did the *Wasp* and her escort suffer any losses. On the 15th of May the American carrier was back at Scapa. Soon afterwards she sailed for her own country and the Pacific, leaving behind her deep British gratitude for her achievement, and admiration for her efficiency. Mr Churchill typically remembered that insects of her family were unlike other hymenoptera, and signalled 'Who said a wasp couldn't sting twice?'[1]

On the 10th, the day after the *Wasp's* second reinforcements had reached Malta, a superior British fighter force met the enemy attackers for the first time. We had travelled a long way since the three Gladiators, nicknamed 'Faith', 'Hope' and 'Charity', had been Malta's sole fighter defences in June 1940. The gun barrage had also been made far heavier and more effective, and smoke could now be used to shield the harbours and the docks. In fact, after two-and-a-half years of war, that vital naval and air base was at last properly defended[2]; and the long-overdue correction of our pre-war neglect was soon to make itself felt in the realm of Allied strategy.

While the great air battles brought on by the arrival of the last fighter reinforcements were being fought over Malta, the Mediterranean submarines suffered two more losses. On the 8th of May the *Olympus* was mined outside Malta and, as she had on board as passengers many of the crews of the boats previously sunk in harbour, the casualty list was exceptionally heavy. Next day it was known that the *Urge*, another of the outstandingly successful boats of the 10th Flotilla, was overdue. She, too, probably struck a mine when on passage from Malta to Alexandria.

In the middle of May seventeen more Spitfires flown off from the

[1] Churchill, Vol. IV, p. 273.
[2] See Vol. I, pp. 48 and 77.

Eagle arrived safely, bringing the total delivered to the island in four weeks to 123; but six Albacore torpedo-bombers, which would have been a valuable contribution towards rebuilding our air striking power, had to return to the carriers because of engine trouble. The *Eagle, Argus, Charybdis* and destroyers were safely back at Gibraltar by the 20th. Early in June the gallant old *Eagle*, which was approaching her silver jubilee, made two more ferrying trips, which added fifty-five new Spitfires to Malta's defenders. It is hard to see how the island could have survived without the repeated reinforcements carried there by the *Eagle*, which, as long ago as the attack on Taranto, Admiral Cunningham had described as 'this obsolescent aircraft carrier'[1], and the two big contributions by the *Wasp*. Although the problem of defending the island fortress seemed, thanks to all these brilliantly executed emergency measures, now to be near solution, that of supplying it was becoming more acute as each week passed. But before telling the story of the next attempt to run in convoys we must return briefly to the eastern Mediterranean.

While the *Wasp* and other ships were reinforcing Malta from the west the receipt of intelligence regarding an enemy convoy bound for Benghazi led to the despatch of the *Jervis* (Captain A. L. Poland), *Kipling, Lively* and *Jackal* to intercept it. On the 11th of May they were sighted by enemy aircraft and turned back in accordance with their orders. Heavy and exceptionally accurate air attacks followed. We now know that they were carried out by a specially trained and highly efficient unit of the German Air Force stationed at Heraklion in Crete. The thirty-one Ju. 88 dive-bombers which took part had just completed a special course of training in attacks on ships. It is indeed interesting to remark how the Germans, like ourselves, had by this time come to realise that success could only be achieved in highly specialised tasks such as maritime air operations by thorough instruction and constant practice. In the present instance the enemy quickly reaped a substantial reward for his trouble.

The *Lively* was the first to be sunk; then at 8 p.m. the *Kipling* and *Jackal* were both hit, and the former went down. The *Jervis* tried to tow the *Jackal*, which was badly on fire; but early on the 12th she, too, had to be sunk. The *Jervis* alone returned to Alexandria, but she had on board 630 survivors from the lost ships. It had been a tragic experience, reminiscent of Crete, and a stern reminder of the consequences of sailing surface ships to operate in waters where the enemy held command of the air. Admiral Pound felt deeply this recurrence of a disaster, the type of which had grown all too familiar during the preceding two years, but which ought, so he considered, by this time to have become avoidable. When next he was under

---

[1] See Vol. I, pp. 300–301.

pressure from the Prime Minister to send ships to stop the enemy's convoys to the ports of the Western Desert, he spoke up with unusual force. 'May I suggest', he wrote, 'that it is upon the Air Force that pressure regarding these convoys should be directed? The enemy's . . . aircraft make these waters prohibitively dangerous to us by day; the latest example . . . is the sinking of the *Kipling, Jackal* and *Lively*. We have considerable air forces in the Middle East capable of working over the sea, and I cannot see why they should not make these waters prohibitively dangerous to enemy surface ships'. It was certainly true that our air striking power in the Mediterranean had recently been increased; but there were many demands arising, and the R.A.F. was greatly handicapped by the recent loss of the advanced desert airfields when the Army was driven out of Cyrenaica. It was also true that, as one member of the Board of Admiralty said at this time, our heavy casualties were often suffered through trying to help the Army without 'efficient fighter cover'. By way of slight recompense, on the 27th and 28th three destroyers hunted a U-boat for no less than fifteen hours off the African shore, and were finally rewarded for their persistence by the destruction of U.568.

Acting-Admiral Sir Henry Harwood, the victor of the River Plate Battle of 13th December 1939[1], had meanwhile arrived to take over command of the Mediterranean Fleet. He hoisted his flag in the *Queen Elizabeth* on the 20th of May. Very soon reinforcements for the June Malta convoy began to reach him from the Eastern Fleet. The *Birmingham* and four destroyers were the first, and arrived at Alexandria on the 6th and 7th of June; the *Newcastle, Hermione, Arethusa* and six more destroyers were meanwhile coming up the Red Sea towards Suez. By the 9th of June all forces were assembled at Alexandria. One may well ponder on the impossibility of making this typically rapid switch of our maritime power had we not had control of the Suez Canal.

The plan for operation 'Vigorous', to revictual Malta in June, was to send eleven supply ships there from the east, while six more sailed simultaneously from the west in operation 'Harpoon'. The two convoys were to reach the island on successive days. We will first follow the fortunes of the western one, which was conducted on similar lines to the three convoy operations successfully carried out during 1941.[2] The 'Harpoon' convoy sailed from Britain with an escort of Home Fleet ships on the 5th of June, and passed the Straits on the night of the 11th–12th. As not all the ships of Force H had yet returned from the assault on Diego Suarez, Madagascar[3], and the

---

[1] See Vol. I, pp. 118–121.

[2] See Vol. I, pp. 421–2, 521–3 and 530–1.

[3] See pp. 185–192.

Eastern Fleet had recently been heavily reinforced, escorts for the Malta convoy had to be specially collected from several stations. The battleship *Malaya*, the carriers *Eagle* and *Argus*, the cruisers *Kenya* (flag of Vice-Admiral A. T. B. Curteis, who commanded the whole operation), *Liverpool* and *Charybdis*, and eight destroyers formed the main escort and covering force. They were to take the convoy as far as 'the Narrows' between Sicily and Tunisia.[1] The close escort to go right through to Malta comprised the anti-aircraft cruiser *Cairo* (Acting-Captain C. C. Hardy), nine more destroyers and four fleet minesweepers. Six minesweeping motor-launches were included in the convoy. They and the fleet minesweepers were not only to sweep the convoy through the dense enemy minefields recently laid off Malta, but were to stay there to solve the island's acute minesweeping problems. The fast minelayer *Welshman* was to go through ahead of the convoy with another cargo of ammunition and special stores; a fleet oiler with her own escort was to cruise independently near the convoy route to fuel the escorts at need, while four submarines patrolled off the enemy's main bases. The merchant ships taking part were the *Troilus*, *Burdwan* and *Orari* (all British), the Dutch *Tanimbar*, and the *Chant* and *Kentucky* (American). Their combined capacity was about 43,000 tons of cargo.

By the morning of the 12th of June all forces were well inside the Mediterranean. Next day they were shadowed from the air and reported by submarine. The short-endurance ships fuelled from the oiler *Brown Ranger* or from the *Liverpool*. By the morning of the 14th, which was fine and calm, they were within range of the enemy air bases in Sardinia. The two carriers, both of them old and slow, were handicapped in working their aircraft, because what little wind was blowing was from astern. If they hauled right round into the wind to fly their fighters on and off quickly, they would have to leave the safety of the destroyer screen; and after flying operations it was bound to be a slow business for them to overtake the convoy. Air attacks began at 10.30, firstly by dive-bombers and a little later by a strong force of high-level bombers and torpedo-bombers. All were Italian. The *Liverpool* was hit in the engine room, and practically disabled; the merchantman *Tanimbar* was sunk. The carriers could not put up more than half a score of fighters at a time, and they were inadequate to drive off so many attackers. The *Liverpool* eventually reached Gibraltar safely on the 17th, having been towed most of the way by the destroyer *Antelope*, and having survived several more air attacks. By the evening of the 14th the convoy was within range of the Sicilian airfields; nor were German bombers slow in appearing. This time, after a preliminary attack by Ju. 88s, a mixed force of

---

[1] See Map 9 (opp. p. 65).

German and Italian dive- and torpedo-bombers came in. Many ships, but especially the carriers, had narrow escapes; but none was hit. In the middle of the air attack the destroyers found time to force down and harry a U-boat whose periscope had been sighted. The carriers' fighters claimed eleven enemies destroyed;[1] but seven of their own small number were lost.

At 9 p.m. that evening 'the Narrows' were reached; Admiral Curteis and the heavy ships then hauled round to the west for the position in which they were to wait for the return of the light forces from Malta. Captain Hardy of the *Cairo* took over command of the convoy and its escort. A dusk air attack, made while they were steering south-east to keep close to the Tunisian coast, did no damage. So far all had gone pretty well. The determined and heavy air attacks of the last two days had not caused heavier losses than had to be expected on such an operation. But the next day, the 15th, told a different story. In previous Malta convoys we had sent cruisers right through with the merchantmen[2], and the Italians had never dared to send their surface ships to attack them closely. Now we had no cruisers to spare for such a duty. Admiral Curteis needed his last two, the *Kenya* and *Charybdis*, to cover and support his carriers; but he has stated that had the *Liverpool* still been with him he would have sent a cruiser back to support the destroyers as soon as he learnt that enemy cruisers were leaving Palermo.

At 6.30 a.m. on the 15th the convoy was about thirty miles south of Pantelleria.[3] One of our Beaufighters from Malta had just reported to Captain Hardy that two enemy 6-inch cruisers and four (actually five) destroyers were only fifteen miles to the north of him. They had sailed from Palermo the previous evening. Ten minutes later the enemy was in sight and the *Bedouin* (Commander B. G. Scurfield) at once, and in complete character with the tradition of her class, led out the fleet destroyers to attack the superior enemy. The *Cairo* and the smaller escorts meanwhile covered the convoy with smoke. The gun action between the Italian cruisers and the British destroyers opened outside the range of the latter's 4·7-inch and 4-inch guns. The *Bedouin* and *Partridge* were soon hit and disabled; but the other three pressed on and managed to hit one enemy destroyer. As soon as the convoy was well shielded by smoke the *Cairo* and the four 'Hunts' joined in the surface action. The convoy thus had no air protection when, at about 7 a.m., it was dive-bombed. The *Chant* was sunk and the tanker *Kentucky* hit, but taken in tow. The Commo-

---

[1] It has proved impossible to check contemporary claims against actual enemy aircraft losses in this operation.

[2] See, for example, Vol. I, pp. 521–3 and 530–1.

[3] See Map 9.

F

dore turned the surviving ships from their southerly course towards Malta, but the Italian squadron, which had gained greatly on the convoy, now closed to threaten them from ahead. The *Cairo* and destroyers laid another smoke screen, and soon the enemy stood away to the north-east.

Except for the damaged *Bedouin* and *Partridge*, which had to be left behind, and for the effects of the luckily-timed bombing attack made while the convoy was unescorted, matters had so far not gone too badly. But at about 11.20 another air attack, made while the convoy was still at the extreme range of the Malta Spitfires, disabled the *Burdwan*. Captain Hardy decided that to sacrifice her and the lame *Kentucky* gave the best hope of getting the last two ships in. Orders were therefore given to sink them. Then the Italian squadron came back to try to pick up our detached ships and stragglers. The *Cairo* and destroyers covered the return of the ships which had stayed behind to sink the damaged merchantmen, but could not go back as far as the *Bedouin* and *Partridge* without endangering the convoy. The *Partridge* had managed to get under way again, and she was towing the wholly crippled *Bedouin*. At about 1.30 p.m. the Italian squadron again came on the scene, at a moment when many enemy aircraft were about. The *Partridge* slipped her tow, made smoke round her consort and engaged the enemy single-handed. But it was of no avail. A torpedo-bomber finally despatched the *Bedouin* at 2.25 p.m. The *Partridge* received yet more damage in an air attack, but miraculously survived all these dangers and got back to Gibraltar on the 17th, the same day as the damaged *Liverpool*.

The Captain of the *Bedouin* and many of his company were picked up by the Italians. While a prisoner of war Scurfield sent an account of his ship's last fight to his wife. In it he said: 'This was what I had been training for, for twenty-two years, and I led my five destroyers up towards the enemy. I was in a fortunate position in many ways, and I knew what we had to do. The cost was not to be counted. The ship was as ready for the test as we had been able to make her. I could do no more about it.'[1] One is reminded of Nelson's words when he heard the cheering with which his fleet greeted his famous signal on the 21st of October 1805. 'Now I can do no more. We must put our trust in the great Disposer of Events, and in the justice of our cause'. Unhappily the story of the *Bedouin* had a tragic ending. When Italy surrendered, Scurfield and most of his men were in a camp in the north, and they fell into German hands. In 1945, when our advancing armies were approaching the camp where he was then held, the Germans marched the prisoners elsewhere. While on the

---

[1] Commander Scurfield's letter was first printed in Blackwood's Magazine for September 1945 under the heading 'The End of a Tribal'.

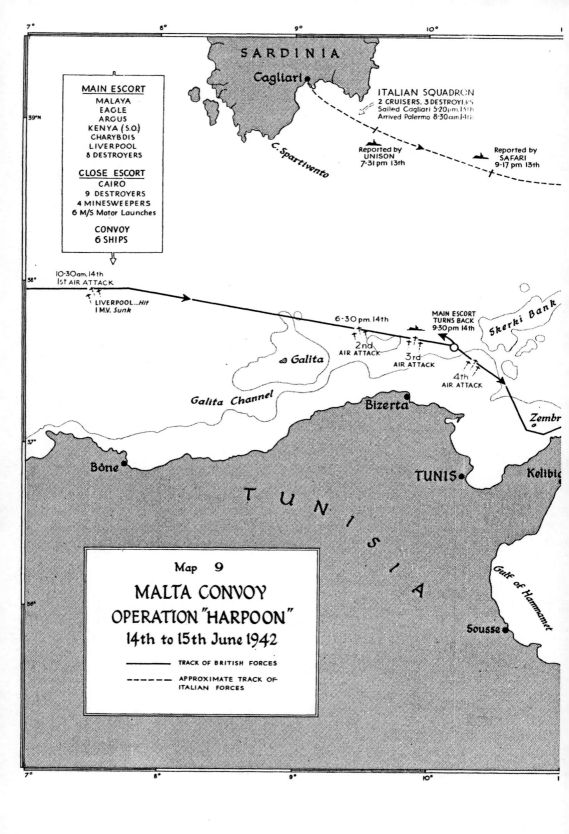

SARDINIA

Cagliari

ITALIAN SQUADRON
2 CRUISERS, 3 DESTROYERS
Sailed Cagliari 5·20 pm. 13th
Arrived Palermo 8·30 am. 14th

C. Spartivento

Reported by
UNISON
7·31 pm 13th

Reported by
SAFARI
9·17 pm 13th

MAIN ESCORT
MALAYA
EAGLE
ARGUS
KENYA (S.O.)
CHARYBDIS
LIVERPOOL
8 DESTROYERS

CLOSE ESCORT
CAIRO
9 DESTROYERS
4 MINESWEEPERS
6 M/S Motor Launches

CONVOY
6 SHIPS

10·30 am. 14th
1ST AIR ATTACK

LIVERPOOL...Hit
1 M.V. Sunk

6·30 pm. 14th

MAIN ESCORT
TURNS BACK
9·30 pm 14th

Skerki Bank

2nd
AIR ATTACK

3rd
AIR ATTACK

4th
AIR ATTACK

Galita

Galita Channel

Bizerta

Zembr

Bône

TUNIS

Kelibi

T U N I S I A

Gulf of Hammamet

Sousse

Map 9

MALTA CONVOY
OPERATION "HARPOON"
14th to 15th June 1942

———————— TRACK OF BRITISH FORCES

– – – – – – – – APPROXIMATE TRACK OF
ITALIAN FORCES

7°   8°   9°   10°

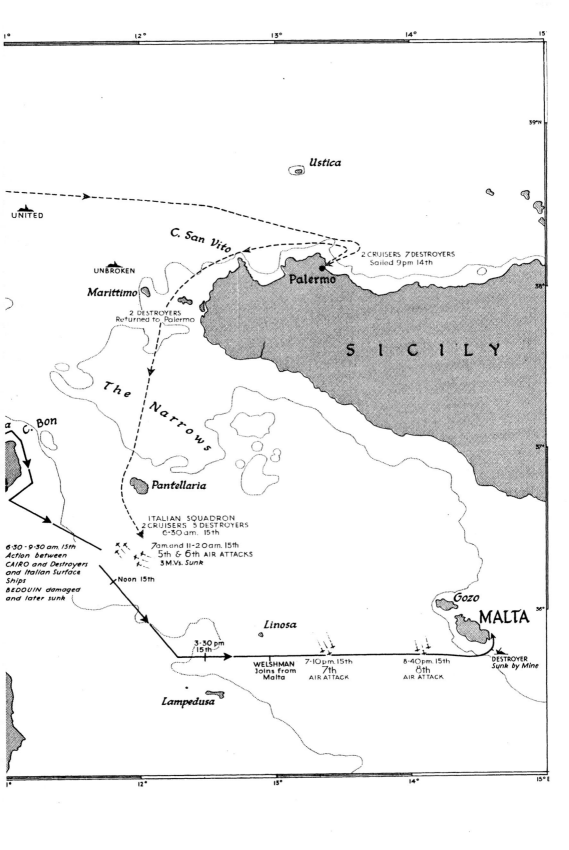

UNITED

C. San Vito

UNBROKEN

Marittimo

2 CRUISERS 7 DESTROYERS
Sailed 9pm 14th

Palermo

2 DESTROYERS
Returned to Palermo

Ustica

S I C I L Y

The

Narrows

a C. Bon

Pantellaria

ITALIAN SQUADRON
2 CRUISERS 5 DESTROYERS
6·30 a.m. 15th

7am.and 11·2 0am. 15th
5th & 6th AIR ATTACKS
3 M.Vs. Sunk

6·30 - 9·30 a.m. 15th
Action between
CAIRO and Destroyers
and Italian Surface
Ships
BEDOUIN damaged
and later sunk

Noon 15th

Gozo

MALTA

3·30 pm
15th

Linosa

WELSHMAN
Joins from
Malta

7·10pm.15th
7th
AIR ATTACK

8·40pm.15th
8th
AIR ATTACK

DESTROYER
Sunk by Mine

Lampedusa

road the column was machine-gunned by our own aircraft, and Scurfield was among those killed. His spirit was, it is true, only typical of the British destroyer service throughout the war. Again and again did their Captains and ships' companies unhesitatingly sacrifice themselves to defend their charges against hopeless odds; and the stories of some of their last fights have appeared in these pages. But the *Bedouin's* name and her Captain should be remembered with those of the *Glowworm, Acasta, Ardent*[1] and the many, many destroyers lost in the Arctic, at Dunkirk, off Crete and in a hundred other fights.

The *Cairo* and the rest of the escort rejoined the convoy at 3.30 p.m. Two hours later the *Welshman*, which had meanwhile arrived at Malta, unloaded her cargo and sailed again, joined up with them. Several more air attacks were foiled by the Malta Spitfires and the escorts' guns. After all these perilous adventures it was, perhaps, understandable that the organisation to receive the convoy did not work as intended. The route used for the final approach had not been fully swept. Three destroyers, a fleet minesweeper and the *Orari* struck mines; luckily four of the five made harbour, but the Polish destroyer *Kujawiak* was sunk. The *Cairo* and the four remaining destroyers sailed again late on the 16th, and met Admiral Curteis the next evening, after surviving yet more air attacks. The *Malaya* and the carriers had already been sent back to Gibraltar, and the *Kenya, Charybdis* and the survivors of Captain Hardy's force also made that base in safety. Thus ended operation 'Harpoon'. Two out of six merchant ships had arrived; but we had lost two destroyers, while a cruiser, three more destroyers and a minesweeper had been seriously damaged.

In Malta Admiral Leatham ordered an enquiry into certain aspects of the operation. When the full report of the 'Harpoon' convoy reached London the Admiralty reviewed the question whether one of Admiral Curteis' two surviving cruisers should have been sent to reinforce Captain Hardy's light forces. The feeling was that had the *Charybdis* been sent the *Burdwan* and *Kentucky* might have been saved and the loss of the *Bedouin* avoided; but that in the very difficult circumstances prevailing at the time, and in view of the widely divergent responsibilities which had to be met, criticism of the Admiral's action could not be sustained.

We must retrace our steps for a few days to see how Operation 'Vigorous' had meanwhile been faring in the eastern basin. It has already been mentioned that the escorting force, once again commanded by Rear-Admiral Vian, had been substantially reinforced from the Eastern Fleet. He had in all seven cruisers, one anti-aircraft

[1] See Vol. I, pp. 158 and 195–196.

cruiser and twenty-six destroyers, in addition to corvettes, mine-sweepers and rescue ships. But there was no heavy-ship covering force capable of dealing with the Italian fleet, should it show fight; nor were there any fleet carriers to carry the convoy's fighter protection along with it, and to strike at the enemy main forces if they came within range. The *Illustrious* and *Indomitable* had only recently completed the Madagascar operations[1], the *Victorious* was with the Home Fleet and the *Formidable* was in the Indian Ocean. It will be remembered that in April consideration had been given to bringing the Eastern Fleet carriers through the Canal to help fight the convoy through[2]; but when the need actually arose none could be made available. There being thus no proper battle fleet to support the operation, the old *Centurion*, which had been the fleet's pre-war wireless-controlled target ship, was sent to masquerade as a battleship. As she was ancient (launched 1911) and virtually unarmed, it was not very likely that the enemy would be taken in by her presence. The real hope was that our air striking forces, and to some extent our submarines, would act as sufficient substitutes for a battle fleet. Admiral Cunningham had long ago declared that, if heavy ships could not be spared for the Mediterranean, our only hope lay in providing 'really adequate air forces'[3]; and many naval and R.A.F. bombers and torpedo-bombers had been sent out to the Middle East and to Malta. But the calls on them had been so varied and so numerous, and the wastage so heavy, that our air striking forces had in reality never yet been able to build up decisive strength. On the present occasion we employed torpedo-carrying Wellingtons and Beauforts from Malta, Beauforts from Egypt and a small force of American Liberators from the Suez Canal—some forty aircraft in all. The sum of their accomplishments was one torpedo hit on the heavy cruiser *Trento*, which damaged her severely and led to her being sunk by the submarine *Umbra* (Lieutenant S. L. C. Maydon) on the 15th of June, and one bomb and one torpedo hit on the battleship *Littorio*. In addition to the lack of heavy ships and the inadequacy of the air striking forces, there were other weaknesses which vitiated the reliance placed on this occasion on air power. To hold off the enemy surface forces and defeat their intentions, good reconnaissance was essential. Neither the submarines nor the air striking forces could carry out their tasks unless the enemy's movements were accurately reported; but we did not possess enough reconnaissance aircraft to watch the enemy continuously. Secondly, fighter protection had, after the first day of the operation, become

---

[1] See pp. 185–192.
[2] See p. 60.
[3] See Vol. I, p. 539.

far more difficult because the Axis army's advance into Libya had deprived us of the use of the advanced airfields. Hurricanes from Egypt, and then Beaufighters and Kittyhawks, flew many sorties right out to the limit of their endurance; but strategic considerations, including the heavy demands of the land battle, prevented their cover being really effective. To try to reduce the enemy's air potential, sabotage parties landed in Crete from submarines just before the surface forces finally sailed west. Though some of the raiders seem not to have found their targets, and contemporary claims of losses inflicted were certainly too high, the enemy's records do show that damage was done to Ju.88 bombers on Heraklion airfield during the night of 13th–14th of June; but it was not enough to tip the scales in our favour during the convoy operation.

As regards our submarines, it had been intended that nine of them should form a screen to the north of the convoy's route, moving westwards as the convoy steamed towards Malta. In the event this proved impracticable, chiefly because the Italian fleet sailed earlier than we had expected. Only one submarine got in an attack as the main Italian force came south. It thus came to pass that the only safeguards provided against heavy-ship attack—namely air striking forces and submarines—both proved illusory. Admiral Vian very well knew that in the long days and calm, clear weather of the summer months he could not hope to bluff and mislead the enemy as he had done so successfully in March.[1] Admiral Harwood and Air Marshal Tedder moved into a special 'combined operations room' in the headquarters of No. 201 Naval Co-operation Group, in order to conduct the intricate movements in intimate collaboration.

The first ships to sail left Port Said on the 11th of June in a 'diversionary convoy' of four merchantmen, escorted by the *Coventry* and seven *Hunt*-class destroyers. They were to go west as far as the meridian of Tobruk, and then turn back and meet the main convoy. It was hoped that this deception would bring the enemy fleet south prematurely; but events did not work out that way.

The main convoy had assembled in two parts at Haifa and Port Said, and they and their escorts were sailed to rendezvous with the returning 'diversionary convoy' off Alexandria on the 13th. Admiral Vian and the rest of the warships (seven cruisers and seventeen destroyers) left Alexandria that same evening to overtake the merchantmen off Tobruk. Enemy aircraft quickly found the real convoy, one of whose number was damaged and sent to Tobruk on the 12th. Another could not keep up, and was sent back to Alexandria; but she never got there. About forty German bombers found and sank her on the 14th.

---

[1] See pp. 51—54.

Throughout the night of the 13th–14th enemy aircraft kept touch with the convoy, and dropped flares continuously around it. When daylight came, fighters from the Western Desert broke up at least one strong formation of enemy bombers. That afternoon, the 14th, one merchantman was sunk and another damaged by bombs. A new threat developed at sunset when enemy motor torpedo-boats approached from the north. By 11.15 p.m. Vian knew that Italian heavy warships had left Taranto, and that they could make contact with him at about 7 a.m. next morning. To hold them off throughout a long summer day was an impossible proposition, so he asked the Commander-in-Chief whether he was to retire. Admiral Harwood, hoping first to make as much distance as possible towards the west, told Vian to hold on until 2 a.m. and then reverse course. That difficult manoeuvre—for there were about fifty ships involved—was safely executed, but it gave the E-boats their chance.[1] Shortly before 4 a.m. one of them torpedoed the *Newcastle*. Not long afterwards the destroyer *Hasty* was struck by a torpedo, and had to be sunk by a consort.[2]

At dawn on the 15th the Italian fleet, consisting of their two newest battleships, the *Vittorio Veneto* and the *Littorio*, two heavy and two light cruisers and about a dozen destroyers, was some 200 miles north-west of the retiring convoy. Shortly before 7 a.m., on the Commander-in-Chief's instructions, the convoy turned again to the west. At about the same time the Malta-based torpedo-bombers attacked the enemy and, as already mentioned, hit and disabled the 8-inch cruiser *Trento*. Our submarines were meanwhile making strenuous, though vain, endeavours to get into position to attack the Italian battleships. Next, between 9 and 10 o'clock the Liberators and torpedo-bombers from Egypt attacked; although both striking forces reported several hits, in fact the only one scored was a bomb hit on the *Littorio's* forward turret, which did her no serious injury. The Italian battleships still held on to the south. At 9.40, with the enemy only 150 miles away, Admiral Harwood ordered the convoy to turn east for the second time; then, just before noon, after hearing the Beauforts' claim to have hit both battleships, he ordered it to resume the course for Malta. Finally, at 12.45 p.m., realising that the air reports might have been incorrect, that our reconnaissance aircraft were not in touch and that he could not assess the true

---

[1] For simplicity both Italian and German motor torpedo-boats are here referred to by the German classification of E-boats.

[2] There is some doubt regarding what enemy fired the torpedo which caused the loss of the *Hasty*. No U-boat claimed doing so, nor does scrutiny of the war diaries of those which were near the scene lend any support to the assumption that she was the victim of a submarine. The probability is that she was torpedoed by the German torpedo-boat S.55 of the 3rd S. Boat Flotilla, then operating from Derna. It was certainly one of this flotilla which hit the *Newcastle*, and it is known that S.55 fired torpedoes at our destroyers a little later. She, however, did not claim any hits.

situation, Admiral Harwood signalled that he must leave it to the cruiser Admiral's discretion whether to hold on or retire. Vian received this message at 2.20 p.m. The *Birmingham* had meanwhile been damaged by a bomb hit, and a little later the destroyer *Airedale* suffered severely in a heavy dive-bombing attack. She had to be sunk by our own forces. Though no more of the convoy had been damaged, the detachment of another ship which could not keep up had reduced its numbers from the original eleven to six.

Our reconnaissance aircraft had meanwhile regained touch, and the enemy fleet, having reached a point only about 100 miles from the convoy, was reported at 4.15 to have set course for Taranto. As soon as this was clear the Commander-in-Chief signalled 'Now is the chance to get [the] convoy to Malta', and asked what was the state of the escorts' fuel and ammunition supplies. This message arrived during a heavy air attack, and the information requested was difficult to collect. 'All known forms of attack' were, in Admiral Vian's words, being made on the convoy and escorts. They lasted from 5.20 until about 7.30 p.m. and, although fighter cover was but intermittent, only the Australian destroyer *Nestor* was seriously damaged. When Vian reported that less than one-third of his ships' ammunition remained, and that what was left was going fast, the Commander-in-Chief recalled all ships to Alexandria.

That, unfortunately, was not quite the end, since in the early hours of the 16th U.205 torpedoed and sank the cruiser *Hermione*, and the damaged *Nestor* had to be scuttled. The other ships were back in Alexandria on the evening of the 16th. On the enemy's side, a Malta-based Wellington scored a torpedo hit right forward on the *Littorio* in a night attack made at about the same time as the *Hermione* was sunk. But she was not seriously hurt and was able to maintain her speed. All the Italian ships returned safely to Taranto on the afternoon of the 16th, at about the same time that Admiral Vian's force reached Alexandria.

Apart from the failure to revictual Malta we had lost a cruiser, three destroyers and two merchant ships. The Italians lost the *Trento* and had the *Littorio* damaged. The enemy's success was undeniable, and no further attempt was made to run a convoy to Malta from Egypt until the Army had driven the Axis forces out of Libya.

As we look back today it seems that a primary cause of the failure was the unfavourable strategic situation on land. That by itself made any fleet operations in the central basin very hazardous. While the convoy was actually at sea the Army had to make a further withdrawal, involving loss of one of the vital desert airfields. Secondly, in the words of Admiral Harwood's report, 'our air striking force had nothing like the weight required to stop a fast and powerful enemy force, and in no way compensated for our lack of heavy ships'. In the

March convoy, for all the brilliance of Admiral Vian's action, it was the lack of heavy cover which delayed the arrival of the merchantmen and gave the Luftwaffe the chance to destroy the *Breconshire* and *Clan Campbell* close off Malta.[1] In the June operation the lack of the same element of maritime power was decisive. Finally, it must be remarked how forcibly these operations drove home the fact that, with enemy shore-based aircraft established in strength close off the flanks of a convoy route, success or failure was to a very large extent decided in the air.

It remains to mention the influence of these operations on the Eighth Army's struggle with Rommel, which was proceeding at the same time. The German Air Commander's War Diary makes it plain that almost the whole of his bomber strength was directed against the convoys, and it seems probable that the successes he achieved at sea were purchased at the price of easing the pressure on the Eighth Army at a critical time during its retreat to El Alamein. It is, of course, conjectural whether, had the enemy not diverted his air strength, it would have been decisive on land; but it is certain that the trials endured and the losses suffered by the two convoys helped the successful withdrawal and subsequent stand of the Army.

As this was the last attempt made during the present phase to revictual Malta on a large scale, it will be a convenient moment to summarise the results achieved and the losses suffered. Compared with the three convoys run from the west in 1941, the degree of success achieved in the first half of the following year was very meagre. In 1941 thirty-one supply ships sailed for Malta from Alexandria or Gibraltar, and all but one arrived safely.[2] In the first seven months of 1942 twenty-one ships sailed in major convoy operations and another nine took part in the smaller attempts from the east made in January and February. Of these thirty ships ten were sunk at sea (seven of them in the major convoys), ten turned back because of damage, or for other reasons such as inability to keep up with their convoys; and of the ten which reached Malta three were sunk after arrival. Thus only seven of the original thirty survived intact with the whole of their cargoes. Moreover, in this period the naval losses had been heavy. Quite apart from the large number of ships damaged we lost a cruiser, eight destroyers and a submarine. The seriousness of these losses can best be realised by mentioning that the whole evacuation of the B.E.F. from Dunkirk in 1941 cost the Royal Navy two less destroyers than were lost in these Malta convoy operations.[3]

---

[1] See p. 55.

[2] See Vol. I, Table 21. The figures for transports and merchant ships in that table included the eight brought out from Malta during Operation 'Excess'.

[3] See Vol. I, p. 228.

Table 2. Malta Convoys, 1st January–31st July, 1942

(Major operations only)

Naval forces employed	From East. Convoy 'M.W.10' (March)			From West. Operation 'Harpoon' (June)			From East. Operation 'Vigorous' (June)		
	No.	Sunk	Dmgd.	No.	Sunk	Dmgd.	No.	Sunk	Dmgd.
Capital Ships . .	Nil	—	—	1	—	—	—	—	—
Aircraft Carriers .	Nil	—	—	2	—	—	—	—	—
Cruisers . . .	4	—	3	3	—	1	7	1	2
A.A. Ships . .	1	—	—	1	—	1	1	—	—
Destroyers . .	18	3	2	18	2	3	26	3	—
Minesweepers and Corvettes .	—	—	—	4	—	1	6	—	1
Submarines . .	5	1	—	4	—	—	9	—	—
Transports and Merchant Ships .	4	1	—	6	4	—	11	2	2
No. of Transports and Merchant Ships which arrived in Malta .	3 (All sunk after arrival)			2			Nil		

While the double attempt to supply Malta was actually in progress, things were going badly for us on land in Africa, and preparations were in train to evacuate Tobruk. On the 17th of June all merchant vessels were ordered to leave the port. Three days later enemy tanks suddenly broke through and reached the harbour. Demolitions were not completed, and some small ships did not sail in time to avoid capture or destruction. By the 21st the enemy was in full possession of the base which had been so stubbornly held throughout the long siege of 1940–41.[1] For the Mediterranean Fleet the implications were most serious. The Naval Staff warned the First Sea Lord that 'in view of the news that Tobruk has fallen we must prepare for the worst'—namely the loss of Alexandria. Preparations were put in hand to move some of the fleet to Haifa and others south of the Suez Canal. After the passage of the latter the Canal was to be blocked. Once before, in April 1941[2], we had prepared to face these dire consequences of defeat on land, but this time the threat was far more serious.

On the 24th Sollum was evacuated and the Army of the Nile fell back to Mersa Matruh[3]; possession by the enemy of the frontier airfields endangered the naval base at Alexandria, which could now be attacked by fighter-escorted bombers. Admiral Harwood therefore sent all unessential warships and merchant ships south of the

---

[1] See Vol. I, pp. 519–520. For a full account of the circumstances surrounding the fall of Tobruk see I. S. O. Playfair, *The Mediterranean and Middle East*, Vol. II. (H.M.S.O. 1956).

[2] See Vol. I, pp. 431–433.

[3] See Map 31 (opp. p. 313).

Suez Canal. On the 27th the battleship *Queen Elizabeth* was undocked and sailed for Port Sudan. Her temporary repairs had been successfully finished by the dockyard staff under most difficult conditions.[1] By the middle of July she was well on her way to America for permanent repairs. The destroyer depot ship *Woolwich*, the fleet repair ship *Resource* and six destroyers also moved south of the Canal. The rest of the fleet was divided between Haifa and Port Said, except for the 1st Submarine Flotilla which moved to Beirut. It should here be remarked that, had we not possessed the use of the rearward bases in Egypt, Palestine and Syria at this difficult juncture, there could have been no alternative but to withdraw the whole fleet through the Canal. Possession of these bases gave us room, albeit very little room, in which to maintain our tenuous hold on the eastern basin. When the ships sailed east, movement of the shore staffs to the Canal Zone was started, and preparations to demolish stores and facilities at Alexandria and to block the harbour were put in hand. By the last day of June the Eighth Army had withdrawn to the defence lines at El Alamein, only sixty miles from Alexandria. On that same day, which marked the nadir of our fortunes in the Middle East, the very valuable submarine depot ship *Medway* was sunk by U.372, who believed she had hit a transport, off Port Said. Many of our reserve torpedoes, weapons of which we had never had an adequate supply, were lost in her.

One of the many serious difficulties which now had to be faced was the future of Admiral Godfroy's squadron of French warships, which had been immobilised in Alexandria since June 1940[2], in the event of our having to evacuate the base. The agreement governing the future of the ships had been a personal one made by Admiral Cunningham with his French colleague, and Godfroy was entitled to be consulted regarding its renewal with Cunningham's successor. A new agreement was negotiated on instructions from London, and signed in June by Admirals Harwood and Godfroy; but discussions regarding the removal of the French ships from Alexandria, should the need arise, proved fruitless. Fortunately the turn of events on land made it unnecessary for the issue to be pursued.

The Eighth Army having held Rommel's first attacks on our position at El Alamein early in July, the rest of the month passed in comparative quiet at sea. A happy augury for the future was that, on the 5th, Admiral Leatham reported that the 10th Submarine Flotilla could now profitably return to Malta. Air attacks had died down, and the approach channels were at last clear of mines. No less than 206 had been cut or exploded off the harbour entrances

---

[1] See Vol. I, p. 538, regarding the damage sustained by the *Queen Elizabeth* and *Valiant* from Italian human torpedoes in December 1941.

[2] See Vol. I, p. 242.

since the clearance work was started early in May. Meanwhile our aircraft and surface ships continued to take a steady toll of the U-boats. On the 1st of May U.573 was sunk by a Hudson of No. 233 Squadron. Next day an aircraft of No. 202 Squadron and the destroyers *Wishart* and *Wrestler* together accounted for U.74; and on the 9th a pleasant success was the capture of the Italian submarine *Perla* by the corvette *Hyacinth* off Beirut. After the fall of Massawa in March 1941 she had escaped back to Italy by way of the Cape of Good Hope—a journey for which her crew must be given full credit. Two days after this success the Italian submarine *Ondina* was sunk by two South African A/S Whalers aided by a naval Walrus amphibian aircraft. However critical our strategic situation might be, the little ships and the air escorts could still hit hard any U-boat which threatened their convoys. On the 10th of July a daring and original attack was made by ten naval Albacores on an enemy supply convoy between Crete and Tobruk. They first flew to a landing ground well inside the enemy's lines, some forty miles south of Sollum. There they were refuelled by R.A.F. transport aircraft, before taking off for the attack. No enemy ships were actually sunk, but the arrival of the torpedo-bombers must have been something of a surprise to the enemy. Next, by way of showing that our offensive spirit had not been dimmed by recent disasters, Admiral Vian's cruisers and destroyers made a daylight bombardment of Mersa Matruh.

The onslaught on the enemy's supply traffic continued even while most of the fleet's attention was being devoted to the Malta convoys, but it was to be expected that, while Malta was under heavy attack and after the 10th Flotilla had to leave, our submarines' successes would diminish; on the other hand, with the re-establishment of the Malta-based striking forces, sinkings by aircraft rose substantially in July. The total results of all our offensive measures against Axis-controlled shipping in this phase are shown in the next table.

For Malta the phase ended with the reassuring arrival of two more fighter reinforcements, of thirty-one and twenty-eight Spitfires, flown off yet again by the *Eagle*; and the *Welshman* arrived on the 16th with certain key men for the defences, and a cargo of concentrated foodstuffs and 'edible oils'. Then came the submarine *Unbroken*, to signalise the return of the famous 10th Flotilla to its proper home, and to warn the enemy that, even if he thought he had effectively neutralised the island, it had made a remarkably sharp recovery.[1] The erstwhile seriously injured patient was quickly to show a remarkable capacity to harm those who had inflicted the injuries. By way of underlining the point an Italian flying boat landed in one of Malta's bays just before the end of the month. It had

---

[1] A graphic account of the passage of this submarine back to Malta, through the enemy minefields, is contained in *Unbroken* by Alastair Mars (Frederick Muller, 1953), pp. 96-7.

been seized by the crew of an R.A.F. Beaufort, who were being taken in it as prisoners from Greece to Italy. Incidents such as these, though trivial in themselves, must surely have appeared as the writing on the wall to an enemy who knew that he was, strategically-speaking, stretched too far; saying once again, 'God hath numbered thy Kingdom and finished it'.[1] Nor were Hitler and Mussolini to escape the fate of Belshazzar, King of the Chaldeans.

Table 3. Enemy Merchant Shipping Losses, 1st January to 31st July, 1942

These tables are mainly derived from 'La Marina Italiana nella Segonda Guerra Mondiale', the Italian Admiralty's published statistics. A close scrutiny of these tables and comparison with other sources have, however, revealed a few small errors in the Italian statistics and these have been corrected in this and subsequent tables.

1. Italian (includes losses outside Mediterranean)

Number of ships: Tonnage

Month	By Surface Ship	By Submarine	By Air Attack See Note (2)	By Mine	By Other Causes	TOTAL
January	—	8: 22,131	2: 18,839	—	1: 25	11: 40,995
February	2: 810	7: 31,220	1: 319	1: 1,334	4: 1,571	15: 35,254
March	—	6: 17,298	1: 1,086	2: 6,008	4: 151	13: 24,543
April	—	6: 14,229	—	2: 1,157	3: 384	11: 15,770
May	—	6: 12,211	1: 6,836	—	6: 5,305	13: 24,352
June	—	2: 2,565	1: 6,837	1: 750	4: 1,216	8: 11,368
July	—	1: 792	7: 9,841	—	1: 54	9: 10,687
TOTAL	2: 810	36: 100,446	13: 43,758	6: 9,249	23: 8,706	80:162,969

2. German and German-controlled (Mediterranean only)

Number of ships: Tonnage

Month	By Surface Ship	By Submarine	By Air Attack	By Mine	By Other Causes	TOTAL
January to July	1: 1,397	2: 3,594	5: 18,934	1: 1,778	1: 2,140	10: 27,843

NOTES: (1) Of the ninety ships sunk in this phase, 51 were of more than 500 tons and 39 were of less than 500 tons.

(2) Of the total tonnage sunk by air attack in this phase, 7 ships of 46,924 tons were sunk at sea, and 11 ships of 15,768 tons in port.

[1] Daniel v, verses 25–28.

CHAPTER III

THE PRIORITY OF
MARITIME AIR OPERATIONS, 1942

'Not by rambling operations, or naval duels,
are wars decided but by force massed and
handled in skilful combination'.
A. T. Mahan (*Sea Power in its Relation to the War of* 1812).

In order fully to understand the discussions on the contribution of the Royal Air Force to the war at sea which lasted throughout 1942, it is necessary to review how matters stood as the previous year drew to a close.

When Air Chief Marshal Bowhill turned over his responsibility for Coastal Command to Sir Philip Joubert de la Ferté in June 1941 the strength of his command was thirty-five squadrons, nominally of 582 aircraft. This was about double the strength which he had commanded on the outbreak of war; but the number of aircraft available on any day for operations was only about half his actual strength.[1] On giving up his command Bowhill stressed the urgent need for new types of aircraft. He wanted Mosquitos to work off the enemy's coasts instead of the obsolescent Hudsons; Beaufighters to replace the Blenheims, and a real force of long-range aircraft for anti-submarine work instead of his mixed lot of Whitleys, Wellingtons and Hudsons. Air Chief Marshal Joubert promptly reassessed his needs—including aircraft for anti-invasion reconnaissance, shipping reconnaissance and attacks on shipping—and arrived at a total of 818 aircraft for all purposes in the home and Atlantic theatres only. His hopes were short-lived. In October the Prime Minister proposed to transfer his bombers to the attack on Germany, and when the First Lord demurred Mr Churchill merely postponed the question till the New Year. All the new long-range bombers were meanwhile being allocated to Bomber Command; prospects for deliveries of new flying boats to Coastal Command were also very bad. As a final blow, just before the end of the year the Air Ministry rejected almost completely the expansion proposals of the Commander-in-Chief. In January 1942 the Admiralty's anxiety about the Command's strength (its daily availability was then only 156 aircraft) was increasing, and Air

---

[1] Appendix C shows the growth of the established strength of Coastal Command from 1st September 1939 to 1st July 1943.

Chief Marshal Joubert renewed his attempt to get some modern long-range bombers. Plainly the clash between the rival purposes of bombing Germany or helping to sink the U-boats and to bring our convoys safely home had now reached a point where the matter had to be weighed and decided by the Cabinet and the Defence Committee.

The very serious losses suffered by the Navy in the closing months of 1941, the ever-increasing strain of maritime operations now become world-wide, the pressure of new and heavy commitments such as the Russian convoys, the extreme peril in the Indian Ocean and the rapidly rising tempo of the Atlantic Battle all combined to make the early months of 1942 among the most anxious of the whole war. As the First Lord said early in March, 'if we lose the war at sea we lose the war'. The strains from which we were suffering at sea, and the heavy anxieties about the future, focused the Admiralty's attention on the one direction from which it seemed that some fairly prompt easement might be obtained. This was considered to lie in the diversion of more long-range aircraft to Coastal Command, and in accepting the inevitable decline in our bombing offensive against Germany. Readers of our first volume will remember that the question who should control our maritime aircraft and who should supply and train their crews ran like a thread—and a somewhat inflammable thread—through the whole story of relations between the Navy and the R.A.F. since 1918.[1]

Early in 1942 a match was set to this powder-train by a paper sent to the Cabinet by the Secretary of State for Air in which he stated that 40 per cent of our bombing effort was being directed at the enemy warships in Brest, that it was difficult to hit those 'extremely small targets', and that the effort to do so was causing us heavy losses and so reducing the effect of our bomber force in its attacks on industrial Germany. Two days after this paper was written the question of bombing the warships in Brest was actually removed from the agenda of all committees by the ships themselves escaping back to Germany.[2] But the paper from the Air Ministry put the whole machinery of the Naval Staff into a state of intense activity—and of some indignation. Ever since 1940 we had been losing warships all over the world for lack of air cover, our losses of merchantmen had been particularly heavy in the waters where aircraft could not reach out to our convoys, and the Ministry of War Transport had several times warned the Admiralty and the Cabinet that losses above a certain rate were bound to affect the morale of the Merchant Navy. It was, in the Admiralty's eyes, hard to believe that all these troubles could best be cured by bombing German towns. Their reaction to

---

[1] See Vol. I, Chapter III.
[2] See pp. 149–161.

the Air Ministry's paper was prompt—and, perhaps, slightly sarcastic. There could not, wrote the First Lord, be any objections in his department to the Air Ministry's proposal. Indeed, the heavier bombing of Germany would be warmly welcomed. But before such a programme was embarked on, the Admiralty had two outstanding and urgent needs which the Air Ministry might be able to fill. The first was for improved long-range reconnaissance in the Indian Ocean and Bay of Bengal; about ninety-four merchant ships were at sea on any one day between Calcutta and Ceylon and they were now exposed to sudden attacks by Japanese warships. Two long-range reconnaissance and three more flying boat squadrons were needed to give warning of such raids. The second need was for far more intensive anti-U-boat patrolling in the inner and outer zones of the Bay of Biscay.[1] This required the transfer to Coastal Command of six-and-a-half Wellington squadrons and eighty-one of the American Fortress aircraft, so the Admiralty calculated. The tinder ignited by the Secretary of State for Air now blew rapidly into flame. On the First Sea Lord's desk a vast file of arguments and counter-arguments began to collect. He called this 'The Battle of the Air'. Even at a time of crisis and strain Sir Dudley Pound could show a quiet, sardonic touch of humour. The battle ebbed to and fro for the next six months in the Chiefs of Staff and Defence Committees, and before the Cabinet. At the risk of irritating the reader an attempt must be made to summarise the arguments used by both sides. For on the findings of a successful solution victory at sea may well have depended.

On the 5th of March the First Lord followed up his first reply to the Air Ministry's view regarding the relative importance of the war at sea and the bombing of Germany with a full statement of what Admiral Pound called 'The Needs of the Navy'. Certain ancient and fundamental strategic principles were first restated. Thus it was pointed out that if our merchant shipping tonnage, particularly in tankers (of which we and the Americans had recently been suffering what the First Lord elsewhere called 'frightful losses'), fell below the point needed to bring in our essential imports and maintain our armed forces, we should lose the war. The best and quickest way of rectifying matters, said the First Lord, was by 'largely increasing the strength of our land-based air forces working over the sea'. This dictum could hardly be disputed and, indeed, the Air Ministry later expressed its cordial agreement. However, the First Lord widened the issue by also claiming that 'if we are not to conduct the war at sea at a disadvantage we must have naval operational control of all aircraft employed on sea operations, on lines similar to those now in

[1] See Map 39 (opp. p. 369).

force with Coastal Command in home waters'. The question of the organisation of sea-air co-operation was thus thrown into the arena simultaneously with the different question of providing adequate strength for that purpose. A third demand by the Admiralty was that the Navy should henceforth be 'intimately associated' with the training of Coastal Command aircrews in work over the sea. The last point arose through the Admiralty's dissatisfaction over the standard of training in Coastal Command. As the First Sea Lord expressed it a little later, the real difficulty had been' to persuade air personnel that there was, in fact, any real difficulty in attacking a U-boat . . . Once this simple fact is absorbed and the airman has determined to learn and, more important still, to practise, the situation changes completely and the efficiency of air attack on U-boats bounds upwards'. Although it was certainly the case that in the early days R.A.F. aircrews had lacked training in anti-U-boat warfare, the Air Ministry had entirely revised its instructions in July 1941.[1] But it was, of course, bound to take time before the beneficial effects of the new tactics made themselves felt at sea.

The world-wide air strength deemed necessary by the Admiralty is shown below.

Table 4. The Admiralty's Assessment of Maritime Air Requirements, March 1942

Station	Flying Boats	General Reconnaissance (Long and Medium Range)	Photographic Reconnaissance	Striking Forces	Long-range Fighters	TOTAL
Home Waters	50	410	30	160	140	790
Central and South Atlantic	20	70	—	20	—	110
Indian Ocean	90	250	20	120*	90*	570* (40 R.N.)
S. and W. Australia	20	60	—	40	—	120
Mediterranean	—	100	30	120*	100*	350* (70 R.N.)
TOTAL	180	890 (250 Long-range, 640 Medium-range)	80	460 (70 R.N.)	330 (40 R.N.)	1,940 (110 R.N.)

* These figures included a proportion of naval aircraft provided by the Admiralty as shown in the totals columns.

[1] See Vol. I, p. 461.

The size of the gap between the requirements of the Admiralty and the actual number of aircraft available in the various theatres is shown in the next table, which gives the contemporary strength of the Empire's Air Forces mainly employed on maritime work. It will be seen that only the first three horizontal items in the table affected the Battle of the Atlantic.

Table 5. British Empire Aircraft employed mainly on Maritime Operations, March 1942

(Fleet Air Arm aircraft excluded—See previous table)

Theatre	G.R. Flying Boats	G.R. V.L.R. and L.R. Recce.	G.R. Medium- and Short- range Recce.	G.R. Anti- Shipping	L.R. Fighters	Photo Recce.	TOTALS	
Western Atlantic (R.C.A.F.)	25	20	40	Nil	Nil	Nil	85	⎫
E. Atlantic and Home Waters (R.A.F. Coastal Command)	51 (plus 11 float planes)	16	121	147 (also used on A/S work)	91	60	497	⎬ Total available for Battle of Atlantic—604
Gibraltar (R.A.F. Coastal Command)	6	Nil	10	Nil	Nil	6	22	⎭
West Africa (R.A.F.)	14	Nil	20	Nil	Nil	Nil	34	
Indian Ocean (R.A.F., R.I.A.F. and S.A.A.F.)	6	Nil	30	6	Nil	Nil	42	
Australasia (R.A.A.F., R.N.Z.A.F.)	16	Nil	120	12	Nil	Nil	148	
Mediterranean (R.A.F., R.A.A.F. and S.A.A.F.)	4	Nil	27	40	40	8	119	
TOTALS	122 plus 11 float planes	36	368	205	131	74	947	

NOTES:
1. In addition to the foregoing totals, the ordinary bombers of the Royal Air Force and, in some cases, of the Commonwealth Air Forces were used on various operations concerned with the war at sea, such as mine-laying, attacks on ports, anti-shipping and anti-submarine work. As they were not allocated to or controlled by the authorities responsible for the maritime war, and it is impossible to give a realistic figure to represent their contribution, they have been omitted from this table.

2. Abbreviations used:
G.R.	General Reconnaissance	S.A.A.F.	South African Air Force
L.R.	Long Range	R.A.A.F.	Royal Australian Air Force
R.C.A.F.	Royal Canadian Air Force	R.N.Z.A.F.	Royal New Zealand Air Force
R.I.A.F.	Royal Indian Air Force		

G

The Air Ministry, however, generously accepted the Admiralty's estimate of its needs and affirmed that it was 'incumbent on us to do our utmost to meet them'. They pointed out that, provided deliveries from American production reached the planned totals, they would all be met by the end of the year. It had to be accepted that, for the first six months of 1942, Coastal Command would be 'seriously under strength' in long-range reconnaissance aircraft. The Admiralty's needs would, therefore, be met 'in quantity though not in time'. This was, perhaps, rather chilly comfort to the department which was responsible for protecting the country's merchant shipping, and knew that it was disappearing at a rate which would render it inadequate within a very definite period of time. The help of the R.A.F. might well be coming. But would it come in time?

The Air Ministry would not consider diverting bombers to long-range reconnaissance until they were fitted with radar, because without it their reconnaissance work could not, so they maintained, be effective. So the radar supply programme, which had fallen badly in arrears, was considered to be the limiting factor. To use bombers without radar for reconnaissance would be 'a dispersion of our bombing resources'; and the 'considered view' of the Air Ministry was that the biggest contribution Bomber Command could make to the defeat of the U-boats was to bomb industrial areas in Germany.

On the 18th of March the Defence Committee approved the transfer of three Catalina Squadrons to the Indian Ocean. The need for them there was certainly urgent, but the consequence was still further to reduce the strength of Coastal Command at home. In London the argument between the Admiralty and the C.-in-C., Coastal Command, on the one side and the Air Ministry and Bomber Command on the other centred around the allocation of the American Fortress and Liberator aircraft now coming across, though still in small numbers, under Lend-Lease. At the end of the month Air Chief Marshal Joubert found that his position was getting impossible. He was, he said, 'kicked by the Admiralty for not asking enough and blamed by the Air Ministry for asking impossibilities'.

The War Office had meanwhile joined in the argument, and on the 1st of April the Air Ministry took the Navy and Army's proposals together and placed its views before the Defence Committee. The issues at stake were, firstly, the provision of larger forces and, secondly, the organisation for the control of those forces. Meeting the first was, said the Air Ministry, only a matter of time, and would be done. But, in their view, the other services' proposals under the second heading constituted in substance if not in name the division of the R.A.F. into three separate services. There may have been some grounds for the feeling that the patient who, in 1941, had been saved from 'a surgical operation' of this nature, was now once again being forced towards the operating table.[1] And the reason for it was, in the opinion of the Air Ministry, that lack of co-operation was being confused with the lack of the means to co-operate. Was it sound, they asked, to make acute shortages a reason to change the organisation? The Admiralty had, in its statement of the Navy's needs, praised the German sea-air organisation and had argued, from the fact that it appeared to be more effective than our own, that 'Coastal Commands' were needed on every station. Actually the Luftwaffe's organisation was, so argued the Air Ministry, the antithesis of the Admiralty proposal; for they had no 'Coastal Commands' at all, and very little naval air strength. Our post-war knowledge certainly does not indicate that the Germans achieved a better system of organisation than our own, nor that co-operation between their Navy and the Luftwaffe was at all good. In fact, the lack of it was a constant cause for complaint by Admiral Raeder and the German Naval Staff. The Air Ministry prophesied that, with American help, we were going to subject the Axis powers to the full rigour of an overwhelming air superiority, which they expected to prove decisive. But to accomplish that the R.A.F. must not be split up. On the issue of the control of Coastal Command aircraft they argued that, whereas at home it was vested in the Admiralty and not in the naval Commanders-in-Chief, abroad, where there was no organisation equivalent to that of the Admiralty, the position was different. On no account would the Air Ministry agree to the R.A.F. squadrons serving on foreign stations being placed under the naval Commanders-in-Chief. The Air Ministry also described the employment of aircraft at sea as a predominantly defensive rôle, and here they were perhaps on less firm ground; for not only were the offensive capabilities of aircraft of decisive importance to the maritime war, but the prosecution of the entire Allied offensive strategy depended on control of sea communications. As Mr Churchill put it early in 1943, 'the defeat of the U-boat and the improvement of the margin of shipbuilding resources are the prelude to all effective aggressive operations'.[2]

The basic issue which had to be settled by the Cabinet was, therefore, whether, taking account of the prevailing shortage of aircraft, a balance could be struck between the accepted Allied policy of bombing Germany and Italy as heavily as possible and the urgent need to improve the protection of our convoys. One fundamental requirement was to estimate just how effective the bombing of Germany had already been, and also how effective it was likely to become. Lord Cherwell forecast that in 1943 bombing of built-up districts would deprive about one-third of the population of Germany

---

[1] See Vol. I, pp. 360–361.
[2] Speech to the House of Commons on the war situation, 11th February 1943.

of their homes, and that this might be decisive. In mid-April the Prime Minister requested Mr Justice Singleton to survey the problem and estimate the results likely to be achieved in six, twelve and eighteen months' time. His conclusion was that, although little could be expected in the first period, the effect in a year or eighteen months would be substantial.

In the middle of April the Chiefs of Staff decided that four squadrons (Wellingtons and Whitleys) should be transferred from Bomber to Coastal Command for anti-submarine work in the Bay of Biscay and the North-West Approaches. This did not satisfy the Admiralty, and in the following month the First Sea Lord told his air colleague that he could 'find very little cause for satisfaction in the present state or future prospects of Coastal Command'—a conclusion with which its Commander-in-Chief could but agree. Nor was the employment of the long-range bombers the only issue; the old problem of Coastal Command's lack of anti-ship striking power was again to the fore.[1] Its Beauforts had mostly been sent abroad, the Hampdens had proved unsuitable for such work, and in June Beaufighters had to be converted to carry torpedoes. But it was plain that little improvement in striking power could be realised before the end of the year.

The enemy had meanwhile strengthened his fighter resources in Holland and Norway, and our reconnaissance aircraft and Hampden torpedo-bombers were suffering heavy losses from his Me. 109s and F.W. 190s. Long-range fighter protection for the air striking forces, and a better photographic reconnaissance aircraft than the Spitfire were urgently needed. Next, the last two Beaufort squadrons went abroad, and Coastal Command was left with virtually no striking force at all. Not until September were plans made to restore to it a force of torpedo-bombers, and then it was decided that it must consist of converted Beaufighters.

In the early summer the Admiralty's anxiety deepened. U-boat sinkings remained very high, in the Mediterranean 'the situation was precarious', the Far East 'was in a state of disintegration', and our ability to hold the Indian Ocean 'was in balance'. 'Ships alone', they said, were 'unable to maintain command at sea' . . . 'a permanent and increased share in the control of sea communications had to be borne by [the] air forces'. The requirements were once again analysed, and a deficiency of 800 aircraft was arrived at. But the Air Ministry still felt that 'to dissipate the Royal Air Force's strength' in order to reinforce Coastal Command would be a strategic error. They held that, as the bombing of Germany gained momentum the threat to our sea communications was bound to diminish. By reducing the

---

[1] See Vol. I, p. 338.

weight of our bombing we might merely postpone the day when the rising curve of Allied merchant ship construction would overtake our losses. To this argument the Admiralty's reply was that, quite apart from the great value of the ships lost, every one of their cargoes was of immense importance to the nation's war effort; that there was a real danger of our war production and transport slowing down, or even coming to a stop, through failure to bring in the essential imports of food and raw materials; that losses on the present scale could not continue without the morale of the Merchant Navy suffering, and finally that unless stronger air escorts were provided the enemy's rising U-boat strength would overwhelm the defenders of our convoys.

The Air Staff fully agreed over the shortage of suitable aircraft to help in the maritime war, but did not see how it could be quickly overcome. However, they considered that it might be mitigated by making better use of what aircraft we possessed. It was indeed plain that, for one reason or another, the difference between established strength and daily availability was far too great. From the investigation of this problem was developed the system known as 'Planned Flying and Maintenance', whose object was to extract the greatest possible operational benefit from every man-hour spent on aircraft maintenance. Though the scheme was ultimately adopted throughout the Royal Air Force, it was more fully applied in Coastal than in the other commands. It contributed much to improving the availability of aircraft for operations.

Meanwhile the views of the naval Commanders-in-Chief had been obtained from meetings in the Admiralty. They, of course, shared to the full the anxiety of the department to which they were responsible; but they were, perhaps, not well placed to view the whole complex problem in all its aspects, as could the inter-service and ministerial committees in London. To Admiral Tovey, Commander-in-Chief, Home Fleet, a situation had arisen which demanded, and could only be resolved by drastic action. He considered that 'substantial reinforcement of Coastal Command both at home and abroad [was] absolutely vital', and that reinforcement and re-equipment of the Fleet Air Arm was no less important. We had, so he considered, reached a point where the Board of Admiralty should resign rather than allow matters to continue as they were—a recommendation which, in spite of the distinguished source from which it emanated, the Board found unwelcome.

In addition to the need to obtain more and better shore-based aircraft to work with the Navy, the Admiralty was also at this time beset by many difficult problems arising out of the great expansion of its own Fleet Air Arm. At the end of 1941 it had consisted of 2,665 aircraft of all types, but it was estimated in June 1942 that by the end of that year its needs would reach the formidable total of 6,350 aircraft. This great expansion was mainly required to equip the thirty-one escort carriers then under construction or ordered. In particular the Navy was in a very bad plight for carrier-borne fighters. The prototype Firefly (2-seater reconnaissance anti-submarine aircraft) had crashed, the new single-seater Firebrand fighter was still an unknown quantity, and the American Martlets were too slow to deal with the Ju. 88s commonly used to attack our shipping. The only remedy was to obtain more Seafires (converted Spitfires) and Hurricanes, and the Admiralty asked the Air Ministry for 500 more of the former and a few of the latter. In July the matter was considered by the Defence Committee (Supply) and it was agreed that the Navy's needs must somehow be met.

Strike squadrons of torpedo-bombers were also expanding. In March the Navy had twenty-eight squadrons of Swordfish and Albacores, and the R.A.F. six squadrons of Beauforts. Torpedo production, which was an Admiralty responsibility, was now about 440 a month; the Navy took three-quarters for its own many and varied purposes, and allocated the remainder to the Air Force. This was enough to expand the latter's strength to six squadrons at home, and a like number in the Mediterranean and Indian Oceans. In April the Chief of the Air Staff agreed to plan for a total of fourteen squadrons that year. The Navy attached great importance to the torpedo-bomber equipment of the sister service, because of its striking power against enemy surface forces.

To return to the basic conflict between strategic bombing and the needs of the maritime war, by May little had been done to allay the Admiralty's anxieties, and an appeal to the Cabinet to divert some of Bomber Command's aircraft to Coastal Command was being planned. On second thoughts, however, it was decided that, even if such an order was given, it was unlikely to produce the desired result unless it had the willing support of the sister service in general, and of the Air Staff in particular. Accordingly the appeal to the Cabinet was shelved, and a new attempt made to reach direct agreement. Discussions between Rear-Admiral E. J. P. Brind and Air Vice-Marshal J. C. Slessor (Assistant Chiefs of Naval and Air Staffs) therefore took place. They did not lead to any transfer of aircraft, but did produce agreement that a fixed number of sorties should be flown weekly by bombers against U-boats crossing the Bay of Biscay. The Admiralty accepted this half measure, though with reluctance.

In August papers reached the War Cabinet from the hands of the Commander-in-Chief, Bomber Command, and Lord Trenchard. They had not been considered by the Chiefs of Staff Committee, and represented only the views of the writers. The Prime Minister did not endorse the views expressed and indeed, when he circulated the papers to his colleagues, he added a rider that, in his opinion, a good case was spoilt by overstatement. We, with many of the enemy's records in our possession, are able to see how near the mark the Prime Minister was. But to the Admiralty the optimistic results claimed, particularly from bombing U-boat yards and bases, were not borne out by the trend of the Atlantic battle; and Lord Trenchard's statement that 'the two-dimensional [air] operations in the Atlantic . . . are purely defensive' and that 'the place to hit the submarines is where they are made and to mine the seas where they emerge, instead of only hunting them over the illimitable sea' read a little strangely. For the fact was that hardly any damage had as yet been done to U-boats by bombing raids, and their numbers at sea in the Atlantic were increasing rapidly[1]; moreover, all our experience since 1939 had shown that it was the sea and air convoy escorts which destroyed most U-boats, and it was chiefly for more of these that the Admiralty was pleading—not to hunt for U-boats 'over the illimitable sea'. The Naval Staff prepared a sober and moderate reply, which was used by the Chiefs of Staff when they placed their views before the Cabinet. At the meeting of the latter on the 12th of August Mr S. M. Bruce, the 'accredited representative of the Government of the Commonwealth of Australia', said that he did not consider adequate data had been furnished by the Chiefs of Staff to enable the Cabinet to reach sound decisions on so difficult a matter. He said that he was disturbed to find that we were apparently working on the basis of providing the minimum air strength needed to secure our vital sea communications, and that he felt that a task of such paramount importance demanded a much higher priority. In particular he was profoundly disturbed by the lack of maritime air strength in the Indian Ocean, where the defence of Ceylon was now 'a matter of importance second only to that of the British Isles'. In general he felt that there had been' a lack of drive and determination' in meeting the urgent needs of the maritime war. He had placed a memorandum of his own before the Cabinet, but it must not be read 'as in any sense an attack on the policy of bombing Germany'. He did, however, consider that the urgent needs of the maritime war should be met, even at the cost of accepting some delay in building up the bombing offensive. The Cabinet therefore instructed the Chiefs of Staff to provide the full data which Mr Bruce considered to have been so far lacking.

In his reply the Secretary of State for Air restated the agreed Allied policy that the defeat of Germany was the key to victory, and said that, in order to implement that decision, diversions to safeguard other vital interests must be kept to the minimum. Only a month earlier the Combined Chiefs of Staff had, he continued, recorded

---

[1] See Appendix K.

their recommendation that, for the years 1942 and '43 'Allied air strength should continue to be built up in the United Kingdom to provide a constantly increasing intensity of air attack on Germany'. He also reminded the Cabinet of the many and varied ways in which Bomber Command had recently contributed and was still contributing to the war at sea by lending squadrons to Coastal Command, by bombing U-boat bases and building yards, by laying thousands of mines, and in other ways, too. His report was accepted by the Cabinet as evidence that in the circumstances then prevailing the best was being done with the aircraft available. It thus came to pass that no definite change of policy was ordered by the Cabinet; but the Prime Minister took action to obtain a shift of emphasis in the allocation of our air effort.

In the previous June and July Mr Bruce had suggested that a small committee, composed of those best equipped with knowledge and experience, those responsible for policy and those capable of rapidly translating policy into action, was necessary to resolve the conflicting needs of the maritime war and the bombing offensive. At the Cabinet meeting on the 12th of August this suggestion was accepted, and the necessary measures, including the explanation of our purpose to the Americans, were put in hand. The fact that the Committee had Cabinet status enabled decisions to be quickly reached, and priorities firmly decided and enforced. On the 4th of November Mr Churchill took the chair at the first meeting of the body, which was called the Cabinet Anti-U-boat Warfare Committee. His colleagues were the Ministers and Service chiefs most concerned in the maritime war, and a number of prominent scientists. Mr Harriman and Admiral H. R. Stark, U.S.N., represented the United States. Mr Churchill described the Committee's purpose as being 'to give the same impulse to anti-U-boat warfare as had been applied to the Battle of the Atlantic[1] and night A/A defence'; its meetings were to be held weekly. At the first meeting the First Lord estimated that 243 U-boats were then operational and that production of new boats was running at the rate of twenty to thirty a month. Since the start of the war he considered that we had sunk or captured 159 and probably sunk 44 more.[2] In other words, we were not destroying more than one-third of the monthly output of new U-boats. The first need was to fill the 'air gap' in mid-Atlantic[3],

---

[1] The Prime Minister was presumably here referring to the Battle of the Atlantic Committee which he had formed in March 1941 to deal with all aspects of the struggle (see Vol. I, p. 364), as distinct from the Cabinet Anti-U-boat Committee now created.

[2] By 1st November 1942, the Germans had actually lost from all causes 135 U-boats and the Italians 53. The number of operational U-boats was then about 200, but a further 170 were undergoing trials or training crews. The Admiralty's estimate of the current rate of production was correct.

[3] See Map 20 (opp. p. 205).

for which we required about forty long-range radar-fitted aircraft; the other need was for more and longer-range air patrols in the Bay of Biscay. The outstanding issues were thus at once placed in the foreground of the Committee's deliberations.

It must be emphasised that there was no disagreement between the Admiralty and the Air Ministry regarding the needs. What was difficult was to provide the V.L.R. aircraft quickly. The only British aircraft comparable to the American Liberator was the Lancaster, which had only just started to come off the production line, and was in every case fitted for land bombing. It was therefore plain that only by allocation of Liberators from the United States could the need be met quickly.

By the middle of October some improvement in the strength of Coastal Command could be shown. There were now forty-four squadrons, compared with thirty-nine twelve months previously. But the increase was really owed to loans from Bomber Command, which could at any time be recalled, and to the four squadrons of naval Swordfish lent by the Admiralty. There were still only two squadrons of Liberators—the most urgently needed aircraft of all— though two more were forming. Deliveries of this type under Lend-Lease had been very disappointing, because the Americans now claimed the lion's share for their own purposes—including the Pacific war.

At the third meeting of the Anti-U-boat Warfare Committee on the 18th of November, the Chief of the Air Staff made clear and definite proposals whereby the Admiralty's needs regarding air patrols in the Bay of Biscay would be met in the very near future. To cover the outer zone he proposed to transfer thirty Halifaxes to Coastal Command, while the Wellingtons already patrolling the inner zone would be re-equipped with more modern aircraft fitted with Leigh Lights[1] and, gradually, with improved radar which the U-boats would be unable to detect. To mitigate the loss of strength to Bomber Command the Prime Minister agreed to ask the U.S.A. to release thirty Liberators, a request which the Americans fulfilled to the extent of two U.S. Army Air Force squadrons.

These measures satisfied, to a considerable extent, the needs which the Admiralty had been pressing since the previous March. One of the Assistant Chiefs of Naval Staff remarked to the First Sea Lord on returning to the Admiralty after this meeting that he had 'sensed the relief of the committee that agreement had been reached'. Doubtless that same sense of relief was felt, in even greater measure, by Admiral Pound himself. It may, therefore, be said that the 'Battle of the Air' of 1942 was closed by the meeting of the Anti-U-boat Committee on

---

[1] See Vol. I, p. 358 regarding the introduction of these searchlight-fitted aircraft.

the 18th of November. It will be told in a later chapter how the crisis in the Atlantic in the early spring of 1943 caused the same issues to be reopened.[1] Meanwhile, Coastal Command remained an integral part of the R.A.F., and its part in the Atlantic struggle grew with the improvement of what the Chief of the Air Staff had aptly called 'the means to co-operate' with the Navy.

In conclusion it must be stressed that the divergent views described in this chapter were both sincerely held opinions regarding the best way of accomplishing the defeat of Germany. In Whitehall the matter was repeatedly and frankly argued in committee and on paper, but never in such a way as to indicate or arouse ill-feeling between the two services. In the Naval and Royal Air Force commands concerned with the day-to-day prosecution of the struggle, there was a deep and mutual sympathy with and understanding of each other's difficulties and problems; and the good sense of the officers and men of both services prevented the natural differences in their outlook affecting the conduct of operations.

---

[1] See Chapter XIV.

CHAPTER IV

THE BATTLE OF THE ATLANTIC

The Campaign in American Waters
1st January–31st July, 1942

'Each and every convoy now involves the
Naval Staff in intricate operations, all carefully planned and brilliantly executed'.
W. S. Churchill. Extract from statement at a Conference of Ministers,
20th April 1943.

A T the beginning of the year the three great operational bases
of the Western Approaches Command (Liverpool, Greenock
and Londonderry) controlled twenty-five groups of escort
vessels totalling some seventy destroyers, eighteen sloops, sixty-seven
corvettes and ten ex-American coastguard cutters.[1] In addition to
these ships American destroyers were still escorting certain North
Atlantic convoys, and were using Londonderry as their base. The
British groups were divided into four categories. Firstly, the 'Special
Escort Groups', composed of short-endurance destroyers, looked after
WS. and PQ. convoys[2] during the first part of their passages, met the
'monster' liners when they started to bring American troops across
the Atlantic, and undertook any unusual requirements which might
arise. Secondly, there were the groups of long-range destroyers and
corvettes, which provided the ocean escorts for the North Atlantic
convoys from the Western Ocean Meeting Point right home to
Britain, and also escorted the Gibraltar convoys. There were now
sufficient long-range ships to avoid, save in exceptional circumstances, the complication of having to send escorts to Iceland to
refuel while on passage, as had been necessary in 1941.[3] Indeed, the
importance of Iceland as a refuelling base for the Atlantic escorts
had declined just when its importance as an air base came to be fully
exploited. These first two categories of escort groups were based on
Liverpool, Greenock and Londonderry. The third class of escort

---

[1] See Vol. I, p. 454, regarding the transfer of the American coastguard cutters to the
Royal Navy.
Full details of our Escort Vessel strength and dispositions on 1st January 1942, 1st
August 1942, and 1st January 1943 are given in Appendix G.
[2] See Appendix F for particulars of the code letters allocated to all convoys.
[3] See Vol. I, pp. 456–457.

group was composed of long-range sloops, destroyers and ex-American cutters. There were six of these groups, and they usually worked from Londonderry to escort the SL/OS convoys to and from the rendezvous with the Freetown local escorts. Lastly, there were anti-aircraft groups, which consisted mainly of auxiliary A.A. ships and worked .in the Irish Sea, besides escorting the Arctic and Gibraltar convoys. The Greenock, Londonderry and Liverpool groups were theoretically interchangeable, but every endeavour was made to keep each individual group intact and to employ them on one route, thereby gaining the advantage of familiarity not only with each other but with the problems peculiar to that route.

At Gibraltar there was a force amounting to about two groups to provide local escorts. The South Atlantic Command possessed one destroyer flotilla, five sloops and some two dozen corvettes in the Freetown Escort Force, while in the Western Atlantic there were fourteen destroyers and about forty corvettes of the Royal Canadian Navy (or lent to that service from the Royal Navy) forming the Newfoundland Escort Force, plus about a score of escort vessels for western local escort purposes.

While transfers of complete groups from one command or station to another occurred fairly frequently, the same general organisation, based on the broad principles described above, continued in the Western Approaches Command throughout the period covered by this volume. Appendix G shows the strength available on different dates, and how changes in allocations were made to meet the varying needs of the war.

Not long after this phase started—to be precise in March—the British and American authorities reviewed their needs of escort vessels. The table below shows the results.

Table 6. British and American Escort Vessel Requirements, March 1942

	British	*American*
Required .	725	590
Available .	383	122
Shortage .	342	468

It was agreed that new ships should be allocated in proportion to each nation's deficiency. There were now 300 escort vessels building on British account in the United States (known as British Destroyer Escorts or B.D.Es, and later called Frigates by the Royal Navy). Delivery of 200 was expected by the end of 1943; but they did not actually enter service fast enough to meet the ever-rising calls for escorts, and the severe shortage from which we had suffered since the beginning of the war continued. It remained indeed a permanent feature of the Atlantic struggle almost to the end. The main factor

'Convoy Air Cover'. By Norman Wilkinson.

German Type IXB (1,050 ton) Atlantic U-boat.

U.71 under attack by Sunderland U. of No. 10 Squadron R.A.A.F. on 5th June 1942. The U-boat dived when sighted, and was forced to the surface by depth charges. The Sunderland then engaged with machine guns, as can be seen in the photograph.

which delayed completion of the new escort vessels was the over-riding priority for labour, steel and engines given in America to the landing craft needed for the cross-Channel operation, which they still hoped to launch in 1943. It was at British insistence that this was finally postponed, and American history has since accepted that our judgment was sound[1]; but the priority given to landing craft certainly contributed greatly to the continuing weakness of our Atlantic escorts, and to the heavy shipping losses we suffered at this time. In July it was agreed with the Americans that all 'Destroyer Escorts', as well as the new twin screw corvettes and minesweepers, whether building in America, Canada or Britain, should be 'thrown into a common pool' and 'assigned between us according to our strategic requirements'. But difficulties soon arose in deciding which 'strategic requirement' should have the highest priority.

During the winter of 1941–42 our convoys were, in general, using the northerly Atlantic route in order to gain the greatest possible protection from the air bases in Iceland. Furthermore, by keeping close to the 'great circle' track between Newfoundland and the North-West Approaches our escorts were able to conserve their fuel as much as possible. But the northerly route was extremely trying to the merchantmen and their escorts in mid-winter, and the Admiralty much desired to move the convoys further south. Not until nearly the end of the phase now to be described did this general shift of the shipping routes become practicable; and even then it had the disadvantage that it reduced the effectiveness of the cover afforded by aircraft working from Iceland. Throughout the whole of the winter and spring our convoys had to contend with the very severe conditions of the high latitudes.

Long before the entry of the United States into the war the German Naval Staff had realised that our shipping was far more vulnerable in the Western Atlantic than in the more easterly parts of that ocean. Although the HX and SC convoys, and also their outward counterparts, now had ·continuous anti-submarine escorts throughout their journeys, it was inevitable that, after reaching the Canadian coast, many ships from west-bound convoys had to be routed onwards independently. These, and the great flow of American shipping off the east coast of the United States, which was still sailing in peacetime fashion, offered inviting targets to the U-boats. Well before Pearl Harbour the Germany Navy had been watching the increasing American participation in the Atlantic struggle with concern, and had repeatedly, though vainly, asked to be allowed to retaliate. Although U-boats had, in the previous September, been sent to work off southern Greenland and in the Straits of Belle Isle,

[1] Churchill, Vol. IV, pp. 510–13 and 586–91, and Morison, Vol. IX, pp. 8–9.

and had there been involved in incidents with American warships[1], Hitler had then refused to allow them greater freedom. To Admiral Dönitz and his staff the entry of the United States into the war brought not only the welcome lifting of such restrictions, but an opportunity again to find virtually undefended targets, such as they had not enjoyed since 'the happy time' of July–October 1940.[2] They knew, moreover, that they had somehow to improve greatly on the results achieved in 1941 if they were to succeed in bringing Britain to her knees. Their estimate was that if sinkings averaged 700,000 tons per month we should soon be defeated. Yet in 1941, although they believed the figure to be much higher, they had actually only managed to sink an average of 180,000 tons every month. America's entry into the war therefore brought new hope as well as new opportunities to the U-boat command, especially as it occurred at a time when its strength was at last beginning to increase rapidly. The decision to send U-boats to the American seaboard was taken on the 12th of December—the day after Germany declared war on the United States—and the movement was given the somewhat histrionic name of 'Paukenschlag' (Roll on the drums). But because Japan's intentions had not been known in Berlin, the sudden arrival of an opportunity which they had long desired took the Germans by surprise, and they were not able at once to make the most of it. They had suffered heavy losses in the Mediterranean and off Portugal in the last month of 1941, and still had a number of boats caught in what Dönitz had accurately described as the 'Mediterranean trap'.[3] Moreover, the German Naval Staff still clung to their determination to help avert a collapse in Africa by keeping a number of U-boats in the Mediterranean. The consequence was that when Dönitz proposed to send twelve of the large (1,100-ton) U-boats to American waters the number was reduced by his superiors to half that figure. Those six boats sailed on the 2nd of January. Three were finally ordered into the Mediterranean to replace losses, while the other three were kept on patrol between Gibraltar and the Azores.

A month later the enemy realised that the Western Atlantic offered far better prospects than the Gibraltar area, where his recent experiences had proved unfortunate. In mid-January Convoy HG. 78 had been attacked by three U-boats, and one of them (U.93) was sunk by the escorting destroyer *Hesperus*; and when the troopship *Llangibby Castle* was torpedoed on the 16th and put into Horta in the Azores to effect temporary repairs, U.581 was sunk by the destroyer *Westcott*, one of the three escorts sent to bring the damaged ship home. Between January and March about five U-boats worked between the

---

[1] See Vol. I, p. 472.
[2] See Vol. I, p. 348.
[3] See Vol. I, pp. 474–475.

Gulf of St. Lawrence and Cape Hatteras, and three more soon reached the waters off the Chesapeake. They immediately achieved such substantial success (forty-four ships were sunk in the Canadian Coastal Area in January and February) that the enemy decided to send every available boat to follow them. The 'Roll on the drums', whose start had been somewhat muffled, was now reverberating menacingly around the western ocean.

By mid-January seven of the medium-sized (750-ton) U-boats had arrived off Newfoundland. There they found conditions much less to their liking. Most of the shipping was strongly escorted, air cover was better and the weather was intensely cold. In February they were therefore moved to the south of Halifax, where it was again found to be both cold and dangerous. In March they started to cruise off New York. Dönitz was pleasantly surprised to find that the endurance of the smaller boats permitted them to stay two or three weeks on patrol in these distant waters.

From the foregoing account of the enemy's policy it will be seen that the Americans were granted about five weeks' grace (7th December 1941–mid-January 1942) before attacks started in earnest. In assessing the reasons for their slowness in starting convoy and getting their anti-submarine defences in order, it is important to remember that many of their escorts were employed in the Pacific until after the Battle of Midway had removed the Japanese threat to the life-line between the west coast of America and Australia. Yet it seems undeniable that even the simplest arrangements for the better control of coastal shipping were very slow in being adopted. As an example of the favourable conditions encountered by the U-boats, we may quote from the war diary of Lieutenant-Commander Hardegen (U.123), who spent a very happy night on the 18th–19th of January off Cape Hatteras. In his diary he wrote: 'It is a pity that there were not . . . ten to twenty U-boats here last night, instead of one. I am sure all would have found ample targets. Altogether I saw about twenty steamships, some undarkened; also a few tramp steamers, all hugging the coast. Buoys and beacons in the area had dimmed lights which, however, were visible up to two or three miles'. It appears that the actual result of that night's work by U.123 was three ships of about 17,000 tons sunk and one damaged.

Not until the 1st of April was even a partial convoy system started; and in the meanwhile innumerable factors such as the lighted channel marks, the complete lack of a coastal 'blackout' and the unrestricted use of ships' wireless, gave the U-boats all the help they needed. Thus began what the American historian has ironically described as 'a merry massacre'[1], and the enemy called his second

---

[1] See Morison, Vol. I, p. 125 *et seq.*

'happy time'. The U-boats generally lay submerged not far offshore
by day, and moved inshore to attack with guns or torpedoes on the
surface by night. Few north Atlantic convoys were sighted, let alone
attacked at this time. The enemy had, in truth, no need to invite
retaliation from their escorts; for he could find all he needed with
much less risk to himself elsewhere. An exception did, however, occur
at the end of February when convoy ON. 67 was sighted by a U-boat
600 miles north-east of Cape Race. Five U-boats (four of which were
outward-bound from their Biscay bases) were called to the scene and
in a three-day battle sank eight ships, six of which were large tankers,
without loss to themselves.

One of the most surprising facts regarding the havoc wrought off
the American coast in the early days of 1942 is that there were never
more than about twelve U-boats working in those waters at any one
time—no greater strength than the enemy had sometimes mustered
to make a 'pack attack' on a single one of our convoys in 1941. Yet
in the first two weeks of the new campaign they sank 13 ships of
nearly 100,000 tons, and in February the sinkings in the American
Eastern Sea Frontier Command alone exceeded that tonnage.[1] In
the following month twenty-eight ships of 159,340 tons were sunk in
the Eastern Sea Frontier and fifteen more of 92,321 tons in the Gulf
and Caribbean commands; and no less than 57 per cent of the tonnage sunk was tankers. Not until April were defensive measures
started by the Americans in earnest.

From the 12th of December 1941 until the following 17th of
January the First Sea Lord himself was in America to review the
whole maritime war with our new Allies, and to co-ordinate with
them the many fields in which the naval forces of the two nations
would be working together. Shortly before Admiral Pound's return
to London discussions between the Admiralty and the U.S. Naval
Mission were started on this side of the Atlantic. The first U-boat
attack off the American coast had just taken place. Arising out of
these discussions the American mission in London asked the U.S.
Navy Department the following questions:

  1. What help could be given by Britain to provide escorts
  from the American Atlantic ports to Halifax or Bermuda, or to
  the Western Ocean Meeting Point? The reply was that 'no
  effective assistance' could be given.

  2. What was the Navy Department's estimate of the effectiveness of their anti-submarine surface and air defences on the
  Atlantic seaboard? The reply was that they were 'inadequate'.

  3. Whether it would be possible to keep a coastal lane reasonably free from U-boat attack? The reply was negative.

---

[1] See Map 10 (opp. p. 97) for the limits of the U.S. Navy's command areas.

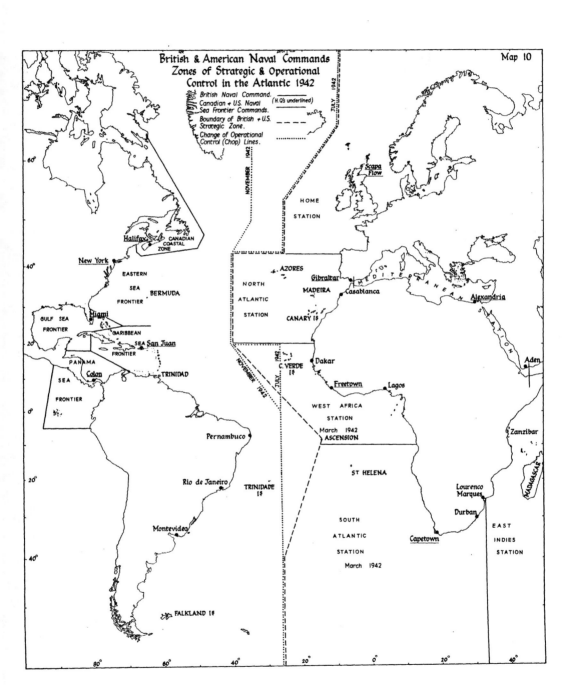

British & American Naval Commands
Zones of Strategic & Operational
Control in the Atlantic 1942

Map 10

British Naval Command.
Canadian + U.S. Naval
Sea Frontier Commands.   (H.Q's underlined)
Boundary of British + U.S.
Strategic Zone.
Change of Operational
Control (Chop) Lines.

JULY 1942

NOVEMBER 1942

Scapa Flow

HOME
STATION

Halifax
CANADIAN
COASTAL
ZONE

New York

EASTERN
SEA
FRONTIER   BERMUDA

AZORES

Gibraltar
MADEIRA
Casablanca

MEDITERRANEAN

Alexandria

NORTH
ATLANTIC
STATION

CANARY IS

GULF SEA
FRONTIER

Miami

CARIBBEAN

SEA San Juan
FRONTIER

PANAMA

Colon

SEA

FRONTIER

TRINIDAD

NOVEMBER 1942   JULY 1942

C. VERDE IS

Dakar

Freetown   Lagos

Aden

WEST AFRICA
STATION

March 1942
ASCENSION

Zanzibar

MADAGASCAR

Pernambuco

Rio de Janeiro   TRINIDADE IS

ST HELENA

Lourenco Marques

Durban

Montevideo

SOUTH
ATLANTIC
STATION

March 1942

Capetown

EAST
INDIES
STATION

FALKLAND IS

60°

40°

20°

0°

20°

40°

60°

80°   60°   40°   20°   0°   20°   40°

In spite of these discouraging replies the British Government had not forgotten what Admiral Pound called 'the two great pre-war gestures' made by the Americans, namely the provision of fifty destroyers when we were at our lowest ebb for escorts, and American participation in Atlantic convoys.[1] Admiral Pound had, while in the United States, offered to turn over ten of our corvettes to them. Early in February the British mission in Washington suggested offering two dozen of our anti-submarine trawlers, and the Admiralty promptly put the proposal into effect. By the end of March most of them had arrived on their new station, and Professor Morison has recorded that 'these rugged little coal burners . . . were a great help'.[2] Loan of some of our bombers was also discussed, but the Air Ministry found itself unable to spare any. However, in June, with Admiralty agreement, No. 53 Squadron of Coastal Command went to Rhode Island and then on to Trinidad, off which sinkings had become serious. The First Sea Lord hoped that we had thus 'responded with equal generosity when the American need for reinforcement became urgent'.

None the less to the British authorities it seemed that the Americans were both slow and unwilling to start coastal convoys. On the 19th of March the First Sea Lord told Admiral King that he 'regarded the introduction of convoy as a matter of urgency', and that convoys with weak escorts were preferable to no convoys. Mr Churchill telegraphed his 'deep concern'[3], but the President suggested palliatives such as reducing the British import programme; while Admiral King considered that 'inadequately escorted convoys were worse than none'—the exact opposite to all that our experience had taught.

The release of escorts from the mid-ocean groups was constantly discussed, and on the 16th of April the Halifax convoy cycle was opened out from six to seven days so that two escort groups could be sent to the east coast of America. Mr Hopkins was at that time in London, and on the 14th of April he telegraphed to President Roosevelt that in the preceding three months Allied losses had totalled 1,200,000 tons, over half of which had been tankers. The First Lord had, in fact, just told the Prime Minister that for the preceding week our tanker losses 'had been frightful'. 'We are', said Hopkins prophetically, 'going to need all these ships desperately in the next few months . . . I doubt very much that anything short of convoy is going to do this job . . . They [i.e. the British] whose island is so dependent on imports realize full well the significance of

---

[1] See Vol. I, pp. 347–348 and 471–473.
[2] Morison, Vol. I, p. 131.
[3] Churchill, Vol. IV, p. 103.

H

these sinkings to the future of the war'. The Admiralty's Director of Anti-Submarine Warfare (Captain G. E. Creasy) and the Air Officer Commanding No. 19 Group of Coastal Command (Air Vice-Marshal G. R. Bromet) had meanwhile gone to the United States to advise on the formation, training and organisation of air and surface anti-submarine forces.

In March, when Admiral Stark was appointed to command the American naval forces in Europe, the First Sea Lord had a review of the whole Atlantic battle prepared for him. Our anti-submarine experiences 'over the past thirty months' were there summarised under the following four headings:

1. The comparative failure of hunting forces.
2. The great value of aircraft in convoy protection.
3. The supreme importance of adequate training and practices.
4. The value of efficient radar.

As to the first the Admiralty said that 'this is one of the hardest of all the lessons of the war to swallow. To go to sea to hunt down and destroy the enemy makes a strong appeal to every naval officer. It gives a sense . . . of the offensive that is lacking in the more hum-drum business of convoy protection. But in this U-boat war . . . in the oceans the limitations of hunting forces have made themselves very clear'. We ourselves had travelled a long and hard road, and had wasted much effort in hunting for U-boats since 1939.[1] One may hope that the conclusion quoted above will prove the final epitaph of the U-boat hunting group.

The Americans, however, certainly seem to have been slow in putting much of our experience into practice. They first tried every conceivable measure—except convoy and escort. Even 'Q Ships' were sent out, and one cannot but agree with Professor Morison's description of them as 'the least useful and most wasteful of all methods to fight submarines'.[2] Yet the most surprising thing about American unreadiness is that, ever since Admiral R. L. Ghormley, U.S.N., arrived in London in August 1940 with a strong mission composed of some of his service's ablest officers, the policy of the Admiralty had been to give to the American Navy virtually the whole of our knowledge and experience, not excepting our latest radar developments. The writer of this history happened to be one of the members of the Naval Staff instructed to put that policy into effect; and he is confident that Admiral Ghormley himself, and the individual officers who accompanied him to deal with their own specific subjects, will agree that nothing of importance was ever

---

[1] See Vol. I, pp. 10, 357 and 481.
[2] Morison, Vol. I, p. 286. For British experience with 'Q Ships' see this author's Vol. I, pp. 136–137.

withheld from them.[1] In fact Ghormley soon told the Washington authorities that he 'was obtaining information fresh from the laboratory of war, of priceless value to national defence'.[2]

In July 1942 the First Sea Lord wrote to Sir Arthur Salter, then head of the British Merchant Shipping Mission in America, reviewing 'the critical situation in the Battle of the Atlantic'. Admiral Pound said that he 'hoped and believed that we have taken them [i.e. the U.S. Navy] fully and frankly into our confidence and have given them all the information available, both on tactical and technical matters'. It is therefore plain that British and American records agree that all we had learnt from more than two years of war was given to the Americans; and it is also the case that numerous publications containing British doctrine and experience were issued by the Navy Department to United States' ships and establishments well before their country was at war. Whether our organisation for the control and protection of shipping could have been imitated earlier by a country which suddenly found itself plunged into a great maritime war may remain a matter for dispute. It is, however, justifiable to quote the German post-war comment that 'the U.S. Navy failed to profit from Britain's war experience'; and to remember that the cost of that failure (if such it was) in terms of tonnage sunk and lives lost was certainly not light.

The American historian has stated his conclusions regarding this disastrous period in such forthright terms that there is no need for us to dwell on them further here.[3] From the British point of view the position was, however, very serious. Not only were the American escort vessels and aircraft, which had so recently begun to take a real share in the Atlantic battle, now needed in their own coastal waters, but British-controlled merchant vessels were being sunk in waters where the Admiralty's writ did not run, and after they had loaded for the long haul to the east or survived a westward passage of the Atlantic. As Admiral Noble put it to the First Sea Lord, 'The Western Approaches Command finds itself in the position today [8th of March 1942] of escorting convoys safely over to the American eastern seaboard, and then . . . finding that many of the ships thus escorted are easy prey to the U-boats . . . off the American coast or in the Caribbean'. Even though much of the shipping was not our own we could not remain passive in face of such a holocaust.

---

[1] The method of sweeping the British magnetic mine was the only subject which the Board of Admiralty specifically ordered should not be given to the American Mission.

[2] Morison, Vol. I, p. 41.

[3] Morison, Vol. I, pp. 200–201. 'This writer cannot avoid the conclusion that the U.S. Navy was woefully unprepared, materially and mentally for the U-boat blitz on the Atlantic coast. He further believes that . . . this unpreparedness was largely the Navy's own fault . . . [Furthermore, the ultimate victory] does not alter the fact that it had no plans ready for a reasonable protection to shipping . . . , and was unable to improvise them for several months'.

Returning now to the enemy's onslaught, the time which U-boats could spend in the more distant waters was greatly extended by the use of U-tankers (or 'milch cows' as the German Navy called them). The first of these (a converted 1,000-ton ex-Turkish boat) left Lorient on the 14th of March and fuelled three operational boats in the Western Approaches. She was followed a fortnight later by U.459, of 1,600 tons and the first proper U-tanker. Between March and August 1942 no less than six 'milch cows' made fuelling trips, and sometimes two or three were engaged on supply operations at the same time. These measures had the effect of about doubling the endurance of the 750-ton boats. They were now worth nearly the same to the enemy as the large 1,100-tonners. Torpedo capacity and expenditure, rather than fuel supply, now became the limiting factor in the length of U-boat cruises in the Western Ocean.

After the initial onslaught off the east coast of America the enemy's intention was to send all his larger boats to the Caribbean, and five of them had arrived there by the middle of February. They sank many ships, especially tankers, in the first few days; one worked off Aruba, another penetrated into the harbours of Port of Spain (Trinidad) and Castries (St Lucia), while U.126 sank nine ships in fourteen days between the Windward Passage and the Old Bahama Channel.[1] Happily no large boats were available to relieve those of the first wave.

Meanwhile the enemy tried to prevent us concentrating our counter-measures in the west by renewing his assaults off Freetown— an area which the U-boats had not visited since the abortive operation of October 1941.[2] Early in March two U-boats arrived there and sank eleven ships (64,391 tons); but the American coast was seen to be the more profitable theatre, so no more boats were sent to west Africa for a time.

One of Hitler's 'intuitions' now caused a fortunate relaxation of pressure in the western Atlantic. At his conference on the 22nd of January he announced his conviction that Norway was 'the zone of destiny', and demanded 'unconditional obedience to all his commands and wishes concerning the defence of this area'. He decided that every warship and U-boat would be needed off that country's coast. Next day, however, in a manner typical of Hitler's desire always to have things both ways, he ordered that operations off the American coast were none the less to continue. On the 25th Dönitz received a totally unexpected order to send eight boats to the waters between Iceland, the Faeroes and Scotland to protect Norway from the anticipated invasion; and the final German defence plan envisaged the disposal of no less than twenty of the medium-sized boats

[1] See Map 11 (opp. p. 105).
[2] See Vol. I, p. 470.

for that purpose. Though Dönitz himself protested vigorously against the diversion of his U-boats, the German Naval Staff seems to have made no serious attempt to counter Hitler's obsession by a reasoned argument against its probability. Nor did they even represent what the consequences would be in the Atlantic. Inevitably the weight of the offensive off the American coast declined, just at the time when it had proved highly profitable. In actual fact, the U-boats stationed between Iceland and the North Channel accomplished little in February and March, though two homeward convoys (SC. 67 and HX. 175) and two outward ones (ON. 63 and ONS. 76) were attacked in those waters. In passing, it is of interest to remark that in April 1942 Mr Churchill did tell the British Chiefs of Staff to examine the feasibility of a landing in Norway, with the object of relieving enemy pressure on our Arctic convoys.[1] His proposal, however, never reached the stage of serious planning, because it conflicted with the basic Allied strategy, which was to strike first in North Africa.

After the successes of the first two months of 1942 it was natural for Dönitz to want to send every U-boat he could find to the American seaboard; but the vacillations among the higher German authorities diverted a substantial proportion of his strength to other waters. None the less the months of March and April saw the climax of the U-boats' successes in the west, in spite of the fact there were rarely more than six to eight boats actually operating at any one time. A new crop of U-boat 'aces', similar to the one which we had successfully harvested in March 1941[2], sprang into being. Between mid-March and the 20th of April Hardegen (U.123) sank eleven ships and Mohr (U.124) nine, while Topp (U.552), Müzelburg (U.203) and Lassen (U.160) each had five or six to his credit. They found most of their victims between New York and Cape Hatteras, but it was off the latter that, on the 14th of April, the American destroyer *Roper* achieved the first success for his country by sinking U.85. Gradually the U-boats now began to be driven from the shallow, profitable coastal waters; more and more did they find it necessary to retire further to seaward, especially on moonlight nights, to recharge their batteries.

While the enemy was achieving enormous, and one may feel largely avoidable, destruction in the west, three thousand miles away to the east his experiences were very different. British anti-submarine tactics and weapons, both surface and air, were improving rapidly; and, unknown to the enemy, radar had arrived in a form capable of being fitted in escort vessels and aircraft. The activities of our aircraft over the Bay of Biscay transit routes and the counter-

[1] Churchill, Vol. IV, pp. 288–291, 312–316 and 510.
[2] See Vol. I, pp. 364–365.

blows of our air and surface convoy escorts were causing the enemy serious losses and much anxiety. The surface escort of convoy OS. 18 sank U.82 on the 6th of February, that of the troop convoy WS. 17 dealt similarly with U.587 in March, and in April U.252 was destroyed by the escort of OG. 82.

The increasing importance now attached to Coastal Command's anti-submarine activities, and the slowly rising tide of their success, are indicated by the fact that in March, when the Chief of the Air Staff asked for statistics of the latter, the Admiralty replied that 'the steadily increasing efficiency of air attack' had been brought about chiefly by changes in tactics, by improved training and by the shallow-set depth charge. 'This increased potency' continued the Admiralty, 'will not only be maintained but should be further increased'.

After the first three months of 1942 had passed, American anti-submarine measures at last began to make themselves felt. This led to the U-boats being allotted to specific areas, instead of being allowed to rove where they wished in search of targets. On the 20th of April the first 'milch cow' (U.459) arrived 500 miles off Bermuda. There were at the time about a dozen boats in American and Caribbean waters. Refuelling them started on the 22nd; twelve medium and two large submarines were soon replenished. It was thanks to this measure that, early in May, the enemy's strength reached a peak of some sixteen to eighteen boats operating between Cape Sable and Key West.[1] The degree of success which Dönitz had expected from them was not, however, achieved—chiefly because a partial convoy system had by now been introduced. Only off Florida could the U-boats still stay in the shallow coastal waters, and there three U-boats sank ten ships. Further north the aggregate results accomplished by a much greater number of enemies were no larger.

The reasons for this long-awaited change for the better are not far to seek. On the 20th of May Admiral King, U.S.N., the Chief of Naval Operations, wrote to the First Sea Lord to say that 'because of your recent addition to [the] Caribbean Escort [Forces] and the inauguration of coastal convoys, I have hopes that matters can be got in hand to a better degree'. But he added that there were, as yet, no escorts for 'the vital Gulf of Mexico part of our common oil transport, which is now seriously threatened'. He therefore asked for fifteen to twenty more British corvettes to be lent for use on the American east coast, so that their own flotilla vessels might be released to the Gulf of Mexico. This request was carefully considered in London, and it

---

[1] See Map 11 (opp. p. 105).

may be appropriate to review the employment of our corvettes at this time.

There were now two hundred of these little ships in service, including those of the Canadian Navy; but ten of them had already been permanently transferred to the Americans. Of the remaining 190 corvettes:—

47 were at Gibraltar, at Freetown, in the Mediterranean, in South Africa, on the American Pacific Coast or in the Indian Ocean.

6 were working with the Russian Convoys.

37 were with the United Kingdom-based Atlantic Escort Groups.

78 were with the Atlantic Escort Groups based on Canada and Newfoundland. But two groups from these bases had already been allocated to the U.S.N.'s coastal escort forces, and four other corvettes were working with the special tanker convoys then running between the Dutch West Indies and Canada.

8 had been lent to the U.S.N.'s Caribbean Escorts.

14 were working with the Gibraltar Convoys.

It will be seen from the foregoing how widely our escort forces had to be dispersed to deal with the U-boat threat, and that the new commitments in the western Atlantic had already absorbed a substantial proportion of the corvettes. None the less Admiral Pound decided that he must try to do something to meet King's request. At the beginning of May we had, in response to an earlier American request, lent a British group for the Trinidad-Aruba convoys by reducing our mid-ocean groups (that is the Western Approaches ships which worked between the Western and Mid-Ocean Meeting Points) from twelve to eleven. Admiral Pound now proposed to meet the new American request by robbing the mid-ocean escorts of one more group. This, of course, meant that the remainder would have to be driven even harder; they would now average twenty-four out of every thirty days at sea, and we should have no margin to allow for foul weather or diversions. The First Sea Lord made the offer conditional on 'U.S. and Canadian escorts being equally hard-worked'. A conference was held in Washington, and it was then found that by adjustments to the Caribbean convoys the diversion of further strength from the Atlantic could be avoided, provided the group already sent to those waters remained there.

To return now to the Caribbean, after the first attacks a month passed before it was again visited by the U-boats. In mid-April three were once again cruising in the profitable waters between Trinidad and Curaçao, and off the Lesser Antilles.[1] On the 18th one of them bombarded the oil storage tanks at Curaçao; and by the 10th of May some nine boats were concentrated, chiefly off Trinidad. There shipping still moved in peacetime fashion, and a lot of it got sunk.

[1] See Map 11 (opp. p. 105).

In May the German Naval Staff reviewed the U-boat war as a whole. Sinkings off the American coast had started to decline, while in Arctic waters poor results had been achieved. In the attack on PQ. 16 for example, five U-boats had been damaged for a return of only one ship sunk.[1] Dönitz wished to call off such operations, but his views did not prevail—unhappily for our next Russian convoy, the ill-fated PQ. 17.[2] The severe winter of 1941–42 had delayed U-boat training in the Baltic, with the result that only thirty-nine boats had been made ready for operations in the first quarter of 1942 and only thirty in the second quarter. Of these sixty-nine, twenty-six were sent to the far north and two to the Mediterranean. Twelve were lost in the first six months of 1942, so the nett gain in the Atlantic fell far below German hopes, and was actually only twenty-nine boats. After the middle of the year the enemy's operational strength was increasing at the formidable figure of about twenty boats per month[3]; but the small total available early in the year, combined with diversions to unprofitable purposes, now seems to have been a decisive factor in the Atlantic battle. Dönitz's staff reviewed the Allied shipping position as well as this time. They believed that the Axis powers were between them more than accomplishing their aim of destroying 700,000 tons a month, the total considered necessary to bring about our defeat. But in truth the exaggerated claims put forward, especially by the Luftwaffe and the Japanese, misled them badly. The true rate of loss inflicted on us is shown in the table below.

Table 7. British, Allied and Neutral Merchant Shipping sunk by U-boats in all theatres January–July 1942[4]

	No. of Ships	Gross Tonnage
January . . .	62	327,357
February . . .	85	476,451
March . . .	95	537,980
April	74	431,664
May	125	607,247
June	144	700,235
July	96	476,065
TOTAL . . .	681	3,556,999
Monthly Average .	97·3 ships	508,143 tons

[1] See pp. 131–132.
[2] See pp. 134–145.
[3] See Appendix K.
[4] Appendix O shows the total shipping losses suffered.

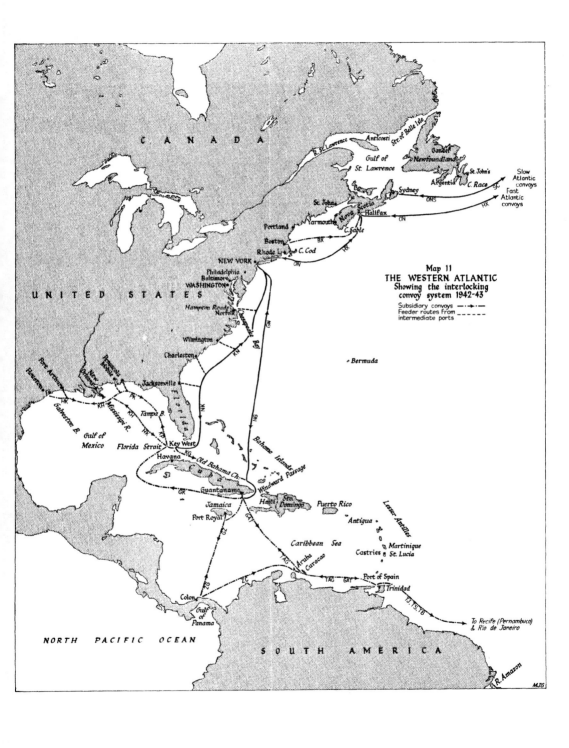

Map 11
THE WESTERN ATLANTIC
Showing the interlocking
convoy system 1942-43

Subsidiary convoys ——→——
Feeder routes from ——————
intermediate ports

Between May and July the U-boats gradually deserted the American seaboard, and concentrated in the Caribbean, though one entered the St Lawrence estuary and sank two ships on the 12th of May. A few attacks were made in these months on Atlantic convoys, and three supply U-boats were now at sea. On the 14th and 15th of May the first north- and south-bound convoys sailed between Hampton Roads and Key West.[1] This measure sounded, at long last, the knell for the U-boats' offshore operations on the American coast; but to accomplish it the entire carefully dovetailed British and Canadian Atlantic escort system had to be recast, and most of the recently gained help from American ships sacrificed.

Since easy torpedo targets had virtually disappeared, minelaying was tried by the U-boats off Boston, and in two other areas further south in July; but only three ships of some 19,000 tons were lost in the minefields. A second penetration into the St Lawrence took place in June, but convoy had now been introduced there as well, and air escorts were much stronger than earlier in the year. By mid-July three enemies had been sunk and several others damaged, and on the 19th the last two were withdrawn from the American coast.

Unfortunately, this success to the Allied anti-submarine forces was not the end of the story, for sufficient enemies were thereby released to make the Caribbean and Gulf of Mexico highly dangerous. About a dozen U-boats, supplied by 'milch cows', worked there in May and June, and they were soon reinforced by others which were sent down from the north. Sinkings became very widespread in those two months, but declined when the convoy system was extended to those waters. By early July most of the U-boats were working cautiously on the perimeter of the Caribbean, but there were still four of them in the Gulf of Mexico. It was plain that, just as the introduction of convoy and improved anti-submarine methods had forced the U-boats away from the American coast, the same process was now taking place further south.

In March and April Italian submarines appeared off the coast of Brazil, and early in May they were joined by three German boats. Two new supply U-boats were ordered to those waters, but they did not prove very profitable and the German boats were soon diverted to the Caribbean.

While these events were taking place in the west, the North Atlantic had been fairly quiet. No planned pack attacks had taken place since the previous November, and our convoys were only molested by U-boats based on Norway and by those on passage to the American coast. Early in May, however, a group of eight boats

[1] See Map 11.

allocated to the western Atlantic was ordered to move north and attack the convoys. The enemy had found out, from our wireless traffic, that we were again using the shorter 'great circle' route across the North Atlantic, and this meant that the U-boats need only shift their operational area a short distance. On the 11th of May convoy ONS. 92 was sighted on a south-westerly course, and seven of its ships were sunk during one night. Contact was then lost by the U-boat pack. After refuelling from a supply U-boat the group continued operations and, on the 11th of June, attacked convoy ONS. 100. A corvette and four ships (19,500 tons) were sunk. In the same month, with the idea of preventing us from further reinforcing the anti-submarine forces on the American coast, a group was sent to the waters off Gibraltar. Convoy HG. 84 was attacked on the 14th, and lost five ships in one night; but the strength of the escorts and the effectiveness of our long-range air cover were greater than the enemy had expected, and he soon called off the U-boats.

On the 21st of June Hitler ordered that a U-boat group should be held ready in case we seized the Atlantic Islands—a project which had been as often discussed in German circles as in the British War Cabinet.[1] Dönitz protested, though once more in vain, against this dispersal of his forces from what he knew to be their most profitable theatre; nor does there now seem to be any doubt that, but for Hitler's frequent diversions, the tonnage sunk by U-boats in the first half of 1942 would have been substantially greater. In spite of this the sinkings in June continued, from the enemy's point of view, to be highly satisfactory. There was a decline in the Gulf of Mexico, but this was offset by heavy sinkings in the Caribbean and off the eastern approaches to the Panama Canal.

In July the convoy system, started between Key West and Hampton Roads and between New York and Halifax in May, was extended further south. The 'Convoy and Routeing' section under the Commander-in-Chief, U.S. Fleet, which was analogous to the Admiralty's convoy-control organisation, had now been made responsible for the entire United States Strategic Area.[2] These initial steps towards the 'interlocking convoy system', which finally covered the western Atlantic routes as completely as the British coastal system ringed these islands, comprised the convoys shown in Table 8, page 107.

---

[1] See Vol. I, pp. 380–381.

[2] See Map 11 (opp. p. 105). The offices of Chief of Naval Operations (C.N.O.) and Commander-in-Chief, U.S. Fleet (Cominch) were combined on 12th March 1942. From 26th March Admiral King filled both positions. On 15th May the Convoy and Routeing Section, which had been formed under C.N.O. in June 1941, became a part of his headquarters as 'Cominch'. (Information from U.S. Navy's Office of Naval History.)

Table 8. *Western Atlantic Coastal Convoys, July 1942*

Convoy	Remarks
Halifax–Aruba and reverse (AH–HA)	There were only four of these convoys. They were superseded in September 1942.
Trinidad–Key West via Aruba and reverse (TAW–WAT)	These were replaced after two months by Guantanamo–Aruba–Trinidad (GAT–TAG) convoys.
Panama–Guantanamo and reverse (PG–GP)	These were renamed GZ–ZG later.
Trinidad–eastwards (TE)	There were 17 of these convoys. They stopped in September 1942.

The above convoys, and also many others introduced later, linked in with the main flow of coastal shipping proceeding to and from New York. When the 'interlocking system' reached its final form the termini of the trans-Atlantic fast (HX–ON) and slow (SC–ONS) convoys were shifted from Halifax and Sydney respectively to New York, which then became the greatest *entrepôt* of shipping in the world. The main north-bound coastal convoys, which had been fed from many secondary routes in the Gulf and Caribbean, and from as far south as Rio de Janeiro, were timed to reach New York on the day before the trans-Atlantic convoys to which they were dovetailed were due to sail. But at the end of the phase with which we are now concerned only the first steps had been taken in this direction, and many ships were still sailing independently, especially off the coast of central America.

In June an important measure which had long been desired by the Admiralty was introduced; convoy escorts began to be refuelled by tankers sailing in the convoy. It had been slow to arrive because, firstly, we had suffered (and still were suffering) from a chronic shortage of tankers; and secondly because special gear had to be supplied to the tankers and to the escorts, and their crews trained in its use. But as soon as tankers could be spared and the equipment provided, it was started, though at first in a small way. It simplified the organisation of escorts enormously, because it saved the wasteful process of sending groups out to overtake convoys at meeting points which, in bad weather, might be missed, and of the relieved groups either returning to base without a convoy or having to wait at a rendezvous for their next commitment. It also reduced the likelihood of escorts having to leave a delayed convoy for lack of fuel, and enabled us to begin again to use the more southerly, and shorter, Atlantic routes, which had been barred to us because they took the escorts too far from their halfway fuelling base in Iceland.

In spite of favourable trends such as those described above, the ebb and flow of the Atlantic battle was still, in the middle of 1942, evenly balanced between the contestants. Though we now had short-wave radar, high-frequency direction finding, the Leigh Light, and air depth charges fitted with a new and more powerful explosive, and were using larger and deeper depth charge patterns, the enemy's strength was increasing rapidly.[1] It was obvious to the Admiralty that the U-boats were still completing far faster than we were sinking them. To Dönitz and his staff the time appeared ripe to renew the pack attacks against our Atlantic convoys on an even greater scale. In reaching this decision he was much influenced by the need to send his U-boats to waters where air cover was still lacking, or was only spasmodic. The Gibraltar route had proved expensive, and the American coastal waters had become untenable. The central Atlantic 'air gap' plainly offered the best prospects, and plans were made to keep at least two U-boat groups permanently at sea in those waters. Thus was restarted the ding-dong battle between the U-boat packs and our Atlantic escort groups.

Convoy OS. 33 was first attacked on the 18th of July, and lost five ships of some 32,000 tons. But the escorts sank U.136. The next outward Sierra Leone convoy was found by the same pack and lost two ships; but in this case the enemy noted with concern that aircraft were still with the convoy when it was nearly 800 miles out. In actual fact this was an exceptional accomplishment by Coastal Command, which had managed to scrape together only one squadron of American Liberators. Air escort at such ranges was not to become a common practice for another nine months. The month of July thus brought no marked success to either side on the Sierra Leone route, and attacks on two outward North Atlantic convoys (ON. 113 and 115) produced similar results; in each case a few ships were sunk and the escorts destroyed one U-boat. In that same month the U-boats did, however, find one soft spot. Much of the traffic across the central Atlantic from Trinidad or New York still sailed independently, and two U-boats, having failed to do any damage off Freetown, sank a number of ships 500 miles further west.

As was inevitable the organisation for the protection of the Atlantic convoys was modified as the battle swung to and fro. By the middle of 1942 the usual practice was for American or Canadian groups to provide the first escorts of a convoy starting from New York. They would take it to the Halifax Ocean Meeting Point (HOMP) in about 61° West. There other Canadian groups took over duty and escorted the convoy eastwards to the Western Ocean Meeting Point (WESTOMP) in about 49° West. Then the mid-ocean groups, which might be Canadian or British from St John's, or American from Argentia, took over for the deadliest part of the journey. During this passage an American-escorted convoy from Iceland might be met at the Iceland Ocean Meeting Point (ICOMP) in about 23° West; but the mid-ocean groups continued to the

---

[1] See Appendix K.

Eastern Ocean Meeting Point (EASTOMP) near Oversay Island in the North-Western Approaches. There the last of the five escorts, the British local groups, took over; and the mid-ocean group went into Londonderry to fuel and, perhaps, to rest before taking out an outward convoy.

The Atlantic convoy cycles in use at this time meant that, on an average, four HX and two SC convoys sailed homeward every month, while an equal number of their outward counterparts (ON and ONS) left British ports: the number of ships in these convoys averaged about fifty, and each convoy needed at least seven escorts. To provide escorts for these twelve convoys as and when required at each stage of their journeys was a very intricate problem[1]; and often the carefully worked-out schedules were wrecked by unforeseen developments, by diversions, or by bad weather. The number of escort groups needed to fulfil the requirement is best shown in tabular form.

Table 9. The Organisation of North Atlantic Escort Forces, June 1942
(The full strength of an Escort Group was 9 ships and the average composition of groups was 3 destroyers and 6 corvettes).

Escort Force	Zone of Responsibility	Strength needed (on basis of 6 Homeward and 6 Outward convoys per month)	Nationality	Usual Bases
Western Local	Departure Port to 61° W (HOMP)	} 8 Groups	British or Canadian	Halifax or Boston
Western Local	61° W (HOMP) to 49° W (WESTOMP)			
Mid-Ocean	49° W (WESTOMP) to 22° W (EASTOMP)	8 Groups	British, Canadian or American	St. John's Argentia.
Iceland	Iceland Ports to 25° W (ICOMP)	2 Groups	American	Argentia, Londonderry and Hvalfiord
Eastern Local	22° W (EASTOMP) to arrival port	8 Groups	British	Liverpool or Clyde

To turn to the parallel development of air cover over the Atlantic, Coastal Command squadrons were now working regularly from Northern Ireland, from bases in the west of Scotland and from Iceland. On the other side aircraft of the R.C.A.F.'s No. 1 Group were based on Yarmouth (Nova Scotia), Halifax, Sydney and

[1] Although the average number of HX/ON and SC/ONS convoys totalled about twelve per month, it was usual for troop convoys and other special movements of shipping to increase the monthly total of convoys run between North America and Britain to about fifteen.

Gander (Newfoundland)[1]; U.S. naval aircraft worked from Argentia
and Iceland. But the range of the Catalinas, Wellingtons, Whitleys
and Hudsons did not enable continuous air escort to be provided,
and the Atlantic 'air gap' was little, if at all, smaller than it had been
in the previous phase.[2] Not for another year could it be closed by
shore-based aircraft. On the American seaboard a mixed and inadequately trained collection of U.S. Army, U.S. Navy and even of
civil aircraft under the Commander, Eastern Sea Frontier, tried to
counter the U-boats—and at first made very little impression on
them.[3] Not until mid-1943 did the American Chiefs of Staff order
the withdrawal of army aircraft from anti-submarine duties, and
place the whole responsibility on the Navy.[4]

On the eastern side of the Atlantic the organisation of the Coastal
Command's Groups had not changed since the middle of 1941[5], but
their strength had increased and some new types of aircraft had
entered service. It will be convenient to show these in tabular form.

Table 10. The Strength and Disposition of Coastal Command, June 1942
(Squadrons on loan from other commands included. Meteorological, Photographic,
Air-Sea Rescue and Training Squadrons omitted)

Station	No. of Squadrons	Duty	Type of Aircraft
Gibraltar	1	Flying Boat	Catalina and Sunderland
Iceland	Part of 1	General Reconnaissance	Hudson
	3	General Reconnaissance	Hudson and Whitley
	Part of 1	Flying Boat	Catalina and Northrop
15 Group (H.Qs. Liverpool)	3	General Reconnaissance	Hudson
	4 (1 forming)	Flying Boat	Sunderland and Catalina
16 Group (H.Qs. Chatham)	2	Long-range Reconnaissance	Liberator and Fortress
	3	Long-range Fighter	Beaufighter and Blenheim
	3½	General Reconnaissance	Hudson
	2	Torpedo-bomber and Mine-laying	Hampden
18 Group (H.Qs. Rosyth)	3	Long-range Fighter	Beaufighter and Blenheim
	2	General Reconnaissance	Hudson
	1	Torpedo-bomber	Beaufort
	1½	Flying Boat	Catalina
19 Group (H.Qs. Plymouth	1	Long-range Reconnaissance	Liberator
	6	General Reconnaissance	Hudson, Whitley, Wellington
	2	Long-range Fighter	Beaufighter
	3	Flying Boat	Sunderland

[1] See Map 11 (opp. p. 105).
[2] See Vol. I, p. 459, and Map 20 (opp. p. 205) in this volume.
[3] Morison, Vol. I, pp. 237–247.
[4] *Ibid.*, pp. 245–246.
[5] See Vol. I, pp. 461–462.

The actual strength of the operational squadrons at that time was fifty-four flying boats and 490 reconnaissance and fighter aircraft. Of these, the average numbers available on any day were twenty-eight and 201 respectively. The Photographic, Meteorological and Air-Sea Rescue squadrons (about nine squadrons in all) totalled 137 aircraft and there were, in addition, four naval squadrons of thirty-six aircraft on loan to Coastal Command.

It will be seen that the growth and development of our surface and air Atlantic escorts, described in the preceding paragraphs, followed logically on the change in conditions brought about by the entry of the United States into the war. But whereas the British Admiralty had, under the old arrangements, carried the whole responsibility for the control of Atlantic shipping, there was now a clear necessity for the Americans to take a full share of that heavy burden. Planning for this eventuality had, in fact, started in January 1941 when the first British–American staff conversations took place in Washington.[1] A year later—to be precise in February 1942—it was plain to both parties that clearer definition of their strategic responsibilities was necessary. Further conferences took place and, as a result, on the 1st of July a 'Change of Operational Control' line (or 'Chop Line' as it came to be called) was established in the Atlantic. At first it corresponded approximately to the division between the U.S.A.'s and the British strategic areas—in general following the meridian of 26° West.[2] Before a convoy sailed the anticipated time of crossing the 'Chop Line' was worked out; this was included in the sailing telegram addressed to all the authorities concerned in its movements. The routeing authority on the arrival side took over control at the time stated in the message, regardless of whether the convoy had or had not then crossed the 'Chop Line'. The line was altered from time to time as the requirements of the war necessitated; but the principle on which control was passed back and forth across the Atlantic remained unchanged to the end.

To sum up the results of the first seven months of 1942, the enemy had reason to be satisfied over the achievements of his U-boats. They had sunk an enormous tonnage of Allied shipping (681 ships of 3,556,999 tons in all, of which 589 ships of over three million tons were sunk in the Atlantic and Arctic theatres)—and at astonishingly small cost to themselves. Only 3·9 per cent of the U-boats at sea had been destroyed, and the rate of sinking inflicted on the Allies had been kept at the high figure of some 300 tons per U-boat per day throughout the period. A great proportion of the tonnage had, however, been sunk in American waters, and it was hardly to be expected that the very favourable conditions found in the western

---

[1] See Vol. I, pp. 471–472.
[2] See Map 10 (opp. p. 97).

Atlantic and Caribbean would continue. In fact, as has already been told, American anti-submarine defences and methods had begun to improve well before the end of the present phase.

In other waters the performance of the U-boats had been in-different, and the outlook for the enemy was not favourable. In particular the fitting of radar sets in Coastal Command aircraft was now general, though the Germans remained sceptical of this achieve-ment until many months later, when night attacks proved that they must be so fitted. The pressure of our patrolling aircraft, particularly in the Bay of Biscay, became far heavier in the spring. The first Leigh-Light squadron (No. 172) was formed early in March and by the beginning of June had four aircraft ready for work.[1] The first 'dark night' attack quickly took place and the squadron's success was as rapid as the enemy's surprise was complete. A second squad-ron (No. 179) was formed at the beginning of September. Whereas for the first three months of the year no U-boat casualties had been caused in the Atlantic by British aircraft and only two by the Americans, in June three boats were severely damaged in the Bay. Dönitz's diary for the 11th of that month contains a remark that 'there being no defence against aircraft in the Bay of Biscay, the R.A.F. can do as it pleases'. The Germans guessed, correctly, that it was some new British development which was causing them surprise and discomfiture, and then set about devising counter-measures. It was not, however, until the next phase that U-boats were fitted with search receivers which could detect the approach of an aircraft using radar. In countering our wireless direction-finding the enemy showed less imagination. He knew that we listened to and measured the direction of the 'homing' signals which, under Dönitz's centralised control system, the U-boats were obliged to transmit; but no counter to our methods was devised. Actually it was in July that we first fitted high-frequency direction-finding sets in our escort vessels, and by the end of the year it was a standard item of their equipment. It made the location of U-boats much more effective than by listening from shore stations only. None the less, and in spite of the success of these new measures, it is disconcerting to find that after two-and-a-half years of war the enemy was still able to read many of our cyphered convoy control signals.

Though the enemy was, we now know, very disturbed by the increasing effectiveness of our defences, the Admiralty was far from satisfied—particularly over the small number of U-boats sunk by our aircraft in relation to the numbers sighted by them. However, by the middle of 1942 certain technical developments, to be referred to more fully later[2], were at last beginning to give Coastal Command's

[1] See Vol. I, p. 358.
[2] See p. 205.

aircrews what the First Sea Lord's adviser on anti-submarine warfare called 'the means whereby they can deliver a deadly attack', and it was plain that better results would soon be achieved. The handling of our surface escort groups was also improving steadily. The Tactical School at Liverpool, in which all escort commanders underwent brief periods of training, contributed a great deal to this process. It was there that U-boat methods were studied, and counter-measures devised; by the introduction of standard procedures to be followed in the event of attack the flexibility and cohesion of our groups, and the speed and confidence with which individual ships reacted to any sudden emergency, all benefited greatly.

As to the enemy's strength, he started the present phase with 249 U-boats in commission; ninety-one of them were operational (sixty-four based on the Atlantic, twenty-three in the Mediterranean and four in the Arctic theatre). By the 1st of March the operational total had increased to 111, eighty of which were in the Atlantic; and by the end of June he had 140 at work. And, throughout the phase dealt with in this chapter, British, American and Canadian forces had only sunk thirty-two U-boats—approximately the equivalent to one month of the enemy's current production.[1] It could not be doubted that the real crisis of the battle was still to come.

---

[1] See Appendix J for particulars of these U-boat sinkings.

I

CHAPTER V

HOME WATERS AND THE ARCTIC
1st January–31st July, 1942

'These Russian convoys are becoming a
regular millstone round our necks, and
cause a steady attrition in both cruisers and
destroyers'.
Admiral Pound (First Sea Lord) to
Admiral King, U.S.N. (Chief of
Naval Operations), 18th May 1942.

AT the beginning of the year Admiral Tovey commanded, in
the Home Fleet, the battleships *King George V* and *Rodney*, the
battle cruiser *Renown*, the aircraft-carrier *Victorious*, four 8-inch
and six 6-inch cruisers and about eighteen destroyers. The new
battleship *Duke of York*, which was not yet fully 'worked up', had
taken the Prime Minister to America; the *Nelson*, three cruisers and
some destroyers were refitting. Very heavy demands on destroyers
were arising in connection with the Russian convoys, and the
Commander-in-Chief was, as ever, concerned over the perpetual
shortage of ships of that class. As to the enemy, it was believed that
the new battleship *Tirpitz*, the pocket-battleship *Admiral Scheer*, the
heavy cruiser *Admiral Hipper*, four light cruisers and about a score of
destroyers were ready for sea. Most of them were known to be in the
Baltic. The *Scharnhorst*, *Gneisenau* and *Prinz Eugen* were still in Brest,
and constituted a permanent threat to our Atlantic convoys. They
were all believed to have repaired damage received in the previous
year[1], and to be ready for sea, though in need of further training.
The increasing signs of the Brest squadron's readiness caused the
Admiralty to press for renewed bombing on a heavy scale, and in
January 612 aircraft of Bomber Command dropped 908 tons of
bombs on the base; but no further damage of a serious nature was
done to any of the ships. The story of the squadron's escape back to
its home waters up the Channel between the 11th and 13th of
February will be told in the next chapter.

The readiness for sea of the enemy's Baltic and Brest forces
compelled Admiral Tovey to keep as close a watch as possible on the
northern passages. One cruiser, therefore, stayed on patrol in the

---

[1] See Vol. I, p. 487.

Denmark Strait, and she was supported by a battleship and two American heavy cruisers, based on Hvalfiord. The Iceland-Faeroes passage was now closed by the minefield which had been laid by stages during the previous eighteen months. It was by no means an impenetrable barrier and needed reinforcement with more mines; but it was now better watched by the patrolling aircraft of Coastal Command's No. 18 Group, and it was far less likely that enemy warships would attempt to break out that way than it had been during the first two years of the war. Offensive measures were constantly considered, and Admiral Tovey wished by frequent coastal raids 'to turn the mind of the enemy to defence'. In this our strategy was more successful than could possibly have been realised at the time, because of Hitler's 'intuition' that we intended to invade Norway.[1] It was actually the German dictator's insistence on the defence of Norway which caused the next movement by the enemy's main forces, for at his conference on the 12th of January he gave orders for the *Tirpitz* to be moved to Trondheim. 'Every ship', he declared at this time, 'which is not stationed in Norway is in the wrong place'. The German Naval Staff knew from recent experience that the movement of the great battleship from the Baltic to the North Sea by the usual passages was almost certain to be reported by British intelligence.[2] They therefore brought the *Tirpitz* through the Kiel Canal to Wilhelmshaven whence she sailed to Trondheim, escorted by four destroyers, on the night of the 14th–15th of January. The German plan was successful, and on the 16th she reached her destination undetected. But the destroyers were at once needed in the south to help bring the two enemy battle cruisers up-Channel. Thus the lack of adequate escorts, added to the serious shortage of oil fuel in Norway, reduced the offensive possibilities of the new German dispositions from the start.

On the 17th of January the Admiralty gave warning that the *Tirpitz* might be at sea. Though it was not expected that she would this time attempt to break out into the Atlantic, Admiral Tovey was taking no chances. He shifted his main concentration to Iceland to cover the northern passages, postponed the sailing of the next Russian convoy (PQ.9) and cancelled an operation off the Norwegian coast. On the 23rd of January, after much strenuous searching, our reconnaissance aircraft at last found the battleship at anchor, camouflaged and heavily protected by nets in Aasfiord, fifteen miles east of Trondheim. Whether her purpose was to assist in the expected return home of the Brest squadron, to threaten our Russian convoys, to deter us from raiding the Norwegian coast or to break out into the Atlantic was still obscure; but from the Admiralty's point of view it

---

[1] See Vol. I, p. 514, and this volume, pp. 100–101.
[2] See Vol. I, pp. 373, 395 and 484.

was plainly desirable to drive her away from a position in which she could exert any or all of these threats, or to immobilise her where she lay. As long as she was present in Norway her influence was bound to make itself felt in all the waters, from Murmansk to the American seaboard, for which the Home Fleet was mainly responsible. For a start it was decided that the Russian convoys should continue, though not more than one should ever be at sea between 10° West and 15° East; secondly, that the Northern passages must meanwhile be left uncovered, and lastly that raids on the Norwegian coast, 'which had so annoyed the German High Command' should continue.

On the 25th the Prime Minister drew the Chiefs of Staffs' attention to the cramping influence exerted by the battleship, and asked for plans to be prepared to attack her with shore-based and carrier-borne aircraft. He considered that 'the entire naval situation throughout the world would be altered' by her successful destruction.[1] Unfortunately she was a difficult target to attack. Carrier-borne aircraft could not use their torpedoes in the narrow, steep-cliffed inlet, and Bomber Command's longest-range aircraft could only reach her from bases in Scotland at the limit of their endurance. The bombing plan was approved on the 28th of January, and was carried out by nine Halifaxes and seven Stirlings on the night of the 29th–30th. No damage was done.

There now followed a trying period for Coastal Command. They had to watch the *Tirpitz* continuously at a range and in conditions which made it almost essential to employ Mosquitos, of which the command possessed very few; secondly, 'break-out' patrols had to be flown in case she escaped from Trondheim unseen and made either for the Atlantic or for the Arctic convoy routes. At the same time it was becoming daily more urgent to watch the Brest squadron's movements. There is little doubt that the need to attempt so many duties at the same time was the main cause of the failure to have the Command's torpedo-bombers ready and at southern bases when the Brest squadron's expected move up-Channel took place. We shall return to that matter later.[2]

Between the 14th and 19th of February, by which time the Brest squadron had reached its home bases, great enemy air activity was noticed in Norway. On the latter date the *Tirpitz* was seen to be under way and exercising in the fiord. Air patrols were at once strengthened, submarines were stationed off-shore and Admiral Tovey left Hvalfiord with his main strength and steamed towards Tromsö. If nothing of greater moment took place, he intended to attack enemy shipping in that port. His anxieties had been made

---

[1] Churchill, Vol. IV, p. 98.
[2] See pp. 153, 156 and 160.

heavier because a big WS. troop convoy was due to leave the Clyde for the Middle East on the 15th and a strong escort, partly drawn from ships of Force H which had specially returned home, and partly from the Home Fleet and Western Approaches commands, had to be provided. After the Brest squadron had successfully reached its home waters, Admiral Tovey reviewed the future outlook and found it little to his liking. 'In a few months' time', he wrote in his despatch, 'the enemy would be able to confront us with a considerable battle fleet'. He did not expect the enemy to risk the *Tirpitz* by herself in an Atlantic foray, but that they would 'gradually assemble the rest of the fleet round her'. In this forecast he was soon to be proved correct, though the actual strength which the enemy could 'assemble round the *Tirpitz*' was less than the Commander-in-Chief feared. Though Admiral Tovey considered the outlook to be 'profoundly changed', he none the less realised that a period of quiescence was likely, while the battle cruisers were repairing the damage sustained during their dash up-Channel. He therefore seized the opportunity to refit some of his own ships. Moreover, the removal of the threat from Brest at once reduced his escort commitments. No longer need a battleship be sent with each important south-bound convoy.

On the 20th of February the Admiralty received indications of another intended warship movement from Germany to Norway. Air patrols were maintained, and the torpedo-bomber squadrons of Coastal Command came to immediate readiness. At 11.10 a.m. the next day two large warships (actually the *Admiral Scheer* and *Prinz Eugen*) and three destroyers were sighted off the Dutch coast, steering north at high speed. Relays of reconnaissance aircraft were sent out to keep in touch, and all the available Beauforts were despatched to catch the enemy force off Utsire that afternoon.[1] Unhappily, the weather worsened, contact was lost and none of the torpedo aircraft found the enemy who had, we now know, turned back on his tracks for a time and so threw our searchers off the scent. Early next morning, the 22nd, two of our aircraft employed on other missions, did, somewhat luckily, sight the enemy squadron as it was entering the Inner Leads. By 3 p.m. the ships were located at anchor in Grimstad Fiord, just south of Bergen.

Admiral Tovey had meanwhile cancelled his intended attack on Tromsö and sent the *Victorious*, *Berwick* and four destroyers to a position 100 miles off Stadlandet[2], whence the carrier's aircraft were to attack the north-bound warships at 1 a.m. on the 23rd. He himself followed in the flagship *King George V* to cover the lighter forces, and four submarines were sent to patrol off Trondheim. Though snow-storms and bad weather again defeated the air searches and strikes,

---

[1] and [2] See Map 37 (opp. p. 363).

the submarine *Trident* (Commander G. M. Sladen) torpedoed the *Prinz Eugen* at 6 a.m. on the 23rd as she approached the entrance to the Leads off Trondheim. She was badly damaged and, for a time, stopped. The *Scheer* went on to Aasfiord and took up a berth not far from the *Tirpitz*. The *Eugen* managed to limp into the same sheltered anchorage at about 11 p.m. that evening. Though less damage had been inflicted than we would have wished, the enemy's plan to form a squadron composed of the *Tirpitz, Admiral Scheer* and *Prinz Eugen* 'to conduct offensive and defensive operations from Trondheim in northern waters' had not gone exactly as he intended. Admiral Tovey was, however, anxious, because 'no disposition of the Home Fleet could adequately protect both the Russian convoys and the northern passages from this threat'—that is to say from a powerful squadron based in Norway.

We must now turn to the Russian convoys, which occupied so large a place in the plans and operations of the Home Fleet at this time. Admiral Tovey was reluctant to use his full strength to cover them throughout their long, outflanked passage, because he could only do so if the northern passages to the Atlantic were left unguarded. The Admiralty, however, considered the risk acceptable and pressed the Commander-in-Chief to afford the convoys the most powerful cover possible.

The early convoys of 1942 fared well. PQ.7, which had been delayed by defects and sailed finally from Hvalfiord in two parts on the 31st of December 1941 and the 8th of January 1942, consisting of two and nine ships respectively, lost only one of its number. PQ.8 had one ship damaged by torpedo off Kola Inlet, but all the eight merchantmen managed to reach their destination. The *Matabele*, one of the two escorting destroyers was, however, sunk on the 17th of January; and from her company there were only two survivors— an unpleasant reminder of the very poor prospects for the crews of ships sunk in those ice-bound waters. The next three convoys, PQ.9 and 10 (which sailed from Hvalfiord together on the 1st of February and totalled only ten ships), and PQ.11 of thirteen ships from Loch Ewe, were never located by the enemy, and got through unscathed. But it was realised that this run of good luck could not last much longer. The lengthening days were steadily depriving the convoys of the friendly shield of darkness; yet for two or three more months they would be forced by ice to pass close off the enemy coast. To Admiral Tovey it was as unacceptable as it was unnecessary that U-boats should be able to lie in wait off the entrance to Kola Inlet, The Russians should, in his opinion, easily be able to make such confined waters untenable to them; and he considered that proper fighter protection should be given to the approaching convoys by our Ally from his shore airfields. The cruiser *Nigeria* (flagship of Rear-Admiral

H. M. Burrough, commanding the 10th Cruiser Squadron) was at Murmansk all February with the object of representing these needs to the Russians, and of covering convoys between Bear Island and Kola Inlet or *vice versa*.

Then occurred the concentration of enemy surface forces at Trondheim already described. In Admiral Tovey's opinion attack by any or all of them was now to be expected between Jan Mayen and Bear Island[1], while the eastern part of the route would, he considered, probably be left to U-boats and aircraft. This meant that cover by heavy ships had to be given throughout the first half of the journey; and to accomplish this at the minimum of added strain the Commander-in-Chief asked, on the 26th of February, for the outward and homeward convoys to be sailed simultaneously. PQ.12 and QP.8, which sailed from Iceland and Kola Inlet on the 1st of March, and were both comparatively large convoys of sixteen and fifteen ships respectively, were the first to be covered by the main Home Fleet. At the same time close escorts were strengthened, Coastal Command took special steps to watch the Trondheim fiords closely, and Liberators flew long-range patrols to the north-east from Iceland. Nor were these measures introduced a moment too soon. On the evening of the 6th the *Seawolf*, one of our submarines on patrol off Trondheim, reported that a large enemy warship, either a battleship or a heavy cruiser, had sailed. It was actually the *Tirpitz*, flying the flag of Vice-Admiral Ciliax, with three destroyers in company. Her departure was missed by our air patrols. We now know that a long-range Focke-Wulf had given the enemy the position of the outward convoy at noon on the 5th of March, and that it was her report which caused the squadron to put to sea.[2] That, however, was the end of the usefulness of the German air reconnaissance.

On the forenoon of the 6th the *King George V* (fleet flagship), *Duke of York*, *Renown* (flagship of Vice-Admiral A. T. B. Curteis, second-in-command, Home Fleet), *Victorious*, *Berwick* and twelve destroyers had concentrated under Admiral Tovey. Until the following afternoon the main fleet patrolled on a line some 50–100 miles south of the convoys' routes, during the dangerous period when they were passing each other. Soon after midnight on the 6th–7th Admiral Tovey received the *Seawolf's* report, relayed to him by the Admiralty. At 8 a.m. the main fleet raised steam for full speed and turned more to the east. The *Victorious* had been warned to be ready to make an air search to the south of the convoy routes, but unhappily—for such a search 'would almost certainly have located the *Tirpitz*'—the weather prevented flying all day. Meanwhile, the *Tirpitz*, which was

---

[1] See Map 12 (opp. p. 121).
[2] See Map 12. Phase 1.

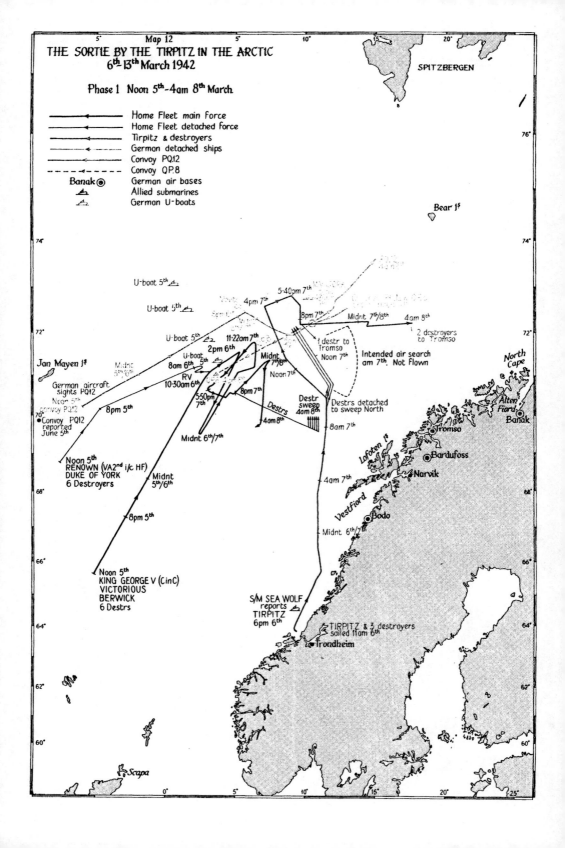

Map 12

THE SORTIE BY THE TIRPITZ IN THE ARCTIC
6th–13th March 1942

Phase 1 Noon 5th–4am 8th March.

Home Fleet main force
Home Fleet detached force
Tirpitz & destroyers
German detached ships
Convoy PQ.12
Convoy QP.8
Banak ⊙ German air bases
⏄ Allied submarines
⏄ German U-boats

SPITZBERGEN

Bear I.

U-boat 5th
U-boat 5th
U-boat 5th
U-boat 5th
RV 10·30am 6th
8am 6th
2pm 6th
11·22am 7th
4pm 7th
5·40pm 7th
8pm 7th
Midnt 7th/8th
4am 8th
2 destroyers to Tromso
1 destr to Tromso Noon 7th
Intended air search am 7th. Not flown
Midnt 7th/8th
Noon 7th
5·50pm 7th
Midnt 6th/7th
Destrs
8pm 7th
4am 8th
Destr sweep 4am 8th
Destrs detached to sweep North
8am 7th

Jan Mayen I.

German aircraft sights PQ12 Noon 5th
Convoy PQ12
8pm 5th
Midnt 5th/6th
Convoy PQ12 reported June 5th

Noon 5th
RENOWN (VA2nd i/c HF)
DUKE OF YORK
6 Destroyers
8pm 5th
Midnt 5th/6th

4am 7th
Midnt 6th/7th

Noon 5th
KING GEORGE V (CinC)
VICTORIOUS
BERWICK
6 Destrs

S/M SEA WOLF reports TIRPITZ 6pm 6th

TIRPITZ & 3 destroyers sailed 11am 6th
Trondheim

North Cape
Alten Fiord
Banak
Tromso
Bardufoss
Narvik
Lofoten
Vestfiord
Bodo

Scapa

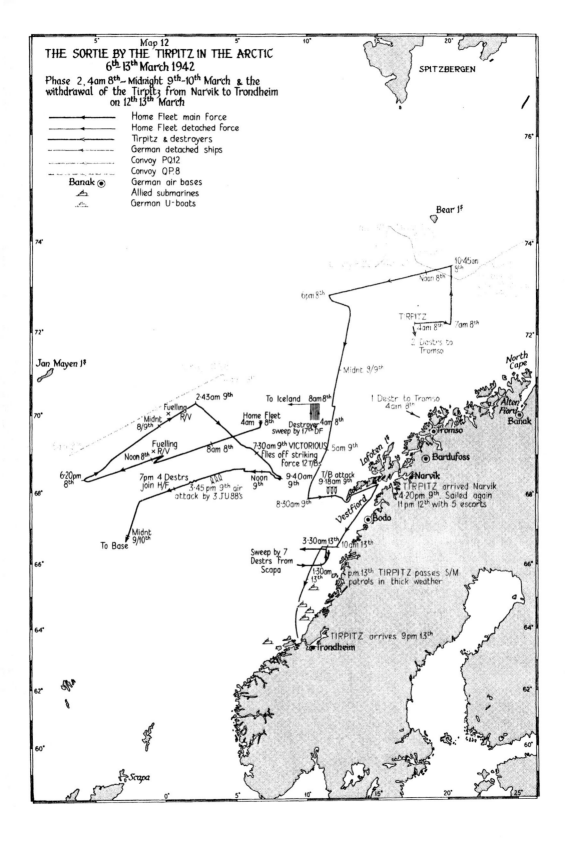

Map 12
THE SORTIE BY THE TIRPITZ IN THE ARCTIC
6th–13th March 1942

Phase 2, 4am 8th – Midnight 9th–10th March & the
withdrawal of the Tirpitz from Narvik to Trondheim
on 12th 13th March

⟵———	Home Fleet main force
⟵———	Home Fleet detached force
⟵———	Tirpitz & destroyers
⟵······	German detached ships
·········	Convoy PQ.12
– – – –	Convoy QP.8
Banak ⊙	German air bases
⌂	Allied submarines
⌐	German U-boats

SPITZBERGEN

Bear I.ᵗ

Jan Mayen Iˢ

North Cape

10·45am 9th
Noon 8th
6pm 8th
TIRPITZ
4am 8th   7am 8th
2 Destrs to Tromso

Midnt 9/9th

1 Destr to Tromso
4am 8th

Alten Fiord
Banak
Tromso

2·43am 9th
Fuelling × R/V
Midnt 8/9th
Home Fleet 4am 8th
To Iceland   8am 8th
Destroyer 4am 8th
sweep by 17th DF

Fuelling × R/V
Noon 8th
8am 8th
7·30am 9th VICTORIOUS
flies off striking
force 12 T/Bs   5am 9th

Bardufoss

Lofoten Iˢ

Narvik

6·20pm 8th
7pm 4 Destrs
join H/F
3·45 pm 9th air
attack by 3 JU.88's
Noon 9th
9·40am 9th
T/B attack
9·18am 9th
8·30am 9th

TIRPITZ arrived Narvik
4·20pm 9th Sailed again
11pm 12th with 5 escorts

To Base
Midnt 9/10th

Vestfjord
Bodö

3·30am 13th   10am 13th
Sweep by 7
Destrs from
Scapa
1·30am 13th
4 p.m.13th TIRPITZ passes S/M
patrols in thick weather

TIRPITZ arrives 9pm 13th
Trondheim

Scapa

also unable to use her reconnaissance aircraft, was closing our main fleet.

At noon on the 7th, when the two convoys were passing each other some 200 miles south-west of Bear Island, they, the enemy and the Home Fleet were all within about eighty or ninety miles of each other.[1] Ciliax had no idea that powerful British forces were at sea, let alone so close to him. He, on the other hand, passed only a few miles astern of PQ.12 and ahead of QP.8. In the prevailing low visibility neither side's forces saw anything of the other's. The German destroyers, which had been detached to search separately to the north, also passed very close to the homeward convoy. At 4.30 that afternoon, the 7th, one of them sank a Russian merchantman, which had dropped astern of the homeward convoy. Not long afterwards Ciliax sent his destroyers back to fuel. He continued to search with the *Tirpitz* alone.

The Russian merchantman's distress message was intercepted by Admiral Tovey, but the sender's position was not clear to him. However, wireless bearings of an enemy vessel, which might be the *Tirpitz*, caused the Commander-in-Chief to alter to the east at 5.50 and to the north-east at 8 p.m. At the latter time he detached six destroyers to spread and sweep along the enemy's most probable return route. They searched to the north from 2 a.m. to 6 a.m. on the 8th, but sighted nothing. It will be seen from Map 12 (Phase 1) that while this game of blind man's buff was in progress the *Tirpitz* was actually still some 150 miles to the north of the Home Fleet. She was now a long way astern of QP.8, and the outward convoy's north-easterly course was taking it away from the enemy. As the gap between the convoys widened, so did the greatest danger recede.

Having heard nothing more of his quarry Admiral Tovey turned south at midnight on 7th–8th, to get his carrier aircraft within striking range off the Lofoten Islands at dawn. Four hours later he came to the conclusion that he had missed the enemy and, having no destroyers to screen his ships in these dangerous waters, he turned towards Iceland 'to collect some destroyers'. This westward movement temporarily took the fleet directly away from the enemy, and the Commander-in-Chief's guess that the *Tirpitz* had already slipped home past him was wrong. Nor was the outward convoy by any means yet out of danger, to the south of Bear Island, since Admiral Ciliax searched to the north during the forenoon of the 8th, and then turned west.[2] At noon he passed only about eighty miles south of the convoy, which thus had a second narrow escape. The Admiralty had meanwhile ordered that convoy to pass north of Bear Island; but ice conditions determined the senior officer of the escort and the Com-

[1] See Map 12. Phase 1.
[2] See Map 12. Phase 2.

modore to disregard an order which could not even be attempted
without grave risk of damage to the ships; for heavy pack-ice had
been encountered while still to the south of the island. In fact, from
noon on the 8th till early next morning the convoy steered east or
south-east, more or less along the edge of the pack-ice. By the
afternoon of the 8th the Home Fleet was some 500 miles to the
south-west of the outward convoy. The Admiralty, however, considered that the *Tirpitz* might still be seeking it in the waters south
of Bear Island—as in fact she was. At 5.30 p.m. a signal from London
to that effect caused the Commander-in-Chief to turn back to the
north-east. It was, we now know, at 8 o'clock that evening that
Ciliax abandoned the search and turned south towards the Lofoten
Islands. The Admiralty's intelligence again proved accurate later
that night, when they told Admiral Tovey that his quarry was now
moving south. Accordingly at 2.40 a.m. on the 9th the Commander-
in-Chief altered towards the Lofotens and increased speed. He was
then about 200 miles to the west of the enemy.[1] Reconnaissance aircraft were flown off from the *Victorious* at 6.40 a.m., followed by
twelve torpedo-carrying Albacores. 'A wonderful chance' Admiral
Tovey signalled to the latter: 'God be with you'. One of the searching
aircraft sighted the *Tirpitz* at 8 a.m., and her report was picked up
by the leader of the torpedo-bombers; forty minutes later the striking
force itself made contact. The enemy, we now know, sighted the
Albacores a few minutes after they had sighted him. Surprise was
thus not achieved, and although the German account says that the
attackers showed great 'determination and dash', it is a fact that
their tactics lost a great deal of the advantage of conditions which
were unusually favourable. The aircraft came in from astern and to
leeward, which meant that, with the *Tirpitz* steaming into the wind,
their relative speed of approach was far less than would have been
the case had they attacked from ahead and to windward. The enemy
thus gained time to take skilful avoiding action, and all the torpedoes
missed. Two Albacores were lost, and the chance of bringing the
battleship to action off the Lofoten Islands, in the waters where the
Renown had fought the *Scharnhorst* and *Gneisenau* in April 1940, was
lost to the Home Fleet.[2] The *Tirpitz* anchored off Narvik that
evening, and Admiral Tovey reached Scapa next day.

The failure of the striking force to slow down the *Tirpitz*, so that
the heavy ships could bring her to book in the same manner as
happened with the *Bismarck*[3], was most disappointing. In fact, such
an opportunity was never to recur. The tactics employed were undoubtedly open to criticism, but it is only right to mention that the

---

[1] See Map 12 (opp. p. 121), Phase 2.
[2] See Vol. I, pp. 165–6 and Map 14 of this volume (opp. p. 141).
[3] See Vol. I, pp. 413–415.

leader of the Albacores had only just taken over command, and had not even flown with his squadron previously. Moreover, both he and the other aircrews lacked the intensive training so necessary to success in air torpedo attacks. To be called on to carry out so critical an operation in such circumstances was a very severe, even unfair test. The only lesson that could be drawn from the failure was the well-known one that success in such attacks could only be achieved after prolonged individual and squadron training, and by experienced as well as gallant leadership.[1] The rapid expansion of the Fleet Air Arm then in progress made it inevitable that its squadrons should be constantly diluted by semi-trained crews, but steps were now taken to ensure that a higher standard of training in torpedo attacks was achieved before individual pilots, or complete units, became operational.

There remained the possibility of catching the *Tirpitz* if and when she left Vestfiord to return to Trondheim. Eight destroyers were sent to sweep along the Norwegian coast south of Vestfiord early on the 13th; and submarines were disposed to catch her at the points where she had to leave the shelter of the Leads. But the *Tirpitz* actually sailed at 11 p.m. on the 12th and steamed south in very bad visibility at high speed, close to the coast.[2] Although she certainly passed very near to some of our submarines none managed to get in a shot. She reached Trondheim at 9 p.m. the next evening; but the weather continued so persistently bad that it was not until the 18th that a Coastal Command reconnaissance aircraft located her in her old berth once more.

Thus ended the first foray by enemy heavy forces in the far north. The results gave the naval authorities of both sides much to ponder on. Although this time our convoys had come through almost unscathed, the realities of the danger in which they lay during the whole of the eastern section of their 2,000-mile journeys received new emphasis. It was plain that by the mere presence of his heavy forces in Norwegian waters the enemy would force us to hold great strength in readiness to deal with them. Reinforcements which were urgently needed elsewhere, and especially in the Indian Ocean, could not be sent out; and every convoy to North Russia would now involve us in a major fleet operation.[3] The enemy, on the other hand, realised that it was only 'sheer good fortune' which had this time saved the battleship from damage, and that such luck would probably not be repeated. Admirals Ciliax and Raeder both stressed the risks they

---

[1] Cf. experience of *Ark Royal's* aircrews in the action off Cape Spartivento, 27th November 1940 (Vol. I, pp. 302–303).

[2] See Map 12 (opp. p. 121), Phase 2.

[3] For a valuable account of the influence of the enemy battleship on Allied maritime strategy and naval dispositions see *Tirpitz* by David Woodward (William Kimber, London, 1953).

ran in such sorties, chiefly because they lacked both an aircraft carrier and effective co-operation from shore-based aircraft. In consequence the German Naval Staff decided on a more cautious policy in the future. Their last battleship would be held in reserve against the anticipated invasion of Norway, and only their lesser ships would be committed in the north. Hitler, however, who always insisted that he could and would have the best of both worlds, ordered that the offensive against the supply route to Russia was to be intensified by air and U-boat attacks, as well as by raids by surface forces. With typical lack of realism he also ordered the lack of carrier aircraft to be rectified by the completion of the *Graf Zeppelin* 'forthwith', and other ships to be converted to auxiliary aircraft carriers.[1]

But the German command was not alone in finding difficulties in operations of this type. Admiral Tovey was critical of the Admiralty instructions that the protection of the convoys must be his main object, and that he was to provide fighter protection for all capital ships within range of enemy shore-based aircraft. Such orders appeared to him a radical departure from the tradition that the destruction of the enemy's principal forces should be the object of our fleet. To carry out such instructions he was forced to work his carrier and capital ships as one unit, often without a destroyer screen, in highly dangerous waters. On the present occasion Admiral Tovey, who considered the sinking of the *Tirpitz* 'of incomparably greater importance to the conduct of the war than the safety of any convoy', had found himself 'seriously embarrassed' by these instructions. Secondly, the Commander-in-Chief criticised in forthright terms 'the detailed instructions for the handling of his forces' which had been signalled from London. This was an old issue, from which Admiral Tovey's predecessor had also suffered, and which was fully discussed in our first volume.[2] The circumstances of the Arctic convoys do, however, appear to have been somewhat different from those earlier cases in which the Admiralty's interventions had aroused the critical comment of Commanders-in-Chief. In the first place the intelligence derived by the Admiralty and sent to the fleet flagship was, we now know, more accurate than the appreciations made afloat. Neither the signalling of the intelligence, nor the issue of orders when the intelligence available in London indicated that the assumptions on which our forces' movements had been based were wrong (as happened on the evening of the 8th of March), is open to criticism. Secondly, communications in those waters were proved to be so difficult that Admiral Tovey himself had once broken wireless silence to ask the Admiralty to operate the cruisers and destroyers of his

---

[1] See Vol. I, pp. 57 and 368. Actually work on the *Graf Zeppelin* was never seriously proceeded with, and in the spring of 1943 it was again suspended.

[2] See Vol. I, pp. 26-7 and 201-203.

fleet. True, some of the Admiralty's messages (such as that ordering the convoy to pass north of Bear Island) now seem to have been unnecessary, and even dangerous; but the conduct of the whole operation produced many novel problems for the Admiralty as well as for the Commander-in-Chief and his staff. If any conclusion is to be drawn, it is perhaps that, as was suggested in an earlier context, it is the extent to which interventions are made from London, rather than the principles involved in making them, which requires constant watchfulness ashore.[1]

We will now take leave temporarily of the distant and dangerous waters across which the war supplies, on which our Russian allies so greatly depended, had to be carried, in order to glance briefly at an operation which took place at this time further south. Readers of our first volume will remember how in January 1941 five Norwegian merchantmen, loaded with valuable cargoes, broke out from Sweden and safely reached British ports.[2] In spite of the greater difficulties inherent in repeating a successful *coup*, plans to do so had long been brewing. On the 11th of March the Admiralty issued definite orders to those concerned; but several postponements were caused by the weather and by the enemy's obvious alertness to what was in the wind. Finally, in the small hours of the 1st of April ten Norwegian ships sailed from Gothenburg. It was not possible to give them surface ship protection for the first day's passage, but for the second day six destroyers were sent out, as well as Coastal and Fighter Command aircraft. The Germans reacted strongly, and many fierce air combats resulted over the North Sea. The final result was that five of the ships were sunk in the Skagerrak by surface forces, grounded, or were scuttled to avoid capture; one was so badly damaged by air attack that our destroyers had to sink her, two returned to Gothenburg and only two reached Britain safely. The results were disappointing after such a determined effort.

The next pair of Russian convoys, PQ.13 and QP.9, sailed from Reykjavik and Murmansk on the 20th and 21st of March respectively. The enemy had brought his revised plans into force and was organising heavier attacks by aircraft and U-boats. Moreover, his policy of concentrating his heavy ships in Norway had just been carried one step further by the transfer of the *Hipper*. She left Brunsbüttel on the 19th and, although our intelligence had once again detected what was afoot, neither our reconnaissance aircraft nor the torpedo striking force of Coastal Command Beauforts managed to find her. On the 21st she anchored in a small fiord near to the *Tirpitz*, and next morning the Home Fleet sailed from Scapa to restart the long and arduous process of covering two Russian convoys.

---

[1] See Vol. 1, pp. 201–203.
[2] See *Ibid*, p. 391.

During their passage Coastal Command did its utmost to watch the four big ships lying in the Trondheim fiords. The weather greatly hindered our aircraft, and the enemy could certainly have evaded their patrols had he wished to do so. In fact, this time none of the four ships put to sea.

The arrangements to protect PQ.13 and QP.9 (both consisting of nineteen ships) were similar to those made for the preceding pair of convoys. The homeward convoy had a safe and comparatively uneventful passage. The only serious encounter with the enemy ended in the ramming and destruction of U.655 by the minesweeper *Sharpshooter* of the close escort. The passage of the outward convoy told a very different story; but all went well until the 24th. The cruiser *Trinidad* was providing close cover, and two destroyers from Iceland had by that time reinforced the close escort. Then a violent gale scattered the convoy far and wide. By the 27th not a single merchantman was in sight of the escort. Next morning the convoy was strung out over about 150 miles of the Arctic Ocean south of Bear Island; and the enemy's searching aircraft had reported its presence. Air attacks soon started, and the wide dispersal of the ships made their protection very difficult. In spite of this only two ships, both stragglers, were sunk by bombs that day, the 28th. But three German destroyers had sailed from Kirkenes on the strength of the first air reports and by the evening of the 28th were sweeping westwards along the presumed track of the convoy. Very early on the 29th they picked up a Panamanian straggler, whose survivors disclosed to the enemy a good deal about the composition and progress of the convoy and its escort. The enemy adjusted his sweep accordingly and, just before 9 a.m. encountered the *Trinidad* and the destroyers *Fury* and *Eclipse* of the escort. A series of sharp actions followed, in conditions of atrocious difficulty—low visibility, snow, and the spray freezing solid as fast as it came aboard. One enemy, the Z.26 was finally sunk. Unhappily, the *Trinidad* was hit by a torpedo and suffered serious damage. After a good deal of difficulty she made Kola Inlet on the 30th under her own steam. The subsequent removal of debris from her boiler rooms produced, quite unexpectedly, a relic from which it was established beyond doubt that she had, in fact, been hit by one of the torpedoes which she herself had fired at the German destroyers during the surface actions. It is almost certain that the extreme cold caused its steering mechanism to behave erratically. But, as Admiral Tovey remarked, 'it was cruel hard luck' for a ship which had just successfully fought off the enemy 'to torpedo herself'.

Meanwhile the convoy, still in several groups, plodded slowly eastward. Two ships got caught in the ice, and one gallant British merchantman, the *Induna*, towed a disabled comrade for more than a day, only to be sunk herself by a U-boat on the 30th. Another fell victim to the same cause a short time later. On the 30th of March and 1st of April the fifteen surviving ships reached their destination. Five had been sunk—two by aircraft, one by destroyers and two by U-boats. Though the escort had sunk one enemy destroyer and also a U-boat (U.585, by the *Fury* on the 29th), the *Trinidad* and *Eclipse* had themselves been badly hurt. And there remained the comfortless fact that one quarter of the convoy had gone down.

Again both sides reviewed the Arctic struggle. The Germans were satisfied, and even claimed a 'notable success' in the operations just described. Admiral Tovey urged the need for stronger close escorts, and more destroyers and corvettes were promised for the next convoys. He also wanted to reduce the number of convoys during the spring and summer, when conditions would increasingly favour the enemy; but he realised that political considerations would probably make this unacceptable. He realised that the enemy was 'determined to do everything in his power to stop this traffic'. Yet efforts to persuade the Russians to make the air and anti-submarine protection more effective at their end of the route continued to produce 'little response'.

On the last day of March Bomber Command made another attempt to reduce the threat from the *Tirpitz* to the Arctic convoys. Thirty-three Halifaxes of No. 4 Group set out to attack her; but the weather was exceedingly bad, and the majority of the bombers failed to identify the target. Those that managed to drop their bombs did no damage, and five aircraft were lost.

The First Sea Lord himself had no illusions regarding the difficulties and dangers of the northern route. Early in April he represented the matter forcefully to the Defence Committee, and ended with a warning that geographical conditions were so greatly in favour of the Germans that losses might become so great as to render the running of these convoys uneconomical. But pressure in the opposite direction was being exerted in the highest quarters, in particular from President Roosevelt to the Prime Minister, and in consequence the next convoy (PQ.14) was made a larger one, of twenty-four ships. It sailed on the 8th of April and soon ran into heavy ice. Sixteen ships returned, and of the eight which went on one was sunk by U-boat. The corresponding homeward convoy, QP.10 of sixteen ships, lost four of its number. The German destroyers again tried to intervene, but the very bad weather frustrated their two attempts.

On the 28th and 29th of April our heavy bombers again attacked the *Tirpitz*, but on both occasions they were met by a very heavy volume of anti-aircraft fire, and had to attack through the dense smoke screen in which the Germans shrouded the battleship. No hits were obtained, and in these two operations we lost seven bombers.

Early in May, after the Admiralty had repeatedly represented the need for the Russians to accept a larger share of the responsibility for the safety of the convoys during the latter part of their journeys, the Prime Minister telegraphed to Stalin pointing out how essential this was. Stalin replied that his 'naval and air forces would do their utmost' on the section of the route east of the meridian of 28° East, but pointed out how small were the forces which he could make available. Though there are no grounds for suggesting that, within the limits imposed by their somewhat primitive conceptions of maritime war, the Russians did not do what they could with what they had, it is none the less the case that they never relieved the Home Fleet of any appreciable share of the responsibility for defending any Arctic convoy.

PQ.15 and QP.11, of twenty-five and thirteen ships respectively, sailed at the end of April. The dispositions followed in general those made for their predecessors, but an anti-aircraft ship joined the close escort, and the covering force included American as well as British warships. We will briefly follow the homeward convoy first. The covering cruiser was the *Edinburgh* (flagship of Rear-Admiral S. S. Bonham-Carter, commanding the 18th Cruiser Squadron), and the close escort comprised six destroyers, four corvettes and a trawler— far greater strength than had so far been employed. In addition British minesweepers and two Russian destroyers kept company for the first stretch of the convoy's passage. On the 29th its presence was reported by enemy aircraft and U-boats, and next afternoon the *Edinburgh* was hit while zig-zagging ahead of the convoy by two torpedoes fired by U.456. Her stern was blown off, and she started back towards Murmansk, 250 miles away, at slow speed escorted by two destroyers. The U-boat meanwhile shadowed the lame cruiser, and the weakening of the convoy escort encouraged the enemy to send three destroyers to sea that night. On the afternoon of the 1st of May, after an air torpedo attack had been unsuccessful, the German destroyers appeared on the scene. They made no less than five separate attempts to reach the convoy, but were each time foiled by the aggressive tactics of the far weaker British escort, which was most ably led by Commander M. Richmond in the aptly-named *Bulldog*. One of our small force, the *Amazon*, was damaged, and one Russian merchant ship, which had straggled, was sunk by an enemy destroyer's torpedo.[1] But that was all. Throughout the afternoon, from 2.0 p.m. till nearly six o'clock, the enemy's repeated lunges at the convoy were successfully driven off. Finally, the Germans abandoned the attempt and went off to find the damaged *Edinburgh*. To Com-

---

[1] The four British destroyers remaining after the *Amazon* had been damaged only mounted six 4·7-inch and three 4-inch guns between them, against the three German ships' ten 5·9-inch and five 5-inch. The gun armaments of many British destroyers had recently been reduced by half to enable more anti-submarine equipment to be fitted for the Atlantic battle.

H.M.S. *Duke of York* in a heavy sea inside the Arctic circle, while covering Convoy PQ.13, March 1942. (See pp. 126–127).

Destroyers for Arctic Convoys. H.M.S. *Onslow* (nearer the camera) and H.M.S. *Ashanti*, March 1942. (See pp. 293–299).

Torpedo-Bomber attack on the *Tirpitz* by Albacores from H.M.S. *Victorious*, 13th March 1942. (See p. 122). Three torpedo tracks can be seen crossing the battleship's wake in the upper photograph. Taken from the *Tirpitz*.

(*Photos.: Captain H. J.*

mander Richmond's congratulatory signal to his consorts one of them instantly replied, 'I should hate to play poker with you'; and there is indeed no doubt that he thoroughly outfought the enemy's 'three of a kind'. QP.11 reached home without further trouble.

Meanwhile the *Edinburgh*, unable to steer except with her engines, and also unable to be towed, was making very slow progress eastwards. On the evening of the 1st she was joined by four minesweepers, but early the following morning the German destroyers found her. A series of confused fights followed, and the cruiser herself, for all her disablement and grievous trouble, managed to hit and stop the large destroyer *Hermann Schoemann*. But the *Forester* was also heavily hit, just at the moment when the enemy had fired torpedoes. By ill luck one of these, almost at the end of its run, hit the *Edinburgh*, which was unable to take any avoiding action, amidships on the opposite side to her earlier damage. The ship was thus almost cut in two. She continued to fight her armament—and one enemy described her gunfire even then as being 'extraordinarily good'—but she was plainly doomed. Another misfortune followed quickly, when the *Foresight*, the last effective destroyer, was badly hit and brought to a standstill. There were thus three British ships all lying stopped at the same time, and all with much of their armament out of action. The two surviving enemies could have finished them off at leisure, but chose instead to take off the crew of the damaged *Schoemann*. This they successfully accomplished, the *Schoemann* sank and the other German destroyers then withdrew. The *Forester* and *Foresight* next managed to get under way at slow speed, the minesweepers took off the *Edinburgh's* crew, among whom casualties were remarkably light, and the cruiser was then sunk by one of our own torpedoes. The enemy had undoubtedly scored a success; but he might have annihilated our whole force had he not mistaken the minesweepers for destroyers and, we now know, greatly overestimated the opposition by which he was faced.

Meanwhile the east-bound convoy PQ.15 had entered the critical part of its passage. It was powerfully escorted, and covered by Admiral Tovey's full strength. Up to the 2nd of May no losses had been suffered. On that day the west-bound convoy (QP.11) was passed, and a gloomy prognostication of what probably lay ahead was received from its escort. Enemy shadowing aircraft were soon in touch, and in the half light of the small hours of the 3rd six torpedo-bombers came in low. They sank three ships. The U-boats never succeeded in getting in an attack, and subsequent bombing caused no more losses. On the 4th, visibility closed right down, and shielded the convoy for the rest of its passage. Of the thirty-eight merchantmen involved in this double movement only four were lost; but casualties among the escorting warships had been heavy. In addition

K

to the loss of the *Edinburgh* and the damage to the *Foresight* and *Forester*, the destroyer *Punjabi* had been rammed and sunk in low visibility by the *King George V* on the 1st of May, and the Polish submarine P.551 was destroyed by our own forces when she was suddenly encountered nearly 100 miles from her patrol area, near to PQ.15, on the 2nd. Nor was the story of our losses yet ended, for on the 13th the damaged *Trinidad* left Murmansk escorted by four destroyers and covered by powerful forces. She was quickly sighted by enemy reconnaissance planes, and on the evening of the 14th air attacks started. Some twenty-five bombers and one torpedo attack failed to damage her, but at 10.45 p.m. a lone Ju.88 dived out of low clouds, and scored a hit with a bomb not far from where she had previously been damaged. This started a serious fire, which spread rapidly; her condition was made more precarious by a near miss blowing a temporary patch off her side and causing flooding. She was still able to steam, but by midnight the fire was out of control and it was decided that, situated as she was far from any friendly port, in the presence of U-boats, and in certain danger of renewed attack by aircraft, salvage was impossible. She was sunk by our own torpedoes at 1.20 a.m. on the 15th. Thus did Admiral Bonham-Carter suffer the loss of two valuable cruisers, both of them his flagship, within a matter of two weeks. Admiral Tovey fully endorsed his recommendation that unless the airfields in north Norway could be neutralised, or some cover obtained from darkness, the convoys should be stopped. 'If', he went on, 'they must continue for political reasons, very serious and heavy losses must be expected'. Nor did the First Sea Lord disagree. On the 18th of May he wrote to his American colleague, Admiral King, about these convoys, saying that 'the whole thing is a most unsound operation with the dice loaded against us in every direction'; and Admiral King replied in sympathetic agreement. Mr Churchill has revealed the extent to which political pressure overruled such strong professional opinion.[1]

It thus came to pass that, far from the convoys being suspended, the next one (PQ.16) of thirty-five ships was the largest yet sailed— and that despite the time of year being now even less favourable. It was plain to all involved in the work of planning the convoys and the associated fleet movements and in the long-drawn anxieties of their execution, that we were gambling with fate to an extent which was bound, sooner or later, to provoke nemesis. All realised that a disaster was likely; but when and on which convoy would it fall?

Though, as we realised, the threat from German destroyers was now more or less eliminated, the *Scheer* had moved north to Narvik, and had been joined there by the *Lützow* on the 26th of May. To

---

[1] Churchill, Vol. IV, pp. 230–234.

escort the convoys with cruisers throughout the passage was therefore deemed less essential, but four cruisers and three destroyers were detailed for close cover against the pocket battleships west of Bear Island. The battle fleet again provided more distant cover against the *Tirpitz*. PQ.16 sailed on the 21st, as did QP.12 of fifteen ships. Early on the 25th the covering cruisers *Nigeria*, *Norfolk*, *Kent* and *Liverpool*, under Rear-Admiral H. M. Burrough, with three destroyers, had joined the east-bound convoy and greatly reinforced its escort. The first shadower promptly arrived, and thereafter for five continuous days the convoy was hardly ever unaccompanied by a watchful enemy reconnaissance plane. On the afternoon of the 25th it passed the homeward convoy, and soon afterwards there began an air battle which lasted throughout virtually the whole of the rest of the journey. Torpedo-bombers (He.111s) alternated with dive attacks by Ju.88s; but the first victim fell to a U-boat early on the 26th. A Catapult Aircraft Merchantman (C.A.M. Ship), the *Empire Lawrence*, had been included in the convoy, and her single Hurricane destroyed one enemy and damaged another.[1] The gunfire of the powerful escort proved effective in holding off the attackers and in destroying some of them, while the anti-submarine escort constantly harassed and chased away the U-boats. But on the 27th, after the cruiser force had left the convoy, yet heavier air attacks took place. The A.A. ship *Alynbank* recorded, with, as we now know, complete accuracy, attacks by 108 aircraft that day. They were generally pressed well home; four merchantmen, including the C.A.M. ship, were sunk, and two others and the Polish-manned destroyer *Garland* badly damaged. The small escort vessels rescued survivors, even while they themselves were being bombed.

Late in the evening heavy attacks were renewed. Two more ships went down and the Commodore's ship, the *Ocean Voice*, was set on fire and badly holed. 'I had little hope of her survival', wrote Commander R. Onslow, senior officer of the escort, 'but this gallant ship maintained her station, fought her fire, and with God's help arrived at her destination'. In the escorts ammunition was beginning to run low; yet there were three more days, and twenty-four hour days, too, to be endured. 'We were all inspired', continued Commander Onslow, 'by the parade-ground rigidity of the convoy's station-keeping, including the [damaged] *Ocean Voice* and the *Stari Bolshevik* [a Russian merchantman], who were both billowing smoke from their foreholds'.

However, the worst was actually over. One more damaged ship went down on the 28th, but a welcome reinforcement of three Russian destroyers arrived. More attacks followed, but no more

---

[1] See Vol. I, p. 477, regarding C.A.M. ships and the demands made on the pilots of their Hurricane fighters.

losses were suffered. Next evening six British minesweepers from Murmansk arrived, and the six ships destined for Archangel were detached. The expected U-boat attacks did not occur, and on the afternoon of the 30th convoy PQ.16 'reduced in numbers, battered and tired, but still keeping perfect station' entered Kola Inlet.[1]

While the east-bound convoy was being subjected to this prolonged ordeal, the fifteen ships of the west-bound QP.12 had a comparatively uneventful passage. Apart from one Russian ship which had to return, it arrived intact at Reykjavik on the 29th of May. Of the fifty ships which started out on the double journey only seven were lost. 'This success was beyond expectation', wrote Admiral Tovey, and gave high praise to the officers and men of both escorts and merchantmen. Dönitz himself paid tribute to the work of the Allied escorts, and admitted that his favourite weapon (the U-boat) had failed him. The Luftwaffe had, with great exaggeration, claimed that the convoy had been totally destroyed. This misled Dönitz into recommending that aircraft rather than U-boats should be used against the summer convoys. On our side, Commander Onslow urged that many more C.A.M. ships or an escort carrier, and more A.A. ships as well should be included in the escort of future convoys. It was indeed realised that, in face of the air strength now deployed by the enemy in north Norway, anti-aircraft defence must take equal precedence with anti-submarine measures and protection against surface attack.[2] Thus was catastrophe in the Arctic deferred—but not for long.

When, in the spring of 1942, the Russian convoys loomed so large in the responsibilities of the Home Fleet and the problems of their defence were of constant concern to the Admiralty, it was natural that the eyes of the British authorities should once more be turned towards the island of Spitzbergen. It was important to prevent the enemy establishing any form of base there, and especially from stationing aircraft in its bays. In August 1941, after we had evacuated all the Allied inhabitants[3], it was known that a German meteoro-

---

[1] The ships of PQ.16 carried 125,000 tons of cargo. Included in it were:
468 Tanks of which 147 were lost.
201 Aircraft of which 77 were lost.
3,277 Vehicles of which 770 were lost.
The total tonnage lost was 32,400.

[2] The total air strength deployed by the enemy on the airfields around North Cape was at this time as follows:

Ju.88	Long-range bombers	103
He.111	Torpedo-bombers	42
He.115	Torpedo float-planes	15
Ju.87	Dive-bombers	30
Long-range reconnaissance planes (F.W.200, Ju.88 and B.V.138)		74
	Total	264

[3] See Vol. I, pp. 488–489.

logical party had been set up ashore; but we had never been able to spare the forces to turn them out, or to re-occupy the island. Now, in May 1942, after a preliminary and very difficult reconnaissance by a Catalina of Coastal Command, a small Norwegian expedition sailed from Iceland. Unfortunately, enemy bombers sank both its ships before all the stores had been unloaded. There now followed a curious period of hide and seek among the fogs which so often shroud this remote Arctic island; for there were Allied and enemy expeditions ashore in different places, and each side tried to support and supply its own party and attack the other's. On our side the denial of Spitzbergen to the enemy owed much to a series of remarkable flights by a Catalina of No. 210 Squadron of Coastal Command, commanded by Flight-Lieutenant D. E. Healey. In the most difficult conditions conceivable, during flights which generally lasted about twenty-four hours, he carried supplies to the stranded Norwegians, attacked the enemy base on Spitzbergen, picked up some of the Allied party, sighted survivors of ships sunk in Russian convoys and performed a dozen other various duties. Unhappily, he was killed in September, in a chance encounter with a German bomber off Kola Inlet. Warships accompanying Russian convoys were several times diverted to relieve, reinforce and supply the Norwegian expedition. Thanks to all these various measures, by the autumn it was plain that we had prevented the enemy establishing himself in Spitzbergen, and had a reasonable hold on it for our own use.

It must not be thought that Coastal Command's long-range reconnaissance and escort work was the only way in which the Royal Air Force tried to mitigate the dangers of the Arctic route. Bomber Command did its best to put the *Tirpitz* out of action while she lay near Trondheim. It has already been told how, on the last day of March and twice during April, strong forces of from thirty to forty-five heavy bombers were sent to attack her[1]; but no hits were obtained on any of these missions.

Our experiences in defending PQ.16 and earlier convoys to Russia had emphasised how difficult it was to carry out the air patrols off north Norway, which were essential to obtain early warning of enemy warship movements, as long as they had to be sent out from British bases. Early in June the Commander-in-Chief, Coastal Command, suggested to the Air Ministry that the establishment of a flying boat base in Kola Inlet would greatly ease such difficulties. The feasibility of providing a similar base at Advent Bay in Spitzbergen was also discussed, but in that case the difficulties were finally found to be insuperable. Another way of increasing the threat to the German warships in the North was to station torpedo-bombers near Murmansk. The Admiralty told the Senior British Naval Officer, North

---

[1] See p. 127.

Russia (Rear-Admiral R. H. L. Bevan) to investigate the latter, but they insisted that the Russians must not treat such a proposal as relieving them of responsibility for the defence of our convoys at the end of their journeys. On the 7th of June the First Sea Lord also told Admiral Miles, the head of our naval mission in Moscow, that if the convoys were to continue the Russians must make a proper contribution to their defence by such steps as bombing enemy air stations, and keeping submarines on patrol east of Bear Island. One-fifth of our losses were incurred at the Russian end of the Arctic route, and Admiral Pound considered that a large proportion of them had been avoidable. Admiral Miles replied that the Russians would welcome our torpedo-bombers, and intended to devote all their resources in the north to improving the defence of the convoys. Though the acute shortage of torpedo-carrying aircraft in Coastal Command prevented the proposal being carried out[1], by the end of June arrangements had been made for Catalinas of Nos. 210 and 240 Squadrons to patrol off north Norway, land at Russian bases and work from them for a time before returning to Britain.

Owing to the desperate need to relieve Malta, considerable strength had to be detached from the Home Fleet early in June, to help fight through a convoy.[2] It was nearly the end of the month before the survivors returned to Scapa, and meanwhile no Russian convoy could be run. There was thus a lull for the rest of the Home Fleet, during which H.M. King George VI came to Scapa. He stayed in the fleet flagship *Duke of York*, and visited several of the ships present, including the U.S.S. *Washington*, flagship of Rear-Admiral R. C. Giffen, U.S.N., who was in command of the American Navy's Task Force 99. But the interlude was a brief one. PQ.17 and QP.13, of thirty-six and thirty-five ships respectively, sailed on the 27th of June, except for the Archangel section of the latter which started a day earlier.

From what has already been written the reader will have understood the profound misgivings with which the continuation of the Russian convoys throughout the summer, and especially of large convoys, was regarded by the officers responsible for their safety. They accepted the need to carry on with them because the political leaders of the Allied nations desired it, and because they knew that a hard-pressed Russia was clamouring for the munitions which had been promised her, and which were steadily piling up in British and American ports. But they did so without any illusions regarding the dangers of the undertaking. So far our forces had not had to deal

---

[1] Coastal Command had only two fully-trained torpedo-bomber squadrons (Nos. 68 and 415) at this time. The Admiralty would not agree to the command's entire striking power being sent to North Russia.

[2] See pp. 63-67 for the story of Operation 'Harpoon'.

simultaneously with all the enemy's weapons—his heavy ships, his light surface forces, his aircraft and his U-boats. Different convoys had been threatened in the Barents Sea by one, two or even three of these four; but never by all four at once. Now, unknown to the Admiralty, the German Naval Staff had just decided to commit the *Tirpitz* to the attempt. True, the instructions issued with Hitler's approval to Admiral Schniewind, the new Commander-in-Chief afloat, were hedged with such cramping restrictions as would have eased the Admiralty's anxiety, and probably altered their actions, had they known of them. But they could not know that Raeder had given warning that a naval reverse at this time was particularly undesirable, nor that Group Command North had told Schniewind 'on no account to allow the enemy to score a success against the main body of the fleet'. The *Tirpitz* and *Hipper*, with four destroyers, were now at Trondheim; and the *Scheer* and *Lützow*, with six destroyers, were at Narvik. 'The strategic situation', wrote Admiral Tovey, 'was wholly favourable to the enemy'; and apart from submarine attacks off the coast he could see no way of mitigating it, except by tempting the enemy heavy forces to attack further to the west. A suggestion that this might be accomplished by turning the convoy back on its tracks temporarily did not meet with Admiralty favour, though they agreed that in certain circumstances they themselves might order it. Their instructions laid down that, to the west of Bear Island, our surface forces would be responsible for the convoy's protection against attack by heavy ships; to the east of that mark our submarines must meet the need. The cruiser covering force was not to go east of Bear Island, unless the threat to the convoy consisted of a surface force which it could fight—that is to say, a force which did not include the *Tirpitz*; nor in any case were the cruisers to go east of 25° East. These instructions did not altogether appeal to Admiral Tovey; and we now know that the Commander-in-Chief was very near the mark in holding that, particularly after his experiences against PQ.12 and QP.8, the enemy would not again risk committing the *Tirpitz* to an attack on a convoy in the Barents Sea. He and the First Sea Lord discussed the new convoy operation, regarding which they were not wholly in agreement, on the telephone from Scapa to the Admiralty. Admiral Tovey had always disliked sending heavy cruisers into the Barents Sea with the convoys. They could not be given adequate protection against U-boats or air attack and, if they were damaged so many miles from home bases, to extricate them was bound to be difficult; for there were no proper facilities at Murmansk for repairing damaged ships. The recent loss of the *Trinidad* and *Edinburgh* from combinations of these causes had lent support to his view that the risks were too great; but the Admiralty still considered cruiser support for the smaller ships of the close escorts essential.

With particular regard to the forthcoming operation Admiral Tovey represented that, apart from the time of year being unsuitable, the close escort was too weak and the convoy too large. If it must be sent, he considered that it should sail in two sections. The First Sea Lord was, however, insistent that the operation should take place as planned. Though no record was kept of these conversations, Admiral Tovey's recollections are clear on one other important point. He first learnt by this means of the possibility of the Admiralty ordering the convoy to scatter, if it appeared to be in imminent danger. Nor is there any doubt that this suggestion shocked the Commander-in-Chief deeply, because all his experience had been in exactly the opposite sense. It had, in fact, been repeatedly shown in all theatres, and very recently confirmed with respect to the Russian convoys, that so long as close order and disciplined movements were maintained, the merchantmen and escorts could afford each other effective mutual support; but once a convoy lost cohesion, its individual ships fell an easy prey to whatever enemy next found them.

The general dispositions made for PQ.17 corresponded to those which had proved successful on the last occasion. Four cruisers under Rear-Admiral L. H. K. Hamilton, the *London* (flagship) and *Norfolk* and the American ships *Tuscaloosa* and *Wichita* with three destroyers, were to provide close cover as far as Bear Island. The Commander-in-Chief in the *Duke of York* with the *Washington* (American battleship), *Victorious*, *Nigeria*, *Cumberland* and fourteen destroyers formed the distant covering force in the waters north-east of Jan Mayen Island. It should be mentioned that this was the first occasion on which substantial American forces were placed under British orders for an operation of this nature. Mr Churchill later 'surmised' that this new factor may have influenced Admiral Pound's actions[1]; but no indication that this was the case has been found in the Admiralty's subsequent investigations, nor does the memory of staff officers who were close to the First Sea Lord lend support to the suggestion.

An attempt to deceive the enemy by sailing a false convoy ahead of the real one was unsuccessful, because the Germans never sighted it. Meanwhile, Hitler's overriding powers had produced still more precautionary orders, and of such stringency that to attack the convoy at all with the heavy ships was made virtually impossible; for Raeder was told that before the ships sailed he must have ascertained the disposition of our aircraft carriers, in order that the Luftwaffe might attack them. This restriction was almost certain to delay sailing the heavy ships until it was too late to attack the convoy; but the Admiralty could not possibly have been aware of this. Raeder tried to overcome the handicap thus imposed by transferring the ships to a temporary base in the extreme north as soon as

---

[1] Churchill, Vol. IV, p. 236.

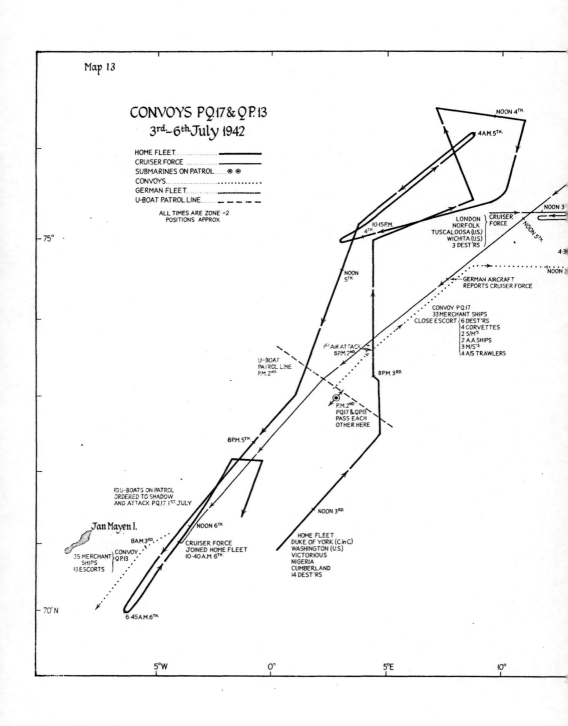

Map 13

CONVOYS P.Q.17 & Q.P.13
3rd.–6th.July 1942

HOME FLEET..................
CRUISER FORCE ....
SUBMARINES ON PATROL ..... ⊙ ⊙
CONVOYS........................
GERMAN FLEET..............
U-BOAT PATROL LINE......

ALL TIMES ARE ZONE –2
POSITIONS APPROX

NOON 4TH.

4 A.M. 5TH.

10·15 P.M.
4TH.

LONDON
NORFOLK
TUSCALOOSA (U.S)
WICHITA (U.S)
3 DEST'RS

CRUISER
FORCE

NOON 3

NOON 5TH.

4·3

NOON
5TH.

GERMAN AIRCRAFT
REPORTS CRUISER FORCE

NOON 3

CONVOY P.Q.17
33 MERCHANT SHIPS
CLOSE ESCORT { 6 DEST'RS
4 CORVETTES
2 S/M'S
2 A.A. SHIPS
3 M/S'S
4 A/S TRAWLERS

1ST. AIR ATTACK
6 P.M. 2ND.

U–BOAT
PATROL LINE
P.M. 2ND.

8 P.M. 3RD.

75°

P.M. 2ND.
PQ17 & QP13
PASS EACH
OTHER HERE

8 P.M. 5TH.

10 U-BOATS ON PATROL
ORDERED TO SHADOW
AND ATTACK PQ.17 1ST. JULY

Jan Mayen I.

NOON 6TH.

NOON 3RD.

8 A.M. 3RD.

CONVOY
Q.P.13

CRUISER FORCE
JOINED HOME FLEET
10·40 A.M. 6TH.

HOME FLEET
DUKE OF YORK (C.in C.)
WASHINGTON (U.S)
VICTORIOUS
NIGERIA
CUMBERLAND
14 DEST'RS

35 MERCHANT
SHIPS
13 ESCORTS

70° N

6·45 A.M. 6TH.

5°W   0°   5°E   10°

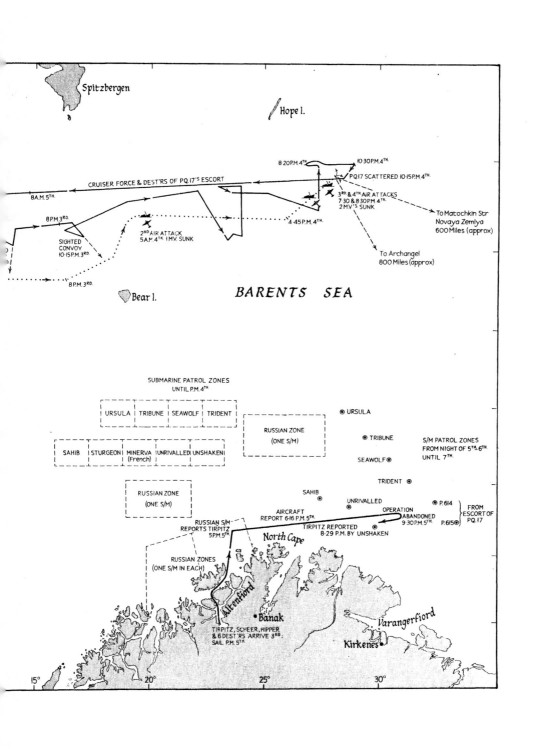

Spitzbergen

Hope I.

CRUISER FORCE & DEST'RS OF PQ.17'S ESCORT

8 A.M. 5TH.

8 20 P.M. 4TH

10·30 P.M. 4TH.

PQ17 SCATTERED 10·15 P.M. 4TH.

3RD & 4TH AIR ATTACKS
7·30 & 8·30 P.M. 4TH.
2 MV'S SUNK

To Matochkin Str
Novaya Zemlya
600 Miles (approx)

8 P.M. 3RD.

4·45 P.M. 4TH.

SIGHTED
CONVOY
10·15 P.M. 3RD.

2ND AIR ATTACK
5 A.M. 4TH. I MV. SUNK

To Archangel
800 Miles (approx)

8 P.M. 3RD.

Bear I.

BARENTS SEA

SUBMARINE PATROL ZONES
UNTIL P.M. 4TH.

| URSULA | TRIBUNE | SEAWOLF | TRIDENT |

URSULA

RUSSIAN ZONE
(ONE S/M)

TRIBUNE

| SAHIB | STURGEON | MINERVA (French) | UNRIVALLED | UNSHAKEN |

SEAWOLF

S/M PATROL ZONES
FROM NIGHT OF 5TH-6TH.
UNTIL 7TH.

RUSSIAN ZONE
(ONE S/M)

TRIDENT

SAHIB

UNRIVALLED

P.614
FROM
ESCORT OF
PQ.17

OPERATION
ABANDONED
9·30 P.M. 5TH.

P.615

RUSSIAN S/M
REPORTS TIRPITZ
5 P.M. 5TH.

AIRCRAFT
REPORT 6·16 P.M. 5TH.

TIRPITZ REPORTED
8·29 P.M. BY UNSHAKEN

North Cape

RUSSIAN ZONES
(ONE S/M IN EACH)

Altenfiord

Banak

Varangerfiord

TIRPITZ, SCHEER, HIPPER
& 6 DEST'RS ARRIVE 3RD.
SAIL P.M. 5TH.

Kirkenes

15°   20°   25°   30°

the convoy was known to have sailed. He hoped to get Hitler's final sanction to the operation while they were there, and thus gain enough time to attack. Admiral Schniewind issued his plan on the 14th of June. As soon as the convoy was known to be approaching, the Narvik force (the *Lützow* and *Scheer*) would move to Altenfiord[1], and the Trondheim force (the *Tirpitz* and *Hipper*) to Vestfiord. The two squadrons would sail as soon as the convoy had passed the meridian of 5° East, and would meet each other 100 miles north of North Cape. The attack would be made when the convoy was between 20° and 30° East. Reconnaissance by U-boats and aircraft was arranged in order to give early warning of our movements.

The convoy was routed further north than before, since the summer limit of the ice made it possible to pass north of Bear Island. This route was, of course, longer, but it kept the convoy further away from the enemy air bases in north Norway. All the merchantmen were destined for Archangel, because Murmansk had been put out of action by bombing. The convoy was in the charge of Commodore J. C. K. Dowding, R.N.R., in the *River Afton*. An oiler was, as usual, included in order to refuel the escorts of the homeward as well as the outward convoy. The escort for the first part of the journey, of three minesweepers and four trawlers, left with the convoy; on the 30th the long-range escort of six destroyers, four corvettes and two submarines under Commander J. E. Broome in the *Keppel* joined up, as did the two anti-aircraft ships *Palomares* and *Pozarica*. There were also three rescue ships. On the 1st of July U-boats and shadowing aircraft made contact, but attacks by the former were all driven off. The outward and homeward convoys passed each other that afternoon in 73° North 3° East, and in the evening an unsuccessful air torpedo attack took place. Admiral Hamilton with his four cruisers had now overtaken the convoy. He was keeping out of sight some forty miles to the north of it in order 'to keep the enemy guessing' as to his whereabouts. From the evening of the 2nd till the following forenoon the convoy was protected by fog. At 7 a.m. on the 3rd course was altered due east, to pass Bear Island and enter the Barents Sea.[2] Shadowing aircraft were temporarily thrown off the scent. Meanwhile the Admiralty had reported that the ice edge was further north than had been anticipated, and the convoy altered somewhat in that direction at Admiral Hamilton's suggestion. Commander Broome, however, was anxious to make eastward progress as quickly as he could, and did not therefore fully accept the cruiser Admiral's proposed northward diversion. By 10.15 that evening, the 3rd, the convoy was thirty miles north of Bear Island. Our reconnaissance aircraft had meanwhile discovered that the

---

[1] See Map 13.
[2] See Map 13.

German Trondheim force had sailed, but no news had yet been obtained regarding the Narvik squadron. Admiral Tovey and the battle fleet were approaching their covering position, and Admiral Hamilton decided to exercise the discretion allowed to him and remain for a time with the convoy after it had passed Bear Island. So far all had gone very well indeed.

But the enemy forces were both meanwhile on the move. The *Tirpitz* and *Hipper* arrived in the Lofoten Islands on the 3rd, and the *Scheer* reached Altenfiord as well. The *Lützow* and three destroyers of the *Tirpitz's* group had all run aground near Narvik, and they took no further part in the operation.[1]

Early on the 4th PQ.17 suffered its first loss when a single aircraft torpedoed an American merchantman 'through a hole in the fog'. At about noon the Admiralty gave Admiral Hamilton discretion to carry on east of the limit of 25° East laid down in his orders 'should [the] situation demand it'. Admiral Tovey, who had no intelligence to justify the change of plan, qualified the Admiralty's message by telling Hamilton 'once the convoy is east of 25° East or earlier at your discretion you are to leave the Barents Sea unless assured by [the] Admiralty that [the] *Tirpitz* cannot be met'. At 6 p.m. Hamilton reported his intention of withdrawing at 10 o'clock, but at 7.30 the Admiralty signalled to him 'Further information may be available shortly. Remain with convoy pending further instructions'. We will return shortly to the 'further information' referred to in the Admiralty's message. The next development was a more serious attack by some two dozen torpedo aircraft at about 8.30 p.m. Three ships were hit, and two of them had to be sunk by the escort; the third, a Russian tanker with at least one woman in the crew, was found, in Commander Broome's words, to be 'holed but happy and capable of nine knots'. She eventually reached port. The convoy and escort defended themselves and each other with splendid discipline, and with good results. All felt that 'provided the ammunition lasted PQ.17 could get anywhere'.

In Germany Hitler's approval for the departure of the heavy ships was still lacking; but Raeder had ordered the *Tirpitz* to join the pocket battleships in Altenfiord, so that no time should be lost if the Führer's approval was forthcoming. The main body of the Home Fleet had not been sighted since early on the 3rd, so that the restriction imposed by Hitler, forbidding the employment of the battleship while the whereabouts of our aircraft carriers was unknown, still held good. Raeder decided he could do no more, and the German ships remained in Altenfiord till the afternoon of the

---

[1] To repair the damage sustained in grounding, the *Lützow* sailed for Germany on the 9th of August. She entered Kiel dockyard on the 21st and remained there until the 5th of November. See p. 290 below for her return to Norway in December 1942.

5th. So much for the enemy's actual dispositions and intentions. Let us now see how they appeared to the Admiralty at the time.

Between the 1st and 4th of July a number of Catalinas of No. 210 Squadron had flown to North Russia, making very thorough reconnaissances off the Norwegian coast on the way. Continuous patrols by these and by home-based aircraft were arranged during the critical period of the convoy's progress. Because of an accident to an aircraft there was, however, a gap in the air patrols from 11 a.m. to 5 p.m. on the 4th of July, and it is likely that the uncertainty produced by this failure influenced the Admiralty's subsequent actions. On the afternoon of the 4th of July our intelligence suggested that although there had been no verification of the photographic reconnaissance which had revealed that the German warships had left Vestfiord, it was 'tolerably certain' that the *Scheer* and *Lützow* were at Altenfiord. There had been no news of the *Tirpitz* and *Hipper* since 2 p.m. on the 3rd, when they were known to have left Trondheim. Thus by the afternoon of the 4th all four heavy warships might have been at sea making for the convoy, and at a time when our long-range air reconnaissance was known to have temporarily failed. The anxiety which this state of affairs must have produced in London is easily to be understood.

At about the time when PQ.17 was repelling the torpedo-bomber attack (8.30 p.m. on the 4th) the First Sea Lord called a staff meeting at which the various possibilities were fully discussed. By that time it was known that the *Tirpitz* had joined the *Scheer* in Altenfiord, and it was therefore considered that surface ship attack might take place at any time after 2 a.m. next morning. It seemed to the Naval Staff that it could only result in Admiral Hamilton's cruisers, the convoy and its escort all being overwhelmed. On the other hand, the convoy still had 800 miles to go, and the enemy aircraft and U-boats would find things much easier for them if the convoy dispersed. The surface attack was held to be the greater of the two dangers and, shortly after 9 p.m. a signal was sent to Admiral Hamilton 'Most Immediate. Cruiser force withdraw to westward at high speed'. This was followed at 9.23 by 'Immediate. Owing to threat of surface ships convoy is to disperse and proceed to Russian ports' and, at 9.36, by 'Most Immediate. My 9.23 of the 4th. Convoy is to scatter'.

Responsibility for the main decision lay, of course, on the First Sea Lord's shoulders. But it must be made clear that so critical a decision was not quickly taken by him.[1] He and the Naval Staff had previously discussed the problem in all its aspects, but memories are not unanimous regarding whether any opposition was then expressed. It is known that the Vice Chief of Naval Staff (Vice-Admiral H. R.

---

[1] Compare Mr Churchill's account (*The Second World War*, Vol. IV, p. 236).

Moore) pointed out that if the convoy was to scatter it must do so soon, because the further east it steamed the less sea-room would it have in which to scatter.

Three important points must be discussed before we turn to the tragic and disastrous sequel. Firstly, the order to disperse was based on anticipation of the enemy's intentions. It was not known whether the enemy surface ships were already at sea and threatening the convoy; but it was reasonable to suppose that such was their intention. To scatter the convoy would certainly incur grave dangers, and the decision to do so gambled on these being less than the risks from surface attack, in spite of the fact that the latter had not yet arisen, and might never arise. Secondly, the Admiralty issued a categorical order without telling those who would have to carry it out whether it was based on positive or negative intelligence. The 'threat of surface ships' mentioned in the second signal was practically meaningless; for such a threat was known to have existed for the past several days. Whilst making every allowance for the strain and anxiety felt in London, it is hard to justify such an intervention, made in such a way. If it was felt that there was a possibility that dispersing the convoy would turn out to be the less perilous action, such a proposal, and the grounds on which it was made, could justifiably have been sent to the responsible officers, for them to carry out or not as they saw fit. It is beyond doubt that had this been done the convoy and escort would have been kept together. Thirdly, the manner in which the decision was signalled by the Admiralty was almost bound to convey a false impression to the recipients of the three messages. In fact, emphasis was placed on the use of high speed in the first signal, only because U-boats were reported to be concentrating on the cruisers' withdrawal route; the distinction between 'disperse' in the second and 'scatter' in the third was merely a technical amendment[1]; and that the final message had a more urgent priority (Most Immediate) than its predecessor appears to have been an error or mischance in the drafting of it. To Admiral Hamilton and Commander Broome, however, the three signals, read together, were bound to signify firstly that they constituted the 'further information' promised to them in the earlier message; secondly, that a moment of extreme urgency, demanding drastic action, had arrived, and thirdly, that the enemy surface forces were really close at hand. None of these deductions was in fact correct. A decision, the wisdom of which was doubtful from the start, was thus made disastrous when translated into action.

---

[1] Convoy instructions laid down that 'to disperse' meant that ships would break formation and proceed to their destinations; they would therefore remain close together for some time. To 'scatter' ordered them to start out in different directions according to a pre-arranged scheme.

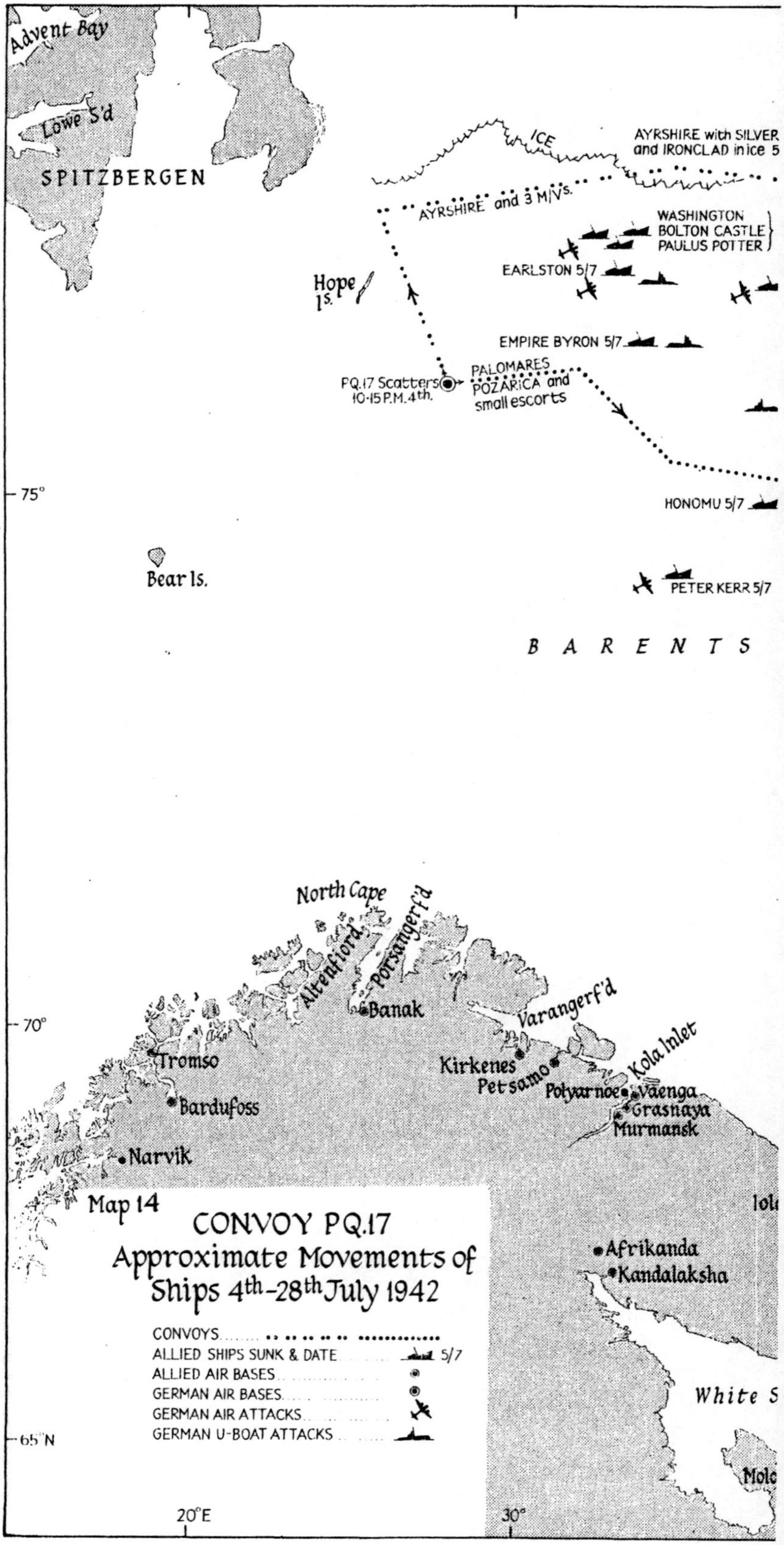

Advent Bay

Lowe S'd

SPITZBERGEN

ICE

AYRSHIRE with SILVER
and IRONCLAD in ice 5

AYRSHIRE and 3 M/V's.

WASHINGTON
BOLTON CASTLE
PAULUS POTTER

EARLSTON 5/7

Hope
1 s.

EMPIRE BYRON 5/7

PQ.17 Scatters
10-15 P.M. 4th.

PALOMARES
POZARICA and
small escorts

HONOMU 5/7

─ 75°

Bear Is.

PETER KERR 5/7

B A R E N T S

North Cape

Altanfiord

Porsangerf'd

Banak

Varangerf'd

Kola Inlet

─ 70°

Tromso

Kirkenes

Petsamo

Polyarnoe

Vaenga

Grasnaya

Bardufoss

Murmansk

Narvik

Iol

Afrikanda

Kandalaksha

Map 14
CONVOY PQ.17
Approximate Movements of
Ships 4th–28th July 1942

CONVOYS...............•• •• •• •• ••••••••••
ALLIED SHIPS SUNK & DATE........ 5/7
ALLIED AIR BASES..................⊚
GERMAN AIR BASES..............✻
GERMAN AIR ATTACKS........✈
GERMAN U-BOAT ATTACKS.......

White S

─ 65°N

Mole

20°E   30°

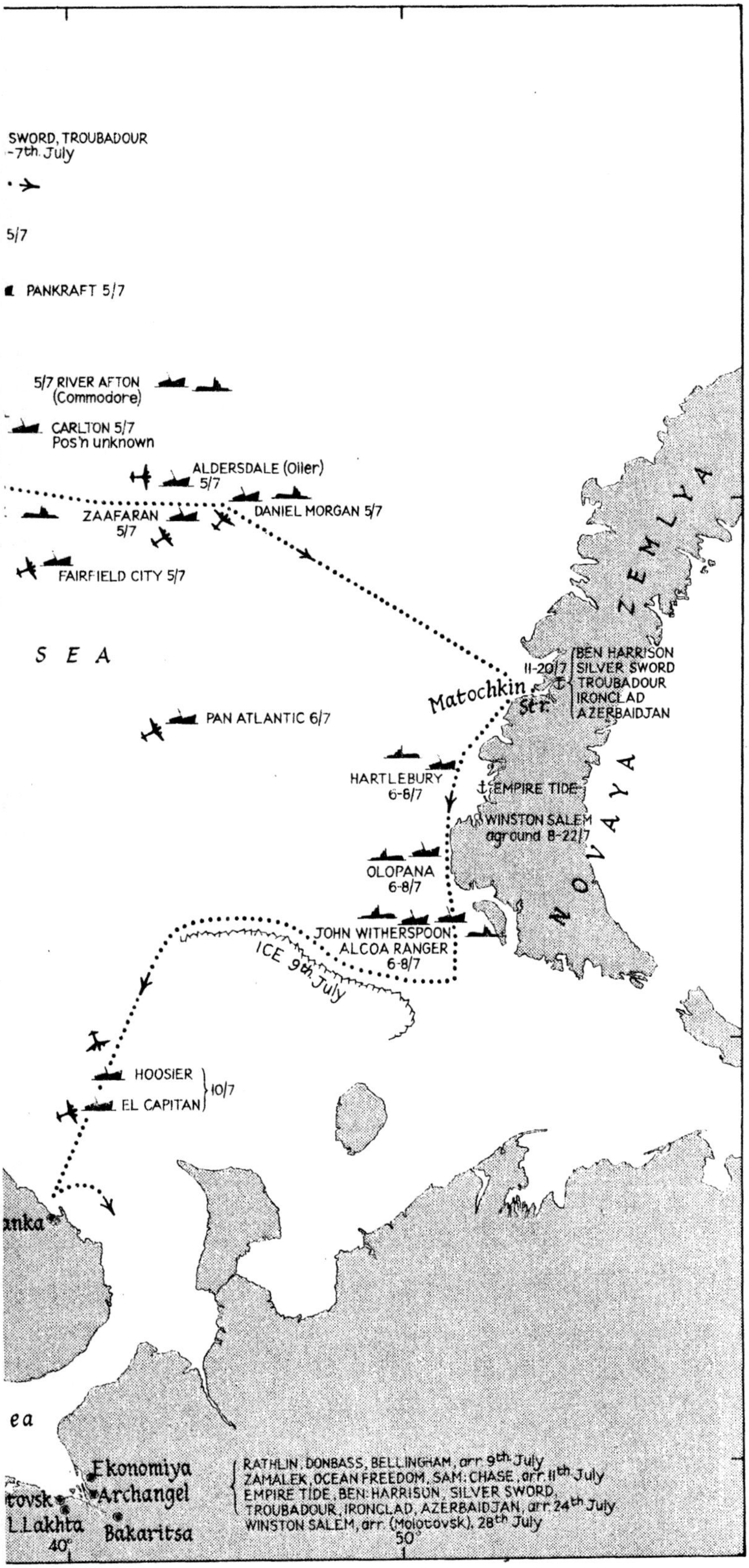

SWORD, TROUBADOUR
-7th July

5/7

PANKRAFT 5/7

5/7 RIVER AFTON
(Commodore)

CARLTON 5/7
Pos'n unknown

ALDERSDALE (Oiler)
5/7

DANIEL MORGAN 5/7

ZAAFARAN
5/7

FAIRFIELD CITY 5/7

S E A

N   O   V   A   Y   A   Z   E   M   L   Y   A

BEN HARRISON
11-20/7   SILVER SWORD
TROUBADOUR
IRONCLAD
AZERBAIDJAN

Matochkin   Str.

PAN ATLANTIC 6/7

HARTLEBURY
6-8/7

EMPIRE TIDE

WINSTON SALEM
aground 8-22/7

OLOPANA
6-8/7

JOHN WITHERSPOON
ALCOA RANGER
6-8/7

ICE 9th July

HOOSIER
}10/7
EL CAPITAN

anka

e a

Ekonomiya
Archangel

tovsk
Lakhta   Bakaritsa
40°   50°

RATHLIN, DONBASS, BELLINGHAM, arr 9th July
ZAMALEK, OCEAN FREEDOM, SAM: CHASE, arr. 11th July
EMPIRE TIDE, BEN: HARRISON, SILVER SWORD,
TROUBADOUR, IRONCLAD, AZERBAIDJAN, arr 24th July
WINSTON SALEM, arr. (Molotovsk), 28th July

The two senior officers both expected the enemy's masts to appear above the horizon at any moment, and for a desperate action to be joined. Commander Broome therefore took his six destroyers to reinforce Admiral Hamilton's cruisers; he left the two submarines of the escort with the convoy to attack the enemy warships, and ordered the rest of the escort (the A.A. ships, minesweepers, corvettes and trawlers) to proceed independently to Archangel.[1] At 10.15 p.m. the order to scatter was passed to the Commodore, and Commander Broome took what he described as the hardest decision of his life— to leave the convoy.

To Commodore Dowding the order to scatter his convoy came as such a surprise that he asked for it to be repeated. 'It must', wrote Broome later, 'have come as a shock to him: he was sharing the wave of confidence which swept through the convoy and escort after the air attack . . . The tails of PQ.17 were well up'. Commander Broome's actions were subsequently fully supported by Admiral Tovey. Fifteen minutes later Admiral Hamilton turned westwards with his four cruisers and the destroyers, passing close to the astonished convoy.

As the hours passed without any drastic developments occurring, Admiral Hamilton and Commander Broome both became increasingly puzzled; but the former had received peremptory orders, and felt bound to continue to carry them out. Moreover, he had no knowledge of the hint given to Admiral Tovey by the First Sea Lord before the convoy sailed, to the effect that the Admiralty might order the convoy to scatter. Broome, on the other hand, 'felt certain that [his destroyers] would be ordered to turn back' to help defend the scattered merchantmen, once the anticipated threat had subsided. The situation was further complicated during the night by thick fog, which persisted until about 6.30 a.m. on the 5th. That afternoon Broome signalled to Admiral Hamilton 'I am always ready to go back', which message he 'intended as a hint as to where I knew my duty lay'; but the cruiser Admiral hoped that he was leading the enemy towards the main British fleet and considered that, since a large-scale surface action might be imminent, 'the most useful service the destroyers could perform would be with the battle fleet'. Not till 6.30 p.m. on the 5th, twenty-one hours after the withdrawal, did a message from Hamilton open the Commander-in-Chief's eyes to the fact that the destroyers of the escort were with the cruisers. He later supported the decision to concentrate the destroyers initially with the cruisers; but he condemned the failure to send Broome's flotilla

---

[1] A note of humour was introduced even at this tense moment. One of the submarines signalled to Broome that he intended to remain on the surface as long as possible. To this the latter replied from the destroyer *Keppel* 'So do I'.

back as soon as it became apparent that the *Tirpitz* was not, in fact, in the offing.

Meanwhile Admiral Tovey had been cruising in the waters north-west of Bear Island. Early on the 5th, he turned towards Scapa. Later that day he received the first firm intelligence of the enemy's movements, from Russian and British submarines and from one of our reconnaissance aircraft. These reports all placed the enemy off North Cape, steering an easterly course, but still some 300 miles from where the convoy had scattered. Actually the enemy's sortie was very brief, for Hitler only gave his permission for the *Tirpitz* to sail during the forenoon of the 5th. She, the *Hipper*, *Scheer*, seven destroyers and two torpedo-boats left Altenfiord between 11 and 11.30 a.m. and steered to the east.[1] When the Allied sighting reports already mentioned were intercepted, and it had become clear that the scattered convoy was suffering heavily at the hands of the U-boats and aircraft, Admiral Raeder cancelled the operation. At 9.30 that evening Admiral Schniewind reversed his course. Though prepara-tions were made to attack him with carrier aircraft, and our sub-marines were redisposed to try to catch the enemy, the *Tirpitz* and her consorts reached Narvik safely. On the 8th the main British forces had also reached harbour.

We must now return to the convoy, whose long-drawn agony began very soon after the cruisers and destroyers had withdrawn. It scattered 'in perfect order', and ships proceeded singly or in small groups, escorted by the A.A. ships *Palomares* and *Pozarica* and screened by the smaller units—so that, in effect the order to scatter was partially, but insufficiently, undone. We cannot here follow the fate of each small group. Their adventures and, all too often, their tragic endings have been told in various eye-witness accounts.[2] Less than half the merchantmen got even as far as Novaya Zemlya.[3] During the next three days seventeen of them, the oiler *Aldersdale* and the rescue ship *Zaafaran* were sunk by U-boats and aircraft. The Commodore's ship, *River Afton*, was among those lost, but happily the gallant and imperturbable Dowding and the ship's Master were both saved, after more than three hours spent on rafts in those icy waters. By the 7th five merchant ships and most of the escorts had reached the Matochkin Strait. They formed themselves into a small convoy and started off on the evening of the 7th to make a hazardous and difficult passage south towards the White Sea. For four hours

---

[1] See Map 13 (opp. p. 137).
[2] See, for example, 'PQ.17' by Godfrey Winn (Hutchinson, 1947), the author of which made the journey in the *Pozarica*.
[3] See Map 14 (opp. p. 141).

during the night of the 9th-10th they were heavily bombed, and two more merchantmen went down. Three ships reached Archangel on the 11th. '*Not* a successful convoy' was the concluding sentence of Commodore Dowding's report—surely one of the classics of understatement. Actually a rescue ship and two merchantmen had already arrived on the 9th, so Dowding's little group was not the first to make port. On the 16th he left Archangel once more, in one of the three corvettes sent to bring in other ships known to be sheltering off Novaya Zemlya. The inhospitable, ice-bound coast was searched; one ship was found aground, another at anchor, and survivors from a third were collected. Then, entering again the Matochkin Strait, he found five more of PQ.17's number at anchor. Three of these—the *Silver Sword* and *Ironclad* (American) and *Troubadour* (Panamanian)—had been collected by the trawler *Ayrshire* (Lieutenant L. J. A. Gradwell, R.N.V.R.) when the convoy scattered, and taken twenty miles into the ice. There they remained for nearly two days, during which they camouflaged themselves by painting their upper works white. They then continued the southward journey and reached the Matochkin Strait safely. The little *Ayrshire's* conduct was, in Admiral Tovey's words 'a splendid example of imagination and initiative'. Her Captain had been a barrister and his First Lieutenant a solicitor before the war; yet they acted as though they had spent a life time acquiring naval outlook and traditions.

As soon as Commodore Dowding arrived off Novaya Zemlya he organised another convoy, and all the ships sailed on the evening of the 20th, with the Commodore leading in a Russian ice-breaker. One more merchantman was collected next day, and they all arrived safely on the 24th. Four days later the American ship *Winston Salem*, which had been aground in Novaya Zemlya, was refloated, and she too made harbour. But that was all. Of the thirty-six merchantmen and three rescue ships which had set out from Iceland, two of the former had returned to the starting point early in the passage; thirteen of the convoy and a rescue ship were sunk by air attack, and ten by U-boats. Only thirteen ships (eleven of the convoy and two rescue ships) survived the ordeal. The figures below give details of the cargo which reached Russia, and the quantity lost:

Table 11. Convoy PQ.17. Cargo Delivered and Lost.

	Delivered	Lost
Vehicles .	896	3,350
Tanks	164	430
Aircraft .	87	210
Other cargo	57,176 tons	99,316 tons

The enemy accomplished his success at trifling cost to himself. Of the 202 attacking aircraft employed[1], only five were lost. The poignancy of the tragedy is only accentuated by our present knowledge of how easily it could have been avoided. Yet the courage, endurance and resource displayed by the merchantmen and by the escorts which went on after the convoy had scattered have never been excelled; and it is they who provide the one redeeming feature in so dark a story. When Admiral Tovey wrote his despatch on the operation he gave it as his opinion that 'the order to scatter the convoy had been premature; its results were disastrous'.

These events had far-reaching repercussions, not least because so many Allied (and especially American) ships were involved. Lurid reports circulated on the other side of the Atlantic, and suggestions were put abroad that the Royal Navy had abandoned its charges at a moment of crisis. It is easy to see how the action of that unhappy afternoon of the 4th of July 1942 could give such an impression to members of the crews of the ill-fated merchantmen. Happily the pertinacity and resource of the A.A. ships and of the little escorts (all British or Free French), who saw things through to the bitter end, give the lie to any such statements. Nor can Admiral Hamilton's withdrawal of the destroyers, now that the full circumstances are known, be regarded as more than an 'error of judgment', as the First Sea Lord described it.

The whole matter was, of course, fully investigated in the Admiralty, and on the 1st of August the First Sea Lord gave to the Cabinet an account of the events which led up to the crucial order being sent. The only new knowledge to be derived from that report is Admiral Pound's statement that on the night of the 3rd–4th July the Admiralty became possessed of intelligence indicating that the *Tirpitz* had eluded our patrolling submarines, and could be in a position to attack the convoy on the morning of the 5th. The existence of such precise intelligence has not been confirmed by post-war research. According to the record of the meeting, Admiral Pound told the Cabinet that the Admiralty had given the orders to disperse, then to scatter the convoy. Mr Churchill's statement that he 'never discussed the matter with him [Admiral Pound]', and that 'so strictly was the secret of these orders being sent on the First Sea Lord's authority guarded by the Admiralty that it was not until after the war that I learned the facts'[2], seems therefore to show a lapse in the Prime Minister's memory.[3]

---

[1] 130 Ju.88s, 43 He.111s and 29 He.115s.
[2] Churchill, Vol. IV, p. 236.
[3] The Prime Minister left London for Cairo and Moscow on the day after this Cabinet meeting (see Churchill, Vol. IV, p. 411), and was away from London for more than three weeks.

H.M.S. *Sheffield* in an Arctic storm. Waves 70 feet high, wind force 12 on Beaufort Scale (Hurricane).

The German battleship *Tirpitz* in north Norway, 1942. In the upper photograph she is concealed in Faettenfiord (near Trondheim), in the lower one she is in an anchorage off Vestfiord.

(Photos.: Captain H. J. Reinick

As we look back on this unhappy episode today, it is plain that the enemy was never likely to risk the *Tirpitz* in close attack on a convoy protected by an escort which was heavily armed with torpedoes. That, as was pointed out earlier, had always been Admiral Tovey's opinion; but the Admiralty had never accepted it. The latter could not, of course, know of the restrictions imposed by Hitler and Raeder on the employment of the battleship. Yet all experience of German warship raiders so far gained had shown how reluctant they were to engage a convoy closely, except when it had scattered or was completely unescorted. The *Scheer's* attack on HX.84[1], the *Hipper's* on WS.5A and SLS.64[2], the wariness of the *Scharnhorst* and *Gneisenau* when they approached, but did not attack, the escorted convoys HX.106 and SL.67[3], all indicated the same unwillingness to accept action except where an escort was very weak, or totally lacking. Furthermore the earlier experiences of German heavy ships had been such as might well make them chary of approaching our destroyers' smoke screens.[4] It may therefore be felt that evidence derived from recent experience was available in London to suggest that, if faced with a similar problem, the *Tirpitz's* actions would probably follow on the same lines as the other raiders. If that be accepted, then the real nature of her threat could have been re-assessed, and it might well have been realised that to scatter was to court far greater perils than to stand on and show fight.

In conclusion the tendency of the Admiralty during Admiral Pound's time as First Sea Lord to intervene excessively in the conduct of fleet operations has been commented on in several other contexts; and it will be remembered that, in spite of the First Sea Lord having expressed quite different intentions early in the war, the practice continued.[5] It was suggested that the First Lord himself bore a share of the responsibility for interventions made in the Norwegian campaign[6]; but the habit persisted, though in varying degrees, long after Mr Churchill had left the Admiralty. There can be no doubt that Admiral Pound himself became markedly prone to make such interventions, often on quite trivial matters, such as telling individual ships to steer a particular course or to steam at a particular speed. Nor did attempts to discourage such practices, made by senior members of the Naval Staff who fully realised the dangers,

---

[1] See Vol. I, pp. 288–289.

[2] See Vol. I, pp. 291–292 and 372.

[3] See Vol. I, pp. 374 and 375–376.

[4] When the *Glowworm* damaged the *Hipper* by ramming and when the *Acasta* torpedoed the *Scharnhorst* (see Vol. I, pp. 158 and 195–196 respectively) the British destroyers attacked in broad daylight through smoke. It can easily be understood how such incidents could have affected German tactics in later engagements.

[5] See Vol. I, p. 27.

[6] See Vol. I, p. 202.

L

meet with any success. When the Russian convoys became such difficult and dangerous operations, signalled interventions from London became very common indeed; and it has been mentioned that Admiral Tovey protested strongly on that score. That, sooner or later a serious misunderstanding would arise seemed all too likely to the Commander-in-Chief and the Flag Officers concerned; and the inevitable nemesis came with the attempt to exercise direct operational control over widely-spread forces, some of which were 1,500 miles or more from London, and working in conditions of which those ashore could not possibly be constantly aware.

The homeward convoy QP.13, of thirty-five ships, had an uneventful passage until one section of it ran into trouble off the northwest corner of Iceland. A large iceberg which suddenly loomed up through thick fog was mistaken for the North Cape of Iceland, and the error caused the Senior Officer of the escort to lead the merchantmen into our own minefield. The Senior Officer's ship—the minesweeper *Niger*—and four merchantmen were sunk, and two more of the convoy were seriously damaged. Coming so soon after the disaster to PQ.17 this was a doubly cruel misfortune.

CHAPTER VI

COASTAL WARFARE

1st January–31st July, 1942

> 'Brest is so placed as though God had made it expressly for the purpose of destroying the commerce of these two Nations' [i.e. Holland and England].
>
> Vauban. *Memorandum regarding war expenditure on which the King might effect economies.* August 1693.

THE concentration of his U-boats in the Western Atlantic did not cause the enemy to neglect our coastal convoy routes, and the New Year saw renewed activity by E-boats and aircraft in laying mines off the east coast. Magnetic and acoustic mines, as well as those worked by a combination of the two influences, were all used; and the new designs enabled them to be laid in deeper water, which meant that many more miles of channel had to be swept. In January we lost eleven small ships (10,079 tons in all) on mines, mostly laid off the east coast, and the destroyer *Vimiera* also fell victim to one when escorting a south-bound convoy. In February our losses dropped to two ships, but E-boats and aircraft constantly appeared on the convoy routes and the vigilance of the escorts could never be relaxed.

Our defences had, however, improved out of all knowledge since the tribulations of the early months of the war.[1] Not only were the escorts better equipped and more experienced, but co-ordination with shore-based aircraft now worked smoothly; and great benefit was beginning to be derived here, as elsewhere, from the radar sets being fitted in escort vessels, and from the unceasing vigil of the shore radar stations. The Thames estuary, with its vital but vulnerable channels into the Port of London, was now comparatively well defended. No less than four commands—the Commander-in-Chief, The Nore (Naval), Fighter Command (R.A.F.), Anti-Aircraft Command (Army) and Balloon Command (R.A.F.)—were concerned in discharging this important responsibility. The plan towards which they all worked was to make minelaying too difficult and expensive for it to continue to be profitable to the enemy. Early in

---

[1] See Vol. I, Chapter VI.

1941 work had been started on constructing forts which could be sunk in the approaches to the Thames, and would be provided with heavy anti-aircraft armaments. The first of them was placed in position in February 1942, and by August there were two in the Thames and two more off Harwich, all manned by naval crews. In addition to these, three more similar forts were manned by the Army.[1] All of them were linked to the Area Combined Headquarters at Chatham and to the naval plot at Harwich. They proved a valuable addition to the defences. Another important contribution to the defence of the Thames estuary was that, by the end of February, no less than twelve of the specially converted anti-aircraft ships known as 'Eagle Ships' were available. They were mostly paddle steamers, built to make excursions in these same waters, and the early ones like the *Royal Eagle* and *Crested Eagle* gave their name to the whole class. Their manoeuvrability, and the good gun platforms obtained from their wide beam, made them very suitable for this class of work. They made many 'excursions' during the war in the waters where, in peacetime, they had carried thousands of trippers between London, Southend, Margate and Ramsgate. Apart from the fixed batteries in the forts and the floating batteries in the 'Eagle Ships', A.A. Command's shore guns were re-disposed, and in some zones they were now allowed to fire by radar at unseen targets, which had been forbidden up to the present because of the danger to our own aircraft; the fighters of Nos. 11 and 12 Groups, controlled by our low-searching coastal radar stations, were sent to intercept enemy minelayers far out at sea; and Bomber Command's No. 2 Group made 'intruder' raids to disturb the peace at the enemy bases. Thus, by a typically British combination of improvisation and adaptation, and by the co-operation of a large number of arms belonging to many commands of all three services, were the enemy's attempts to interfere with the traffic in and out of the Port of London increasingly frustrated.

It will be remembered that the diversion of the main strength of the Luftwaffe to the Russian front in 1941 substantially reduced the air threat to our coastal shipping.[2] None the less, sporadic and widely separated attacks in the Channel and off the east coast still occurred, generally with fast, low-flying fighter-bombers such as the Me.109 and F.W.190. The enemy at this time reduced his day

---

[1] These were called 'Maunsell Forts' after their designer, Mr Guy Maunsell. Their armaments consisted of two to four heavy and many light anti-aircraft guns, searchlights and radar. The four manned by the Navy were: 'Tongue Sand Tower' and 'Knock John Tower' in the Thames approaches, 'Roughs Fort' and 'Sunk Head Fort' off Harwich. The Army's three forts were: 'Great Nore Tower', 'Red Sand Tower' and 'Shivering Sand Tower', in the Thames approaches. The first-named replaced the Nore Light Vessel, which had been withdrawn after the enemy had made many air attacks on such defenceless targets. (See Vol. I, p. 138).

[2] See Vol. I, pp. 463 and 507–508.

attacks in favour of dusk or night raids, and we were still finding these difficult to deal with. Radar sets capable of detecting fast low-flying aircraft were lacking, and new methods of air interception also had to be devised.

It was told earlier how Fighter Command came to shoulder a large share of the burden of defending our coastal shipping.[1] To prevent a wasteful amount of its strength being employed on standing patrols, a system was devised to enable the groups concerned to make their effort proportional to the value and importance of what they were protecting. The ships were divided into five categories, ranging from units of exceptional or irreplaceable value in the first category, through important groups such as the main fleet or troop convoys, down to vessels of minor importance. The protective measures were also divided into grades. 'Fighter escort' was given to the irreplaceable ships; 'sweeps or patrols' were made over the routes taken by important vessels; and distant 'protection' or 'cover', which meant only that aircraft were available if attacks developed, was given to the least valuable ships. The escort vessels communicated with the fighters by radio-telephony, and thus in some measure controlled their movements. This system, which was disliked by Fighter Command, was replaced by control from the shore head-quarters when the coastal radar stations became capable of detecting the low-flying raids already mentioned. Although his 'tip and run' attacks sometimes got through our defences, we now had the measure of his daylight bombing of our coastal shipping, and losses were few. The fighters normally withdrew at dusk, and the ships then had to rely only on their guns. Although this was not entirely satisfactory, the development of night fighter control had not yet reached a point where protection could be given to the convoys during dark hours or low visibility. None the less the general picture regarding air defence of our coastal shipping during the first six months of 1942 is a favourable one. The extent of the enemy's effort throughout this phase, both in direct attacks and in air minelaying, and the shipping losses suffered by both sides will be analysed later.

Before the month of February was many days old all the southern commands became involved in a more exciting event than the daily toil to keep the swept channels open, for it was then that the *Scharnhorst* and *Gneisenau* escaped up-Channel from Brest. It is to that event that we must therefore turn.

The German decision to bring the Brest squadron back to their home waters was part of the plan made at Hitler's instigation to defeat the imagined British intention to invade Norway.[2] Before the end of 1941 Hitler had decided, against Raeder's advice, that the

---

[1] See Vol. I, pp. 138–139 and 322–333.
[2] See Vol. I, p. 514, and this volume pp. 100–101.

Brest squadron should return to Germany, and that this could best be accomplished by 'a surprise break through the Channel'. Should the German Naval Staff declare this to be impossible Hitler would favour paying the ships off, a bitter pill for the creator of the German fleet.

On the 12th of January 1942 Hitler reiterated his views regarding the importance of defending Norway and the movement of the Brest ships. He compared the latter to 'a patient with cancer who is doomed unless he submits to an operation'. The passage up-Channel 'would' he considered, 'constitute such an operation and had therefore to be attempted'. Raeder now agreed to the Führer's proposal, and the plans were sketched in outline at the conference. Since surprise was essential Hitler ordered that the squadron must not leave Brest until after dark; he accepted that this would mean passing through the Dover Straits in daylight. The transfer of the battleship *Tirpitz* to Trondheim, described in the last chapter, was decided by Hitler at the same conference.

The detailed plans for the movement of the two battle cruisers and the *Prinz Eugen* were worked out by Vice-Admiral Ciliax, whose flag was flown in the *Scharnhorst*. Great care was taken over choosing the best possible route, to enable the ships to steam at high speed and yet avoid our minefields. Channels were swept and mark buoys placed to show the way. That the Admiralty was alive to the significance of the enemy's minesweeping activities is shown by the fact that they asked Bomber Command to mine the five areas considered likely to prove 'the most fruitful'. Between the 3rd and the 9th of February ninety-eight magnetic mines were laid in the enemy's swept channels.

To gain as long a period of darkness as possible the enemy timed his movement to take place four days before the new moon, and the squadron was ordered to start from Brest at 7.30 p.m. A spring tide would then be flooding up-Channel to speed the ships' progress and, as it rose, it would reduce the danger from our mines. Fighter protection was very carefully worked out. There were to be sixteen aircraft constantly over the ships during daylight, and cover was to be at its strongest during the mid-day passage of the Dover Straits. Six destroyers were to escort the big ships for the first part of the eastward dash, ten torpedo-boats would join next morning and more torpedo-boats, E-boats, R-boats and small escort craft would meet the squadron off Cape Gris Nez. By the 9th of February all three ships had completed trials inside Brest roads, and the decision was taken to carry out the plan on the 11th.

The preliminary movements of the German ships were not shrouded from the eyes of Coastal Command's watchful aircraft. Enemy activity, including the westward movement of destroyers and his minesweeping in the Channel, made it appear almost certain that a big operation in which all three heavy ships would be involved was imminent. On the 2nd of February the Admiralty distributed an 'appreciation' in which the various alternatives open to the enemy were weighed and considered. The Admiralty concluded, firstly, that an Atlantic sortie was improbable, because after their long spell in harbour the enemy ships could not be fully efficient; secondly that the enemy must wish to get the ships into quieter waters where they could work up efficiency, and thirdly that the most probable route to such waters was up the English Channel. Although, said the Admiralty, 'at first sight this passage appears hazardous' they considered that it was, from the enemy's point of view, greatly to be preferred to the long journey by the northern passages to the North Sea, or to an attempt to force the Straits of Gibraltar and reach an Italian harbour. With remarkable prescience the Admiralty concluded that 'we might well find the two battle cruisers and the eight-inch cruiser with five large and five small destroyers and . . . twenty fighters constantly overhead . . . proceeding up-Channel.'

On the 3rd the Admiralty's appreciation was read to the naval officers attached to the three R.A.F. commands, and they were told to pass it to the Air Officers Commanding-in-Chief. All naval authorities at home were informed by signal, the Nore Command was told to keep six destroyers with torpedo armaments at short notice in the Thames, and to be prepared to reinforce the few motor torpedo-boats already at Dover with six more. The fast minelayer *Manxman* was allocated to the Plymouth command to work in the approaches to Brest and the western end of the Channel, while her sister-ship the *Welshman* was placed under Admiral Ramsay at Dover. Owing to recent heavy calls for submarines for the Mediterranean station, very few were at this time left in home waters. Two old boats normally employed for training purposes were sent on Biscay patrols and, on the 6th, the *Sealion*, the only modern submarine available, was given discretion to penetrate inside Brest roads, to try and catch the German ships in the enclosed waters where they had been seen to carry out their trials and exercises. Lastly, all the six serviceable Swordfish torpedo-bombers of No. 825 Fleet Air Arm Squadron were, at Admiral Ramsay's suggestion, moved from Lee-on-Solent to Manston in Kent[1], to augment the striking power available in the Straits. The Admiralty also asked Admiral Somerville of Force H how he proposed to act if the battle cruisers attempted another Atlantic foray or tried to pass Gibraltar to the east, and told the British mission in Washington that we must know American plans and dispositions well in advance if strategic co-ordination was to be effective in the event. Though the Admiralty

---

[1] See Map 15 (opp. p. 153).

considered the break up-Channel the most probable action they were taking no chances over the safety of our Atlantic shipping.

Having received the Admiralty's broad appreciation of the enemy's probable intention Admiral Ramsay, who was plainly the naval commander most concerned in frustrating the enemy's intention, considered the matter in greater detail. His conclusion was that the Germans would adjust their departure from Brest, and their subsequent movements, so as to arrive in the Straits of Dover at or before daylight. He also expected them to choose a day when high water occurred near the expected time of their passage through the Straits, in order to reduce the danger from mines. It has already been mentioned that Admiral Ciliax was actually planning to pass Dover in daylight.

The reader may, with reason, feel that the British naval forces thus made ready in the south to stop three powerful warships were extremely slender. The Assistant Chief of Naval Staff responsible for home operations later told the Board of Enquiry set up by the Prime Minister to investigate the escape of the enemy ships that no more could possibly have been produced. The Home Fleet was at an extremely low ebb. Admiral Tovey had at Scapa only the *King George V, Renown* and *Rodney* (which was long overdue for refit), the aircraft carrier *Victorious*, four cruisers and thirteen destroyers. The *Tirpitz* was at Trondheim and might at any time attempt to break out into the Atlantic or attack our Russian convoys, and, moreover, a great troop convoy, WS.16 of twenty-six large ships with between forty and fifty thousand soldiers and much equipment on board, was about to sail from the Clyde. It was bound to pass not very far off Brest. The *Rodney* had actually been detached from the Home Fleet to escort this convoy on the first part of its long journey, and the greater part of Force H had been brought home from Gibraltar for the same purpose. Lastly the light forces at Scapa were already inadequate to enable the Home Fleet to perform its principal function, and none could therefore be spared to reinforce the southern commands. But it was realised that a few destroyers, motor torpedo-boats and torpedo-bombers were unlikely to do more than inflict some under-water damage, which might put the enemy ships into dock for a time. Experience had taught that Bomber Command was very unlikely to hit such difficult and fleeting targets, while Coastal Command's striking power was little greater than that of the naval aircraft available.

A plan to deal with a break up-Channel had long since been prepared by the Admiralty and Air Ministry. On the 3rd of February it was brought into force. The naval part of this plan has already been outlined. Simultaneously with the naval dispositions Coastal Command established the pre-arranged reconnaissance patrols, of which

North Coates
407 Sqdn
(6 Hudsons)

Bircham
Newton
500 Sqdn
(5 Hudsons)
Coltishall
Haisbo
Gt.
42 Sqdn
(14 T/Bs) arrived
12/2
Lo

Felixstowe
Harwich
16th & 21st
Destyr. Flotil
(6 Destroyer
825 Sqdn (FAA)
(6 T/Bs)

LONDON
Sheerness
Chatham Ramsgate
5 MTBs 3 MTBs Dover
2 MGBs Folkestone
Manston
Sword
ott
MTB
attack

Brady Head
Newhaven
Shoreham
Thorney Is.
Portsmouth Is.
Yarmouth
Portland
Is of Wight
217 Sqdn
(7 T/Bs)

Straits of Dover

Identified
by Spitfire
10·42am

86/217 Sqdn
(12 T/Bs)
St Eval
Plymouth
Dartmouth

Lyme Bay

The English Channel

6·30am

4·25am

Dieppe
Fécamp
Le Havre
Le T
R. Seine

Alderney
Cherbourg
Guernsey
Jersey
Côte la Hague

11th
8·55pm radar failed
9·56pm returned to base
8·15pm 11th

Brehat Is

7·56pm 11th
8·51pm
0·28am

Ushant
Brest

Midnt
11/12th
11·56 pm 11th

1434 SEALION

Lorient

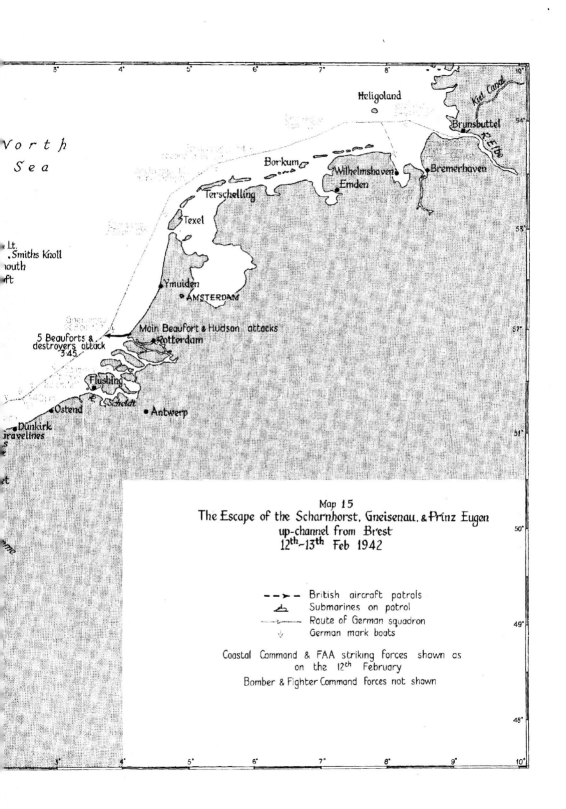

Map 15
The Escape of the Scharnhorst, Gneisenau, & Prinz Eugen
up-channel from Brest
12th-13th Feb 1942

North Sea

Heligoland

Kiel Canal

Brunsbuttel

R. Elbe

Borkum
Wilhelmshaven
Emden
Bremerhaven

Terschelling

Texel

Lt. Smiths Knoll
outh
ft

Ymuiden
AMSTERDAM

Main Beaufort & Hudson attacks
Rotterdam

5 Beauforts &
destroyers attack
3·45

Flushing

R. Schelde

Ostend
Antwerp

Dunkirk
travelines

--▸-- British aircraft patrols
⊿ Submarines on patrol
——∽—— Route of German squadron
↓ German mark boats

Coastal Command & FAA striking forces shown as
on the 12th February
Bomber & Fighter Command forces not shown

more will be said shortly, and prepared its striking forces. One torpedo-bomber squadron (No. 42) of fourteen Beauforts was at Leuchars in Scotland, ready to strike at the *Tirpitz*. It was ordered south to Norfolk on the 11th, but because there was deep snow on the East Anglian airfields, it did not move until next day. Twelve more Beauforts of Nos. 86 and 217 Squadrons were at St. Eval in Cornwall, and seven were at Thorney Island near Portsmouth. About a dozen Hudsons were at airfields on the east coast.[1] Bomber Command possessed about 240 aircraft suitable for day bombing at various airfields all over the country, but none was properly trained to identify and attack warships at sea; and Fighter Command had some 550 aircraft, mostly Spitfires, in the south. On paper the air forces available were therefore considerable. The weakness lay in the small proportion of torpedo-bombers, and in the lack of training of the heavy bombers for the work which might be needed. It was perhaps now that the consequences of the long delay in providing Coastal Command with a properly trained and well-equipped torpedo striking force were most seriously felt[2]; and that the pre-war preference of the Air Staff for the bomb, as opposed to the torpedo, as the main weapon for use against ships was shown to have been mistaken.[3] In passing it is interesting to remark how the enemy realised, though too late, that he had committed a similar error. In July 1943, at a conference with his naval leaders, Hitler commented bitterly on how certain 'cleverly executed demonstrations' carried out by the Navy and Air Force in 1938—'probably the only time they were ever in full agreement'—had made him abandon his intention to build up a strong torpedo striking force. By mid-1943 it was obvious to him that the conclusions 'proven so expertly by those wretched demonstrations' had been wholly erroneous.

As soon as the precautionary orders were issued on the 3rd, Coastal Command started to carry out its planned night air patrols. These comprised three patrol lines. The first was flown off the entrance to Brest, the second from Ushant to the Isle de Bréhat, and the third between Havre and Boulogne.[4] All were flown by Hudsons fitted with a radar set theoretically capable of detecting a large ship at thirty miles' range. We shall see shortly how these patrols fared on the night of the 11th-12th of February. In addition to these Hudson patrols, it was already the practice for fighters of No. 11 Group to reconnoitre the Channel between Ostend and the mouth of the Somme for enemy shipping soon after dawn each day. So much for the naval and air preparations.

---

[1] See Map 15.
[2] See Vol. I, pp. 38, 145 and 338.
[3] See Vol. I, p. 509.
[4] See Map 15.

Admiral Ciliax had intended to sail from Brest at 7.30 p.m. on the 11th, but a British air raid caused a postponement until 10.45 p.m. The night was very dark with a light south-westerly wind and scattered clouds. Just after midnight the three ships, steaming at twenty-seven knots, rounded Ushant and shaped course up-Channel. They passed the island of Alderney at 5.30 a.m. on the 12th, and then altered to a more easterly course.[1] At dawn the first sixteen German fighters appeared overhead.[2] The Hudson aircraft detailed for the British night patrol off Brest on the 11th had returned to its base, because of a radar failure, at about 7.30 p.m. The same crew exchanged into another aircraft and took off again two hours later. They remained on patrol until shortly before midnight, and were then relieved by another Hudson. Post-war analysis reveals that only for a few minutes early on the 12th was the enemy within radar range from this aircraft, and no contact was obtained. A worse misadventure made the second patrol, between Ushant and the Isle de Bréhat, totally ineffective. That Hudson's radar also failed, and at 9.50 p.m. it returned to base. No relief aircraft was sent out, nor was the failure of the patrol reported to Admiral Ramsay. The third patrol, between Havre and Boulogne, functioned normally, but sighted nothing. The enemy squadron never actually passed within its range. It thus happened that the morning of the 12th of February was well advanced, and the enemy squadron had reached the mouth of the Somme at about 10.30 a.m., before any firm intelligence that it had sailed from Brest was received in England. At about 9.20 the enemy started to jam our shore radar stations' reception; but, as this had been happening intermittently for some weeks, no particular significance was attached to it until an hour later, when the interference became continuous. Plots of enemy aircraft to the north of Havre appeared on our radar screens between 8.25 and 10.0 a.m.; but these were a common occurrence and, again, their significance was not realised.

The arrangement for a fighter sweep to be made down-Channel by No. 11 Group soon after dawn each morning has been mentioned. The two Spitfires which made the sweep on the morning of the 12th reported, on landing at their base, a good deal of small craft activity between Ostend and Boulogne. A 'strike' against them was ordered by No. 11 Group at about 10.0 a.m. Meanwhile the radar plots of enemy aircraft caused No. 11 Group to send out a further recon-naissance at 10.20 to search from Boulogne to Fécamp. One Spitfire of this patrol sighted what was thought to be a convoy and its escort

---

[1] See Map 15 (opp. p. 153).

[2] An interesting account, from the German point of view, of the fighter protection afforded to the Brest squadron is to be found in *The First and the Last* by Adolf Galland (Methuen, 1955), pp. 140–167.

(some twenty to thirty vessels) off Le Touquet. Only when the crew was interrogated on return to base was it revealed that an enemy capital ship had been among the vessels sighted. Almost at the same time two other Spitfires, which were not actually looking for enemy shipping but were engaged with German fighters, flew right over the *Scharnhorst* and *Gneisenau*. The time was 10.42 a.m. Because the Spitfires were flying nearly at sea level, and in such conditions a wireless message could not have got through, no report was made until after they had landed at 11.09. Thus it was getting on towards 11.30 a.m. before all the carefully planned machinery to make co-ordinated attacks on these very ships was set in motion on the strength of the reports issued from Fighter Command Headquarters.

But the earlier signs that something abnormal might be afoot in the Channel had not gone unheeded at Dover. Lieutenant-Commander E. Esmonde, commanding No. 825 Squadron at Manston, had been warned, and had brought his six Swordfish to immediate readiness. The need for Coastal Command's Beauforts to attack at the same time was realised, and was discussed between Dover and No. 16 Group; but the slow speed of the Swordfish made such tactics difficult to carry out. Moreover, it was by this time plainly essential to attack as soon as possible with whatever forces were ready. Accordingly it was decided that No. 825 Squadron would attack at about 12.45 p.m. No. 11 Fighter Group had already been asked to cover and escort the slow and vulnerable Swordfish with five squadrons of fighters. They were to meet the torpedo-bombers over Manston at 12.25, which gave very little time for the fighter pilots to be briefed and for the movement of aircraft from other stations. Esmonde was warned that some or all of the fighters would be late. He decided that he could not delay his departure. At 12.28 the first fighter squadron appeared, and Esmonde set course for the targets. Two more fighter squadrons having missed the rendezvous at Manston, made straight for the enemy and were engaged with his fighters during the Swordfish attack. The last two fighter squadrons of Esmonde's intended escort searched for the enemy off Calais, but failed to find him.

The six Swordfish, escorted by ten Spitfires, accordingly flew to a position some ten miles north of Calais, which the German squadron was believed to have reached. Enemy fighters soon got among the Swordfish. Esmonde himself led the first flight and was last seen pressing in over the German destroyer screen towards the battle cruisers, through a hailstorm of fire. He was shot down before he had completed his attack, and all that gallant crew were lost. The next two aircraft got in close enough to release their torpedoes, but were then shot down; five survivors were picked up later. The other three Swordfish were last seen closing in towards the enemy. No survivors were ever found. There can, in the history of forlorn hopes, be few more moving stories than that of the last flight of No. 825 Fleet Air Arm Squadron. Its leader—the same officer who had led the Swordfish from the *Victorious* to attack the *Bismarck* in May 1941[1]—typified all that was finest in the newest branch of the naval service; and the junior members of his squadron followed him faithfully to the end. He was awarded a posthumous Victoria Cross. Unhappily the sacrifice was made in vain, since none of their torpedoes found the targets.

The five serviceable motor torpedo-boats at Dover cleared harbour at 11.55 a.m., and sighted the enemy about thirty minutes later. One boat broke down and, lacking fighter or motor gun-boat escort, the leader decided that it was quite impossible for him to penetrate the powerful enemy screen with the remaining four. Torpedoes were therefore fired at long-range from outside the screen. No hits resulted. Three more M.T.Bs, the Ramsgate flotilla, left harbour at 12.25. They sighted the screening vessels but never found the heavy ships. Worsening weather and engine trouble caused them to return without having attacked.

Of Coastal Command's striking forces the Beauforts of No. 217 Squadron at Thorney Island were closest to the enemy when he was first definitely reported. Only four of the squadron's seven aircraft were immediately available. They left for Manston, to pick up a fighter escort, at 1.40 p.m., but became split up in the process. Attacks were made in ones and twos in bad visibility between about 3.40 and 6.00 p.m. Of the last three Beauforts from Thorney Island one was shot down, but the other two got in attacks. Neither did the enemy any damage. The next effort was made by No. 42 Squadron, from Leuchars in Fife, which had only been ordered south that morning. Nine of its fourteen Beauforts left Leuchars armed with torpedoes, while the other five were ordered to pick them up on an airfield in Norfolk. Unfortunately the thick snow on the Coastal Command stations in East Anglia forced them to land at a fighter station, where there were no torpedoes. Efforts were made to bring the weapons by road to the waiting aircraft, but they arrived too late. The result was that only nine Beauforts left for Manston in Kent, armed with torpedoes, early in the afternoon. At about 3.30 they set course for the target accompanied by five Hudsons. Seven of the Beauforts got in attacks, and some of the Hudsons managed to bomb the enemy in the worsening visibility. Again no damage was done. Lastly the twelve serviceable Beauforts from St. Eval in Cornwall arrived at Thorney Island at 2.30 p.m. and were ordered to Coltishall in Norfolk to pick up a fighter escort. None was, however, found

---

[1] See Vol. I, p. 408.

there, and the squadron commander therefore left at 5.40 to attack without escort. Dusk was already falling by the time they reached the waters where the enemy was now believed to be. No attacks were made, and two of the Beauforts were lost.

The destroyers at Harwich, which had been placed under Admiral Ramsay's orders, comprised two ships of the 21st Flotilla—the *Campbell* and *Vivacious*—and the *Mackay, Whitshed, Walpole* and *Worcester* of the 16th Flotilla. All were of 1914-18 war design and more than twenty years old. Their normal duty was to escort and cover the east coast convoys. Captain C. T. M. Pizey of the 21st Flotilla, in the *Campbell*, was the senior officer present; and the 16th Flotilla was commanded by Captain J. P. Wright in the *Mackay*. The six ships were, by good chance, exercising off Harwich when, at 11.56 a.m., a message was received from Admiral Ramsay to attack in accordance with the orders already issued. At 1 p.m. Dover told Captain Pizey that the enemy's speed was much greater than had been expected. The only chance of catching him lay in crossing the undefined German minefields, and making for a position off the mouth of the River Scheldt. This risk was at once accepted by Pizey. At 3.17 his radar picked up two large ships some nine miles off, and at 3.43 the *Scharnhorst* and *Gneisenau* were sighted at 4 miles range. The *Walpole* had already had to return home with her main bearings run, so only five destroyers remained with the flotilla commander. The worsening visibility had so far shielded them from the greatly superior enemy, but they now came under heavy gun fire. Captain Pizey drove his ships on until, at 3,500 yards he felt that his luck could not last much longer. The *Campbell* and *Vivacious* fired their torpedo salvoes at about 3,000 yards; the *Worcester* pressed in even closer and was severely damaged in doing so. The *Mackay* and *Whitshed*, which were following astern of the others, got in their attacks a little later. The four undamaged ships then went to the help of the *Worcester;* but she managed finally to get back to harbour under her own steam. It had been a fine effort, and deserved better success than it achieved. Though hits were believed to have been obtained, the enemy actually avoided all the torpedoes. However, at 2.31 p.m., while the destroyers were closing to the attack, the enemy received his first check. The *Scharnhorst* struck a mine and came to a stop; but the damage was not serious and she was soon able to go ahead again at about 25 knots.

The main attacks by Bomber Command also developed during the early afternoon, and it is to them that we must now turn. The prevailing low cloud and poor visibility made high-level bombing with armour-piercing bombs impossible, and this eliminated the only means whereby the heavy bombers might damage the German warships seriously. General-purpose bombs could not penetrate the armoured decks, but might do some damage by blast. Most of the bombers which were available when, at 11.27 a.m. all groups were warned to be ready to attack, were armed with general-purpose bombs. The Commander-in-Chief organised his forces to attack in three successive waves, and hoped that this would distract attention from the torpedo attacks by the Navy and Coastal Command. Of the 242 bombers which set out during the afternoon thirty-nine are believed to have attacked some enemy warship; fifteen were lost and the rest were prevented from attacking by low cloud and bad visibility. No damage was done to the enemy, and a heavy price was exacted from the bombers. While all these brave, but ineffective, air and surface actions were in progress Fighter Command was doing its best to protect our torpedo-bombers, the light coastal craft and the heavy bombers, and also to attack the enemy's escort vessels. But the confused nature of the battle made the fighters' work extremely difficult. Many actions took place with enemy fighters, but few were decisive. Of the 398 aircraft sent out seventeen were lost.

As night fell the enemy entered on the last lap of his race for home, and Admiral Ciliax must have felt well satisfied with the result of the air and surface actions fought while he was steaming to the east. But he was not yet clear of the mines which had been laid by the R.A.F. As already mentioned, the *Scharnhorst* had hit one early in the afternoon when to the north of the Scheldt estuary. She had in consequence become separated from her consorts. At 7.55 p.m. the *Gneisenau* was mined off Terschelling, but after a short delay she was able to steam at 25 knots. At 9.34 p.m. in nearly the same position, the *Scharnhorst* hit a second mine, and this time she was seriously hurt. Both main engines stopped, her steering was put out of action and her fire control failed temporarily. Not until 10.23 was she able to go ahead at slow speed. She had shipped 1,000 tons of water and her port engines were useless. She limped into Wilhelmshaven in the early hours of the 13th. The other two ships reached the mouth of the Elbe at 7 a.m. that day.

Apart from the magnetic mines laid in the previous fortnight, Bomber Command had tried to drop others ahead of the enemy ships on the 12th. But the weather made it next to impossible to place mines accurately, and only thirteen more were actually laid. It is not known which lays caused the damage to the enemy; nor was the fact that any damage had been received known in London until much later. The belief that the enemy squadron had passed unscathed through what were almost our home waters, under the very noses of the Royal Navy and Air Force, caused a wave of indignation to pass over the country. Vehement criticisms were made in Parliament and the press. Even *The Times* abandoned its customary restraint and wrote that 'Vice-Admiral Ciliax has succeeded where the Duke of Medina Sidonia failed . . . Nothing more mortifying to the pride of sea-power has happened in home waters since the 17th Century'.[1] The German Naval Staff, however, with a more just realisation of the fundamental issues involved, summarised the outcome as 'a tactical victory, but a strategic defeat', and to-day that judgement must surely be admitted to be the correct one. The gain for Britain lay in the elimination of the long-standing threat to our Atlantic convoys from Brest, and in the fact that the enemy had abandoned his offensive purpose and had concentrated his ships for defence against an expected invasion of Norway.[2]

It remains to discuss the undoubted tactical success achieved by the enemy. The Admiralty's analysis of his intention was proved correct on all important issues. Admiral Ramsay, it is true, had been wrong in his prophesy of the time at which the enemy squadron would sail, and when it would pass through the Straits. But this misjudgement was not important enough by itself to give the enemy his success. It is, however, possible that it contributed to excessive confidence in the measures taken to detect the moment of the actual departure of the enemy squadron. The main cause of the failure to do more damage to the German ships was that they were at sea for twelve hours, four of them in daylight, before they were discovered. And it was undoubtedly the failure of our air patrols, already recounted, which brought that about.

The Prime Minister appointed a Board of Enquiry under Mr Justice Bucknill to investigate the whole circumstances of the escape of the enemy squadron. In their report the Board criticised Coastal Command for the fact that, although it was known that neither the first air patrol off Brest nor the patrol between Ushant and the Isle de Bréhat had functioned correctly on the night of the 11th-12th, no dawn reconnaissance was made down-Channel next morning. Stronger inferences might, they considered, also have been drawn from the enemy's jamming of our radar stations during the forenoon of the 12th. With regard to the heavy bombers' attacks the Board remarked that 'the evidence . . . indicated that the training of the greater part of Bomber Command is not designed for effective attack on fast-moving warships by day'. The reasons, they continued, were clear; rapid expansion of the force, the despatch of much of its strength overseas and the replacement of the heavy casualties suffered had 'enforced concentration of their training on their major rôle of night bombing'. 'Whether', stated the report, 'they should be trained in attacks on moving warships is a matter of high policy, but if they are to be expected to take a more important part in the control of sea communications, large additions to their training would

---

[1] Leading article of 14th February 1942.
[2] See Vol. I, p. 9.

appear to be necessary, and this can presumably only be effected at the expense of their operating capacity in what is now considered their primary, if not their only rôle'.[1]

The Board accepted that it was the delay in finding the enemy which led to the air and surface attacks being made piecemeal; and that the need, at that late hour, to try to inflict some damage quickly eliminated all chance of making co-ordinated attacks. In face of the powerful defences organised by the enemy it was not surprising that those attackers who succeeded in finding the German ships, and pressed in to close ranges, were cut to pieces.

There remains the question of the disposition of our sea and air forces to deal with an event which was predicted with accuracy. The heavy responsibilities which lay upon the Home Fleet at the time have already been mentioned, and it is hard to see how more, and more modern, destroyers could, for example, have been sent south to wait at Plymouth or Portsmouth. Nor, owing to the reconnaissance failure, is it likely that such reinforcements could have attacked early in the enemy's progress. The reinforcement of Coastal Command's torpedo-bombers in the south by No. 42 Squadron from Leuchars was not started sooner because of the Admiralty's insistence on keeping a striking force ready to deal with the *Tirpitz*. When the move was actually ordered the need was already urgent, and every minute mattered. Haste combined with the weather conditions on the airfields in East Anglia produced some understandable confusion. Finally, in summing up the lessons to be learnt from this unhappy event, it seems undeniable that the organisation for the control of all the various sea and air forces involved did not prove adequate to the occasion. The orders designed to deal with a break up-Channel by the enemy ships had been issued as long ago as May 1941, but had not included any special arrangements for placing all ships and aircraft under one unified command as soon as the enemy move occurred, or appeared likely to occur. It now seems that in circumstances such as actually arose a specially created command system was essential to the efficient and flexible control of all our forces.

In the Air Ministry it was realised that co-ordination of their operations by the three commands concerned (Bomber, Fighter and Coastal) had not stood the severe test imposed. On the 20th of March they therefore requested the three Air Commanders-in-Chief to consider the matter, and to make recommendations. Sir Philip Joubert, C.-in-C., Coastal Command, took this opportunity once

---

[1] 'Report of the Board of Enquiry appointed to enquire into the circumstances in which the German Battle Cruisers *Scharnhorst* and *Gneisenau* and Cruiser *Prinz Eugen* proceeded from Brest to Germany on February 12th 1942, and on the operations undertaken to prevent this movement'. Cmd. 6775. (H.M.S.O., 1946.)

The *Scharnhorst* and *Gneisenau* steaming up-Channel, 12th February 1942. Taken from the *Prinz Eugen*. (The plume of water to port of the battle cruisers appears to be from a bomb burst).

Destroyer escort and fighter cover for the German Brest Squadron, 12th February 1942.

The *Prinz Eugen* with A.A. guns in action during the break up-Channel.

(*Photos.: Captain H. J. Reinicke*)

'The attack on the *Scharnhorst* and *Gneisenau* by No. 825 Fleet Air Arm Squadron',
12th February 1942. By Norman Wilkinson.

'Motor torpedo and motor gunboats on patrol', 1942. By R. V. Pitchforth.

again to stress the need for his Command to assume complete responsibility for all anti-shipping activities. His proposal was, however, rejected and a 'combined operational instruction', which had been agreed between the three Commanders-in-Chief, was instead approved by the Air Ministry. A month later Coastal Command renewed its claim, but the frequent transfer of much of its strength abroad (to be discussed shortly) had then made it impossible of accomplishment, and the whole matter was deferred.

After the German battle cruisers reached their home bases, Bomber Command renewed its efforts to destroy them. The *Gneisenau* was hit twice by heavy bombs while in the floating dock at Kiel on the night of 26th-27th of February. Though the British authorities could not, of course, be aware of it, the cumulative effect of the damage received in Brest, of the mine explosion while on passage and of these latest bomb hits was so serious that it was estimated that a year under repair was necessary. In fact her refit was finally abandoned in January 1943, and this fine ship, which had many times caused us trouble and anxiety, thereafter gradually decayed into a disarmed and useless hulk.

Before taking leave of Admiral Ciliax's squadron, and of the unfortunate impression made by what it accomplished almost within sight of England's shores, it must be remarked how it was the selfless efforts of British fighting men—of Esmonde's ancient Swordfish and Pizey's superannuated destroyers, and of the many R.A.F. aircrews involved—which did most to mitigate the failure to stop the German ships. In conclusion it is fair to record that, even allowing for the advantage of the initiative, which in this case was bound to rest with the enemy, his plans were well-conceived, and were carried through with skill and determination.[1]

After these stirring actions and events we must return briefly to the more humdrum work of keeping the coastal convoys running smoothly. From March to the end of July our losses to mines averaged six ships of about 16,000 tons sunk in each month; and it was still off the east coast that most of these losses were suffered.[2] Nor did the escorting destroyers escape the hidden menace. In addition to the *Vimiera*, already mentioned, the *Whitshed*, *Cotswold* and *Quorn* were all mined at this time, but only the *Whitshed* was lost; the *Vortigern*, however, fell victim to an E-boat's torpedo on the 15th of March. E-boats laid about 260 mines in the first six months of 1942, and

---

[1] An interesting account of the planning of this operation and of its execution by the Germans is to be found in the *United States Naval Institute Proceedings* for June 1955. It was written by Captain H. J. Reinicke, formerly of the German Navy, who was Staff Officer to Admiral Ciliax at the time.

[2] Full particulars of our shipping losses from all causes are given in Appendix O.

M

enemy aircraft added a good many more. In that period Nore Command minesweepers swept a total of 460 magnetic or magnetic-acoustic mines, fifty-three acoustics and ninety moored mines. In addition some 450 of our own mines had to be swept for one reason or another. In June the Commander-in-Chief, Admiral Lyon, reported to the Admiralty that his minesweepers had accounted for 2,000 influence type and 400 contact mines since the start of the war.

Actions between the convoy escorts and the E-boats were still fairly frequent. On the night of 19th-20th of February the destroyers escorting a southbound convoy met and engaged a group of eight E-boats engaged in minelaying. One enemy was sunk and another badly damaged. The Germans were dissatisfied over this encounter, and their war diary remarks, doubtless with truth, that 'the British destroyers on the south-east coast knew their job'. It is plain that it was still the destroyers which the German light forces engaged on forays against our coastal convoys chiefly feared. Our motor gun-boats were, however, now making offensive sweeps over on the Dutch coast, and they scored some successes. For example on the night of 14th-15th of March they caught a group of E-boats soon after leaving Ymuiden to attack our east coast shipping. After a series of fierce fights the enemy's purpose was frustrated, and one of his number sunk. Spitfires of Fighter Command joined in the pursuit of the retiring survivors next morning.

So far the share taken by our fighter aircraft in dealing with German E-boats had been of a somewhat fortuitous nature. If, while employed on other missions, the fighters sighted such targets, they would attack; but no operations specifically directed against E-boats had yet been planned. In January, however, Fighter Command began to take part with the other naval and air forces in a co-ordinated offensive, and in the first two months of the year about ninety attacks were made, mostly on E-boats returning to their bases in daylight. In addition to attacks by fighters of No. 12 Group, Coastal Command's Beaufighters also sometimes joined in. But these measures actually yielded no material success. The enemy light craft, though obviously very vulnerable to cannon fire, were elusive targets, and proved extraordinarily difficult to hit from a fast aircraft. None the less an entry in the German Command's war diary does indicate that, by the middle of the year, our air attacks were forcing the enemy to desist from daylight operations, and to send out his light torpedo craft only in darkness.

In the Channel too the initiative was passing into our hands. The Germans realised this, and commented on the growing danger to their convoys and the declining effects of their attacks on our own. They attributed this largely to the work of our shore radar stations. 'The British', so they commented, 'can *see* what is happening . . .

whilst we can only *listen* to the enemy's wireless traffic and warn our boats accordingly'. The fitting of radar sets in our coastal force craft themselves did not actually start until the autumn of 1942. Until then they had to rely on visual sighting, or on listening devices to detect the enemy; but they also received a steady stream of information from the shore plots, which themselves were fed by the radar stations. Thus, off the east coast, a line of M.Ls and M.G.Bs was stationed some miles to seaward of our convoy route, to intercept approaching enemies.

Our light coastal forces were now expanding rapidly. By the middle of the year there were six motor gun-boat flotillas, two of motor torpedo-boats and eight of motor launches in the Nore Command. At full strength each flotilla consisted of eight boats. The M.G.Bs were used to protect our convoys and to attack the enemy E-boats; the M.T.Bs were used offensively against coastal shipping, and the M.Ls performed multifarious services such as minelaying, air-sea rescue work, and escort or patrol duties. As the spring of 1942 changed to summer, attacks on our east coast convoys declined. We now know that early in June the enemy decided that, because his recent experiences had been unprofitable and the short nights so favoured the defence, he would transfer his effort to the Channel. At the end of June two of his flotillas arrived at Cherbourg with the object of attacking our Channel convoys. On the 7th of July they scored a substantial success by sinking six ships of 12,356 tons in Lyme Bay. Then most of the E-boats returned to their Dutch bases, and in August they renewed their attacks on our east coast convoys. These sudden shifts of his coastal craft, to seek weak spots in our defences, were analogous to the constant changes of theatre made by Dönitz with his U-boats, as has been recorded in other chapters.[1]

Though the trend of this 'mosquito' warfare was now favourable to our cause, and it is plain that the spring of 1942 marked the turn from the defensive protection of our own coastal shipping to the onslaught against the enemy's, it is none the less the case that successful attacks on enemy convoys were still few and far between. The German traffic moved along the North Sea and Channel coasts almost entirely by night, and in short stages from one port to the next. Full advantage was taken of bad weather, and for specially important movements very powerful and numerous escorts were provided. It was thus not only hard for our light forces and aircraft to find the enemy, but very difficult for the former to penetrate the screening escorts in order to engage the principal targets. We now know that two disguised raiders passed successfully down-Channel during the present phase. The first one was the *Michel* (Raider H)[2] which left Kiel on the 9th of March and reached Flushing four days later. There

---

[1] See pp. 100 and 269–271.
[2] See Vol. I, p. 278 (note) regarding nomenclature of raiders.

she picked up a strong escort of five torpedo-boats and nine mine-sweepers, and started her passage down-Channel on the evening of the 13th. Early next morning light forces (six M.T.Bs and three M.G.Bs) sent out from Dover were in touch with the convoy; but our wireless traffic had given the enemy warning of their approach. The coastal craft located their quarry close to the French coast, but the enemy had been thoroughly alerted. His shore batteries fired starshell to illuminate the scene, and the attackers were met by such concentrated gunfire that they could not penetrate the screen. Soon after this skirmish five destroyers, which had been on patrol off Beachy Head, arrived and engaged the German escort; the *Windsor* and *Walpole* fired torpedoes, but none of them hit. Little damage was in fact done to either side, and the raider safely reached Havre on the afternoon of the 14th. She then coasted by stages to La Pallice, where she made her final preparations for her cruise. She sailed for the South Atlantic on the 20th of March.

In May another raider, the *Stier* (Raider J), made a successful passage down-Channel. It is to be remarked that whereas in 1940 and 1941 most disguised raiders broke out by the Denmark Strait[1], the enemy had now wholly abandoned that circuitous passage in favour of the much shorter Channel route, where powerful escorts could be provided, and there were many ports of shelter ready to hand. The *Stier* left Rotterdam on the 12th of May escorted as strongly as the *Michel* had been. Very early next morning she was fired on by the Dover long-range guns, but received no damage. Then our coastal force craft gained touch, and a fierce action between them and the numerous escort developed. Two German torpedo-boats, the *Seeadler* and the *Iltis*, were sunk with heavy loss of life. We lost one M.T.B., but the raider herself was unscathed. She entered Boulogne that same morning, and then followed the example of her predecessor by making short coastal journeys by night to the Gironde. We shall recount the adventures of both these ships on their raiding cruises in the next chapter.

To turn now to Coastal Command's efforts to disrupt the enemy's coastwise shipping, the old handicap of lack of really suitable strike aircraft had not yet been overcome, and the Command was only able to continue its campaign by means of loans from other sources.[2] Three squadrons of Bomber Command Bostons and some naval Swordfish were all at this time lent for such purposes. Furthermore the very-low-level bombing attacks, which had been started in the previous autumn, resulted in severe losses being suffered. By July we were losing one in five of the attacking aircraft, a rate of loss which could not be sustained. The very low attacks were thereupon stopped.

[1] See Vol. I, Maps 24 and 27.
[2] See Vol. I, p. 503.

It had long since been brought home that the torpedo was the best weapon for aircraft to use against ships[1]; but it was not easy in the middle of a war greatly to increase the emphasis on torpedo striking power. Not only were we still suffering from a severe shortage of torpedoes, but there were very few suitable modern aircraft capable of carrying them. The Beauforts were excellent for the purpose, but they had not reached Coastal Command in anything like the predicted numbers, largely because new squadrons had been sent to the Middle East as fast as they were formed, in order to meet the urgent need of attacking the enemy's supply traffic to Libya.[2] At the beginning of 1942 Coastal Command still only possessed three squadrons of Beauforts (Nos. 42, 86 and 217). They were allocated to stations from which they could deal with a break-out by the enemy's major warships from Norwegian ports and from Brest. In the spring the situation got worse, for Nos. 42 and 217 Squadrons were ordered overseas. By way of compensation two squadrons (Nos. 415 and 489) of torpedo-carrying Hampdens were formed early in the year, and in April two more similarly equipped squadrons (Nos. 144 and 455) were transferred to Coastal from Bomber Command. They were not, however, ready to start work until July. Nor, apart from its good range, was the Hampden a satisfactory substitute for the Beaufort. It was too slow, not manoeuvrable enough and too vulnerable to fighter attack. In the middle of the year it was decided to try to improve matters by converting Beaufighters to carry torpedoes; but none were available until the autumn.[3]

Table 12. The Air Offensive against Enemy Shipping by Direct Attacks at Sea.
(All Royal Air Force Commands—Home Theatre only)

January–July, 1942

Month 1942	Aircraft Sorties	Attacks Made	Enemy Vessels Sunk		Enemy Vessels Damaged		Aircraft Losses
			No.	Tonnage	No.	Tonnage	
January .	498	52	2	2,152	2	11,131	14
February .	1,674	174	5	1,245	Nil		64
March .	898	63	1	200	Nil		16
April . .	766	83	1	1,494	Nil		18
May . .	960	208	14	31,787	9	30,973	45
June . .	904	240	1	1,497	3	8,172	24
July . .	917	180	6	1,764	Nil		14
TOTAL .	6,617	1,000	30	40,139	14	50,276	195

NOTE: The high figure of sorties flown in relation to losses inflicted on the enemy is partly attributable to the big effort made by Fighter Command over the Channel, where targets were few and were generally only small enemy auxiliary craft.

[1] See Vol. I, p. 509.
[2] See pp. 44, 46 and 48.
[3] These converted Beaufighters were called 'Torbeaus'.

Quite apart, therefore, from the shortage of torpedoes, supply of which was an Admiralty responsibility, there was throughout nearly the whole of the present phase a very severe shortage of torpedo-carrying aircraft in Coastal Command. Only one Hampden squadron was fully operational until the summer. It is certain that the small results achieved and the heavy losses suffered in the air offensive against enemy shipping stemmed from these causes. They are shown in Table 12.

The next table shows how the enemy's parallel effort against our coastal shipping fared. Here again the meagreness of the results accomplished by direct attacks is to be remarked. The losses suffered by the Luftwaffe in this form of warfare cannot, unfortunately, be separated from its other losses.

Table 13. German Air Attacks on Allied Shipping and Royal Air Force Sorties in Defence of Shipping
(Home Theatre only)
January-July, 1942

Month 1942	Estimated German Day and Night Aircraft Sorties for		Allied Shipping Sunk by Direct Attacks (Day and Night)		Royal Air Force Sorties in Defence of Shipping (Day and Night)	Royal Air Force Losses
	(1) Direct Attack	(2) Mine-laying	No.	Tonnage		
January .	452	180	4	9,538	3,643	1
February .	644	160	4	4,776	4,772	4
March .	685	190	2	884	3,868	11
April . .	592	227	Nil		4,509	2
May . .	648	230	Nil		3,956	4
June . .	589	220	2	1,465	4,425	6
July . .	828	93	4	1,868	4,270	6
TOTALS .	4,438	1,300	16	18,531	29,443	34

NOTES: (1) As we cannot distinguish Allied losses due to air-laid mines from losses caused by mines laid by other means, it is impossible to compare the achievements of the enemy's minelaying with those of his direct attacks on shipping.
(2) Allied shipping sunk includes Merchantmen, Naval Vessels and Fishing Craft.
(3) The great majority of the sorties made in defence of Allied shipping was flown by Fighter Command aircraft.

While the give and take in direct air attacks on shipping was thus proving of little profit to either side the Royal Air Force's mine-laying campaign was continuing and expanding, and with very different results. The Admiralty had now raised mine production to 200 per week, and had taken steps to increase it to 300. This created the need to review the number of aircraft available for the purpose. It had always been the case that the more distant, and more fruitful waters could only be reached by Bomber Command's long-range air-craft.[1] That Command now intended gradually to modify all its aircraft to enable them to be so employed. Because it was less

[1] See Vol. I, pp. 509–510.

economical to use the few torpedo-carrying aircraft of Coastal Command, in March it was suggested by Air Marshal Joubert that mine-laying should cease to be a routine duty for his aircrews. This proposal was accepted, and new directives were accordingly issued to both the commands concerned. Bomber Command was instructed that it would take over all minelaying in home waters, but would carry it out with inexperienced crews, as part of their training, or with 'veteran crews' who had been taken off bombing raids. Mine-laying was not to prejudice the command's bombing effort. Coastal Command might still carry out such operations as part of its training in night-flying or for special purposes, but was to consult Bomber Command before doing so.

Accordingly in March bombers of Nos. 1 and 3 Groups (equipped with Wellingtons and Stirlings) were added to those of No. 5 Group, which had formerly been the chief minelayers and had recently received some Manchester squadrons. In that month a total of 355 mines were laid, but in April and May the bombers' accomplishment rose steeply to 559 and 1,027 mines respectively. In all 3,468 mines were laid, nearly all by Bomber Command, in the first six months of 1942 at a cost of sixty-nine aircraft. The waters which were mined stretched from the River Gironde to the Bay of Danzig. At the end of the present phase the Admiralty was ready with an acoustic firing mechanism, but it was decided not to use it until stocks were large enough to cause the enemy serious embarrassment.

The results achieved by the campaign are shown in the table below and it will be seen how, as remarked earlier,[1] the greater economy of minelaying compared with direct attacks on shipping received renewed emphasis.

Table 14.   The R.A.F.'s Air Minelaying Campaign
(Home Theatre only)
January–July, 1942

Month 1942	Aircraft Sorties	Mines Laid	Enemy Vessels Sunk		Enemy Vessels Damaged		Aircraft Losses
			No.	Tonnage	No.	Tonnage	
January .	100	61	5	4,380	Nil		4
February .	319	306	4	11,372	2	62,600	13
March .	266	355	6	6,783	Nil		14
April . .	344	559	7	16,902	2	1,977	12
May . .	456	1,027	25	14,967	2	7,426	16
June . .	516	1,160	15	27,260	4	12,902	10
July . .	434	898	22	22,394	4	14,268	12
TOTALS .	2,435	4,366	84	104,058	14	99,173	81

Before leaving this subject it is relevant to mention that in this same seven month period the British and American air forces flew

[1] See Vol. I, pp. 511–512.

7,476 sorties against enemy ports. The target given to the bombers
was not invariably shipping in those ports, nor the area containing
the docks and wharves. In many cases U-boat building slips, war
industries in the port district, or workers' housing were named as
primary targets. The total losses to enemy shipping in the ports caused
by those raids were eleven ships (17,635 tons) sunk and three (39,851
tons) damaged. Four hundred and seven Allied bombers were lost.

With the *Tirpitz* now known to be operational, the possibility
that she, like the *Bismarck*[1], would be sent on an Atlantic foray and
then make for a base in western France, was one of the Admiralty's
greatest cares. Should she do so there was only one place where she
could be docked—in the great lock at St. Nazaire originally designed
to take the liner *Normandie*, and bearing that ship's name. Access to
this lock, which was 1,148 feet long and 164 feet wide, could be
gained direct from the river Loire.[2] At each end of it were giant
caissons worked by hydraulic machinery which, when in place,
enabled the lock to be pumped dry, and so used as a dry dock. The
suggestion that a surprise attack should be made with the object of
destroying the outer caisson and as much of the dock's operating
machinery as possible originated in the Plans Division of the Naval
Staff, whose Director passed it to Admiral Mountbatten, the Chief of
Combined Operations. The outline plan was then worked out in the
latter's headquarters, and submitted for approval by the Chiefs of
Staff.

It was an exceedingly bold plan, for the attacking forces would
have to make a 400 mile open-sea passage, during which they might
be detected at any time, and then a five mile journey up a closely
guarded river estuary, during which it would be hard to disguise
their presence, and their purpose. The plan was that the ex-
American destroyer *Campbeltown* with three tons of explosive on
board, timed to blow up about two-and-a-half hours after impact,
would be lightened sufficiently to enable her to steam straight up the
river estuary across the numerous sandbanks, instead of keeping to
the tortuous dredged channel. This reduced the navigational
hazards and increased the possibility of surprise; but it meant that
the attack could only take place at the top of a spring tide. The
Campbeltown was then to ram the outer caisson of the lock. Meanwhile Commandos would land from motor launches, and hold a small
bridgehead while demolitions were being carried out. The naval
forces comprised one motor gunboat (M.G.B.) as headquarters
ship, in which were embarked the senior naval officer (Commander

[1] See Vol. I, Chapter XIX.
[2] See Map 17 (p. 171).

R. E. D. Ryder) and the military commander (Lieutenant-Colonel A. C. Newman), sixteen motor launches (M.Ls), some carrying troops and some armed with torpedoes, and one motor torpedo-boat (M.T.B.). The *Campbeltown* (Lieutenant-Commander S. H. Beattie) also carried troops. For the outward passage all the head-quarters staff embarked in the destroyer *Atherstone*. She and her sister ship the *Tynedale* formed the escort force, while two more *Hunt*-class destroyers (the *Cleveland* and *Brocklesby*) were to reinforce the expedition for the homeward passage. After the plan made by the Chief of Combined Operations had been approved by the Chiefs of Staff, the training of the various forces and the meticulous prepara-tion of all the details of the expedition's equipment were done under the direction of Admiral of the Fleet Sir Charles Forbes, now Com-mander-in-Chief, Plymouth.

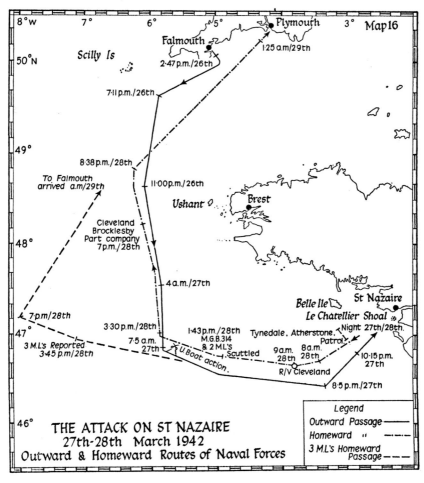

THE ATTACK ON ST NAZAIRE
27th-28th March 1942
Outward & Homeward Routes of Naval Forces

The striking force and its escort sailed from Falmouth on the afternoon of the 26th of March. The *Atherstone* towed the head-quarters M.G.B., and the *Campbeltown* towed the single M.T.B., whose function it was to use her torpedoes against the lock gates if the *Campbeltown* should fail to reach them, or against any other suitable targets which might be found. The southward course was carefully chosen to avoid the enemy's naval and air patrols. German colours were hoisted when Ushant had been passed, but the passage was uneventful except for encounters with French fishing boats, and for an attack on a U-boat by the escorting destroyers early on the 27th. The U-boat (U.593) was not seriously damaged; at 2 p.m. that afternoon she surfaced and reported the presence of our forces. But Commander Ryder considered that the encounter might have com-promised his destination and plan, and to mislead the enemy he altered temporarily to a south-westerly course. The U-boat duly reported his ships to be steering in that direction and the German authorities did not guess that their presence had any connection with St. Nazaire. But it was a narrow escape from loss of surprise, on which so much depended. Detection from the air became less likely when, that same afternoon, the previously clear sky filled with low clouds. One of Commander Ryder's anxieties concerned the move-ments of five German torpedo-boats which had been located at St. Nazaire; but this superior force was removed from his path by the enemy's wrong assessment of U.593's report. The Germans sent their torpedo-boats to sea to make a night sweep off the coast.

Soon after sunset the Force Commanders transferred to the M.G.B., and the light craft took up their dispositions for the approach. The whole force then turned north-east, to pick up the submarine which had been stationed off the river estuary as a navi-gation mark. She was sighted at 10 p.m., and soon afterwards the escorting destroyers parted company. The eighteen coastal force boats and the *Campbeltown* were now entirely on their own. Em-barked in them were sixty-two naval officers and 291 ratings, and forty-four officers and 224 other ranks of the Commandos—a total of 621 men proceeding to attack one of the most heavily defended bases in Europe. At midnight anti-aircraft gunfire was noticed ahead. The R.A.F. had been asked to raid the port in order to divert the enemy's attention; but this actually proved a mixed blessing to the attackers, because the low cloud prevented accurate bombing and the presence of our aircraft brought the enemy garrison to the alert. None the less our forces got to within two miles of their objective before the alarm was given or enemy searchlights were switched on. At about 1.30 a.m. the whole force was brilliantly flood-lit, but fire was not at once opened on it. Commander Ryder gained precious minutes of immunity by making false identification signals and, when the guns did at last open up, at first rather uncertainly, by making protestations of friendliness. But this could not last for long, and very soon 'the full fury . . . was let loose on both sides, [and] the air became one mass of red and green tracer travelling in all directions'. In spite of this, and of the blinding glare of the many searchlights, Lieutenant-Commander Beattie steered the *Campbeltown* well and true for her target. At 1.34 a.m. on the 28th of March (four minutes late on the scheduled time) she rammed the lock gates hard, and stuck there well embedded in them. Her Commandos at once landed and set about their tasks of destruction to good effect.

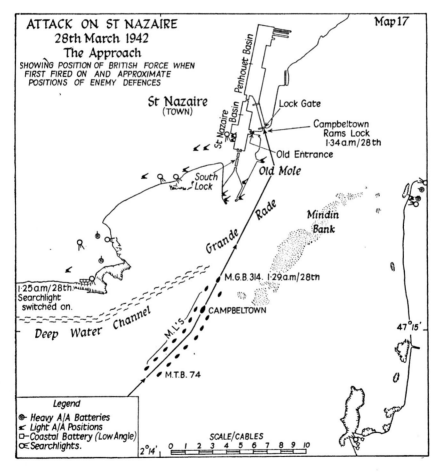

ATTACK ON ST NAZAIRE
28th March 1942
The Approach
SHOWING POSITION OF BRITISH FORCE WHEN
FIRST FIRED ON AND APPROXIMATE
POSITIONS OF ENEMY DEFENCES

Map 17

St Nazaire
(TOWN)

Penhouet Basin

St Nazaire Basin

Lock Gate

Campbeltown
Rams Lock
1·34 a.m/28 th

Old Entrance

South Lock

Old Mole

Rade

Mindin Bank

Grande

1·25 a.m/28th.
Searchlight
switched on.

M.G.B.314. 1·29 a.m/28th

CAMPBELTOWN

M.L'S.

Deep Water Channel

47°15'

M.T.B. 74

Legend
⊕ Heavy A/A Batteries
⊰ Light A/A Positions
□ Coastal Battery (Low Angle)
⊂ Searchlights.

SCALE/CABLES

2°14'   0 1 2 3 4 5 6 7 8 9 10

To land the rest of the soldiers from the motor launches was more difficult, as a torrent of point-blank fire from innumerable weapons, large and small was directed at them. The starboard column of

M.Ls was supposed to land its men at the 'Old Entrance' to the St. Nazaire basin, the port column at the 'Old Mole'.[1] The former suffered heavy casualties; only M.L.177 and M.G.B.314 succeeded in landing their men as planned. At the mole the enemy resistance was even fiercer, and again only one M.L. (No. 457) managed to get her Commandos ashore. M.L.177 and Commander Ryder's M.G.B. rescued many of the *Campbeltown's* crew, but the former was sunk on her way down river and the survivors, including Lieutenant-Commander Beattie, were made prisoner. Ryder himself landed to see that all was well with the blockship's position and, finding that so, told M.T.B.74 to use her torpedoes on the lock gate at the Old Entrance. He then went to support the soldiers on the Old Mole with his M.G.B.; but there matters were going badly. He lay about 100 yards off under a hail of fire, to which his crew answered as long as they could. Around him were many of the M.Ls burning and sinking. Though the demolition parties from the *Campbeltown* could be heard blowing up the buildings and machinery allocated to them, it was obvious that to rescue the soldiers now ashore was impossible, and that the attempt could only lead to the loss of the few surviving coastal craft. At 2.50 a.m. Commander Ryder, whose M.G.B. had 'by the grace of God' [not so far been] set ablaze' but had however been many times hit and was full of badly wounded men, decided to withdraw. He reached the rendezvous with the *Atherstone* five hours later. Meanwhile the five enemy torpedo-boats, which had caused the assault force anxiety the evening before, appeared at last on the scene. At about 6.30 a.m. a short engagement took place between them and the *Tynedale*, while Commander Ryder's much scarred M.G.B. was in the offing; but the enemy was driven off. Seven of our M.Ls, all damaged in varying degree, began the hazardous passage down river. One encountered the German T.B.Ds already mentioned and was sunk. Two others and M.G.B. 314 had to be scuttled by our own forces after the crews had been rescued; only four motor launches got home safely.

We cannot here follow in detail the desperate fighting of the heavily outnumbered Commandos ashore. At the same time as Commander Ryder realised that to rescue them was impossible, Colonel Newman decided to try and break through to the interior of France. After making a determined attempt the survivors were trapped and captured. Shortly before noon on the 28th the *Campbeltown* blew up. With incredibly little imagination a large number of German officers had just gone on board to inspect her, and casualties among them were heavy. M.T.B.74's torpedoes, fired into the lock gates at the Old Entrance, blew up after about one-and-a-half

---

[1] See Map 17 (p. 171).

days' delay.¹ These repeated explosions, combined with the loss of so many of their officers, caused German troops to panic, and in the ensuing indiscriminate firing many hundreds of their fellow-countrymen, and unhappily many French workmen, were killed.

As to the results of the raid, air photographs soon revealed that the main target, the gates of the giant lock, had been totally destroyed. This and the demolition of the working machinery made it certain that the *Tirpitz* could not be docked there—at any rate for a long time. Towards the end of March the German Naval Staff had ordered that all its operational centres should be shifted inland. The reason was that Hitler anticipated an Allied landing in western France. After the raid he ordered U-boat Headquarters to be transferred immediately, and on the 29th of March they accordingly moved from Lorient to Paris.

We lost, in all, fourteen coastal craft, and thirty-four officers and 157 men of their crews; but over half were taken prisoner and returned home after the war. The Commandos lost nearly all the officers and men who landed, but again many were made prisoner. The final totals of British killed and missing were eighty-five to the Navy and fifty-nine to the Army—astonishingly small casualties to have suffered, when it is remembered where the forces went and what they did. The enemy's losses were certainly far higher. But quite apart from the balance sheet of profit and loss, the success of the raid undoubtedly shook the Germans' confidence in their coast defences, and caused them to waste still more men and weapons in sterile garrison duties. Morally the success was as valuable to our own cause as it was detrimental to the enemy's; for in the raid on St. Nazaire were revived the calculated boldness in conception, the calm acceptance of great risks in planning, the steadfastness of purpose in execution and the unflinching courage of performance which has characterised British penetrations into enemy strongholds from Drake's 'singeing of the King of Spain's beard' in Cadiz harbour in 1587, through Cochrane's attack on Aix Roads in 1809 to Keyes 'giving the dragon's tail a damned good twist' at Zeebrugge in 1918.²

---

¹ The delay setting was actually 2½ hours, but the fuzes used were of improvised design, and produced much longer delays than had been intended.

² The Victoria Cross was awarded to Commander R. E. D. Ryder, Lieutenant-Colonel A. C. Newman, Lieutenant-Commander S. H. Beattie (also in recognition 'of the unnamed officers and men of a very gallant ship's company' of the *Campbeltown*), Able Seaman W. A. Savage of M.G.B.314 (posthumously, and also 'in recognition . . . of the valour shown by many others, unnamed, in motor launches, motor gunboats and motor torpedo-boats)' and, also posthumously, to Sergeant J. F. Durrant, Royal Engineers (attached Commandos).

CHAPTER VII

OCEAN WARFARE

1st January–31st July, 1942

> 'The advantage of time and place in all
> martial actions is half the victory; which
> being lost is irrecoverable'.
>
> Sir Francis Drake, 13th April 1588.

EARLY in 1942 Rear-Admiral F. H. Pegram, commanding the South America Division, called at Montevideo in the cruiser *Birmingham*. He found the Uruguayan authorities now willing, even anxious, to afford full facilities for British naval forces to use their country's harbours. This made matters far easier for our patrols in the South Atlantic. It will be remembered how, in the early months of the war, Commodore Harwood's difficulties had been accentuated by the need to adhere strictly to international law in the matter of warships fuelling in the ports of neutral South American countries.[1] As things turned out it was the U.S. Navy which benefited chiefly from these more favourable arrangements, for Admiral Pegram and most of his warships were soon withdrawn from those waters.

With the full maritime power of the United States now available to help protect the ocean shipping routes, it was natural that part of our responsibility for the South Atlantic should be assumed by our Ally. On the 20th of February the whole of the western part of that ocean as far as 40° South was taken over by the U.S. Navy; but the small British cruisers *Despatch* and *Diomede* were placed under the commander of the American Task Force, chiefly to maintain British responsibility for the Falkland Islands. A week after these arrangements came into force the Commander-in-Chief, South Atlantic, Vice-Admiral W. E. C. Tait, was ordered to transfer his headquarters from Freetown to Simonstown, the latter base being now the more conveniently placed centre of the British strategic zone. He sailed in mid-March, and hoisted his flag ashore at Simonstown on the 26th of that month. In the following August Admiral Tait transferred his headquarters from Simonstown to join up with those of the local air authorities at Cape Town. This change was made to facilitate

---

[1] See Vol. I, pp. 116-7.

co-operation with the South African Army and Air Force. It amounted to the establishment of an Area Combined Headquarters, such as had been found essential at home and on other foreign stations, at Cape Town.[1]

As a corollary to Admiral Tait's transfer from Sierra Leone to South Africa, Rear-Admiral Pegram was appointed Flag Officer, West Africa, at Freetown. In the following November his command, extending between 20° North and 10° South and as far west as the line marking the American strategic zone, was made a separate naval command.[2] In the same month the American zone was moved somewhat to the east to take in Ascension Island, where American aircraft were by that time stationed.

It will be appropriate to mention here that in June 1942 the government of the Union of South Africa announced the amalgamation of its Naval Volunteer Reserve and Seaward Defence Force into one service, soon called the South African Naval Service. Another of the Commonwealth countries thus formed its own Navy. Its ships and men continued to work in close co-operation with those of our own South Atlantic Command.

In the early months of 1942 the British forces in the South Atlantic, a few cruisers and armed merchant cruisers, were generally used to escort WS convoys and to patrol for blockade runners or for enemy raiders. In January anxiety was felt for the Falkland Islands, where it was considered that the Japanese might attempt a sudden landing, so the cruiser *Birmingham* and A.M.C. *Asturias* were sent there for a time. To give the impression that we had greater forces in those waters than was actually the case, warships were ordered to appear and disappear off the Patagonian coast with a varying number of dummy funnels in position. Another deceptive ruse was the sailing of imaginary reinforcements from Freetown. That base communicated freely by wireless with them, and it was a nice thought to give the call signs of the battle cruisers *Invincible* and *Inflexible*, victors in the Falkland Islands battle of the 8th of December 1914, to this phantom squadron.

No ocean forays were made by German warships during the present phase. Indeed the close watch now kept by ourselves and our American Allies on the northern exits to the Atlantic, and the far more extensive patrolling by our cruisers and aircraft in the central and southern parts of that ocean, would have made such sorties suicidal. Furthermore it was no longer German policy to employ their warships in such a manner. Though some were being used in the Baltic to give support on the flank of the armies advancing into Russia, the principal units were now kept in Norwegian waters

[1] See Vol. I, pp. 19 and 36.
[2] See Map 10 (opp. p. 97).

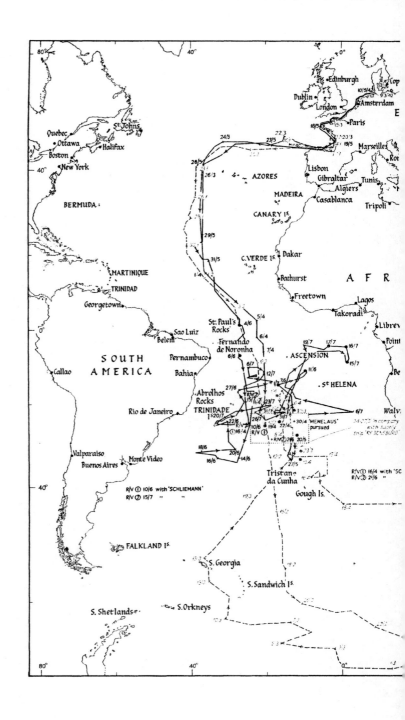

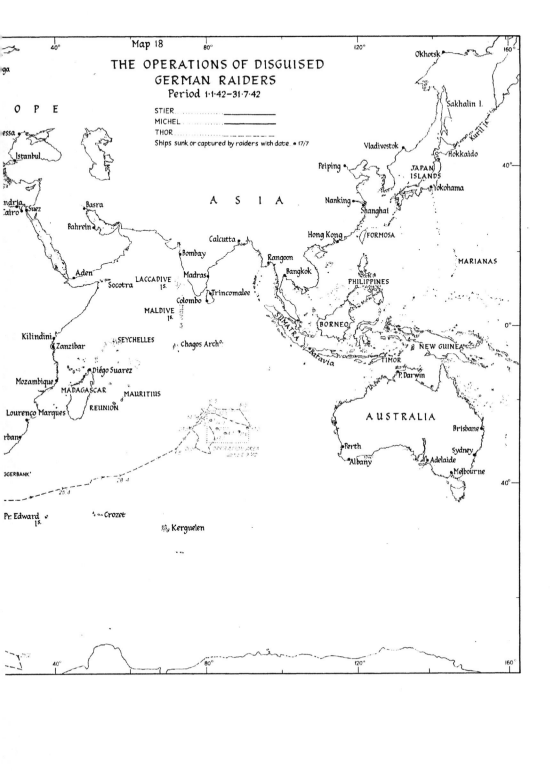

Map 18

THE OPERATIONS OF DISGUISED
GERMAN RAIDERS
Period 1·1·42–31·7·42

STIER .... ▬▬▬▬▬
MICHEL .... ▬▬▬▬▬
THOR .... ▬▬▬▬▬
Ships sunk or captured by raiders with date ● 17/7

to protect the country from the invasion which Hitler's 'intuition' had for some months foretold[1], or to strike against our Arctic convoys. The U-boats, on the other hand, were reaching out ever further, and in the distant waters had now replaced the warship raiders of the first two years. We will return to their depredations later.

Three disguised merchant raiders left German-controlled waters during the first six months of 1942. They were the *Thor* (Raider E), which had completed her first successful cruise in April 1941 and had passed down-Channel from Kiel to the Gironde preparatory to starting her second cruise in the following December[2]; the *Stier* (Raider J), and the *Michel* (Raider H). The last two were new entrants to the *guerre de course*. The *Thor* sailed from the Gironde on the 14th of January, but ran into a heavy gale and had to shelter off the north coast of Spain. A week later she reached the centre of the Atlantic, where she turned south and steamed straight down to the Antarctic, to seek the Allied whaling fleets, against which the *Pinguin* had scored a notable success a year earlier.[3] From late February to the middle of March she searched the Antarctic between 30° East and 30° West, constantly using her aircraft to extend her vision; but she met with no success.[4] On the 11th of March she headed north again, for a rendezvous at which she was to meet the supply ship *Regensburg*. On the 23rd, when very close to the rendezvous, she sighted and sank a Greek ship, her first victim in six weeks' cruising. Next day she met the supply ship as arranged, and obtained fuel and stores from her. She then moved north and rapidly found three victims, two British and one Norwegian, all dry cargo ships. On the 10th April, a little further south, her radar picked up a ship at night, and enabled her to surprise and sink the British *Kirkpool*. On the 16th her aircraft found another ship, but the *Thor's* captain was uncertain whether she might not be the minelayer and supply ship *Doggerbank* (about which more will be said shortly) or the raider *Michel*, both of which might have been in those waters at the time. Before the ship could be identified with certainty contact was lost. The *Thor* next rounded the Cape of Good Hope and entered the Indian Ocean. She had so far sunk five ships totalling 23,626 tons. After first patrolling the Australian-Cape route without success, she moved to a cruising area some 2,000 miles south of Ceylon, where shipping bound from Australia to Ceylon or India might be met. Earlier raiders had found those waters profitable. There, early in May, she again met the *Regensburg* with replenish-

[1] See Vol. I p. 514 and this volume pp. 100–101.
[2] See Vol. I pp. 383 and 505.
[3] See Vol. I p. 384.
[4] See Map 18.

N

ments, in 22° 30′ South 80° East; and on the 10th she encountered the British liner *Nankin* (7,131 tons), bound for Colombo with over 300 persons, including women and children, on board. The liner sent a wireless report, which the raider tried to jam, engaged with her armament and did her best to escape. But it was of no avail, for the *Thor* was the faster ship. The *Nankin* was taken in prize, renamed *Miollnir* and left in company with the *Regensburg*, which was ordered to take on board as much of the captured ship's cargo as possible. On finding that the *Nankin's* distress message had got through to Perth, whence it was re-broadcast, the raider moved further south. The captured ship was sent to Japan, where she arrived on the 18th of July, and her passengers and crew were interned. We have no log of the *Thor* covering this cruise after the 4th of June, but we know that she sank the Dutch ship *Olivia* (6,307 tons) on the 14th, and captured the Norwegian tanker *Herborg* (7,862 tons) five days later. The latter was, like the former *Nankin*, sent in prize to Japan, and was used later as a blockade-runner. In July the *Thor* captured another Norwegian ship and sent her to Japan; and she sank the British ship *Indus* on the 20th. At the end of this phase the raider was still in the central Indian Ocean. The end of her cruise and her final destruction will be told in a later chapter.

The *Stier* (Raider J) had, like the *Michel*, broken out successfully by the down-Channel route. Her passage from Rotterdam to the Bay of Biscay has already been described, and it will be remembered that our light forces sank two of her escort, but failed to harm the raider herself.[1] She reached the Gironde on the 19th of May and sailed next day for the central Atlantic. Her outward passage was not detected.

The *Stier's* first victim, the British ship *Gemstone* (4,986 tons), was sunk in mid-Atlantic just north of the equator on the 4th of June.[2] Two days later she sank a valuable Panamanian tanker of over 10,000 tons. But this good start by the raider was not maintained. Although she cruised many thousands more miles in the South Atlantic, and was several times refuelled by the tanker *Charlotte Schliemann*, which in return relieved the raider of her prisoners, she did no more damage in this phase of ocean warfare. On the 28th of July she met the *Michel* (Raider H) in mid-ocean between Trinidade Island and St. Helena, and there we will take leave of her for the present.

It is worth while briefly to tell the story of the tanker *Schliemann*, which has just appeared as a raider supply ship. She had arrived at Las Palmas in the Spanish Canary Islands on the day before war was declared, with 10,800 tons of oil fuel embarked at Aruba in the Dutch West Indies. There she remained until early in 1942. Though

---

[1] See p. 164.
[2] See Map 18 (opp. p. 177).

her presence and her obvious suitability as a raider or U-boat supply ship was a source of concern to the Admiralty, she seems only to have supplied fuel to one Italian submarine while in Las Palmas. On the 24th of February she left the Canaries to supply the *Stier* and *Michel* during the cruises now being described, and between April and August made at least three rendezvous with each of them in the South Atlantic. At about the end of August, after her last supply operation in these waters, she sailed for Yokohama with the raiders' prisoners. She arrived in Japan on the 20th of October. Her next employment was to carry 'edible oils' from Malaya to Japan, but in mid-1943 she reappeared in the Indian Ocean as a U-boat supply ship.

The *Michel's* departure from Kiel on the 9th of March and her safe passage down-Channel, in spite of attacks by the Dover coastal craft and destroyers, have been mentioned above.[1] Her Captain was that same von Rücksteschell who had been a U-boat captain in the 1914-18 war and had commanded the *Widder* (Raider D) earlier in this one. His ruthless methods have already been commented on, and it has been told how he was ultimately indicted and sentenced as a war criminal.[2] He was well satisfied by the result of the engagement with our light forces in the Channel. His ship came through unscathed and his crew, many of whom were entirely new to sea warfare, had gained valuable experience. However inexcusable von Rücksteschell's conduct may have been towards the crews of his victims, one has to admit his efficiency as a raider Captain. By the beginning of 1942 the *guerre de course* had become far more hazardous than it had been during the preceding two years; yet his cruise accomplished substantial results. While the *Michel* was fitting out, Raeder had allowed him great freedom to introduce improvements based on his experience in the *Widder*. One was to embark a ten-ton motor torpedo-boat with two fourteen-inch stern torpedo tubes and capable of a speed of thirty-seven knots. We shall see later how he made good use of this entirely novel auxiliary. He conducted his whole operations on two principles. The first was to conceal the identity of his own ship at all costs; the second he expressed when he wrote in his diary that ships must be sunk 'with no possibility of "squealing" by wireless'. He greatly favoured attacks on moonless nights.

The *Michel* reached La Pallice safely on the 17th of March, and left three days later for the Atlantic. Her orders were not to make any attacks until she had reached the southern waters of that ocean, so she took avoiding action on sighting no less than five steamers on her way south. In mid-April she met the tanker *Charlotte Schliemann* in

---

[1] See pp. 163–164.
[2] See Vol. I p. 279.

25° South and 22° West. The *Michel* was to live off this supply ship for no less than six months. After fuelling from her von Rückteschell was ready to start work in earnest. On the 19th of April the *Michel* secured her first victim, the British ship *Patella* carrying nearly 10,000 tons of fuel oil from Trinidad to Cape Town. She was sunk in a surprise attack at dawn. Four days days later the raider's M.T.B. was used for the first time in a night attack on the American tanker *Connecticut*, also carrying fuel oil to Cape Town. On the 1st of May an endeavour to repeat these tactics against the British *Menelaus* was unsuccessful. The Alfred Holt ship had a good turn of speed and escaped damage both from torpedoes and from the guns of the raider herself. After meeting the *Schliemann* again and transferring her prisoners to the supply ship, the *Michel* attacked and sank the Norwegian freighter *Kattegat* on the 20th of May by gunfire.

In June the *Michel* moved north, to the waters south of St. Helena, and there, on the 6th, her M.T.B. made a night attack on the American *George Clymer*. This ship had broken down on the 30th of May, since when she had been sending out wireless distress messages. It seems likely that the raider intercepted these, as his course took him some 900 miles north direct to the stopped ship's position.[1] The distress messages were also picked up at Freetown, and the Commander-in-Chief, South Atlantic, detached the A.M.C. *Alcantara* from the escort of convoy WS. 19 to go to the assistance of the *George Clymer*. On the 7th the A.M.C. found her still afloat, and rescued her crew. She then remained in the vicinity of the damaged ship in case salvage should prove possible; but it was finally decided to sink her. This proved unusually difficult, and when the *Alcantara* left on the 12th the derelict was still afloat. The raider, who believed she had sunk the *George Clymer*, appears also to have been quite close during these events, but she and the *Alcantara* never sighted each other.

Five days after this incident the *Michel* sank the British ship *Lylepark* south of Ascension Island. She next met the *Schliemann* and also the converted mine-layer *Doggerbank*. All three ships remained in company for about a week. Having got rid of her prisoners and replenished her supplies the *Michel* moved east, towards the African coast at Walvis Bay, to try her luck against the main shipping route between Freetown and the Cape; she met with no success, so soon shifted further north, to operate against the same route east of Ascension Island. This brought her three valuable victims in quick succession between the 15th and 17th of July. The first was the Union Castle passenger and cargo ship *Gloucester Castle*, bound for Cape Town with military supplies. She was sunk by gunfire and

---

[1] See Map 18 (opp. p. 177).

torpedo, and ninety lives were lost. Next day, the 16th of July, an American tanker returning to Trinidad in ballast was sunk, and the Norwegian tanker *Aramis* was attacked by the M.T.B. and damaged in a night attack. The *Aramis* made raider reports and did her best to escape, but after a twenty-four hour pursuit the *Michel* caught and sank her. After these successes von Rückteschell considered it desirable to move elsewhere. He steamed south once more to the usual rendez-vous and fuelling position in mid-ocean. There he met firstly the raider *Stier*, as has already been mentioned, and subsequently the *Schliemann;* the three ships remained in company for about a week. In the first four months of her cruise the *Michel* had sunk eight ships of 56,731 tons (if the *Clymer* be included among her victims); but her career was to last a long time more.

Although no U-boats or surface raiders visited the great focus of shipping off the Cape of Good Hope at this time, the enemy did not leave those waters entirely unmolested. The density of our traffic there is well indicated by the fact that in the one month of May 1942 Cape Town handled a total of 290 Allied ships and Durban 218. Nor were these figures exceptional. On the 13th of March a Dutch ship was mined and sunk off Cape Town. Our intelligence indicated that the former British ship *Speybank*, which had been captured in the Indian Ocean early in 1941 by the raider *Atlantis* and taken back to Bordeaux in prize, there to be converted to an auxiliary minelayer, might have arrived off the Cape.[1] The intelligence was correct; but we failed to catch her. It is worth briefly following the cruise of the *Speybank* (now renamed *Doggerbank* by the enemy). She had sailed from La Pallice on the 21st of January carrying 280 mines, and equipped in addition to act as a U-boat supply ship. She steamed straight to the Cape, and was sighted on the 12th of March by one of our aircraft about 100 miles west of Cape Town. She identified herself as her sister-ship *Levernbank*, allegedly bound from New York to Cape Town, and was allowed to proceed. That was her first escape, and that night she laid her mines. While actually doing so she was sighted and passed at close range by the light cruiser *Durban*. She again reported herself as the *Levernbank*, and was again accepted as such. Next day the A.M.C. *Cheshire* sighted her further to the south-east, and for the third time a false identity (this time as the *Inverbank*) was accepted. These lost opportunities led to the Admiralty hastening the introduction of the 'check-mate' system, whereby a warship which intercepted a suspicious ship could call for verification from London, and if verification was denied could at once assume the ship to be hostile. The difficulty in introducing this method of calling the enemy's

---

[1] See Vol. I, p. 381.

bluff lay in the fact that the Admiralty had first to know the daily position of every Allied merchantman; otherwise there was a real danger of friendly ships being sunk by our own forces. It had taken a long time to organise the necessary world-wide reporting and plotting, and although the 'check-mate' system was introduced in eastern waters in October 1942, it was May of the following year before it was made world-wide.

The *Doggerbank* next cruised to the east into the Indian Ocean. In mid-April she was back off the Cape, and on the 16th and 17th laid more mines off the Agulhas Bank. These too caused us casualties. One merchantman was sunk, and two others and the fleet repair ship *Hecla* were damaged. In addition to these losses, the mines caused the South Atlantic command considerable anxiety, because besides the many large troopships normally sailing past the Cape in WS convoys, the giant liners *Queen Mary*, *Queen Elizabeth* and *Aquitania* all passed through Cape Town in May. Special arrangements were made to sweep them in and out of harbour.

The *Doggerbank* returned to the South Atlantic after having made this second lay. In mid-May she there met the blockade runner *Dresden*, outward bound for Japan. On the 21st of June she supplied the raider *Michel* in 29° South 19° West, transferred most of her remaining supplies to the tanker *Charlotte Schliemann*, and embarked 177 Merchant Navy prisoners captured by raiders. With these onboard she sailed firstly for Batavia and thence to Japan, where she changed her varied rôles once more and became a blockade runner. The end of her adventurous career did not come until March 1943, when a German U-boat sank her nearly at the end of a blockade running trip.[1]

German attempts to break though our blockade and bring home valuable cargoes of raw materials were discussed in our first volume, and it was there remarked that the enemy's occupation of the ports of western France in 1940 made such journeys much easier.[2] As long as Russia remained neutral a valuable traffic in raw rubber from French Indo-China had been carried to Germany, firstly in Japanese ships to Dairen, and thence by the trans-Siberian railway. But when Hitler's intention to attack Russia became known to his advisers, they had to devise other means for maintaining the supply of a commodity which was essential to Germany's war effort. The Japanese did not at that time want to risk sending their ships to Europe; but they had no objection to carrying cargoes to Japan, where they could be transferred to German blockade runners. The first ship to accomplish such a homeward voyage successfully was the *Ermland*, which reached Europe on the 3rd of April 1941. After two

[1] See pp. 409–410.
[2] See Vol. I pp. 551–552.

more ships (the *Anneliese Essberger* and *Regensburg*) had followed the *Ermland*, the authorities in London considered steps to stop this leak in the blockade. Late in 1941 the Admiralty and the Ministry of Economic Warfare arranged to receive warnings of the movements of all ships likely to be engaged in blockade running, and the Royal Air Force adjusted its patrols in the Bay of Biscay to try to catch them at the end of their journeys. During the first phase of this blockade running, from April 1941 to May 1942, we were occupied with more urgent matters, and the enemy achieved a high proportion of successful journeys. Sixteen ships sailed from the Far East during those thirteen months. They employed many and skilful disguises on passage; but the *Elbe* was identified by aircraft from the *Eagle* and sunk, the *Odenwald* was captured by an American Neutrality Patrol[1], one ship turned back and the *Spreewald* was sunk in error by a German U-boat. Two blockade runners were attacked and damaged by Coastal Command aircraft and one of them, the *Elsa Essberger*, took shelter in the Spanish port of Ferrol for nearly two months. There she transferred some of her cargo to small ships; and she herself finally reached Bordeaux safely. The balance of success undoubtedly lay with the enemy during this period. About seventy-five per cent of the cargoes despatched, including some 33,000 tons of raw rubber and a like quantity of 'edible oils', reached Germany; and six outward-bound blockade runners carried more than 32,000 tons of cargo, much of it valuable machinery, to Japan as well.[2] While on passage the blockade runners were often used to supply U-boats and surface raiders, and to relieve the latter of their prisoners. U-boats invariably escorted them in and out of the Bay of Biscay.

By April 1942 the authorities in London had determined that stronger measures must be taken to stop this traffic, and the various possibilities were reviewed. It was considered that the most economical counter-measure would be for Coastal Command to intensify its patrols and strikes in the Bay of Biscay, as soon as evidence of the approach or departure of a blockade runner became strong. Such operations would be carried out by No. 19 Group and directed from its headquarters at Plymouth; but the provision of aircraft with the necessary range, for it was over 400 miles from the home bases to the approach routes of the blockade runners, proved difficult. In the spring of 1942 the loan of a Whitley squadron and eight Liberators from Bomber Command helped matters, and in June six Lancasters were also temporarily transferred; but long-range aircraft were at this time needed even more to close the 'air gap' on the Atlantic

---

[1] See Vol. I p. 546.
[2] See Appendix N.

convoy routes[1], and it was impossible to make the patrols off Cape Finisterre a matter of high priority. In fact Coastal Command aircraft only damaged one blockade runner at this time; and as five of its long-range aircraft were lost on such operations the exchange was not profitable. The joint sea and air counter-measures designed to improve results against blockade runners will be dealt with in later chapters.

The distant operations by German U-boats in this phase off the American coast and in the Caribbean have already been described.[2] So rich a dividend was reaped in those waters that Dönitz sent out most of his available strength, to the neglect of nearly all other distant operations. The Freetown area had been visited in October 1941, but with small success. Because he expected us, in view of America's entry into the war and the concentration of U-boats in the west, to route more of our South African and South American shipping through Freetown, Dönitz decided in February 1942 to send two U-boats there on a reconnaissance. In March they found a good deal of traffic to the south of that base, and managed to sink eleven ships. But the enemy still considered the western Atlantic by far the most fruitful theatre, so he did not revisit west African waters until the next phase.

The Japanese had meanwhile established their first operational links with their Axis partners, and an agreement with regard to zones of submarine patrols in the Indian Ocean had been included in the Tripartite Pact in December 1941. Later it was several times amended, and in October 1942 the Japanese were supposed only to work to the east of longitude 70° East and the Germans to the west of that meridian. Neither country seems, however, to have regarded itself as rigidly bound by these zones, and U-boats of both nationalities were in fact to be found at work in most parts of the Indian Ocean at different times. It is worth recording that the submarine operations in these waters provided the only known instance of Japanese and German co-operation by land, sea or in the air throughout the war.

In April 1942 five submarines of the I Class (displacement about 2,000 tons) and two auxiliary cruisers (the *Hokoku Maru* and *Aikoku Maru*) left Penang for the west. The latter were to act as supply ships for the submarines, as well as themselves carrying out attacks on merchant ships. In the latter capacity they did little damage, since they only accounted for three Allied ships during their cruise. By mid-May the five submarines had arrived south of Madagascar, while others reconnoitred our various bases as far north as Aden. They were seeking warship targets, but failed to find any. They

---

[1] See pp. 206–207.
[2] See pp. 95–105.

did however achieve one success, which will be recounted shortly, in penetrating Diego Suarez harbour with the midget submarines which some of them carried.[1]

During June and July the Japanese submarines worked mainly in the Mozambique Channel. There our shipping traffic was dense; and because anti-submarine escorts were still almost totally lacking it nearly all sailed independently. Admiral Somerville guessed correctly that a supply ship was working with the Japanese submarines, and wanted to send his carriers to find her; but he was prevented from doing so by the need to try to relieve the pressure on the Americans in the Solomon Islands theatre at this time.[2] All the Commanders-in-Chief, South Atlantic and East Indies, could do to combat this menace was to divert shipping outside of Madagascar, or route it close to the coast to gain what little surface ship or air cover could be provided. The South African Air Force's Venturas flew patrols for this purpose; but we lost fourteen ships of 59,205 tons in those waters in June, and no less than twenty Allied ships of about 94,000 tons altogether, before the Japanese submarines withdrew in the following month.

At the end of the present phase the Japanese submarines once more reconnoitred our Indian Ocean bases, after which they returned to Penang, except for I.30 which arrived at Lorient on a special mission.

As the tide of Japanese success swept south and west in the early months of 1942, it was natural that Allied eyes should be anxiously turned towards the island of Madagascar. Not only did its geographic position command much of the southern Indian Ocean, but from its excellent harbour of Diego Suarez enemy warships and submarines could menace our Middle East convoy route most dangerously.[3] Furthermore the fact that the French authorities in the island owed allegiance to Vichy, whose representatives in Indo-China had so recently and so tamely submitted to Japanese military occupation under the transparent disguise of 'joint defence', increased the potential danger.[4] Of that General Smuts was particularly conscious. The Prime Minister too considered 'that the Japanese might well turn up [at Madagascar] one of these fine days', and that 'Vichy will offer no more resistance to them there than in French Indo-China'[5]; but he and the Chiefs of Staff all felt that a prior strategic requirement was to reinforce India and Ceylon, and that the safety of the latter must take precedence over the occupation of Madagascar. At the end of February the American Chiefs of Staff also

[1] See p. 192.
[2] See pp. 222–223.
[3] See Map 18 (opp. p. 177).
[4] See Vol. I, p. 554.
[5] Churchill, Vol. IV, p. 197.

stressed the desirability of denying the enemy the use of Diego Suarez; almost at the same time General de Gaulle came up with proposals of his own. These, however, found no favour with the Prime Minister or Chiefs of Staff, because the Free French did not possess the forces and equipment necessary to ensure success, and de Gaulle's plan was considered unsound in other respects. Mr Churchill favoured the alternative of doing the job ourselves; but he would not on any account 'have a mixed expedition'. Memories of the fiasco of the mixed expedition of September 1940 were still fresh and, said General Smuts, 'we cannot afford another Dakar'.[1] Early in March the Prime Minister still gave Ceylon first priority, but he declared that Madagascar came next and had to be urgently considered. Definite planning was thereupon undertaken, and by the 14th the Chiefs of Staff had an outline ready. The assault force was to be sent out from England in convoy WS. 17 to Durban; but the necessary warships had mostly to come from Force H at Gibraltar, because the Eastern Fleet had too many and too serious preoccupations elsewhere. Air co-operation and cover were to be provided from the Navy's carriers, aided by a contribution from the South African Air Force; and the Prime Minister asked Mr Roosevelt that the United States Navy should send reinforcements across temporarily, to replace the departed Force H. The President, however, preferred that we should replace the Gibraltar force from the Home Fleet, while his Navy would in turn reinforce the latter temporarily. On the 18th of March the decision to go ahead was taken, and the Defence Committee was informed of the plan. Next day the Admiralty signalled the composition of the forces to all naval authorities, and Rear-Admiral E. N. Syfret of Force H, who had already been warned of what was in train, was appointed Combined Commander-in-Chief for the occupation of Diego Suarez. On the 24th Mr Churchill told General Smuts that 'we have decided to storm and occupy Diego Suarez'[2], a decision which the South African Prime Minister immediately acknowledged with gratitude and relief. The rapidity of the steps taken from first conception, through the planning stage, to operational action is to be admired, as is the flexibility of the maritime power which enabled us to mount such an expedition at so great a distance in so short a time, and moreover, at a very difficult period of the war. For reasons of security it was decided that the Free French were to be kept in the dark. Finally President Roosevelt, on the 29th, promised his country's moral support by delivering to the Vichy Government a statement on the purposes of the expedition on the day when the operation, now called 'Ironclad', was actually launched. There had been some

---

[1] See Vol. I, pp. 308–319.
[2] Churchill, Vol. IV, p. 202.

anxiety in London over possible reactions at Vichy, where M. Laval had just come into power, such as the admission of the Germans to the naval base of Bizerta in Tunisia. American support was calculated to reduce such dangers.

The expedition was not a simple affair from the point of view of those responsible for its conduct and success. Diego Suarez is some 9,000 miles from Britain, and important forces, urgently needed elsewhere, were bound to be locked up for some time. Mr Churchill was determined to limit the commitment to the essential minimum. He knew too well how a requirement such as this could grow, and could absorb increasing numbers of men. 'We are not setting out to subjugate Madagascar', he told the Chiefs of Staff at the end of April, 'but rather to establish ourselves in key positions to deny it to a far-flung Japanese attack'.[1] The troops were to go on to India as quickly as possible after the seizure of Diego Suarez, which was the only thing that mattered.

Admiral Syfret was warned to be ready to leave Gibraltar on the 30th of March, and he received certain reinforcements additional to his normal Force H. In all they comprised the *Malaya*, the aircraft-carriers *Illustrious* and *Indomitable* (which latter replaced the *Hermes* when she was sunk in the Indian Ocean on the 9th of April[2]), the cruisers *Devonshire* and *Hermione*, nine destroyers, half a dozen corvettes and six minesweepers. Most of the corvettes and minesweepers were already in South African waters. All the ships, except those joining later from Admiral Somerville's Eastern Fleet, were to be ready to leave Durban on the 25th or 26th of April. To Major-General R. G. Sturges, R.M., commander of the military forces, three Infantry Brigade Groups and a Commando were finally allocated. Captain G. A. Garnons-Williams was appointed Senior Naval Officer for the actual landings. The five assault ships all sailed with convoy WS. 17, while the motor-transport and stores left Britain in convoys OS. 22 and 23 on the 13th and 23rd of March. Admiral Syfret himself, whose ships were now called Force F, left Gibraltar early on the 1st of April and reached Freetown five days later. There the *Illustrious, Devonshire* and four destroyers joined him. On the 19th of April they all arrived at Cape Town. Next day Admiral Syfret sailed again, reaching Durban on the 22nd. There the battleship *Ramillies*, from Kilindini, joined and the Admiral transferred his flag to her. The next week was devoted to making the final preparations, in close co-operation with the government of the Union of South Africa. Admiral Somerville, Commander-in-Chief, Eastern Fleet, now reported his proposals to cover the assault against surface ship interference from the east, and arranged for the

[1] Churchill, Vol. IV, p. 205.
[2] See pp. 26–28.

Indomitable to join his colleague's force. Thus were all the instruments of maritime power, 'distributed with a regard to a common purpose, and linked together by the effectual energy of a single will'[1], directed towards the critical point. It was, indeed, a classic example of a maritime concentration.[2]

It is now necessary to give the reader some idea of the geography of northern Madagascar, and of the approaches to Diego Suarez Bay, which lies on the east coast near its northern tip. That fine harbour could only be approached from the sea by the narrow Oronjia Pass, three quarters of a mile wide, which was known to be heavily defended.[3] The naval base of Antsirane, our primary objective, lies on a peninsula between two of the four small bays enclosed within the main harbour. But Diego Suarez Bay cuts so deeply into the northern tip of Madagascar (Cape Amber) as almost to sever it from the rest of the island. The isthmus thus formed is only some two and a half to six miles wide, and to the west of it lie several bays which, though very difficult of access through reefs and islands, could accommodate a large fleet. These anchorages are only ten or twelve miles in a direct line from Antsirane, and were much less strongly defended than the Oronjia Pass. It was therefore decided that the landings should be made in the bays on the west coast, at the back door to Antsirane. Two convoys from Durban, one slow and one fast, were to meet ninety-five miles west of Cape Amber on the day before the assault, and from there the minesweepers were to lead the ships into their anchorages. The troops were to land in Courrier and Ambararata Bays, seize the coastal batteries, secure a bridgehead and then advance on Antsirane base and airport.[4] Meanwhile the cruiser *Hermione* was to stage a pyrotechnical diversion on the east coast. The main difficulties were caused by 'the unlit and tortuous channels studded with rocks and shoals' through which the ships had to steam to reach their anchorages, and by the strong and unpredictable currents. For the final approach and landings the ships were divided into five groups. The first was under Admiral Syfret himself in the *Ramillies;* Captain R. D. Oliver of the *Devonshire* was senior officer of the other four groups, in which were included the assault ships; and Captain Garnons-Williams in the *Keren* was to take charge of the actual landings.

The convoys left Durban on the 25th and 28th of April and had a calm passage. Not until the 1st of May were final orders to make the assault on the 5th received from London; in Admiral Syfret's opinion this allowed too narrow a margin of time for the final arrangements

---

[1] A. T. Mahan, *Sea Power in its Relations to the War of 1812*, p. 316.

[2] See Vol. 1, pp. 7 and 11.

[3] See Map 19 (opp. p. 189).

[4] See Map 19.

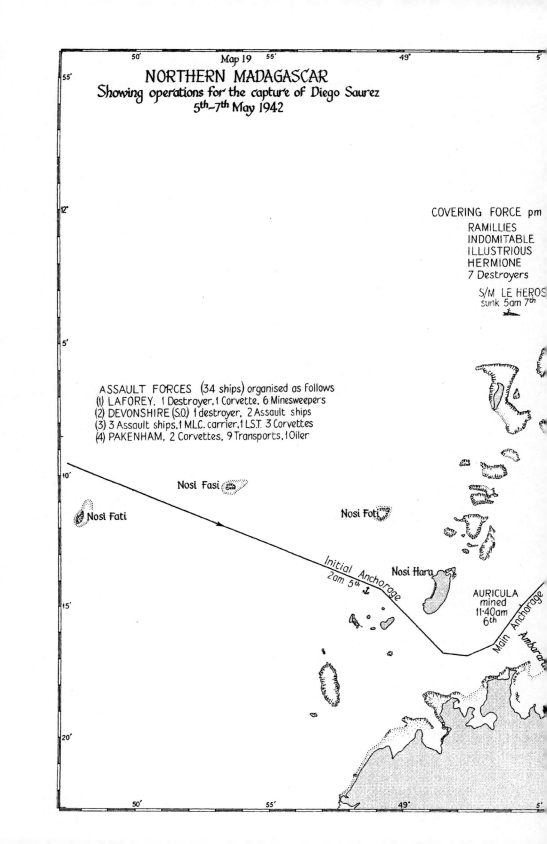

Map 19

NORTHERN MADAGASCAR
Showing operations for the capture of Diego Suarez
5th–7th May 1942

COVERING FORCE pm
RAMILLIES
INDOMITABLE
ILLUSTRIOUS
HERMIONE
7 Destroyers

S/M LE HEROS
sunk 5am 7th

ASSAULT FORCES (34 ships) organised as follows
(1) LAFOREY. 1 Destroyer, 1 Corvette, 6 Minesweepers
(2) DEVONSHIRE (S.O.) 1 destroyer, 2 Assault ships
(3) 3 Assault ships, 1 M.L.C. carrier, 1 L.S.T. 3 Corvettes
(4) PAKENHAM, 2 Corvettes, 9 Transports, 1 Oiler

Nosi Fasi

Nosi Fati

Nosi Foti

Initial Anchorage
2am 5th

Nosi Hara

AURICULA
mined
11·40am
6th

Main Anchorage

Amboran

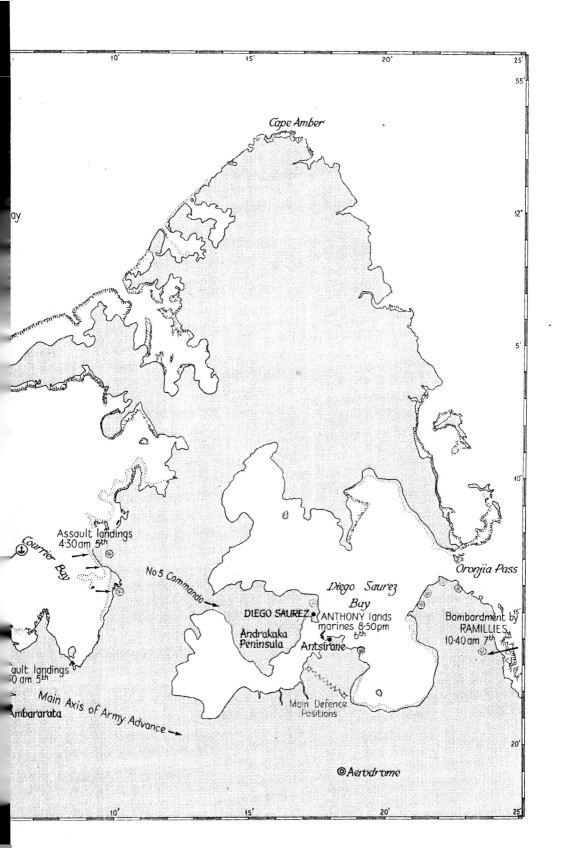

Cape Amber

Courrier Bay

Assault landings
4·30am 5th

No 5 Commando

Diego Saurez
Bay

DIEGO SAUREZ

Andrakaka
Peninsula

Antsirane

ANTHONY lands
marines 8·50pm
6th

Oronjia Pass

Bombardment by
RAMILLIES
10·40 am 7th

Main Defence
Positions

Assault landings
30 am 5th

Ambararata

Main Axis of Army Advance →

◎Aerodrome

to be made. On the 3rd the *Indomitable* (flagship of Rear-Admiral D. W. Boyd) and two destroyers of the Eastern Fleet joined Syfret's force. At 3 p.m. next day, the 4th, the traditional naval executive signal to all ships to 'proceed in execution of previous orders' was made, and they formed up for the final approach. The *Devonshire* was now responsible for the safety of no less than thirty-four ships, some of them large liners like the *Winchester Castle, Sobieski, Duchess of Atholl* and *Oronsay*. The last ninety miles were covered almost entirely in the dark, and as the French considered a night passage through the reefs was impracticable, 'the enemy was', in Captain Oliver's words, 'caught unawares'. Buoys were laid as the channel was discovered, and soon after midnight the destroyer *Laforey* reported its marking completed. She then watched 'with some apprehension' the entry of the transports. Just before 2 a.m. on the 5th they reached the initial anchorage safely, and the assault craft were lowered. Captain Garnons-Williams now took over from Captain Oliver; and the minesweepers swept the eight mile channel to the final anchorage. Though several mines were exploded this did not awaken the defenders. Much to everyone's surprise 'the quiet of the summer night remained undisturbed'. The corvette *Auricula*, which struck a mine and sank later, was the only casualty.

At 3.30 a.m. the dispersal point was reached, and the assault flotillas moved inshore to the three appointed beaches. The assault took place exactly as planned, and without meeting serious opposition. Meanwhile the Swordfish of the *Illustrious*, covered by Martlet fighters, had been attacking shipping in the main harbour, while the *Indomitable's* aircraft dealt with the airport. They too achieved surprise and success.[1] Our aircraft also dropped leaflets in which our objects were defined to the defenders, and the return of Madagascar to France after the war was promised; the reply was, however, that the garrison would 'defend to the last'. Admiral Syfret later described such approaches to the Vichy French as useless and even dangerous; for they made them consider that their 'military honour' was involved.

By 6.20 a.m. 2,000 troops were ashore, and the movement of the transports into the inner anchorage continued. Throughout the day troops and equipment landed steadily, in spite of a rising wind and an unpleasant sea, while the clearance work of the minesweepers continued and naval fighters patrolled over the beaches. The attack on the airport had, however, eliminated serious air opposition. By 5 p.m. most of the troops and vehicles were ashore, and Andrakaka peninsula had been seized; but the army was held up by strong

---

[1] In the air attacks the French submarine *Béveziers* was sunk by depth charges, the auxiliary cruiser *Bougainville* was hit by torpedo and the sloop *d'Entrecasteaux* damaged by bombs and beached.

defences some three miles short of Antsirane, which had not been revealed by the photographic reconnaissances carried out before the operation. In consequence the warships, which had been waiting off Oronjia Pass since early in the forenoon, were still unable to enter the bay.

Early in the afternoon of the 6th the Admiral learnt that the assault on Antsirane was held up. 'Things were not going well', and the unpleasant prospect of prolonged operations, which we were most anxious to avoid, was looming up. General Sturges returned on board the flagship, and a night attack on the troublesome defence line was arranged to take place at 8 p.m. Admiral Syfret promised 'any and all assistance', including air bombardment at zero hour. Actually the situation was not as gloomy as was then believed in the flagship; the army had in fact made good penetrations into the defence line, but bad communications had prevented their accomplishments being fully realised.

At this difficult juncture General Sturges asked if it would be possible to land a small party in the enemy's rear on Antsirane peninsula. The suggestion was no sooner made than acted on. The destroyer *Anthony* (Lieutenant Commander J. M. Hodges) was called alongside the *Ramillies*, and fifty of the latter's Royal Marine detachment under Captain M. Price R.M. were immediately embarked. At 3.45 p.m. the *Anthony* cast off and steamed at high speed round Cape Amber to reach the Oronjia Pass. The sea was rough, and the effects of a destroyer's motion on the landing party did not augur well for such a hazardous undertaking. Soon after 8 p.m. the *Anthony* steamed through the Pass, apparently unobserved until she was almost inside the bay. The batteries then opened fire, and the destroyer's guns immediately replied. It had been hoped that some Commandos would reach the quay where the marines were to land, in time to take the *Anthony's* wires and help to berth her; but they failed to arrive. A first attempt by Hodges to go alongside was frustrated by a strong off-shore wind. He then made a 'stern board' to the quay and by extremely skilful ship-handling, in darkness in a strange harbour and under fire, managed to hold his ship's stern to the quay long enough for the marines to scramble ashore. We cannot here follow the adventures of Captain Price's party in detail. What had started as little better than a forlorn hope ended in an atmosphere of *opéra bouffe*. A few men occupied the French artillery general's house, while others found and seized the naval depot, whose Commandant at once surrendered. British prisoners recently captured were released, including a British agent who was awaiting execution next morning, and Captain Price's chief embarrassment arose from the number of enemies who wished to surrender to him. While the diversionary attack was thus completely successful the main assault had begun from the west. By 3 a.m. on the 7th the army was able to report that it was in complete occupation of the town and its defences, and that the French naval and military commanders had surrendered. The landing in the enemy's rear, made in the finest tradition of the Royal Marines, certainly contributed greatly to the sudden collapse of resistance.

When, in the early hours of the 7th, it was obvious to him that the night attack had succeeded, Admiral Syfret shaped course to join his other ships off the main harbour entrance. One of the watchful Swordfish from the *Illustrious* at this time sank the submarine *Le Héros*, which had reached a menacing position off the northern entrance to the assault ships' anchorage.[1] Having arrived off the Oronjia Pass the *Ramillies*, *Devonshire* and *Hermione* formed line, screened by four destroyers, and prepared to bombard the defences. Fire was opened at 10.40, but ten minutes later it was learnt that Oronjia Peninsula and the main harbour defences had surrendered. By 4.30 p.m. the minesweepers had swept the channel into Diego Suarez Bay, and the main body of the fleet then entered. Barely sixty hours had elapsed since the first landings on the west coast. The warships were soon followed by all the transports and storeships, and thus ended an operation of great importance to our control of the Indian Ocean and of the supply route to the Middle East. In his final report Admiral Syfret remarked that 'co-operation between the services was most cordial'. The success may justly be attributed to this, to the Navy's ability to assemble and escort a great concourse of shipping across many thousands of miles of ocean, to recent developments in landing operations and technique carried out under the Chief of Combined Operations, and to the ability of the Fleet Air Arm to provide air cover and co-operation where shore-based aircraft were lacking. The Prime Minister sent Admiral Syfret and General Sturges his warm congratulations.

At the end of May we suffered a misfortune which marred the amazingly small cost at which this success had been achieved. Most of the warships had by then dispersed to other duties, and anti-submarine patrols were weak. The *Ramillies*, however, had stayed on in Diego Suarez. At 10.30 p.m. on the 29th of May a seaplane unexpectedly flew over the harbour. It was realised that it must have come from an enemy warship of some sort. We now know that it was actually launched by the Japanese submarine I.10. The alert was at once given and the *Ramillies* weighed and steamed round the bay. In spite of these precautions, between 8 and 9 p.m. on the following evening the battleship and a tanker were both torpedoed. The former was considerably damaged and the latter sank. Two

---

[1] See Map 19 (opp. p. 189).

midget submarines launched from the parent submarines I.16 and I.20 had in fact penetrated into the harbour. Their crews must be given credit for accomplishing a daring and successful 'attack at source'. Not until the 3rd of June was the *Ramillies* sufficiently patched up to proceed to Durban.

There remained the need to gain adequate control over the remainder of the 900 miles long island of Madagascar, and especially of the sea ports facing the Mozambique Channel. It was at first hoped that this could be accomplished without further military operations, but Vichy French resistance continued, and in September landings were made at three points on the west coast and at Tamatave on the east coast. On the 23rd British forces entered Tananarivo, the capital of the island. Next month operations moved further south until, on the 5th of November, the Vichy French Governor-General surrendered. So ended a campaign which Mr Churchill has described as 'a model for amphibious descents'.[1]

About twenty-four hours after the Japanese midget submarine attack in Diego Suarez, a similar penetration was made into the great harbour of Sydney, New South Wales. It seems probable that both operations were planned to divert Allied attention from the Central Pacific, in which the great eastward fleet movements from Japan against Midway and the Aleutians had just started.[2] Five submarines, four of them carrying midgets and the fifth a seaplane, took part in the Sydney attempt. The main target was the American heavy cruiser *Chicago*, but the only casualty was an old ferry-boat, serving as an accommodation ship and moored in the naval base. She received a torpedo intended for the *Chicago*. None of the enemy midgets returned to their parent submarines. Japanese claims to have sunk the *Warspite* bore no relation to the truth[3], and the night of the 31st of May–1st of June 1942 is chiefly remembered in Sydney for the pyrotechnics provided by the defending forces, and for the arrival on shore of shells fired by defending Allied warships.

As we look back today at the progress of the whole world-wide struggle, it seems beyond doubt that the month of July 1942 produced the high-water mark of the flood tide of Axis success. In Africa Rommel had reached El Alamein, in Russia the Germans were at Rostov on the Don, in the Pacific the Japanese had occupied the Aleutians and the Solomons, and were threatening the North

[1] Churchill, Vol. IV, p. 212.

[2] See p. 38.

[3] The *Warspite* had actually called at Sydney in February 1942 on her way from Bremerton, where she had been repairing the damage received off Crete (see Vol. I, p. 442), to join the Eastern Fleet.

American and Australasian continents. In the Indian Ocean our command of the sea was precarious; we had recently been driven out of the whole of Burma, and the overland supply route to China was severed; in the Arctic we had just suffered a serious disaster to one convoy, and in the Atlantic our shipping losses had recently been very heavy. Mr Churchill has testified how heavily the cares and anxieties of the phase whose story we have now concluded bore on those in high position at the time.[1] Yet in the eyes of history it is now clear that, for all the defeats and discouragements that we had suffered and were still suffering, the adverse movement of the balance of success had been slowed, then checked, and finally stopped. In the next phase the tendency of the balance to move back to a central position became marked.

---

[1] Churchill, Vol. III, Chapter XXXVII and Vol. IV, Chapters I to XI.

O

CHRONOLOGICAL SUMMARY

OF PRINCIPAL EVENTS

AUGUST 1942–DECEMBER 1942

1942	Atlantic	Arctic	Mediterranean	Indian Ocean	Pacific	Europe
August	U-boat activity transferred from North American coast to convoy routes in North Atlantic, the Freetown area, and Brazilian and Venezuelan waters 22 Brazil declares war on Germany and Italy		10–14 Malta convoy operation 'Pedestal'		7 Americans land on Guadalcanal 9 Battle of Savo Is. 24 Battle of Eastern Solomons	19 Dieppe raid
September	U-boat activity continues against shipping on convoy routes in North Atlantic, Freetown area and Venezuelan waters	2–17 PQ.18 Further Arctic convoys suspended until the successful completion of operation 'Torch'	14 Assault on Tobruk. Operation 'Agreement'		17 Japanese advance on Port Moresby halted 26 Australians start counter-offensive and drive Japanese back	

Month		Arctic Convoys	Mediterranean & N. Africa	Indian Ocean	Pacific	Russia & W. Europe
October	U-boat activity continues in the same waters and also off the west coast of South Africa		23 Eighth Army launches counter-offensive at El Alamein and breaks through Axis defences		11–12 Battle of Cape Esperance 26 Battle of Santa Cruz	
November	U-boat activity continues against convoys in North Atlantic and Venezuelan waters. Collapse of Bay offensive		8 Allied landings in French North Africa Operation 'Torch' 20 Arrival of 'Stoneage' convoy raises the siege of Malta 27 French fleet scuttles itself at Toulon	German U-boat activity off the east coast of South Africa	13–15 Battle of Guadalcanal 30 Battle of Tassafaronga	14 Enemy enters 'unoccupied' France 18 Russian counter-attack at Stalingrad begins
December	U-boat activity continues against convoys in North Atlantic and off the North coast of South America	15–25 JW.51A 22 Dec.–3 Jan. JW.51B Attacked by *Hipper* and *Lützow*	Eighth Army continues advance in Libya			

CHAPTER VIII

THE BATTLE OF THE ATLANTIC
The Second Campaign on the Convoy Routes
1st August–31st December, 1942

> 'I don't think it is even faintly realised the immense, impending revolution which the submarine will effect as offensive weapons of war'.
>
> Admiral Sir J. A. Fisher (later Lord Fisher of Kilverstone). Letter to a friend, 20th April 1904.

SHORTLY before the start of the phase now to be considered the First Sea Lord reviewed 'the present critical situation in the Battle of the Atlantic'. It was plain that the institution of convoy on the American eastern coastal routes had 'produced the anticipated decrease in losses' and that the same measure was now producing identical results in the Caribbean. Admiral Pound 'confidently predicted that the bulk of trade will now pass through these waters in safety;' but he considered it equally certain that we should 'have to face a heavy scale of attack on the focal area to the east of Trinidad'. Measures were in hand to deal with this probability. But the Naval Staff's reasoning and instinct saw even deeper than this into the enemy's mind. 'It is firmly believed', wrote Admiral Pound, 'that another turning point in the U-boat war is approaching'. He considered that at some stage, and probably quite soon, Dönitz would decide that the defences in the western Atlantic had become so strong that 'attack in those waters ceased to pay a return commensurate with the risk . . . and with the lack of economy in this use of his U-boats.' For every boat which Dönitz could send to the western Atlantic, he could keep three at work in our own Western Approaches; for every convoy he could attack in those distant waters, he could deploy four or five times the strength against one in the eastern Atlantic. Meanwhile our own position was none too happy, because we had sent reinforcements to the American side just at the time when attacks on our arctic convoys were increasing; and we needed every escort vessel we could find on that perilous route as well as for the main Atlantic traffic.[1] The events now to be

---

[1] See Chapter V.

recounted will show how extraordinarily accurate was the Naval Staff's prescient reasoning, and how well-founded were its apprehensions. The outlook was, in Admiral Pound's view, made even more foreboding because we and the Americans had not yet managed to make 'our dual control . . . function as a single control based on a single, unified strategy'. No declaration of such a policy had yet been made and he felt grave doubts whether, if his forecast of the enemy's intentions proved correct, 'the United States authorities . . . would be prepared to surrender some of their own forces, or even the British forces which have been helping their own efforts, to meet the new situation'. 'Clearly', continued the First Sea Lord, 'this was a lot to expect', but unless we could expect it we could not 'claim to be fighting on the basis of a unified strategy'. In the event, although the necessary readjustments were not made fast enough or in great enough strength to anticipate the enemy, the general purpose urged by Admiral Pound was carried out between ourselves and the Americans.

On the 27th of July, shortly after the paper summarised above had been produced, a broadcast by Dönitz gave a clear indication of his intentions. The Admiralty called this 'a tip straight from the horse's mouth'. The broadcast and succeeding Press interview were carefully scrutinised in the Admiralty, and the real motives behind them analysed; a great deal was found to confirm the impressions already gathered from other sources. The U-boats had not had a good month in July. Total sinkings had fallen to ninety-six ships of 476,065 tons compared with 144 of over 700,000 tons in June; and eleven U-boats had been sunk in that month (six in American waters and four in the Atlantic, all of them at the hands of the convoy escorts), compared with a total loss of only four in May and three in June.[1] Dönitz's public warnings about the harsh realities of the U-boat war and the certainty that his forces would suffer heavier losses, might therefore reasonably be taken to indicate his intention to attack where losses were most likely to be incurred—namely around the Atlantic convoys.

On the British side it was realised that our escort forces were still too weak, and most of them too slow, to deal as we should wish with a renewed onslaught on a greater scale than in 1941. For lack of numbers the little ships were repeatedly deprived of the possibility of forcing a decision. They simply could not wait to conduct a prolonged and patient hunt, because it would deprive their charges for hours on end of perhaps a quarter of their protecting shield. Thus, when convoy SL.118 was attacked, the senior officer of the escort reported that 'again and again encounters which might have been pursued to a successful conclusion had to be prematurely broken off

---

[1] See Appendix J for the cause of these losses.

The occupation of Madagascar. Assault forces in Ambararata Bay, 8th May 1942.
(See pp. 185–191).

The occupation of Madagascar. General view of Antsirane showing fires started by naval
aircraft, 7th May 1942.

U.597 attacked and sunk
by Liberator H. of
No. 120 Squadron R.A.F.,
5th December 1942. Note
fragments of metal thrown
into the air by depth
charge explosions

German coastal convoy
under attack by Coastal
Command Beaufighters
off the Texel, 18th April
1943. The ship making
smoke was torpedoed
and sunk. Note the A.A.
balloons.

Escort carriers in the Atlantic. H.M.Ss *Biter* and *Avenger*, November 1942. Taken from
H.M.S. *Victorious*.

H.M.S. *Viscount* in
harbour after ramming
and sinking U.619 in the
Atlantic, 15th October
1942. (See pp. 212–213).

'Convoy entering Weymouth'. By John Platt.

in order to maintain a safe minimum escort with the convoy'. As to the speed of our escorts, it was perhaps now that we felt most acutely the slowness of the corvettes. Their margin of speed over the ships they were protecting might be only about four knots, which meant that if they dallied to hunt an attractive contact they might take hours to catch up the convoy again. True, slower convoys allowed them more time to hunt, but then the losses caused to the slower convoys were always far heavier (about 30 per cent) than to the faster ones. The real need obviously was for faster as well as for more escorts—and that could only mean more destroyers, of which we had always suffered a chronic shortage.

To enable us to reinforce the escorts of threatened convoys and then to hunt the U-boats to the death, it was in this phase—to be precise in September 1942—that Support Groups were first formed. The earliest was the 20th Escort Group, of ten flotilla vessels and an oiler, under Commander F. J. Walker.[1] Some of its ships sailed on the 22nd of that month to reinforce the escort of ONS.132, but they were not allowed the chance to work for long together as an integrated group. In the following month the overriding need to provide for the safety of the troop and supply convoys to North Africa led to another postponement of a plan which the Admiralty had long cherished and repeatedly tried to introduce. The opening of the North African campaign also deferred the use of our few escort carriers with the mercantile convoys, for they too were diverted to help guard the invasion forces.[2] The great days of the support groups and escort carriers on the North Atlantic routes were not to come for another six months.

Because the escort carriers were so slow in entering the Atlantic battle, the Admiralty decided at this time to fit a number of merchant ships with a flight deck so that, while still carrying normal cargoes, they could operate a few aircraft in defence of the convoy in which they were sailing. Two types of ship, grain-carriers of 8,000 tons and tankers of 11,000 tons, were chosen for conversion, and as a first step six of each type were taken in hand in October. They could carry three or four Swordfish each, and it was hoped to complete half of them by the early spring of 1943. In actual fact none was ready until May of that year, so that these 'Merchant Aircraft Carriers' (M.A.C. ships) had no influence on the battle during the period covered by this volume.[3]

---

[1] See Vol. I, p. 478.

[2] See p. 317.

[3] The M.A.C. ships, which had flight decks 400-460 feet long, must not be confused with the C.A.M. ships (Catapult Aircraft Merchantment, see Vol. I, p. 477) which were fitted with a catapult and carried only one single-seater fighter. Both classes sailed under the Red Ensign, and were stop-gaps introduced because of the urgent need to mitigate our lack of escort aircraft carriers.

At the start of this phase in August 1942 the enemy had a group of twelve U-boats to the south of Greenland, one of six boats off the Azores and another of the same strength off north-west Africa. There were four or five U-boats off the Canadian coast, some fifteen in or near the Caribbean and half a dozen off Brazil. Finally twenty U-boats were on passage to or from one or other of the theatres already mentioned, and ten new ones were outward bound around the north of Scotland. His total strength had now passed the three hundred mark, of which approximately half were available for operations.[1]

The month of August saw, as the Admiralty had predicted, the last considerable U-boat forays in the Caribbean and Gulf of Mexico. Though air cover had now been greatly improved, the conformation of the islands forced the convoys to use certain well-defined channels, such as the Windward Passage between Cuba and Haiti.[2] It was there and to the east of Trinidad that most successes were now scored by the U-boats; the enemy had, early in August, discovered the focal waters in which the east-west shipping to and from Trinidad and the north-south coastal traffic intersected. Between the 20th of July and the end of August fifteen ships were sunk in the Caribbean and Gulf for the price of three U-boats; but the enemy's successes were steadily declining, and the surviving submarines were withdrawn early in September to the waters around Trinidad, and later to the mouths of the Orinoco. The former yielded a rich harvest in September (29 ships of 143,000 tons, to an average of about eight U-boats at work) and, contrary to the enemy's expectations, remained very fruitful in the two succeeding months. Seventeen ships of 81,742 tons in October and twenty-five of 150,132 tons in November there fell victims to the U-boats, and these remote waters temporarily gave the enemy his greatest successes of the time. The great majority of the ships sunk were still independently-routed. It was not till October, when south-bound convoys from Trinidad (TS convoys) were started, that the southern sections of the Americans' 'Interlocking Convoy System' made their influence felt in this area[3]; and by that time the U-boats had begun to move elsewhere. The squadron of Coastal Command Hudsons mentioned earlier (No. 53) did good patrol work from Trinidad at this time and reported many sightings[4]; but no U-boats were destroyed.

The southward extension of the coastal convoy system was greatly facilitated by Brazil's declaration of war against the Axis powers on the 22nd of August. Although it is true that since the early days of

---

[1] See Appendix K regarding the growth of German U-boat strength.
[2] See Map 11 (opp. p. 105).
[3] See Map 11.
[4] See p. 97.

1942 the Brazilian Government had shown itself to be favourably disposed towards the Allies, the Germans brought its active hostility on themselves by typically callous actions. Brazilian ships had been sunk by U-boats at various times since the beginning of 1942, and tension had been rising. But on the 16th and 17th of August U.507 sank five in rapid succession close off Bahia, and this led immediately to a declaration of war. This may be considered an outstanding example not only of the Germans' political ineptitude, but of their lack of strategic insight. It was of course true that, measured in terms of ships, aircraft and fighting men, Brazil's assistance to the Allied cause was comparatively small; but the enormous length of her coastline and the fact that it juts far out in the South Atlantic were of inestimably greater advantage to us than her material aid. The Allied shipping control organisation could now be extended almost to the great focal area off the River Plate, defence of which was always one of Britain's major anxieties.[1] But an even greater advantage was the stronger strategic control of the whole South Atlantic gained from the use of Brazilian bases. Natal and Pernambuco (Recife) were the closest points on the American continent to our African bases at Freetown, Bathurst and Takoradi[2]; and so our watch was greatly improved over the narrowest part of the ocean, through which all our Middle East troop and supply convoys and a great stream of mercantile traffic still had to pass. U-boats would now find these waters less healthy, surface raiders were almost certainly debarred from them, and enemy blockade runners would be more easily intercepted. The importance to our cause of this development cannot be better demonstrated than by glancing at the maps in our first volume which show the depredations of the enemy's commerce raiders during the first two years of war in the waters from which they were now finally driven.[3]

Though it was an American responsibility and has been fully described in the U.S. Navy's history[4], it may be desirable here to give an outline of the way in which the 'Interlocking Convoy System', already mentioned, worked. In essence it was the same as that organised long before in British coastal waters to feed to and from the main ocean shipping routes, at regular intervals, the traffic which started from, or was destined for ports beyond the ocean terminals. But in the western Atlantic the problem was a good deal more complex, because of the number of subsidiary routes involved.

[1] See Vol I, pp. 116–118.
[2] See Map 18 (opp. p. 177).
[3] See Vol. I, Maps 11, 20, 24, 25, 27, 29 and 42.
[4] Morison, Vol. I, pp. 260–265.

The whole system was governed by two cardinal principles. Firstly the north-bound coastal convoys had to arrive at New York shortly before the Atlantic convoy which its ships were to join sailed for Britain; and secondly the lesser local routes were all linked into the two main coastal routes between Key West or Guantanamo and New York or *vice-versa* (called KN-NK and GN-NG convoys respectively).[1] These 'trunkline' convoys ran on four or five day cycles, and the subsidiary routes generally ran at double those intervals, so that local convoys joined every alternate main coastal convoy. The first of the 'trunkline' convoys sailed in both directions at the end of August or early in September. Concurrently with these new measures the western termini of the trans-Atlantic convoys were shifted from Halifax (HX-ON) and Sydney (SC-ONS) to New York; and the Boston to Halifax convoys (BX-XB), thus rendered redundant, were stopped. It is relevant here to mention that the immense concentration of shipping thus funnelled into and out from New York became more than even that port could manage, and six months later the SC-ONS convoys were therefore transferred to Halifax.[2]

It is unnecessary to detail the many subsidiary convoys which were linked into the main coastal lines already described, but they are shown on Map 11. Professor Morison has given their full particulars and has stated that 'the inter-locking system proved its worth immediately. During the last three months of 1942 the Eastern, Gulf and Panama Sea Frontiers suffered no loss from enemy submarines'.[3] Only off Trinidad (Caribbean Sea Frontier West) did sinkings continue at that time. Professor Morison further records that only thirty-nine ships were sunk between the 1st of July and the 7th of December 1942 out of the 9,064 which sailed in western Atlantic convoys—a proportion of less than one half of one per cent—and concludes that 'this record justified the convoy system'.[4] British historians will no doubt agree with his conclusion; but posterity may well ponder on the combination of circumstances which prevented that achievement being realised many months earlier.

---

[1] See Map 11 (opp. p. 105).

[2] The first convoys to sail under the revised arrangements were as follows:—
(A) When the trans-Atlantic termini were shifted from Halifax and Sydney to New York
HX.208 sailed from New York for Britain 17th Sept. 1942
SC.102   „   „   „   „   „   „   19th Sept. 1942
ON.125   „   „   Britain for New York 28th August 1942
ONS.126   „   „   „   „   „   „   29th August 1942
(B) When the terminus for the slow convoys was shifted from New York to Halifax
SC. 125 sailed from Halifax for Britain 31st March 1943
ONS. 1 (New Series) sailed from Britain for Halifax 15th March 1943
Boston to Halifax convoys (BX-XB) were restarted concurrently, with BX.38 which sailed from Boston on 23rd March 1943.

[3] Morison, Vol. I, p. 264.

[4] Morison, Vol. I, p. 265.

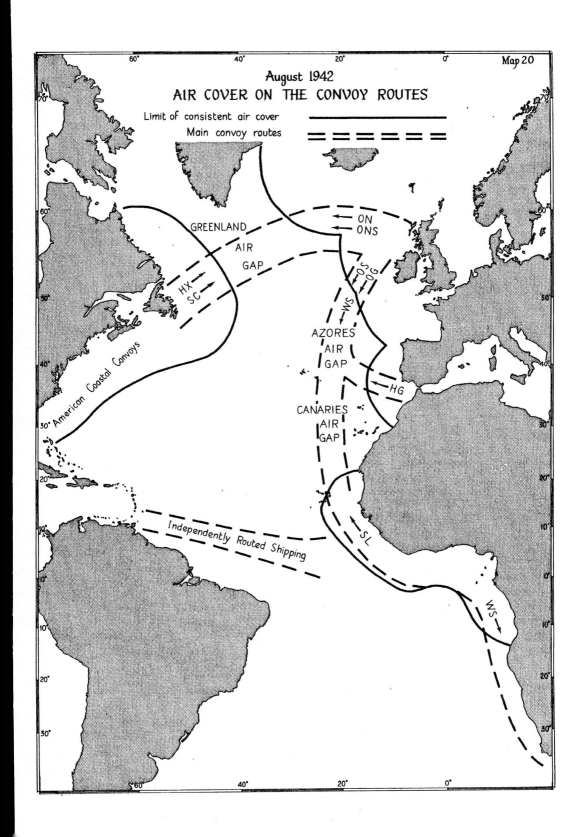

August 1942
AIR COVER ON THE CONVOY ROUTES

Map 20

Limit of consistent air cover
Main convoy routes

GREENLAND
AIR
GAP

ON
ONS

OG
OS

WS

HX
SC

American Coastal Convoys

AZORES
AIR
GAP

HG

CANARIES
AIR
GAP

Independently Routed Shipping

SL

WS

Meanwhile Dönitz had started to re-dispose his forces, very much in the manner foretold by the Admiralty. But before we turn again to the ocean convoy routes it is necessary to make a digression into the technical field, and review the new anti-submarine measures now becoming available to Allied surface and air escorts, and the improvements in his defences which the enemy was concurrently designing. Among our own developments the Leigh Light used in conjunction with airborne radar was of great importance. Together they placed the advantage of surprise in the hands of the attacking aircraft. In July and August the enemy lost three U-boats, all commanded by experienced men to Coastal Command's Bay of Biscay patrols. Furthermore the more powerful depth charge fitted with the new shallow-firing pistol, which entered service in mid-1942, at last enabled our aircraft to exploit their inherent tactical advantage of surprise with deadly effect. The Germans started to fit search receivers in their boats in August. The design was somewhat crude, but they sufficed to give U-boats warning of the approach of our aircraft, which were still equipped with the one-and-a-half metre radar set. Much of our advantage was thus temporarily lost, and it was at once realised that it could only be restored by giving our aircraft the new ten centimetre radar set already being developed.[1] By October the Bay offensive, which had recently seemed to offer such great promise, had come to a halt. To recover the advantage was made more difficult by the fact that production of the new radar set for Coastal Command clashed with manufacture of a set for Bomber Command, from which greatly improved results in bombing Germany were anticipated. The latter command refused at first to forego any part of its claim on the new intruments; but the collapse of the air offensive against U-boats crossing the Bay of Biscay was regarded so seriously that the Air Ministry ordered the diversion of the first forty sets to the Leigh-Light Wellingtons. This, however, could only be a stop gap and was unlikely to be wholly satisfactory, because the set had been designed for a different aircraft employed on a different function. The only adequate solution was to get the new sets from the U.S.A., where they were now being made and fitted to Liberators. The American authorities realised the acute nature of our need, and in October single Liberators began to come across equipped with the ten centimetre set. Inevitably some modifications had to be made on this side, and it was not till the end of January 1943 that No. 224 Squadron began to receive its new

---

[1] The fitting of metric radar sets in the Navy's larger ships for gunnery purposes and in its smaller ships for tactical and search purposes had started in 1940. Reconnaissance aircraft had also been supplied with sets of this type. Certain technical developments made in 1941 enabled a centimetric set to be designed. This needed a smaller and lighter aerial than any earlier set, and was able to pick up much smaller objects, and to show them on a new type of screen. It was eminently suitable for aircraft and coastal force vessels, and had many other uses as well.

equipment. There, for the present, we will leave the Bay offensive, since it was not until the next phase that the initiative was regained by Coastal Command's aircraft.

While Coastal Command's No. 19 Group was trying to deal with the U-boat traffic to and from the Bay of Biscay bases, the aircraft of Nos. 15 and 18 Groups were conducting a parallel offensive against the U-boats which were passing from German ports out into the Atlantic round the north of Scotland. Conditions in this 'northern transit area' were, however, more difficult. Not only were there fewer targets, but they were able to vary their routes far more widely than in the Bay of Biscay; weather conditions were generally far worse, and wireless communication often proved exceedingly unreliable. By the middle of 1942, however, patrols were being flown on a wide arc stretching from the passage between the Shetland Islands and Norway in the east to a line joining Iceland to Ireland in the west.[1] The first success gained from this wider patrolling was the sinking of the valuable 'milch cow' U.464 by a U.S. Navy Catalina on the 20th August. As more searchlight-fitted aircraft became available night patrols were intensified. Many contacts failed to produce results, but on the 15th of September a Whitley of No. 58 Squadron sank U.261, and in the following month a Leigh-Light Wellington accounted for U.412. The Admiralty realised the need to introduce a two-pronged offensive in the waters north of the Shetlands by making surface vessels available to co-operate with the Coastal Command aircraft, but for a long time shortage of ships prevented this being done. At the end of October, however, Admiral Tovey was able to allocate three destroyers, but by then the outward flow of new U-boats had declined and no results were obtained. Next many of No. 18 Group's aircraft were sent south to reinforce the air cover for the invasion convoys for North Africa, and patrols against U-boats in transit declined.

Outside the Bay of Biscay and the 'northern transit area', on the main convoy routes, our surface escorts were now receiving a centri-metric radar set, with the result that the U-boats never felt safe when on the surface and within its range. Moreover they quickly found that our Iceland-based aircraft were reaching further south, thus narrowing the 'Greenland air gap'—the waters in which the U-boats greatly preferred to work.[2] In fact Dönitz's plan was to locate our convoys before they reached the air gap, then to concentrate against them while they were traversing it, and finally to withdraw when air cover returned to the convoys. Although in exceptional circumstances temporary air cover could be given at a distance of 800 miles from our bases, Coastal Command only had one

[1] See Map 37 (opp. p. 363).
[2] See Map 20 (opp. p. 205).

squadron of Liberators (No. 120) able to reach to such distances. The normal range of air cover was still only about 450 miles from the shore bases.

Though the Greenland gap was the most important 'zone of no air cover', there was a similar gap to the east of the Azores, which affected the Gibraltar and Sierra Leone convoys, and another in the neighbourhood of the Canary Islands.[1] These too were used by the U-boats to their advantage. The enemy called the Azores air gap 'the black pit'. In it many ships were sunk; and he was often able there to replenish his U-boats from 'milch cows' as well.

The Germans felt, with good reason, that their own developments were not keeping pace with Allied improvements in anti-submarine tactics and weapons. Dönitz put great faith in the totally new design of submarine known as the Walter boat. In addition to normal means of propulsion these were to have turbines driven by gases produced from the combustion of diesel fuel and hydrogen peroxide. They would be capable of very high under-water speeds for short periods. But this revolutionary design suffered from long delays and troubles, and no Walter boat actually operated against us during the war. Meanwhile their radar lagged far behind our own. To give U-boats a better chance if caught by our aircraft on the surface, heavier anti-aircraft armaments were fitted; and unsuccessful attempts were made to get efficient long-range fighters from the Luftwaffe to protect the U-boats. As to under-water weapons, the enemy was developing acoustic and zigzag-running torpedoes, besides improved magnetic torpedo pistols; asdic decoys, which could be released from a submerged submarine when being hunted, were also tried out, though without any marked success. The greatest improvement given to the U-boats was, without doubt, the ability to dive much deeper. The latest models could dive to 600 feet, or even deeper in emergency. But we were also setting our depth charge patterns to explode at greater depths, and releasing them in greater numbers.

Though the U-boats suffered therefore from tactical and technical handicaps at this time, there were still several important factors which acted in their favour; and of them Dönitz was able to take advantage in planning his new assault on the convoy routes. Firstly he now had a number of 'milch cows' available to refuel his boats and so extend their time on operations. Secondly, our shortage of escorts, and the acute fuel problems with which they were still beset, forced the convoys to keep close to the shortest ('great circle') route across the Atlantic. In the autumn the enemy commented on the way in which this inelasticity in routeing acted in his favour. Lastly his wireless intelligence was still working at a high pitch of efficiency; he was

[1] See Map 20 (opp. p. 205).

once more able to read many of the cyphered and coded signals passing between our shore authorities and the convoys, and so deduce or anticipate their movements. Readers of our first volume will recollect that the initial successes of the German cryptographers were checked when, in August 1940, the Admiralty changed our cyphers.[1] German records leave no room for doubt that, in spite of the change then made, by 1942 the enemy had achieved another substantial penetration of our cyphers; nor was it until the end of that year that our counter-measures began to take effect. Though its runs ahead of the stage now reached in our story, it is relevant to mention that it was not until May 1943 that the discomfiture of the highly skilled German cypher-breakers was made complete and final. The reader should not, of course, assume that we British were meanwhile idle in achieving the opposite purpose. None the less the successes of the enemy, and their long duration, will doubtless surprise those who believed that British cyphers were invariably secure against such encroachments.

Looking back to-day at the enemy's various endeavours to correct an adverse trend of which he was fully aware, one cannot but realise that British scientists had put into our fighting men's hands many developments of inestimable value, and that their accomplishments outstripped the enemy in many directions. But one of their achieve-ments—the centrimetric radar set—stands out above all the others, for it returned to us the initiative in attack by night or in low visi-bility. Though it was, at this stage, only our surface escorts which were benefiting from it, a similar advantage would soon be placed in the hands of Coastal Command's aircrews, and a renewal of the Bay Offensive in greatly improved conditions would then be possible. It is, of course, the human factor rather than any technical develop-ment which is ultimately decisive in war; yet the effect on the fighting man of knowing that he possesses the tactical initiative is immense. And it is precisely that knowledge which, at this critical juncture, the scientists and technicians gave to our anti-submarine escorts and patrols.[2]

Though technical developments were vitally important, they were by no means the only contribution made by scientists to the Atlantic

---

[1] See Vol I, page 267.

[2] A member of the Anti-Submarine Warfare Division of the Naval Staff produced the following doggerel at this time:—

'Gaily the backroom boys,
Peddling their gruesome toys,
Come in and make a noise,
Oozing with science!
Humbly their aid we've sought;
Without them we're as nought,
For modern wars are fought
By such alliance'.

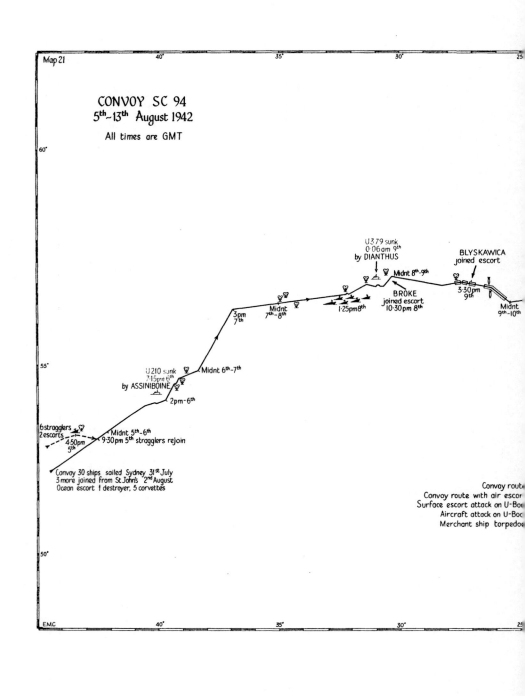

Map 21

CONVOY SC 94
5th–13th August 1942

All times are GMT

60°

U 379 sunk
0·06 am 9th
by DIANTHUS

BLYSKAWICA
joined escort

Midnt 8th–9th

3·30pm
9th

BROKE
joined escort
10·30 pm 8th

Midnt
9th–10th

Midnt
7th–8th

3pm
7th

1·25pm 8th

55°

U 210 sunk
7·15 pm 6th
by ASSINIBOINE

Midnt 6th–7th

2pm 6th

6 stragglers
2 escorts

Midnt 5th–6th

4·50pm
5th

9·30 pm 5th stragglers rejoin

Convoy 30 ships sailed Sydney 31st July
3 more joined from St.John's 2nd August
Ocean escort 1 destroyer, 5 corvettes

Convoy route
Convoy route with air escort
Surface escort attack on U-Boat
Aircraft attack on U-Boat
Merchant ship torpedoed

50°

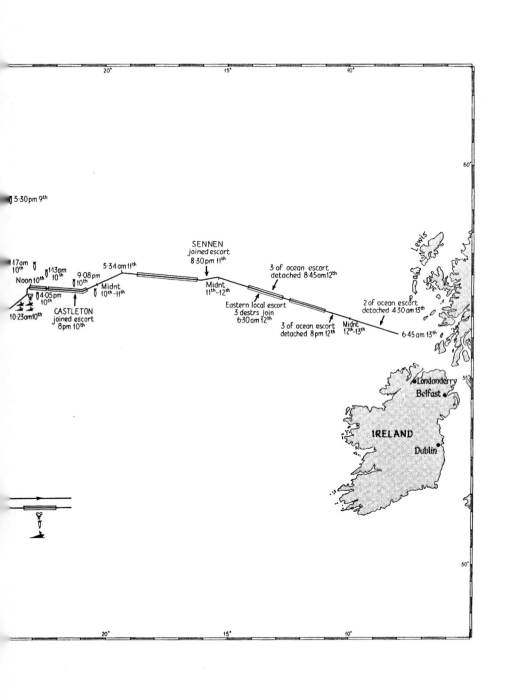

5·30 pm 9th

4·17 am 10th

1·13 pm 10th

Noon 10th

4·05 pm 10th

9·08 pm 10th

10·23am10th

CASTLETON joined escort 8 pm 10th

5·34 am 11th

Midnt 10th-11th

SENNEN joined escort 8·30 pm 11th

Midnt 11th-12th

Eastern local escort 3 destrs join 6·30 am 12th

3 of ocean escort detached 8·45am12th

3 of ocean escort detached 8 pm 12th

Midnt 12th-13th

2 of ocean escort detached 4·30 am 13th

6·45 am 13th

Lewis

Londonderry

Belfast

IRELAND

Dublin

struggle. By mid-1942 a large number of them were working with the Admiralty and Western Approaches operational staffs, studying the results achieved by both sides and recommending strategic and tactical changes which could be deduced from them. 'Operational Research' had indeed been a wholly new development, but under the brilliant leadership of Professor P. M. S. Blackett it had now become a recognized element in planning our moves and disposing our forces.

The first Atlantic convoy to feel the weight of the enemy's new offensive was SC.94. By the time it was attacked on the 5th of August about 450 miles south of Cape Farewell, it consisted of thirty-three ships and had seven escort vessels in company: foggy weather and the distance from our air bases had for the time deprived the convoy of air cover. Next day a series of actions took place.[1] The Canadian destroyer *Assiniboine* rammed and sank U.210, but so injured herself that she had to return to base. Two other U-boats were damaged, and the depleted escort successfully held off all attacks, including those by the substantial reinforcements sent by Dönitz, until the afternoon of the 8th. Then five ships were lost. In the resulting confusion three more crews abandoned their ships under the impression that they had been torpedoed; two of them quickly returned on board, but the third refused to do so and their ship, though still undamaged, had to be left abandoned. She was sunk by a U-boat later. It was a rare event for British merchant seamen to act in such a manner.

The corvette *Dianthus* rammed and sank U.379 on the 8th, and another enemy was damaged. Again the escorts completely foiled many attacks, or forced the enemy to fire at such long ranges that the torpedoes missed. On the 9th Dönitz ordered yet more reinforcements to the scene, but that afternoon Liberators of No. 120 Squadron from Northern Ireland met and escorted the convoy at nearly 800 miles from their base, while the U.S. Navy's Catalinas from Iceland reached south towards the convoy as far as they could. The surface escort was also reinforced, and together they temporarily gained the upper hand. But the advantage was only temporary. Next morning, before the first Liberator had arrived, four ships were sunk; but from noon till dusk air escort was almost continuous and no more ships were lost.[2] Though many enemies were attacked by the Liberators and Catalinas, none was damaged; but it was largely the watchful pressure of the long-range aircraft which forced the U-boats to abandon the operation. On the 13th the surviving twenty-two

[1] See Map 21.
[2] See Map 21.

P

ships reached British ports. Eleven of 53,000 tons had been lost; but considering that all but one of the eighteen U-boats taking part had at one time or another been in touch with the convoy, and that two of them were sunk and four others damaged, the results of the the five day battle were not unfavourable to the Allied cause.

Early in September the outward convoy ON.127 suffered heavily when outside the range of air cover. Seven of its ships and the escorting R.C.N. destroyer *Ottawa* were sunk, and four other merchantmen damaged, without any retribution having been exacted. It is, however, to be remarked that none of the escorts of this convoy had been fitted with radar. The same month saw heavy attacks on two Russian convoys (PQ.18 and QP.14), but we shall tell their story in another chapter.[1] Late in September the enemy failed against HX.209, and lost two U-boats to air attacks south of Iceland. Of the twenty-nine ships sunk in convoy during the month, twenty were lost in the North Atlantic.

On the Sierra Leone route our experiences were very similar. The U-boats waited in the 'Azores air gap' and tried to attack the convoys before they could be reached by shore-based aircraft. For example SL.118, which sailed on the 14th of August, lost three ships between the 16th and 17th. Then it was met by a Liberator from Cornwall, 780 miles out, a U-boat was promptly damaged and only one more ship was sunk. Gibraltar-based aircraft also helped to protect the SL and OS convoys while they were passing within their range.

That Dönitz was by no means happy over the first fruits of his new offensive is shown by entries in his war diary at this time. 'The number of British aircraft in the eastern Atlantic', wrote the Admiral, 'has increased and a great variety of them is seen. They are equipped with an excellent location device. U-boat traffic off the north of Scotland and in the Bay of Biscay is gravely endangered . . . by patrolling aircraft. In the Atlantic the enemy's daily reconnaissance . . . forces us to dispose U-boats far out in the centre of the ocean . . . There are also some aircraft of particularly long-range which are used as convoy escorts. They have been met 800 miles from British bases'. All of which was a true and accurate summary of the capacity and employment of our air escorts and patrols.

It was in this same month of September 1942 that an incident took place which had lengthy repercussions. Four U-boats and a 'milch cow' left Lorient in mid-August to work just south of the equator. There, on the 12th of September, U.156 torpedoed the troopship *Laconia* (19,695 tons), which had 1,800 Italian prisoners on board. Dönitz ordered other boats to go to the rescue, and the Vichy Government was asked to send help from Dakar. While U-boats

---

[1] See pp. 280–287.

were collecting survivors they were bombed by American aircraft, and this led to the issue by Dönitz of the order subsequently known as the 'Laconia order', directing that survivors of ships sunk were not to be rescued. At the Nuremberg trial of Dönitz this was held to have been a violation of the Protocol of 1936[1], even though it was not proved that he had actually ordered the killing of survivors.[2]

We have so far considered only the fortunes of our Atlantic mercantile convoys; but it was during the present phase that the 'monster' liners first started to carry troops (most of whom were American) on the same route, and it is to them that we will now briefly turn. There were six such ships under British control—the *Queen Elizabeth* (83,675 tons), the *Queen Mary* (81,235 tons), the *Aquitania* (44,786 tons), and the *Mauretania* (35,739 tons), all of the Cunard-White Star fleet, the French ship *Ile de France* (43,450 tons) which had been requisitioned in 1940, and the *Nieuw Amsterdam* (36,287 tons) which was on charter from the Dutch. They had already done a prodigious amount of steaming between Australia, New Zealand or India and the Middle East, and from the west coast of America to the Antipodes; and they had carried thousands of troops of many nationalities safely to their destinations.[3] Now the need to move American troops to Europe was so urgent that it was decided not only to accept the risk of employing them in the North Atlantic, but also greatly to increase the numbers carried on each such voyage. Thus the 'Queens', which had carried 6,000 men each formerly, had their carrying capacity increased firstly to 10,500 and then, in June 1942, to no less than 15,000 men. The risks were severe, for one torpedo could bring disaster on an appalling scale. Their safety lay only in their own speed of about 28½ knots; but this itself brought danger, for it prevented them being escorted except at the start and finish of their journeys. No destroyers could maintain such a speed long enough to provide continuous escort right across the Atlantic. Their passages were known as 'operational convoys' and, when in the British strategic zone, they were always controlled by the Admiralty. Special routes were devised for each journey, and diversions from those routes were ordered as soon as any sign of U-boat activity occurred on their tracks. Their progress was continuously and anxiously watched from the Admiralty's Operational Intelligence Centre. A monster liner might thus be routed from New York far south into mid-Atlantic, thence almost due north towards

---

[1] See Vol. I, p. 52.

[2] Cmd. 694. 'Judgment of the International Military Tribunal for the Trial of German Major War Criminals—Nuremberg', p. 109.

[3] See *Merchant Shipping and the Demands of War* (H.M.S.O. & Longmans, 1955) by C. B. A. Behrens, Chapter XI, for a full account of the voyages of monster liners in 1942. Appendix E to this volume gives the totals of fighting men carried across the Atlantic by them in 1942-43.

Iceland, and finally approach the Clyde down the sheltered waters of the Minches off western Scotland.

The liners were escorted out from Halifax or New York by American or Canadian destroyers, but after the first few hours these left, and they then remained entirely on their own until they were met by the Western Approaches escorts, consisting perhaps of an anti-aircraft cruiser and six destroyers, in about 12° West. The *Queen Mary* started work on the north Atlantic route on the 7th of August 1942. A month later the *Queen Elizabeth* joined her sister, and she had made ten Atlantic crossings before the end of the year. The other four great liners continued meanwhile to work on the more distant routes in the south Atlantic, the Indian Ocean and Pacific. Between July and December 194,850 American troops were safely carried across the north Atlantic to Britain.

> 'Bearing her load of lives, over and back,
> The great Queen passes, scorning the deep-sea pack
> Snarling below; in crimson, gold and rose
> The skies salute, waves curtsey as she goes'.[1]

Only one mishap, though a serious one, marred the great liners' accomplishments at this time. On the 2nd of October, just after the Western Approaches escort had joined the *Queen Mary*, she rammed and sank the anti-aircraft cruiser *Curacoa*. This old ship was slower than the liner, and the accident happened while she was escorting from ahead on a steady course, with the *Queen Mary* zig-zagging across her wake. Unhappily 338 lives were lost. On the issue of responsibility, which was taken much later to the House of Lords, it was finally held that blame was attributable to both ships in the proportion of two-thirds against the Admiralty and one-third against the Cunard-White Star Company.

To revert now to the Atlantic trade convoys, after the failure against HX.209 some of the U-boats refuelled, and then two long enemy patrol lines were established, one on each side of the north Atlantic. SC.104, originally of forty-seven ships, was sighted on the 12th of October by the eastern U-boat group, and in the two following nights one of them sank seven of the convoy, including a large tanker. The mid-ocean escort consisted of two destroyers and four corvettes (the latter all Norwegian-manned); but the westerly gale and heavy seas at first gave them a very difficult time. On the 15th the weather moderated and the escorts found their task easier. The destroyer *Viscount* rammed and sank U.619 that night; next afternoon in low

---

[1] *The Queen Mary* by Leonora Speyer. These lines were given to the author of this history by the American poetess shortly before he left New York for the Clyde in the *Queen Mary* in January 1944, to return to Britain with the ship's company of a damaged cruiser, and about 15,000 American troops. They were printed later in the *New York Times*.

visibility the senior officer's ship, the *Fame*, destroyed U.353. As a Coastal Command Liberator of No. 120 Squadron sank a third enemy (U.661) not far from the convoy's track, and only eight of its ships in all were lost, the battle did not go wholly in the enemy's favour.

As October drew to a close the pressure on the convoy routes increased. HX.212 lost six ships, and a few days later a lucky wireless interception enabled the enemy to make a heavy concentration against the slow convoy SC.107. Fifteen ships of about 88,000 tons had been sunk before the air escorts arrived and forced the attackers to desist. Further south SL.125 was attacked off Madeira by ten enemies. In a seven-day battle thirteen of its ships went down, and no U-boats were destroyed. But the ill fortune which overtook this convoy appears to have benefited the Allied cause, quite unexpectedly, in another direction. The first military convoys for North Africa were passing through adjacent waters at the time when the U-boats were occupied in attacking SL.125.[1] Had the enemy not been thus engaged he might well have detected the great movements of troop and supply ships, have attacked them or guessed their purpose and their destinations, and so deprived our landing forces of the important advantage of surprise.

As soon as the enemy realised that we had launched an invasion in North Africa, Dönitz re-deployed a large proportion of his strength off the disembarkation ports. Fifteen U-boats were sent to the Moroccan coast, but they arrived too late; the Allied air and surface defences had been given time to organise themselves, and the enemy inflicted few losses.[2] Early in November one group of U-boats was sent into the Mediterranean to work off Algiers and Oran, and other reinforcements arrived off Gibraltar. There our traffic was heavy, but the air and surface defences were strong and the enemies were kept well in check. We lost a few valuable ships, but the U-boats themselves suffered severely. Three were sunk and six badly damaged to the west of Gibraltar in the second half of the month; and those inside the Mediterranean also fared ill. At the end of the month the U-boats in the approaches to Gibraltar were withdrawn further to the west, in order to catch the troop and supply convoys coming from America direct to North Africa. In this too they failed. None the less our total losses to U-boats in November were very high—119 ships of 729,160 tons; but a great proportion of these, no less than 70 ships, were 'independents', and of that number the majority were sunk in the two 'soft spots' which the enemy had found, off the Cape of Good Hope and in the waters around Trinidad.

---

[1] See p. 320 and Map 32 (opp. p. 317).

[2] See pp. 333–334.

We shall recount later the story of the great movements by sea which preceded the successful launching of operation 'Torch'.[1] Here it is only necessary to consider the effect of those movements on the Atlantic struggle. The British and American Governments and the Combined Chiefs of Staff were all determined that the success of this first major Allied offensive must take priority over all other needs. The demands which it made on the Royal Navy for escorts were, inevitably, very heavy; not less than 125 flotilla vessels and fifty-two minesweepers had to be found. This could only be done by temporarily stopping the Russian, Gibraltar and Sierra Leone convoys, by holding back all reinforcements destined for other theatres and by stripping the Home Fleet and the British coastal convoy routes almost bare of flotilla vessels.[2] Parallel demands were, of course, made on Coastal Command to provide special protection to the 'Torch' convoys which sailed from Britain.

But the opening of the North African campaign did not eliminate the need for large numbers of merchant ships to sail between Britain and the South Atlantic, even though the convoys in which they would previously have sailed were suspended. This need was met by re-casting the routes taken by the whole of this traffic, a feat which would have been quite impossible but for the centralised control of shipping exercised by the Admiralty. Homeward-bound ships from the Cape and from ports in West Africa, and those starting from South American ports north of the River Plate were now routed independently to Trinidad, whence they would join convoys to North America, and ultimately cross the Atlantic in HX or SC convoys. Fast ships of adequate endurance were allowed to miss Trinidad, where congestion was in any case serious, and proceeded direct to the American eastern seaboard. Lastly ships from the River Plate and a proportion of those sailing from South Africa were routed through the Magellan Straits, up the west coast of South America and then by the Panama Canal to the Atlantic convoy assembly ports. After the OS convoys were stopped, outward-bound ships from Britain to the south started in certain ON convoys which

---

[1] See pp. 315–320.

[2] The stopping of convoys before operation 'Torch' and their subsequent restarting (sometimes under different titles) took place as follows:—

  (a) OG. 89 which sailed from Britain on 31st August 1942, was the last of the series before 'Torch'. OG.90, which sailed on 19th May 1943 was also called KX.10. The KX/XK series of 'special slow' convoys between Gibraltar and the United Kingdom had started on 2nd October 1942.

  (b) HG.89 left Gibraltar on 17th September 1942, and was the last of its series. Homeward-bound ships from Gibraltar were thereafter included in the MKS (North Africa—United Kingdom) convoys.

  (c) OS.42, which sailed from Britain on 29th September 1942 was the last before 'Torch'. OS.43 sailed on 14th February 1943.

  (d) SL.125 which, as told above lost thirteen ships, sailed from Freetown on 16th October 1942 was the last before 'Torch'. SL.126 sailed on 12th March 1943.

See also Tables 24 and 25 (pp. 316–317 and 319).

were taking a southerly route, and broke away from them in the vicinity of the Azores. Thence they sailed independently to the west, to South Africa, or to South America.

It will readily be understood how this great re-organisation increased the length of the journeys, and so slowed down the turn-round of the shipping on which the British war effort entirely depended.[1] But the risks and difficulties had to be accepted for the sake of the success of 'Torch'.

It now seems surprising that a heavier price was not exacted from the northern convoys for the successful lighting of the 'Torch'. Their surface escorts had certainly been temporarily weakened, but this may have been balanced by the enemy's diversion (too late) of much of his strength against the overseas expedition.

Air escorts were less affected than the surface escorts, because Coastal Command had sufficient strength in medium-range aircraft to meet the new requirement, and No. 120 Squadron, which possessed the only Liberators in the command, continued to meet emergency calls for long-range air cover. The most important consequences were, perhaps, that all the eight escort carriers (four British and four American) were diverted to meet the needs of the offensive, and that the employment of Support Groups to aid threatened convoys had again to be postponed.

At the beginning of November the enemy had forty-two U-boats between Greenland and the Azores, sixteen in the eastern Caribbean and the 'Atlantic narrows' between Africa and Brazil. Seven were off the Cape of Good Hope and six off the Central African coast; ten were dispersed after attacking SL.125[2], and about twenty-eight were on passage homeward or outward.

Convoy SC.107 had been reported off Newfoundland on the 30th of October. The first attackers were sternly handled by the Royal Canadian Air Force, which sank U.520 and U.658. But seven U-boats made contact on the 1st of November after the convoy had passed beyond the range of air escorts. In two successive nights

---

[1] The average *monthly* number of merchant ships sailed on the South Atlantic routes at this time was as follows:—

Freetown to Cape of Good Hope	77
Cape of Good Hope to Freetown	30
Freetown to South America	27
South America to Freetown	40
U.S.A. to Cape of Good Hope	27
Cape of Good Hope to U.S.A.	57
U.S.A. to South America	36
South America to U.S.A.	17
Cape of Good Hope to South America	25
South America to Cape of Good Hope	16
Total	**352 ships**

[2] See p. 213.

fifteen ships were sunk. Then aircraft from Iceland joined, a Liberator sank U.132 and the attacks were called off. A little later the enemy located ONS.144 when it was out of range of air cover. On the 17th and 18th of November five ships and one of the escorts were lost, but the Norwegian-manned corvette *Potentilla* sank U.184.

By the end of November more U-boats were available to throw into the battle on the convoy routes. Early next month HX.217 was pursued by no less than twenty-two enemies; but it had powerful air protection at a critical time and only lost two ships for an equal number of U-boats sunk by the air escorts. The next convoy attacks were substantial failures, and it was not till nearly the end of December that the enemy again achieved any great success. Then ONS.154 was attacked and lost thirteen ships as well as the special service ship *Fidelity*.[1] The latter, like a good many of our more important merchant-men, had the Admiralty's net defence against torpedoes. This protection was fitted to 768 merchant ships in all, and it certainly saved some of them; but it slowed the ships down and was difficult for the crews to manage in heavy weather. In the *Fidelity's* case it took five torpedoes to sink her.

Towards the end of this present phase an important change took place in the command of the British forces engaged in the Atlantic battle. On the 19th of November Admiral Sir Max Horton, who had commanded our home-based submarines since the early days of 1940, succeeded Admiral Sir Percy Noble as Commander-in-Chief, Western Approaches. Admiral Noble had been Commander-in-Chief since February 1941, when the Western Approaches headquarters were moved from Plymouth to Liverpool.[2] His period of command saw immense progress made in the formation and training of the escort groups, and in the full integration of our sea and air forces. But he accomplished far more than the conquest of many tactical, technical, and administrative problems. He recognized from the earliest days that the Battle of the Atlantic would ultimately be won by the side whose morale was the higher; that to achieve a morale which would overcome all difficulties, and would rise above all tragedies and set-backs, demanded that the Captains of the escort vessels and aircraft should have complete confidence in his shore organisation. So he constantly went to sea in the little ships and flew in the lonely aircraft of Coastal Command, sharing their dangers and their discomforts. Thus the crews came to learn that their Commander-in-Chief understood their difficulties and their problems; and links of mutual confidence of inestimable value were forged.

---

[1] This was the ex-French ship *Le Rhin* which, under Lieutenant de Vaisseau C. A. M. Peri, escaped from Marseilles at the time of the fall of France. She was later commissioned, still under her Free French commander, in the Western Approaches command, and performed many varied services in home waters and the Mediterranean before she was sunk.

[2] See Vol. I, p. 360.

Though the strength which he had been able to deploy had never been sufficient to gain and keep the upper hand over the U-boats and the bombers, he had brought the country safely through the first great crisis, and he turned over to his successor not only the scores of ships which had been commissioned and trained, but also a smoothly running operational organisation in which his own staff and that of No. 15 Group of Coastal Command worked together in intimate harmony. His next appointment was head of the British Naval Mission in Washington and representative of the First Sea Lord on the American side of the Combined Chief of Staff's organisation.

Admiral Horton brought to his new command exceptional experience of submarine warfare dating back to the 1914-18 war, in which he had proved himself an outstanding commander. Moreover, he possessed a deep grasp of all the intricate human and technical problems involved in submarine warfare. There was no living officer who better understood the U-boat commander's mind, nor could more surely anticipate what his reactions to our counter-measures would be. Though the British submarine service to a man deplored his departure from its headquarters, all knew that he had been called to carry even greater responsibilities, and in a crisis which was becoming ever more plain. With his knowledge and insight, his ruthless determination and driving energy, he was without doubt the right man to pit against Dönitz.

During the closing days of 1942 the Admiralty reviewed yet again the problems and prospects of the Atlantic battle. 'Our shipping situation' reported a senior member of the Naval Staff, 'has never been tighter'; and our surface and air escorts were still far too few. In spite of the success of the North African landings, grave anxiety was felt that future offensive plans might be delayed or even frustrated for lack of shipping. In particular, fuel stocks had fallen to a very low figure.

In mid-December there were only 300,000 tons of commercial bunker fuel in Britain, and consumption was running at about 130,000 tons a month. The Admiralty held another million tons which could be used in emergency, but if the naval stocks were allowed to run down the fleet might be immobilised. 'An ample reserve of fuel on this side of the Atlantic is the basis of all our activities' reported the Admiralty; and when the Prime Minister was given the figures quoted above, he minuted on the paper 'This does not look at all good . . .' To expedite and increase fuel imports it was proposed to open up the North Atlantic convoy cycle from eight to ten days, and to use the escorts thereby released to bring across forty-ship convoys of tankers direct from Aruba in the Dutch West Indies on a twenty day cycle. These proposals were put into effect in the next phase, but as we then suffered more heavy losses, it was many months before our stocks of fuel had increased appreciably.

The Admiralty also reviewed at this time the principles on which we should defend our convoys. One member of the Board summed up the problem to the First Sea Lord in these words. 'Experience shows quite clearly that surface escorts without air co-operation cannot give sufficient security to convoys, unless they are in overwhelming strength. It is also clear that air escort unaided by surface vessels is not sufficient. The most effective and economical use of our resources requires a careful balance in the combined use of surface and air escorts'. We had indeed travelled a long way since 1939.[1]

As to the losses we had suffered during the year, it was beyond question that the enemy had done us great damage. At the time he believed that he had destroyed over seven million tons of shipping, and had therefore nearly achieved the target which he considered necessary to bring us to our knees. In fact the U-boats sank, in all waters, 1,160 ships totalling 6,266,215 tons; but his other weapons increased our total losses to no less than 1,664 ships of 7,790,697 tons.[2] To offset this enormous total, just over seven million tons of new Allied shipping had been built. A further deficit of about a million tons of shipping had thus been added in 1942 to the unfavourable balance shown in each year's accounts since the start of the war. British imports fell below thirty-four million tons—one-third less than the 1939 figure.

The U-boats had accomplished their share of this prodigious destruction with less strength than the enemy had hoped to receive; for only seventeen new boats had entered service each month instead of the hoped-for score or more. Yet he had started the year with ninety-one boats operational out of a total strength of 249, and ended it with 212 out of 393.[3] Eighty-seven German and twenty-two Italian submarines had been sunk or destroyed during the year— an insufficient figure to offset the new construction.[4] To the British Admiralty it was plain that the Battle of the Convoy Routes was still to be decided, that the enemy had greater strength than ever before, and that the crisis in the long-drawn struggle was near.

---

[1] See Vol. I, pp. 33–34, and 45–46.
[2] See Appendix O for the division of these losses according to cause and to theatres of war.
[3] See Appendix K.
[4] See Appendix J for the causes of these losses.

CHAPTER IX

THE PACIFIC AND INDIAN OCEANS
1st August–31st December, 1942

'So, reader, if this tale has seemed repetitious
with shock and gore, exploding magazines,
burning and sinking ships and plummeting
planes—that is simply how it was'.
S. E. Morison. *The History of United
States Naval Operations*, Vol. V, p. 315.

W HEN, after the first World War, Admiral of the Fleet Lord
Jellicoe, as Governor General of New Zealand, visited the
Solomon Islands, he remarked that if ever war came to the
South Pacific their geographic position, and the wide stretches of
sheltered water which they enclose, would make them the likely
scene of the decisive struggle for maritime control over the whole
theatre. For the next two decades little happened to disturb the peace
of those remote tropical outposts. Then in 1942 Lord Jellicoe's
prophecy was fulfilled very precisely, and there raged around the
Solomon Islands some of the fiercest sea fighting of all time.

The Solomons group comprises two lines of islands running
approximately north-west to south-east.[1] This double chain is about
600 miles long, but it is with the southern end, and in particular the
waters between the islands of Guadalcanal and Florida that we are
concerned in this phase. The encyclopedia says of the Solomons that
'the climate is hot, the rainfall heavy, and the islands are largely
clothed with thick forest'[2], a description which those who fought
there will probably consider a gross understatement. The Americans
gave to the narrow strip of water between the western and eastern
groups the appropriate nickname of 'the Slot', and it was there that
most of the fighting took place, generally by night. It became the
graveyard of many fine ships, and of thousands of Allied seamen and
airmen. At one time the expectation of life for a cruiser or destroyer
operating in those waters was assessed at about three night patrols.

Long before the Japanese invasion of the Solomons the Australian
Navy enlisted the help of men who had acquired from their peacetime work special knowledge of the islands, and organised them into
a coast-watching service. These brave men, mostly planters or

[1] See Map 22 (p. 220).
[2] Chambers. Vol. 12, p. 696.

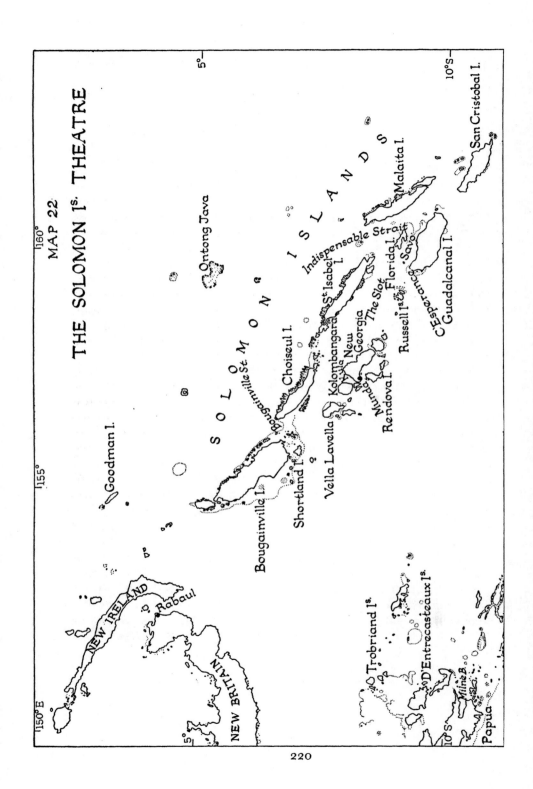

MAP 22

THE SOLOMON Is. THEATRE

150°E
155°
160°

5°

5°S

10°S

10°S

NEW IRELAND

Rabaul

NEW BRITAIN

Goodman I.

Bougainville I.

Bougainville St.

Shortland I.

Choiseul I.

SOLOMON

Ontong Java

Vella Lavella

Kolombangara

Vella
Gulf

New
Georgia

Munda

Rendova I.

The Slot

ISLANDS

St. Isabel
I.

Indispensable Strait

Russell Is.

Savo

Florida I.

C. Esperance

Guadalcanal I.

Malaita I.

San Cristobal I.

Trobriand Is.

D'Entrecasteaux Is.

Milne B.

Papua

belonging to Government services, remained behind the Japanese lines, living in the jungle with their wireless sets and a few faithful Solomon islanders. They kept watch on the narrow waters between the islands, and again and again were they able to send timely warning of enemy movements. When the campaign moved to the northern islands they also rescued and succoured many Allied seamen and airmen, whose ships had been sunk or whose aircraft had been shot down. The Japanese did their utmost to catch the coast-watchers, who had repeatedly to play hide and seek in the jungle with their lives as the forfeit. Some were caught, but none was ever betrayed by the islanders, whose loyalty to their British rulers is one of the most pleasing aspects of the story of the struggle in the Solomons. Among the British who took to the jungle when the Japanese arrived was the Anglican Bishop of Melanesia and his mission staff.[1] They too survived the campaign, and the writer of this history well remembers his astonishment when in mid-1943 an Englishman wearing a pectoral cross, and accompanied by several Solomon islanders and a spaniel, boarded his ship at Tulagi and welcomed her company to his diocese, then mostly still occupied by the enemy. He preached on board the following Sunday, and kept up his association with that ship's officers and men to the end of her career.

To Britain, with her many pressing commitments in the Arctic and Atlantic and in the Mediterranean and the Indian Ocean, the Solomon Islands were very far away; and as most of the fighting was done by the United States Navy the struggle attracted less attention than it deserved. Australia and New Zealand looked at it very differently, for it was happening almost on their front doorstep, and it was obvious to them that, if the enemy became firmly established in the Solomons, communications to and from America would be gravely threatened; and moreover their men of all three services were fighting there, generally under American command.

Because even today it may be difficult for a British reader to grasp the significance of the campaign and the nature of the fighting, it may be permissible to suggest a mythical parallel in our own home waters. If in modern times the British fleet and that of a Continental enemy were contesting the control of the English Channel, much as the Dutch and English fleets repeatedly did in the seventeenth century, the struggle might well centre around the waters enclosed by the Isle of Wight, leading to the great bases of Portsmouth and Southampton. If night after night the two contestants sent their squadrons into the Solent, one from the east and the other from the west, they would probably meet in the narrow waters of Spithead. If inhabitants of Southsea and Ryde can imagine the sight and

---

[1] The Right Reverend Walter Baddeley, D.S.O. M.C. M.A. now (1956) Bishop of Blackburn.

sound of large numbers of cruisers, destroyers and even of heavy-gunned battleships manoeuvring there at high speed in inky darkness, and engaging sometimes at point-blank ranges, they will have formed a fairly accurate mental picture of the fighting in the Solomon Islands 'slot'.

It was told earlier how in July 1942 the Japanese were preparing for a second attempt, this time by a land attack, to capture Port Moresby in New Guinea.[1] To secure their seaward eastern flank in that operation, and in order to prepare for their next lunge to the south-east, they decided to establish an air base on Guadalcanal in the southern Solomons. Almost simultaneously the American Chiefs of Staff decided, as a first step towards the seizure of the islands of New Britain and New Ireland and the ejection of the Japanese from eastern New Guinea, to occupy the Santa Cruz Islands, and to establish bases near Tulagi.[2] The date first intended for these moves was the 1st of August, but it was subsequently postponed until the 7th. Early in July it was reported that the Japanese, who had occupied Tulagi two months earlier, were preparing an air base on Guadalcanal. This made it plain that time was short, and unless the Allies acted quickly the Japanese would become firmly established in the southern Solomons and correspondingly more difficult to dislodge. It will thus be seen that in the early days of July both sides had their eyes focused on the same places. Clearly a major clash was pending.

The Americans moved fast, and before the end of July their expedition was ready. It consisted of an 'Air Support Force' commanded by Rear-Admiral L. Noyes, U.S.N., and an 'Amphibious Force' under Rear-Admiral R. K. Turner, U.S.N. Vice-Admiral F. J. Fletcher, U.S.N., who had commanded the Carrier Task Forces at Coral Sea and Midway,[3] was in charge of the whole operation. The Air Support Force consisted of the carriers *Saratoga, Enterprise* and *Wasp,* supported by one battleship, six cruisers and a large number of destroyers. The Amphibious Force of twenty-two transports supported by four cruisers and eleven destroyers had a separate screening force under Rear-Admiral V. A. C. Crutchley, V.C. Included in it were the Australian cruisers *Australia, Canberra* and *Hobart.* Admiral Crutchley was also second-in-command of Admiral Turner's Amphibious Force.

Towards the end of July the Commander-in-Chief, U.S. Fleet, (Admiral King) asked the Admiralty to stage a diversion in the Indian Ocean early in August to coincide with the American assault on the Solomons. The Admiralty was anxious to help contain

---

[1] See p. 42.
[2] See Map 5 (Opp. p. 33).
[3] See pp. 35–36 and 37–42.

Japanese air and surface forces, but found it difficult to devise an effective way of doing so. They did not consider that hit-and-run raids on the Andaman Islands or on northern Sumatra would deceive the enemy, and they were determined not to run the risk of exposing a fleet, whose fighter defences were bound to be very thin, to attack by shore-based aircraft. In the end it was decided to simulate an expedition against the Andamans by sailing dummy convoys from the east coast of India and Ceylon towards those islands. The movements were started on the 1st of August, and there were indications that the Japanese moved bomber reinforcements to northern Sumatra at about that time; but it is doubtful whether the diversion deceived the enemy, or caused him to move any substantial force in the direction of the Indian Ocean.

To return to the Solomons expedition, the Amphibious Force left New Zealand on the 22nd of July, met the Air Support Force south of Fiji, and carried out rehearsals of the landings in a remote part of that group of islands for four days. On the last night of the month the expedition sailed again, and reached its destination undetected. On the morning of the 7th of August the assaults took place, and were completely successful. The partly-completed airstrip on Guadalcanal, which the Americans renamed Henderson Field, was captured and the Japanese garrison withdrew. Across the 'slot' at Tulagi opposition was stiffer, but the base was in Allied hands by the 8th.[1] It was here that we first learnt how a Japanese garrison would fight until the last man was killed.

Meanwhile the Japanese naval commander at Rabaul, 550 miles to the north-west, had reacted as quickly as was to be expected. Troops were at once embarked in six transports, and sailed to reinforce the garrisons in the south. When, however, an American submarine sank one of the transports on the 8th the rest were recalled. Admiral Mikawa next led down his five heavy and two light cruisers to strike at Admiral Turner's Amphibious Force. Such a possibility had always been allowed for in the American plans, and extensive air searches by shore-based and carrier-borne aircraft were already on the look-out for enemies. On the evening of the 7th Mikawa's squadron was reported off the north of New Ireland, and an American submarine sighted it south-bound at high speed later that night. Special air searches were sent out next morning, but a combination of errors and ill-fortune enabled Mikawa to accomplish the one thing that it had been hoped to prevent, namely a surprise arrival near to the scene of the assaults. It is worth while studying in some detail how this came to pass.

A Hudson of the R.A.A.F. sighted the Japanese squadron at 10.26

---

[1] See Morison, Vol. V, for a full account of the seizure of Guadalcanal and Tulagi and of the fighting which followed.

a.m. on the 8th, but made no report until it returned to base in the afternoon. Not till 6.40 p.m. did the report reach Admiral Turner, and even then it was misleadingly inaccurate as regards the composition of the force sighted. Only three cruisers were mentioned, which was too small strength with which to attack the Allied covering forces; and the inclusion of two imaginary seaplane tenders led Admiral Turner to deduce that the enemy intended to set up a floating air base in a sheltered bay about 150 miles to the north, and to renew air attacks on his force in the morning. Nor was this chain of mistakes and mischances the end of the story. The aircraft ordered to make the special search in the most likely direction of approach by the enemy had been forced by bad weather to return; but this critical information never reached Admiral Turner, so that he remained in ignorance of the fact that the most likely approach route had not been fully covered. One is reminded of the failures in intelligence and communications which marked the opening hours of the Norwegian campaign in 1940.[1] That evening Turner heard, to his dismay, that the Air Support Force was withdrawing almost at once. This would leave the transports to face the next day's air attacks without any carrier air support. Admiral Turner at once called a conference with Admiral Crutchley and General Vandegrift, who was in command of the assault troops, and it was decided that in such circumstances the transports must be sailed at daylight on the 9th, whether they were unloaded or not.

Meanwhile the ships of the screening force had taken up their patrol positions for the night, though without any information to indicate that attack was imminent. The seven-mile-wide southern channel between Savo Island and Guadalcanal was patrolled by the heavy cruisers *Canberra* (R.A.N.) and *Chicago* (U.S.N.) and two American destroyers.[2] Admiral Crutchley's flagship, the *Australia*, formed part of this force, but at 8.30 p.m. she withdrew to the transport anchorage off Lunga Point, because the Admiral had been urgently summoned to attend the conference already mentioned.

To the north of Savo Island the other approach channel was patrolled by the three American cruisers *Vincennes*, *Astoria* and *Quincy*, and two destroyers. Further east were the light cruisers *San Juan* (U.S.N.), *Hobart* (R.A.N.) and two more destroyers. Finally, as extended radar look-outs, two destroyers patrolled outside Savo Island. In retrospect this division of the substantial forces available to cover the approach routes certainly seems to have been mistaken; but, as the Admiral lacked accurate information of the enemy's strength and intentions, it must have seemed at the time the natural thing to do.

---

[1] See Vol. I, pp. 158–160.
[2] See Map 23 (opp. p. 225).

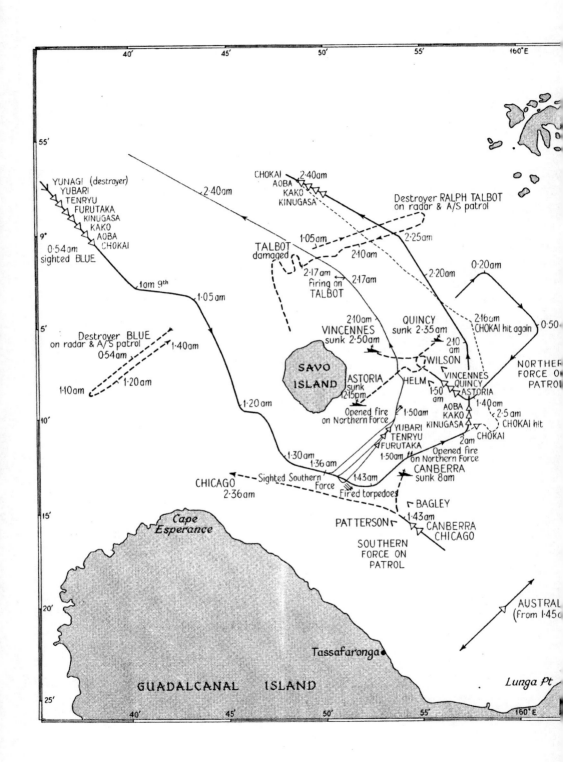

YUNAGI (destroyer)
YUBARI
TENRYU
FURUTAKA
KINUGASA
KAKO
AOBA
CHOKAI
0·54 am
sighted BLUE

1 am 9th

1·05 am

2·40 am

CHOKAI — 2·40 am
AOBA
KAKO
KINUGASA

Destroyer RALPH TALBOT
on radar & A/S patrol

1·05 am

2·25 am

TALBOT
damaged

2·10 am

2·20 am

0·20 am

2·17 am
firing on
TALBOT

2·17 am

Destroyer BLUE
on radar & A/S patrol
0·54 am

1·40 am

1·20 am

1·10 am

2·10 am
VINCENNES
sunk 2·50 am

QUINCY
sunk 2·35 am

2·16 am
CHOKAI hit again

0·50

SAVO
ISLAND

WILSON

2·10
am

NORTHER
FORCE O
PATROL

ASTORIA
sunk
1·15 pm

HELM

VINCENNES
QUINCY
ASTORIA

1·20 am

Opened fire
on Northern Force

1·50 am

1·50
am
AOBA
KAKO
KINUGASA

1·40 am

2·5 am
CHOKAI hit

2 am
CHOKAI

1·30 am

1·36 am

YUBARI
TENRYU
FURUTAKA

1·50 am

Opened fire
on Northern Force

CANBERRA
sunk 8 am

CHICAGO
2·36 am

Sighted Southern
Force

1·43 am

Fired torpedoes

BAGLEY

1·43 am

PATTERSON

CANBERRA
CHICAGO

Cape
Esperance

SOUTHERN
FORCE ON
PATROL

AUSTRAL
(from 1·45 a

Tassafaronga

Lunga Pt

GUADALCANAL   ISLAND

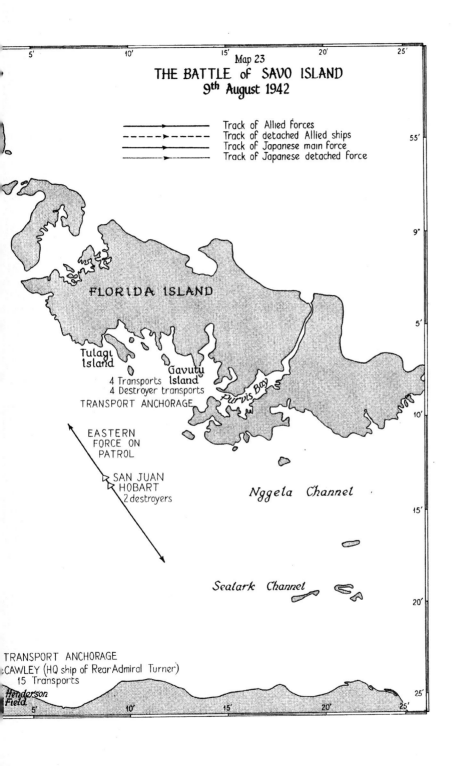

Map 23
THE BATTLE of SAVO ISLAND
9th August 1942

——————▶——————	Track of Allied forces
——— —▶— ———	Track of detached Allied ships
———————▶———	Track of Japanese main force
———————▶———	Track of Japanese detached force

FLORIDA ISLAND

Tulagi
Island
Gavutu
Island
4 Transports
4 Destroyer transports
TRANSPORT ANCHORAGE

Purvis Bay

EASTERN
FORCE ON
PATROL

SAN JUAN
HOBART
2 destroyers

Nggela Channel

Sealark Channel

TRANSPORT ANCHORAGE
CAWLEY (HQ ship of Rear Admiral Turner)
15 Transports

Henderson
Field

Shortly before 1 a.m. on the 9th the leading Japanese cruiser sighted, but was not herself seen by, one of the destroyers on extended look-out. Mikawa then led his column of five heavy and two light cruisers through the southern channel and turned to the north-east. At 1.34 the Japanese sighted strange ships on a closing bearing, and they fired torpedoes a few minutes later. Not till 1.43 did an American destroyer give the alarm, by which time it was too late for the Allied cruisers to do much to save themselves. A dense, tropical rain cloud had passed between them and the enemy at a critical time, and helped to conceal the Japanese squadron's approach. The *Canberra* was hit by two torpedoes and many shells. Within a few minutes her Captain was mortally wounded, all power had failed and she was badly on fire. Although strenuous efforts were made, it proved impossible to get the fires under control. At about 8 a.m., on Admiral Turner's instructions, her survivors were taken off and she was sunk. The *Chicago*, next astern of the *Canberra*, was a good deal luckier. She sustained no serious damage; but she did none to the enemy, who rapidly disappeared to the north-east. Unfortunately no enemy reports were made by the southern force, and as the rain cloud entirely concealed the surface action, the northern squadron unwisely assumed the gunfire to have been directed against aircraft. The three American cruisers *Vincennes*, *Astoria* and *Quincy* were thus also caught by surprise when at 1.49 they came under heavy fire from two directions. Within a few minutes all three were hit and blazing fiercely. The *Quincy* and *Vincennes* soon capsized, and the *Astoria* sank the following afternoon after a magazine explosion. It was a crushing defeat, brought about by faulty intelligence leading to faulty dispositions, and sealed by tactical errors. But the reader who feels strongly regarding the inadequate readiness of the ships, the failures of communications and the poor look-out maintained should himself experience the strain of trying to remain alert for several successive nights, after long and anxious days in the deadening, exhausting heat of the Solomon Islands' climate.

The ending of this disastrous episode was at least happier than it might have been, for the Japanese Admiral, after reducing the northern force to a shambles, decided to retire from the scene without attacking the transports, although they had been named as his primary objective. As only the *Australia*, *San Juan* and *Hobart* and about half a dozen destroyers, all of them very scattered, remained for their defence, Mikawa undoubtedly thereby sacrificed the chance of inflicting a defeat which would have brought disaster to the whole Allied expedition. Perhaps the price paid to avoid that was not excessive. Finally an American submarine did something towards restoring the balance of losses, by sinking the heavy cruiser *Kako* of Mikawa's squadron on her way back to base on the 10th.

Q

As the day after the Battle of Savo Island dawned Admiral Turner's position was indeed difficult, while the outlook for the 11,000 U.S. Marines so far landed was, to say the least of it, unenviable. Turner, however, took the bold decision to continue unloading the transports. He thus assured the marines of sufficient supplies for a short time; but their position was still precarious.

The next fortnight was a very anxious one for the Americans. Though they had possession of the Henderson airfield, the Japanese had regained a measure of control over the adjacent waters, and could reinforce their garrison far more easily than the Americans could. Luckily the Japanese at first only landed troops in driblets, and so failed to drive home their temporary advantage. One thing was plain—that neither side intended to give up the fight and withdraw. Thus was the stage set for one of the longest and fiercest sea struggles in history.

On the 19th of August the Japanese sailed four transports from Rabaul with 1,500 troops to assault Guadalcanal. One light cruiser and four destroyers escorted the transports, but the movement was powerfully covered by Admiral Kondo, who had three carriers, two battleships, five cruisers and seventeen destroyers, which had come south from Truk in the Caroline Islands. Intelligence warned the Americans of these moves, and once more they formed a Task Force of three groups built around the well-tried carriers *Saratoga*, *Enterprise* and *Wasp*, again commanded by Admiral Fletcher. By the 21st they were in the waters south and east of the Solomons awaiting developments. Not till the 24th did the expected sightings take place, and by then the *Wasp's* group had been detached to fuel further south. Kondo's plan rather resembled that adopted at Coral Sea.[1] The small carrier *Ryujo* was to be offered as a bait to attract the main American carrier air blows, thus giving Nagumo the chance to strike back heavily from the fleet carriers *Zuikaku* and *Shokaku*, which were kept away to the westward. At the start this worked out as intended, for the *Saratoga* and *Enterprise* did send their striking forces against the *Ryujo*, and they sank her at 3.50 p.m. on the 24th. But Nagumo's force had also been sighted by then, and the American carriers had their full strength of fighters in the air to meet the expected counter-attacks. The *Enterprise* was hit by three bombs, but she escaped serious damage; and a heavy toll was exacted from attackers. That night Fletcher withdrew southwards, not wishing to risk a night encounter, and Kondo retired in the opposite direction to escape renewed air attacks next day. This fight, called the Battle of the Eastern Solomons, was indecisive; but the advantage lay with the Americans. The enemy landing force which precipitated the

---

[1] See pp. 35–36.

encounter went on towards Guadalcanal, but was attacked from the air on the 25th and suffered some loss. It was then recalled, and the troops were transferred to destroyers, which landed them by night a short time later.

There now ensued a period of balance of an unusual nature in the Solomons. By day command of the air gave the Americans sufficient maritime control to bring in stores and reinforcements, but by night the Japanese light forces commanded those narrow waters; and they could bombard shore positions, land men and hold off any surface ships encountered. Meanwhile the grim struggle on land continued with unabated fury, in appalling conditions.

On the last day of August, while the *Saratoga* was patrolling 260 miles south of Guadalcanal, she was torpedoed by a Japanese submarine. Her aircraft were flown off and sent to reinforce the Henderson Field, but the ship had to return to Pearl Harbour for repairs. It was an unlucky moment to have this valuable and experienced ship put out of action. Fifteen days later worse occurred. The *Wasp*, which we had known so well from her two reinforcements of Malta at a critical time[1], was hit by three torpedoes fired by another enemy submarine. Uncontrollable fires broke out, and this splendid ship had to be abandoned and sunk. At about the same time the battleship *North Carolina* and a destroyer were both hit and damaged by torpedoes, and the carrier *Hornet* was narrowly missed. Although there was a second Japanese submarine in the vicinity she does not seem to have fired any torpedoes, and it is therefore likely that all these successes were achieved by one salvo fired from the submarine I.19. Had this convincing demonstration of the performance of the Japanese torpedoes been realised at the time, we might have been spared some of the losses caused later by them. As the *Enterprise*, like the *Saratoga*, was repairing battle damage, there was now only one carrier left in the South Pacific; and only one modern battleship, the *Washington*, remained. Nor was the solitary carrier *Hornet* destined to survive many days longer. These were two of the comparatively few occasions when Japanese submarines scored important successes. In fact among the many mistakes made by the Japanese must be numbered that of dispersing their substantial submarine strength far and wide in the Indian Ocean and Pacific, in pursuit of quite unimportant targets, instead of concentrating it for use in the vital areas.[2] Now if ever was the chance for the Japanese to avenge Midway; but they entirely failed to seize it.

---

[1] See pp. 59 and 61.

[2] For example the 'midget' submarine attacks on Diego Suarez and Sydney (see p. 192) accomplished little, and absorbed a substantial number of submarines for long periods. Many long and almost fruitless submarine reconnaissances were also made at this time in the Indian Ocean. (See pp. 185 and 271).

Throughout September and early October the battle swung to and fro on land, on the sea and in the air. Heavy losses were suffered by both sides, but neither could oust the other from Guadalcanal. The Americans determined to stop the nightly runs down the 'slot' by Japanese cruisers and destroyers carrying reinforcements, locally known as 'Tokyo Expresses'. Accordingly a Task Force was formed for the purpose, and on the night of the 11th-12th of October it intercepted a Japanese squadron of three heavy cruisers and two destroyers. On this occasion the battle of Savo Island was reversed, for the Japanese were caught unprepared for battle, and lost a large cruiser and two destroyers in those same waters. This encounter, called the Battle of Cape Esperance, was the second of the many deadly night actions between surface forces in the 'slot'; but it did nothing to curb the enemy's efforts. Indeed the Japanese quickened the pace with a heavy bombardment of the Henderson Field by two battleships on the 14th of October, while substantial reinforcements were being landed from transports. The land fighting reached its climax between that date and the 26th, but the Americans managed to cling to the Henderson Field. Meanwhile the *Enterprise* had returned to the South Pacific, where Admiral W. F. Halsey relieved Admiral Ghormley on the 18th as Commander-in-Chief. But the advantage still lay heavily with the enemy, had he but known how to use it; for Yamamoto's main fleet in these waters and in support consisted of no less than five carriers, five battleships, fourteen cruisers and forty-four destroyers.

The sinking of the *Wasp* made no difference to Halsey's determination to give the hard-pressed marines on Guadalcanal every support that lay within his power. His fleet was once again organised in three main groups. The first consisted of the *Enterprise* and the new battleship *South Dakota*, the second of the *Hornet* and cruisers, while the third was composed of the battleship *Washington* and more cruisers. Each group had its own destroyers for screening. Rear-Admiral T. C. Kinkaid in the *Enterprise* was the senior officer afloat. A powerful Japanese force, which included four carriers, was operating near the Santa Cruz Islands with the same broad purpose as Halsey's relative to the fighting on Guadalcanal. Early on the 26th of October Kinkaid was ordered to attack it. Each side's search aircraft sighted the other's carriers at about 6.30 a.m., and the Americans started with the good luck of putting the *Zuiho* out of action with the first of the many bombs dropped that day. Then the main carrier air battle was joined. The *Shokaku* was so severely damaged that she was out of action for nine months; but the Japanese got her home. When the turn came for the *Hornet* and *Enterprise* to shield themselves, the defending fighters were overwhelmed and both ships were hit. The *Enterprise*, after some anxious moments got her damage under control; but the *Hornet* was repeatedly hit, caught fire and had to be abandoned. She finally sank in the small hours of the 27th. The Japanese once again suffered heavy losses in aircraft, but the Battle of Santa Cruz, the fourth carrier air battle to be fought in six months, left the Americans for the second time with only one carrier in the South Pacific, and she was considerably damaged.

The Americans estimated that by the beginning of December the Japanese would have three or four carriers with about 250 aircraft ready for service in the South-West Pacific, besides powerful battleship and cruiser strength. Their assessment of Japanese naval air forces was, we now know, somewhat exaggerated, but the prospective disparity in aircraft carriers caused the United States Navy to turn to its principal Ally with an appeal for help. We will therefore take leave temporarily of the men fighting desperately in, over and around the embattled Solomon Islands to review the messages which passed between London and Washington on the subject. They show how easily two Allies, even two as closely tied together by blood, language and friendship as we and the Americans, can get at cross purposes.

On the 23rd of October the First Sea Lord signalled to Admiral Sir Charles Little, the head of our mission in America and Admiral Pound's representative on the Combined Chiefs of Staff Committee, that Admiral Stark (the head of the American mission in London) had suggested that 'now was a golden opportunity for positive action [by the Eastern Fleet] against the Bay of Bengal or along the Malay barrier'. Professor Morison tells us that this suggestion originated in a letter from Admiral Nimitz to Admiral King.[1] The Admiralty quickly followed up its first message to Washington with another saying that they 'could not discover what they could do to relieve the pressure', and pointed out that Operation 'Torch', which was about to be launched in North Africa, and which had been given overriding strategic priority by both governments, had 'reduced the Eastern Fleet to one carrier and two battleships'. Admiral King was apparently away from Washington when this message arrived, and Admiral Little discovered that his Chief of Staff was wholly in the dark as to who had originated the request for help. However Admiral Little persevered in discovering the American needs, and the reasons for them, and on the 27th he signalled to the First Sea Lord urging that 'one or more of the Eastern Fleet's carriers be sent to Halsey's command'. 'This', said Little, 'is a real cry for immediate help', because the *Hornet* had been sunk and the *Enterprise* was only fifty per cent efficient. Next day Admiral Pound replied that the

[1] See Morison, Vol. V, p. 184.

matter 'raises issues of the gravest importance concerning the ultimate command of the sea'. 'What', he asked, 'are the American dispositions? When and how was the *Hornet* sunk?'[1] Admiral Little was instructed to 'tell King that we are most anxious to help, but must have a clear picture of the whole situation'. In retrospect it does seem surprising that the highest naval authorities in London should have been kept so very much in the dark regarding American dispositions, and events in the Pacific.

On the 30th Little signalled that he had seen King that day, that the American Admiral had resented what he had called 'the catechism' given to him which, so he said, did not make it appear that we wished to help; further that King had said 'he had not asked any questions over giving us Task Force 99'.[2] 'Both of us' said Admiral Little 'were rather ruffled'. None the less that same day Little was able to signal a full statement of American dispositions, and their assessment of the enemy's strength. On the last day of the month the Admiralty tentatively offered a fleet carrier, but asked a lot of technical questions about what aircraft she was to operate. It was they said, impossible to be more definite until operation 'Torch' had been launched, and we knew whether we had suffered any carrier losses in it. Meanwhile Admiral Somerville, Commander-in-Chief, Eastern Fleet, had been asked how he viewed being deprived of his last carrier—a proposition which did not appeal to him at all. On the 6th of December, by which time the success of 'Torch' was well assured, the Admiralty signalled that the *Victorious* was being sent to the Pacific, which left the Home Fleet without a carrier. Admiral Cunningham was therefore asked to release the *Formidable*, since 'two carriers with Force H are a luxury in face of the inactivity of the Italian Fleet'. Finally on the 8th Admiral Little was instructed to tell King that the *Victorious* and three destroyers would be ready to leave the Clyde on the 19th. We will return to the period of her service in the Pacific in a later chapter. By the time she got there and had been re-equipped to use American aircraft, the crisis had, in fact passed.

In retrospect it seems that much of this signalling and most of the misunderstanding would have been avoided had the Admiralty been fully informed of the progress of the Pacific war. Nor was the Admiralty the only place where the lack of information regarding American accomplishments, plans and intentions was felt. Admiral Somerville had quite recently told the First Sea Lord that he was only able to glean such information through unofficial channels in

---

[1] The *Hornet* was actually sunk at 1.35 a.m. (local time) on 27th October in the Battle of Santa Cruz. This was equivalent to 12.35 p.m. on the 27th London time, only about twelve hours before Admiral Pound's signal was despatched.

[2] This was the force commanded by Admiral R. C. Giffen, U.S.N., which came to Scapa in April 1942 (see p. 134). It was originally called Task Force 39.

Australia. It also seems certain that Admiral Nimitz's suggestion about sending a British carrier to the Pacific was passed to London without the American Navy Department having considered all aspects of the problem. Nimitz, of course, could not know all the details of operation 'Torch', though he must have known that it was about to be launched. Admiral King and the Navy Department certainly knew all about it, knew that it had first claim on Allied resources, and that it involved the Royal Navy in very heavy commitments so long as the outcome was in the balance. Had these factors been carefully weighed in Washington, the problem might, even in face of the crisis which had arisen in the Pacific, have been viewed rather differently from the beginning. To send an aircraft carrier to fight on the other side of the world with a strange fleet is, of course, a very different matter from sending one to undertake short ferry operations such as the *Wasp* twice did to reinforce Malta.[1] If the *Victorious* took out her own aircraft complement, she would find no spares or replacements in the Pacific; so it was obviously preferable that she should be re-equipped with American aircraft. Yet her aircrews would certainly have to be re-trained to fly the latter. The technical and human problems involved were undoubtedly serious. That such a transfer was not as simple a matter as Washington seems to have felt, is shown by the fact that after her arrival at Pearl Harbour early in March 1943 some time elapsed before, even with all the help the Americans could give, the *Victorious* was ready to work with their Pacific Fleet.[2]

After this digression we must return to the bitter contest on Guadalcanal. In spite of the failure of their October assaults the Japanese stuck to their intention of capturing the Henderson Field, cost what it might. Early in November cruisers and destroyers poured in reinforcements almost every night. At the same time troops and transports were being concentrated near Rabaul. For the next major attempt the Japanese planned to put the airfield out of action by battleship bombardment, and then run in powerfully escorted transports by day. The Americans were no less determined that their marines should be reinforced, and the enemy's plan defeated. On the 11th and 12th of November seven American transports successfully landed troops and stores under cover of a powerful naval force commanded by Rear-Admiral D. J. Callaghan, U.S.N., and in face of heavy air attacks. The empty transports were sent south on the evening of the 12th. Meanwhile Admiral Callaghan learnt that a large enemy force was coming down the 'slot', so he returned to the anchorage recently vacated by his transports, and prepared to meet the enemy. In the very early hours of the 13th the two forces met

---

[1] See pp. 59 and 61.
[2] See p. 415.

almost head-on, and a furious night battle took place. As is all too likely in such circumstances there was much confusion, and the Americans lost two light cruisers and four destroyers. All their other ships were damaged, and Callaghan's flagship the *San Francisco* received so many hits that her upper works were riddled; but she survived. Admiral Callaghan was killed, as was Admiral Scott of the *Atlanta*, and casualties were very heavy. The Japanese battleship *Hiyei* was crippled in the night action, and was scuttled next day after numerous air attacks[1]; and two Japanese destroyers were also sunk. Though the balance of losses in the first phase of the Battle of Guadalcanal was in the enemy's favour, his intended bombardment of the airfield was frustrated. This enabled American aircraft to destroy all eleven Japanese transports during the next two days, a clean sweep which amply compensated for the warship losses suffered. Two nights later the battle was renewed, and there took place one of the few night actions in which capital ships were involved on both sides. The *Enterprise*, whose damage received on the 26th of October had been hastily patched up, and the 16-inch battleships *Washington* and *South Dakota* under Rear Admiral W. E. Lee, U.S.N., were on their way north from Noumea. The carrier was to support the defenders of Guadalcanal, and the battleships were to dispute control of the waters leading to the island. On the night of the 13th-14th a Japanese cruiser and destroyer force plastered the airfield with shells. On the afternoon of the 14th the *Enterprise's* aircraft sank the heavy cruiser *Kinugasa*, and damaged several other ships which were escorting a troop convoy. Meanwhile the Guadalcanal shore planes attacked the transports and sank seven out of eleven of them. Still the survivors came on, for Kondo was determined to bombard the airfield that night with great strength—the battleship *Kirishima*, four cruisers and nine destroyers. Admiral Halsey had signalled to Lee on the 13th that his 'objective [was the] enemy transports expected . . . for Guadalcanal plus targets encountered'. Thus was the stage set for the meeting between the big ships. Shortly after 10 p.m. Admiral Lee led his two battleships round the north of Savo Island and into the narrow waters where the Japanese had gained their substantial success in the early hours of August the 9th.[2] The encounter was even fiercer than its immediate predecessor. The *Kirishima* was so damaged that she had to be abandoned and sunk, three American and one Japanese destroyer went to the bottom, and the *South Dakota* was heavily hit; but she

---

[1] It is interesting to recall that the *Hiyei* and her three sister ships (laid down 1911–12 in Japanese yards) were designed by Sir George Thurston, one of the most distinguished British naval architects of the time. The large amount of punishment she withstood more than thirty years later, without sinking or blowing up, appears to be a remarkable tribute to the men who designed her. But see p. 236 footnote (1) regarding American torpedo failures.

[2] See pp. 223-225.

managed to withdraw safely. This may justly be claimed as the first solid Allied victory in the Solomons campaign. Apart from his loss of another battleship, the enemy's bombardment was frustrated, and his intention to reinforce his garrison shattered. The four troop-ships which had survived the earlier air attacks were beached, and although 2,000 men got ashore all the stores were lost. In a short time the beached ships too were destroyed. Admiral Lee and the supporting American aircraft had dealt most adequately with the 'plus targets encountered' described in Halsey's terse definition of the battleships' objective.

These hard-fought battles put an end to Japanese attempts to dis-pute control of the narrow waters with their major warships, and they reverted to their earlier practice of sending down destroyers by night with stores and men. To deal with this renewal of the 'Tokyo Expresses' the Americans quickly assembled another strong cruiser and destroyer force. It was not long before it saw action. On the last night of November five American cruisers and six destroyers inter-cepted a column of eight enemy destroyers, which were carrying supplies for Guadalcanal. Although the Americans held the tactical advantage of surprise the Japanese destroyers got away deadly sal-voes of torpedoes, and several found their marks. The heavy cruiser *Northampton* was sunk, and three other cruisers were severely damaged. The American historian has described this action, called the Battle of Tassafaronga, as 'a sharp defeat inflicted on an alert and superior cruiser force by a partially surprised and inferior destroyer force'.[1] The principal error was without doubt to hold the destroyers rigidly in column with the cruisers, instead of freeing them to act independently as a striking force; this led inevitably to the destroyers firing their torpedoes at excessive ranges. But in addition to this the cruisers' gunnery was wildly erratic. We had learnt during the 1914-18 war, and especially from the last phase of the Battle of Jutland[2], that night fighting demanded the most thorough and careful tactical and technical training if confusion was to be avoided; and in the Battle of Cape Matapan, the action off Cape Bon and in many other encounters we reaped the benefits of the constant training undertaken between the wars.[3] It is difficult to say whether the special needs and difficulties of night action had been brought home as forcibly to the United States Navy; but, while admiring the way in which our Allies at once admitted and took energetic steps to rectify their errors, it is certain that the tactical handling of the American squadron was gravely at fault in the Battle of Tassafaronga.

---

[1] Morison, Vol. V, p. 313.

[2] See Sir Julian Corbett, Naval Operations, Vol. III (Longmans, Green & Co., New Edition, 1940), pp. 391-406.

[3] See Vol. I, pp. 427-31 and 534, respectively.

Lastly the Japanese had shown that, in spite of their lack of modern instrumental aids to fire control, their destroyer torpedo, with its long range and exceptionally heavy explosive head, was a weapon to be feared. Many more Allied ships were to experience its effects before 'the slot' was finally cleared of enemy warships.

Tassafaronga was the last of the series of desperately fought night encounters which took place in the southern Solomons. In spite of their success on that occasion the Japanese had, taking the series of battles as a whole, undoubtedly tasted defeat. That they were aware of it is shown by their Navy's desire to withdraw from Guadalcanal towards the end of the year. It was the Japanese Army which insisted that the fight must be continued until a final decision was gained. Accordingly small reinforcements were run down in December; but these only led to more losses among their fast dwindling number of destroyers, and at the end of the year they were reduced to sending in supplies by submarine, much as we had been forced to do for Malta at the crisis of its fortunes.[1] Gradually the condition of the Japanese land garrison deteriorated, and early in 1943 the decision was taken that Guadalcanal should be evacuated within a month. Once again the assertion of maritime control over adjacent waters brought decisive consequences on land.

While all these gruelling sea fights were happening in the Solomons an equally stubborn struggle was taking place in New Guinea for control of the Papuan peninsula. It will be remembered that the Battle of the Coral Sea had frustrated the enemy's purpose of capturing Port Moresby from the sea, and that after that check he decided instead to attack the base overland by crossing the wild and precipitous Owen Stanley mountains.[2] To further this purpose a base and an airfield on the north coast of New Guinea was essential, and the Japanese selected the small port of Buna for these purposes.[3] By the end of August 12,000 men had been landed there, and the advance across the mountains towards Moresby begun. After fierce fighting the Australians stopped the enemy in the mountains, and by the end of September he was in full retreat. Meanwhile the Allies had occupied Milne Bay on the south-east tip of Papua, and were thereby able to repel a Japanese landing on the flank of the defenders of Port Moresby. By October a strong offensive against Buna had been started by the Australians and Americans. As so often in these island campaigns, possession of an airfield, or even of a jungle landing strip was the critical object. That near Buna was the key to the hold on the Papuan peninsula, and its possession was most stubbornly contested. In spite of appalling conditions, fighting in as

[1] See pp. 60, 301, 308 and 312.
[2] See pp. 35–36 and 42.
[3] See Map 5 (opp. p. 33).

bad a climate as can be found anywhere in the tropics, and having to endure the ravages of disease, the Allied troops persevered. On Christmas Day the surviving remnants of the Japanese garrison of Buna received orders to evacuate the base.

In the New Guinea campaign the chief problem of the maritime services was to provide adequate and suitable sea transport for the support and supply of the troops. The naval forces in General Mac-Arthur's command were very slender, and almost wholly lacked the light craft so essential to combined operations. To employ transports and to escort them with cruisers and destroyers, even had these been available, would have tempted providence too far; for command of the air off the New Guinea coast was certainly not assured to the Allies. The solution was found in using Dutch and Australian coasting vessels, whose crews were familiar with those waters, and also native craft. Their services were of great value in ferrying troops along a coast which had only been inadequately surveyed many years previously. They were supported by light warships of the Royal Australian Navy, and together they proved adequate, if extemporised, substitutes for specially designed and properly equipped landing craft.

Before leaving the Pacific theatre it may be well to survey briefly the far-reaching campaign against the enemy's sea communications. In the first six months of the Pacific war the Japanese had gained control of a vast and scattered empire. Conquest had proved comparatively easy, but to exploit the resources of the captured territories and to sustain garrisons thousands of miles away from their home bases demanded a very large merchant navy. This simple need, so well known to Britain from her centuries of experience of the connection between imperial requirements and the sea, seems to have been inadequately understood by the Japanese. They embarked on their plan of aggression with only some six million tons of merchant shipping, which was barely sufficient to support their peace time economy. Though Japan gained about 800,000 tons of shipping from captures in the Far East, she still possessed nothing like adequate tonnage to meet her greatly increased commitments. Her losses in the first year's fighting reached the considerable total of a million tons; but in spite of this her rulers made little effort to build new merchant ships, or even to protect adequately those that they possessed. Surprising though it is in a maritime nation like Japan, merchant navy tonnage seems to have been regarded as readily expendable, and not as a vital war asset. To the Americans, as to ourselves, the vulnerability of Japan's long lines of communications was very plain, and our Ally immediately embarked on a large programme of submarine construction in order to attack them. There were over seventy American submarines in the Pacific at the beginning, and about the same number of new boats were building; but their accomplishments remained disappointing for a long time. One factor which contributed to this was the poor performance and unreliability of American torpedoes.[1] Immediate steps were taken to rectify these defects, but the results did not become apparent until the next phase. It is a curious fact that two nations as skilled in engineering design and production as Germany and the United States both entered the war with inefficient torpedoes.[2] By contrast the Japanese torpedo was, as was mentioned earlier, a deadly weapon. It thus happened that at the end of 1942 the Achilles' Heel of the whole structure of Japan's strategy had not yet been subjected to sustained and effective attack.

While all the bitter fighting so far described was taking place in the Pacific, the Indian Ocean remained relatively quiet. But after the shock which we had suffered from Nagumo's and Ozawa's forays in the preceding April[3], the Admiralty was bound to feel anxious lest a repetition should be attempted. In retrospect it seems that the effects of the American victory of Midway, the consequences of the many battles fought near the Solomons, and Japan's obvious preoccupation with the campaign in those waters were not fully allowed for in London. Be that as it may, it is now abundantly plain that after the middle of the year there was never any real possibility of the Japanese making another foray in force into the Indian Ocean. The Admiralty, however, with the vulnerability of the vital WS convoys always in its mind, felt bound to reinforce Admiral Somerville as powerfully as possible. In May the aircraft carrier *Illustrious* joined his flag, but much of his strength was detached for the attack on Madagascar.[4] Moreover, the *Indomitable* and several destroyers were then ordered home to help fight the August convoy through to Malta.[5]

The diversionary movement staged in the Indian Ocean at the end of July to coincide with the launching of the American assault on the southern Solomons was mentioned earlier.[6] Soon after the Eastern Fleet returned to harbour from that operation, the Admiralty called home another of Somerville's carriers to replace the *Indomitable*, which had been damaged in the Malta convoy and could not be ready again in time to play her part in the invasion of North

[1] For example Morison V pp. 221–222 describes the difficulty experienced in sinking the crippled *Hornet*. No less than sixteen torpedoes were fired at her, and nine of them hit. The Japanese battleship *Hiyei* also survived numerous hits by American torpedoes (see p. 232). At least two were seen to hit, but rebounded off her side without exploding.
[2] See Vol. I, p. 164, regarding early German torpedo failures.
[3] See pp. 23–31.
[4] See pp. 185–191.
[5] Operation 'Pedestal'. See pp. 302–308.
[6] See pp. 222-223.

Africa. The *Formidable* therefore left the Eastern Fleet on the 24th of August and, although the battleship *Valiant* had meanwhile joined Admiral Somerville's flag, his strength remained at a low ebb.

It thus happened that the Admiralty's many other pressing commitments from the Arctic to the Mediterranean prevented Somerville gaining any permanent and substantial increase in strength. By the end of August the fast squadron which provided the main deterrent against another Japanese incursion into the Indian Ocean consisted only of the *Illustrious, Warspite, Valiant* and two or three cruisers; and he had less than half a dozen destroyers with which to screen his fleet. Nor did matters improve in the autumn, when Somerville was first required to support the extension of operations southward from Diego Suarez in Madagascar, and then had to detach most of his destroyer strength to counter the heavy U-boat attacks which had just started off the Cape of Good Hope.[1] As Somerville remarked at this time to the First Sea Lord 'the carrier striking force is at present a very poor thing. Much as I dislike having to hold off at all, I do feel very strongly that we must try to exploit our *night* striking to the utmost. I am convinced we have the advantage there, but I realise that good luck as well as good management will be wanted to bring off a night strike before the enemy can strike by day'.

The Prime Minister had for some time shown impatience over the apparent inactivity of the Eastern Fleet, and on the 15th of October he urged the First Sea Lord to consider whether its big ships could not be put to more profitable use in the Mediterranean. In his reply Admiral Pound said that 'the absence of Japanese surface ships in the Indian Ocean has, I think, given us an unjustified feeling of security. The Eastern Fleet is desperately weak. Every further detachment is an invitation to the Japanese to operate in the Indian Ocean. I am of the opinion therefore that we have reached a position in which we should risk neither capital ships nor carriers except to achieve some great purpose'. The Prime Minister replied that in accepting Admiral Pound's view he must not be deemed to agree with all the Naval Staff's arguments, and that in his opinion idle ships were a reproach. A week later came the request from the Navy Department for the loan of one or two British carriers to tide over the crisis which had arisen in the Pacific.[2]

As we look back today at these events it is very hard to see what more Admiral Somerville and the Admiralty could have done in the Indian Ocean. It was not as though the Commander-in-Chief possessed a well-trained, stable and properly integrated fleet. Ever since he arrived on the station ships had been taken away as often

---

[1] See pp. 269–271.
[2] See pp. 229–231.

as others had joined his flag; and in April he had been shown in no uncertain way what sort of opposition he might have to contend with. His deficiencies in such vital matters as bases and the shore-based air element of maritime power have already been recounted, as have the numerous extraneous commitments which he had some-how to meet. The truth is that we were still trying to fight a five-ocean war with, at the best, a two-ocean Navy. In such circumstances Somerville could only cling to the essential need to keep the WS convoys inviolate, and to preserve the flow of shipping in and across the Indian Ocean. Offensive operations must wait on an increase in his strength and a better balance in its composition.

The Admiralty's heavy cares are even more easily understood. Quite apart from the everlasting struggle in the Atlantic, in the Arctic we had taken a heavy knock in the disaster to PQ. 17 in July[1]; and we were faced with a very powerful German surface squadron permanently threatening the exposed flank of the Russian convoy route. In the Mediterranean the August convoy to Malta had fared ill, and we had suffered heavy losses.[2] Anxiety for the safety of the island on which so much, including the fate of our armies in Africa, depended was at its most acute. And looming daily nearer was the launching of operation 'Torch'. We simply could not afford to take a gamble over the success of 'Torch' by risking elsewhere the many and powerful ships which were needed for it. In war it is sometimes hardest of all to refrain from activity; yet the need to conserve one's strength for concentration at the vital point remains paramount. In the autumn of 1942 'Torch' was the accepted first priority, and what the Admiralty was trying to do was to ensure its success without sacrificing any other essential. Surely that must be assessed as the essence of sound strategy. Somerville's weakness and his enforced inactivity was one of the prices we had to pay to accomplish a greater purpose than anything that could be gained in his theatre. No-one who knew that forceful commander would ever suggest that he accepted inactivity willingly.

---

[1] See pp. 136-145.
[2] See pp. 302-308.

CHAPTER X

COASTAL WARFARE

1st August–31st December, 1942

'At half-past one a.m. we got within half
gunshot of the Mole head, without being
discovered, when the alarm bells rang and
30 or 40 pieces of cannon, with musketry
from one end of the Town to the other,
opened upon us'.

Nelson's Journal, 25th July 1797. (The
unsuccessful attack on Santa Cruz,
Tenerife).

THE well-known capacity of a maritime power to fling small
bodies of well trained men ashore for short periods at widely
separated points on an enemy-held coastline, and the way in
which its continental enemies are thereby forced to hold quite dis-
proportionate numbers of troops in useless garrison duties, were
commented on earlier[1]; and some of the raids made in accordance
with this principle have already appeared briefly in this history. In
the spring of 1942 a number of factors, political and moral as well as
military, contributed to the decision to undertake a cross-Channel
raid on a much larger scale than had so far been attempted. There
was at that time a widespread, if ill-informed, agitation, fostered by
persons whose political opinions lay far to the left, to form 'a second
front now'.[2] In so far as this agitation was a sincere and genuine
expression of admiration for the stubborn courage of the Russian
soldiers, and of appreciation of the fact that it was they who were
doing most of the fighting against the German army, our Government was in full sympathy with it. Measures to take some of the
weight off Russia were constantly discussed by the Cabinet and
Chiefs of Staff.

By August operation 'Sledgehammer', which was in effect the
'second front now' in western Europe demanded by the agitators,
had been abandoned as militarily impracticable in 1942.[3] Neither
trained men nor specialised equipment were available in anything
like the quantities needed to assault a powerfully fortified coastline,

[1] See Vol. I, pp. 513–4.
[2] See Darke. *The Communist Technique in Britain* (Collins, 1953), pp. 77–8.
[3] See Churchill, Vol. IV, pp. 288–291 and 391–392.

let alone to establish a large army there hard on the heels of the assault troops. Such considerations were, however, no hindrance to the demands of the amateur strategists, few of whom had any idea of the carnage which past failures in combined operations had entailed, or had stopped to consider how much costlier a failure might be in the face of the fire-power of modern weapons. The agitators could wage their campaign, and daub their slogans on walls, in the safe knowledge that it would not be their bodies which would be heaped up on the beaches, below gun positions which had not been put out of action before the assault. Moreover those same enthusiasts would probably have been the leaders of an outcry against the responsible authorities, had a disastrous failure, such as their demands invited, been incurred. The Cabinet and Chiefs of Staff, were, of course, fully aware of all these perils; and, although the agitations of the left had no influence upon their deliberations, there remained in their minds a desire to do all they could to discourage the Germans from reducing their garrisons in the west to reinforce their armies in the east.

There was stationed in Britain at this time a large number of troops many of whom, and especially Canadians, had come over-seas to fight the Germans, and had not yet seen any fighting, or any Germans. Idleness in war can destroy the morale of the finest units, and the desire to help Russia fitted in well with the need to find active employment for these fine but as yet untried soldiers. Further-more the War Office was insistent that, before a full scale invasion was launched in Europe, it was essential to gain up-to-date experience by making a raid in force against the enemy-held coastline. The Chief of Combined Operations was accordingly ordered to use the Canadian troops in such an operation. Lastly there was no longer the acute shortage of weapons and equipment which had cramped our strategy everywhere throughout the first thirty months or so of the war; and a great deal of new material, some of it not yet tried out in battle, was being produced specifically for overseas assaults. Ex-perience under action conditions might produce valuable data, to the benefit of the later and much larger landings.

After careful discussion of alternatives it was decided, in April, that Dieppe alone 'provided worth while' military objectives, while ful-filling certain other essential needs. There were in its vicinity a radar station, a fighter airfield and four heavy-gun batteries, besides the port, docks and shipping, and various naval or military installations the destruction of which would be an embarrassment, if a minor one, to the enemy. And Dieppe lay within easy range of our shore-based fighters—a condition which we had learnt at no small cost to be essential to the success of any combined operation. But there were other factors which made Dieppe far from an ideal place to choose for an assault. It was heavily defended on both sides of the harbour, and there were high cliffs from which the sea approaches were easily commanded. Except at the town itself openings in the cliffs were few and small, the beaches were narrow, and rocky ledges restricted the state of the tide at which landing craft could approach. Lastly a wall with no breaches in it defended the town itself against invasion from the sea, as well as from encroachments by the sea.

In April planning was begun in Combined Operations Head-quarters. Two alternatives were discussed at length. The first was to make a frontal assault on Dieppe itself, and to support it by seaborne and airborne landings on both flanks, while in the second plan there would be no frontal assault. The Army favoured the frontal assault, chiefly because the flank landings had to be made so far away from the town that surprise was bound to be lost by the time the attack on the main object took place. Naval opinion was worried about the hazards of a frontal assault, but considered it possible to land the soldiers for that purpose, if the risks to the latter were acceptable. Another difficult question was whether to bomb the town and har-bour just before the landing. British policy then was to avoid bombing French towns by night and, although the Prime Minister agreed to relax the rule in this instance, it was finally decided not to bomb the place. The reasons were that the bombing might merely alert the enemy—as was believed to have happened in the case of the St. Nazaire raid[1]—and that the destruction of houses might prevent our own tanks penetrating into the town. Later experience leads one to believe that these arguments against air bombardment were not altogether sound; and their acceptance may well have contributed to the failure of the raid. Be that as it may, the decision to cancel the bombing did not lead to a demand to increase cor-respondingly the naval supporting gunfire. It seems that this was partly because there was still marked reluctance in naval circles to expose heavy ships to the inevitable risks from bombs and mines, and partly because our long experience of engaging coast defences with warships' guns had not generally produced happy results. After it was all over, the Naval Force Commander and the Commander-in-Chief, Portsmouth, both independently expressed a regret that a battleship had not been present; and the former considered that one 'would probably have turned the tide in our favour'.

There now followed a series of alterations to the plan, and post-ponements of the operation. Then, on the 7th of July enemy aircraft hit with bombs the two assault ships, which were lying with their troops on board off Yarmouth (Isle of Wight). At the time it was feared that the attack might indicate fore-knowledge by the enemy of our intentions; but it is now known that this was not the case. As the

---

[1] See p. 170.

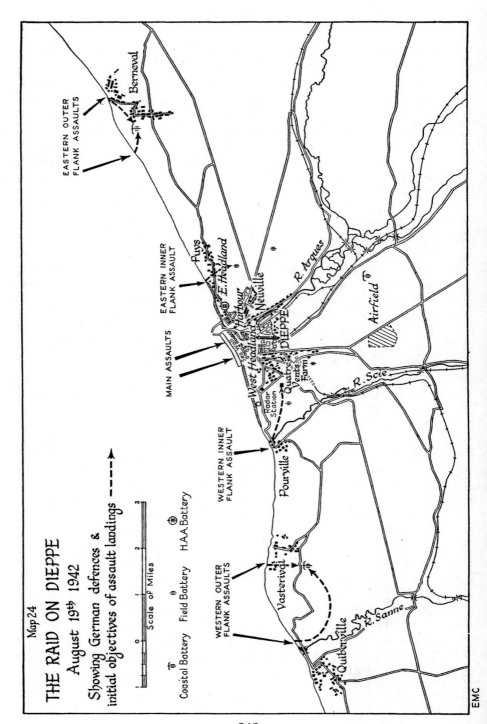

Map 24

THE RAID ON DIEPPE
August 19th 1942
Showing German defences &
initial objectives of assault landings - - - ▶

Scale of Miles
0   1   2   3

⫟ Coastal Battery   ⫟ Field Battery   ⊕ H.A.A. Battery

EASTERN OUTER
FLANK ASSAULTS

Berneval

EASTERN INNER
FLANK ASSAULT

Puys

E. Headland

Harbour

Neuville

R. Arques

Airfield

MAIN ASSAULTS

West Headland

DIEPPE

Radar
Station

Quatre
Vents
Farm

R. Scie

WESTERN INNER
FLANK ASSAULT

Pourville

WESTERN OUTER
FLANK ASSAULTS

Vasterival

Quiberville

R. Sanne

EMC

weather continued unsuitable for the employment of airborne troops, the operation was now cancelled.

Later in July revival of the operation in a modified form was discussed. Mr Churchill was strongly in favour of going ahead, but the security risk was serious, because of the large number of men who had been briefed for the attack before it was cancelled. To mitigate this risk nothing was committed to paper, and the decision to remount the operation was taken by the Prime Minister in consultation only with Admiral Mountbatten, the Chief of Combined Operations, and the Chiefs of Staff.

There were now to be three landings on each flank of Dieppe, and two in the main frontal assault.[1] The airborne landings were cancelled—a fact on which the enemy later commented with surprise—and Commandos were introduced in substitution. On the 17th of July Captain J. Hughes-Hallett was appointed Naval Force Commander. The Military and Air Force Commanders, Major-General J. H. Roberts, commanding the 2nd Canadian Division, and Air Vice-Marshal T. Leigh-Mallory respectively, had already been appointed.

The naval forces taking part can be summarised as follows:

Destroyers	8
Landing Ships Infantry	9
Coastal Craft (Gunboats, Launches, etc.)	39
Landing Craft	179
Miscellaneous	2
TOTAL	237

This fleet was to carry across, land and re-embark a total of 4,961 officers and men of the Canadian Army, 1,057 Commandos and a small number of United States Rangers. The air forces allocated to support and protect the raiding forces comprised 67 squadrons, all but seven of them composed of fighters. In its final form the plan provided for two landings to be made on each side of Dieppe at dawn 'nautical twilight' (i.e. when the sun was 12 degrees below the horizon), followed half an hour later by the main assault on the town. The outer flank attacks were to capture the heavy gun batteries near their landing points, and those on the inner flanks were to seize another battery and a strong-point, after which the troops were to assault the heights commanding the town from the rear. Certain units from the flank landings were to move inland against the enemy fighter airfield and his local headquarters, while the main frontal attack was to capture, and for a time hold the town.

Supporting bombardments would only come from the destroyers' 4-inch guns, but certain specially equipped landing craft would give

---

[1] See Map 24 (p. 242).

close support during the landings.[1] None of these, however, mounted
a larger gun than 4-inch, and most of them only had much smaller
weapons. The five enemy coast defence batteries near the town were
known to mount a total of about twenty guns, many of them 5·9-
inch naval weapons[2]; and in addition to these there were many
anti-aircraft batteries, some of which could be put to low-angle use,
and also dozens of automatic weapons sited in well-defended strong
points.

Air bombardment of the town having been declined, the co-
operation of the R.A.F. was limited to attacking the headlands above
the town and the enemy batteries, and to shrouding the headlands
in smoke which, so it was hoped, would mask their fire. The enemy,
in his subsequent study of British actions and motives, found 'the
behaviour and employment of British air strength strange'. He considered it 'incomprehensible why, at the beginning of the landing,
the bridgehead of Dieppe and other points of disembarkation were
not subjected to continuous air bombardment, to prevent or at
least delay the arrival of local reserves'.

In retrospect it is plain that the plan suffered from several serious
defects. The first was the excessive reliance placed on surprise, in
conditions where complete surprise was unlikely to be achieved.
Even if the flank attacks caught the enemy unprepared, the town's
defenders were bound to be fully alerted before the main assault was
launched. Secondly the weight and strength of supporting fire—
both close and distant—was nothing like adequate to deal with
defences of such power and density. Lastly the plan was extremely
complicated. Not only were a great number of different objects
defined and allocated, and great exactitude of timing demanded,
but there was a lack of flexibility in many directions. For example
the main landings' success obviously depended on that of the flank
attackers, and on our aircraft and ships neutralising the guns on the
commanding headlands; the tanks could not get into the town until
the sappers had blown up the anti-tank obstructions on the promenade behind the sea wall; if the tanks did not get into the town to
deal with enemy strong points the infantry must be pinned to the
beaches. If anything considerable went awry in timing, or in
achieving the initial objects, the whole operation must be jeopardised. The enemy, who captured and quickly translated and circulated complete copies of the operation orders, considered that
'their detailed nature contained the germs of failure should unforeseen

---

[1] The contemporary names of these types of landing craft were:—

L.C.F.(L).   Landing Craft Flak (Large). Converted Landing Craft Tank, of about
                400 tons mostly armed with eight 2-pounder guns.
L.C.S.(M).   Landing Craft Support (Medium). Mounted one 4-inch smoke mortar
                and a twin 0·5-inch machine gun.

[2] See Map 24 (p. 242).

difficulties arise' and that 'the operation was executed with almost too much precision and detailed arrangement'. There is a certain irony in this German criticism of British excess of detail and inflexibility in planning; for we are inclined to consider such faults essentially teutonic.

The Naval Force Commander seems to have been uneasy over the risks involved. Shortly before sailing he described the operation as 'unusually complex and hazardous'. This was probably a reflection of the feeling among the naval planners ever since the early days that, while the frontal attack could certainly be carried out, the risks were very high. Centuries of experience, and many failures, had taught the Royal Navy the dangers of assault from the sea against intact defence works manned by an alerted garrison.

On the morning of the 17th of August orders were given for the expedition to sail on the night of the 18th-19th. The flank attacks were to take place at 4.50 a.m. and the main landings half an hour later. Embarkation of the troops and of fifty-eight 'Churchill' tanks took place on the 17th and 18th, and went according to plan. Two flotillas of minesweepers sailed first, to clear a channel through the enemy minefield, and by the time the main expedition arrived this had been completed. The naval forces were divided into thirteen groups, mostly composed of various types of landing ships and craft, and sailed from Portsmouth, Newhaven and Shoreham. In addition to these there was the escorting and supporting force of eight *Hunt*-class destroyers, and a number of coastal craft (motor gunboats and motor launches). The Naval and Military Force Commanders embarked in the destroyer *Calpe*. As the moon set before midnight most of the passage was made in darkness. In spite of this there were few deviations from the intricate time-table. Once clear of the minefield the ships and craft started to form up for the approach.

The reader will understand more clearly what followed if a somewhat detailed description of the situation at about 3 a.m. on the 19th is given. In the van with their escorting craft were the landing ships shown in Table 15 (p. 246). Astern of these came the destroyers *Calpe* and *Fernie*, the gunboat *Locust* with the Royal Marine Commando, and then motor launches carrying the reinforcements for the western inner flank attack (the Cameron Highlanders of Canada) and the floating reserve (the Fusiliers Mont Royal). The tank landing craft followed in the rear.

The landing ships now made for their allotted positions about ten miles offshore. Between 3.0 and 3.20 a.m. they lowered their craft, and the assault troops transferred to them. The landing ships then turned for home, their task completed almost exactly on time, while the assault craft formed up ready to be led to their various beaches. A diversion was meanwhile being staged off Boulogne.

Table 15. *The Raid on Dieppe. Operation 'Jubilee'*

Forces taking part

Landing Ships Infantry	Troops	Landing
Prins Albert . . .	No. 4 Commando	Western Outer Flank
Prinses Beatrix ⎫ . . *Invicta* . ⎭	South Saskatchewan Regiment	Western Inner Flank
Queen Emma ⎫ . . *Prinses Astrid* ⎭	Royal Regiment of Canada	Eastern Inner Flank
One group of landing craft	No. 3 Commando	Eastern Outer Flank
These were followed by:		
Glengyle . ⎫ *Prince Charles* ⎬ . . *Prince Leopold* ⎭	Royal Hamilton Light Infantry and Canadian Essex Scottish	Dieppe beaches
Duke of Wellington . .		Reinforcements for eastern inner flank

Just when all seemed set to achieve surprise—for the enemy had still shown no sign of life—an unfortunate chance encounter took place. At 3.47 a.m. a group of landing craft carrying the commandos destined for the eastern outer flank attack suddenly ran into an escorted German convoy, and a sharp engagement followed. The landing craft were delayed and fell into considerable disorder. It is not clear how far this engagement alerted the enemy at Dieppe. The German naval headquarters at first considered it to be only another affray between light forces, but the German army's report says that it caused 'the alarm [to be] given to the coastal defence', and attributes our loss of surprise to this encounter.

The senior officer of the British group's escort tried to fight his way through, but was disabled. The destroyers, whose function it was to protect the landing craft, did not intervene because their senior officer mistakenly thought the gunfire came from the shore. Of the twenty-three landing craft in the group only seven reached their allotted beach and landed their troops.

An unexplained feature of this sudden and confusing encounter is that no radar set in the warships seems to have picked up the enemy convoy as it closed the expedition. It is true that it was our practice in Channel operations to rely mainly on information regarding enemy movements being relayed to our ships from the shore radar stations; furthermore the presence of so many friendly vessels may have confused the ships' radar screens. None the less one hour before the clash the Commander-in-Chief, Portsmouth, warned the Naval Force Commander of the presence of unidentified vessels on a course which would probably bring them into contact with the group of landing craft. The significance of this warning seems to have been realised in the destroyer *Fernie* (stand-by H.Q. Ship), but not in the

Calpe. The most serious result was the crippling of the attack on the eastern outer flank, for the small number of men landed could not possibly accomplish the seizure of the 'Goebbels' battery which was the target allotted to No. 3 Commando.[1]

On the eastern outer flank there thus was an almost total failure, though a small party did get close to the battery. They engaged it most gallantly, subdued it temporarily and then managed to re-embark. On the eastern inner flank, on which the success of the main landing greatly depended, the landing craft were sixteen minutes late, and daylight was breaking. Here complete reliance had been placed on surprise, and no covering bombardment had been arranged. The troops quickly came under a withering fire, and suffered heavy casualties. Only a very small number even succeeded in getting off the beach. The failure was complete; and its effect on the frontal assault was bound to be serious. Desperate but vain attempts at evacuation were made, and the Royal Regiment of Canada suffered terrible losses—all but three of the twenty-nine officers taking part and 459 out of 516 men were killed, wounded or missing.

In happy, but unfortunately not in decisive contrast to these failures on the eastern flank, a complete success was obtained on the western outer flank. Lieutenant-Colonel Lord Lovat and 250 men of No. 4 Commando landed on time without opposition, and finally captured the 'Hess' battery at the bayonet's point. At 7.30 the commandos re-embarked, bringing their wounded with them. It had been 'a model for future operations of this kind', and the casualties had been light.

On the western inner flank the South Saskatchewan Regiment and the Cameron Highlanders of Canada landed successfully and moved off to attack their objectives, some of which they captured; but the initial success could not be maintained in face of enemy reinforcements and the failure of the intended junction with troops and tanks coming from the town. We will return shortly to the gallant but largely unsuccessful attempt to evacuate these troops later in the forenoon, for it is necessary first to recount the outcome of the main landings. The failure on the eastern flank, and the partial success on the western one had left the enemy in full possession of the batteries and strong points on the heights commanding the Dieppe beaches from both sides. None the less the main assault was proceeded with.

The landing craft beached almost exactly on time. As soon as the destroyer bombardment and air attacks had stopped, the enemy opened up a murderous fire on the beaches, which were enfiladed from concealed weapons in the cliffs. The tanks followed the assault

---

[1] See Map 24 (p. 242).

parties; but they were slightly late—and even that small delay had the most serious consequences. The tank landing craft suffered heavily, but twenty-seven of the thirty tanks in the 'first wave' were landed. At the time it was believed that the sea wall had proved a serious obstacle to the tanks, but it is now known that this was not the case except in the centre, where a ditch had been dug in front of the wall. The tanks had no great difficulty in surmounting the wall at either end, where it was only about two feet high. About half of the twenty-seven tanks which got ashore successfully gained the promenade behind the sea wall; but there they were stopped by road blocks, which the sappers tried valiantly but unsuccessfully to breach. No tanks succeeded in forcing their way off the promenade into the town.[1] The failure of the tanks sealed the fate of the infantry. The destroyers, landing craft and coastal craft did their best to support the troops and silence the enemy weapons, but their guns were not big enough to accomplish much. 'At no time was the support which the ships were able to give sufficient for the purpose'. The result was a costly failure. Not even the whole of the beaches could be properly secured. None the less at about 7 a.m. General Roberts, who was throughout severely handicapped by lack of accurate information about how matters were going on shore, sent in his floating reserve—the Fusiliers Mont Royal. Most of them were put ashore, but under such heavy fire that they could accomplish little and suffered cruelly. The Royal Marine Commando, originally intended for a cutting-out expedition into the harbour, was now placed at the disposal of the Military Force Commander. It seems that in the Headquarters Ship there was no clear idea of how desperate the situation was on shore; for it was decided to use the marines to reinforce the main landing beaches. They moved in at 8.30 escorted by Free French patrol craft. It was in truth 'a sea parallel of the Charge of the Light Brigade', for as soon as they cleared the smoke the landing craft came under a murderous fire from every conceivable weapon. Lieutenant-Colonel J. P. Phillipps, who was in command of the marines managed, at the cost of his own life, to signal to the rear landing craft to return, and so saved about 200 of his men. That marked the end of the frontal assault on Dieppe. It remained only to try to rescue the survivors. By 9 a.m. the Military Force Commander considered that capture of the headlands was unlikely, and so the main attack must fail. The rest of the tanks were therefore sent home. The time laid down in the orders for withdrawal was 11 a.m.; but when the Force Commanders wished to advance it by half an hour it was pointed out that this

---

[1] See Colonel C. P. Stacey *The Canadian Army 1939–45*, (Published by authority of the Minister of National Defence, Ottawa, 1948) for a full account of the landing of the Churchill tanks.

The Raid on Dieppe, Operation 'Jubilee', 19th August 1942. Naval forces on passage.

The Raid on Dieppe, 19th August 1942. Assault craft making for the beaches under cover of smoke.

The scene on the beach at Dieppe after the raid, 19th August 1942.

would upset the R.A.F.'s time-table for laying the protective smoke screen. The lack of flexibility in the orders thus condemned the troops ashore to a prolongation of their agony.

Shortly before 11 a.m. about a dozen of the larger and better protected landing craft were sent to rescue the troops which had landed on the western inner flank. Under very heavy fire the survivors of the South Saskatchewan Regiment and the Cameron Highlanders tried to reach the landing craft. Many waded out to sea, which made embarkation much too slow. When a landing craft reached the beach there was sometimes a rush, and the ramps became choked with dead and wounded. Some craft were disabled and abandoned on the beach, others were hit and sunk on the way off. Destroyers and gunboats did their best to cover the withdrawal, but there were too few of them, and their guns were not heavy enough. None the less two assault landing craft (L.C.As 250 and 315) each made three trips into this inferno, while the South Saskatchewan's Commanding Officer (Lieutenant-Colonel C. C. I. Merritt) formed a rearguard, and kept the enemy off the beach itself. They fought until their ammunition was exhausted. At 12.15 the last landing craft approached the beach. There was then no movement on it.

Off Dieppe itself the attempt to fetch away the troops fared no better. Smoke, blowing inshore, shrouded the landing craft until they were close to the beaches, and also partially obscured the vision of the enemy gunners; but it blinded the gunfire of our own covering warships as well. As soon as the landing craft cleared the smoke they came under withering fire. The plan was to ferry troops off in the assault craft to the larger tank landing craft, which were to lie a mile out. But many of the former were sunk, and some of the larger vessels, which tried to help matters by moving closer inshore, suffered a similar fate. Again, understandably if disastrously, soldiers rushed a vessel as soon as it beached. At 11.30 the destroyers moved in closer to give stronger supporting fire; but the result was that the *Brocklesby* and *Fernie* were both soon hit. L.C.A. 186 visited both the Dieppe landing beaches at about noon. She picked up thirty men swimming in the water. Only two were seen alive on the beaches, which had become a shambles of wrecked landing craft, burning tanks and equipment—and of British or Canadian dead. She was the last vessel to leave.

At 12.20 the officer in charge of the evacuation reported that no more could be done; ten minutes later he withdrew the surviving landing craft. They had, under conditions of utmost difficulty and danger, rescued over 1,000 men. When one considers the tornado of fire that was being directed at the beaches, their accomplishment appears all the more astonishing. At 12.40 the *Calpe* closed the shore to see if there was any possibility of further rescue. She too came under heavy fire; and no troops could then be seen in a position from which they might be picked up.

At about 1 p.m. a general withdrawal of the surviving ships and craft began. German air attacks were now almost continuous. The destroyer *Berkeley* was so damaged that she had to be sunk by our own forces, and the *Calpe* also was hit. Thereafter, as the main body of landing craft and coastal craft steamed away, they were effectively shielded by Royal Air Force fighters. Fresh forces met the returning expedition, and escorted the small vessels to Newhaven. The destroyers and the gunboat *Locust* reached Portsmouth soon after midnight, with over 500 wounded aboard.

The air fighting, which had started on a comparatively small scale, increased in fury and intensity as the day progressed. Our bombing was only on a very small scale, and did not succeed in hampering the enemy shore guns substantially. Enemy bombers concentrated their attention on our ships but, except for sinking the *Berkeley*, did us no great damage. Our fighters did splendid work in attacking shore positions, but their weapons were not heavy enough to influence the fighting decisively. Their protection of the expedition during the withdrawal was, however, most successful. We lost 106 aircraft, eighty-eight of them fighters, while the enemy's losses were twenty-five bombers and twenty-three fighters. The disparity between our own and the enemy's aircraft losses can partly be accounted for by the distance from their home bases at which ours were operating.

The casualties among the Canadian Army and the commandos were very heavy. Of the 4,961 Canadians engaged 3,363 (68 per cent) became casualties, as did 247 of the 1,057 commandos. About 2,200 of the British and Canadian 'missing' were, however, taken prisoner. In addition the Navy lost one destroyer and thirty-three landing craft and had 550 casualties, while the Royal Air Force had 190 casualties. We lost all the thirty tanks which reached, or tried to reach, the shore. The enemy's losses, were, comparatively speaking light, and amounted to only about 600 from all three Services.

The enemy was, not unnaturally, jubilant at having 'repelled' an expedition (it was actually never intended to stay ashore for more than a few hours) which he considered might have been the advance-guard of a larger force. He was, as already mentioned, critical of our detailed planning, of our failure to bomb the perimeter of the bridgehead continuously and heavily, of the main forces of troops and tanks being thrown into the frontal attack on Dieppe, and of our failure to use parachute or airborne troops. He considered that, if airborne troops had landed on the eastern flank, and tanks had supported the western attack (which we had actually considered doing but had rejected), things might have turned out very differently; and one must admit that in the wisdom of after events his judgement on those points now seems sound. But in one important respect the conclusions drawn by the enemy were wholly erroneous. The Germans decided that the Dieppe raid indicated that, when the time came for the Allies to invade the European continent in earnest, their initial thrust would be aimed at capturing a large port. It is likely that this false deduction contributed greatly to the successful landing on the Normandy beaches in June 1944.

On our own side the lessons learnt were many, and were promptly put into practice. We had learnt at no small cost in Norway, Greece, Crete, Malaya and indeed in all theatres of the war, that command of the air was an essential pre-requisite for success in landings from the sea. We put those hard-bought lessons to good effect in the Dieppe raid by allocating great fighter strength to the operation. But we seem perhaps to have allowed this new and essential need to obscure an older and just as essential one—namely that enemy fixed defences must be destroyed, or at least neutralised, before troops are flung ashore within range of their guns. The supporting fire provided was nothing like adequate. Off Dieppe the heavy guns of long-range bombarding ships and the rocket and gunfire of close support vessels were shown to be as essential as adequate air cover. Though it anticipates events, it is perhaps permissible here to remark that the landing at Salerno in September 1943 might have ended in disaster on a vastly greater scale than the failure at Dieppe had not the gunfire of the heavy warships, in Admiral Cunningham's words, 'held the ring when there was danger of the enemy breaking through to the beaches'.[1]

From the naval point of view the biggest 'lesson learnt' from this raid was that the practice of collecting together, from all sorts of sources, the ships and vessels required for such an intricate purpose as a combined operation was quite unacceptable. It was recommended, and the Admiralty finally agreed, that 'permanent naval assault forces' should be formed, and that they must possess 'a coherence comparable to that of any other first line formation'.

As to the conduct of the raid itself, the gallantry of the troops and of the crews of the landing craft was beyond all praise, and the enemy paid just tribute to it in his study of the results. Weak points such as the inflexibility of our planning have already been mentioned, and it may perhaps have been this feature which prevented the abandonment of the frontal attack as soon as it was known that the flank attacks had achieved only slight success. No commander willingly gives up an enterprise on which he has embarked; and in

---

[1] Despatch of Admiral of the Fleet Sir Andrew Cunningham. Supplement to the London Gazette, 2nd May, 1950, para. 30.

this case the decision to commit the floating reserve was undoubtedly influenced by the lack of accurate information from the beaches. None the less it now seems plain that the reinforcement of the frontal attack with the reserve and the commandos took place after all prospect of success had vanished.

At a meeting of the War Cabinet on the 20th of August, the Chief of Combined Operations stressed the value that the lessons learnt at Dieppe would have in planning the invasion of Europe; and the Vice-Chief of the Imperial General Staff (Lieutenant-General A. E. Nye) wisely reminded the Cabinet how past experience had shown that a landing regardless of cost could always be achieved, but that the second stage—exploitation—had invariably proved more difficult than the landing itself. This was exactly what had been found at Dieppe. Though the price there paid had been heavy, the recommendations made in the combined report were all put into effect by the time the great landings of later days took place; and it may well be that, but for the sacrifices made in operation 'Jubilee', operation 'Husky' (Sicily) or the later landings in Italy might have produced a terrible failure.

To return now to the coastal convoy routes, it was in this phase that the many and varied measures taken since the outbreak of the war to defend our coastal shipping against U-boats, E-boats, mines and bombs started to gain a clear ascendancy over the attack. Our light forces had increased greatly in numbers, and in quality. In the Coastal Forces there were now 1,294 officers (mostly of the R.N.V.R.) and 7,721 ratings. The disposition of its strength is shown below.

Table 16. Coastal Forces. Strength and Dispositions on 1st November, 1942

	Steam Gunboats	Motor Gunboats	Motor Torpedo-boats	Motor Launches
Nore	—	45	24	35
Dover . . .	—	20	7	17
Portsmouth . . .	6	15	16	28
Plymouth . . .	—	—	8	19
Western Approaches .	—	—	—	25
Orkneys and Shetlands .	—	—	8	24
Miscellaneous and Training	—	10	7	35
Abroad . . .	—	—	31(1)	80(2)
TOTALS . . .	6	90	101	263

NOTES: (1) All in the Eastern Mediterranean.
(2) All over the world.

The strength of the minesweeping service also was enormously greater than in the early days[1]; and ships were now fitted to deal with all the many types of mine laid by the enemy. As an indication of the size of the effort involved it is worth tabulating the composition and disposition of our minesweeping forces after three years of war.

Table 17. British Minesweeping Forces in September 1942, and losses suffered September 1939–September 1942

I. HOME WATERS

Class	Numbers	Losses
Fleet Minesweepers:		
Algerine Class	5	—
Bangor Class	33	—
Hebe and *Halcyon* Classes	13	4
Albury Class (twin screw)	9	3
Exe Class(1)	5	—
Corvettes fitted for minesweeping(2)	20	—
Paddle Minesweepers	6	9
Mine Destructor Ships	2	3
Minesweeping/Anti-Submarine Trawlers	54	8
Commercial Type Trawlers(3)	240	54
L.L. Trawlers and Whalers(4)	187	34
'B.Y.M.S.' (British 'Yard Minesweepers')(5)	2	—
Motor Minesweepers	95	3
L.L. Drifters and Tugs(4)	103	7
Skid towing vessels, yachts, etc.	30	15
TOTALS	**804**	**140**

II. ABROAD

Class	Numbers	Losses
Fleet Minesweepers:		
Hebe and *Halcyon* Classes	2	—
Bangor Class(6)	9	—
Bathurst Class(7)	21	—
Albury Class (twin screw)	5	5
Corvettes fitted for minesweeping	13	3
Mine Destructor Ships	5	—
Minesweeping/Anti-Submarine Trawlers	21	1
Various types fitted for moored minesweeping	115	10
Various types fitted for magnetic minesweeping	100	13
Motor minesweepers	29	—
Skid towing vessels	33	1
TOTALS	**353**	**33(8)**

NOTES: (1) Only used temporarily for minesweeping.
(2) These were more commonly used for anti-submarine work.
(3) Fitted for moored-minesweeping.
(4) L.L. craft were magnetic minesweepers.
(5) Built in U.S.A. under Lend-Lease.
(6) In addition the Royal Canadian Navy had 36 and the Royal Indian Navy 3.
(7) In addition the Royal Australian Navy had 15 and the Royal Indian Navy 3.
(8) Losses shown do not include 59 minesweepers of various types scuttled to avoid capture or sunk by the enemy in the Far East.

[1] See Vol. I, pp. 47–48 and 329.

It will be seen that 1,157 minesweepers were now in commission all over the world (excluding the Commonwealth countries' ships), and that 173 of all types had so far been lost (excluding the 59 lost in the Far East). Throughout the fourth year of the war production from American and Canadian ship yards increased. In particular a new American-designed type of fleet minesweeper, called the 'A.M. 100 Class' by them and 'B.A.M.S.' (British A.M. Ships) if built for us under Lend-Lease, and an improved type of motor minesweeper had begun to enter service. The former had a good turn of speed, and were fitted to deal with moored and 'influence' mines. From British yards came more of the new fleet minesweepers, trawlers and motor minesweepers. A point had now been reached at which vessels fitted for anti-submarine work as well (the *Exe* class and corvettes) could be released to this latter duty, and a number of minesweepers could also be turned over to the smaller Allied nations. There was no doubt that, like the Coastal Forces, the minesweeping service was now getting on top of the enemy. Research work, designed to anticipate enemy developments, continued all the time, and new sweeping technique and tactics were constantly being developed. It was, for example, at this time that we turned our attention to the problem of clearing the assault area of an overseas expedition of all types of mine. In fact the whole vast problem of planning, organising and providing special equipment for such operations now loomed large in British and Allied councils. Our Combined Operations organisation also expanded rapidly in 1942. Bases for training purposes were established at Boston, Sheerness, Lowestoft and Harwich. That at Boston in Lincolnshire was called H.M.S. *Arbella*, a name provided by the Vicar of the parish, who remembered that the flagship of the fleet which had sailed for America in 1630, bearing many emigrants from East Anglia, had been so called; and that it was they who gave its name to the city of Boston in Massachusetts.

In August the German E-boats, which had transferred their main effort to the Channel in the previous May, returned to the east coast routes. The patrol line of motor gunboats and motor launches which we had established some eight miles to seaward of the shipping lanes has already been mentioned.[1] Our short-wave shore radar and the 'Very High Frequency' wireless stations now played a big part in keeping the patrol craft informed of enemy movements. By the end of the year the whole of the Nore Command's coastal area was covered by these radar stations' beams, and the enemy could be detected and plotted while still some twenty miles off-shore; and added to this great advantage was the fact that radar sets were now being fitted in the Coastal Force vessels themselves.

---

[1] See p. 163.

In August the convoy channel off Yarmouth, known as 'E-boat alley', saw many fierce actions, fought at close range. But only rarely did the enemy achieve substantial success. Once in mid-December E-boats penetrated our patrol line undetected, and sank five ships of convoy FN.889.[1] By the end of the year, however, his minelaying and E-boat attacks had declined, and it was plain that a turning point in coastal warfare had been reached. In 1942 the E-boats only sank twenty-three ships of 71,156 tons in all theatres.

From the outbreak of war up to the 14th of November 1942, no less than 63,350 ships had sailed in the east coast FN, FS and EC convoys[2], and only 157 (0·247 per cent) had been lost from all causes. When serious losses had been suffered in the early months they had nearly always been among independently-routed ships. As to mines, in the whole of 1942 we lost twenty-one ships of about 43,000 tons on the east coast, and fifty-one Allied ships of 104,588 tons in all waters.[3] The Nore Command minesweepers had swept 707 ground and 157 moored mines in the same period. By the end of 1942 this menace too had plainly been overcome to a great extent.

Before leaving our defensive measures we must again briefly mention the state of our various mine barriers. It will be remembered that since the early days of the war we had steadily strengthened the mine field along the whole of our east coast, whose purpose it was to prevent incursions by enemy U-boats or surface forces on to our shipping lanes; and that in 1940 the 1st Minelaying Squadron had started to lay an enormous mine field between the Faeroes and Iceland.[4] In the present phase the minelayer *Adventure* once reinforced the east coast barrier, and the 1st Minelaying Squadron twice laid fields south-west of the Faeroes. It was, however, inevitable that, as the first phase of our maritime strategy receded, purely defensive measures such as these should be regarded as less important, and that the authorities should become more and more unwilling to devote men and resources to them. The 1st Minelaying Squadron was, however, kept in being until October 1943. In retrospect it seems that, although the Dover and to a lesser extent the east coast barrier accomplished the purposes for which they were designed, the great effort put into the Iceland-Faeroes minefield was a singularly unprofitable venture, and yielded little or no return.

In October our coastal convoys were reorganised. Between

---

[1] To simplify signalling, convoys were, after February 1940, referred to only by their last two numbers. Thus in contemporary records Convoy FN.889 may be referred to as FN.89. As, however, there were several convoys which had the latter designation during the war, it has been thought best to give each one its full number here.

[2] See Vol. I, Map 38.

[3] See Appendix O.

[4] See Vol. I, Map 10.

Plymouth and the Bristol Channel ports PW/WP convoys, each of about twenty ships, now sailed every two days[1]; and small convoys of about seven ships were run at the same interval between Portsmouth and Plymouth. Between the Thames and Portsmouth the CW/CE convoys of about eighteen ships still continued, but now on a shorter and more regular six day cycle.[2] On the east coast itself the FN and FS convoys, of about thirty-six ships, still sailed between the Thames and the Forth on six days out of every seven. These changes, which ringed the British Isles with regularly running and interlocking coastal convoys, were made possible by our improved control in the Channel and by our increasing ascendancy over the enemy's attacks on our coastal shipping.

It was to be expected, now that matters were going far better on our own coastal routes, that we should turn increasingly to the offensive against the enemy's. It took many forms. Firstly there were attacks by Coastal Force craft on enemy convoys off the Dutch and Belgian coasts and in the Channel. In the preceding phase, although many operations were carried out, successes against the heavily escorted German convoys had been few. It will, for example, be remembered that in March and May 1942 the two raiders *Michel* and *Stier* both passed down-Channel successfully, in spite of being heavily attacked.[3] In October the enemy tried it again, with the *Komet* (Raider B), which had returned from her first cruise in November 1941[4]. She left Flushing for Boulogne on the first stage of her outward journey at midnight on the 7th-8th of October.[5] Her first trouble occurred next morning when four of the minesweepers of her escort were mined, in spite of the route having been swept four hours earlier. The raider therefore put into Dunkirk on the 8th. Four days later she left, and reached Boulogne; then she coasted from Boulogne to Havre, whence she sailed on the evening of the 13th. She passed Cherbourg in the early hours of the following morning.

In the Admiralty it had meanwhile been realised that an unusually important movement was afoot on the other side of the Channel. A destroyer force was therefore assembled at Portsmouth, and air searches and strikes were arranged. After the enemy had passed successfully as far west as Havre, the Portsmouth destroyers and motor torpedo-boats also moved down-Channel. On the night of the 13th-14th of October five *Hunt*-class destroyers under Lieutenant-Commander J. C. A. Ingram in the *Cottesmore*, and also eight M.T.Bs, sailed from Dartmouth to patrol off Cape de la Hague; four more

---

[1] These convoys started in July 1941.

[2] See Vol. I, p. 323 regarding the start of CW/CE convoys. They originally ran between the Thames and Bristol Channel ports.

[3] See pp. 163–164.

[4] See Vol. I, p. 547.

[5] See Map 25 (inset) (opp. p. 265).

'*Hunts*' were sent out from Plymouth. The first group gained contact just before 1 a.m. on the 14th, engaged at once and set the raider and two of her escorts on fire. M.T.B.236 (Sub-Lieutenant R. Q. Drayson, R.N.V.R.) then appeared and set the seal to the destroyers' work by torpedoing the *Komet*. The other group of our destroyers had meanwhile got among the enemy escort craft, every one of which was damaged. This dangerous raider was eliminated at a cost to ourselves of two men wounded.

We were less successful in dealing with the next raider, or rather ex-raider, to appear in these coastal waters. She was the *Orion* (Raider A of the Admiralty's original catalogue) which had returned safely to the Gironde in August 1941, after a not very successful cruise.[1] Though the German Naval Staff had wanted to bring her back to Germany earlier and intended to use her as a gunnery training ship, they found it impossible to do so. She actually stayed in the Gironde, and was used for deception purposes in connection with the arrival and departure of blockade runners. On the 8th of March she left Bordeaux, and on the 17th reached Havre, where she was extensively damaged in an air raid. Her repairs lasted till November. On the 9th of that month she left for Boulogne under escort and, on the night of the 10th-11th, sailed from that port to pass through the Dover Strait under cover of thick fog. Though the Dover batteries fired on her, and coastal forces and aircraft searched, she reached Dunkirk safely. Her log contains an entry that she listened to the pilots of our aircraft apostrophizing the fog, so she must have had someone on board who was well versed in Royal Air Force vernacular. She reached the Elbe on the 15th, and so passes out of our story.

To summarise this phase of the struggle to control the coastal routes through the Channel, there was very little enemy traffic by day. By night it was heavily escorted, and our aircraft and coastal forces were only rarely successful in stopping the enemy ships. Though our offensive measures achieved few positive successes, our defences were now adequate and well enough trained to prevent the enemy repeating his earlier successes against our own shipping.

Against the enemy's shipping off Norway we employed a large number of different forms of surface attack. Long-range motor-torpedo and motor gunboats had now started to make raids into the 'Leads' from the Shetlands. The 30th M.T.B. Flotilla, which was Norwegian-manned, sank two ships in November, and Admiral Tovey asked to be given four flotillas to exploit the opportunities more fully. But the stormy North Sea weather made it difficult to do much with these small vessels in winter. Our home-based submarines too, though mostly needed to help protect Russian convoys

---

[1] See Vol. I, pp. 278–9 and 546–7.

S

from enemy surface ship attacks, made a few patrols off Norway. The *Junon* (Free French) and *Uredd* (Norwegian) both scored successes in October. Sabotage parties and agents were also landed from submarines. In that same month a most original and gallant, though unsuccessful, attempt was made to attack the *Tirpitz* in a fiord near Trondheim. For some time we had been developing a one-man torpedo known as a 'Chariot', and volunteers had been training at a Scottish base in their use.[1] On the 26th of October the fishing trawler *Arthur* left the Shetlands, commanded by the famous Norwegian resistance leader Leif Larsen, with two Chariots secured underneath her and their crews concealed onboard. Larsen bluffed his way past all the German patrols into the fiord, and got within about ten miles of his target. Then a sudden and most unlucky squall caused the Chariots to break adrift, and the operation had to be abandoned. The crews landed and all but one man got safely into Sweden, and thence back to Britain. The *Tirpitz* and *Scheer* were both seen by them in fiords adjacent to Trondheim.

To turn now to the air side of our anti-shipping campaign in coastal waters, by the middle of the year the enemy's increased escorts, and the formidable anti-aircraft gunfire which his vessels could throw up, had forced Coastal Command to abandon low-level attacks, because the losses we were incurring could not be sustained. This eased the enemy's shipping problems just when, for the first time since the outbreak of war, he was finding it difficult to meet all civil and military needs. The decision thus forced on Coastal Command produced a temporary impasse. Low-level attacks were too expensive; medium-level attacks remained inaccurate, for lack of an efficient bomb sight; and torpedo attacks were rare events, because the command possessed few suitable aircraft and there was still a severe shortage of torpedoes. In the summer replacement of the slow and unwieldy Hampdens, of which there were four squadrons in Coastal Command, was realised to be an urgent matter. Aircraft of the Beaufighter type, which was fast, manoeuvrable and had good fire power, were what was needed. Conversions were started, but No. 254 Squadron, the first to be re-equipped, did not receive its 'Torbeaus' till November. Meanwhile Coastal Command had to continue to make do with the Hampdens.

The period from July 1942 to February 1943 was, for these reasons, chiefly one of tactical and technical development for Coastal Command. Its actual accomplishments in the anti-shipping war were small. In retrospect it seems that the progress of the Royal Air Force from almost complete dependence on the bomb for use against ships to full acceptance of the torpedo for such purposes was slow. At the

---

[1] A full account of the development and employment of 'Chariots' is given in *Above us the Waves* by Warren and Benson (Harrap 1953).

end of July a joint Admiralty and Air Ministry Committee, composed of high officers of both services with the Commander-in-Chief, Coastal Command, as its chairman, was set up with the purpose of doing everything possible to improve tactical and technical efficiency in this matter. Thus once again, under stress of circumstances, the two services put their heads together to produce the best solutions; and the prejudices which had so long hindered progress in this, as in other similar problems, were buried.[1]

The first Beaufighter and 'Torbeau' operation against shipping off the Dutch coast took place on the 20th of November. It was a costly failure, caused partly by bad weather and partly by the inexperience of the aircrews. In consequence of this the Commander-in-Chief withdrew the squadrons for more intensive training, and they do not reappear in our story until April 1943.

It thus happened that for the rest of this phase the outdated Hampdens were all that could be used off the Norwegian coast; Hudsons continued to make bombing attacks from medium heights, at which they were unlikely to be effective, off the German and Dutch coasts; the four-engined Stirlings, Halifaxes and Lancasters tried, with little success, to attack blockade-runners in the Bay of Biscay and to interfere with the contraband traffic from Bilbao to Bayonne[2]; and Fighter Command, assisted by naval aircraft, flew many sorties against traffic through the Channel, but did the enemy little damage. Bomber Command's contribution to the offensive against coastal shipping was, at this time, confined to minelaying, to which we shall return shortly.[3]

Fortunately the decline in our offensive was, to some extent, off-set by the Germans' mistaken outlook towards the importance of their merchant shipping. Between July 1940 and July 1942 they had lost about one quarter of the tonnage available to them (originally some 4,200,000 tons). Yet wasteful requisitioning by the Navy was not checked, and only a very small replacement programme was put in hand. Even in the Baltic, the only waters where German traffic flowed in anything like normal fashion, and where Swedish ships carried many German cargoes, there was now a sharp decline—particularly in Germany's vital iron ore imports from Sweden. The appointment of a very capable 'Reich Commissioner' for merchant shipping (Kaufmann) and the drastic measures which he introduced, tided our principal enemy over difficulties which, had we been able to prosecute a more deadly air offensive, might have been made critical. It is, perhaps, worth remarking that when Dönitz proposed

---

[1] c.f. the story of the anti-submarine bomb and the air depth charge. See Vol. I, pp. 135–6.

[2] See Vol. I, p. 503 and pp. 274–275 of this volume.

[3] See pp. 263–264.

that the German Navy should take over complete control of merchant shipping, as the British Admiralty had done before the outbreak of war[1], Hitler insisted on keeping all such powers in his own hands.

The results accomplished in the R.A.F.'s offensive against enemy shipping in this phase are tabulated below. Between July 1942 and February 1943 (eight months) German shipping losses in the home theatre from all causes amounted to 250 ships of 261,154 tons. The R.A.F. flew 4,659 sorties against enemy shipping, and made 849 direct attacks; but they accounted for only eighteen enemy ships of 28,556 tons. Our losses in the same period amounted to 78 aircraft—about 4·3 aircraft for each of the ships sunk. The reasons for the small results so far accomplished have already been suggested; but the introduction of the new Strike Wing, composed of Beaufighters and 'Torbeaus', the emphasis now placed on the training of the aircrews employed on this highly specialised form of warfare, and the development of carefully co-ordinated attacks all combined to give hopes of achieving better results in the succeeding phases.

Table 18. The Air Offensive against Enemy Shipping by Direct Attacks at Sea

(All Royal Air Force Commands—Home Theatre only)

August–December 1942

Month 1942	Aircraft Sorties	Attacks Made	Enemy Vessels Sunk		Enemy Vessels Damaged		Aircraft Losses
			No.	Tonnage	No.	Tonnage	
August. .	781	121	2	594	Nil		17
September .	614	149	3	10,258	1	8,998	8
October .	551	72	2	4,129	3	6,515	7
November .	821	129	3	4,227	2	15,426	23
December .	482	94	2	1,681	1	937	9
TOTALS .	3,249	565	12	20,889	7	31,876	64

During the latter part of 1942 the enemy's air offensive against our own coastal shipping underwent a steady decline both in the 'tip and run' fighter-bomber raids, which had been a marked feature in the previous phase, and in his minelaying.[2] In fact a large part of his effort was transferred from our coastal convoys to attacks on concentrations of shipping in our harbours; and with defence of the latter we are not here concerned. It will be remembered that between March and June 1941 we suffered heavy losses on our coastal routes.[3] Then, just when he might have gained a real

---

[1] See Vol. I, pp. 21 and 45.
[2] See Table 19 (p. 262).
[3] See Vol. I, Table 9.

ascendancy, the enemy transferred a great proportion of his forces to the Russian front.[1] In retrospect it seems that the Germans never fully realised the possibilities of achieving valuable, perhaps decisive, results by air attacks on our coastal waters—particularly with torpedoes. They often frittered away their available strength by bombing land targets of doubtful importance, and with little effect. Because of this, by the end of 1942 they no longer possessed the strength to make a sustained effort. Once more the tendency of the Germans not to adhere to one purpose and one object for long enough to produce decisive results is to be remarked. There can be little doubt that Hitler's unstable temperament, his insistence on keeping all powers of decision in his own hands, and his intuitive 'inspirations' prevented the formulation and maintenance of sound strategic purposes. None the less the weakness of his Service advisers stands fully revealed by repeated abandonments of their objects just when results were beginning to be obtained.

In spite of the weakness of the policies whereby the German fighting services were guided, it must none the less be admitted that their campaign against our coastal shipping forced us to keep large numbers of fighter aircraft and escort vessels permanently in home waters, at a time when the former were desperately needed in the Mediterranean and Far East, and the latter in the Atlantic. But for his offensive in home waters, Malaya and Egypt could have been reinforced in better time, the agony of Malta, soon to reach its climax, might have been greatly shortened, and our ocean convoys could have been better defended earlier.

The results of the air fighting on the coastal routes during this phase are shown in the table overleaf.

The reader will notice several very striking features in this table, particularly when it is compared with similar tables covering earlier phases.[2] The first is the steady decline of the enemy's offensive effort against our shipping, especially in minelaying. The causes were his increased attention to our Russian convoys, which demanded most of the aircraft he could spare from the eastern front, and, secondly, the much stronger defences which he now met in his sorties against our shipping. We suffered no merchant ship losses at all from direct attacks in this phase, and the sinking of three small naval craft was the sum of his entire accomplishment by this means. It was natural that Fighter Command's sorties in defence of shipping should decrease with the enemy's effort, but the small number of fighters lost is a sign of the degree to which the air defences had now mastered the attack against our coastal routes.

---

[1] See Vol. I, pp. 463 and 502.
[2] See Table 13 (p. 166), and Vol. I, Tables 9 and 16.

Table 19. *German Air Attacks on Allied Shipping and Royal Air Force*
Sorties in Defence of Shipping
(Home Theatre only)
August–December 1942

Month 1942	Estimated German Day and Night Aircraft Sorties for		Allied Shipping Sunk by Direct Attacks (Day and Night)		Royal Air Force Sorties in Defence of Shipping (Day and Night)	Royal Air Force Losses
	Direct Attack	Mine-laying	No.	Tonnage		
August. .	887	28	2	203	3,253	1
September .	667	11	1	378	2,909	Nil
October .	696	12	Nil		2,274	1
November .	457	14	Nil		2,008	5
December .	373	70	Nil		1,622	4
TOTALS .	3,080	135	3	590	12,066	11

NOTES: (1) As we cannot distinguish Allied losses from air-laid mines from losses caused by mines laid by other means, it is impossible to compare the success of the enemy's minelaying with that of his direct attacks on shipping.
(2) Allied shipping sunk includes merchantmen, naval vessels and fishing craft.
(3) The great majority of the sorties made in defence of Allied shipping was flown by Fighter Command aircraft.

While, therefore, our air attacks on the enemy's coastal shipping were producing only small results and his own parallel effort had become almost negligible, the R.A.F.'s air minelaying continued to expand, and to good effect. Production of mines had increased enormously. In September 1942 1,600 were produced, and the Admiralty was planning to increase the figure to 4,000 a month by the middle of the following year. Coastal Command had temporarily faded out of the minelaying campaign, for lack of suitable aircraft; but Bomber Command was laying about 1,000 mines each month, in waters which reached from the Baltic to the Spanish frontier. A special effort was now made against the routes used by U-boats entering and leaving their Biscay bases. While our aircraft mined the inshore waters, submarines and surface minelayers infested the routes with moored mines, which they laid as far out as the 100 fathom line. This forced the U-boats to travel on the surface a long way from the coast, and, moreover, in order to avoid surprise attacks by our Leigh-Light aircraft, they had to do so in daylight. U-boats on passage thus suffered many delays. In September an outward-bound U-boat (U.600) was badly damaged off La Pallice, and on the 28th the inward-bound U.165 was sunk off Lorient. On the 9th of October U.171 suffered a similar fate.[1] Though the delays caused to the enemy, and losses such as these, were a valuable contribution, it

---

[1] See Map 39 (opp. p. 369).

must be emphasised that at no time during the war did the damage and losses caused to the U-boats by our mines compare in importance with what was achieved by our air and surface convoy escorts.[1]

On the 9th of August minelaying by Coastal Command, to whom two naval Swordfish squadrons had been lent for the purpose, was renewed. In October two more naval squadrons joined No. 16 Group. The whale-oil factory ships *Ole Wegger* and *Solglimt*, prizes captured by the raider *Pinguin* in the Antarctic in January 1941[2], were identified at Cherbourg, and mines were laid to catch them if they tried to slip up-Channel. All three whale-oil factory ships and eight of the eleven captured whalecatchers had been safely taken to France by German prize crews in March 1941. The former had on board over 21,000 tons of whale oil, a valuable addition to Germany's food reserves. The *Solglimt* was sunk in Cherbourg on the 15th of September 1942, salved in the following year and finally scuttled in June 1944; the *Ole Wegger* was scuttled in the Seine in August 1944, and the third one, the *Pelagos* was still afloat at Narvik at the end of the war.

By September, production of British acoustic mines had reached a point at which the Admiralty was able to recommend that we should begin to lay them. The temptation to use them in small quantities as they became available, which would probably have reduced their surprise effect and have given the enemy more time to develop countermeasures, had been resisted. On three consecutive nights between the 19th and 24th, 457 of the new mines, mixed in with some of those of older design, were laid. It is, of course, impossible to separate the sinkings caused by the acoustic mines from those attributable to others; but it seems likely that they contributed to the rise in enemy losses in October. They certainly caused some increase in his sweeping problems, with consequential delays to shipping.

The last table of this chapter sets out the accomplishments of the air minelayers during what was their most successful phase up to date. It will be seen that the enemy's losses were substantial, and that the cost in British aircraft was not unduly heavy. In conclusion the effectiveness of our minelaying cannot be better demonstrated than by noting the fact that in this same phase *all* other forms of air attack on shipping, in port as well as at sea, only caused the enemy the loss of twenty ships (36,882 tons) sunk and a further ten (52,185 tons) damaged; and the aircraft losses in accomplishing these modest figures amounted to no less than 197.

---

[1] U-boats sunk from all causes during the period covered by this volume are tabulated in Appendix J.

[2] See Vol. I, p. 384.

R.A.F. MINELAYING

Table 20. The R.A.F.'s Air Minelaying Campaign
(Home Theatre only)
August–December 1942

Month 1942	Aircraft Sorties	Mines Laid	Enemy Vessels Sunk		Enemy Vessels Damaged		Aircraft Losses
			No.	Tonnage	No.	Tonnage	
August. .	408	981	21	27,898	2	10,633	19
September .	487	1,081	21	12,167	7	9,632	21
October .	510	1,052	23	25,107	4	6,437	20
November .	626	1,219	23	18,308	4	6,906	20
December .	441	1,012	15	10,067	1	1,444	13
TOTALS .	2,472	5,345	103	93,547	18	35,052	93

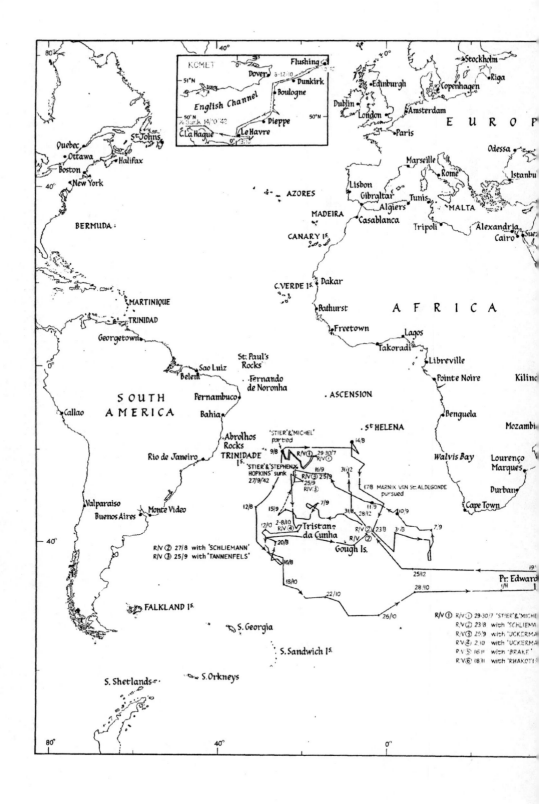

KOMET

English Channel

Flushing
Dover
Dunkirk
Boulogne
Dieppe
Le Havre
C. La Hague

80°   40°   40°   0°

Stockholm
Edinburgh   Copenhagen   Riga
Dublin   Amsterdam
London
Paris   E U R O P E

Quebec   St Johns
Ottawa   Halifax
Boston
New York

Odessa
Marseille   Rome
Istanbul
Lisbon   Gibraltar   Tunis   MALTA
Algiers
Casablanca   Tripoli   Alexandria
Cairo   Sue

BERMUDA

AZORES
MADEIRA
CANARY IS.

MARTINIQUE
TRINIDAD
Georgetown

C. VERDE IS.   Dakar
Bathurst   A F R I C A
Freetown   Lagos
Takoradi   Libreville
Pointe Noire   Kilin

St. Paul's Rocks
Sao Luiz   Fernando
Belém   de Noronha   ASCENSION
S O U T H
A M E R I C A   Pernambuco
Callao   Bahia

St HELENA
Benguela
Walvis Bay   Mozambi
Lourenço Marques

Rio de Janeiro   Abrolhos Rocks
TRINIDADE IS.
'STIER' & 'MICHEL' parted   9/8   R/V① 29-30/7   14/8
R/V①
'STIER' & 'STEPHEN X HOPKINS' sunk   16/9
27/9/'42   R/V③ 25/9   31/12
25/9   17/8 MARNIX VAN St ALDEGONDE
R/V③   pursued
12/8   15/9   7/9   31/8   11/9
Valparaiso   Monte Video   2-8/10   28/12   10/9
Buenos Aires   12/10 R/V④   Tristan   31/8   7/9
da Cunha   R/V② 23/8
20/8   Gough Is.   R/V②
R/V② 27/8 with 'SCHLIEMANN'   Durban
R/V③ 25/9 with 'TANNENFELS'   Cape Town

16/8
18/10   25/12   Pr. Edward
28/10
FALKLAND IS.   22/10   26/10

S. Georgia   R/V① R/V① 29-30/7 'STIER'&'MICHE
R/V② 23/8 with 'SCHLIEMA
R/V③ 25/9 with 'UCKERMA
S. Sandwich IS.   R/V② 2/10 with 'UCKERMA
R/V⑤ 16/11 with 'BRAKE'
S. Shetlands   S. Orkneys   R/V⑥ 18/11 with 'RHAKOTI

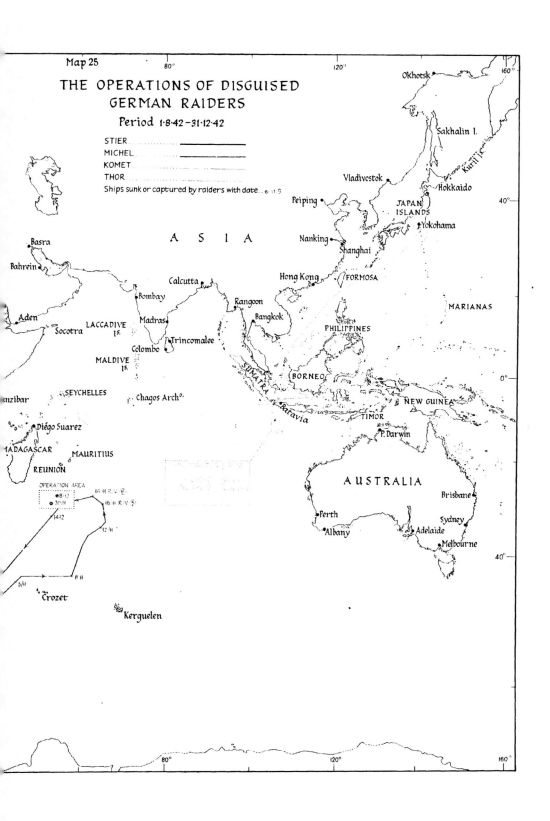

Map 25

THE OPERATIONS OF DISGUISED
GERMAN RAIDERS
Period 1·8·42 – 31·12·42

STIER .... ──────────
MICHEL .... ──────────
KOMET ....
THOR ....
Ships sunk or captured by raiders with date.. ● 11·9

A S I A

Okhotsk
Sakhalin I.
Kuril Is.
Vladivostok
Hokkaido
Peiping
JAPAN
ISLANDS
Yokohama
Nanking
Shanghai
Hong Kong
FORMOSA
MARIANAS
Basra
Bahrein
Calcutta
Bombay
Rangoon
Aden
Socotra
LACCADIVE Is.
Madras
Bangkok
PHILIPPINES
Colombo
Trincomalee
MALDIVE Is.
SUMATRA
BORNEO
NEW GUINEA
nzibar
SEYCHELLES
Chagos Arch°.
Batavia
TIMOR
P. Darwin
Diégo Suarez
MADAGASCAR
MAURITIUS
REUNION

OPERATION AREA
● 8·12
● 30·11
14·12
16·11 R.V. ⑥
16·11 R.V. ⑤
12·11

AUSTRALIA
Brisbane
Perth
Sydney
Albany
Adelaide
Melbourne

5·11
8·11
Crozet
Kerguelen

80°   120°   160°
40°
0°
40°

CHAPTER XI

OCEAN WARFARE
1st August–31st December, 1942

> 'The strength of Great Britain, however, lay
> in her great body of merchant seamen'.
> A. T. Mahan. *The Influence of Sea
> Power on the French Revolution and
> Empire.* Vol. I, p. 70.

THOUGH it may reasonably be claimed that by the beginning
of this phase the days of the German armed raiders were
numbered, there were still three of them at sea—the *Thor*
(Raider E), the *Stier* (J) and the *Michel* (H). A fourth, the *Komet*
(Raider B), which had returned home after her first successful
cruise at the end of November 1941[1], now attempted to make a
second; but, as was told in the last chapter, she got no further than
the English Channel.[2]

On the 1st of August the *Stier* and *Michel*, which had met three
days previously, were still in company in the south Atlantic, and
their Captains now decided to try joint operations.[3] On the 9th the
Stier, when to the east of Trinidade Island, sighted the *Dalhousie* in
ballast from Cape Town to Trinidad. The British ship might have
escaped had she not first altered course towards the *Stier*, and so
brought herself within range of the raider's guns. As soon as the
merchantman realised what was up she turned away, and began to
send raider reports. The *Stier* thereupon opened fire, and soon sank
the ship. The *Michel* turned up while survivors were being rescued,
and the two raiders decided that the *Dalhousie's* wireless reports made
an immediate departure from the scene advisable. They thereupon
separated.

The *Stier* steamed further south, to seek traffic between Cape Town
and the River Plate. She spent some six weeks cruising in the remote
waters around Tristan da Cunha and Gough Island, and she fuelled
again from the *Schliemann* on the 27th of August. The tanker then
left for Japan. On the 4th of September the raider sighted a large
and fast passenger ship in about 33° 30′ South and 15° 45′ West,

---

[1] See Vol. I, pp. 505 and 547.
[2] See pp. 256–257.
[3] See Map 25.

which she identified as the liner *Pasteur* (29,253 tons). She had been expecting her ever since Berlin had wirelessed that the liner had left Cape Town for Rio on the 30th of August.[1] The identification was almost certainly correct, but the liner's speed was sufficient to keep her out of harm's way.

Having obtained no success in the south the *Stier* moved north again in mid-September. On the 24th she met the *Michel* once more, and next day found the blockade runner *Tannenfels*, which was acting as a supply ship, in about 24° 50′ South 22° 10′ West. At about 9 a.m. on the 27th of September in hazy weather in 24° 44′ South 21° 50′ West, she sighted a steamer on her starboard bow.[2] The *Tannenfels*, which was still in company, was cast off and a signal was made ordering the steamer to stop. The raider's would-be victim, the American merchantman *Stephen Hopkins* (a 'Liberty ship', of 7,818 tons armed with one four-inch gun) was however very alert. She at once opened fire on the *Stier* at close range and quickly obtained about fifteen hits, two of which were 'disastrous' and set the raider on fire. The *Tannenfels* also joined in what Professor Morison has aptly described as 'an old-time sea battle . . . that recalls the war of 1812'. An attempt by the blockade runner to tow the damaged and burning raider was unsuccessful, and at about noon the latter sank. The *Tannenfels* rescued all her survivors, and later reached Bordeaux with them safely. The fate of the crew of the *Stephen Hopkins* was less happy. The ship sank after three hours of unequal combat. One boat, with fifteen of the crew still alive, reached Brazil after a thirty-one day journey, made without any navigational aids. All the rest were lost; but they fought an action of which all the Allied navies and merchant navies should be proud, and had rid the oceans of one of the heavily armed and dangerous German raiders.

Meanwhile the *Thor* was still in the Indian Ocean, where we last left her.[3] Though some uncertainty still surrounds her movements we

---

[1] The Sea Transport Officer at Durban sent a signal on the 28th of August saying that the *Pasteur* would sail from that port on the 30th for Rio de Janeiro, whence she was routed to Halifax. As the Berlin message to the *Stier* mentions Cape Town instead of Durban as the departure port, it seems unlikely that the enemy intercepted this message. His intelligence was, possibly, derived from careless talk about shipping movements, of which there was a good deal in South African ports at this time. At 22 knots the *Pasteur* could very well have reached the position in which the raider believed she had sighted her on the 4th of September.

[2] See Morison, Vol. I, pp. 398–9. There is a considerable discrepancy, both as regards the time and the position of this epic encounter, between Professor Morison's account, which appears to be mainly derived from the reports of the *Hopkins*' survivors, and the War Diary of the *Stier*. The former says the enemy was sighted at noon, in 28° 08′ South and 20° 01′ West. The latter gives the start of the battle as 8.55 a.m. and the sinking of the *Stier* as taking place at 11.59 a.m. It is not known whether the discrepancy in times can be accounted for entirely by differences in the Zone Times kept by the two sides. As regards position it seems likely that the German one is the more accurate, observing that they saved most of their records and instruments, while the *Hopkins*' crew lost all theirs.

[3] See p. 178.

know that at the end of August she met the blockade-runner *Tannenfels*, en route to Bordeaux, in 27° South 76° East. The *Thor* was next given a new operational area and worked between 20° and 30° South, 80° and 100° East, from the 8th of August to the 20th of September; but she found no victims there. She next passed through the Sunda Strait and arrived at Balikpapan in Borneo on the 25th.[1] There she fuelled, and then set course up the China Sea for Yokohama, which she reached on the 9th of October. On the 30th of November she was lying there alongside the supply ship *Uckermark*, whose fuel tanks were being cleaned. At 2 p.m. a heavy explosion occurred in the *Uckermark*, caused, so the German enquiry concluded, by ignition of fumes in the tanks. The supply ship blew up and the raider was burnt out. Another German ship (the *Leuthen*) which was in harbour also caught fire and became a total loss. Thus passed off the stage yet another German raider and, moreover, one which in her early career had done us considerable harm.[2]

The *Michel* (Raider H) was meanwhile continuing her cruise in the South Atlantic. After she had refuelled from the *Schliemann* early in August off Trinidade Island, she moved east and savagely attacked the British ship *Arabistan* south of St. Helena on the 14th. The raider only picked up one survivor. Her next exploit was to chase the large Dutch liner *Marnix van St. Aldegonde* (19,355 tons), then serving as an Allied troopship, which luckily had sufficient speed to shake off the pursuit. Later in the month the raider again met the faithful *Charlotte Schliemann* east of Tristan da Cunha and replenished her tanks.[3] On the 10th/11th of September, by night attacks typical of von Rückteschell's methods, she sank the *American Leader* and the British *Empire Dawn*, after which she returned once more to the mid-ocean rendezvous and again met the *Stier*. On the 25th she replenished from the supply ship *Uckermark*, which was kept in company with the raider until the 5th of October.

On the 27th of September the *Michel*, while still taking in stores from the *Uckermark*, intercepted firstly the *Stephen Hopkins'* distress message, and then a signal from the *Stier* asking that her sister raider should close her position. The *Michel's* captain did not guess that an action fatal to his colleague was being fought near by, but he considered it advisable to move away from rather than towards the *Stier's* position. Not till mid-October did he learn from Germany of the *Stier's* fate.

The *Michel* next steamed far south into the Antarctic—not, apparently, to seek Allied whaling ships, but to make a safe passage to his new operational area in the Indian Ocean. According to von

---

[1] See Map 25 (opp. p. 265).
[2] See Vol. I, pp. 284–286, 383–384 and Appendix M.
[3] See pp. 178–179.

Rückteschell's diary, Berlin's order to him to move east was prompted by anxiety lest his continued activities in the South Atlantic might provoke strong Allied reactions, and so endanger the supply arrangements made for the U-boat group which was at the time southward-bound for the Cape of Good Hope.[1]

The *Michel* cruised slowly east in the Antarctic and, at the end of October in 53° South, passed into the Indian Ocean.[2] In mid-November she replenished stores and fuel from the *Brake* in 30° South 65° East, and met the homeward-bound blockade runner *Rhakotis* south of Rodriguez Island. The *Michel's* log for the preceding months was lost when the *Rhakotis* was sunk[3], and this has made the raider's cruise in the South Atlantic difficult to piece together.

On the 29th of November, in 29° South 54° East, the *Michel*, by another typical night attack, secured her first victim in the Indian Ocean—an American freighter bound from Colombo to Cape Town. About a week later, still in the waters east of Madagascar, she sank a Greek ship. In both these cases the M.T.B. was used for reconnaissance and to take part in the attack.[4] In mid-December she returned once more to the former hunting ground in the South Atlantic, and early in the New Year we find her again south of St. Helena. On the 20th of December the German Naval Staff told the *Michel's* Captain to plan his return to the Gironde for early February 1943, but on the 6th of January this was changed. Because of our greatly strengthened air reconnaissance in the Bay, Berlin considered that an attempt to return there was too risky and advised von Rückteschell to proceed instead to Japan. It thus happened that his cruise, which had already lasted nine months, was greatly extended. In this phase he sank five ships of 30,591 tons, and so brought the *Michel's* total score to thirteen of 87,322 tons.

The German Naval Staff must have realised that, by the end of 1942, the days when surface ships could profitably be sent out to attack our merchant shipping in the broad oceans had passed and were not likely to return. No attempt to use warships in the Atlantic had been made since the disastrous *Bismarck* episode of May 1941; and the withdrawal home of the Brest squadron in February 1942 had marked the final defeat of the strategic purpose for which the battle cruisers and heavy cruisers had so long been stationed there.[5] Now, in the closing months of 1942, it must also have been plain that the days of the disguised raiders were fast drawing to a close. The *Stier* was sunk in the South Atlantic in September, the *Komet* in the

---

[1] See pp. 269–271.
[2] See Map 25 (opp. p. 265).
[3] See p. 276.
[4] See p. 179.
[5] See pp. 149–161.

Channel in October and the *Thor* blew up in Yokohama in November. Only the *Michel* survived, and she, as has been told, was on her way to Japan, because it was considered unsafe to try to bring her back to Europe. In these circumstances the enemy's hope of continuing sporadic warfare in remote waters could only lie with the U-boats. It is not surprising, therefore, to find that they now come to replace the surface raiders of the first three years of the war.

In October 1942 two U-boats were sent to the mouth of the Congo River to attack shipping which the enemy believed to be passing to and from adjacent West African ports. In fact such traffic was of small dimensions, but on the 23rd of October one of the U-boats encountered the cruiser *Phoebe* which, with her sister ship the *Sirius*, was proceeding to Pointe Noire in French Equatorial Africa, and torpedoed her.[1] She was badly damaged and had to be sent to America for repairs. The U-boats, finding the Congo delta unrewarding, next moved north to the Gulf of Guinea, to try their luck off Lagos and Takoradi. But they accomplished very little there either.

Meanwhile the Admiralty's long-felt anxiety regarding the great concentration of ill-defended shipping entering and leaving Cape Town and passing round the Cape of Good Hope was justified by events. It will be remembered that the enemy's earlier attempts to attack these focal waters had been defeated by the interception of the U-boats' supply ships.[2] He did not repeat the attempt to use such ships. As early as the 21st of September the Submarine Tracking Room had, with prescient accuracy, given warning that a southward movement of U-boats appeared imminent. All shipping was routed further west, away from the African coast, and east-bound traffic was, if possible, sent to Durban instead of Cape Town. Orders were issued for those west-bound ships which had to call at Cape Town to be escorted clear of the danger area. These arrangements were the best that could be organised quickly; it will be told shortly how they failed to save us from heavy losses.

Actually it was not until the 7th of October, nearly three weeks after the Submarine Tracking Room's warning had been given, that the first five U-boats reached the waters off Cape Town. Although U.179, the first of the new 'U-cruisers' of 1,600 tons with a radius of action of 30,000 miles, was quickly sunk by the destroyer *Active*, and Cape Town roads were found empty, the other enemies reaped a rich harvest between that base and Durban. By the end of the month they had sunk twenty-four ships of 161,121 tons, many of which were loaded with important military cargoes. For the first time on the WS convoy route we lost several of the large and valuable liners which had served us so well as troop carriers. The *Oronsay* (20,043 tons) fell

[1] See Map 25 (opp. p. 265).
[2] See Vol. I, pp. 470, 479–480, 542 and 546.

victim to a U-boat just north of the equator on the 9th of October, and on the following day the *Orcades* (23,456 tons) was sunk off the Cape, while the *Duchess of Atholl* (20,119 tons) was caught by another 'U-cruiser' north of Ascension Island. These were grievous losses, for such fine ships could never be replaced during the war. Fortunately there were comparatively few casualties among their passengers and crews.

Anti-submarine reinforcements had to be sent out, even though the enemy's widely separated lunges had already forced us and the Americans to disperse our still inadequate strength to a dangerous degree. The Admiralty ordered out twelve anti-submarine trawlers from the Western Approaches, and asked the U.S. Navy Department to release the last eighteen of those which we had lent them in the previous February.[1] The Americans agreed, and they soon began the long passage to Cape Town; but it was nearly the end of the year before they arrived. Other reinforcements were sent from home and from the Halifax Escort Force; refits of destroyers at Simonstown were postponed, while six destroyers and four corvettes were detached from the Eastern Fleet to the South Atlantic station. Substantial escort-vessel strength was thus assembled at Simonstown, but it did not make its presence felt until after serious losses had been suffered. The South African Air Force contributed anti-submarine patrols with its Venturas and Ansons; British naval aircrews training in South Africa were also pressed into service, and four Catalinas of the R.A.F.'s No. 209 Squadron soon arrived to make long range patrols from Saldanha Bay near Cape Town, and from Durban.

The Admiralty told Admiral Tait (Commander-in-Chief, South Atlantic) to sail ships through the dangerous waters in organised groups, even if they could only be weakly escorted. But he could do little until the destroyers, corvettes and trawlers mentioned earlier had become available.

In November German U-boats moved to the southern approaches to the Mozambique Channel, the waters where their Japanese allies had wrought considerable havoc in the previous June and July.[2] Twenty-four ships of 127,261 tons were sunk. It was the worst month in the Indian Ocean since Japanese warships had scoured the Bay of Bengal in the previous April.[3] The port of Lourenço Marques had twice to be closed, with serious effects on the coal traffic for the Middle East theatre; and again troopships were among the victims. In December enough escorts had arrived to enable convoys to be sailed between Cape Town and Durban (CD–DC Convoys), and in some cases northwards to Lourenço Marques as well. This, and

---

[1] See p. 97.
[2] See pp. 184–185.
[3] See pp. 25–32.

the fact that the U-boats now started to make their way homewards, caused a drop in sinkings to five ships of 23,251 tons. A crisis, which might have assumed serious proportions had the enemy been able to reinforce the attackers, thus subsided. Though the U-boats' foray into these distant waters had been short, it had been very fruitful. They had done more damage than the disguised raiders, which were their predecessors in the *guerre de course* in these waters, and at vastly less effort. Indeed it was in these months that Dönitz's policy of constantly probing for weak spots in our defences, even at the cost of sending his U-boats thousands of miles away, reaped its greatest reward. Thus, just when the first group was withdrawing from the Indian Ocean, another of nine U-boats, aided by a 'milch cow' which fuelled them off St. Paul rocks, found easy targets between those islets and the Brazilian coast. In December they sank seven ships, but the Americans then strengthened the air patrols, and the surviving U-boats withdrew, after suffering losses.

The arrival of Japanese submarines and armed raiders in the Indian Ocean was mentioned in an earlier chapter.[1] In July and early August they reconnoitred many Allied island bases, such as Reunion, Mauritius, Seychelles and Diego Garcia in the Chagos Archipelago[2], but did no damage at any of them. They returned to Penang in August. The shipping routes off East Africa were thus left to the German U-boats throughout the present phase.

It has already been told how two Japanese surface raiders, the *Hokoku* and *Aikoku Maru* cruised in the southern Indian Ocean, in co-operation with a number of submarines, from May to July 1942; and how the submarines then wrought considerable havoc among our unescorted shipping, while the surface raiders achieved little success.[3] The latter returned to their base at Penang in July and did not reappear until the autumn. Not only was the second Japanese attempt at the *guerre de course* no more successful than the first, but it led to one of the most remarkable actions ever fought by a small escort vessel in defence of a merchant ship.

On the 11th of November the *Bengal*, an Australian-built mine-sweeper of 733 tons manned by the Royal Indian Navy, under Lieutenant-Commander W. J. Wilson, R.I.N.R. and armed with one twelve-pounder gun, was escorting the Dutch tanker *Ondina* (armament one four-inch gun) from Fremantle to the island of Diego Garcia. Shortly before noon 'on a beautiful sunny day with a calm sea' in about 23° South 93° East two strange ships were sighted nearly ahead on a closing course. The *Bengal* quickly identified them as enemy, ordered the *Ondina* to 'act independently' and steered

---

[1] See pp. 184–185.

[2] See Map 25 (opposite p. 265).

[3] See pp. 184–185.

straight for the approaching strangers. Enemy reports were made with a speed and efficiency which would have been commendable in a much larger ship. Soon after noon both enemies opened fire, to which the *Bengal* promptly replied with her one little gun at about 3,500 yards range. She soon obtained a satisfactory hit which caused a large explosion and a fire, but herself sustained two hits.[1] As the tanker had now opened the range to about seven miles the *Bengal's* Captain decided 'to break off the engagement against uneven odds' and retire under cover of smoke towards his charge. His ammunition was now running very short. The undamaged raider pursued and continued the fight, firing broadsides of four quite heavy guns (about six-inch). At 1.12 p.m. a second and heavier explosion was seen on board the first enemy, which had been burning continuously since she had first been hit. Shortly afterwards she was seen to sink. The *Ondina* had meanwhile also been under fire, and had suffered severe hits. But 'Ah Kong' (the Chinese helmsman) 'remained at his post throughout the action', and the enemy fire was returned by the four-inch gun's crew. After firing about twenty rounds the *Bengal* obscured the range for the tanker, whose fire was therefore checked. 'Gunlayer Hammond', states the tanker's report, 'told his crew to carry on smoking, and gave them each a cigarette from his packet. As soon as the range was clear he carried on the action'. What the gun's crew then did with their cigarettes is not recorded.[2]

The enemy had now closed the range, and a hit on the *Ondina's* bridge killed her Master, William Horsman. As she herself had fired all her ammunition, the order to abandon ship was given. The raider fired two torpedoes and several shells into the tanker, then machine-gunned the boats at point blank range, killing the Chief Engineer and several of the crew. She then returned to the scene of her sister ship's destruction, presumably to rescue the crew.

The *Ondina's* survivors now believed the *Bengal* to have been sunk, the latter believed the *Ondina* to have escaped, and the second raider obviously believed the tanker to be doomed; for she had been seriously holed by shells and torpedoes, was on fire and had taken a heavy list. All three beliefs were actually incorrect. By 4.30 p.m. the raider had disappeared over the horizon, and the survivors of the tanker's crew, under the second officer, boarded their ship once more. They put out the fire, got the list off the ship, raised steam again and by 9 p.m. on the next day had set course to return to Fremantle. She arrived there safely on the 18th of November. The *Bengal* had meanwhile given her wounds first aid and set course for Colombo,

---

[1] The Japanese account says that the *Ondina* hit the first raider, but the *Bengal's* report is emphatic that it was her own gunfire which did the damage.

[2] Able Seaman H. Hammond was a Royal Australian Naval Reserve rating.

which she too reached safely. She had fought a most gallant and successful action, and well might one of her officers record his pride and astonishment 'that a small ship with only one twelve-pounder gun, should engage two raiders, both more than ten times her size and each with about twenty times her gun power, and so enable the tanker to escape, sink one raider, and then get away herself'. The young Indian Navy had good reason to feel proud 'of their little *Bengal* tiger'. In conclusion it should be mentioned that the *Ondina's* gun's crew consisted of three British soldiers of the Royal Artillery, four Able Seamen of the Royal Navy and a Dutch Merchant Navy gunlayer. This was typical of the mixed crews provided to merchantmen by the Admiralty's Trade Division, which was responsible for their defensive arming[1]. The Japanese ships were armed with half a dozen guns of six-inch calibre, as well as torpedo tubes, and they carried two seaplanes. It was the *Hokoku Maru* (10,438 tons) which was sunk by the *Bengal* and *Ondina*.

It will be remembered that up to the middle of 1942 the Germans had been comparatively successful in their attempts to get home cargoes of essential raw materials, and especially rubber, from the Far East.[2] In the present phase the enemy's early successes were not repeated. One important factor was the constant photographic air reconnaissance of the French ports to and from which blockade runners habitually sailed. From these photographs the enemy's intentions and expectations could often be deduced. Since the use of Coastal Command's few and precious long-range aircraft to find and attack enemy ships off the north-west corner of Spain had proved expensive and not very successful, in September it was agreed that joint action by aircraft and submarines should be tried. The aircraft would patrol and report enemy movements, and the submarines attack any ships identified as blockade runners. The new arrangements came into force in mid-October.

For homeward blockade running in this phase the enemy had originally planned to use thirty-two German and Italian ships, nine of which were tankers. At first he hoped to bring back 440,000 tons of cargo between August 1942 and May 1943, but his hopes soon had to be drastically modified and the final programme aimed at bringing to France only 210,000 tons. Thirteen dry cargo ships and two tankers actually left the Far East for Europe, but four of them turned back early in their voyages and seven were sunk. Seventeen ships, four of them tankers, sailed outwards from France during the same period, but only ten of them reached Japan; and they carried

[1] See Vol. I, pp. 21–22 and 140–141.
[2] See pp. 182–184.

T

no more than some 24,000 tons of cargo.[1] In September, when it appeared that at least five ships were loading at Bordeaux, we tried to bomb them while in port, but none was damaged. It was in that month that the light cruisers *Sirius* and *Phoebe* arrived on the South Atlantic station.[2] They and some South African minesweepers made patrols to the south of the Cape to catch blockade runners coming from Japan or Indo-China; but they met with no success. American warships and those allotted to our own West African Command patrolled likewise in the South Atlantic, and kept watch on the Cape Horn route.

In October the Air Ministry formed a squadron of Wellington torpedo-bombers (No. 547) in order to accomplish better results in the Bay of Biscay. It was no easy matter at this stage to find aircraft capable of striking effectively against escorted ships at distances of 350 to 480 miles from their bases. The Lancasters' attempts had not proved at all successful; in fact, when they were used to strike at an outward-bound blockade runner on the 19th of August, no results were obtained, and the cost to us was four of these valuable aircraft. The Commander-in-Chief, Coastal Command, hoped to employ a combined torpedo and bombing strike force to better purpose; but it proved impossible to make the Wellingtons available, and the idea came to nothing.

Although there was a good deal of enemy traffic in both directions in October, no blockade runners were sunk, or even forced to abandon their journeys. In November the tempo quickened; more ships were sighted inward or outward-bound, generally with war-ship and powerful air escorts, and more offensive sweeps were flown by Coastal Command. Mines were laid in the approaches to the Gironde, and when a concentration of shipping was observed off the entrance to the river a heavy bombing attack was made by Coastal and Bomber Command aircraft on the 7th. This resulted in one outward-bound blockade runner, the *Elsa Essberger*, being put out of action. Another, the *Anneliese Essberger* was also attacked from the air but continued her journey, only to be caught by the American cruiser *Milwaukee* in the South Atlantic on the 21st of November. This month saw heavy activity by both sides, but our only other success was to damage the *Spichern* so seriously by air attack that she put into Ferrol. Errors in sighting reports, faulty wireless communications and inadequate training of aircrews in this specialised task were all found, by enquiry at Coastal Command Headquarters, to have contributed to our poor results. It had been shown once again that

---

[1] See Appendix N. In addition to the blockade runners the tanker *Charlotte Schliemann*, which had been acting as a supply ship for raiders and U-boats (see pp. 178–179) also reached Japan at this time.

[2] See p. 269.

aircraft trained in one duty could not successfully be switched suddenly to a totally different function. The lesson was clear, to the Germans as well as to the British. Maritime air operations demanded a high degree of tactical and technical skill, which could only be acquired after long training and much practice. Further, the assimilation of such work into the general pattern of sea warfare required the most careful planning and co-ordination, if success was to be achieved and losses kept as small as possible.

Another difficulty which had to be faced and accepted lay in operating our own submarines in among the enemy U-boats' approach routes to his Biscay bases. Restricted bombing zones were established in the submarines' patrol areas, but it was difficult, especially in bad weather, for our aircraft to navigate with such accuracy that they could be sure whether a submarine sighted near the limits of a restricted area was a friend or an enemy. It is possible that the loss of the *Unbeaten* on the 11th of November, some twelve miles within an area where total restriction of night attacks was in force, was attributable to a navigational error by one of our own aircraft, which reported making an attack on a submarine in a position only a few miles from that of the *Unbeaten*.

At the end of November the departure of the outward-bound Italian ship *Cortellazo* caused us to bring into force the arrangements for combined air and submarine action already described. Four submarines, including the captured and renamed *Graph* which we first encountered as U.570[1], took part in the chase, and many air searches were flown. None the less the blockade runner would probably have escaped had she not accidentally run right into the the south-bound 'Torch' convoy KMF.4. She was sunk by its escort on the 1st of December. Neither Coastal Command nor the Flag Officer, Submarines, was satisfied with the performance of their forces on this occasion; and the Commander-in-Chief, Plymouth, considered that success in such intricate operations would continue to prove elusive until firm and centralised control of all units taking part was established.

On the 7th of December a new form of attack was carried out against the enemy blockade runners lying in the Gironde River. A small party of Royal Marine Commandos under Major H. G. Hasler landed by canoe from the submarine *Tuna* and successfully fixed limpet mines to the hulls of four large ships. They were all seriously damaged by flooding, and were put out of action for several months. Major Hasler and one of the commandos then escaped successfully into Spain and so back to Britain.[2]

---

[1] See Vol. I, p. 467.

[2] The damaged ships were the *Alabama, Tannenfels, Dresden* and *Portland*. See Bruce Lockhart *The Marines were there*, pp. 80–84 (Putnam, 1950) for a full account of this attack.

The next outward-bound ship, the tanker *Germania*, met a some-what similar fate to the *Cortellazo's*; for she encountered one of our north-bound convoys on the 12th of December and scuttled herself. Another success was achieved on New Year's Day, 1943. Intelligence had indicated that an inward-bound ship was approaching the Bay and, as the cruiser *Scylla* and an escorted convoy (MKS.4) from Gibraltar were in the vicinity, it was possible to add surface ships to the more usual submarine and air pursuers. After many hours of searching a Sunderland of No. 10 (R.A.A.F.) Squadron sighted the ship. The flying boat then made contact with the *Scylla*, and guided her to the quarry by the unorthodox but effective method of laying flame floats along the course to be steered. The cruiser finally sank the enemy ship, which was the *Rhakotis*, about 140 miles north-west of Cape Finisterre on the evening of the 1st of January. The opera-tion showed how much more could be done when a fast surface ship was available to co-operate with Coastal Command's aircraft.

The adventures of the remaining ships which the enemy had organised to break through our blockade will be told in a later chapter, in which the results of his second wave of blockade running will also be summarised.

CHAPTER XII

HOME WATERS AND THE ARCTIC
1st August–31st December, 1942

'How . . . could anyone who had really
studied imagine that . . . a vast number
of light craft of all kinds would not be
needed in war?'
Richmond. *National Policy and Naval
Strength* (1928).

A BRIEF review of the strength available to both sides shortly
before the start of this phase will help the reader to understand the difficulties which the Home Fleet had to face. In
mid-July the American contribution to the war in the eastern
Atlantic had been reduced by the withdrawal of the battleship
Washington and four destroyers. Admiral Giffen, U.S.N., then transferred his flag to the heavy cruiser *Wichita*, which, together with the
Tuscaloosa, remained part of Admiral Tovey's fleet for a short time
longer. In August the *Wichita* was recalled. The *Tuscaloosa* carried out
one more operation in the Arctic (to be recounted shortly), and then
she too left British waters. 'Task Force 99', which had, in Admiral
Tovey's words, been 'a welcome reinforcement to the Home Fleet',
thus came to an end. Before these withdrawals took place the *King
George V* had completed her refit and rejoined the fleet, which then
comprised two battleships (*King George V* and *Duke of York*) and one
battle cruiser (*Renown*). The new battleship *Anson* was, however,
working up efficiency and would soon be ready to play her full part.
On the enemy side the *Tirpitz*, *Scheer* and *Hipper* were all fit for service
and were now using Narvik instead of Trondheim as their main base.
On the 13th of July the light cruiser *Köln* sailed north from Oslo,
and on the 6th of August she too joined the Narvik squadron; on the
10th the pocket-battleship *Lützow*, which had been damaged by
grounding near Narvik on the 3rd of July[1], returned from Trondheim to Germany. Two of our submarines tried unsuccessfully to
catch her off Egersund, while No. 18 Group's intended air attacks
were frustrated by fog.

Meanwhile the urgency of getting a convoy through to Malta was
considered by the Cabinet to override all other tasks, including the

---

[1] See p. 138.

despatch of another convoy to Russia. The story of that operation ('Pedestal') will be told in another chapter.[1] Here we need only note that the *Nelson* and *Victorious*, the cruisers *Nigeria*, *Kenya* and *Manchester* and eleven destroyers of the powerful escort all came from the Home Fleet. The convoy left the Clyde on the 4th of August and passed the Straits of Gibraltar six days later. In the heavy fighting which marked its eastward progress the old aircraft carrier *Eagle*, the *Manchester* and one Home Fleet destroyer were sunk, while the *Nigeria* and *Kenya* were both damaged. It was the end of August before the surviving ships rejoined Admiral Tovey.

The only merchant ships to sail for Arctic ports in August were two Russians, which left independently from Iceland and got through unscathed after a very long passage. Meanwhile preparations to run a big convoy in September were being pressed ahead. The Prime Minister had urged on the Admiralty the need for 'a further and intense effort . . . to solve the problem of running convoys by the northern route'. He suggested fighting the next one through by a more southerly course, 'not hugging the ice', but under an air 'umbrella' provided from all our available fleet and escort carriers.[2] But to the Naval Staff, which had always to consider each requirement in relation to its other world-wide commitments, this meant hazarding our entire carrier strength for a purpose which could not justify taking such risks with irreplaceable ships. The idea was therefore dropped.

To run a September convoy by more conventional methods required, firstly, the replacement of the stores and ammunition for our ships in North Russia, much of which had been lost in PQ.17. On the 20th of July four destroyers sailed to Archangel for this purpose, and arrived safely. Secondly arrangements had to be made to improve our air cover and striking power, particularly at the Russian end of the route. We could deal with the Narvik squadron from the air only by sending heavy bombers from England to attack it in harbour, and by keeping a torpedo-bomber force in North Russia to strike at the German ships if they followed our convoys into the Barents Sea. Attack with heavy bombers depended on our Allies furnishing a base at which they could land in the far north after their strike; while a torpedo-bomber force would need a properly organised base and ground staff if it was to work efficiently. Admiral Tovey agreed to send out the ground staff and R.A.F. stores as soon as Russian co-operation was obtained. The American cruiser *Tuscaloosa* and three destroyers accordingly sailed from Greenock on the 13th of August with the men and equipment for Nos. 144 and 455 Hampden Squadrons, and landed them safely. They also carried a

---

[1] See pp. 302–308.
[2] See Churchill, Vol. IV, p. 239.

British medical unit to look after our sick and wounded in North Russia, who had been suffering severe privations. Moscow flatly declined to allow the medical personnel to be landed at Archangel, a decision for which no reasons were given, and which Admiral Tovey described, with moderation, as 'astonishing' behaviour by the ally in whose cause our men had been disabled. The medical unit came back in the next westward convoy.

Early in September thirty-two Hampden torpedo-bombers left Sumburgh for North Russia. They were routed first to Afrikanda, a base further behind the front line than Vaenga, from which they would actually operate.[1] Six of the bombers crashed in Norway or Sweden during the outward flight, and of two others which lost their way one was seriously damaged in making a forced landing and the other was shot down by Russian fighters when it unluckily arrived over Kola Inlet during an air raid. By the 5th of September twenty-four Hampdens had reached Vaenga safely. At about the same time four photographic reconnaissance Spitfires flew to Vaenga. Finally No. 210 Catalina long-range reconnaissance squadron followed. They were to work from Lake Lakhta and Grasnaya, and their equipment was flown out in advance by other Catalinas. It thus came to pass that, in spite of the great difficulties of climate and distance, a balanced force of reconnaissance planes and strike aircraft was set up by us in North Russia by early September 1942, under the command of Group Captain F. L. Hopps. Finally, after various conferences had been held in Russia, an Area Combined Headquarters was established at Polyarnoe, where the Senior British Naval Officer, now Rear-Admiral D. B. Fisher, was already installed. In London it had meanwhile been agreed that the most important duty for the Catalinas was to watch the enemy surface warships; escort for PQ.18 came second, and, for the westbound QP.14, third in priority.

Before the convoys sailed the *Scheer* made a brief sortie to attack Russian shipping believed to be using the route north of Siberia. She left Narvik on the 16th of August, passed north of Novaya Zemlya and went as far as about 78° North 100° East; but the only victim she found was one ice-breaker. By the 30th the pocket-battleship was back in Narvik again. His wireless intelligence service had revealed to the enemy our intentions regarding where the next pair of convoys should cross over, and where the escort was to change from the outward to the homeward convoy. He accordingly sent U-boats, destroyers and an auxiliary minelayer to infest the entrance to the White Sea and the shallow waters off Novaya Zemlya with mines. The minelayer *Ulm* was employed on this purpose during the

---

[1] See Map 14 (opp. p. 141).

Scheer's cruise; but she was caught by the destroyers which, with the *Tuscaloosa*, were returning home after taking men and stores to North Russia, and was sunk south-east of Bear Island on the 25th of August.[1] Towards the end of September and again in early November the *Hipper* and destroyers made more minelaying sorties along the Barents Sea route, between Novaya Zemlya and Spitzbergen; but the only success achieved by all this minelaying appears to have been the sinking of one Russian tanker.

For the passage of PQ.18 the naval plans were entirely recast. In Admiral Tovey's opinion covering the convoy with the battle fleet after it had passed Bear Island did not provide really effective protection, and he was strongly opposed to taking his heavy ships into the Barents Sea. If the battle fleet was kept at sea a large number of long-endurance destroyers was absorbed in screening it, and he much preferred to use them to strengthen the convoy's escort. The Commander-in-Chief was confident that, provided the inevitable losses were accepted, we could fight a convoy through, but he thought it essential that it should take its chief defence against surface ship attack along with it; and that meant a very powerful escort of destroyers armed with torpedoes. These would reinforce the close anti-submarine and anti-aircraft escorts until such time as enemy surface ships appeared, when they would at once devote their full effort to attacking them. He considered that 'a fighting destroyer escort' of twelve to sixteen ships would probably deter the enemy surface ships altogether; if they persisted in trying to attack the convoy, it was strong enough to defeat them. Rear-Admiral R. L. Burnett, flying his flag in the light cruiser *Scylla*, was accordingly put in command of the whole escort, including the sixteen additional fleet destroyers allocated to accompany the outward and the homeward convoys during the critical parts of their journeys. Furthermore an escort carrier, the *Avenger* (Commander A. P. Colthurst), which carried a dozen fighters and three anti-submarine Swordfish, was included in the escort for the first time. The size of the operation which these convoys and the concurrent reinforcement of Spitzbergen involved will be best indicated by tabulating all the ships taking part.

Table 21. *Convoy PQ.18. Escort and Covering Forces.*

(1) *Convoy.* Thirty-nine merchantmen, a rescue ship, an oiler and three minesweepers bound for Russia, and two fleet oilers. Under Commodore (Rear-Admiral, Retired) E. K. Boddam-Whetham.

(2) *Close Escort.* Two destroyers, two anti-aircraft ships, two submarines, four corvettes, three minesweepers and four trawlers.

---

[1] It is interesting to record that the last appearance of the *Ulm* in this history was when, in April 1940, she had laid mines undetected on our east coast convoy routes. See Vol I, p. 128.

(3) *Carrier Force. Avenger* and two destroyers.

(4) *'Fighting Destroyer Escort'. Scylla*, and sixteen destroyers, divided into two separate forces.

(5) *Spitzbergen Fuelling Force.* Two fleet oilers and four destroyers, for Lowe Sound.

(6) *Cruiser Covering Force. Norfolk* (flag of Vice-Admiral S. S. Bonham-Carter), *Suffolk* and *London.*

(7) *To carry reinforcements and stores to Spitzbergen. Cumberland, Sheffield* and one destroyer.

(8) *Distant Covering Force* (from Akureyri in north Iceland) *Anson* (flag of Vice-Admiral Sir Bruce Fraser, Second-in-Command Home Fleet), *Duke of York, Jamaica* and five short-endurance destroyers.

(9) *Submarine Patrols.* Four off Lofoten Islands, three off north Norway.

The Commander-in-Chief himself stayed at Scapa in the *King George V*, and controlled the operation from that base. He reported later that he found this arrangement advantageous. The sea-keeping capacity of the distant covering force was naturally much restricted by the lack of a proper screen; but that handicap had been deliberately accepted. One other change was made in the plans. To give both convoys full protection while they most needed it, namely in the Barents Sea, the earlier custom of sailing them so that they crossed in the neighbourhood of Bear Island had to be abandoned. The west-bound convoy, QP.14, was therefore ordered not to sail till the east-bound convoy had nearly reached its destination. This, of course, greatly extended the whole operation, with all the addition-al strain on ships and crews. Furthermore at this time of year the ice edge had receded far to the north, which permitted the convoys to pass north of Bear Island, but also lengthened their time on passage. It was the increased duration of the operation caused by these factors which made it necessary to send so many oilers with, or ahead of, the convoy. The escorts were to refuel from the two oilers in the convoy, or would be sent in turn to replenish from the two in Lowe Sound, Spitzbergen. It has been mentioned that the enemy became aware, from our wireless traffic, of the revised plans for the next pair of convoys.

The main body of the outward convoy sailed from Loch Ewe on the 2nd of September. To conserve the long-range escorts' fuel, ships from the Western Approaches command looked after it as far as the Denmark Strait. On the 7th the long-range escort relieved the Western Approaches group, and two days later Admiral Burnett joined with the *Scylla, Avenger* and half the 'fighting destroyer escort'. The other half of the latter had gone ahead to Lowe Sound to fuel from the oilers, which had left Scapa on the 3rd.

The enemy was determined to do his best to repeat his success against PQ.17.[1] He first devoted a great deal of flying to the attempt

---

[1] See pp. 136–145.

to find PQ.18, before it had actually sailed; but on the 8th of September his air searches succeeded in locating it north of Iceland. Twelve U-boats were disposed in three groups along its anticipated course. On the 10th the *Scheer, Hipper, Köln* and some destroyers moved from Narvik to Altenfiord. They were sighted by our submarine patrols, but only the *Tigris* got in an attack, and she missed. The *Tirpitz* stayed behind in Narvik. On the 13th the German Group Command, North, wished to sail the Altenfiord squadron to attack QP.14; but Hitler warned Raeder that, because the ships were so important to the defence of Norway, he must not accept undue risks. Raeder thereupon cancelled the operation, and the surface ships remained idle throughout the convoys' passages. The Luftwaffe, on the other hand, was ordered to make a great effort against PQ.18. Once again the German failure to integrate sea and air operations is to be remarked. There were now ninety-two German torpedo-bombers and 133 long-range and dive-bombers in north Norway. The enemy knew that a carrier was accompanying the convoy, and decided to single her out as the chief target.

Between the 9th and 13th of September the escorts refuelled by

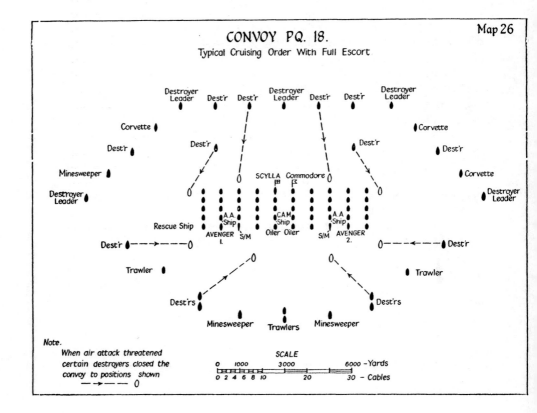

CONVOY PQ. 18.

Typical Cruising Order With Full Escort

Map 26

Note.

When air attack threatened certain destroyers closed the convoy to positions shown — -→ -- — 0

SCALE

detachments in Lowe Sound or from the convoy oilers, and by the afternoon of the latter date all had rejoined; the escort was thus at full strength for the most hazardous stretch. The convoy was then about 150 miles north-west of Bear Island. A typical formation of the convoy and its unusually powerful and assorted escort when at full strength is shown on the diagram on page 282.

So far things had gone well. The *Faulknor* had sunk U.88 ahead of the convoy on the 12th, but next morning two ships in the starboard wing column were torpedoed and sunk. Other U-boat attacks were foiled by the destroyers and air patrols. Foggy weather, rain and snow storms had so far shielded the convoy from the air, but by the 13th enemy shadowers were in continuous touch with it. The *Avenger's* Sea Hurricanes could do little against the heavily protected German aircraft.[1] The first air attack took place that afternoon, and what was very ominous about it was that the convoy was then at least 450 miles from the German shore air bases. It was evident that even with the ice edge at its furthest northern limit our convoys could not be kept outside air striking distance from north Norway. After preliminary and ineffective bombing by a number of Ju.88s, about forty torpedo planes came in low on the convoy's starboard bow, in line abreast 'like a huge flight of nightmare locusts'. The merchantmen and escorts threw up an intense barrage and the Commodore ordered an emergency turn to starboard which, in the excitement of the moment seems not to have been executed. The enemy pressed in very boldly, and the attack was over in seven or eight minutes. In the two starboard wing columns of the convoy only one ship survived. Eight ships in all were sunk, at a cost to the enemy of five aircraft. Two more attacks, but of a much less dangerous nature, were beaten off later that evening without further loss; but the convoy had taken a hard knock in the massed attack. The *Avenger's* aircraft were engaged with shadowers or high-level bombers at the time, and thus no fighter defence was available. Her Captain decided in future to reserve his small fighter strength to break up large formations. In the early hours of the 14th the oiler *Atheltemplar* in the convoy was damaged by a U-boat, and had to be sunk. But she was avenged when, not many hours later, co-ordinated action by one of the *Avenger's* Swordfish and the destroyer *Onslow* led to the destruction of U.589.

Meanwhile the possibility that the *Tirpitz* was at sea was causing anxiety in London. On the 14th a reconnaissance aircraft sent from Britain found that she was not in her usual berth in Narvik, while a similar reconnaissance from North Russia had only located the

---

[1] The *Avenger's* Hurricanes were of the earliest type (Mark I). Admiral Tovey represented to the Prime Minister and Sir Stafford Cripps that to use these old aircraft to defend merchantmen carrying much later types of Hurricane (Marks X or XI) to Russia was illogical. As a result improved types were sent to the carriers.

Scheer, Hipper and *Köln.* In fact the *Tirpitz* was only exercising inside Vestfiord, but the uncertainty as to her whereabouts, and a gap in the long-range patrols off north Norway during the night of the 13th-14th, led to the Hampden torpedo striking force being sent out on an offensive sweep. However they sighted nothing. Doubts regarding the *Tirpitz's* movements were not dispelled until she was seen back in her old anchorage on the 18th.

In the early afternoon of the 14th the air battle around the convoy was renewed by a torpedo attack similar to that which had wrought such destruction the previous day, but smaller. This time the torpedo-bombers concentrated against the *Avenger* and the escorting warships. The carrier and the A.A. ship *Ulster Queen* stood out from the convoy to gain freedom of manoeuvre, and the former flew off half a dozen Hurricanes. The fighters drove off some enemies, while the escorts' gunfire forced others to drop their torpedoes at long range. No ships were hit and thirteen torpedo-bombers were shot down. 'It was a fine sight', wrote Admiral Burnett, 'to see [the] *Avenger* peeling off Hurricanes whilst streaking across the front of the convoy . . . Altogether a most gratifying action'. Next came more bombing by Ju.88s. Though some ships, including the invaluable carrier, had narrow escapes, none was hit. Then more torpedo-bombers arrived, and again they made a dead set at the *Avenger;* but she was ready for them, and by clever organisation managed to get ten of her twelve Hurricanes in the air at the critical moment. They and the escorts' guns destroyed nine enemies. One merchant-man—again in the ill-fated starboard wing column—was torpedoed and blew up, and three Hurricanes were lost when they most gallantly accepted the risk of flying through our own ships' barrage. Happily all the pilots were rescued. The last event of the day was another ineffectual bombing attack.

Next day, the 15th, was comparatively quiet—if such an expression can ever be used to describe a day with a Russian convoy in the Barents Sea. Only about half a hundred bombers attacked, and they were well harried by fighters and gunfire. No ships were hit. Though a lull in the air battle followed, there were still a large number of U-boats to contend with. About a dozen were in contact with the convoy, but their attempts to penetrate the screen were promptly and successfully countered. The presence of escorting Catalinas after the 15th of September certainly contributed to this favourable result. No attacks got home, and early on the 16th the destroyer *Impulsive* sank U.457.

That same afternoon Admiral Burnett and the greater part of his force left PQ.18, to take over protection of the homeward convoy. PQ.18 received, however, a welcome reinforcement of four Russian destroyers by way of replacement. On the 18th, when at the entrance to the White Sea, the convoy was again attacked by a combination of bombers and torpedo-bombers. One ship was lost, but four enemies were destroyed—one of them by the Hurricane of the C.A.M. ship *Empire Morn*.[1] The fighter pilot (Flying Officer A. H. Barr) then drove off other enemies by making dummy attacks, and finally flew 240 miles to an airfield near Archangel. He landed with four gallons of petrol left. A last enemy attempt was made on the 20th while the convoy, as though it had not already endured enough, was trying to shelter from a full gale which had blown up. Luckily no damage was done.

So ended the battle of PQ.18. It had been chiefly fought between the escorts and the Luftwaffe, and the latter, urged on personally by Marshal Göring, had done its worst. Though enemy aircraft sank ten ships, they lost about forty of their number in doing so; and they entirely failed in their purpose of breaking up the convoy in the way that they had, as they erroneously believed, broken up PQ.17. U-boats sank three more ships, but lost three of their number in the battle. Twenty-seven of the original forty ships in the convoy reached Archangel.

Convoy QP.14, of fifteen ships, left Archangel on the 13th of September under Commodore Dowding, R.N.R., who had been in charge of the ill-fated PQ.17 and had seen it through its agony most heroically.[2] QP.14 had an escort of two anti-aircraft ships and eleven corvettes, minesweepers and trawlers. It was joined by Admiral Burnett's force on the 17th in about 75° North and 48° East. The next three days were comparatively uneventful. The weather was thick at first, and this, combined with a diversion made up the west coast of Spitzbergen, defeated shadowing aircraft and U-boats. The two fleet oilers which had been with the outward convoy had by this time emptied their tanks in supplying the escorts, so one of the Spitzbergen oilers was fetched out by destroyers to join the homeward convoy.

After the relative quiet of the first week the luck changed on the 20th. Firstly the fleet minesweeper *Leda* was torpedoed and sunk by a U-boat. Though the *Avenger's* Swordfish and the destroyers hunted and harried the enemies which were trailing the convoy, they did not actually succeed in destroying any of them at this time. In the evening a merchantman, the *Silver Sword*, which had survived PQ.17, was sunk. As the danger from air attack had now passed Admiral Burnett transferred his flag to the destroyer *Milne*, and sent home the *Avenger* and *Scylla* escorted by three destroyers. He considered that to keep these valuable ships longer with the convoy would only offer tempting targets to the U-boats; but his decision deprived the

---

[1] See Volume I, p. 477 regarding C.A.M. ships.
[2] See pp. 136–145.

merchantmen of the regular air anti-submarine escort which only a carrier could provide, and the consequences were quickly felt. Hardly had the warships parted company when the destroyer *Somali*, which was with the convoy, was torpedoed. Her sister ship, the *Ashanti*, took her in tow, and they struggled west for eight hours. Then, when 420 miles had been covered, a gale blew up and the *Somali* broke in half. Another of the splendid pre-war Tribal class destroyers, originally sixteen strong had gone.[1]

Very soon after the *Avenger* had been detached Admiral Burnett signalled for long-range shore-based aircraft 'to escort QP.14 and assist in keeping submarines down'. Next day, the 21st, Catalinas and Liberators from the Shetlands and Iceland were with the convoy for about four hours; but the slow Atlantic convoy SC.100 was meanwhile being subjected to heavy U-boat attacks, and was in urgent need of air escort. This made it more difficult than ever for Coastal Command to look after QP.14.

Admiral Burnett in the *Milne* parted company with the convoy on the 22nd, leaving it in charge of Captain Scott-Moncrieff in the *Faulknor*. He had eleven destroyers and nine smaller ships left to screen the merchantmen, but weather conditions made it impossible for shore-based aircraft from either the Shetlands or Iceland to fly any sorties that day. An hour after the *Milne* had gone three ships were sunk by U.435 in a matter of a few minutes. One was the *Bellingham*, another survivor of PQ.17, one was the Commodore's ship and the third was a fleet oiler. This was a hard blow, coming after so many trials and perils had been successfully surmounted. The lack of air cover and the inevitable exhaustion of the crews of the escorting warships, which had been at sea in conditions demanding perpetual vigilance and producing unparalleled physical and mental strain for about eighteen continuous days and nights, both probably contributed to the U-boat getting inside the screen.

---

[1] Only four of the sixteen *Tribal*-class destroyers now survived. The very heavy losses suffered by them, as by all the pre-war destroyer flotillas, can best be illustrated by tabulating the losses.

Gurkha	Sunk by enemy aircraft off Norway, 9th April 1940.
Afridi	Sunk by enemy aircraft off Norway, 3rd May 1940.
Mohawk	Torpedoed by Italian destroyer off North Africa, 16th April 1941 and sunk by our own forces.
Mashona	Sunk by enemy aircraft in the North Atlantic, 28th May 1941.
Cossack	Sunk west of Gibraltar, 27th October 1941, after being torpedoed by U-boat on the 23rd.
Matabele	Sunk by U-boat in Barents Sea, 17th January 1942.
Maori	Sunk by enemy aircraft in Malta, 12th February 1942.
Punjabi	Rammed and sunk by the *King George V*, 1st May 1942 during the passage of convoy PQ.15.
Bedouin	Sunk by enemy aircraft in the central Mediterranean, 15th June 1942.
Sikh	Sunk by shore battery fire off Tobruk, 14th September 1942.
Zulu	Sunk by enemy aircraft in eastern Mediterranean, 14th September 1942.
Somali	Torpedoed by U-boat in the Arctic, 20th September 1942, and sank whilst in tow on the 24th.

Happily it was the last attack. On the 23rd air escorts reached the convoy, a Catalina of No. 210 Squadron sank U.253, and the U-boat attacks ceased. The twelve survivors of QP.14 reached Loch Ewe on the 26th.

It remains to mention that the main battle force of the Home Fleet had put to sea for two periods from Akureyri to try to produce the illusion that heavy ship cover was being afforded while the convoys were east of Bear Island; that the cruiser covering force had revictualled the Spitzbergen garrison for the winter and had then covered the returning convoy; that photographic aircraft had kept a constant watch on the German warships, and that Catalinas had patrolled off north Norway throughout the convoys' passages.

There was certainly ground for reasonable satisfaction over the outcome of these operations. True, the losses of merchantmen and warships had been serious, but the escorts had hit back hard and effectively. Not only did the enemy lose a total of four U-boats, but out of 337 air sorties flown by the Luftwaffe against PQ.18, thirty-three torpedo planes, six long-range bombers and two reconnaissance aircraft were destroyed. Moreover it seemed clear that, in Admiral Tovey's words, 'the constant [air] reconnaissance [of Altenfiord], together with the strength of the destroyer covering force, the presence of torpedo aircraft in north Russia and of our submarines off the coast, probably all contributed to the enemy's decision not to venture on a surface attack'. Lastly special mention must be made of the *Avenger's* work. Just as the *Audacity* had first closed the 'air gap' on the Gibraltar route in September 1941[1], and others of her class were soon to close the 'Atlantic air gap'[2], so had the *Avenger* first performed the same inestimable service on the North Russia run. The meeting of the need for convoys to carry their own air defences along with them had been abundantly justified.[3]

After QP.14 had been brought home, the Coastal Command Catalinas were recalled from Russia. Only one had been lost, and they had done invaluable work escorting the outward convoy and watching for the enemy surface ships. The surviving Hampdens, of which ten had been destroyed in air raids on Vaenga, and also the photographic reconnaissance Spitfires, were turned over to the Russians with all their equipment. We do not know anything about their subsequent services. The light cruiser *Argonaut* and two destroyers were sent to Kola Inlet in mid-October, calling at Spitzbergen on the way; they landed a medical unit, which the Russians had now permitted to come out to look after our sick and wounded,

---

[1] See Vol. I, p. 478.
[2] See pp. 366–367.
[3] See Vol. I, p. 476.

and returned with the Royal Air Force Hampden crews. They all reached Scapa without incident on the 28th of October.

Though the Admiralty could not possibly have realised it at the time, we now know that the success achieved in the passage of PQ.18 and QP.14 was, in a way, decisive. Never again did the enemy deploy such great air strength in the far north. Before the next pair of convoys sailed, events in Africa had forced him to send south his entire heavy bomber and torpedo striking forces of Ju.88s and He.111s. Thus did a strategic success obtained thousands of miles away, when Allied soldiers landed in North Africa, have favourable repercussions inside the Arctic Circle; and because the African landings drew the Luftwaffe south more British and American tanks, vehicles and aircraft were before long helping the Russians in their great counter-offensive on the eastern front.

Finally it is worth recording the enemy's post-war comment regarding his failure to repeat the success achieved against PQ.17. He considered that 'the smaller successes [against PQ.18 and QP.14] were due to the fact that the convoys maintained their close formation in the face of heavy and persistent attacks'. Though it is of course undeniable that in certain circumstances, of which the *Jervis Bay's* action in defence of HX.84 against the *Scheer* is a notable example[1], a convoy should undoubtedly be ordered by the senior officer present to scatter, it is interesting to find the enemy stressing the advantages of maintaining formation.

Although, therefore, in terms of strategy the developments of the autumn of 1942 were favourable to the Allied cause, in terms of meeting Russia's pressing needs the immediate consequences were less favourable. Because the North African landings caused a great proportion of the Home Fleet's strength to be diverted south, it was impossible to run another convoy to North Russia for a time. Forty ships were ready loaded by the end of September, but to send them would have meant postponing Operation 'Torch' for three weeks. Very heavy pressure was applied by the Russians to get us to send the convoy; but the Prime Minister and the War Cabinet held firmly to the need to place first strategic requirements first. On the 22nd of September Mr Churchill told President Roosevelt that the time had come to tell Stalin that there would be no PQ.19, and that we could not run any more PQ convoys until January. The President, however, considered this 'a tough blow for the Russians' and urged that the convoy should be sailed in several successive groups, which Mr Churchill described as impossible of fulfilment. By way of compromise, from the end of October onwards a number of ships were sailed independently from Iceland to Russia, taking advantage of the

---

[1] See Vol. I, pp. 288-289.

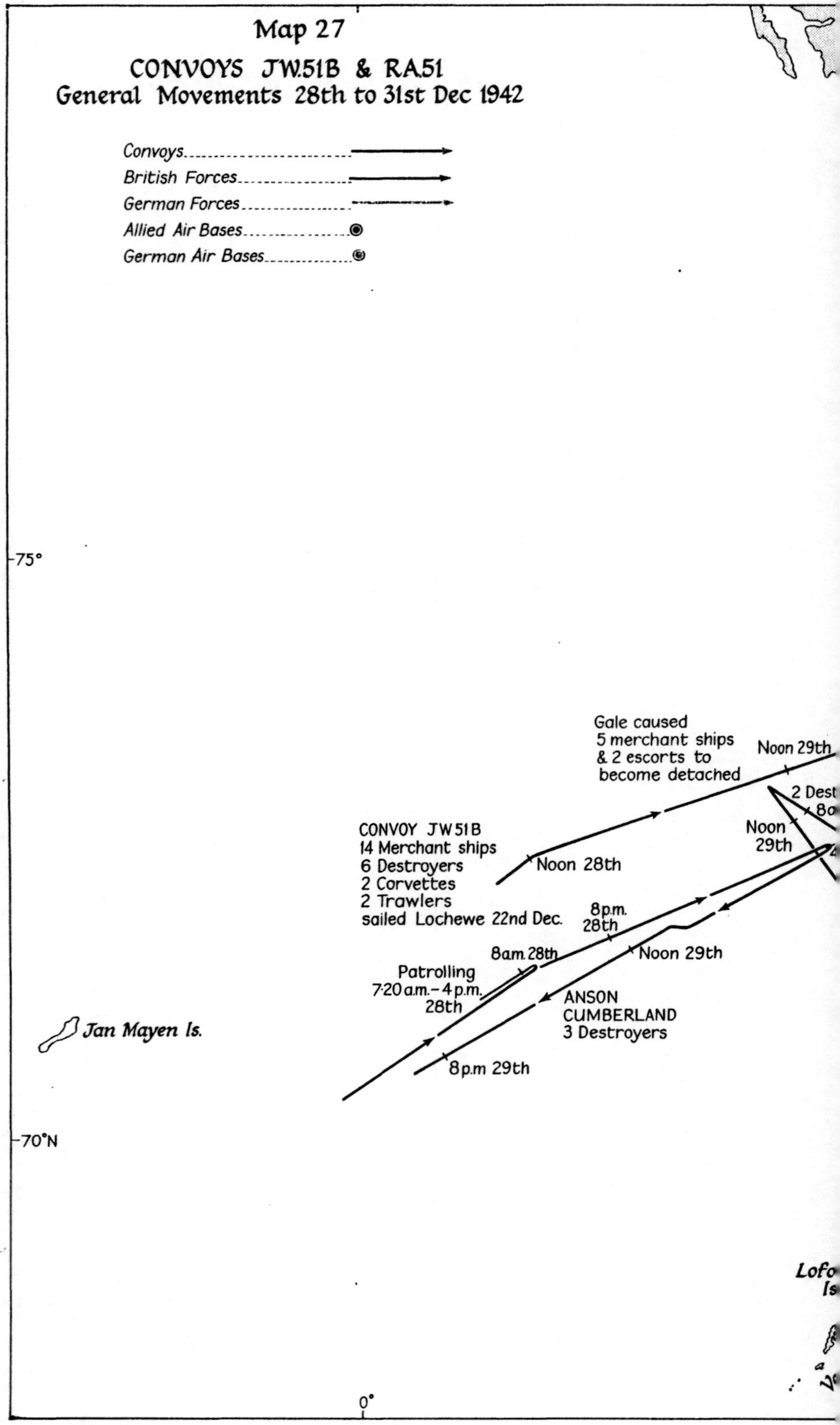

Map 27

CONVOYS JW.51B & RA.51
General Movements 28th to 31st Dec 1942

Convoys........................⟶
British Forces.................⟶
German Forces.................⟶
Allied Air Bases.............◉
German Air Bases............◉

Gale caused
5 merchant ships
& 2 escorts to
become detached

Noon 29th

2 Dest
8a

Noon
29th

CONVOY JW51B
14 Merchant ships
6 Destroyers
2 Corvettes
2 Trawlers
sailed Lochewe 22nd Dec.

Noon 28th

8p.m.
28th

8am.28th

Noon 29th

Patrolling
7·20 a.m.– 4 p.m.
28th

ANSON
CUMBERLAND
3 Destroyers

Jan Mayen Is.

8 p.m 29th

75°

70°N

Lofo
Is

0°

Advent Bay

...e Sound

...PITZBERGEN

Hope Is.

BARENTS SEA

Bear Is.

CONVOY J.W.51B
Noon 30th
...ched to U.K.
8.30 p.m. 30th
7.45 a.m. 31st
8.30 a.m. 31st
9.55 a.m.
10.30 a.m. 31st
6 a.m. 30th
10.20 a.m. 31st
10.45 a.m. 31st

Action of
31st Dec '42
see Maps
28 & 29

Noon 28th
SHEFFIELD
JAMAICA
2 Destroyers
left Kola Inlet
27th Dec

8 p.m. 28th
8 p.m. 29th

HIPPER & 3 Destr's
8 a.m. 31st
Noon 30th
6 p.m. 30th

LÜTZOW & 3 Destr's
2.40 a.m. 31st

1 a.m. 31st
GRAPH UNRULY TRESPASSER SEADOG
North Cape
Submarine patrols
29th Dec – 4th Jan.

9.45 p.m. 30th

Banak

Altenfiord

Tromso

Kirkenes
Petsamo
Polyarnoe
Vaenga
Kola Inlet

11.45 a.m. 31st
7 a.m. 31st

CONVOY RA.51
14 Merchant ships
6 Destroyers
1 Minesweeper
4 Trawlers
sailed Murmansk
30th Dec.

Bardufoss

Narvik

Murmansk

30°

long nights. British and American ships were sent off alternatively at intervals of about 200 miles. Trawlers were spaced out along the route for life-saving purposes, and submarines were sent to patrol north of Bear Island. These independent sailings were more successful than some people had expected. They are tabulated below:

Table 22. Independent Sailings to North Russia,
October–December 1942

	Sailed	Turned Back	Sunk	Wrecked	Arrived
To Russia .	13	3	4	1	5
From Russia .	23	Nil	1	Nil	22

As large numbers of Allied merchantmen had been waiting many months in Russian ports for homeward escort, in November it was decided to mount a comparatively small operation to bring home about thirty of them. The passage would be made in almost continuous darkness, the ice conditions still permitted a route to be taken north of Bear Island, and the Luftwaffe's strength was known to be greatly reduced. Accordingly on the 17th of November convoy QP.15, of which twenty-eight ships actually got to sea, sailed from Archangel. The escort consisted of an A.A. ship and ten smaller vessels. It was to be reinforced by five destroyers in the Barents Sea, and they were to be relieved by five others later. The cruisers London and Suffolk, with three destroyers, provided cover west of Bear Island while four submarines patrolled off Altenfiord to discourage the Hipper and Köln from sailing.

The convoy was severely buffeted by a succession of gales which, combined with the almost continuous darkness, caused it to become very scattered. It was not found by either of the destroyer reinforcements, and by the time it reached Bear Island it was broken up into a number of small groups. Fortunately the weather not only defeated the German air reconnaissance but also prevented German surface ships putting to sea, as had been intended. U-boats sank two ships, but all the rest ultimately reached Iceland, whence they were escorted on to Loch Ewe.

This was the last of the convoys in the famous PQ-QP series. For security reasons their designations were now changed to JW and RA, both starting at number 51.

Before continuing with the Home Fleet's story, it is perhaps worth reviewing German strategic purposes as 1942 drew to a close. Hitler's obsession about a pending invasion of Norway, or of north Europe, was still the dominant factor; and it had been enhanced by our raids on the French and Norwegian coasts. Troops were moved

U

west in large numbers, and fortifications started on a pro
scale. His restrictive orders regarding the use of the surface sh
especially of the *Tirpitz*, remained in force. Finally the sho
fuel was now seriously cramping all German maritime purpo
operations. The *Scheer* went back to Germany to refit e
November, but the *Nürnberg* arrived at Narvik on the 2nd of De
in her place. Early in the same month the *Lützow* came fr
Baltic firstly to Narvik and then, on the 18th, joined the *Hip*
Köln in Altenfiord, where there were also from three to
destroyers. The *Tirpitz* sailed from Narvik to Trondheim
23rd of October, and remained there for the rest of this pha
was suffering from numerous defects and was badly in ne
dockyard refit, but Hitler's insistence on her remaining in :
prevented her being brought back to Germany for dockir
repair facilities at Trondheim were therefore employed, an
yard workmen were sent there by ship from Germany to ha:
great ship's refit as much as possible.

The appearance of the *Lützow* in the north caused Admira
to re-establish the Denmark Strait patrol, which had more
lapsed on account of the shortage of cruisers, and to m
battleship *Anson* to Hvalfiord. The enemy did actually in
send the pocket-battleship out into the Atlantic, but not un
the next operation against our Arctic convoys.

During the interval between the passage of PQ.18 and t
convoy, the Admiralty and the Commander-in-Chief onc
reviewed the whole question of these intricate and ha
operations. The Admiralty wished to sail one large convoy as
fully escorted as PQ.18 had been; but the Commander-i
pressed for two smaller ones. He considered that the lack of e
during the winter months would put a stop to the enen
reconnaissance, and that small, easily-handled convoys migh
for escape both air and submarine attacks. The possibility
weather breaking up a large convoy into scattered groups e
many miles of ocean, as had occurred with QP.15, was
present at that time of year; if that happened it would be ea
the enemy to find and attack the merchantmen. Small e
were, in Admiral Tovey's view, more easily kept together, ar
more easily re-formed if scattered by storms. The Admiralty a
his views on the size of the convoys, but the First Sea Lord
that the covering force of two cruisers should not turn back a
25° East, but should go well into the Barents Sea with the c
Events were to show that in this matter the Admiralty's ju
was correct.

The chief danger to the convoys now came from U-bo
which there were more in the far north than ever before. Se

them came the surface ships in the Norwegian fiords. As usual the latter made it necessary that the main Home Fleet should cover the operation from a position some 350 miles north-west of Altenfiord. Submarines patrolled off north Norway as before.

Convoy JW.51A, of fifteen ships and a fleet oiler, escorted by seven destroyers and five smaller ships, sailed from Loch Ewe on the 15th of December and had a fine passage, passing south of Bear Island. It was not sighted at all and arrived safely and appropriately off Kola Inlet on Christmas Day. Admiral Burnett, with the *Sheffield* (Captain A. W. Clarke), the *Jamaica* (Captain J. L. Storey) and two destroyers, went right through with the merchantmen. Convoy JW.51B, of fourteen ships, left a week after JW.51A, with an escort of six destroyers and five smaller ships under Captain R. St. V. Sherbrooke in the *Onslow*.[1] The first six days passed quietly, but then a gale caused two of the escort and five merchantmen to lose touch with the remainder. The minesweeper *Bramble* (Commander H. T. Rust), one of the only two ships in the escort fitted with radar, was detached to look for the missing merchantmen on the 29th, but she never found them, and was finally caught and sunk in unequal combat with the *Hipper* on the 31st. Four of the merchantmen and one escort actually rejoined the convoy; the fifth and the other escort reached Kola Inlet separately, but safely.

Meanwhile Admiral Burnett had sailed from Kola on the 27th to cover and support the convoy. He first swept well to the west, then sent his two destroyers home while he himself with the two cruisers turned east again on the 29th, keeping some way to the south of the convoy route. Next day, in the longitude of Kola Inlet, he turned north-west, with the intention of crossing the convoy's route early on New Year's Eve.[2] His plan was to cover the convoy from a position about forty miles astern, thus avoiding the U-boats which might well be trailing it. The Admiral's guess was that the enemy would know the approximate course of JW.51B, but would not know how far along it the convoy had steamed. The most likely action by the surface ships from Altenfiord would be to sweep along the route from west to east. Admiral Burnett considered that the last day of the year would be the most critical. By covering the convoy from its northern flank he would gain 'the advantage of light', because enemy ships would stand out against such daylight as there was in the southern sky. Things did not, however, turn out at all as the Admiral expected, chiefly because an estimated position of the convoy signalled by the Commander-in-Chief at 4 p.m. on the 29th was

---

[1] It is interesting to recall that the last destroyer to bear the name H.M.S. *Onslow* was commanded by Lieutenant-Commander J. C. Tovey, and fought with great distinction in the Battle of Jutland. See *Corbett*, Naval Operations, Vol. III (Longmans Green & Co.) Revised Edition, 1939, pp. 344, 357 and 363.

[2] See Map 27 (opp. p. 289).

considerably in error. Admiral Burnett was thereby led to believe that the convoy was 150 miles further east, and slightly further north than was actually the case. In consequence the cruisers crossed ahead instead of astern of the convoy, and at 8.30 a.m. on the 31st were about thirty miles due north of it.[1] So far our forces had received no indication that the enemy knew anything about the convoy's progress. That, in spite of all scientific advances, conditions at sea can still leave plenty of room for doubt and confusion is well shown by the fact that, throughout all the confused fighting which followed, Admiral Burnett never sighted the convoy which he was protecting, and never discovered exactly where it was. Our ships were constantly plagued by uncertainty whether a radar contact, or a ship dimly discerned in the Arctic twilight, was a friend, an enemy, or a straggler from the convoy. Knowledge that the recent gale might well have scattered the merchantmen, as in fact it had, made the uncertainties still more acute.

We will now temporarily take leave of JW.51B and its covering force to see what the enemy knew, and what he was doing. A U-boat had reported the convoy south of Bear Island on the 30th, and the *Hipper* (flying the flag of Vice-Admiral Kummetz), the *Lützow* and six destroyers at once put to sea. The German Admiral knew nothing about Admiral Burnett's covering cruisers; and he had received orders to the effect that he must not accept action with equal or superior forces, nor risk his heavy ships in a night battle in which our escorts might use their torpedoes. The German Naval Staff, though no doubt pressed in that direction by Hitler, seems to have shown remarkable aptitude for depriving its sea-going commanders of all initiative. But quite apart from the effect of these cramping restrictions, the German plan lacked singleness of purpose; for the *Lützow* was under orders to break out into the Atlantic after the attack on the convoy, and this may well account for the marked timidity with which she was handled in the fighting shortly to be described.

Admiral Kummetz intended to approach the convoy from astern, as his British opponent had anticipated. The attack was, however, to be made from both flanks, for which reason the German forces were divided. The *Hipper* and three destroyers were to approach from the north-west, the *Lützow* and the other three destroyers from the south. Kummetz hoped that the British escorts would be drawn off by the first attackers, and so leave the convoy at the mercy of the second. Though the German Admiral has been criticised for dividing his forces, it is to be remarked that events worked out almost exactly as he planned; the *Lützow's* force passed very close indeed to the south of the convoy while almost all its escorts were engaged with

---

[1] See Map 27 (opp. p. 289).

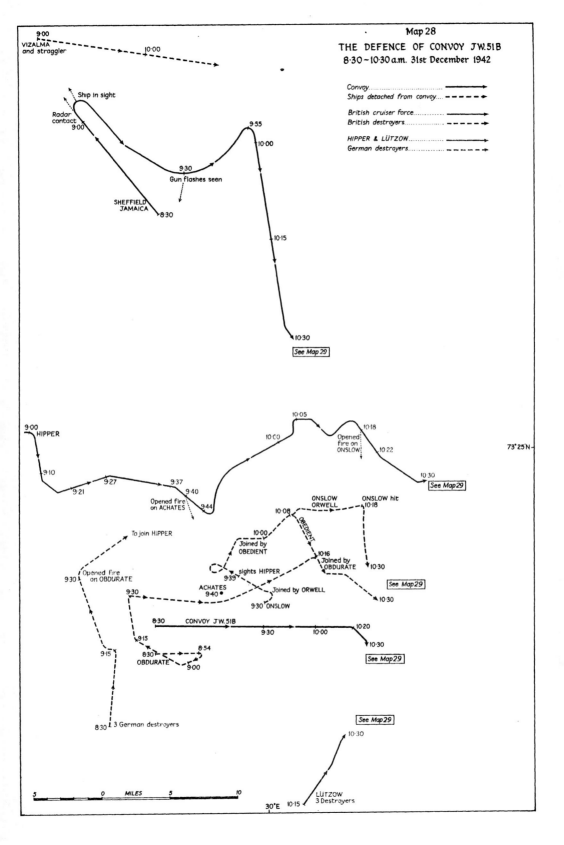

Map 28

THE DEFENCE OF CONVOY JW.51B
8·30~10·30 a.m. 31st December 1942

Convoy.................................... →
Ships detached from convoy.... --→

British cruiser force.............. →
British destroyers.................. --→

HIPPER & LÜTZOW.................. →
German destroyers................. --→

9·00
VIZALMA
and straggler
10·00

Ship in sight
Radar contact
9·00
9·55
10·00
9·30
Gun flashes seen
SHEFFIELD
JAMAICA
8·30
10·15
10·30
See Map 29

9·00 HIPPER
9·10
9·21
9·27
9·37
9·40
Opened fire
on ACHATES
9·44
10·00
10·05
10·18
Opened
fire on
ONSLOW
10·22
10·30
See Map 29
73°25′N

ONSLOW
ORWELL
ONSLOW hit
10·18
10·08
10·00
Joined by
OBEDIENT
OBEDIENT
10·16
Joined by
OBDURATE
10·30
See Map 29
To join HIPPER
sights HIPPER
ACHATES
9·40
Joined by ORWELL
9·30 ONSLOW
10·30
Opened fire
on OBDURATE
9·30
9·30
9·15
8·30 CONVOY JW.51B
9·30
10·00
10·20
10·30
See Map 29
9·15
8·30
OBDURATE
8·54
9·00
8·30 3 German destroyers

See Map 29
10·30

5   0   MILES   5   10
30°E 10·15
LÜTZOW
3 Destroyers

the *Hipper's* force on the other flank. It seems that only the over-caution of the *Lützow's* Captain then saved the convoy from utter destruction.

At 8.30 a.m. on New Year's Eve there were four groups of British ships all in the vicinity of about 73° North 29° East, none of which knew the exact position of the others. The main convoy of twelve ships with eight escorts was steering about east; some forty-five miles north of it was the trawler *Vizalma* with one merchantman, while the minesweeper *Bramble* was about fifteen miles north-east of the convoy. Finally Admiral Burnett, with the *Sheffield* and the *Jamaica*, was about thirty miles north of the convoy and fifteen miles south-east of the *Vizalma*.[1] Quite unknown to all our forces the *Hipper's* group had just passed across the convoy's wake, twenty miles astern of it, while the *Lützow's* was fifty miles away and closing from the south. The weather was clear, except during snow squalls, and visibility varied between seven and ten miles. It was freezing hard, and although the sea was calm the spray which swept over the destroyers when they steamed at more than about twenty knots was freezing as it came on board. This made it very difficult for them to fight their forward guns.

Before sailing Captain Sherbrooke had decided what his tactics would be if the convoy was attacked by enemy surface forces, and he had described them at the convoy conference. The fleet destroyers would, in such an event concentrate with their flotilla commander on the threatened flank of the convoy, while he would at once steer to intercept the enemy, keeping between the attackers and the merchantmen. The convoy was to turn away from the enemy and drop smoke floats, while the remaining escorts would form a close screen and lay smoke between the enemy and the convoy. When the moment arrived all ships acted precisely as Sherbrooke had prescribed, and his foresight reaped a splendid reward in saving the merchantmen from a most dangerous situation.

At about 8.20 a.m. the corvette *Hyderabad*, one of the close escort, sighted two strange destroyers. She took them to be the expected Russian reinforcements, and therefore made no report. Ten minutes later the destroyer *Obdurate*, which was on the starboard beam of the convoy, sighted and reported the same ships crossing astern of the convoy. Sherbrooke at once answered the *Obdurate's* report with an order to her to 'investigate', and she thereupon hauled round towards the unidentified ships. At the same time Sherbrooke sent his own ship's company to breakfast and ordered them to change into clean underclothing. It must have been one of the few occasions when that traditional order before battle was actually given during the last war.

---

[1] See Map 28.

The *Obdurate* was meanwhile closing at her best speed and trying to identify the ships, which were actually the three destroyers of the *Hipper's* group, against a background of dark snow-laden clouds. Though she was cutting off a corner as she closed, it was not until 9.30 that she was within four miles of the ships, which then identified themselves as enemies by opening fire on the *Obdurate*.[1] The British destroyer turned away towards the convoy, and the enemy made no attempt to follow her. Captain Sherbrooke saw the gun flashes, at once altered course towards them and told the *Orwell*, *Obedient* and *Obdurate* to join him. At 9.41 Sherbrooke made the first definite enemy report. It was received in the cruiser flagship five minutes later, and as a previous message had given the destroyer leader's position Admiral Burnett now knew that enemy forces were in contact with the convoy escorts, and also the whereabouts of the latter.

The movement of Captain Sherbrooke's four ships towards the enemy left only the destroyer *Achates* (Lieutenant-Commander A. H. T. Johns) and three smaller escorts with the convoy. They moved out to lay a smoke screen between the merchant ships and the enemy. At 9.39 a more formidable opponent—actually the *Hipper*—was sighted by the *Onslow*, which at the time only had the *Orwell* with her. The German heavy cruiser opened fire on the *Achates*, and Captain Sherbrooke's two British destroyers followed round and engaged her. For half an hour the two forces skirmished in and out of the smoke, while Sherbrooke took every opportunity to threaten the enemy with his torpedoes. The convoy, shielded by the escorts' smoke screen, meanwhile held on to the east. Captain Sherbrooke was now anxious lest the three German destroyers should get among the merchantmen, so he sent the *Obedient* and *Obdurate* back to rejoin the convoy. Soon after 10 a.m. a signal came from the *Sheffield* that she was approaching on a southerly course. This news was received 'with acclamation' by the destroyers, which had believed Admiral Burnett's cruisers to be a long way off. But in fact, for reasons to be discussed later, reinforcement of the small ships was not yet close at hand.

The *Hipper* had meanwhile conducted herself in a very uncertain manner, though this may have been partly done intentionally in order to conform to Kummetz's plan to lure our escorts away to the north. But her gunnery had so far been 'aimless and erratic'. True, light conditions were very difficult with 'sea and cloud all merging into a uniform silver-grey', against which the camouflaged ships of Sherbrooke's flotilla showed up but dimly. Furthermore a lame tanker straggling astern of the convoy seems to have distracted the *Hipper's* attention and disorganised her gunnery control. However at

---

[1] See Map 28 (opp. p. 293).

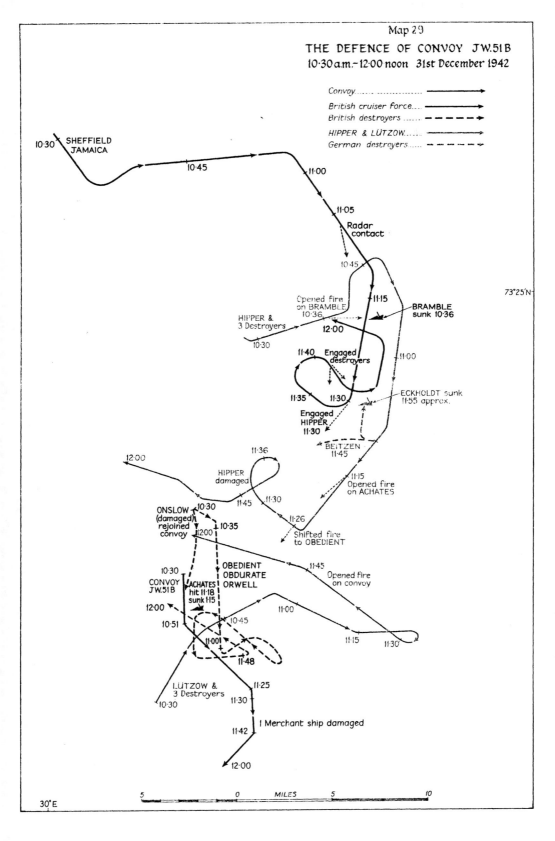

Map 29

THE DEFENCE OF CONVOY JW.51B
10.30 a.m.–12.00 noon 31st December 1942

Convoy ....
British cruiser force ....
British destroyers ......
HIPPER & LÜTZOW ......
German destroyers ......

about 10.20, in the words of Lieutenant-Commander D. C. Kinloch of the *Obedient*, 'she suddenly pulled herself together', quickly found the *Onslow's* range, put half Sherbrooke's armament out of action, holed his ship in the engine room, set her on fire—and severely wounded her Captain. He, however, continued to direct his ships until another hit forced him to disengage. Only when he had learnt that Kinloch had effectively taken over command of his flotilla did he leave his bridge. Captain Sherbrooke was awarded the Victoria Cross in recognition of his gallant and determined leadership, and of his successful defence of the merchantmen in this action. The *Hipper's* report also pays tribute to the skill with which the British destroyers shielded their charges. It was 10.35 a.m. when Lieutenant-Commander Kinloch learnt that he was in command of the close escort. His main adversary, the *Hipper*, disappeared in a snow squall at about the same time.

To turn now to the covering cruisers, Admiral Burnett's southward movement towards the convoy was first delayed by investigation of a radar contact, which was actually the *Vizalma* and her single merchantman. At 9.30 the cruisers sighted gun flashes over the southern horizon, but the Admiral thought that they must come from 'H.A. fire, probably at Russian aircraft'. At 9.46 heavy gunfire was observed to the southward, and Captain Sherbrooke's first definite enemy report, already mentioned, was received at about the same time. Nine minutes later the cruisers hauled round to a southerly course, increased speed to twenty-five knots and signalled their approach to the destroyers.

As the *Sheffield* and *Jamaica* steamed south and worked up speed to thirty-one knots, they caught glimpses of the fight between the destroyers and the *Hipper*, but could not make out friend from foe. Nor did two radar contacts obtained at long range help to elucidate matters. At 10.32 the Admiral felt the need to identify and track these contacts. He therefore turned from the course which would have brought him rapidly into touch with our destroyers, and steered in an easterly direction.[1] Then came a burst of fire on his starboard bow—probably caused by the *Hipper* sinking the unfortunate little *Bramble*—and the Admiral closed towards it. An enemy ship was sighted by the flagship at 10.45, and Admiral Burnett 'followed [this target] around' to the south nine minutes later. At 11.05 the cruiser flagship obtained another radar contact to starboard. We shall return shortly to this ship. At about the same time Commander Kinloch gave the Admiral his position, and reported that he would 'home' the cruisers by wireless.[2] It is therefore evident that neither

---

[1] See Map 29.

[2] Lieutenant-Commander Kinloch was promoted on New Year's Eve 1942, while the battle here described was in progress in the Arctic.

force at that time knew the position of the other. At 11.12 the cruisers returned to a southerly course. Though the situation with which Admiral Burnett was confronted was certainly very confusing, and allowance must be made both for the arctic conditions and the uncertain efficiency of the radar sets then in use, it does now seem that the British cruisers should have been able to intervene earlier. The failure of the *Hyderabad* to report the first unidentified ships sighted, and the long interval which elapsed before the *Obdurate* was certain that they were enemies, both contributed to the cruiser Admiral's perplexities; but the main cause was the two easterly diversions made by Admiral Burnett from 9 to 9.55 a.m. and from 10.35 to 10.55.[1] The reason why these changes of course were made has already been explained.

The hour following on Kinloch's assuming command of the escort was a very anxious one for him. After disengaging from the *Hipper* he steered south with his three destroyers to overtake the convoy, which had altered to the south-east at 10.20 a.m. and was still shielded by the *Achates* with her smoke. The damaged *Onslow* had meanwhile taken station ahead of the merchantmen.

The next development came quickly, but in no way lessened the escort commander's anxieties. At 10.45 the corvette *Rhododendron* reported unidentified ships close at hand to the south. Actually the *Hyderabad* had sighted these—the *Lützow's* force—a little earlier, but again had made no report. Only a providential snow squall, and the timidity of the German pocket-battleship's Captain, saved the convoy from a most unpleasant predicament; for the powerful German force had got within a couple of miles of its quarry before being sighted. Fortunately the *Lützow* stood away, 'to wait for the weather to clear'.

While the convoy was thus narrowly escaping destruction by the *Lützow*, the *Hipper* was steering E.N.E. at high speed. It was this movement that led to the destruction of the *Bramble*, already mentioned. Her enemy report was picked up by the *Hyderabad*, but once more the latter maintained silence.

At about 11 a.m., by which time Kinloch's destroyers had overtaken the convoy, the weather cleared and the *Lützow's* force was once again sighted.[2] The *Obedient* and her consorts at once steered to keep between her and the convoy, and shielded the latter with smoke. Then the *Hipper* also suddenly loomed up, just when the *Achates* was getting clear of her own smoke and setting course to join the *Onslow* ahead of the convoy. The German cruiser opened fire on her second diminutive adversary, quickly crippled the *Achates*, killed her Captain and caused many casualties among her crew.

---

[1] See Map 29 (opp. p. 295).
[2] See Map 29.

Admiral Sir Max Horton (left), Commander-in-Chief Western Approaches, 19th November 1942 to 15th August 1945, and Admiral Sir John Tovey, Commander-in-Chief, Home Fleet, 2nd December 1940 to 8th May 1943, on board H.M.S. *King George V*.

Convoy to North Russia PQ.18, September 1942. Destroyer *Eskimo* in foreground.
(See pp. 280–285).

Convoy PQ.18, September 1942. A merchant ship blows up. Taken from
H.M.S. *Avenger*.

Then she shifted fire to Kinloch's *Obedient*, which apparently, and understandably, thought she was again engaged with the *Lützow*. Though she escaped serious damage from her redoubtable adversary, the *Obedient's* wireless was put out of action, and Kinloch therefore ordered the *Obdurate* (Lieutenant-Commander C. E. L. Sclater) to take over command, while he himself took station astern of the *Orwell*. Meanwhile the threat from the destroyer's torpedoes caused the *Hipper* to haul off.

So far the *Hipper* had had things too much her own way. It was therefore an unexpected shock when she suddenly came under heavy gunfire from the north. The British cruisers had sighted her at 11.30, engaged at about seven miles range and quickly obtained a hit which reduced the German cruiser's speed to twenty-eight knots. She was slow to reply, turned towards the British force, made smoke and then altered right away—receiving two more hits as she did so. Kummetz thus found the tables suddenly turned on him, for he was caught between the British destroyers and cruisers. He ordered all his ships to disengage and retire to the west. The *Sheffield* and *Jamaica* at once followed, and the range fell to as little as 8,000 yards. Unluckily the German ship became obscured for several precious minutes, just when a decisive fire might have been poured into her at close range. She escaped without receiving further damage. At 11.43 two German destroyers suddenly appeared about 4,000 yards from our cruisers, in an ideal position to use torpedoes. The *Sheffield* at once steered for the nearer one, the *Friedrich Eckholdt*, and quickly reduced her to a shambles. The *Jamaica* fired on the other, but she turned away unharmed.

At about 11.40 yet another engagement in this long series of quickly-changing, confused actions took place. The *Lützow* opened fire on the convoy at about nine miles range. One merchantman was damaged—the only casualty suffered by the stubbornly defended ships. The Commodore made an emergency turn away, and it was now Sclater's turn to lead the surviving destroyers out to attack, and to lay more smoke. As soon as the smoke screen was effective the pocket-battleship ceased fire. No sooner had that threat been countered than the *Hipper* appeared yet again. The three British destroyers at once turned towards the new enemy, and in doing so they came under accurate fire; but the *Hipper* did not persist. At 11.49 Kummetz repeated his order to withdraw, and that was the last of their two big adversaries seen by our destroyers. Soon after noon, as 'night was drawing on' they steered south to overtake the convoy, which the sinking *Achates* had all this time continued to shield with smoke. Not till 1.15 p.m. did she call for assistance, but before a rescuing trawler had closed her she suddenly capsized. The last fight of Lieutenant-Commander John's *Achates*, and the splendid devotion of her crew in continuing to shield the convoy right to the end, were justly described by Admiral Tovey as 'magnificent'. Her name may worthily be placed alongside those of her sister-ships the *Acasta* and *Ardent*, lost in heroic endeavour to defend the *Glorious* in June 1940.[1]

The British cruisers had one more brief engagement with both the heavy German ships at about 12.30; but no damage was done to either side. The enemy held on to the west, and Admiral Burnett followed until about 2 p.m. when he finally lost touch. He then swept south, keeping between the convoy and the retiring enemy.

So ended the fighting. We had lost the *Achates* and the *Bramble*; but the sinking of the *Eckholdt* and the damage to the *Hipper* balanced the material losses fairly evenly; and the convoy had escaped virtually unscathed. The *Lützow's* account ends with the remark that 'in spite of the general situation being at first satisfactory, we had not succeeded in getting at the convoy or in scoring any successes at all'—an admission which a little more thrustfulness and determination on her own part might have substantially altered. The pocket-battleship's intended sortie into the Atlantic was abandoned, and the *Hipper*, though her damage was repaired, was never again sent on active service.

Convoy JW.51B had no more adventures. The main body entered Kola Inlet on the 3rd of January 1943, and the Archangel detachment reached port three days later.

The west-bound convoy RA.51, of fourteen ships with eleven escorts, sailed from Murmansk on the 30th of December. It was covered in turn by Admiral Burnett's cruisers and by a new force sent out under Rear-Admiral L. H. K. Hamilton, which took over on the 2nd. The Commander-in-Chief put to sea to provide additional cover with the *King George V, Howe, Bermuda* and six destroyers, as soon as he received reports of the New Year's Eve fighting. But such precautions were in fact unnecessary, for the enemy forces returned direct to Altenfiord. All RA.51's ships arrived safely at Loch Ewe on the 11th of January.

There is no doubt at all that the passages of PQ.18 and of the first two JW convoys, combined with the safe return of most of the ships in the corresponding westward convoys, were important successes to our cause—particularly with regard to the fighting on New Year's Eve. As Admiral Tovey said, 'that an enemy force of at least one pocket-battleship, one heavy cruiser and six destroyers, with all the advantages of surprise and concentration, should be held off for four hours by five destroyers, and driven from the area by two 6-inch cruisers is most creditable and satisfactory'. Nor is the reason far to seek. Whereas the Germans had shown themselves

[1] See Vol. I, pp. 194-5.

LESSONS OF THE BATTLE 299

hesitant of purpose and unwilling to accept risks, our own destroyers
had been handled with splendid determination and had protected
the convoy in their charge with selfless devotion typical of their class
and tradition. The faults in German outlook and in German operational plans were certainly reflected in their individual ship's conduct.
Yet, even when every allowance has been made for this, the inactivity
of the six enemy destroyers appears, by British standards, quite extra-
ordinary. It was a combination of the German failings and the
manner in which our own ships were fought, which resulted in our
being let off lightly from the consequences of our mistakes. But in
pointing out the latter one should never forget how severe a strain
the Russian convoys imposed on the officers and men who took part
in them. In such conditions it is indeed surprising that so many
difficult decisions were taken with such correct and rapid judgment.
The enemy certainly had no illusions, for he later described the
engagements as 'obviously unsatisfactory to the Germans, but a
complete success for the British'.

The enemy learnt one lesson from this sortie—that no sea commander could possibly fight successfully if he was tied by restrictions
such as were imposed on Admiral Kummetz. Because Dönitz was on
easier terms with Hitler than his predecessor, he succeeded in obtaining the Führer's agreement to giving senior officers greater freedom.
But it was a long time before the new policy was tested in action; for
the events here described produced in Hitler the ungovernable rage
which led to his 'firm and unalterable resolve' to pay off the big
ships. And this brought about the resignation of Grand Admiral
Raeder—a considerable seismic disturbance in the enemy camp to
result from an action fought by two British cruisers and half a dozen
destroyers in the Arctic twilight.

In conclusion the results of the Russian convoys which sailed
during this phase are tabulated below:

Table 23. Russian Convoys, 1st August, 1942–11th January, 1943

Convoy	No. of Ships	Ships Turned Back	Ships Sunk	Ships Arrived	Escort Losses	Enemy Losses
PQ.18 .	40	Nil	13	27	Nil	3 U-boats 41 Aircraft
QP.14 .	15	Nil	3	12	1 Destroyer 1 Fleet Oiler 1 Minesweeper	2 U-boats
QP.15 .	28	Nil	2	26	Nil	Nil
JW.51A	16	Nil	Nil	16	Nil	Nil
JW.51B	14	Nil	Nil	14	1 Destroyer 1 Minesweeper	1 Destroyer
RA.51 .	14	Nil	Nil	14	Nil	Nil

CHAPTER XIII

THE AFRICAN CAMPAIGNS
1st August–31st December, 1942

> 'If anyone wishes to know the history of this War, I will tell them it is our maritime superiority gives me the power of maintaining my army, while the enemy are unable to do so'.
>
> Duke of Wellington to Rear-Admiral T. Byam Martin. (Quoted by the latter in his Report of Proceedings to Lord Keith dated 21st September 1803. *Letters and Papers of Admiral of the Fleet Sir Thomas Byam Martin.* Vol. II, page 409. Navy Records Society.)

THE failure of the June attempt to revictual Malta on a large scale from both ends of the Mediterranean was followed by reinforcement of the island's fighter defences by numerous ferry operations from the west. These were highly successful, and set the final seal on the substantial defeat suffered by the Luftwaffe and the Regia Aeronautica over Malta in the middle of May.[1] Meanwhile emergency measures to run in essential supplies such as aviation spirit, anti-aircraft ammunition and torpedoes by submarines and by exceptionally fast surface ships were continued. These sufficed to keep the defences in action, but did little to ease the ever-tightening siege conditions which had to be imposed on the Maltese people. Another attempt to pass in a surface-ship convoy had to be made in August, and the British Cabinet decided that this requirement should take priority over the many other demands now arising in all the waters for which the Royal Navy was responsible, from the Arctic to the Far East.

The losses suffered for the slight relief gained by the June convoy had in no way weakened the British Government's determination that Malta should not fall. Mr Churchill told the Admiralty that 'the fate of the island was at stake', and that he must be able to tell the Government that 'the Navy would never abandon Malta'. The First Lord and First Sea Lord fully shared Mr Churchill's view that 'the loss [of Malta] would be a disaster of [the] first magnitude to the

---

[1] See p. 61.

British Empire, and probably [would be] fatal in the long run to the defence of the Nile Valley'[1]; and they were equally determined to accept the inevitably heavy risks in order to achieve a success 'worthy of the effort'. The new attempt was to be made from the west, and great strength was to be provided to fight the convoy through. This was made easier by the suspension of the Arctic convoys after the disaster to PQ.17 in July[2], since a large part of the Home Fleet could thus take part.

The plan was basically the same as that which had governed the June convoy[3], except that this time only a 'diversionary convoy' was sailed from Egypt. Indeed geographical conditions in the Mediterranean made it difficult to vary from a stereotyped plan in these operations. Until the strategic situation in Africa had once more moved in our favour, all we could do was to ring the changes on the various deceptive ruses which could be employed, conceal our actual intentions up to the last possible moment, and provide enough force to counter all the different threats which the enemy could so easily exert from his excellently placed air and naval bases in Sardinia, Sicily, southern Italy and Tripolitania.

The chief change made for the August convoy, which was called operation 'Pedestal', was the increase in carrier-borne air strength by the inclusion of the *Victorious* (flagship of Rear-Admiral A. L. St. G. Lyster), *Indomitable* and *Eagle*. Between them they could put up seventy-two fighters. While the plans were being discussed the Chief of the Air Staff raised the need once again to reinforce Malta's fighter defences. There were, so he told Admiral Pound at the end of July, eighty effective Spitfires there; but losses were being incurred at the high rate of seventeen a week. The First Sea Lord at once agreed to make the *Furious* available for another ferry trip, and the plans were altered to include flying off thirty-eight more Spitfires from the carrier to Malta. In addition the only two ships of the June convoy which had got through safely were to be brought out from the besieged island during the operation.

The forces taking part were all to be commanded by Vice-Admiral E. N. Syfret, who had, in addition to the three carriers already mentioned, the battleships *Nelson* and *Rodney*, six cruisers, one anti-aircraft cruiser and two dozen destroyers. A proportion of his strength, namely the cruisers *Nigeria*, *Kenya* and *Manchester*, the anti-aircraft cruiser *Cairo*, and half the total of destroyers were to go right through to Malta under Rear-Admiral H. M. Burrough, who had already gained experience of the Malta run in 1941.[4] Provision

---

[1] Churchill, Vol. IV, p. 275.
[2] See pp. 136–145.
[3] See pp. 64–67.
[4] See Vol. I, pp. 530–531.

was made for two oilers, with their own escort of four corvettes, to enter the Mediterranean with the main force, and then wait near the convoy route to refuel the escorts at need. Eight more destroyers were detailed to look after the *Furious*, and then to strengthen Admiral Syfret's main body while it was cruising to the west of 'the Narrows' between Sicily and Tunisia to await the return of Admiral Burrough's ships from Malta.[1] Finally, among the warships taking part were eight submarines. Some were ordered to patrol off the Italian bases, while others were to form a screen in 'the Narrows' to the north of the convoy route, where they might be able to intercept enemy surface forces coming south to attack the convoy at that critical stage in its passage.

It will be seen how thoroughly the lessons of previous Malta convoys, and in particular those of the June attempt, were applied on this occasion. In particular Admiral Burrough's cruisers and the submarines would prevent the interference of the surface forces which had contributed a good deal to the last convoy's difficulties; and the Malta-based mine-sweepers, which had gone through in June, were to sweep channels and to take the merchantmen into the Grand Harbour, thus avoiding losses from mines such as had been suffered right at the end of the preceding convoy's journey.[2] So determined was the War Cabinet that the Italian Fleet should not be allowed this time to interfere that they even discussed sending the battleships and carriers right through with the convoy.

Admiral Syfret and the main body of the escort met the convoy off the Clyde on the 3rd of August. The fourteen merchantmen, including two American ships and the tanker *Ohio*, were called convoy WS.21S. The Commodore of the convoy was Commander A. G. Venables, R.N. (Retired), in the *Port Chalmers*. All forces passed Gibraltar in dense fog in the small hours of the 10th. That same day Admiral Harwood sailed the dummy convoy already mentioned from Port Said, escorted by Admiral Vian's cruisers and destroyers. Next day they all turned back to the east, greatly to the disappointment of the merchantmen, who had been expecting to go on to Malta. Admiral Vian then went off to keep the enemy still more busy and guessing by bombarding Rhodes early on the 13th, and that was the end of the part played in the main operation 'Pedestal' by the Mediterranean Fleet.

It was the afternoon of the 10th before the enemy received definite warning of the big movement taking place in the west. Early next morning his aircraft gained touch and thereafter they shadowed the convoy more or less continuously, in spite of the attention devoted to them by the carrier-borne fighters. The *Furious* started to fly off

---

[1] See Map 30 (opp. p. 305).

[2] See p. 67.

her Spitfires when 550 miles from Malta on the afternoon of the 11th, but at 1.15 p.m. the *Eagle* was struck by four torpedoes fired by U.73 which had successfully penetrated the screen.[1] The faithful old carrier, which had made no less than nine aircraft ferry trips and had despatched 183 Spitfires to Malta in 1942, sank in eight minutes. If we had to lose her it was appropriate that her grave should be in the Mediterranean, whose waters she had known so well. Happily the destroyers rescued about 900 of her company of 1160, including Captain L. D. Mackintosh. That evening the *Furious*, her task completed, turned back for Gibraltar with a special destroyer screen. One of the latter, the *Wolverine*, rammed and sank the Italian submarine *Dagabur* on the way.

Late that evening, the 11th, the first air attacks on the main forces took place. About three dozen German bombers and torpedo-bombers came out of the dusk. Though they escaped our fighters in the failing light they scored no hits at all, and the escorts' guns destroyed several of their number.[2] Next morning air attacks were renewed, but this time the carrier fighters intercepted at a good distance from the convoy, and few enemies got past them. Again no damage was done. These attacks were, however, only a preliminary tuning up by the Luftwaffe and its allies. Their big effort, made from the Sardinian airfields, started at noon, and was intended to be a combined attack by a total of some eighty torpedo-bombers, dive-bombers and fighter-bombers, using every conceivable air-borne weapon and one (called a 'motobomba', apparently a new sort of aerial torpedo) which we had not met before. Perfect timing was not achieved, but the enemy plan was in general carried out. The attacks lasted from 12.15 to 1.45 p.m.[3] Though the *Victorious* had a narrow escape when a heavy bomb hit, but broke up on her armoured flight deck, the only ship seriously damaged was a merchantman, the *Deucalion*. She had to leave the convoy, and was finally destroyed by the enemy that evening close in to the Tunisian coast. The carrier fighters and ships' gunners did splendidly to defeat these skilfully made attacks.

That afternoon the convoy passed through the main enemy submarine concentration. There were innumerable contacts and attacks, and after several destroyers had hunted one contact the Italian submarine *Cobalto* came to the surface, and was rammed and sunk by the *Ithuriel*. Many torpedoes were fired at our ships but, thanks to the vigilance of the escort and the precision with which the merchantmen carried out numerous emergency turns, none found their

---

[1] See Map 30 (opp. p. 305).

[2] The contemporary claim was four enemy aircraft destroyed in this attack. It has proved impossible to verify this figure from enemy records, but his total losses make it clear that our claims were in excess of actual achievements.

[3] See Map 30.

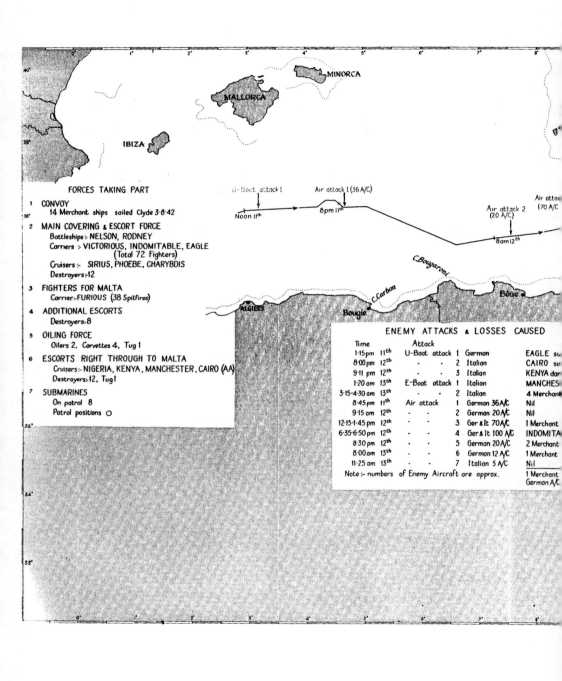

FORCES TAKING PART

1. **CONVOY**
   14 Merchant ships sailed Clyde 3·8·42

2. **MAIN COVERING & ESCORT FORCE**
   Battleships:- NELSON, RODNEY
   Carriers :- VICTORIOUS, INDOMITABLE, EAGLE
            (Total 72 Fighters)
   Cruisers :- SIRIUS, PHOEBE, CHARYBDIS
   Destroyers:-12

3. **FIGHTERS FOR MALTA**
   Carrier:-FURIOUS (38 Spitfires)

4. **ADDITIONAL ESCORTS**
   Destroyers:-8

5. **OILING FORCE**
   Oilers 2, Corvettes 4, Tug 1

6. **ESCORTS RIGHT THROUGH TO MALTA**
   Cruisers:- NIGERIA, KENYA, MANCHESTER, CAIRO (AA)
   Destroyers:-12, Tug 1

7. **SUBMARINES**
   On patrol 8
   Patrol positions O

Noon 11th   U-Boat attack 1   Air attack 1 (36 A/C)   8pm 11th   Air attack 2 (20 A/C)   Air atta (70 A/C)   8am 12th

MINORCA
MALLORCA
IBIZA

C.Bougaroni
C.Carbon
Bône
ALGIERS
Bougie

ENEMY ATTACKS & LOSSES CAUSED

Time		Attack			
1·15pm 11th	U-Boat attack	1	German		EAGLE su
8·00 pm 12th	" "	2	Italian		CAIRO su
9·11 pm 12th	" "	3	Italian		KENYA dar
1·20 am 13th	E-Boat attack	1	Italian		MANCHES
3·15-4·30 am 13th	" "	2	Italian		4 Merchant
8·45 pm 11th	Air attack	1	German 36 A/C		Nil
9·15 am 12th	" "	2	German 20 A/C		Nil
12·15-1·45 pm 12th	" "	3	Ger & It 70 A/C		1 Merchant
6·35-6·50 pm 12th	" "	4	Ger & It 100 A/C		INDOMITA
8·30 pm 12th	" "	5	German 20 A/C		2 Merchant
8·00 am 13th	" "	6	German 12 A/C		1 Merchant
11·25 am 13th	" "	7	Italian 5 A/C		Nil

Note :- numbers of Enemy Aircraft are approx.

1 Merchant
German A/C

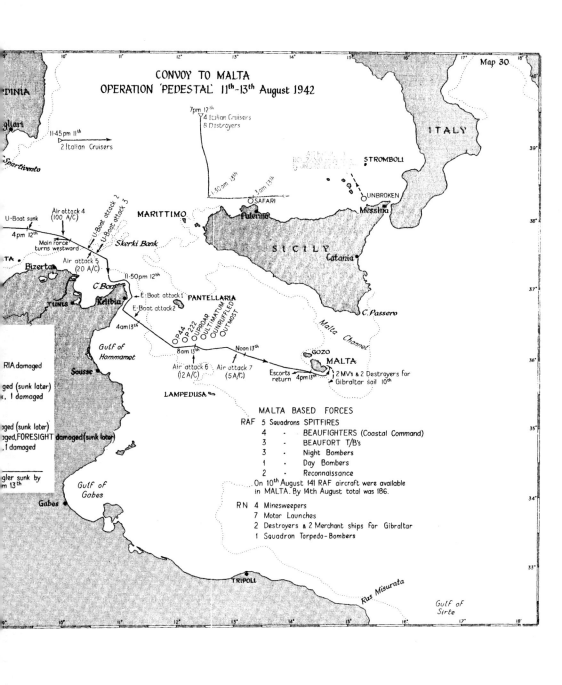

CONVOY TO MALTA
OPERATION 'PEDESTAL' 11th–13th August 1942

Map 30

SARDINIA

Cagliari

Spartivento

ITALY

7pm 12th
4 Italian Cruisers
8 Destroyers

STROMBOLI

11-45 pm 11th
2 Italian Cruisers

MARITTIMO

1-30 am 13th   3 am 13th   UNBROKEN

SAFARI   Messina

Palermo

U-Boat sunk

Air attack 4
(100 A/C)

U-Boat attack 2
U-Boat attack 3

4 pm 12th

Main Force
turns westward

Skerki Bank

S I C I L Y   Catania

Bizerta

Air attack 5
(20 A/C)

C. Bon

11-50 pm 12th

Kelibia

E-Boat attack 1   PANTELLARIA

E-Boat attack 2

C. Passero

Malta Channel

4 am 13th

OP44
OP222
OUPROAR
OULTIMATUM
OUNRUFFLED
OUTMOST

Gulf of
Hommamet

8 am 13th   Noon 13th

GOZO

MALTA

Air attack 6
(12 A/C)   Air attack 7
(5 A/C)

Escorts
return   4pm 13th

2 MV's & 2 Destroyers for
Gibraltar sail 10th

Sousse

TUNIS

LAMPEDUSA

...RIA damaged

...ged (sunk later)
... 1 damaged

...ged (sunk later)
...ged, FORESIGHT damaged (sunk later)
... 1 damaged

...gler sunk by
...m 13th

Gulf of
Gabes

Gabes

MALTA BASED FORCES

RAF 5 Squadrons SPITFIRES
    4   -   BEAUFIGHTERS (Coastal Command)
    3   -   BEAUFORT T/B's
    3   -   Night Bombers
    1   -   Day Bombers
    2   -   Reconnaissance
On 10th August 141 RAF aircraft were available
in MALTA. By 14th August total was 186.

RN 4 Minesweepers
    7 Motor Launches
    2 Destroyers & 2 Merchant ships for Gibraltar
    1 Squadron Torpedo-Bombers

TRIPOLI

Ras Misurata

Gulf of
Sirte

mark. At 6.35 p.m. air attacks were renewed in a dangerous synchronised effort by torpedo- and dive-bombers. The destroyer *Foresight* was hit by a torpedo and disabled. She had to be sunk later by our own forces. A worse blow was that the *Indomitable* suffered three heavy bomb hits, which put her flight deck out of action; her aircraft had to land on the *Victorious*, now the only effective carrier remaining. It will be an appropriate moment to summarise the shipborne fighters' achievement. Since the loss of the *Eagle* about sixty fighters had remained to Admiral Syfret, and by the evening of the 12th thirteen had been lost. Though it has even now proved very difficult to estimate accurately the losses inflicted by them on the enemy it appears that they and the ships' guns between them destroyed about thirty of all types during the entire operation.

The convoy had nearly reached the Skerki Channel by the time the evening air attacks were over, and Admiral Syfret hauled round to the west at 7 p.m.[1] Admiral Burrough now took charge of the convoy. At 8 p.m. his flagship, the *Nigeria*, and the *Cairo* were both hit by torpedoes, fired we now know by the Italian submarine *Axum*. The Admiral transferred his flag to the destroyer *Ashanti*, and the *Nigeria* headed back for Gibraltar; but the *Cairo* had to be sunk. The tanker *Ohio* was hit at the same time, but remained with the convoy. The attacks took place just when the convoy was changing its formation from four columns into two, to pass through the Skerki Channel. This manoeuvre, and the subsequent alterations of course away from the submarine danger, caused the ships temporarily to lose their disciplined formation, and to become bunched up. At this dangerous moment enemy aircraft attacked out of the dusk. The two fighter-direction ships (the *Nigeria* and *Cairo*) had gone, the long-range fighters from Malta had just returned home, and the ships were thus caught at a grave disadvantage. Two merchantmen (the *Empire Hope* and *Clan Ferguson*) were lost. The *Brisbane Star* was also hit, but eventually reached Malta. Next the cruiser *Kenya* was hit by a torpedo fired by the Italian submarine *Alagi*. Luckily she was not seriously damaged and was able to carry on with the convoy.

After this setback the scattered ships gradually struggled back into formation, with the minesweeping destroyers ahead and the surviving cruisers and merchantmen following; but the latter had become somewhat strung out. Admiral Syfret had sent the *Charybdis* and two destroyers to replace the lost and damaged ships, but the reinforcements had not yet joined Admiral Burrough's force. The main body rounded Cape Bon at midnight, and turned south, keeping close to the Tunisian Coast.[2] Soon afterwards our ships became aware that enemy E-boats (motor torpedo-boats) were on

---

[1] See Map 30.
[2] See Map 30.

W

the prowl. At 1.20 a.m. on the 13th the *Manchester* was hit by a torpedo fired at very close range by one of them, and was brought to a standstill with all her four propellor shafts temporarily out of action and three of the four permanently disabled. The destroyer *Pathfinder* took off some of her crew. When he learnt of the *Manchester's* predicament Admiral Burrough sent back two more destroyers, but they did not arrive in time to help save the ship. Meanwhile the Captain of the *Manchester* was faced with a very difficult situation. In July 1941 he had got the same ship back to Gibraltar on only one shaft after being hit by torpedo in an earlier Malta convoy[1]; but he thought it would prove far more difficult to extricate her from her present situation. By 5 a.m. the *Manchester* had not yet been able to move, and her Captain therefore ordered the ship to be sunk, and the crew to make their way to the Tunisian coast. The majority of them were there interned by the French until after the invasion of North Africa in the following November.[2]

The *Manchester* was not the only ship to suffer at this time. Five of the merchantmen which were following some distance behind the main body were also hit, and four of them (the *Wairangi*, the *Almeria Lykes* (*U.S.*), the *Santa Elisa* (*U.S.*) and probably the *Glenorchy*) were sunk between 3.15 and 4.30 a.m. There is little doubt that this succession of disasters was mainly caused by the loss of cohesion brought about by the cleverly organised and well executed enemy attacks of the previous evening. But the circumstances were singularly favourable to motor torpedo-boat attack, and it seems unlikely that, even had the convoy been able to maintain proper formation, its large ships could all have been successfully defended in such constricted waters on a dark night. But it was a cruel blow suddenly to suffer such heavy casualties, after the convoy had come so far with such success.

Soon after daylight on the 13th German bombers reappeared. The *Waimarama* was hit and blew up, and other ships had narrow escapes. The *Ohio*, already damaged, was crashed into by an enemy aircraft which had just released its bomb. Beaufighters and long-range Spitfires from Malta were now patrolling overhead; but still more damage was to be suffered. At 10.50 the *Ohio* was disabled, the *Rochester Castle* set on fire and the *Dorset* hit and stopped. Destroyers went back to look after the cripples, while the survivors, now only three strong, struggled on to the east. Soon they came within reach of the short-range Malta Spitfires, whose protecting wings held off subsequent attacks. At 2.30 p.m. the Malta minesweepers and motor-launches

---

[1] See Vol. I, p. 522.

[2] The loss of the *Manchester* led to the trial by Court Martial of certain of her officers and men after they had been released from internment in French North Africa. The findings of the court were to the effect that the decision to scuttle the ship had been premature.

met the main convoy. It consisted only of the *Port Chalmers*, the *Melbourne Star* and the damaged *Rochester Castle*. They entered Grand Harbour two hours later. Three damaged ships the *Dorset*, *Ohio* and *Brisbane Star* were still astern, and a great effort was being made to get them in. The *Ohio* and the *Dorset* were hit yet again in dusk attacks, and the latter sank. The destroyer *Penn* and the minesweepers *Rye* and *Ledbury*, supported by the splendid determination of the Master and crew of the *Ohio*, towed in turn and fought off air attacks from about 11 a.m. on the 13th until the morning of the 15th. Their efforts were finally crowned with success, when the grievously wounded, almost unmanageable but still indomitable *Ohio* entered harbour. The fuel which she carried enabled air strikes to be restarted from Malta just when Rommel was preparing for the offensive intended to drive the Allies finally out of Egypt. The enemy's shipping losses to air attacks at once increased[1], and the offensive had to be postponed because of shortage of supplies. The *Ohio's* Master, Captain D. W. Mason, was awarded the George Cross. The *Brisbane Star* survived the unhelpful attentions of French boarding officers during her unpremeditated stay in Tunisian waters, and reached Malta safely shortly before the *Ohio*. Thus did five ships out of fourteen reach their destination, and two of them were so much damaged that they very nearly sank. Admiral Syfret said in his report that he and all officers and men of the Royal Navy who saw 'the steadfast manner in which [the merchantmen] pressed on their way to Malta through all attacks . . . will desire to give first place to the conduct, courage and determination of their Masters, officers and men'. In addition to the nine merchant ships lost, the *Eagle*, *Manchester*, *Cairo* and *Foresight* had gone to swell the long tale of warships sunk in the many attempts to supply Malta; and the *Indomitable*, *Nigeria* and *Kenya* had all been damaged.

The only form of attack not made on the convoy was by enemy surface ships. Yet cruisers and destroyers from Cagliari, Messina and Naples had put to sea on the 11th and 12th.[2] The R.A.F. in Malta conducted a skilful and convincing bluff, to deceive them into the belief that strong air striking forces were on the way to deal with them. No enemy surface ships actually ventured south of Sicily, and the submarine *Unbroken* (Lieutenant A. C. G. Mars) scored a success on the 13th by hitting both the heavy cruiser *Bolzano* and the light cruiser *Muzio Attendolo* with torpedoes.[3] The former was taken to Spezia for repairs and fell into German hands at the Italian surrender. In June 1944 she was finally destroyed in that harbour by one of the

---

[1] See Table 26 (p. 344).

[2] See Map 30 (opp. p. 305).

[3] See *Unbroken* by Alastair Mars (Frederick Muller, 1953) pp. 115–127.

two British 'human torpedo' crews carried to Spezia in an Italian M.T.B.[1]

By the 22nd of August 32,000 tons of cargo had been unloaded from the five surviving ships of the convoy, and removed to comparative safety. This duty, which chiefly fell to the soldiers of the Malta garrison, was called operation 'Ceres'. Unhappily the goddess of harvest had not proved nearly as bountiful as had been hoped, and it was a sadly dwindled cornucopia which she emptied into Malta's hungry storehouses. The enemy made no attempt to interfere with the unloading. Thus ended what was to prove the last of the many major operations undertaken to save Malta. The First Sea Lord summed up the results in a letter to Admiral Cunningham. 'We paid a heavy price' he wrote, 'but personally I think we got out of it lightly considering the risks we had to run, and the tremendous concentration of everything . . . which we had to face'. Taken together, the Malta convoys of 1941-42 succeeded in their purpose; for the island held out, as it certainly could not have done without them. Yet the cost had been very heavy, especially to the British maritime services, and to the people of Malta. If ever in the centuries to come students should seek an example of the costliness in war of failure by a maritime nation properly to defend its overseas bases in time of peace, surely the story of Malta's ordeal in 1941-42 will provide the classic case.

It remains to mention that, on the 17th of August, just after the completion of operation 'Pedestal', the *Furious* flew another batch of Spitfires to Malta. All but three of the thirty-two arrived safely. The carrier and her escort were safely back at Gibraltar on the 19th.

While Operation 'Pedestal' was in progress in the west, three more submarines (the *Otus*, *Rorqual* and *Clyde*) carried urgently needed ammunition, torpedoes and aviation spirit to Malta. Fuel for the Spitfires had become the island's most urgent need, and it could only be taken there by submarines. There was too small a chance of survival to send a surface ship loaded with such a cargo, until the Army had regained possession of the advanced airfields in Libya. The supply trips by submarines had therefore to be continued in September and October.

The early days of August brought two successes to our anti-submarine forces. On the 4th U.372, which had sunk the *Medway* in June[2], was herself destroyed off the coast of Palestine after a combined hunt by a radar-fitted Wellington and several destroyers. This reduced the number of German U-boats in the Mediterranean to fifteen. Six days later the Italian submarine *Scire* was sunk by the trawler *Islay* in the approaches to Haifa. There were indications

---

[1] See *Above us the Waves* by Warren and Benson (Harrap 1953), pp. 171–181.
[2] See p. 74.

that both these enemies had intended to attack our shipping in Haifa, or the valuable oil installations near that base; but the Levant escort forces, which now included one all-Greek and one all-Free-French group of ships, had proved too alert. The First Submarine Flotilla's new base at Beirut was now in working order; but the flotilla's strength was low, and the need to make storing trips to Malta reduced its capacity for offensive patrols. The surface forces remaining to Admiral Harwood were still divided between Haifa and Port Said, but a few *Hunt*-class destroyers and an M.T.B. flotilla had returned to Alexandria. On the 8th of August the Commander-in-Chief and his operation staff moved back to that base from the Canal Zone. The opportunity afforded by this comparatively quiet period in the eastern Mediterranean was used to dock the ships of the 15th Cruiser Squadron at Massawa in Eritrea. The Italian floating dock there had been raised after scuttling, and was now put to our own use. Once again the value of our control of the Suez Canal and of the rearward bases, at a time of acute difficulty inside the Mediterranean, is to be remarked.[1]

Early in August the Commanders-in-Chief, Middle East, considered ways and means of relieving the pressure on the Army, and forcing Rommel to divert a proportion of his strength from the front near El Alamein. General Auchinleck had signalled from his headquarters in the desert that he considered 'any and every means' of accomplishing that purpose was justified. It was indeed a most anxious period for the Army. The plans discussed in Cairo included an attack from the sea on Tobruk, then some way behind the German lines. On the 13th of August General Montgomery assumed command of the Eighth Army, and two days later General Alexander replaced General Auchinleck as Commander-in-Chief, Middle East. On the 21st the three Commanders-in-Chief approved the plan finally presented to them. It is therefore plain that the genesis of operation 'Agreement' was an urgent request for help from the Army, that the intentions remained unaltered after the changes in command had taken place, and that the plan was accepted by all three services. Copies of the plan were certainly sent to the Eighth Army Commander, and although he was critical of the operation after it had failed, he does not appear to have expressed any disagreement with it while it was in process of preparation. Admiral Harwood described it later as 'a desperate gamble', which could only be justified by the perilous situation prevailing on land at the time.

The planning and preparation were not completed until early in September. The assault on Tobruk from the sea was to be synchronised with a sudden lunge by a mobile land column from the desert.

[1] See p. 74.

On the 13th the *Sikh* (Captain St.J. A. Micklethwait) and *Zulu*, with 350 marines embarked, sailed from Alexandria to meet the anti-aircraft cruiser *Coventry* and the *Hunt*-class destroyers of the 5th Flotilla at sea. Another force comprising eighteen M.T.Bs and three motor launches had left a day earlier with 150 troops on board. The intention was to land the marines on the north side of Tobruk harbour, while the troops carried by the coastal craft landed on the south side in support of the land column already mentioned. Having gained possession of the coast defences the destroyers were to enter the harbour 'covered by the enemy gun positions manned by us', destroy shipping and port facilities and then re-embark the marines and soldiers. A frontal assault on a heavily defended base with such very slender forces certainly now appears unduly hazardous. The results were disastrous. The Royal Air Force made heavy air attacks to cover the landings on the night of the 13th-14th of September and, as soon as it was known that the mobile column had gained possession of the gun positions to the south of the harbour, the landing of the marines was attempted. Only two of the twenty-one coastal craft got their troops ashore; and the assault craft from the destroyers never returned after landing, or trying to land, the first flight of marines. The *Sikh* moved close inshore to find the assault craft; at 5.30 a.m. on the 14th she was disabled by gunfire from the shore batteries. The *Zulu* tried to tow her to seaward, but the accurate enemy fire made it impossible. Captain Micklethwait therefore told the *Zulu* to leave him. The *Sikh* sank close inshore, and many of her crew as well as the surviving marines were made prisoners. At 9 a.m. the *Coventry* and the 'Hunts' were ordered west again to support the *Zulu*. The anti-aircraft ship was hit by a bomb, caught fire and had to be abandoned. At 4.15 p.m. the *Zulu* was hit by the last bomb dropped in the last attack, and sank after dark. Six of the coastal craft were also lost. When the report on this expensive failure reached London the Prime Minister, for all his admiration of offensive intentions, was gravely disturbed. Today one cannot but feel that, even making full allowance for the circumstances which caused it to be carried out, the operation was rash in conception, and that an assault from the sea on a strongly fortified port must require far stronger forces and far more specialised equipment and training than were available on this occasion. Coming so soon after the loss of three other valuable fleet destroyers in circumstances which some felt had been avoidable[1], the operation aroused serious misgivings in London.

September 1942, which marked for the British people the start of the fourth year of the war, brought some easement of the acute anxieties which, particularly since July, had beset all three services

[1] *Jackal, Kipling* and *Lively*. See pp. 62–63.

fighting in the Middle East. In the first place the Army held all the attacks made on their position at El Alamein. The continuous night air attacks, for which two naval Albacore squadrons (Nos. 821 and 826) were lent to the Royal Air Force, were, in the opinion of the Air Officer Commanding-in-Chief (Air Chief Marshal Sir Arthur Tedder), 'one of the decisive factors' in holding Rommel's assaults; and he foretold that this accomplishment 'may well prove to be a turning point in the war in Africa'. While British eyes were focused chiefly on the Army's battle front at El Alamein, the Navy could only contribute by ensuring that the flow of men and supplies continued without interruption up the Red Sea, and that the Levant convoys came through with their precious cargoes of fuel. Early in the month enemy submarines had appeared in the Gulf of Aden, for the first time since the Italians had been eliminated in 1941.[1] They were probably Japanese boats from Penang.[2] They sank two ships, and anti-submarine reinforcements had to be sent south through the Canal. These sinkings, and attacks by German aircraft on the exposed anchorages at the head of the Red Sea, caused us some anxiety; but neither became seriously troublesome. In the Levant our surface escorts, which often had the benefit of co-operation from the Royal Air Force, took a steady toll of the U-boats. August had been a particularly successful month, especially against the Italian submarines, three more of which were sunk. On the 14th of September a Royal Air Force Sunderland from Gibraltar added the *Alabastro* to the score on the same day that, as a portent of happier times, the headquarters of No. 201 Naval Co-operation Group moved back to Alexandria. Our submarines meanwhile slowly increased in numbers, and steadily continued their pressure against the Axis supply lines to Africa. The 10th Flotilla was now able to keep about nine boats on patrol in the central basin; and its strength was still increasing. On the night of the 19th-20th of October five of them worked together against a valuable convoy, from which two ships and an escort were sunk. A few days later sustained attacks were made by R.A.F. Beauforts against another convoy of a tanker and two merchant ships making for Tobruk. The tanker was left ablaze. The month of October marked a climax in the relentless pressure exerted by all arms, but especially by our submarines and aircraft, against the enemy's supply line to Africa. Axis shipping losses rose steeply, and it is now known that Rommel was thereby deprived of precious fuel and supplies at a critical juncture.[3]

Then, at 10 p.m. on the 23rd of October, the Eighth Army launched its assault at El Alamein. In hopeful expectation the fleet

---

[1] See Vol. I, p. 426.
[2] See pp. 184–185.
[3] See Table 26 (p. 344).

had for some time been preparing the staff, ships and equipment needed to re-open the Cyrenaican ports, and the Inshore Squadron (now commanded by Captain C. Wauchope) had been strengthened to prepare for its great task of keeping the advancing Army supplied. After the battle had been won General Montgomery signalled his gratitude 'for the valuable assistance afforded by the naval operations on D night', which, so he considered, 'had influence on our main objective'.

At Malta the fighters had defeated the renewed enemy air attacks, aimed especially at our own airfields. At the end of the month twenty-nine more Spitfires were flown off the *Furious*, all of which arrived safely. Thus, while the Navy kept our land forces supplied and, with the Royal Air Force, hammered at the enemy's sea communications, the Army launched itself with renewed vigour and determination in the offensive which was to drive Rommel finally out of Egypt, regain to us the Libyan airfields, and so restore our command of the central basin. On the night of the 4th-5th of November General Montgomery's men, after twelve days and nights of gruelling fighting, made a complete break in the Axis defences.

One serious anxiety remained inside the Mediterranean. Malta was desperately short of aviation fuel, food and ammunition. Though an attempt was made to get a disguised merchant ship through early in November, it failed. Once again the submarines and fast minelayers had to fill the breach. The *Parthian, Clyde, Traveller* and *Thrasher* all contributed, and the *Welshman* dashed in from Gibraltar with a vital cargo of concentrated food and torpedoes. Between them they saved the situation, and enabled Malta to play its part in operation 'Torch'.

For the story of the protracted discussions between the British and American authorities regarding the opening of a new front in Europe or in Africa in 1942 the reader must be referred to other volumes of this series.[1] Here it is only necessary to state that the final decision to invade French North Africa was taken at a meeting of the Combined Chiefs of Staff held in London on the 25th of July. Detailed planning by a joint British and American staff began forthwith in Norfolk House, London. On the 14th of August General Eisenhower was appointed Allied Commander-in-Chief, and Admiral Sir Andrew Cunningham 'Allied Naval Commander Expeditionary Force' for operation 'Torch', the first major Allied overseas offensive. The plans were approved by the American and British Chiefs of Staff on the 29th of September and the 2nd of October respectively, and the orders were issued on the 8th of October.

---

[1] See *Grand Strategy*, Vol. III, by J. M. A. Gwyer. (In preparation)

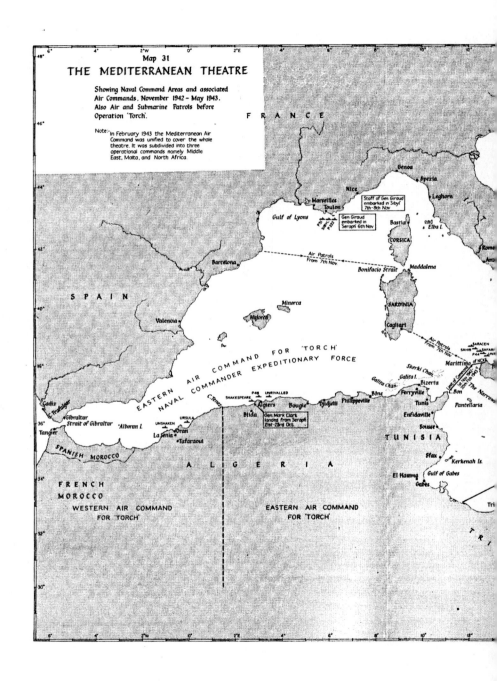

Map 31

THE MEDITERRANEAN THEATRE

Showing Naval Command Areas and associated
Air Commands, November 1942 – May 1943.
Also Air and Submarine Patrols before
Operation 'Torch'.

Note:- In February 1943 the Mediterranean Air
Command was unified to cover the whole
theatre. It was subdivided into three
operational commands namely Middle
East, Malta, and North Africa.

FRANCE

Genoa
Spezia
Nice
Leghorn
Marseilles
Toulon
Gulf of Lyons
Staff of Gen Giraud
embarked in Sibyl
7th–8th Nov
Bastia
Elba I.
Gen Giraud
embarked in
Seraph 6th Nov
CORSICA
Rome

Barcelona
Air Patrols
From 7th Nov.
Bonifacio Strait
Maddalena

SPAIN
Minorca
SARDINIA
Valencia
Majorca
Cagliari
Air Patrols
From 7th Nov.

SARACEN
SAHIB
SAFARI
P44
UNA of NCXF
Marittimo
Skerki Chan.
Galita I.
Galita Chan.
Bizerta
Ferryville
Tunis
Bône
C. Bon
Pantellaria

EASTERN AIR COMMAND FOR 'TORCH'
NAVAL COMMANDER EXPEDITIONARY FORCE

Cadiz
Trafalgar
Gibraltar
Strait of Gibraltar
Alboran I.
Tangier
SHAKESPEARE
UNRIVALLED
Algiers
Bougie
Djidjelli
Philippeville
Enfidaville
Sousse
Blida
Gen Mark Clark
landing from Seraph
21st–23rd Oct.
UNSHAKEN
URSULA
La Senia
Oran
Tafaraoui

SPANISH MOROCCO
ALGERIA
TUNISIA

Sfax
Kerkenah Is.
El Hamma
Gulf of Gabes
Gabes

FRENCH
MOROCCO
WESTERN AIR COMMAND
FOR 'TORCH'

EASTERN AIR COMMAND
FOR 'TORCH'

Tri

TRI

Admiral Cunningham, whose connection with operation 'Torch' had been kept a closely-guarded secret, sailed from Plymouth in the cruiser *Scylla* at the end of October, and arrived at Gibraltar on the 1st of November.[1] There he hoisted his flag as Commander of the whole naval side of the immense undertaking. His deputy, Admiral Sir Bertram Ramsay, whose name will always be connected with the Dunkirk evacuation of 1940[2], remained in London and acted as Admiral Cunningham's direct link with the home authorities. When General Eisenhower reached Gibraltar by air from England on the 5th of November, the preliminary movements from both sides of the Atlantic were in full swing.

On Admiral Cunningham's return to the Mediterranean, that theatre was divided into two commands. Admiral Harwood's responsibility was restricted to the waters east of a line drawn from Cape Bon in Africa to the island of Marittimo off Sicily and thence up the west coast of Italy[3], while the 'Torch' Commander took over the whole of the western Mediterranean, in addition to his responsibility for the safety, supply and support of all three landings. The Naval Staff insisted that there should be no possibility of confusion arising through divisions of responsibility, or vagueness regarding the chain of command. 'Only by placing the whole naval side of the entire undertaking under Admiral Cunningham', they said, 'can one force be speedily reinforced by another'. The consequences of divided command earlier in the war had not been forgotten.[4]

We are not concerned here with the detailed planning of this great expedition, nor with the fortunes of the British and American forces after they had been landed. It is, however, essential to describe how our maritime control was exploited to carry the armies and their multifarious equipment and supplies to their destinations, and how they were supported after the landings; and to enable the reader fully to understand that vital accomplishment it is necessary to give the Allied plan in outline.

There were to be three landings, at Algiers and Oran inside the Mediterranean, and at Casablanca on the Moroccan coast. About 70,000 assault troops were to be used to capture the three ports. The landing at Algiers by a mixed British and American force under American command was to be followed up by the British First Army; Oran was to be assaulted by American troops, who would be followed up by more of their own countrymen; while the Casablanca landing was planned in and executed from the United States, and was entirely carried out by American troops. At Algiers and Oran the naval

---

[1] See *A Sailor's Odyssey* by Viscount Cunningham of Hyndhope (Hutchinson, 1951), pp. 481 *et seq.*
[2] See Vol. I, pp. 217–228.
[3] See Map 31.
[4] See Vol. I, pp. 199–201 and 309–311.

forces for escorting, and supporting the troops were British, and were commanded by Vice-Admiral Sir Harold Burrough (Eastern Task Force) and Commodore T. H. Troubridge (Central Task Force) respectively; at Casablanca they were composed entirely of the American ships of the Western Task Force, commanded by Rear-Admiral H. K. Hewitt, U.S.N. Responsibility for air support for the landings was divided between the Eastern Air Command under Air Marshal Sir William Welsh, with headquarters at Gibraltar, who looked after the assault on Algiers, and the Western Air Command under Major General Doolittle of the U.S. Army Air Force, who was responsible for Oran and Casablanca.[1]

The Admiralty was, as was natural, anxious about possible repercussions in France and Spain. It would indeed have been rash to assume that the Germans would not take violent action in the unoccupied zone of France and in the Iberian Peninsula, as soon as they realised that we had invaded French Morocco and Algeria. We could not look to Vichy to resist the Germans, and the attitude of the Spanish Government if their country were invaded was doubtful. It was therefore essential both to watch the French Toulon fleet and to cover the expedition against interference from that base and from Dakar, where the *Richelieu* and several cruisers still lay. If the Germans invaded Spain, the safety of Gibraltar and our control of the Straits might ultimately be imperilled. It was estimated that, if Spain did not resist, the Germans could station three or four hundred aircraft in the south of that country within three months. The only possible counter to such a move would have been for us to enter Spanish Morocco.

The original date for the assaults had been the 30th of October. Various causes contributed to postponement, in mid-September, until the 4th of November, and on the 21st of September it was postponed until the 8th—principally because the U.S. Army could not be ready in time for the earlier date. Then, on the 26th of September, a Catalina crashed off the Spanish coast, and the body of an officer carrying a letter in which the date of the assault was given as the 4th of November, was washed ashore near Cadiz. The succeeding days were anxious, for it was realised that our plan might have been compromised. When, however, no signs of a leakage became apparent it was decided that the date of the assault should remain unaltered. Although it is known that on a later occasion information derived from such a source reached Germany[2], no trace of this earlier incident has been found in enemy records. The high degree of success obtained from the strict secrecy in which the assembly and loading of the great convoys was shrouded, and from

---

[1] See Map 31 (opp. p. 313).
[2] See *The Man Who Never Was* by Ewen Montagu. (Evans Bros. 1953).

our various deceptive ruses, is indicated by a German 'appreciation' dated as late as the 4th of November. In it their Naval Staff remarked that 'the relatively small number of landing craft, and the fact that only two passenger ships are in this assembly at Gibraltar, do not indicate any immediate landing in the Mediterranean area or on the north-west African coast'. There can be few more revealing examples of the German failure to realise the possibilities of what was earlier described as 'the use of maritime power suddenly to descend on widely separated parts of the enemy-held coastline'.[1]

The British warships needed for the operation, about 160 in all, could only be provided by removing a substantial part of the Home Fleet's strength, by stopping the Russian convoys, by reducing our Atlantic escort forces and by temporarily suspending the mercantile convoys running between Britain and the south Atlantic.[2] Force H, under Vice-Admiral Sir Neville Syfret, which was to be specially reinforced from the Home Fleet, was responsible for covering the Algiers and Oran landings against the French and Italian fleets, while a small squadron of British cruisers and destroyers covered the American landing at Casablanca against the possibility of surface ship interference from the Atlantic. In addition to these a special fuelling force was organised to replenish ships inside the Mediterranean, and to save them from having to return to Gibraltar. It will easily be realised how complex a matter was the organisation of the numerous convoys and assault forces required to carry the invasion troops, and their great quantities of vehicles and supplies, to the one centrally placed base available until such time as the ports of entry had been captured—namely Gibraltar. It is no exaggeration to say that the rock fortress itself, its airfield, its dockyard, its storage and communication facilities and the anchorage available for the great assembly of ships in the adjacent Bay of Algeciras, formed the hub around which the wheel of the whole enterprise revolved.

The plan provided for sailing from Britain to Gibraltar in October a number of Advance Convoys (KX), in which were included the colliers, tankers, ammunition ships, tugs and auxiliary craft needed by the warships and the assault forces which would follow. Later in October and early in November four large Assault Convoys (KMF and KMS) sailed southward[3], carrying the troops and landing craft for the initial landings. On approaching Gibraltar these were to divide into the sections destined for Algiers (KMF.A) and for Oran (KMF.O). Meanwhile the American Assault Convoy UGF.1 and its escort (together called Task Force 34) had started out from the United States on the long haul across the Atlantic to Casablanca,

---

[1] See Vol. I, pp. 11–12 and 513.
[2] See pp. 214–215.
[3] The Suffixes F and S in the designation letters of these convoys indicated Fast or Slow convoys, as on other routes.

and was followed by supply and reinforcement convoys (UGF and UGS). The slowest convoys had, of course, to be sailed the earliest, and this meant that the collection and loading of the necessary shipping had to be started long before the operation was launched. The organisation of the Advance and Assault convoys is shown in the table below.

Table 24. Operation 'Torch'. Advance and Assault Convoys

NOTE: Suffix F and S in convoy designations, means Fast and Slow respectively.
Suffix A and B in convoy designations indicates division into two sections.
Suffix (A) and (O) in convoy designations means Algiers and Oran destinations.

I. BRITISH ADVANCE CONVOYS

Convoy	Composition and Escort	Speed	Sailing Date	Departure Port	Date Due Gibraltar	Remarks
KX.1	5 ships / 7 escorts	7½ knots	2/10/42	Clyde	14/10/42	Included 3 colliers and an A/S Trawler Group.
KX.2	18 ships / 13 escorts	7 knots	18/10/42	Clyde	31/10/42	Included 5 Ammunition ships, 3 with cased aircraft, and 4 tankers.
KX.3	1 ship / 2 escorts	13 knots	19/10/42	Clyde	27/10/42	Personnel for Gibraltar only.
KX.4A	20 ships / 8 escorts	7½ knots	21/10/42	Clyde	4/11/42	Included 3 Landing Ships Tank.
KX.4B	8 ships / 2 escorts	6½ knots	25/10/42	Milford-Haven	3/11/42	Included tugs, trawlers, 4 fuelling coasters and cased petrol ships.
KX.5	32 ships / 10 escorts	7 knots	30/10/42	Clyde	10/11/42	Included 15 Coasters, 3 tankers, 5 colliers and 7 cased petrol ships.

II. BRITISH ASSAULT CONVOYS

Convoy	Composition and Escort	Speed	Sailing Date	Departure Port	Date Due Gibraltar	Remarks
KMS(A).1 KMS(O).1	47 ships / 18 escorts	8 knots	22/10/42	Loch Ewe and Clyde	5/11/42 / 6/11/42	Included 39 MT/Store ships. Algiers and Oran sections divide west of Gibraltar.
KMS.2	52 ships / 14 escorts	7 knots	25/10/42	Loch Ewe and Clyde	10/11/42	Included 46 MT/Store ships.
KMF(A).1 KMF(O).1	39 ships / 12 escorts	11½ knots	26/10/42	Clyde	6/11/42 / 6/11/42	Included 2 H.Q. Ships and 31 L.S.Is. Algiers and Oran sections divide west of Gibraltar.
KMF.2	18 ships / 8 escorts	13 knots	1/11/42	Clyde	10/11/42	Included 13 Personnel ships for Oran and Algiers.

Subsequent to the above, KMF and KMS convoys both sailed at approximately 15 day intervals from Britain. KX convoys continued for a time at irregular intervals of between 15 and 35 days.

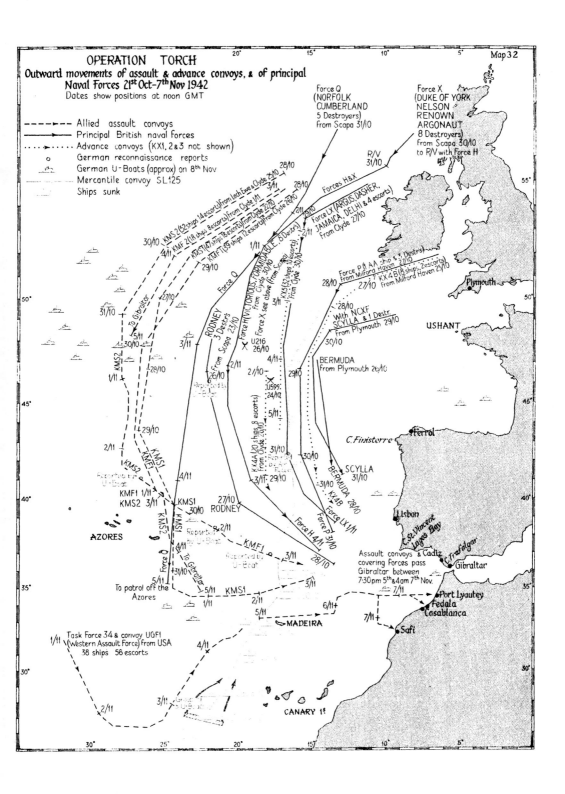

OPERATION TORCH
Outward movements of assault & advance convoys, & of principal
Naval Forces 21ˢᵗ Oct-7ᵗʰ Nov 1942
Dates show positions at noon GMT

Map 32

------►--- Allied assault convoys
━━━━━━━► Principal British naval forces
·········► Advance convoys (KX1,2&3 not shown)
o   German reconnaissance reports
         German U-Boats (approx) on 8ᵗʰ Nov
         Mercantile convoy SL125
         Ships sunk

Force Q
(NORFOLK
CUMBERLAND
5 Destroyers)
from Scapa 31/10

Force X
(DUKE OF YORK
NELSON
RENOWN
ARGONAUT
8 Destroyers)
from Scapa 30/10
to R/V with Force H

R/V
31/10

Forces H&X

28/10
3/11
28/10

Force LX (ARGUS, DASHER,
JAMAICA, DELHI & 4 escorts)
From Clyde 27/10

30/10 KMS 2 (52 ships 14 escort)s from Loch Ewe & Clyde 26/10
KMF 2(18 ships 8 escorts) from Clyde 27/10
4/11 KMS1 (47 ships 18 escorts) from Clyde 22/10
KMF1 (39 ships 12 escorts) from Clyde 26/10
29/10

Force Q

Force P(1 A.A. ship & 5 Destrs)
From Milford Haven 27/10
KX4B(8 ships 2 escorts)
27/10 From Milford Haven 25/10
28/10

28/10 With NCXF
SCYLLA & 1 Destr.
From Plymouth 29/10
30/10

RODNEY
3 Destr's
From Scapa 23/10

Force H (VICTORIOUS, FORMIDABLE, 5 Destrs)
From Clyde 30/10
Force X, see above (from Clyde 30/10)
KX5 (53 ships 7 escorts)
From Clyde 30/10

BERMUDA
From Plymouth 26/10

U216
26/10
2/11
4/11
26/10

To Gibraltar
27/10
31/10
5/11
30/10
28/10

KMS2
1/11

2/10
29/10

2/11
U599
24/10
5/11

KX4A (20 ships, 8 escorts)
From Clyde 20/10
From Scapa
3/11 29/10

C. Finisterre

Ferrol

BERMUDA
From D.R.
31/10
3/11
KX4B

SCYLLA
31/10

Ferrol

29/10

30/10

KMS1
KMF1
2/11
29/10

Reported by
U-Boat

KMS1 30/10

27/10
RODNEY

Force LX 1/11
Force P 3/11
KX4B 28/10

Lisbon

Azores

KMF1 1/11
KMS2 3/11

KMS1
30/10

Reported
by U-Boat

2/11

KMF1
3/11
28/10

Assault convoys & Cadiz
covering forces pass
Gibraltar between
7:30pm 5ᵗʰ & 4am 7ᵗʰ Nov.

C. St. Vincent
Lagos Bay
C. Trafalgar
Gibraltar

Force Q
4/11
31/10

To Gibraltar

Reported by
U-Boat

5/11
To patrol off the
Azores

KMS1
1/11
2/11
5/11
3/11
6/11

7/11

Port Lyautey
Fedala
Casablanca

7/11

Safi

Task Force 34 & convoy UGF1
1/11 (Western Assault Force) from USA
38 ships 56 escorts

4/11

MADEIRA

2/11
3/11
Group
U-Boat

CANARY Iˢ

USHANT

Plymouth

55°

50°

45°

40°

35°

30°

III. AMERICAN CONVOYS

Convoy	Composition	Designation	Date Due Casablanca	Remarks
UGF.1 (Assault Convoy)	38 ships 56 escorts	Task Force 34	8/11/42	The main western invasion force.
UGF.2	24 ships 10 escorts	Task Force 38	13/11/42	Entered Casablanca 18/11/42.
UGS.2*	45 ships 9 escorts	Task Force 37		
—	29 Miscellaneous ships and small craft	Task Force 39	25/11/42	

* No convoy UGS.1 was run.

Subsequent to the above, the UGF convoys of 15–20 ships (13½ knots) and UGS convoys of about 45 ships (9 knots) both sailed from the U.S.A. at approximately 25 day intervals.

The British 'Torch' convoys were operated by the Commander-in-Chief, Western Approaches, in a similar manner to WS convoys, until such time as they entered the area of responsibility of the expeditionary force commander. The necessary air co-operation was arranged between the Admiralty and the Air Ministry. It included reconnaissance of enemy harbours, protection of the convoys against air and U-boat attacks, and strikes at any enemy surface ships which might intervene. The slow convoys were routed down the meridian of 18° West and so kept within range of No. 19 Group's normal patrols; but the fast convoys were kept further out in the Atlantic, along 26° West, and were thus out of range from British air bases for a large part of their journeys. Air escorts were therefore provided by carriers. The *Biter* sailed with KMF.1 and the *Avenger* with KMS.1.[1]

The possibility of a heavy U-boat concentration attacking the convoys was the cause of great anxiety to the Admiralty. The Naval Staff estimated that, if the enemy got wind of our intentions, fifty U-boats could be deployed against the expedition by the end of October, and another twenty-five by the 6th of November. The First Sea Lord told the Prime Minister that the U-boats 'might well prove exceedingly menacing' . . . to 'the most valuable convoys ever to leave these shores', and asked for more long-range aircraft for the Bay of Biscay patrols. All possible escort vessels, in all about a hundred, were allocated to the convoys, without regard to the risks accepted on other routes. It will be told later how it came to pass that the U-boat menace proved much smaller than was anticipated.

The arrival of the Assault Convoys at their destinations was, of

---

[1] See Map 32.

course, the beginning rather than the end of the responsibility of the Navy for supporting the other services and keeping them supplied. In our first volume it was explained that in a combined operation the maritime services' functions differ from those which they bear for normal mercantile convoys since, after the disembarkation of the troops, they have to remain to support and supply the Army, and to guard its seaward flank.[1] Admiral Cunningham expressed this ancient requirement forcibly when, as soon as the initial assaults had succeeded, he told all his forces that 'Our task is not finished. We must assist the Allied armies to keep up the momentum of the assault'.

In the case of operation 'Torch' not only was this essential, but a long series of Follow-up Convoys (KMF, KMS and KX) had to be taken out from Britain to Gibraltar or the newly captured ports, local Mediterranean Follow-up Convoys (TF and TE) had to be run from Gibraltar to the same destinations, and a series of local (ET, FT and CG) and ocean (MKF and MKS) homeward convoys had to be started to bring empty ships back again; and escorts had, of course, to be provided for every one of these commitments. The Americans did much the same with Follow-up Convoys from their own continent (UGF and UGS), and with their homeward counterparts to the United States (GUF and GUS).

The Eastern and Centre Naval Task Forces were, as has been said, responsible for the landings at Algiers and Oran respectively, and for providing the necessary cover and support. The two attacks were to take place simultaneously at 1 a.m. on the 8th of November, and the Task Force Commanders were ordered to mislead the enemy by acting as though they were carrying out a large operation for the relief of Malta. The composition of the naval forces involved in the whole operation is summarised in Table 25 (opposite).[2]

The southward movement of the warships began on the 20th of October with the departure of the *Furious* and three destroyers from the Clyde. Three days later the *Rodney* and her escort left Scapa; on the 27th two carriers, two cruisers and four more destroyers left the Clyde.[3] On the 30th they were followed by the main British support and covering forces of two battleships, one battle cruiser, two carriers, one cruiser and thirteen destroyers from Scapa and the Clyde. No. 15 Group of Coastal Command escorted all convoys and warship squadrons as far west as possible, while No. 19 Group reinforced its Bay offensive with loans of long-range aircraft from Bomber Command. Only one U-boat was sighted by the convoy air escorts and she, U.599, was sunk by a Liberator of No. 224 Squadron

---

[1] See Vol. I, pp. 11–12.

[2] Appendix H gives full particulars of the naval forces employed in operation 'Torch'.

[3] See Map 32 (opp. p. 317).

on the 24th of October. Another, U.216, was destroyed by a Bay air patrol on the 20th. We now know that enemy aircraft and U-boats made several chance sightings of our various forces and convoys. The *Rodney* was reported by one U-boat (as an American battleship) on the 26th, the carrier force was sighted by a Focke-Wulf west of Finisterre on the 31st, and a convoy, which was probably KMS.2, was reported by another U-boat on the 2nd of November. Finally a large body of ships, which undoubtedly must have been the vital assault convoy KMF.1, was reported by yet other U-boats in 38° North 22° West on the 2nd and again in the small hours of the next morning, when it was steering east for Gibraltar.[1] But in spite of all these reports of exceptionally heavy southward movements between the 26th of October and the 3rd of November the enemy did not guess what was in train.

Table 25.   Operation 'Torch'. Maritime Forces Engaged

	Force H and fuelling force (Admiral Syfret)	Centre Task Forces (Commodore Troubridge)	Eastern Task Forces (Admiral Burrough)	Western Task Forces (Admiral Hewitt, U.S.N.)
H.Q. Ships . .	–	1	1	–
Battleships and Battlecruisers	3	–	–	3
Aircraft Carriers .	3	–	1	1
Escort Carriers .	–	2	1	4
Cruisers . .	3	2	3	7
Monitors . .	–	–	1	–
A.A. Ships . .	–	2	3	–
Destroyers . .	17	13	13	38
Cutters . .	–	2	–	–
Fleet Minesweepers	–	8	7	8
Sloops . . .	–	2	3	–
Corvettes . .	1	6	6	–
Trawlers (A/S-M/S)	4	8	8	–
Minelayers . .	–	–	–	3
Seaplane Tender .	–	–	–	1
Motor launches .	–	10	8	–
Submarines . .	–	2	3	4
Landing Ships Infantry	–	15	11	–
Combat Loaders .	–	–	4	23
Landing Ships Tank	–	3	–	–
Landing Ships Gantry	–	1	2	–
Mechanical Transport and other ships	–	28	16	8
Tankers . .	2	–	–	5

Ships which were to take part in the actual landings were allocated to the special 'Inshore Groups', from which the assaults were to be mounted. Each of these groups was given a particular beach on to

---

[1] See Map 32 (opp. p. 317).

which its troops, tanks, guns and equipment were to be landed. Air support was to be provided in the first instance by the carriers; but special arrangements were made to seize shore airfields as quickly as possible, in certain cases with paratroops flown from Britain. As soon as that had been accomplished shore-based fighters were to be flown in from Gibraltar. Early fighter support was, of course, more important in the case of the Algiers landing than for the two more westerly ones, which were considerably further from German and Italian air bases.

The British maritime forces comprised in all about 340 ships, and each unit had to approach Gibraltar in the correct sequence and then pass on to the east, most of them between 7.30 p.m. on the 5th of November and 4 a.m. on the 7th. The ocean passages were made in almost complete safety, not least because the only U-boat group in the approaches to Gibraltar had been fortuitously attracted to a Sierra Leone convoy, which was passing east and north of the invasion fleet between the 27th and 30th of October.[1] Though the merchantmen suffered severe losses, it was then that the three great troop and supply convoys KMS.1 and 2 and KMF.1, slipped through unscathed. The Commodore of SL.125 (Rear-Admiral C. N. Reyne, Ret'd.) later remarked to the author that it was the only time he had been congratulated for losing ships. One American 'Combat Loader', was torpedoed after entering the Mediterranean; but she ultimately reached harbour safely.[2] Her assault troops showed such indomitable determination not to miss the landings that they set off in their landing craft when their parent ship was damaged, although they were about 200 miles from Algiers at the time. The troops were finally picked up by escort vessels, and landed on the day following the assault.

The success of the whole operation depended, after the ocean passages had been safely made, on exact timing of the arrival of each convoy, ship or group of ships at Gibraltar, on the efficiency of the fuelling arrangements in that base, and on the punctuality with which every unit set out again on its eastward journey. This was the responsibility of Vice-Admiral Sir F. Edward-Collins, the Flag Officer, North Atlantic Station, and his special assistant Commodore G. N. Oliver.

As darkness descended on the Rock on the evening of the 5th of November the invasion fleet approached the Straits.

No waters in all the wide oceans of the world, not even those which wash the shores of Britain herself, have played a greater part in her history, or seen more of her maritime renown than these, where the rolling waves of the Atlantic approach the constricting passage of

---

[1] See p. 213 and Map 32 (opp. p. 317).
[2] See Map 34 (opp. p. 323).

Convoy to Malta. Operation 'Pedestal', August 1942. Aircraft carriers *Eagle* (nearest camera), *Victorious, Indomitable* and cruisers of the escort. Convoy in the background. (See pp. 302–308).

Convoy to Malta, Operation 'Pedestal' H.M.S. *Eagle* sinking after being torpedoed by U.73, 11th August 1942. (See p. 304).

Convoy to Malta, Operation 'Pedestal' August 1942. H.M.S. *Indomitable* on fire after receiving three bomb hits. (See p. 305).

The merchant ship *Dorset* under heavy air attack in Malta Convoy, Operation 'Pedestal', 12th August 1942. She was disabled, and sunk in a later attack. (See p. 307).

The tanker *Ohio* hit by torpedo in Malta Convoy, Operation 'Pedestal', 12th August 1942. She finally reached Malta safely. (See pp. 306–307).

Merchantmen in Malta Convoy, Operation 'Pedestal', under heavy air attack. (See pp. 302–308).

the Pillars of Hercules. Here it was that in 1587 Sir Francis Drake raided Cadiz and 'singed the King of Spain's beard'; through these waters sailed the ships of Sir George Rooke to the capture of Gibraltar itself in 1704, those of Admiral Rodney which fought the Moonlight Battle and relieved the Rock in 1780, and Lord Howe's fleet which finally raised the three-year siege in 1782. Over there Boscawen led his battleships into Lagos Bay and, by destroying de la Clue's squadron, added one more laurel to those gathered all over the world by British seamen in 1759—the 'annus mirabilis'. It was here that on St. Valentine's day 1797 John Jervis, 'old heart of oak', to whom England owed so much in an earlier crisis which had shaken her maritime power to its foundations, gained the victory by which his name is still chiefly remembered—the victory which, as he said, was 'very essential to England at this moment'.

It was in these narrows that a young Captain Nelson, for once pursued instead of pursuing, backed his topsails in the face of a superior enemy to pick up his friend and Lieutenant, with the remark 'by God, I'll not lose Hardy'. Through these straits passed Nelson's ships which finally ran Brueys to ground in Aboukir Bay, and those which chased Villeneuve to the West Indies and back again; and it was here that, on a calm and misty morning in October 1805, he and Collingwood led their two lines of battleships down towards the widely-stretched crescent of the combined French and Spanish fleets. It was in that bay near Cape Trafalgar, on that same afternoon, that a dying admiral urged that his victorious but shattered ships should be anchored at once, to meet the storm he felt approaching from the Atlantic.

> 'Nobly, nobly Cape St. Vincent to the North-West died away;
> Sunset ran, one glorious blood-red reeking into Cadiz Bay;
> Bluish mid the burning water, full in face Trafalgar lay;
> In the dimmest North-East distance dawned Gibraltar grand and grey;
> 'Here and here did England help me: how can I help England?'—say.[1]

For the last two years and more Cunningham's, Somerville's and Syfret's ships had passed and re-passed through these same waters, escorting supplies for Egypt or Malta, holding off a superior enemy and harassing his own sea communications; and, throughout the defensive phase, they had again and again at Taranto, Matapan, Sirte, Crete, Spartivento and in a hundred lesser fights, won fresh renown on the station where Nelson hoped for, and found, 'a bed of laurels'. It was they who had kept the torch burning, albeit sometimes dimly, through all the desperate days of 1940 and 1941. Now that same torch was to be fanned into full flame by the men of the troopships, landing craft, escort vessels and covering warships,

---

[1] Robert Browning. *Home-thoughts, from the Sea.*

X

commanded once again by Cunningham and sailing through those same historic waters on Operation 'Torch'. And, although none of them probably thought of the poet's rhetorical question, all of them now combined to answer it. For what they did marked the passing of the Defensive Phase.

At Gibraltar the programme was carried out without any serious hitches and, by daylight on the 7th of November, the Central and Eastern Task Forces, with the assault convoys and the covering warships of Force H, were all well inside the Mediterranean, steering towards the rendezvous at which their various components would assemble and from which they would, at their allotted times, steam inshore to the assault areas. The Task Force Commanders took over complete responsibility on passing the meridian of 3° West.

Meanwhile our submarines of the 10th (Malta) Flotilla were patrolling off Italian naval bases, while three of the 8th (Gibraltar) Flotilla waited off Toulon for any movement by the French fleet.[1] Another British submarine, the *Seraph*, had already landed General Mark Clark west of Algiers with the object of getting into touch with the French military authorities. On the 6th of November the same submarine embarked General Giraud from a beach near Toulon, and transferred him to a Catalina which brought him to Gibraltar, while another, the *Sibyl*, collected his staff on the 7th and 8th. But these hazardous crepuscular undertakings actually had little influence on the launching and progress of operation 'Torch'.

It will perhaps make it easier for the reader to understand the account which follows, if a brief digression is first made to explain the method of mounting such operations, as practised by the British services in 1942. One of the main lessons derived from the Dieppe raid was the need to create special naval assault forces under their own senior naval officers.[2] These comprised the landing ships and craft required by a specific Army formation, at this time a Division; and the naval force commander, the military commander and a representative of the air command were jointly responsible for planning their operation and for carrying out the necessary training.

A Headquarters Ship, usually a converted passenger liner, was allocated to each assault force. The commanders and their staffs were embarked in these ships, and directed the assault from them. The final composition of the assault force depended, of course, on the plan to be carried out, and additional ships or craft might be added to meet special circumstances. There was not, and could not

---

[1] See Map 31 (opp. p. 313).
[2] See p. 251.

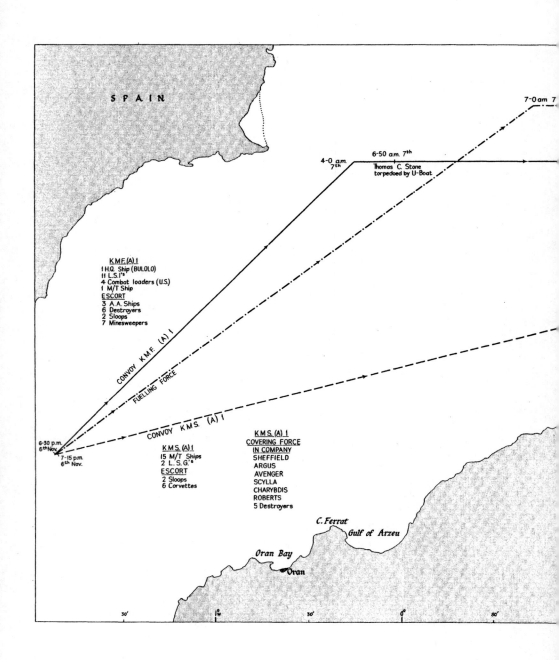

SPAIN

7-0 am 7

4-0 a.m.
7th

6-50 a.m. 7th
Thomas C. Stone
torpedoed by U-Boat

K.M.F.(A) 1
1 H.Q. Ship (BULOLO)
11 L.S.I's
4 Combat loaders (U.S.)
1 M/T Ship
ESCORT
3 A.A. Ships
6 Destroyers
2 Sloops
7 Minesweepers

CONVOY K.M.F. (A) 1

FUELLING FORCE

CONVOY K.M.S. (A) 1

6-30 p.m.
6th Nov.

7-15 p.m.
6th Nov.

K.M.S. (A) 1
15 M/T Ships
2 L.S.G.'s
ESCORT
2 Sloops
6 Corvettes

K.M.S. (A) 1
COVERING FORCE
IN COMPANY
SHEFFIELD
ARGUS
AVENGER
SCYLLA
CHARYBDIS
ROBERTS
5 Destroyers

C. Ferrat
Gulf of Arzeu

Oran Bay
Oran

30'   1° W   30'   0°   30'

FUELLING FORCE
2 Oilers
1 Corvette
4 Trawlers

Fast convoy KMF(A)1
Slow convoy KMS(A)1
Fuelling force
Beacon submarines

FUELLING FORCE
Cruising in this area
7th-8th Nov.

4-0 pm 7th

6-0 pm 7th

Joined by 8 trawlers
and 8 M.L.'s from the
fuelling force

7-0 pm 7th

MAIN
COVERING
FORCE

DUKE OF YORK
RENOWN
FORMIDABLE
VICTORIOUS
3 Cruisers
16 Destroyers

Cruising NORTH of this line night of 7th-8th November
Cruising SOUTH of this line night of 7th-8th November

K.M.S.A(1)
COVERING
FORCE

3 Cruisers
1 Carrier
1 Escort carrier
5 Destroyers

Central and Eastern sectors assault forces

Eastern sector assault forces

6-0 pm 7th

Western sector assault forces

Western and Central sectors

9-30 pm 7th

P 48

Central sector
landing beaches

BROKE and MALCOLM
attack harbour

UNRIVALLED
10-30pm 7th

C. Sidi 10-30pm
Ferruch 7th

Matifu

SHAKESPEARE
10-45 pm 7th

ALGIERS

4 am 8th

Eastern sector
landing beaches

Western sector
landing beaches

MAISON BLANCHE
Airfield

C. Tenez

BLIDA
Airfield

WESTERN LANDING GROUP	CENTRE LANDING GROUP	EASTERN LANDING GROUP
3 L.S.I.'s	1 H.Q. Ship	3 Combat loaders (U.S)
1 L.S.G.	7 L.S.I's	1 L.S.I.
4 M/T. Ships	9 M/T. Ships	3 M/T Ships
	1 L.S.G.	
ESCORT	ESCORT	ESCORT
1 A.A. Ship	4 Destroyers	1 A.A. Ship
2 Sloops	1 A.A. Ship 1 Sloop	2 Destroyers
2 Corvettes	2 Corvettes	
3 Trawlers	3 Minesweepers	4 Minesweepers
3 M.L.'s	3 Trawlers	2 Trawlers
	3 M.L.'s	2 M.L.'s

30'   2°   30'   3°   30'

be, exact standardisation in operations of such infinite variability; but the principles outlined above applied to all of them.

The assault convoys were divided into fast and slow groups and one or more groups of major landing craft, each with its own escort. The Headquarters Ship and Landing Ships Infantry (L.S.Is.) would be in the fast group, which would overtake the slower groups, perhaps on the evening before the assault. The fast group, supported and covered by warships, would lead the assault. A submarine was usually stationed off the landing beach to serve as a navigational mark.[1] After passing it the L.S.Is. would disperse to their 'lowering positions', about seven miles off-shore. There they would stop or anchor, and lower the assault craft (L.C.As) with the first wave of troops embarked in them. These would then form up in flotillas, and move inshore so as to 'touch down' exactly at Zero Hour. The assault craft would then return to the ships to embark the subsequent waves of troops.

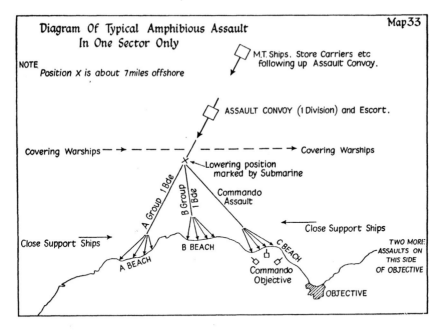

It was the British practice generally to make the first assault by night, accepting the navigational risks involved in order to achieve surprise. There would probably be no preliminary bombardment, but small support ships might move close inshore just before the 'touch down' to give fire support.

---

[1] See Map 33.

If possible the L.S.Is would move closer inshore after the first wave had left, in order to speed up the arrival of later waves on the beaches. Meanwhile a small number of the most urgently needed vehicles would be landed in such craft as L.C.Ms (Landing Craft Mechanised).

After daylight the various groups carrying guns, tanks, vehicles and supplies of all kinds would be sent inshore. Landing Ships Tank (L.S.Ts) and Landing Craft Tank (L.C.Ts) were specially designed to disembark their loads direct on to the beaches. This called for considerable skill, judgement and training. Various devices were introduced later to make this difficult task easier and safer; in particular vehicles were water-proofed, so that they could negotiate shallow water under their own power.

Though favourable weather must always be a cardinal necessity in a combined operation, meticulously careful planning, accurate timing and thorough training were essential to success. The risks were always great, and success in the actual assault landing was by no means a guarantee of final success; for the Army remained highly vulnerable to counter-attack for some hours, even days, after the assault. The speed with which its strength was built up was therefore as important as the successful execution of the first landings.

Off Algiers the ninety-three warships and merchantmen in Admiral Burrough's Task Force passed through the successive rendezvous, at which they divided and then re-divided to arrive finally at the 'lowering positions' of the landing craft.[1] The landings were to be made in three sectors, one to the east and two to the west of Algiers; and within each sector the assault units from various ships were allotted to different beaches. Three submarines marked the release positions of the landing craft, and specially trained pilots went inshore by boat to mark the several beaches in each sector.

The landings in the westernmost sector at Algiers took place punctually. In the central sector matters did not go so well. There was a considerable westerly set, which soon caused the landing ships and their craft to get out of position. This and a pilotage failure combined to cause a breakdown of the procedure for locating the various beaches, and many troops landed in the wrong place. Happily serious resistance was only encountered at one beach in this sector; had it proved otherwise the results might have been unfortunate. In the eastern sector as well there was some confusion and delay; but in spite of these mishaps good progress was made as soon as the assault parties got ashore.

---

[1] See Map 34 (opp. p. 323).

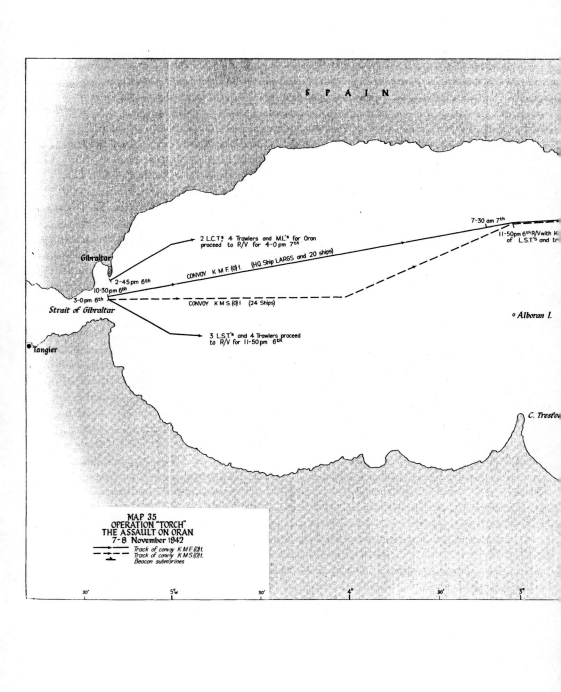

S P A I N

7-30 am 7th

11-50pm 6th R/V with K
of L.S.T.'s and tr

2 L.C.T.'s 4 Trawlers and M.L.'s for Oran
proceed to R/V for 4-0 pm 7th

Gibraltar

2-45 pm 6th   CONVOY K M F. (O) 1.   (H.Q. Ship LARGS and 20 ships)
10-30 pm 6th

3-0 pm 6th   CONVOY K M S. (O) 1   (24 Ships)

Strait of Gibraltar   o Alboran I.

Tangier   3 L.S.T.'s and 4 Trawlers proceed
                        to R/V for 11-50 pm 6th

                                                                                            C. Tresfo

MAP 35
OPERATION "TORCH"
THE ASSAULT ON ORAN
7-8 November 1942
———————— Track of convoy K M F. (O) 1.
– – – – – – – Track of convoy K M S. (O) 1.
▸——▸   Beacon submarines

30'   5°w   30'   4°   30'   3°

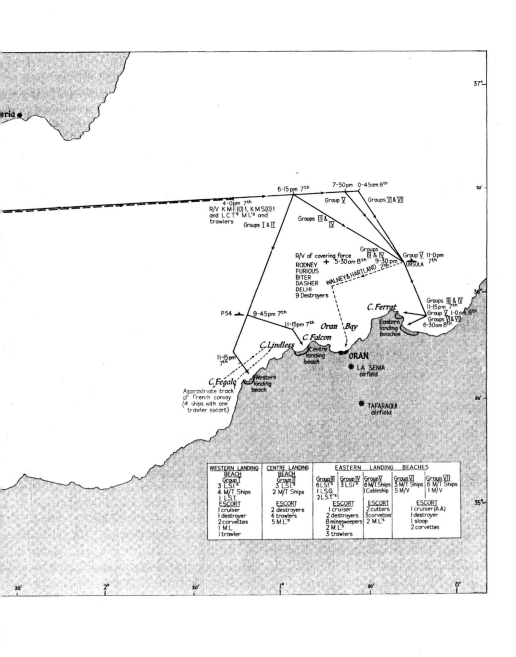

37°

ria ●

30'

6-15 pm 7th   7-50pm   0-45am 8th

Group V   Groups VI & VII

4-0pm 7th
R/V KMF(0) I, KMS(0) 1
and L.C.T.s M.L's and
trawlers
Groups I & II

Groups III &
IV

R/V of covering force
RODNEY
FURIOUS
BITER
DASHER
DELHI
9 Destroyers

Groups
III & IV
9-30 pm
7th

Group V 11-0pm
7th
URSULA

36°

WALNEY & HARTLAND

Groups III & IV
11-15pm 7th
Group V 1-0am 8th
Groups VI & VII
6-30am 8th

C. Ferrat

Eastern
landing
beaches

P 54   9-45pm 7th

11-15pm 7th   Oran Bay

C. Falcon

C. Lindless

Centre
landing
beach

ORAN

11-15
7th

Western
landing
beach

LA SENIA
airfield

C. Fegalo

Approximate track
of French convoy
(4 ships with one
trawler escort)

TAFARAOUI
airfield

30'

35°

30'   2°   30'   1°   30'   30'   0°

WESTERN LANDING BEACH	CENTRE LANDING BEACH	EASTERN LANDING BEACHES				
Group I	Group II	Group III	Group IV	Group V	Group VI	Group VII
3 L.S.I.s	3 L.S.I.s	6 L.S.I.s	3 L.S.I.s	6 M/T Ships	3 M/T Ships	6 M/T Ships
4 M/T Ships	2 M/T Ships	1 L.S.G.		1 Cableship	5 M/V	1 M/V
1 L.S.T.		2 L.S.T.s				
ESCORT	ESCORT	ESCORT		ESCORT		ESCORT
1 cruiser	2 destroyers	1 cruiser		2 cutters		1 cruiser (A.A)
1 destroyer	4 trawlers	2 destroyers		3 corvettes		1 destroyer
2 corvettes	5 M.L's	8 minesweepers		2 M.L's		1 sloop
1 M.L.		2 M.L's				2 corvettes
1 trawler		3 trawlers				

At 6.40 a.m. on the 8th of November a U.S. Regimental Combat Team captured the Maison Blanche airfield—the more important of the two near Algiers—and R.A.F. fighters from Gibraltar landed there soon after 9 o'clock. Fuel was available, and they immediately established patrols over the Algiers landing beaches. The second airfield, near Blida, was captured at about 8.30 a.m. by Martlet fighters of the Fleet Air Arm, a handful of which under Lieutenant B. H. C. Nation of the *Victorious* held it until the Commandos arrived. Probably this was the first time in history that naval aircraft captured a shore airfield.

Meanwhile a frontal attack on Algiers harbour by the destroyers *Broke* and *Malcolm*, whose object was to prevent the French scuttling their ships and demolishing the port installations, had not gone according to plan. They failed to find the entrance in the darkness, and came under heavy fire. The *Malcolm* was badly hit and withdrew, but at 5.20 a.m., at her fourth attempt, the *Broke* charged the boom and broke through. She berthed successfully and the American troops on board her were disembarked; but she was soon forced by heavy and accurate fire to leave the harbour. The *Broke* suffered much damage, and sank the next day. It was perhaps appropriate that a gallant old veteran, who bore a name made famous by her predecessor in close action in the Straits of Dover in the 1914-18 war[1], should find a grave in the Mediterranean after having broken into a hostile harbour in the second.

By the afternoon the forts guarding the harbour had been silenced by bombardment and bombing; but enemy aircraft had made a first appearance, and attacked our warships and transports off the coast. Damage was not, however, serious. At 7 p.m. French resistance ceased, and we were soon in control of the harbour. At dawn next day, the 9th, Admiral Burrough's flagship the *Bulolo* entered harbour. Her arrival was, perhaps, rather more sensational than intended, because a near-miss bomb threw off her electrical engine-room telegraphs at a critical moment. In consequence, when the order to go astern was given nothing happened, and she overshot her intended berth. She ultimately brought up undamaged on a convenient mud bank. The transports and store ships soon followed her in. The speed with which possession of the harbour was gained was fortunate, since the freshening wind had caused unloading delays and heavy losses of landing craft on the beaches, especially in the eastern sector.

The general plan which the Centre Task Force under Commodore Troubridge was to carry out against Oran was similar to that executed at Algiers. The fast and slow convoys KMF.(O)1 and KMS.(O)1 met at 4 p.m. on the 7th of November, and then divided

---

[1] See Henry Newbolt, *Naval Operations*, Vol. IV. (Longmans, Green and Co. 1928) pp. 377-8.

into the seven groups detailed for the three assault areas. Again there was to be one assault to the east and two to the west of the port.[1] All groups continued together towards Malta until, at appropriate moments after darkness had fallen, they broke off individually and turned south towards their real objectives. Cruisers were ordered to provide supporting fire at the beaches, and to patrol off Oran to intercept any ships which attempted to escape. The *Rodney*, which was to protect the transports against surface ship attack, three aircraft carriers and the anti-aircraft cruiser *Delhi* met at 5.30 a.m. twenty-five miles to seaward of Oran, and thereafter operated in support of the expedition. The position through which the assault ships had to pass, to approach the points where their landing craft would be lowered, were again marked by submarines, and the beaches themselves were marked by pilots. By midnight on the 7th-8th all the great fleet of over seventy warships and thirty-two transports was moving silently inshore. The night was calm and dark, but, as at Algiers, a westerly set was experienced, and again this had disconcerting results for the landing craft, some of which missed their proper beaches. In the western sector a chance encounter with a small French convoy further delayed the assault, and produced indirectly 'no little confusion'. One may compare this incident and its consequences with the equally fortuitous encounter made by the expedition to Dieppe with the German Channel convoy.[2] Both showed how easily a slight mischance could upset the intricate timing essential to success in night assaults from the sea. Luckily off Oran there were no very dire consequences, though the western assault did not take place until thirty-five minutes after its appointed time. None the less by the 11th over 3,000 men, 458 tanks and vehicles, and more than 1,100 tons of stores had been landed in the western sector, a large proportion of them in a small well-sheltered cove which had not been intended to take such heavy traffic.

In the centre sector, unlike the western one, the landings took place on the correct beaches, though not without unforeseen troubles. Chief among these was a sand bar which extended over the whole length of the sector a few yards off-shore, and had not been revealed by photographs or preliminary reconnaissances. Many of the forty-five landing craft were damaged on it and some were lost, while vehicles disappeared under water as they tried to drive ashore from landing craft grounded on the bar. The assault was late and, understandably, ill co-ordinated. It was fortunate that there was no opposition.

The eastern landings were by far the biggest of the three made against Oran. In that sector 29,000 men, 2,400 vehicles and 14,000

[1] See Map 35 (opp. p. 325).
[2] See p. 246.

tons of stores were to be put ashore from thirty-four ships. The total of landing craft involved was eighty-five, of which sixty-eight were for the initial assault (L.C.As). The landings were made unopposed, and in general on time, though the armoured vehicles were very late in reaching the shore—an error which would probably have proved expensive had there been serious resistance.

To prevent the French scuttling ships and destroying the port, a frontal assault by two ex-American coastguard cutters, the *Walney* and the *Hartland* under the command of Captain F. T. Peters, had been included in the plan. Their job was similar to that of the *Broke* and *Malcolm* at Algiers. Two motor launches were included in the force to provide smoke cover, while the light cruiser *Aurora* was detailed to support them with her guns. American troops were to be put ashore by the cutters to seize key points and prevent sabotage. This attack had originally been timed for 1 a.m., simultaneously with the assault landings; but the Task Force Commander had been given discretion over sending the cutters in, and he did not do so until two hours later. By that time the harbour defences had, of course, been thoroughly aroused. Just after 3 a.m. on the 8th the *Walney*, followed closely by her consort, charged the boom and broke into the harbour. She at once came under withering fire from ships and shore, was totally disabled, had most of her company killed and finally sank. The *Hartland* fared no better; she too was soon disabled, caught fire and suffered very heavy casualties. At about 6 a.m. she blew up. Captain Peters and Lieutenant-Commander Billot, R.N.R., the Captain of the *Hartland*, were among the very few survivors from the two ships. The former survived the assault but, by a tragic piece of irony, was killed a few days later in an aircraft accident. He was awarded a posthumous Victoria Cross.

While this gallant but unsuccessful attack was taking place the *Aurora* (Captain W. G. Agnew), which had made her name as leader of Force K from Malta in 1941[1], and several of our destroyers fought a hot action outside the harbour with French destroyers, which had come out of Oran and appeared intent on attacking our transports. One Frenchman was sunk, one driven ashore, and the third retired back to harbour. Admiral Cunningham remarked in his despatch that 'the *Aurora* polished off her opponents with practised ease'.

By 9 a.m. the tanks were landing on the Oran beaches, and naval aircraft from the three carriers had done good work in putting the nearest shore airfield (La Senia) out of action; but the paratroop operation to capture the main airfield at Tafaroui, fifteen miles south of Oran, went badly awry.[2] Not until noon were our land forces in possession of it. In the afternoon Spitfires from Gibraltar

---

[1] See Vol. I, pp. 532—533.
[2] See Map 35 (opp. p. 325).

landed there. Meanwhile the French coastal guns had opened on our transports, damaged two of them and forced others further away from the coast. The *Rodney* bombarded with her 16-inch guns in reply.

Throughout the 8th the landing of troops, vehicles and stores went on, though not without difficulties and losses caused by an increasing swell. Fighting continued on land and sea all the next day, which was marked by another engagement with French destroyers. The troops were by that time closing in on Oran from both sides, but resistance was still stubborn. By the evening of the 9th we had a firm hold on the airfield at La Senia, and were preparing for a final assault on the town of Oran next morning. The attack was launched at 7.30, and by 11 a.m. armoured units had penetrated into the city. At noon the French capitulated, and thus, fifty-nine hours after the first assault, a base which had been a source of trouble and anxiety to us ever since June 1940 passed into Allied hands.[1]

While these important successes were being won on land, Admiral Syfret's main covering force was patrolling to and fro further north. When it was plain that no interference by the Italian Fleet was likely, he took most of his ships back to Gibraltar. They arrived on the 15th, and the *Duke of York* and *Victorious* promptly returned to the Home Fleet, to which they properly belonged. The only important incident during Force H's patrol occurred when the submarine *Unruffled* (Lieutenant J. S. Stevens) hit and severely damaged the Italian cruiser *Attilio Regolo*. A detachment of Admiral Syfret's original force had meanwhile proceeded under Rear-Admiral C. H. J. Harcourt in the *Sheffield* to take part in the assault on Bougie, the next important port to the east on the road to the final Allied objective at Tunis.[2] We shall return to that operation, and to the still more easterly one against Bone, later, for it is time to take the reader outside the Straits of Gibraltar to see how the concurrent American assault on Casablanca had fared.[3]

For the landings on the Moroccan coast Admiral Hewitt's forces were divided into a Covering Group, composed of a battleship, two heavy cruisers and four destroyers, an Air Group of four carriers with a cruiser for support and flotilla vessels for screening purposes, and three Attack Groups. The latter each comprised a battleship and a cruiser, or two of the latter, and numerous transports, auxiliaries and escort vessels. To each Attack Group were also allocated beacon submarines, to mark the approach to the landing beaches, minesweepers and tankers. It will be observed that the American Western Naval Task Force took its attack transports along with it,

---

[1] See Vol. I, pp. 242–245.

[2] See Map 31 (opp. p. 313).

[3] A full account of the American landings in Morocco is contained in Morison, Vol. II.

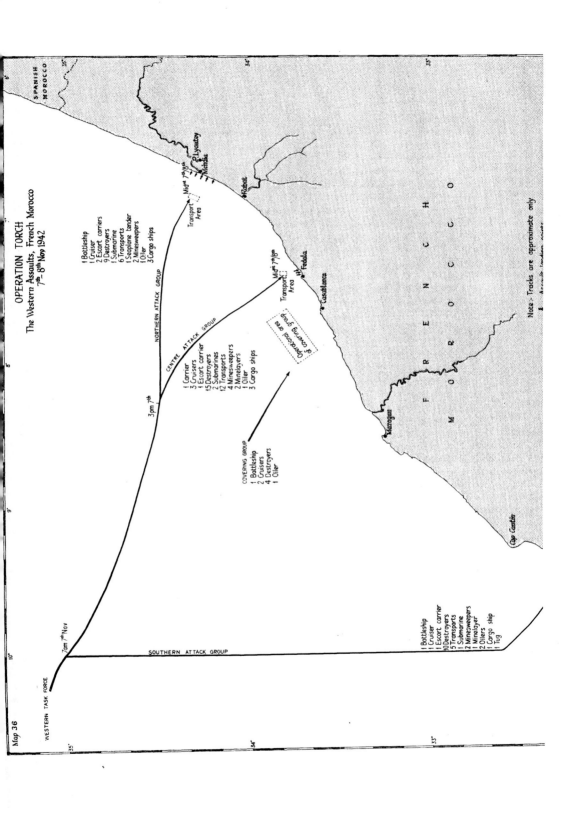

Map 36

OPERATION TORCH
The Western Assaults, French Morocco
7th–8th Nov 1942

WESTERN TASK FORCE

SOUTHERN ATTACK GROUP

7am 7th Nov

CENTRE ATTACK GROUP

NORTHERN ATTACK GROUP

3pm 7th

Transport Area
Midt 7th/8th

Transport Area
Midt 7th/8th

Transport Area
Midt 7th/8th

Operational area of covering group

COVERING GROUP
1 Battleship
2 Cruisers
4 Destroyers
1 Oiler

1 Battleship
1 Cruiser
2 Escort carriers
9 Destroyers
1 Submarine
6 Transports
1 Seaplane tender
2 Minesweepers
1 Oiler
3 Cargo ships

1 Carrier
3 Cruisers
1 Escort carrier
15 Destroyers
2 Submarines
12 Transports
4 Minesweepers
2 Minelayers
1 Oiler
3 Cargo ships

1 Battleship
1 Cruiser
1 Escort carrier
10 Destroyers
5 Transports
1 Submarine
2 Minesweepers
1 Minelayer
2 Oilers
1 Cargo ship
1 Tug

SPANISH MOROCCO

FRENCH MOROCCO

Pt Lyautey
Mehdia

Rabat

Fedala

Casablanca

Mazagan

Cap Cantin

Note:- Tracks are approximate only

35°

34°

33°

10°

9°

8°

6°

35°

34°

33°

whereas our own Centre and Eastern Task Forces met their assault convoys, which had sailed separately from Britain, off Gibraltar, and then joined up with them for the passages to their destinations.

Admiral Hewitt's flag was flown in the cruiser *Augusta*. By the 24th and 25th of October his various groups were at sea and heading east. The Air Group left Bermuda on the 26th, and two days later all the ships of the American expedition, in all some sixty warships and forty transports and tankers, had concentrated in 40° North 51° West. Fuelling was carried out twice at sea, and on the 7th of November all forces were approaching the African coast. Not a ship was lost on the way.

The three attack groups were to make their assaults in separate places. By far the most important of the three was the landing of 18,700 men at Fedala, some fifteen miles north of Casablanca.[1] This was the responsibility of the Centre Attack Group, and the outcome of the whole Moroccan operation depended on its success. The Northern Attack Group was to land 9,000 men near Port Lyautey, about sixty-five miles north-east of Casablanca, and bore the important responsibility for quickly capturing the adjacent air-field, which was the best in Morocco. The Southern Attack Group was to land at Safi where the expedition's Sherman tanks were to be disembarked. If serious resistance were encountered at Casablanca the tanks were to come north and master it.

By midnight on the 6th-7th of November Admiral Hewitt had to take a difficult decision. The weather forecasts from Britain and America had been consistently pessimistic regarding the practicability of a landing in Morocco on the 8th. The plans had provided for the Western Task Force to make alternative landings inside the Mediterranean should the surf-bound Moroccan coast prove un-approachable; but this alternative was strategically unattractive, for it eliminated the possibility of winning Morocco and Algeria simultaneously. After crossing the 'Chop Line'[2], Admiral Hewitt came under the control of the Naval Commander, Expeditionary Force, and there is no doubt that Admiral Cunningham and General Eisenhower considered whether, in view of the unfavourable weather, the Moroccan landings should be cancelled. The matter was, however, left in Admiral Hewitt's hands and, as the forecasts of his Task Force meteorologist predicted moderating winds, he decided to adhere to his original plan. His decision was to be abundantly justified.

We will first follow the fortunes of the Southern Attack Group at Safi. The assault was based on the use of two old American destroyers, the *Bernadou* and the *Cole*, to land small bodies of troops (about

---

[1] See Map 36.
[2] See p. 111.

400 in all) inside the harbour and seize the port facilities, so that the ship in which the Sherman tanks were embarked could at once enter and unload. Simultaneously beach landings were to be made to the north and south of the harbour. The approach of the attack group passed without incident. Zero hours for all the landings in Morocco was 4 a.m. on the 8th of November, three hours later than those at Oran and Algiers; but all three of the Western Task Force's assaults were, for various reasons, somewhat delayed. The *Bernadou* opened the ball at Safi by entering the harbour at about 4.30, and quickly came under heavy fire. The *Cole* got temporarily lost in the darkness outside, but she and a wave of assault craft followed in, about forty minutes later. Meanwhile the heavy ships of the covering force smothered the shore defences with their gunfire, and this, by diverting French attention from the harbour, undoubtedly helped the destroyers to land their troops with surprisingly few casualties. In very little time all the harbour works had been secured.

The southernmost beach landing was badly delayed, chiefly by an accidental explosion among landing craft, and it was nearly 9.30 before the first assault wave got ashore. They met no resistance, and were soon moving north against the town. The naval bombardment was successful beyond expectations in silencing the coast defences, the other landings went well, and by 2.30 p.m. Safi was in American hands. The *Lakehurst*, with the Sherman tanks on board, entered harbour soon afterwards. The speed with which success was achieved had been remarkable, and there is no doubt that it owed much to the daring and skill of the two old destroyers whose small landing parties caught the French entirely by surprise. The discharge of cargo inside the harbour continued uninterruptedly during the succeeding days. By the 13th the operation was completed, and a homeward-bound convoy of empty ships sailed for the United States. Safi had been captured for the loss of an insignificant number of landing craft and, which was even more astonishing, at a cost of only about ten men killed and seventy-five wounded. But the slowness of the French reaction from the air, from Marrakesh airfield, was very fortunate, because only here did the American carrier-borne air co-operation prove inadequate to the task placed upon it.

To turn now to the much stronger and all-important central attack in the neighbourhood of Casablanca itself, at midnight on 7th-8th of November the transports had reached the position where the landing craft were to be lowered; but slow work in getting the craft away delayed the assault until just after 5 o'clock. For a time the fate of the whole expedition hung in the balance. Although the night was fine and calm, a heavy surf was breaking on the beaches exposed to the Atlantic rollers. Nearly half the landing craft used in the initial assault were wrecked; some missed their allotted beaches and ended up on the rocky coast several miles away. Fortunately most of the men managed to scramble ashore, and in the first hour 3,500 were landed. There was little resistance until, at daylight, the shore batteries opened fire on the ships. Then French aircraft, warships from Casablanca and the shore guns all attacked the transports, the beaches and the landing craft. The American covering warships fought two sharp actions during the forenoon with the French cruiser *Primauguet* and seven destroyers, and handled them very roughly. No less than six destroyers were sunk, or disabled and driven ashore, and the cruiser was reduced to a wreck. Eight French submarines also left harbour early in the forenoon to attack the invasion fleet; but only one of them returned to her berth undamaged. Two reached Dakar, and one made Cadiz; of the other four, one was bombed and beached and three were never heard of again. No did they do any damage to American ships, though the battleship *Massachusetts* and the cruiser *Brooklyn* narrowly avoided torpedoes fired at them. There were moments of anxiety over the possibility of the powerful French squadron in Dakar intervening; but the *Richelieu*, *Gloire* and *Montcalm* did not attempt to reach the scene of the landings.

Thus was the threat from the sea countered by the covering forces, and in no uncertain manner; but there was an element of high tragedy in the French Navy's sacrifice, at Algiers and Oran as well as at Casablanca, of so many good ships and lives in attacking those whom most Frenchmen must in their hearts have known to be their best friends and, moreover, the only people who could liberate their enslaved homeland. None the less it must be counted to the credit of the French Navy that its ships went out to fight overwhelmingly superior strength with great gallantry.

On the same forenoon that the covering force was dealing with the French warships which had put to sea, the American carrier aircraft and the heavy guns of the bombarding ships did severe execution among those which had remained in harbour. The 16-inch shells of the *Massachusetts* put the *Jean Bart* out of action, while three submarines and many merchantmen and auxiliaries were destroyed within the confines of the port. Only against the French shore batteries was the warships' gunfire comparatively ineffective, and the old lesson of the doubtful ability of ships to deal effectively with such defences was once again demonstrated; but on this occasion it did not influence the outcome of the operation.

Meanwhile the heavy surf continued to cause serious difficulties in landing reinforcements of men and supplies over the beaches at Fedala. Happily the situation was eased by the capture of its small port at 2.30 in the afternoon. By nightfall 7,750 men had landed, and unloading in the harbour had begun to replace the use of the beaches. About two thirds of the 140 landing craft used in this operation were wrecked or out of action by that time.

On the 10th American air attacks finally eliminated the French air force, and did more damage to the French ships. The Army had meanwhile encircled Casablanca, and was awaiting the arrival of the Sherman tanks from Safi. But it was on that day that Admiral Darlan broadcast an order to all French forces in North Africa to cease resistance. At a conference held in Casablanca that afternoon it was agreed that hostilities should be suspended.

Well before that happened the Northern Attack Group had landed its assault forces on either side of the mouth of the winding river which led to Port Lyautey. This group, commanded by Rear-Admiral Monroe Kelly, U.S.N., had remained in company with the Centre Group until 3 p.m. on the 7th of November, when the two forces parted and steered for their respective assault areas.[1] By about 11.30 p.m. the northern group and its transports had arrived off the town of Mehedia at the river entrance, but difficulty was experienced in fixing the ships' position relative to the landing beaches. Then, soon after midnight, an unlucky encounter with a coastal convoy revealed the presence of Admiral Monroe's force to the French defences. Zero hour for the landings was 4 a.m., but the trouble experienced in making contact with the beach-marking boats, and slow disembarkation from the transports, delayed the assaults by more than an hour.

The main defence of the approaches to Port Lyautey was a battery of six 5·5-inch coastal guns sited near the river entrance, and it had been intended that it should be captured immediately the troops got ashore. This was not, however, accomplished; nor was good use at first made of the ample naval supporting fire available. Not for forty-eight hours was the battery put out of action. The trouble experienced in fixing the transports' position and contacting the mark boats, the delays in manning the assault craft, and the heavy swell on the beaches combined to make the landings what the American general called 'a hit-or-miss affair that would have spelled disaster against a well-armed enemy intent upon resistance'.[2] Soon after daylight on the 8th French aircraft attacked the beaches, the coastal battery opened fire on the transport area, and French reinforcements with tanks and artillery arrived from Port Lyautey. Furthermore the plan to send the destroyer *Dallas* quickly up the river with a raider detachment to capture the airfield went awry. On the 8th and 9th stubborn resistance was encountered by the American troops. Not until early on the 10th was the dash up-river by the *Dallas* successful. The airfield was then seized, and by 11

---

[1] See Map 36 (opp. p. 329).
[2] Morison, Vol. II, p. 123.

a.m. that morning the first American aircraft had landed on it. At about the same time the troublesome coast defence battery at the river mouth was captured. The transports could then move close inshore and land the urgently-needed reinforcements, vehicles, and supplies. At midnight on the 10th-11th the French defenders received Darlan's order to stop fighting, and thereafter no difficulty was experienced in taking full control of the whole district. The Northern Attack Group had to overcome the stiffest resistance of any of the Moroccan assault forces.

The reactions of the German Naval Staff and U-boat Command to the launching of Operation 'Torch' were, to say the least, somewhat tardy. The first firm intelligence did not reach U-boat headquarters until 6.30 a.m. on the 8th of November. A total of fifteen boats was then ordered to steer for the Moroccan coast at high speed. Later all those on convoy operations west of Ireland were ordered to the approaches to Gibraltar; but the enemy realised that he was probably already too late to interfere with the actual landings. His purpose therefore became the interruption of the stream of supplies and reinforcements. One U-boat arrived off Morocco on the 9th, but accomplished nothing. Not until two days later, by which time the defences were well organised, did others appear on the scene; and it was the evening of the 11th before one of them (U.173) accomplished the first success by sinking a transport off Fedala. She herself was, however, sunk by American escort vessels off Casablanca on the 16th. Next day, the 12th, U.130 destroyed three more transports, but thereafter, although nine U-boats were present, the increasing use of the ports for unloading reduced the enemy's chances of success, and no more sinkings were achieved offshore. The intervention of the U-boats had come too late to threaten the invasion fleet at its most critical time.

By the middle of November about a dozen German U-boats had concentrated to the west of Gibraltar, and another group of seven had penetrated the Straits while our escorts were fully employed guarding the Algiers and Oran convoys. This temporarily raised the number of German U-boats inside the Mediterranean to twenty-five, the highest total ever reached by them. But in this same month we sank no less than five of their number so that, at the end of November, their strength was reduced again to twenty.[1] In the following month three out of five more U-boats ordered into the Mediterranean by Dönitz succeeded in getting through the Straits. At the end of the year there were thus twenty-three working in the narrow sea, out of a total operational strength of 212. In addition to the arrival of German reinforcements, ten Italian submarines left

---

[1] See below p. 336 (footnote 2) and Appendix J for details of these U-boat sinkings.

Cagliari for the North African coast as soon as they learnt of the invasion. We will return to them later. To the west of Gibraltar a few successes were obtained by the Germans but, considering the great flow of traffic passing in both directions through those waters, they were surprisingly small. On the 12th U.515 sank the destroyer depot ship *Hecla* and damaged the destroyer *Marne*. Three days later the escort carrier *Avenger* and the transport *Ettrick* (11,279 tons) fell victims to U.155, while a chance encounter with a north-bound convoy off Lisbon on the 14th led to the loss of the valuable troop-ship *Warwick Castle* (20,107 tons). In general, however, the rapid strengthening of our anti-submarine defences off the Straits after the invasion had been launched made that great focus highly dangerous to the enemy, and the U-boats were soon forced further west. Three U-boats were sunk and six others seriously damaged in those waters in November, and for comparatively small accomplishments. In December the Germans therefore tried instead to catch the supply convoys from the United States (UGF and UGS). On the 6th the troopship *Ceramic* and three other independent ships were sunk west of the Azores; but the convoys were actually routed further south than the enemy believed, and he failed to find them. The great stream of shipping from America to Casablanca continued to pass on its way unhindered.

But with the Americans firmly installed in Morocco it is time to return inside the Mediterranean, where greater difficulties were meanwhile being encountered.

As soon as the Eastern and Centre Task Forces had secured Algiers and Oran harbours and sufficient troops had been landed, the race for Tunis began. Both sides realised that command of 'The Narrows' of the Mediterranean, and so the ultimate fate of the armies in North Africa, depended on holding the northward-jutting promontory on which stand Tunis and the important French naval base of Bizerta.[1] In Algeria the land communications were not nearly good enough to enable the First Army to make a rapid advance, so long as it had to be supplied from Algiers. Hence arose the need to seize and bring into use as quickly as possible the more easterly harbours of Bougie and Bone. Those two ports had to per-form for the First Army the functions that Tobruk and Benghazi had often fulfilled for the Eighth Army; and the need to seize them quickly had always taken an important place in the 'Torch' plans.

The assault on Bougie had originally been planned for the 9th of November, but bad weather caused its postponement for two days. At dawn on the 11th Rear-Admiral C. H. J. Harcourt, flying his flag in the cruiser *Sheffield*, safely escorted three transports there,

---

[1] See Map 31 (opp. p. 313).

and the troops landed unopposed. It had been intended to make another landing further east to seize Djidjelli airfield simultaneously, but it was frustrated by a heavy swell on the beach. The airfield was actually captured by paratroops, but the petrol for the aircraft was in the assault convoy, which had returned to Bougie. This seriously delayed getting our own fighters, one squadron of which arrived there early on the 12th, into service. It thus came to pass that for two days the ships in Bougie had no air cover, and they were subjected to heavy bombing. The monitor *Roberts* was hit and badly damaged; and serious losses were suffered by the exposed troopships. The *Cathay*, *Awatea*, and *Karanja* were all sunk by air attacks, and the anti-aircraft ship *Tynwald* was torpedoed or mined, and lost. 'The essential importance of establishing properly directed fighter protection at the earliest moment was', said Admiral Cunningham, 'a lesson well learnt in the Western Desert campaigns, which now had to be demonstrated again by bitter experience in a new theatre'. By the 13th R.A.F. Spitfires were operating from Djidjelli, and thereafter the port of Bougie was worked in comparative immunity. At Bone, 230 miles east of Algiers, the initial landings were made by Commandos carried there in two destroyers. The port and nearby airfield was quickly seized, but again there were heavy bombing attacks. 'The tide of our advance reached little beyond the port' of Bone, remarked Admiral Cunningham; and the chief reason was that our air forces in Algeria were not yet fully established. As soon as fighter protection could be given, Bone proved a valuable advanced base for use by our light forces in attacking the enemy's supply traffic to Africa. But at the end of November the First Army was still building up strength about forty miles west of Bizerta, and it was plain that Axis reinforcements and supplies were reaching Tunisia by sea and air in sufficient quantities to deprive us of first place in the race for Tunis.[1]

Admiral Cunningham regretted this deeply. He considered that had the French in Tunisia offered even weak resistance between the 9th and 15th of November 'Our gamble would have succeeded'. 'The timidity and vacillation of the French in Tunisia' in his view 'cost the Allies much time and effort'. He has also left on record his opinion that, in spite of the serious risks involved, a bold lunge by a part of our invasion forces straight for Bizerta would have succeeded in forestalling the enemy at that crucial point.[2]

While we were thus building up our land forces and reaching out to the east, the enemy's bombers were ranging up and down the African coast seeking suitable targets; and his U-boats were closing

[1] See Map 31 (opp. p. 313).
[2] Viscount Cunningham of Hyndhope, *A Sailor's Odyssey*, p. 501.

in on the concentration of shipping passing in and out of the expedition's bases, much of it sailing independently. Though we lost some valuable ships, including the transports *Viceroy of India* and *Nieuw Zeeland* (Dutch) on the 11th of November to U-boat attacks, and the *Narkunda* from bombing, such losses among big ships employed in advanced waters where our maritime control was not complete were inevitable. They continued in the following month when the *Strathallan* (23,772 tons), a splendid ship and the last pre-war addition to the P. and O. Company's fleet, was torpedoed in Convoy KMF.5 when she had 5,000 troops on board. She sank on the 22nd of December, the day after she was hit. Happily the loss of life was small. The *Cameronia*, in the same convoy, was hit by an aircraft torpedo, but survived. Regrettable though the loss of such fine ships was, it did not influence the campaign.[1]

The U-boats also took a toll of the escort vessels protecting the 'Torch' convoys. The destroyer *Martin* and the Dutch destroyer *Isaac Sweers*, which had given long and distinguished service on this station, fell victims to them in November; but they were amply avenged, since no less than seven German and a like number of Italian submarines were destroyed in the Mediterranean or off Gibraltar between the 7th of November and mid-December.[2] Special mention must be made of a few of these successes. The trawler *Lord Nuffield*, which had been ignored by the Italian submarine *Emo* as too small fry to engage her attention, sank her disdainful adversary and rescued most of the crew; U.331, commanded by Tiesenhausen, who had sunk the *Barham* a year earlier[3], was dealt with entirely by aircraft. She was sighted and damaged by Hudsons of No. 500 Squadron, and surrendered. Naval aircraft from the *Formidable* which, unfortunately, had not seen the surrender signals, then torpedoed and sank her. Survivors were finally picked up by a

---

[1] The total losses to Allied merchant ships during the assault phase of operation 'Torch' were sixteen ships of 181,732 tons.

[2] The complete list of U-boats sunk in the Mediterranean and its approaches at this time is as follows:

7th November	*Antonio Sciesa* sunk by United States air raid at Tobruk.
9th November	*Granito* sunk by S/M *Saracen* off N.W. Sciily.
10th November	*Emo* sunk by H.M.T. *Lord Nuffield*—off Algiers.
12th November	U.660 sunk by *Lotus* and *Starwort*—Western Mediterranean.
13th November	U.605 sunk by *Lotus* and *Poppy*—off Algiers.
14th November	U.595 sunk by aircraft of No. 500 Squadron—N.W. Mediterranean.
15th November	U.411 sunk by *Wrestler*—Western approaches to Mediterranean.
15th November	U.259 sunk by aircraft of No. 500 Squadron—off Algiers.
17th November	U.331 sunk by carrier and land aircraft—Western Mediterranean.
19th November	U.98 sunk by Gibraltar air patrol of No. 608 Squadron—Western approaches to Mediterranean.
2nd December	*Dessie* sunk by *Quiberon* (R.A.N.) and *Quentin* off Bone.
6th December	*Porfido* sunk by S/M *Tigris*—South of Sardinia.
13th December	*Corallo* sunk by *Enchantress*—off Bougie.
15th December	*Uarsciek* sunk by *Petard* and *Queen Olga*—South of Malta.

[3] See Vol. I, p. 534.

The heavy ships of the covering force in Operation 'Torch', November 1942.
H.M.Ss *Duke of York, Nelson, Renown, Formidable, Argonaut.* (See pp. 314–328).

The assault convoy K.M.F.1 for Operation 'Torch' on passage to Gibraltar,
November 1942.

Operation 'Torch'. Landing craft leaving for the beaches off Algiers, 9th November 194
(See pp. 324–325).

Algiers harbour in use as the main Allied base, April 1943. The ships shown include
H.M.Ss *Formidable, Dido, Maidstone, Carlisle, Oakley, Vienna* and *Ashanti.*

Walrus amphibian. No. 500 Squadron, which had achieved two other successes against U-boats in the preceding days received a signal of congratulations from the Admiralty. The corvettes *Lotus* and *Starwort* disposed of U.660 on the 12th of November. Next day the *Lotus* had a different companion, the *Poppy*, when they attacked another promising contact off Algiers. After several depth charge attacks the *Lotus* used her 'hedgehog'.[1] There were no visible effects, but the Captain of the corvette found himself best able to describe the resulting underwater noises by quoting an onomatopoeic line from Aristophanes in his Report of Proceedings. That his anti-submarine tactics were as good as his knowledge of the classics is shown by the fact that enemy records confirm the destruction of U.605 in that position on that day. The Naval Staff evidently appreciated receiving so erudite a report, for they reproduced it, with suitable translation and explanations for those less well educated than the corvette's officers.[2]

On the 11th of November Admiral Darlan sent a message to Admiral de Laborde, who was in command of the French fleet at Toulon, urging that his ships should come to North Africa immediately[3]; but in his conversations with Admiral Cunningham Darlan admitted that he was doubtful whether his suggestion would be adopted. In the first place de Laborde was known to be fanatically anti-British, and in the second place he was able to argue that Darlan's proposal had no backing from the Vichy government to which he (de Laborde) was responsible. Subsequent events were to prove that Darlan's estimate of his countrymen's reactions was accurate. Although Admiral Auphan, the Minister of Marine at Vichy, supported Darlan, de Laborde's attitude made it impossible

---

[1] An ahead-throwing weapon firing mortar bombs which exploded on contact with a submarine. See Vol. I, p. 480 regarding the introduction of this weapon.

[2] The Report of Proceedings used the word πομφολυγοπαφλάσμασιν to describe underwater bubbling noises. It is taken from 'The Frogs' lines 246–249.

ἢ Διὸς φεύγοντες ὄμβρον
ἔννδρον ἐν βύθῳ χορείαν
αἰόλαν ἐφθεγξάμεσθα
πομφολυγοπαφλάσμασιν

which have been translated as:

'Or when fleeing the storm, we went
Down to the depths and our choral song
Wildly raised to a loud and long
Bubble-bursting accompaniment'.

[3] It is believed that Darlan sent two messages to the commander of the Toulon Fleet at this time, but the text of the first one does not appear to have been preserved. The second message was sent from Algiers at 3.47 p.m. on 11th November. The full text is printed in '*Le Sabordage de la Flotte*' by Pierre Varillon (Amiot–Dumont, Paris, 1954) p. 55.

Y

for the ships to move until it was too late. On the 14th of November, German and Italian forces entered 'unoccupied France', and on the 27th the French Navy destroyed and scuttled its ships in Toulon harbour.[1] Though it is true that Admiral Darlan's 1940 promise that his country's ships should not fall into Axis hands was thus in the main part carried out, and that the act relieved us of a serious anxiety, there was stark tragedy in the self-immolation of so many fine ships without having struck a blow for the cause of their country's freedom. The Royal Navy had known many of those same ships and their crews, as comrades-in-arms in the early days of the war, and had always looked forward to the time when they would again work together as Allies. It had been the harsh realities of our own danger which had forced us at Oran, at Dakar, at Madagascar, and often on the high seas to treat the French Navy as enemies; and we well understood how our acts of violence had aroused passionate hatred in the breasts of many patriotic French officers. Yet, if one looks back today at those tragic events, it will surely be agreed that the basic cause lay in the terms of the French surrender of 1940, and in the refusal of the government which succeeded to M. Reynaud's to continue the fight against Germany from its African possessions. Had that amount of faith been shown in the justice of our cause, and in our ultimate victory, the succession of tragedies which reached their climax in Toulon harbour on the 27th of November 1942 might all have been avoided.

In Alexandria the destruction of the Toulon Fleet had no immediate effect on Admiral Godfroy's reconsideration of the position of his squadron. In spite of pressure from British and American officers and visits by those of his own service from Algiers, he continued to vacillate over the issue of joining forces with Admiral Harwood. The Prime Minister, who had for some time shown discontent over what he considered to be the inactivity of the Eastern Fleet, wished to bring the *Warspite* and *Valiant* through the canal to add the force of their presence to the persuasions of Godfroy's visitors. But the First Sea Lord demurred, and pointed out that our control of the Indian Ocean depended on the presence of the fleet rather than on the violence of its activities. To have jeopardised that control for the sake of getting Godfroy's squadron on to our side was not, in Admiral Pound's view, a profitable proposition.

A minor but happy result of the successful invasion of North Africa

---

[1] Out of all the French warships in Toulon only three submarines succeeded in reaching Allied ports. About half a dozen destroyers and a like number of submarines remained comparatively undamaged in the base. The sunk or seriously damaged ships included one battleship, two battle cruisers, four heavy and three light cruisers, twenty-four large and small destroyers and ten submarines. There had been no such self-destruction by the major part of a once great Navy since the German High Seas Fleet scuttled itself in Scapa Flow in June 1919.

was the release from internment of a large number of British servicemen, including the crews of the *Havock* and *Manchester*.[1] In spite of our having repatriated many thousands of French soldiers and sailors from England in 1940 and from Syria in the following year, these unfortunate men had been held in very bad conditions in a desert camp ever since falling into the hands of our former Allies.

So ended the assault phase of 'Torch'. Its success had been remarkably complete, even allowing for the weak French resistance offered at some, though not at all of the points of disembarkation. The First Sea Lord sent Admiral Cunningham his very warm congratulations, and one can sense from that letter his relief that all had gone well. 'I am sure' he wrote 'that you had as anxious a time as we did here. I had visions of large convoys waltzing up and down inside as well as outside the Mediterranean, with the weather too bad to land, and the U-boats buzzing around. We really did have remarkable luck'.

Admiral Cunningham in his despatch attributed the success to many causes. Secrecy was well maintained, and so surprise was achieved; the planning had proved sound, and inter-service co-operation had been as good in execution as in preparation; the great base at Gibraltar had fulfilled its vital functions excellently, and the officers and men of the fleet had shown 'a high standard of seamanship and technical efficiency'. He paid warm tribute to 'the courage, determination and adaptability of the Merchant Navy'; but it was to the 'spirit of comradeship and understanding . . . exemplified in our Commander-in-Chief, General Eisenhower', that he attributed the greatest share of the credit. 'We counted it', modestly concluded Admiral Cunningham, 'a privilege to follow in his train'; and although the Naval Commander's tribute was certainly echoed throughout the expeditionary force as sincerely as he expressed it, history must surely record the immense share due to Admiral Cunningham's own leadership and determination.

At the end of November the First Lord summarised the strategic gains from the success of Operation 'Torch' in a letter to the Prime Minister. Airfields for flying boats and shore-based aircraft were now available to our use in West Africa, and a sorely needed naval air base for escort carriers' aircrews could be provided at Dakar. The same port could be used as advanced base by the escorts of OS and SL convoys, instead of Freetown, which had always suffered from many disadvantages.[2] Continuous air cover for our convoys was now practicable all the way from Gibraltar to Freetown, and it might be possible to combine the Sierra Leone and Gibraltar convoys. Many French warships had fallen into our hands, and although most of

---

[1] See pp. 58 and 306.
[2] See Vol. I, p. 273.

them had to be refitted and modernised they would ultimately join Allied fleets and squadrons.[1] Finally in Dakar and French ports to the south of it, which came into Allied hands when Darlan ordered resistance to cease, we had seized fifty-one merchant ships of 169,954 tons. These were substantial gains; but the greatest benefits of all lay in the additional security of our Atlantic shipping, and in the prospect that the Mediterranean would soon be opened to our use.

While these great events were taking place in the western Mediterranean, Admiral Harwood's principal concerns were to keep the Eighth Army supplied during its rapid advance, and to relieve Malta. Mersa Matruh was retaken on the day of the 'Torch' landings, and the first convoy was at once sailed there from Alexandria. On the 11th of November the fast minelayer *Manxman* and six destroyers left for Malta with urgently needed stores. Her sister-ship the *Welshman* had just made a similar dash from the west under cover of the 'Torch' landings.[2] Both got in safely, but two disguised merchantmen routed through French territorial waters just before the invasion were less fortunate, and both were interned at Bizerta. On the 20th of November, the minelayer *Adventure* sailed from Plymouth with an urgently needed cargo of 2,000 aircraft depth charges, which she landed at Gibraltar for onward passage to Malta. She made a second trip in the following month. These measures sufficed to tide over Malta's most urgent military needs until such time as regular convoys could again be sent there.

Bardia was recaptured on the 12th and Tobruk on the following day, and again the most energetic steps were taken to bring the ports into use for our own purposes. The enemy's retreat was so rapid that he had no time to carry out effective demolitions; but our own bombing had done a good deal of damage, and it was no easy matter to restore the ports sufficiently to unload the Army's requirements. The first convoy reached Tobruk on the 19th, and on that day 1,000 tons of stores were unloaded. Our land forces once again entered Benghazi on the 20th of November, and were quickly

---

[1] Apart from the French warships already under Allied surveillance at Alexandria and Martinique (See Vol. I, pp. 241 and 276) the following were the principal units which gradually joined Allied fleets and squadrons after the invasion of North Africa.
    Battleship *Richelieu*
    6-inch Cruisers *Montcalm*, *Georges Leygues* and *Gloire*
    Large destroyers 3
    Small destroyers 3
    Submarine depot ship *Jules Verne*
    Submarines 17
    Escort vessels and minesweepers 11
    Miscellaneous smaller ships—about 24
The battleship *Jean Bart* was raised at Casablanca in January 1943, but was too badly damaged to be restored to service during the war.
[2] See p. 312.

followed by the naval parties needed to clear and work the port. The entrance channel had been swept clear of mines by the 26th, and the first two merchant ships entered that same day. Early in December, Admiral Harwood was able to report that 'Benghazi was getting well into its stride', and the unloading rate had reached 2,000 tons a day by the 10th. Enemy air attacks on both Tobruk and Benghazi were fairly frequent, but no serious damage was caused. Meanwhile our still-advancing armies needed more supplies yet further ahead, and a start was made with unloading stores over the beaches in the Gulf of Sirte. Thus did the Navy carry out its traditional function of guarding and supporting the Army's seaward flank, and of carrying its supplies ever further forward on the line of advance. The Eighth Army's gratitude was nicely expressed by its commander's message: 'We send to the Navy our thanks for the part they have played . . . in safeguarding the passage of troops and supplies, without which the offensive would not have been possible'.

Meanwhile a convoy for Malta (called operation 'Stoneage') was being organised. On the 17th of November four ships (two American, one Dutch and one British) arrived off Alexandria from the Canal. The 15th Cruiser Squadron (Rear-Admiral A. J. Power) and seven destroyers sailed from Alexandria to overtake the convoy on the 18th, and then escorted it to the west. That morning enemy air attacks started. None of the convoy were damaged, but at 6 p.m. the light cruiser *Arethusa* was torpedoed. After a very long stern-first tow, and a battle with serious fires and a rising gale of wind, she was got back safely to Alexandria on the evening of the 21st; but she had 155 men killed. It is pleasant to record that this was the last serious casualty suffered by the sorely-tried little cruisers of the 15th Cruiser Squadron during their long and tenacious fight to hold the eastern Mediterranean, and also the last of the tragically heavy list of naval casualties suffered during the struggle to keep Malta supplied.

In spite of heavy weather and air attacks, most of which were broken up by the excellent fighter cover sent from the desert airfields, the 'Stoneage' convoy reached Malta safely in the small hours of the 20th. Admiral Power and most of the escort had already returned to the east, but the *Euryalus* and ten *Hunt*-class destroyers berthed alongside the battered wharves of the Grand Harbour. By the 25th the merchantmen were unloaded, and Malta was at last adequately supplied with aviation spirit. Supply trips by submarines were now discontinued, for the arrival of the 'Stoneage' convoy marked the final and effective relief of Malta. But the margin had been very narrow. Quite apart from the serious danger of the island being neutralised militarily for lack of petrol, ammunition and torpedoes, even the siege scale of food rations forced on its people could not have been continued after the middle of December.

The offensive consequences of the relief of Malta were immediately reaped. More submarines were available to work against the Axis supply lines; at the end of the month, No. 821 Squadron of naval Albacores moved there; the famous Force K, the Malta-based surface-ship striking force, was at the same time reconstituted by the arrival of Admiral Power with the *Dido*, *Euryalus* and four fleet destroyers, and finally a motor torpedo-boat flotilla was sent to work from the island. Taken together with the rising tempo of the Royal Air Force's attacks, and the stationing of another surface-ship striking force at Bone, the outlook for Axis convoys attempting the short passages to Tunis or Tripoli had suddenly become grim indeed. The submarines had a very profitable month in October, but in the following month their collective results showed a decline, and the *Utmost* and the Greek *Triton* were lost. The air offensive was now taking a heavier toll of enemy shipping. Indeed it is interesting to see how, just as the surface ships' weakness had proved 'the submarines' opportunity'[1], the re-born air and surface ship offensives had, by the last month of the year, drawn level with the submarines' accomplishments. But it should never be forgotten that, throughout the whole of the long twelve months of our grave maritime weakness in the Mediterranean theatre, it had been the submarines of the 1st, 8th and 10th Flotillas which, at times almost alone, had played the chief part in prosecuting the offensive against the Axis supply routes. The Admiralty's message at the end of the year expressing 'admiration for the Mediterranean submarines' tenacity and ingenuity in maintaining their offensive' was certainly well merited.

By the last month of the year, the 10th Flotilla had been reinforced to a strength of twelve boats, and there were in all twenty-two in the Mediterranean (including four Greek and one Yugoslav boat). Their sinkings rose to the high figure of nineteen Axis ships of 43,868 tons. It was now that the *Safari* (Commander B. Bryant) added to her already formidable reputation; but three boats, the *Traveller*, P.222 and P.48, were lost in December. The same month saw the start of another form of under-water offensive when British human torpedoes, or 'Chariots', arrived at Malta under another distinguished submarine officer, Commander G. M. S. Sladen, who had been in charge of training the volunteers for this extremely hazardous work at a base in Scotland. They sailed from Malta to strike their first blows at Palermo and Maddalena just before the end of the year. Though P.311 and her two 'chariots' were lost with all hands, others carried by the *Trooper* and *Thunderbolt* penetrated into Palermo harbour. The new light cruiser *Ulpio Traiano* (3,362 tons) was sunk in the port and a large liner damaged on the night of the 2nd-3rd

---

[1] See Volume I, p. 525.

January 1943; but none of the 'chariot' crews reached the rendezvous with the rescue submarine. Attacks of this nature had so far been something of an Italian speciality. Motor boats carrying explosives had achieved a success when they penetrated Suda Bay and damaged the heavy cruiser *York* in March 1941[1]; and Italian human torpedoes had damaged the *Queen Elizabeth* and *Valiant* in Alexandria later that year.[2] Similar attempts had several times been made on our shipping at Gibraltar in 1940 and 1941, though only on one occasion (in September 1941) had they achieved any success. In 1942 the human torpedo attacks on Gibraltar were replaced by swimmers specially trained in under-water sabotage. A party of these was sent overland through Spain to Algeciras. There they boarded an Italian steamer, the *Olterra*, and from her they made no less than four assaults on our shipping in Gibraltar Bay between July 1942 and September 1943. Out of the total of ten merchant ships attacked, four were sunk and six damaged. In the small hours of the 12th of December the Italians used human torpedoes against our shipping in Algiers Bay, and they sank two merchantmen. Though the successes they achieved in this form of assault had no influence on the progress of the African campaigns, it is right that the Italian crews should be given credit for the gallantry and persistence with which they undertook such operations.[3]

The first offensive sweep by the new British striking force of cruisers and destroyers based on Bone took place on the night of the 1st-2nd December, with deadly effect. A convoy was attacked about forty miles north of Cape Bon; all its four ships and one of the escort were destroyed; but the destroyer *Quentin* was sunk by an aircraft torpedo on the way back to harbour. On the following night the new Malta-based striking force was at sea searching for a convoy which had already been severely handled by the Malta air forces and the submarine *Umbra*. Our various forces sank four more merchant ships and a destroyer. To increase the pressure the Admiralty next ordered the *Dido* to join the Bone squadron, thus giving it sufficient strength to send out a force of two cruisers and several destroyers on successive nights. The *Aurora* and *Argonaut* worked in one group from Bone, and the *Sirius* and *Dido* in another, while the *Cleopatra*, *Euryalus*, *Orion* and about four destroyers continued to strike from Malta. In December sweeps were repeatedly carried out against enemy convoys, and it was rare for them to yield no results. Though the striking forces did not have matters all their own way, and the *Argonaut* was badly damaged by aircraft

[1] See Vol. I, p. 424.
[2] See Vol. I, pp. 538-539.
[3] J. Valerio Borghese, *Sea Devils* (English translation, Andrew Melrose, 1952) contains a full account of Italian human torpedo and underwater sabotage operations.

torpedoes in the middle of the month, the combined effect of their work and that of the submarines and aircraft was decisive. The next table shows the results achieved in terms of shipping losses suffered by the enemy, and it will be seen that the year ended on a note of high accomplishment by all British arms.

Table 26. Enemy Merchant Shipping Losses.
1st August–31st December, 1942

(1) Italian (includes losses outside Mediterranean)

Number of ships : Tonnage

Month	By Surface Ship	By Submarine	By Air Attack (See Note 2)	By Mine	By Other Cause	TOTAL
August	—	7 : 31,794	4 : 20,346	1 : 4,894	2 : 382	14 : 57,416
September	—	8 : 10,209	8 : 22,262	:	4 : 1,099	20 : 33,570
October	—	14 : 35,698	11 : 20,142	:	4 : 329	29 : 56,169
November	—	3 : 1,968	21 : 41,061	2 : 5,540	20 : 3,906	46 : 52,475
December	5 :13,279	15 : 33,400	14 : 23,669	3 : 1,755	4 : 4,040	41 : 76,143
TOTAL	5 :13,279	47 :113,069	58 :127,480	6 :12,189	34 : 9,756	150 :275,773

(2) German and German-Controlled (Mediterranean only)

Number of ships : Tonnage

Month	By Surface Ship	By Submarine	By Air Attack	By Mine	By Other Cause	TOTAL
August to December	1 : 548	9 : 25,818	5 : 9,937	3 : 7,389	6 : 738	24 : 44,430

NOTES: (1) Of the 174 ships sunk in this phase, 91 were of over 500 tons and 83 of less than 500 tons.
(2) Of the ships sunk or destroyed by air attack, 33 ships of 100,762 tons were sunk at sea and 30 ships of 36,665 tons in port.

The successful arrival of the 'Stoneage' convoy in Malta was quickly followed by others. On the 1st of December four more merchantmen sailed from Port Said, and a tanker was added from Benghazi to meet Malta's urgent need for furnace fuel for the surface forces. They all arrived safely, escorted by the 15th Cruiser Squadron and no less than seventeen destroyers. The enemy did not interfere at all with this convoy, either at sea or while it was unloading. By the 9th its ships had all been cleared of their cargoes. As a result of this convoy's easy passage it was decided to sail merchantmen in pairs with the normal western desert convoys to a point off Benghazi, where they would be met by escorts from Malta. The 15th

Cruiser Squadron covered the latter part of the journey against Italian forces from Taranto, but the precaution proved unnecessary. In December and January four pairs of merchantmen were thus successfully passed into Malta, and at the same time empty ships from earlier convoys, including four survivors of the 'Pedestal' operation of the previous August[1], were safely brought out to the east. During December Malta received 58,500 tons of general cargo and over 18,000 tons of fuel oil. 'The supply situation', noted Admiral Harwood, 'from being most precarious became . . . established on a firm basis'. And, in addition, convoys kept running steadily to Tobruk and Benghazi, where over 3,000 tons were unloaded daily before the end of the month, and also to the Levant. Our maritime control over 'this ancient waterway', as Admiral Cunningham had called it, had been completely reasserted; and the ever-precarious dependence of the enemy's African armies on the routes across the central basin had been made correspondingly more precarious. The balance had come central in this theatre with astonishing rapidity. The extent to which this was attributable to the Army's advance in Cyrenaica, and to the relief of Malta thereby made possible, is well illustrated by the next table, showing the effort made and the losses suffered in supplying Malta in August, compared with the results of the last two months of 1942. Before the end of the year it was decided that Malta was to be supplied solely from the east, and the ships held loaded and ready in the west were placed at Admiral Cunningham's disposal.

[1] See pp. 302–308.

Table 27. Malta Convoys, 1st August–31st December, 1942. The Last Phase and the Relief of Malta

Naval Forces Employed	From West — Operation 'Pedestal' (August)			From East — Operation 'Stoneage' (November)			From East — Operation 'Portcullis' (December)			From East — Operations 'Quadrangle' 'A', 'B', 'C' and 'D' (December 1942-January 1943)		
	No.	Sunk	Damaged	No.	Sunk	Damaged	No.	Sunk	Damaged	No.	Sunk	Damaged
Capital Ships	2	0	0	–	–	–	–	–	–	–	–	–
Aircraft Carriers	3	1	1	–	–	–	–	–	–	–	–	–
Cruisers	6	1	2	4	0	1	4	0	0	1	– See Note below	–
A.A. Ships	1	1	0	–	–	–	–	–	–	–	–	–
Destroyers	31	1	0	17	0	0	10	0	0	5	–	–
Minesweepers and Corvettes	8	0	0	–	–	–	–	–	–	–	–	–
Submarines	8	0	0	–	–	–	–	–	–	–	–	–
Transports and Merchant Ships	14	9	3	4	0	0	5	0	0	8	0	0
Number of Transports and Merchant ships which arrived Malta	5			4			5			8		

TOBRUK RECAPTURED 13TH NOVEMBER
BENGHAZI 20TH NOVEMBER

THE RELIEF OF MALTA

NOTE: Operation 'Portcullis' was the last convoy to be sent straight through from Egypt. For Operations 'Quadrangle,' 'A', 'B', 'C' and 'D' the merchantmen sailed with the normal western desert convoys, and were met at sea by Malta-based escorts of Force 'K'. The strength of these escorts varied for the three operations, but was approximately as shown in the table.

CHRONOLOGICAL SUMMARY

OF PRINCIPAL EVENTS

JANUARY 1943–MAY 1943

1943	Atlantic	Arctic	Mediterranean	Indian Ocean	Pacific	Europe
January	U-boats mainly operating in the central Atlantic and off the north coast of South America. Heavy bombing attacks started on Biscay U-boat bases	17–27 JW.52	23 Tripoli captured 29 Eighth Army crosses Tunisian frontier		2 Japanese driven out of Papua	
February	Heavy U-boat attacks against shipping on North Atlantic convoy routes	15–27 JW.53			7 Japanese withdraw from Guadalcanal	2 German capitulation at Stalingrad 14 Russians recapture Rostov
March	Heavy shipping losses on North Atlantic convoy routes. Five support groups operating	Further Arctic convoys postponed because escorts were needed to reinforce Atlantic convoys			2 Battle of the Bismarck Sea	

April	Continued shipping losses on North Atlantic convoy routes and off Freetown 26 April–5 May Battle of convoy ONS.5	29 Eighth Army breaks through Mareth Line		7–11 Japanese air offensive against Allied positions in the Solomons and Papua is a complete failure
	Atlantic 'air gap' closed Introduction of 10 cm. radar revitalises Bay offensive			
May	Battle of Atlantic turns in Allies' favour 37 U-boats destroyed in North Atlantic Shipping losses greatly reduced Bay of Biscay offensive takes a heavy toll.	7 Tunis and Bizerta captured 13 Axis surrender in Tunisia 17–26 First through Mediterranean convoy since 1941		11 Attu recaptured by the Americans

CHAPTER XIV

THE BATTLE OF THE ATLANTIC

The Triumph of the Escorts
1st January–31st May, 1943

'These were the men
who were her salvation
who conquered the waters and the underwaters
who
in storm and calm
taught England to live anew,
and fed her children'.

From the Solemn Bidding to the Service of
Celebration at Liverpool Cathedral, 9th
August 1945.

IT was told in the last chapter dealing with the Battle of the Atlantic how the year 1942 had been one of continuous and heavy Allied shipping losses.[1] The balance sheet of profit and loss in mercantile tonnage was one of the most disturbing issues which confronted the Casablanca Conference when it opened on the 14th of January 1943. Until the U-boats were defeated the offensive strategy to which the Allies were committed could not succeed. Europe could never be invaded until the Battle of the Atlantic had been won, and the latter purpose had therefore to be made a first charge on all Allied resources.

The bomb-proof U-boat shelters at Lorient and La Pallice, each designed to protect two flotillas, were in use by the end of 1941; by the middle of 1942 those at Brest and St. Nazaire, which would accommodate two flotillas, were about half-finished. At Bordeaux a shelter for one flotilla was being built, but it was not ready to receive its occupants until March 1943. Ever since the summer of 1940 the Admiralty and Coastal Command had pressed for the bombing of the Biscay U-boat bases[2], and Bomber Command had in fact deployed a considerable proportion of its effort against them and against other naval targets. It is now plain that the most favourable time to attack the shelters was while they were being constructed behind water-tight caissons, as was revealed by our constant photographic air reconnaissances[3]; but neither the Admiralty nor the

---

[1] See Chapter VIII.
[2] See Vol. I, pp. 459 and 468.
[3] See Vol. I, p. 459.

Air Ministry appears to have suggested this at the time. Early in December 1942 the bombing of the Biscay bases was considered by the Cabinet Anti U-boat Committee. The Air Staff then represented that, as the submarine pens themselves could not be penetrated by bombs, it would be necessary to achieve the object by devastating the adjacent towns and dockyards. This was bound to cause heavy casualties among the French civilian population, with possibly unfavourable political repercussions. The Foreign Office supported the view that the infliction of such suffering on the French should if possible be avoided, and the attacks were therefore postponed. On the 7th of January 1943, however, the First Sea Lord circulated a memorandum stressing the view that the situation in the Atlantic was so critical that 'area bombing' of the towns and installations near the U-boat bases was justified, and the Cabinet thereupon decided to go ahead. On the 14th orders were accordingly issued to Bomber Command to give first priority to the Biscay ports, and to start by attacking Lorient. The French population was warned of our intention, and on the night of 14th-15th of January a raid was made by 101 aircraft. Next night an even greater strength of 131 bombers was sent out. American bombers made 'precision' daylight attacks on the actual submarine pens concurrently. On the 20th of January the Cabinet decided to carry on with attacks on the other bases without pausing to study the effects on Lorient, as had at first been intended. This decision conformed with a directive issued by the Combined Chiefs of Staff at the Casablanca Conference on the 21st, making the U-boat building industry and the Biscay operational bases the primary objects of the Allied bomber offensive. On the 23rd and 27th of January the Commander-in-Chief, Bomber Command, wrote to the Air Ministry protesting that the new offensive was a waste of effort, and could not contribute effectively to reducing the depredations of the U-boats against our Atlantic convoys. But the Air Staff felt bound to give the policy a fair trial, and in the two following months heavy raids were therefore made on St. Nazaire. Not until mid-April, by which time the Atlantic struggle appeared to be moving more in our favour, was Bomber Command relieved of the duty to attack the Biscay ports. The American 8th Air Force, however, continued to make daylight attacks on the U-boat pens until mid-summer, and the offensive was continued sporadically right up to the end of the war. We now know that at no time was a submarine shelter in any Biscay port penetrated by a bomb.[1]

Apart from one U-boat being damaged and slightly delayed at Lorient in December 1940, no loss was inflicted by bombing a U-boat base until U.622 was destroyed in Trondheim by U.S. Army bombers

---

[1] The roof of one of the U-boat assembly yards at Hamburg was penetrated by a bomb right at the end of the war.

on the 24th of July 1943. Nor do the U-boat crews seem to have suffered appreciably from the raids, for they were accommodated out in the country; and our losses of bombers on these operations were heavy. As to attacks on the U-boat building yards, a substantial proportion of Bomber Command's effort was devoted to trying to put the yards themselves out of action and to destroy the U-boats completing in them. Heavy attacks had been made on Hamburg, Bremen and Wilhelmshaven, and on Vegesack, Flensburg and Lübeck in the autumn of 1942, but with little effect on the yards themselves, or on the U-boats in them. Not until April 1944 was a completed U-boat destroyed in a German building yard. We shall return to the effect of bombing raids on U-boat production in our final volume. Here it is only necessary to point out that their effect on the Battle of the Atlantic during the present critical phase was not appreciable. The size of the air effort involved and the losses suffered during the first half of 1943 are shown in the table below.

Table 28. Bombing Operations against U-boat Bases and Building Yards,
(R.A.F. and U.S.A.A.F.)
January–May 1943

Month 1943	BISCAY BASES			GERMAN YARDS		
	No of. Aircraft Sorties	Tons of H.E. Bombs dropped	Aircraft Losses	No. of Aircraft Sorties	Tons of H.E. Bombs dropped	Aircraft Losses
January	666	744	31	167	317	13
February	1,744	2,184	30	1,119	1,550	46
March	646	1,250	6	539	981	15
April	148	544	9	1,041	1,572	59
May	364	707	22	548	1,152	35
TOTAL	3,568	5,429 (Plus 3,704 tons Incendiaries)	98	3,414	5,572 (Plus 4,173 tons Incendiaries)	168

It was in the first month of the year that the long-smouldering conflict between Admiral Raeder and Hitler on the functions of maritime power and the employment of the German Navy came to a head. Since this had important repercussions on the Battle of the Atlantic it is best considered now, before we turn to the convoy routes. The immediate cause of the rupture was the unsatisfactory action fought on New Year's Eve 1942 in the Arctic by the *Hipper*, *Lützow* and six destroyers against the far weaker British escort of the Arctic convoy JW.51B.[1] The breach might have been postponed, or even avoided, had not Göring, who could never miss a chance to exploit the Navy's difficulties to his own aggrandisement, assiduously fanned the flames of Hitler's schizophrenic rage. The critical

[1] See pp. 291–299.

conference between Raeder and Hitler took place on the 6th of January. It opened with a ninety minute diatribe by the Führer castigating the conduct and impugning the courage of the German Navy, past, present and future. He called the recent failure in the Arctic 'typical of German ships, just the opposite of the British who, true to their tradition, fought to the bitter end'—a tribute which the Royal Navy would probably appreciate more had it come from any other source. Raeder, who 'rarely had an opportunity to comment', was finally told to make proposals to pay off all the big ships. On the 15th he submitted a paper in which he ably argued the true meaning, purpose and significance of maritime power. He warned Hitler that the order he had given 'will be a victory for our enemies, gained without any effort on their part'. But such abstract reasoning was beyond Hitler's comprehension, and he remained adamant. On the 30th of January Raeder resigned the post he had held since October 1928, and Hitler appointed Dönitz in his place. Raeder's soundness in strategic outlook is, perhaps, clearer today to his former enemies than it ever was to the people whom he so long served. It is true that he had earlier shown that he lacked the moral courage to press his convictions very far against the weight of the Führer's opinions; and that he suffered, though to a lesser degree than many of his Army contemporaries, from the common German failing of excessive veneration for authority—even to the point of sycophancy.[1] But it is none the less fair that a British history should record that had he got his way in building the German Navy he wanted to build[2], and, had he then been allowed to use it as he wished to do, it cannot be doubted that the Allied victory at sea would have been more hardly won.

On the 13th of February, at Hitler's conference, the new Commander-in-Chief outlined his proposals for putting the Führer's views into effect. Most of the big ships were to be paid off, complete priority was asked for the construction, repair and manning of U-boats, and adequate air support from the Luftwaffe (which Raeder had so long and vainly requested) was demanded. To all Dönitz's proposals Hitler gave 'his complete and definite approval'. In spite of the categorical nature of these decisions it was less than a fortnight later, on the 26th of February, that the German Commander-in-Chief sought and obtained substantial modification of

---

[1] See for example Raeder's evidence at his trial. (The Trial of German Major War Criminals. Proceedings of the International Military Tribunal sitting at Nuremberg. Part 14. H.M.S.O. 1947)

p. 164   'Further warnings therefore . . . were completely without purpose, as one knew from experience'.
'Once the Führer had issued a directive . . . it was, in general, useless to produce objections against it'.

p. 210   'But what one could not do was to throw up the job and give the impression of being insubordinate . . . I would never have done that'.

[2] See Vol. I, p. 53.

the order to pay off the big ships. The *Tirpitz* and *Lützow* were to stay in Norway 'for the present', and the *Scharnhorst* was to be sent there to provide between them 'a fairly powerful task force'. One may well ponder on the consequences of such violent and erratic changes in high policy and strategic purpose, both to the fighting service concerned and to the German nation as a whole.

Thus was the stage set for Germany to fling into the Atlantic struggle the greatest possible strength, directed by the man who had from the beginning of the war controlled the U-boats and had always been their protagonist. It was plain to both sides that the U-boats and the convoy escorts would shortly be locked in a deadly, ruthless series of fights, in which no mercy would be expected and little shown. Nor would one battle, or a week's or a month's fighting, decide the issue. It would be decided by which side could endure the longer; by whether the stamina and strength·of purpose of the crews of the Allied escort vessels and aircraft, watching and listening all the time for the hidden enemy, outlasted the will-power of the U-boat crews, lurking in the darkness or the depths, fearing the relentless tap of the asdic, the unseen eye of the radar and the crash of the depth charges. It depended on whether the men of the Merchant Navy, themselves almost powerless to defend their precious cargoes of fuel, munitions and food, could stand the strain of waiting day after day and night after night throughout the long, slow passages for the rending detonation of the torpedoes, which could send their ships to the bottom in a matter of seconds, ór explode their cargoes in a searing sheet of flame from which there could be no escape. It was a battle between *men*, aided certainly by all the instruments and devices which science could provide, but still one that would be decided by the skill and endurance of men, and by the intensity of the moral purpose which inspired them. In all the long history of sea warfare there has been no parallel to this battle, whose field was thousands of square miles of ocean, and to which no limits in time or space could be set. In its intensity, and in the certainty that its outcome would decide the issue of the war, the battle may be compared to the Battle of Britain of 1940. Just as Göring then tried with all the forces of the Luftwaffe to gain command of the skies over Britain, so now did Dönitz seek to gain command of the Atlantic with his U-boats. And the men who defeated him—the crews of the little ships, of the air escorts and of our tiny force of long-range aircraft—may justly be immortalised alongside 'the few' who won the 1940 battle of the air.

In the North Atlantic the month of January produced its customary tempestuous weather. This and the successful use of evasive routeing caused an immediate drop in sinkings. Only one convoy (HX.222) was attacked, and it only lost one ship, but further south a total of eleven 'independents' or stragglers were sunk; and a tanker convoy from Trinidad to Gibraltar (TM.1) was cut to pieces between the 9th and 11th when out of range of air cover south of the Azores. It was escorted by only one destroyer and three corvettes, and they were handicapped by failure of their radar sets; only two of the nine tankers comprising the convoy survived.

The enemy was now steadily increasing his strength in the Atlantic, and by the end of the month there were thirty-seven U-boats waiting on the limits of the 'Greenland air gap'[1], eleven between the Azores and the Bay of Biscay and twenty-five stretching down from the Azores, past the Canaries to the west coast of Africa. With twenty-seven more on passage in or out, his total of U-boats at sea in the north and central Atlantic reached the formidable figure of 100. The effects of this concentration were soon felt.

Early in February convoy HX.224 was intercepted, but by no great number of enemies. Two ships were lost, but a Fortress of No. 220 Squadron sank U.265 in return. U.632 picked up one lone survivor from a British straggler which she had sunk from this convoy. He told his captors that a large, slow convoy was following along astern of his own faster one, and by the same route. With this gratuitous aid the enemy was able to concentrate great strength against SC.118. The informant must have sacrificed many of his comrades' lives, for that convoy, which consisted originally of sixty-three ships and ten escorts, was attacked by no less than twenty U-boats and lost thirteen ships between the 4th and 9th of February. The battle with the sea and air escorts was, however a furious one; three-quarters of the enemies suffered depth charge attacks at one time or another, three U-boats were sunk and two more seriously damaged by the escorts. The Germans, who believed—as so often— that the U-boats had done far better than they had, were satisfied with the results of this battle. We on our side learnt that even continuous escort by long-range aircraft in daylight could not prevent some enemies catching up and attacking the convoys during the long winter nights. It was plain that the Fortresses and Liberators needed to be fitted with Leigh-Lights as soon as possible. A disturbing feature of this convoy's passage was that heavy losses were suffered in spite of the unusually numerous surface escort; thanks to American reinforcements from Iceland there were twelve warships with the convoy at the height of the attack—double the strength of a normal escort group. But the reinforcements could not pull their full weight, because they lacked training as part of an integrated group; we had long since learnt that training was more important than mere

---

[1] See Map 20 (opp. p. 205).

numbers.[1] A further lesson was that in such a prolonged and severe battle expenditure of depth charges was enormous; replenishments for the escorts must therefore be carried in the merchantmen. And still more weight was added to the arguments in favour of support groups being used to reinforce threatened convoys. They were, in Admiral Horton's words, 'vital to ensure reasonable safety'.

Although by mid-February the north Atlantic routes were well covered by the four groups of U-boats then formed or forming, their next operation was not a success. The slow, outward convoy ONS.165 was located about 350 miles east of Newfoundland and attacked in very stormy weather. Only two ships were sunk, and the destroyers *Fame* and *Viscount* accounted for U.201 and U.69 respectively. These were the same ships of the Liverpool Escort Force which had destroyed two other enemies in the heavy attack on SC.104 in the previous October.[2] Their double success was an example of what a well-trained and experienced escort group could do. As Admiral Horton put it at an Admiralty conference at this time, 'it could not be too often stressed that the trained group was the basis of protection, not mere numbers of escort vessels'. That training also counted for more than modernity is well brought out by the fact that, although the *Fame* was a comparatively modern ship (1932 Programme, completed 1935), the *Viscount* dated back to the First World War and was about to celebrate the silver jubilee of her entry into service (March 1918). Nor was she by any means the only ship of the 1914-18 War's 'V-and W-Classes' still to be fighting in the Atlantic.

His next operation brought the enemy even more substantial success. ON.166 was located by wireless interception early in its passage, and was pursued from the 21st to the 25th of February across 1,100 miles of ocean. Fourteen ships of some 85,000 tons were sunk, and only one U-boat was destroyed. The next slow outward convoy was also attacked, but suffered less severe losses.

These successive attacks on three outward convoys (ONS.165, ON.166 and ONS.167) were made possible by the two 'milch cows' U.460 and U.462. They lay between 400 and 600 miles to the north of the Azores and replenished no less than twenty-seven operational U-boats between the 21st of February and 5th of March. On our part the escort of ON.166 was fuelled from tankers accompanying the convoy—a practice which was now becoming common.

January, with its bad weather, had seen a big drop in sinkings to thirty-seven ships of 203,128 tons by U-boats, and fifty of little more than a quarter of a million tons in all; but the next two months told a very different story. In February the U-boats' score shot up to sixty-three ships of 359,328 tons. March was even worse with 108

[1] See Vol. I, pp. 358–360.
[2] See pp. 212–213.

ships of 627,377 tons sunk by U-boats. Enemy aircraft also improved their performance and we lost in all 120 ships of about 693,000 tons— the worst month since November 1942.[1]

On the 1st of March an 'Atlantic Convoy Conference' was opened between the United Kingdom, the Americans and the Canadians in Washington. The matters to be discussed included revision of the arrangements for the operational control of Atlantic convoys, the provision of air and surface escorts, and adjustment of the 'Chop Line' to coincide with the Western Ocean Meeting Point in 40° West.[2] The senior British representatives were Admiral Sir Percy Noble, head of the British Admiralty Delegation in America, and Vice-Admiral Sir Henry Moore (Vice Chief of Naval Staff). The Commander-in-Chief, Coastal Command, was represented by Air Vice-Marshal A. Durston. Early in the discussions it became apparent that the Americans wished to withdraw entirely from sharing the protection of the North Atlantic convoys (HX/ON and SC/ONS). The main reasons for the American proposal appear to have been that Admiral King disliked escorts of mixed nationality, and that he desired to concentrate his country's ships on the more southerly convoy routes, which served the United States forces in the Mediterranean theatre. But it is evident that the suggestion to withdraw from the North Atlantic took the British delegates by surprise. It was, however, finally agreed that the U.S. Navy would compensate for the increased strain thereby placed on Britain and Canada by taking over responsibility for the important tanker convoys (CU/UC) running between Britain and the Dutch West Indies, and by providing a support group, consisting of an escort carrier and five destroyers, to work under British control with the North Atlantic convoys.[3] This difficulty out of the way, the rest of the agenda was, with one exception (to be referred to shortly), dealt with fairly easily. It was decided that Britain and Canada would take complete charge of all convoys running between Britain and New York, or ports north of the latter; Canada would create a North-West Atlantic Command to exercise full control on her side of 47° West (to which meridian the 'Chop Line' would be shifted), in the same way that the Commander-in-Chief, Western Approaches, controlled all movements to the east of that line.[4] In addition new convoy cycles were agreed for the North Atlantic, and it was decided that the number of long-range aircraft in Newfoundland would be

---

[1] See Appendix O for details of these losses.

[2] See Map 10 (opp. p. 97). J. Schull *The Far Distant Ships* (Dept. of National Defence, Ottawa, 1950), pp. 166–168 gives a full account of this conference from the point of view of the Royal Canadian Navy.

[3] This group, formed around the U.S.S. *Bogue*, the first escort carrier to work with the North Atlantic convoys started work in March 1943, when she escorted Convoy SC.123. See p. 366.

[4] The first Commander-in-Chief was Rear-Admiral L. W. Murray of the Royal Canadian Navy, whose headquarters were at Halifax.

increased to four squadrons (forty-eight aircraft). The long-range aircraft, no matter of which country, were to work to the limit of their endurance without regard to the 'Chop Line'; and the support groups were also to have freedom to move wherever they might be needed, under the general strategic control of the command to which they belonged.

These arrangements (with minor variations) came into force on the 1st of April 1943. Canada thereafter became responsible not only for all movements within the Canadian coastal zone, but for the routeing and diversion of HX/ON and SC/ONS convoys westward of 'Chop', provided they were outside the American Eastern Sea Frontier. Independently-sailed troopships and also merchantmen plying between Canadian, Newfoundland and British ports came within her jurisdiction as well. It will thus be seen how the Royal Canadian Navy, having started the war with such very small strength, and having so long shared with the Royal Navy the heat and burden of the Atlantic Battle, now came into full partnership in controlling the forces deployed in this vast theatre.[1] To help Canada meet her increased responsibilities the R.C.N. corvettes lent to the United States Navy to work in the Caribbean, and those which had come across to take part in operation 'Torch', returned to their own country. Furthermore Britain transferred to Canada six of her older fleet destroyers.

The only matter which could not be resolved satisfactorily at the Atlantic Convoy Conference concerned the control of Allied aircraft at Gibraltar and in Morocco. For the North African landings control of the Royal Air Force at Gibraltar and of the aircraft allocated to the three Task Forces had passed to the Allied Commander-in-Chief of Operation 'Torch' (General Eisenhower), who exercised it through the Eastern and Western Air Commanders (Air Marshal Sir William Welsh and Major-General J. Doolittle, U.S.A.A.F. respectively).[2] The British Chiefs of Staff undoubtedly expected the special arrangements made for the assault to lapse at some convenient date after its completion; but this did not take place. It is certain that the British authorities never agreed to, and would not have accepted, a permanent and independent American command within the British Strategic Zone. None the less this came to pass when, on the 17th of February, Admiral King set up a Moroccan Sea Frontier Command responsible direct to Washington. The Royal Air Force at Gibraltar was meanwhile still under the 'Torch' Commander. This and the new organisation in Morocco at once produced difficulties over the air protection of British military and trade convoys in the eastern

---

[1] See Vol. I, pp. 49–50 and 451–453 and J. Schull *The Far Distant Ships* (Dept. of National Defence, Ottawa, 1950) pp. 166–168.

[2] See pp. 313–314 and Map 31 (opp. p. 313).

Atlantic, for which the Admiralty and Coastal Command were responsible. The unsatisfactory nature of these arrangements was raised at the Atlantic Convoy Conference in March. The Sub-Committee appointed by Admiral King to investigate the problem then proposed that a naval officer should be in charge of all air operations; but the Air Ministry resisted this, because it was contrary to the long-established British practice of all the services working in and through an Area Combined Headquarters in which they were all equal. The Conference next proposed that General Eisenhower should decide whether the British Admiral at Gibraltar or the American one in Morocco should be the controlling authority. It was then the turn of the Admiralty to protest, on the grounds that the air co-operation supplied for them by the Royal Air Force should not be controlled by an American naval officer.

In June the question was examined by the Allied Anti-Submarine Survey Board[1], which recommended that the Moroccan Sea Frontier should be abolished, and that control of all maritime aircraft in the area should be vested in the Area Combined Headquarters at Gibraltar. The British Chiefs of Staff, and also Admiral Cunningham and Air Marshal Tedder agreed to this readily enough; but the U.S. Navy Department turned it down. The consequences of the failure of the protracted attempts to achieve unification of the anti-U-boat air offensive in these waters were that confusion persisted and that much wasteful flying was undertaken. Control of the Royal Air Force at Gibraltar did not revert to Coastal Command until October 1943; and the American enclave within the British Strategic Zone remained until the end of the war. The needs of our Atlantic shipping were, however, meanwhile met by the Gibraltar aircraft flying surreptitiously to meet the requirements of the Admiralty and Coastal Command.[2]

Having thus made one digression from the field of battle into the

---

[1] The original members of this Board were Rear-Admiral J. C. Kauffman, U.S.N. and Rear-Admiral J. M. Mansfield, R.N. (lately Chief of Staff to C.-in-C., Western Approaches). In March 1942 U.S. Naval Aviation and British Coastal Command representatives were added. The Board travelled round various theatres and made its recommendations to the Combined Chiefs of Staff; but it had no executive authority. It was disbanded in September 1943, and so ended the only attempt to achieve a measure of combined strategy and a standard operational procedure in the Atlantic.

[2] It should be recorded that the American historian's view on this intricate problem is that 'we refused to give exclusive control of the Straits of Gibraltar to Coastal Command because there were too many U.S. convoys going through' and that this was done for the same reasons that 'Britain could never have given up control of the Western Approaches to us' (Professor S. E. Morison to the author, June 1955). But to this writer the analogy suggested above does not seem valid; for the Moroccan Sea Frontier and the approaches to Gibraltar from the west were never within the U.S.A.'s area of strategic responsibility (see Map 10 opp. p. 97). It would therefore have been just as logical for the Americans to have claimed control in the Western Approaches to the British Isles as in the Moroccan Sea Frontier, especially when a steady stream of transports carrying American troops, and of supply ships with their stores and equipment, was coming to Britain. As the Americans were apparently satisfied to leave the protection of their ships crossing the North Atlantic to the Admiralty and Coastal Command, why should it have been deemed necessary to make special arrangements for those approaching Africa from the west?

Series of photographs showing the destruction of U.465 by Liberator P of No. 86 Squadron R.A.F. while escorting Convoy HX.236 on 4th May 1943. (See p. 381).

Top photograph. The U-boat sighted and starting to dive.

Middle photograph. Depth charges exploding.

Bottom photograph. Wreckage and oil comes to the surface.

U-boat base at Lorient under attack by Fortress aircraft of the U.S.A.A.F.,
6th March 1943. (See pp. 351–353).

The minelaying U-boat U.119 under depth charge attack by two R.A.A.F.
Sunderlands, 29th April 1943. In spite of the accuracy of the attacks the U-boat
was only slightly damaged.

homeward-bound Atlantic convoy, probably SC.105, as seen from a Coastal Command
Fortress, October 1942.

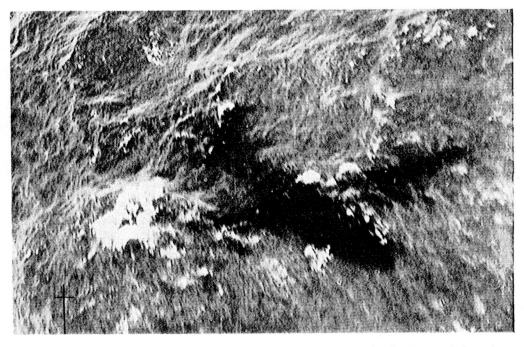

The shadow of a Sunderland over the spot where the combined efforts of aircraft
from Nos. 58 and 22 Squadrons had just destroyed U.563 on 31st May 1943.

'Clear Flight Deck' and 'An Escort Carrier' by Stephen Bone.

field of policy, it will be convenient to make another before returning to the convoy routes. Between the months of February and April 1943 proposals were received in London from various sources urging that a 'Super-Commander-in-Chief' should be appointed to assume strategic responsibility for all forces involved in the Atlantic battle and, secondly, that a 'Super-Air Officer Commander-in-Chief' should be appointed to take charge of the entire Allied air effort involved in that struggle. Field Marshal Smuts had made suggestions to Mr Churchill for achieving unified strategic control and, although the U.S. Navy certainly opposed the idea of a Supreme Commander, it is plain that the U.S. Army Air Force and some members of the United States Government were in favour of it. The First Sea Lord asked his staff to advise on all the different aspects of the problem. The Naval Staff's advice was, broadly speaking, that, while unified strategic control was undoubtedly a need 'devoutly to be wished' and one that might be achieved by gradual stages, a new authority could not possibly be suddenly super-imposed on the whole complicated structure of British-American-Canadian operational practice. To attempt to do so would cause endless confusion and, moreover, would almost certainly slow up the day-to-day, even hour-to-hour, prosecution of the war against the U-boats. A second and no less important consideration was that some Americans appeared to envisage an officer of their nationality being appointed. To Britain victory in the Atlantic was a matter of life or death; to America it was only one part of a world-wide struggle. How could the British Admiralty delegate its responsibility to a national of another country? And what asked the Naval Staff, would be the reaction of the House of Commons, the Press and the British people to such an idea? The Allied Anti-Submarine Survey Board had recently been formed with the chief duty of 'making recommendations as regards the distribution of forces', and the Naval Staff considered that this first step towards unified strategic control was all that could be prudently undertaken at that time.

A similar proposal to that which was now being discussed had been made by Air Chief Marshal Joubert, C.-in-C. Coastal Command, in the autumn of 1942, and the Air Staff seems all along to have looked on it with greater favour than the Naval Staff.

As to the second high appointment, that of a 'Super-Air Officer Commander-in-Chief' to achieve 'unified air control of the Atlantic', the proposal emanated from Mr Stimson in mid-April 1942, and was fully discussed between the Prime Minister, the First Sea Lord and the Chief of the Air Staff. The British authorities were, of course, well aware of the confusion then reigning on the American side of the Atlantic[1], caused by failure to integrate air operations over the sea

---

[1] See Morison, Vol. I, pp. 240–246.

or to place control of maritime aircraft in the hands of one service and one command. Not until June 1942 had General Marshall ordered the U.S. Army Air Force to leave the anti-submarine field entirely to the Navy. That being the case the Chief of the Air Staff, Sir Charles Portal, whilst not by any means averse to the principle involved, considered that the essential preliminary was for the Americans to put their own house in order. The First Sea Lord, on the other hand, was 'very definitely against a supreme commander either for surface ships or air forces for the whole Atlantic' and gave his full reasons. The Prime Minister himself felt that 'there comes a point . . . in the development of all large commands where one must consider whether the general advantages of unity will outweigh the practical difficulties of administration, as the size of the command and the complexity of the arrangements increase . . . When all this is taken into account, it is clear that the best practicable arrangement is to have separate commands working in close co-operation and unison on either side of the Atlantic.'[1]

These matters were much debated in the spring of 1943, and at one time it seemed that at least a unified air command for all anti-submarine work might be achieved. All such proposals seem, however, to have foundered on the unwillingness of Britain or the United States to surrender any measure of sovereignty within their own strategic zones, and on the very real difficulty of integrating the functions of the British Admiralty and Ministry of War Transport with the corresponding American departments. Moreover the Chiefs of Staff of both nations felt that, on questions of major strategy which concerned the forces for which they were responsible to their own Governments, they could not share their responsibility with anyone else. The outcome was that the proposal was not pursued, and it was left for the post-war Governments of the North Atlantic Treaty Organisation to accept and introduce measures similar to those here discussed.

Concurrently with the discussions on the control of the sea and air forces engaged in the Atlantic battle, outlined above, the long-debated question of providing adequate numbers of 'Very Long Range' (V.L.R.) aircraft came to a head. In February 1943, when Air Marshal Sir John Slessor succeeded Sir Philip Joubert as C.-in-C., Coastal Command still possessed only one V.L.R. Liberator Squadron (No. 120), though another (No. 224) was working in the Bay of Biscay with Liberators which had not been modified to give extended endurance. At the Casablanca Conference of the previous month the Combined Chiefs of Staff had recommended that eighty V.L.R. aircraft should be allocated to cover the Greenland 'air gap',

---

[1] The full text of Mr Churchill's letter from which this extract is taken is given in Appendix P.

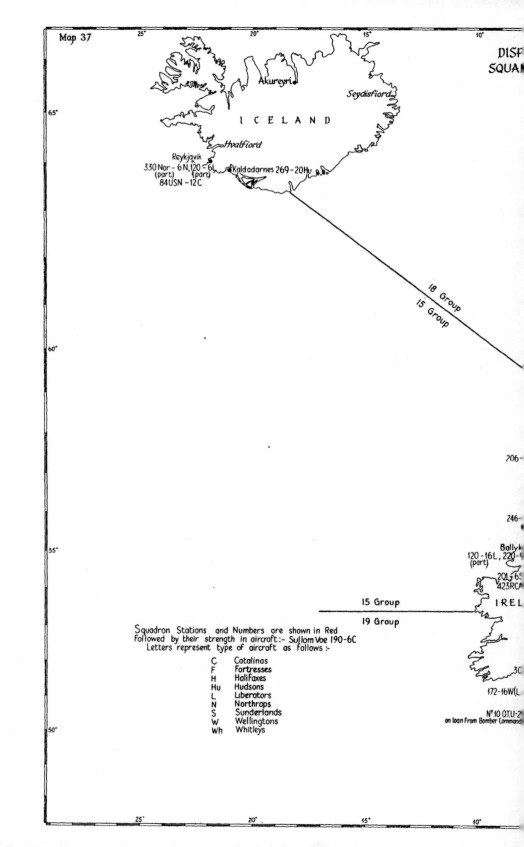

Map 37

25° 20° 15° 10°

DISP
SQUA

65°

Akureyri

ÁSN

Seydisfiord

I C E L A N D

Hvalfiord

Reykjavik
330 Nor – 6 N, 120 – 6 L Kaldadarnes 269 – 20 Hu
(part) (part)
84 USN – 12 C

18 Group
15 Group

60°

206 –

246 –

55°

Bally
120 – 16 L, 220 – 9
(part)
201 6 S
423 RCA

15 Group I R E L

19 Group

Squadron Stations and Numbers are shown in Red
followed by their strength in aircraft :- Sullom Voe 190 – 6 C
Letters represent type of aircraft as follows :-

C	Catalinas
F	Fortresses
H	Halifaxes
Hu	Hudsons
L	Liberators
N	Northrops
S	Sunderlands
W	Wellingtons
Wh	Whitleys

30

172 – 16 W (L

N° 10 O.T.U – 2
on loan from Bomber Command

50°

25° 20° 15° 10°

NS & STRENGTH OF COASTAL COMMAND
EMPLOYED IN THE BATTLE OF THE ATLANTIC
FEBRUARY 1943
Showing Group Boundaries

but deliveries had lagged sadly. The urgency of the matter was raised at the Washington Convoy Conference in March, when Canada reported that she possessed trained crews for the purpose, but no aircraft. It was agreed that twenty Liberators should be transferred from the British allocation to the R.C.A.F., to work in the western Atlantic; but they could not be made ready at once.

Meanwhile the U.S. Navy had, under earlier agreements, been receiving large allocations of the sorely-needed Liberators. By the end of 1942 they had received fifty-two, and by the 1st of July, 1943 (when Coastal Command possessed thirty-seven V.L.R. aircraft) the U.S. Navy's total was 209.[1] Moreover many of the U.S. Navy's Liberators were working in the Pacific, and were apparently being used for reconnaissance purposes.[2] The air strength available to the Allies for the war against the U-boats on the North Atlantic convoy routes in February 1943 is shown in the next table.

Table 29. Allied Maritime Air Forces available for the Battle of the Atlantic Convoy Routes, February 1943

EASTERN SIDE OF THE ATLANTIC

Location	Very Long Range	Long Range	Medium Range	Short Range	Total No. of Squadrons	Approx. Strength
Iceland	9	11	12	24	3½	56
No. 15 Group	9	60	—	—	6½	69
Gibraltar and Morocco	—	43	20	42	6+1 flight	105
West Africa	—	18	—	20	4	38
South Africa	—	—	—	32	2	32
TOTAL	18	132	32	118	22+1 flight	300

WESTERN SIDE OF THE ATLANTIC

Greenland	—	2	8	4	3 flights	14
Newfoundland and Canada	—	34	24	70	12+2 flights	128
Bermuda	—	12	—	—	1	12
Eastern Sea Frontier	—	70	100	144	25+4 flights	314
Gulf Sea Frontier	—	12	24	56	6+5 flights	92
Caribbean Sea Frontier	—	30	108	70	12+16 flights	208
Brazilian Coast	—	20	20	12	3+3 flights	52
TOTAL	Nil	180	284	356	59+33 flights	820

NOTES: The Western Atlantic figures include both U.S.N. and U.S.A.A.F. aircraft. In the Eastern Atlantic figures are included two squadrons of U.S.N. flying boats in Morocco, and one in Iceland.
Aircraft employed against U-boats passing through the Bay of Biscay and the northern transit area from Germany are not included in this table.

[1] See W. F. Craven and J. L. Cate *The Army Air Forces in World War II*, (University of Chicago Press, 1948) p. 551 f.n.
[2] By 19th March 1943, 112 Liberators had been delivered to the U.S. Navy, and more than 70 of them were operating in the Pacific.

At the end of March the Navy Department at last realised the seriousness of the situation, and underwent a change of heart. It seems that the President enquired where its Liberators were operating at the time when the recent heavy losses in the Atlantic were suffered; furthermore the Allied Anti-Submarine Survey Board had just reported that air cover in the North Atlantic was 'totally inadequate', and had drawn attention to the fact that *not one* V.L.R. aircraft was to be found at any Allied air base west of Iceland. The result was that the Americans agreed that 255 Liberators (seventy-five from the U.S. Army Air Force, sixty from the U.S. Navy and 120 from British allocations) should be provided for the North Atlantic. This could not, of course, take effect at once, and the full benefits were not felt until the next phase. At the end of March we had twenty V.L.R. aircraft operational, and by mid-April the maximum was only forty-one—all of them flown by British crews.

In other directions Coastal Command's strength was increasing more satisfactorily. All its Whitley and all but three of its Hudson squadrons had by mid-May been rearmed with Leigh-Light Wellingtons or ordinary (not V.L.R.) Liberators.[1] Apart from Bomber Command, Fighter Command or Naval aircraft on loan, it then possessed twenty-eight anti-submarine and eleven anti-shipping squadrons, 619 aircraft in all—a striking change since September 1939.[2]

The difficulty experienced by the enemy in locating our convoys during the early days of 1943 led him to make a full investigation of the sources from which the British Admiralty was presumed to derive its intelligence regarding U-boat movements and dispositions. The U-boat command was seriously disturbed over the evidence regarding the efficiency of our intelligence. After examining all possibilities they concluded that there was no evidence of treachery, and that their cyphers were secure. Our successes must, they considered, be achieved by constant search and patrolling by radar-fitted aircraft. On their own side they were still deriving great benefit from the daily 'U-boat situation' and convoy-control signals sent by the Commander-in-Chief, Western Approaches, or the Admiralty; and such successes as they achieved in intercepting our convoys were largely brought about through the undoubted efficiency of the German wireless intelligence service. Yet the U-boat Command was harassed and anxious about what they believed to be the principal

---

[1] See Map 37 (opp. p. 363).
[2] See Vol. I, pp. 35–36. In September 1939 the total strength of Coastal Command had been 298 aircraft of all types, of which about 170 were available for operations on any one day.

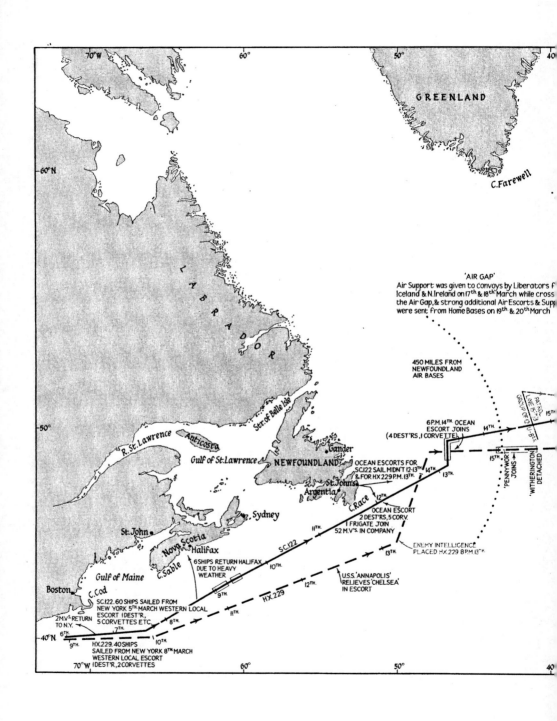

'AIR GAP'

Air Support was given to convoys by Liberators f
Iceland & N.Ireland on 17ᵗʰ & 18ᵗʰ March while cross
the Air Gap, & strong additional Air Escorts & Supp
were sent from Home Bases on 19ᵗʰ & 20ᵗʰ March

450 MILES FROM
NEWFOUNDLAND
AIR BASES

GREENLAND

C.Farewell

LABRADOR

Str.of Belle Isle

R.St.Lawrence

Anticosta

Gulf of St.Lawrence

NEWFOUNDLAND

Gander

St.John's

Argentia

C.Race

Sydney

St.John

Nova Scotia

Halifax

C.Sable

6 SHIPS RETURN HALIFAX
DUE TO HEAVY
WEATHER

SC.122

6 P.M.14ᵀᴴ OCEAN
ESCORT JOINS
(4 DEST'RS, I CORVETTE)

OCEAN ESCORTS FOR
SC.122 SAIL MIDN'T 12-13ᵀᴴ 14ᵀᴴ
& FOR HX.229 P.M.13ᵀᴴ

OCEAN ESCORT
2 DEST'RS, 5 CORV.
I FRIGATE JOIN
52 M.V's. IN COMPANY

ENEMY INTELLIGENCE
PLACED HX.229 8 P.M.13ᵀᴴ

'PENNYWORT'
JOINS

'WITHERINGTON'
DETACHED

PAT
LINE I
GROUP OF 12

Gulf of Maine

Boston

C.Cod

2 M.Vˢ RETURN
TO N.Y.

SC.122.60 SHIPS SAILED FROM
NEW YORK 5ᵀᴴ MARCH WESTERN LOCAL
ESCORT IDEST'R,
5 CORVETTES ETC.

HX.229

U.S.S.'ANNAPOLIS'
RELIEVES 'CHELSEA'
IN ESCORT

HX.229.40 SHIPS
SAILED FROM NEW YORK 8ᵀᴴ MARCH
WESTERN LOCAL ESCORT
IDEST'R, 2 CORVETTES

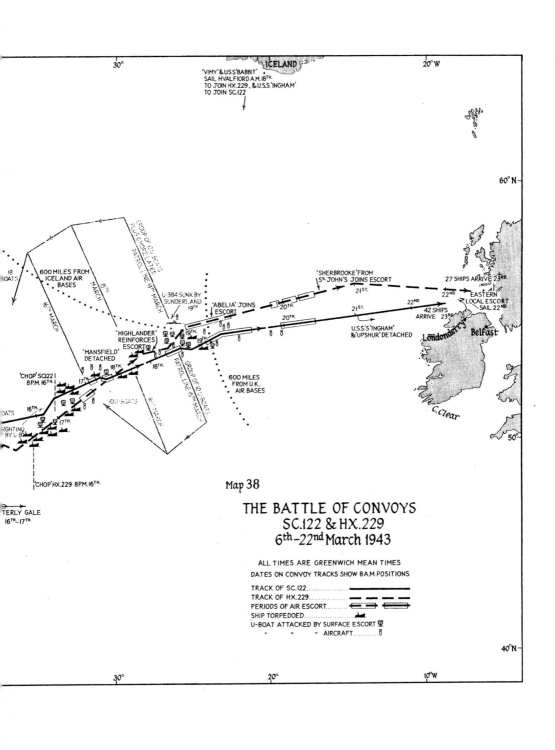

ICELAND

'VIMY'&U.S.S'BABBIT'
SAIL HVALFIORD A.M.18TH.
TO JOIN HX.229,&U.S.S'INGHAM'
TO JOIN SC.122

30°   20° W

60° N

'SHERBROOKE'FROM
St.JOHN'S JOINS ESCORT   27 SHIPS ARRIVE 23RD.
GROUP OF 29 BOATS   21ST.   22ND.   EASTERN
PLUS 8 MORE LATER   LOCAL ESCORT
PATROL LINE 11TH MARCH   'ABELIA' JOINS   42 SHIPS   SAIL 22ND.
                               ESCORT   ARRIVE 23RD
18   20TH.   21ST.   22ND.
BOATS   600 MILES FROM   Londonderry Belfast
        ICELAND AIR   U-384 SUNK BY
        BASES   SUNDERLAND
                                   19TH.   20TH.
                              19TH.   U.S.S'S'INGHAM'
                        19TH.   &'UPSHUR' DETACHED
        'HIGHLANDER'
        REINFORCES
        ESCORT
    'MANSFIELD'   GROUP
    DETACHED   OF 10 U-BOATS
                    18TH.   PATROL LINE 15TH MARCH
'CHOP' SC122   17TH. 18TH.
8 P.M. 16TH.   600 MILES
                               FROM U.K.
BOATS 16TH.   40 U-BOATS   AIR BASES
            17TH.
SIGHTING   C. Clear
BY U.B.

'CHOP'HX.229 8 P.M.16TH.   50°

TERLY GALE   Map 38
16TH-17TH.
                    THE BATTLE OF CONVOYS
                         SC.122 & HX.229
                      6th–22nd March 1943

                ALL TIMES ARE GREENWICH MEAN TIMES
                DATES ON CONVOY TRACKS SHOW 8A.M.POSITIONS

                TRACK OF SC.122..................
                TRACK OF HX.229..................
                PERIODS OF AIR ESCORT..........
                SHIP TORPEDOED....................
                U-BOAT ATTACKED BY SURFACE ESCORT
                 "   "   " AIRCRAFT..........

40° N

30°   20°   10° W

cause of our successes in locating U-boats and in evading their concentrations; namely our wide use of and superiority in radar, and the efficiency of our air patrols. On the 5th of March they ordered that as soon as a U-boat became aware of radar transmissions she was to dive for half an hour. The enemy was also conscious of the great increase in our escort strength, often permitting a convoy to be given an outer as well as an inner screen, made possible by fuelling the little ships from tankers in the convoy. They tried to find new tactics with which to defeat our radar and our swelling escort strength; and for a time they continued to achieve a very serious degree of success.

At the end of February the enemy made a determined attempt to catch convoy SC.121, using two groups of U-boats for this purpose; but the convoy slipped through their patrol line unsighted. There followed a pursuit by seventeen enemies which lasted from the 7th to the 11th of March. Several ships straggled from the convoy in the prevailing heavy weather, and provided easy targets. In all thirteen ships (about 62,000 tons) were sunk without loss to the U-boats. The next operation (7th to 14th of March) against HX.228 was less successful, and only four of its number were sunk. In the course of this battle the Senior Officer of the escort, in the *Harvester*, rammed and sank U.444, but the destroyer received such damage herself that she was disabled and fell an easy prey to U.432. The latter was then sunk in turn by the Free French corvette *Aconit*—a good example of the relentless giving and taking of lethal blows which was such a marked feature of the struggle. The *Harvester's* Commanding Officer (Commander A. A. Tait), 'an outstanding leader of a group of British, Polish and Free French escort vessels', was lost with his ship.

There now followed one of the biggest convoy battles of the whole war. No less than forty U-boats were concentrated against HX.229 and SC.122.[1] By noon on the 16th of March eight enemies were in touch with the former convoy, originally composed of forty ships, and in the course of the next three days they sank twelve of its number. Meanwhile SC.122 had been located some 120 miles ahead of the sorely beset Halifax convoy. As the leading convoy was the slower, the two convoys were gradually closing each other, and so ultimately formed a large mass of shipping in a relatively confined space of ocean. Although air cover became available for part of the 17th, the enemy was able to exploit these favourable circumstances. Attacks were continued during the two succeeding nights, the HX convoy suffering the more heavily. Not till the 20th did the increasing air support force the attackers to desist. The U-boats claimed thirty-two ships of 136,000 tons. In fact we lost only twenty-one, but their

---

[1] See Map 38.

tonnage was no less than 141,000; and only one U-boat was lost by the enemy in the course of all these attacks, in which about a score participated. It was a serious disaster to the Allied cause. The Commodore of HX.229, who had already had much experience of Atlantic convoys, imperturbably remarked in his report that 'apart from U-boat attacks the voyage was fairly average'.

Happily such misfortune was not repeated with the next Halifax convoy (HX.230). The enemy made strenuous endeavours to intercept both it and the corresponding outward convoy. Once again a storm of such violence as to warrant classification as a hurricane raged around the embattled convoys. Even the normally stormy North Atlantic excelled itself in the weather which it provided throughout this winter and early spring. Storm succeeded storm, and ships were often overwhelmed by the mere violence of the elements. True, the weather handicapped the U-boats, but our escorts and aircraft suffered as much and more; the convoyed ships were forced to scatter and straggle, and so fell easy victims to the pursuers when the weather abated. Losses from 'marine causes' rose so high as to be second only to those caused by U-boats. For example, the Commodore's ship of one convoy capsized, and was lost with all hands. HX.230, however, had a fortunate passage, and lost only one straggler. The American escort carrier *Bogue* accompanied the slow convoy SC.123, which was passing eastwards at the same time, as far as a position some 175 miles south-east of Cape Farewell. Furthermore a support group, led by the destroyer *Offa*, was sent to the convoy's help until such time as it had passed through the danger zone, when the group was switched back to reinforce HX.230; and, lastly the direction-finding wireless in the escorts enabled them to find the reporting U-boat and force her under, so that 'a hole was punched in the [U-boat patrol] line and the convoy passed safely through'. The successful passages of HX.230 and SC.123 thus did something to offset the disaster to their immediate predecessors.

It thus came to pass that the appearance of the long-awaited escort carriers on the Atlantic convoy routes coincided with the introduction of support groups. It will therefore be convenient to analyse the strength and composition of the latter. The reader will remember how the first escort carrier, the *Audacity*, closed the air gap on the Gibraltar route in September 1941.[1] Now other ships of the same class were to perform the same vital function in the Atlantic. At the end of March Admiral Horton had five support groups at his disposal. The 1st and 2nd Groups were composed of experienced flotilla vessels of the Western Approaches command; the 3rd and 4th of destroyers lent from the Home Fleet, and the 5th comprised the escort carrier *Biter* and three destroyers. In addition to the *Biter*

---

[1] See Vol. I, pp. 478–9.

and the U.S. Navy's *Bogue*, mentioned above, the carriers *Archer* and *Dasher* also came to the Western Approaches during the month. Admiral Horton reported on the 13th that 'much depends on the successful employment of these carriers, especially the first two'.[1] Unhappily the *Dasher* was destroyed by an internal petrol explosion while carrying out exercises on the 27th of March.[2]

The detailed organisation of the support groups is shown below.

Table 30. Atlantic Support Groups, March–May 1943

1st Escort Group (Commander G. N. Brewer) *Pelican Sennen Rother Spey Wear Jed.*

2nd Escort Group (Captain F. J. Walker) *Cygnet Starling Wren Kite Whimbrel Wild Goose Woodpecker.*

3rd Escort Group (Captain J. A. McCoy) *Offa Obedient Oribi Orwell Onslaught*

4th Escort Group (Captain A. K. Scott-Moncrieff) *Inglefield Eclipse Impulsive Icarus Fury.*

5th Escort Group (Captain E. M. C. Abel Smith) *Biter Pathfinder Obdurate Opportune.*

NOTE: The Composition of the above groups varied constantly. The table only shows a typical allocation of ships.

At the end of 1943, when the Admiralty cast their eye backward to the crisis of the previous spring, they recorded that 'the Germans never came so near to disrupting communication between the New World and the Old as in the first twenty days of March 1943'. Even at the present distance of time one can sense the relief which the dawning realisation that the crisis of crises had come, and had been successfully surmounted, brought in London. Nor can one yet look back on that month without feeling something approaching horror over the losses we suffered. In the first ten days, in all waters, we lost forty-one ships; in the second ten days fifty-six. More than half a million tons of shipping was sunk in those twenty days; and, what made the losses so much more serious than the bare figures can indicate, was that nearly two-thirds of the ships sunk during the month were sunk in convoy. 'It appeared possible' wrote the Naval Staff after the crisis had passed, 'that we should not be able to continue [to regard] convoy as an effective system of defence'. It had, during three-and-a-half years of war, slowly become the lynch

---

[1] See Rear-Admiral W. S. Chalmers. *Max Horton and the Western Approaches*, p. 186 (Hodder and Stoughton, 1954).

[2] It seems unlikely that British and American opinions regarding the cause of the loss of this ship will ever be wholly reconciled. The Admiralty, commenting on the Board of Enquiry's report, remarked that 'safeguards against accidents of this nature are, by our standards, practically non-existent in the petrol arrangements and hangars of these American-built escort carriers', and decided to take steps to rectify the matter. The Americans seem to have attributed the disaster to inexperience on the part of British officers in handling bulk petrol, and it is true that after the loss of the *Dasher* a warning was issued by the Admiralty describing the sources of danger in her class of ship. It is however, a fact that the later escort carriers had their petrol systems modified in America for greater safety before they entered service.

pin of our maritime strategy. Where could the Admiralty turn if the convoy system had lost its effectiveness? They did not know; but they must have felt, though no one admitted it, that defeat then stared them in the face. Apart from the indomitable spirit of the seamen and airmen engaged in the battle, it was the advent of the Support Groups, the Escort Carriers and the Very Long Range Aircraft which turned the tables on the U-boats—and did so with astonishing rapidity.

Next there took place a series of actions with HX, SL and ON convoys in which neither side gained great advantage. We lost some, though not many, ships; and the U-boats suffered some, though not decisive, losses. Nor did the enemy's attempts to find and attack the supply convoys passing further south, direct from America to the North African supply bases, yield more substantial results. Sinkings on that important route remained small. By the end of March the pendulum had swung back central again. An attempt by six U-boats to strike again off the American coast and in the Caribbean had produced only slight returns, because almost all ships were convoyed, and the American sea and air forces were now well-trained and watchful. And in the North Atlantic we only lost fifteen ships during the last eleven days of this fateful month, compared with 107 sunk during the first twenty days. Yet the collapse of the enemy's offensive, when it came, was so sudden that it took him completely by surprise. We now know that, in fact, a downward trend in the U-boats' recent accomplishments could have forewarned him, but was concealed from him by the exaggerated claims made by their commanders.

We must now take temporary leave of the convoy routes to review the ebb and flow of Coastal Command's offensive against outward-bound U-boats from Germany and in the Bay of Biscay. In the 'northern transit area', through which all new U-boats bound for the Atlantic had to pass, the patrols flown by Nos. 15 and 18 Groups at first followed the same general pattern as in 1942[1]; but until March the heavy calls for aircraft for other purposes, and in particular for escort duties in the Atlantic, prevented a constant watch being kept on the routes used by the enemy. In that month reinforcements began to reach the R.A.F. groups concerned. Of the twenty-four U-boats now known to have traversed those waters in March, two (U.469 and U.169) were sunk by a Fortress of No. 206 Squadron. In April more aircraft were available, but out of the twenty-one U-boats which passed through only one (U.227) was sunk by an air patrol. May brought further air reinforcements, but again only one enemy was sunk in the transit area. Not until the U-boat packs withdrew from the convoy routes in June was it possible sub-stantially to increase the patrols in the north.

[1] See p. 206.

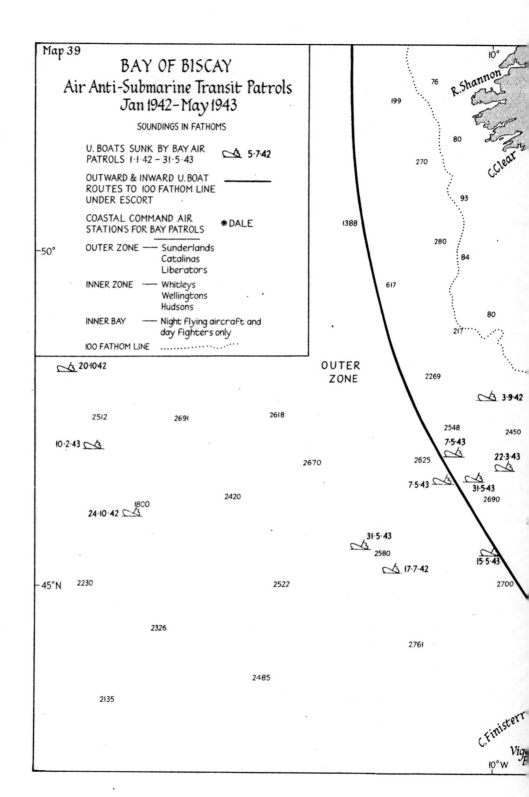

Map 39

BAY OF BISCAY
Air Anti-Submarine Transit Patrols
Jan 1942 – May 1943

SOUNDINGS IN FATHOMS

U. BOATS SUNK BY BAY AIR
PATROLS 1·1·42 – 31·5·43   5·7·42

OUTWARD & INWARD U. BOAT
ROUTES TO 100 FATHOM LINE
UNDER ESCORT

COASTAL COMMAND AIR   ● DALE
STATIONS FOR BAY PATROLS

OUTER ZONE —— Sunderlands
              Catalinas
              Liberators

INNER ZONE —— Whitleys
              Wellingtons
              Hudsons

INNER BAY —— Night flying aircraft and
              day fighters only

100 FATHOM LINE ....·······

R. Shannon

76
199
80
270
93
280
84
617
80
217
1388

OUTER
ZONE

2269

20·10·42

3·9·42

2512   2691   2618   2548   2450
                                                    7·5·43
10·2·43   2625   22·3·43

                          2670   7·5·43   31·5·43
                                                              2690
                    2420
          1800
24·10·42   31·5·43
                                           2580
                                                15·5·43
                                    17·7·42
45°N 2230   2522   2700

          2326

                                              2761

                    2485

     2135

C. Finisterre
10°W   Vigo

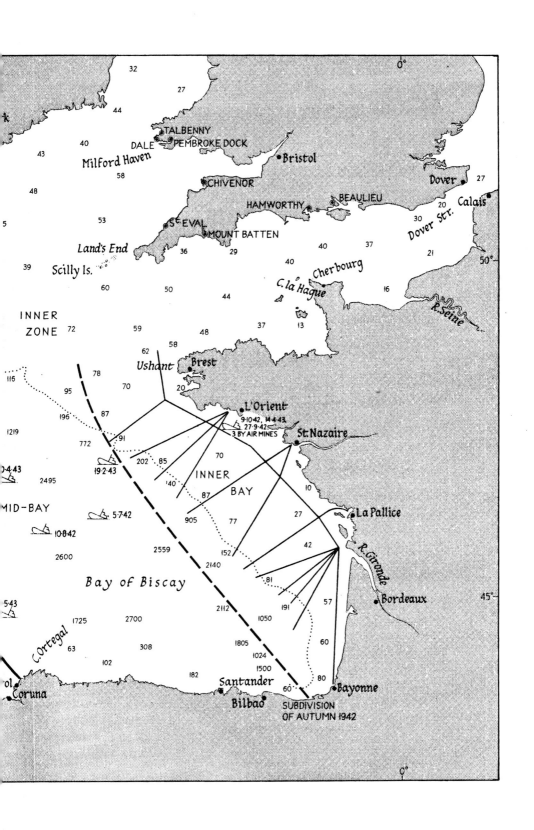

32

27

44

TALBENNY
DALE ● ● PEMBROKE DOCK
Milford Haven

40

43

48

5

58

53

● Bristol

CHIVENOR

St EVAL
Land's End

Scilly Is.

39

60

50

44

INNER
ZONE 72

59

48

37   13

62   58

Ushant   Brest

78

95

196

116

1219

772

91

202   85

19·2·43

140

2495

0·4·43

2600

2700

63

102

Bol
● Coruna

C. Ortegal

MID-BAY

10·8·42

2559

905

152

2140

2112

1725

308

182

1805

1024

1500

Santander

Bilbao

Bay of Biscay

HAMWORTHY

BEAULIEU

MOUNT BATTEN

36   29

40

40

44

C. la Hague

Cherbourg

Dover

Calais

20

30   Dover Str.

21

16

R. Seine

50°

70

20

L'Orient
9·10·42, 14·4·43
27·9·42
3 BY AIR MINES

St. Nazaire

70

INNER

BAY

87

77

10

27

42

5·7·42

81

191

57

1050

60

80

60°   Bayonne

La Pallice

R. Gironde

● Bordeaux

45°

SUBDIVISION
OF AUTUMN 1942

0°

0°

The reader will remember that, after achieving some initial successes when airborne one-and-a-half metre radar was first introduced, the offensive against the U-boats passing to and from the Bay of Biscay bases had entirely collapsed in October 1942, because the German search receiver gave ample warning of the approach of an aircraft, and so enabled the U-boats to get well below the surface before an attack could be delivered.[1] The initiative could only be regained by Coastal Command when the early radar sets had been replaced by the new ten-centimetre model. The extent of the decline of our offensive is best indicated by the fact that, although U-boat traffic was heavy in January 1943, the number of aircraft sightings was the lowest ever recorded. In February the patrols were reorganised and a big effort was made by No. 19 Group from the 6th to the 15th. It resulted in eighteen of the forty U-boats now known to have crossed the Bay being sighted; but only U.519 was sunk. She fell victim to a United States Army Liberator fitted with ten-centimetre radar—the first success in these waters to the new equipment. After this improvement another recession occurred, partly because the convoy battles had become so violent that aircraft could not be spared to carry out patrolling. However, on the night of the 19th-20th of February a Leigh-Light Wellington of No. 172 Squadron sank U.268 in the 'Inner Bay'.[2] Then, early in March, No. 19 Group's only two Liberator squadrons were moved by the Americans to Port Lyautey in Morocco, in spite of vigorous protests by the British Chiefs of Staff, to help combat the U-boats which had appeared off that coast.[3]

At about the same time a Wellington fitted with the new ten-centimetre radar located and attacked a U-boat, but was shot down in the process. This enemy (U.333) reported that her search receiver had failed to detect the aircraft's radar; and that report, combined with her success in destroying her attacker, was to have important results.

For eight days towards the end of March No. 19 Group, which now had more aircraft fitted with the new radar set, made a fresh effort. Forty-one U-boats passed across the patrol lines; one was sunk and one seriously damaged. Both successes were achieved by Leigh-Light Wellingtons fitted with the new radar set. It was at this time that Dönitz noted the increasing effectiveness of our air patrols and prophesied, correctly, 'that there will be further losses'.

There now followed a period of controversy and discussion, chiefly in the Prime Minister's Anti-U-Boat Committee, regarding the conflicting needs of the Bay patrols, of convoy protection and of

[1] See p. 205.
[2] See Map 39.
[3] See pp. 333–334.

2A

bombing Germany. The Admiralty pitched its requirements in additional aircraft for the Bay at the high figure of 190, and wanted at the same time to have the bases and their U-boat accommodation continuously bombed. The Air Ministry declared that to meet the former need would drastically reduce the offensive against Germany, and said (we now know correctly) that the 10,000 tons of bombs recently dropped on Lorient and St. Nazaire had not produced the desired results.[1] The Chief of the Air Staff proposed instead to increase patrols in the Bay by some seventy aircraft, by making loans to Coastal Command and by re-deploying certain of its forces. As a long-term measure, he would ask the Americans to provide additional radar-fitted aircraft to start 'an all-out offensive . . . in the Bay of Biscay' in July. The story of the harvest gathered from this offensive will be told in our third volume.

The conflict between the desire to devote the maximum strength to bombing Germany and the Admiralty's deep anxiety regarding our losses from U-boats was thus reopened in March 1943.[2] As the Admiralty saw it, the whole grand strategy of the Allies depended on defeating the U-boats. 'The people of Britain can tighten their belts', said Professor P. M. S. Blackett, Chief of Operational Research in the Admiralty, 'but our armies cannot be let down by failure to provide equipment, guns and tanks, This means ships and more ships, and safe escort for them'. In addition to bombing the U-boat bases more intensively the crucial needs were, in the Naval Staff's opinion, to provide more Very Long Range aircraft, to expedite the entry of escort carriers into service, and to gain the use of bases in the Azores. Bomber Command and the Air Staff considered that the 'softening process', which could only be applied to Germany by the persistent use of the heavy bombers against land targets, was the essential preliminary to victory. Against that the Admiralty argued that the art of grand strategy was to employ all our forces in further-ance of a common aim, that the accepted aim was the strategic offensive by all arms into Europe, and that the destruction of the U-boats was the necessary prelude to the successful mounting and maintenance of our offensive plans. Such was the problem which the Cabinet, working through the Prime Minister's Anti-U-Boat Com-mittee, had to resolve. In effect it was resolved by something in the nature of a compromise. The Admiralty's needs were met, though not as quickly as that department wished, the U-boats were defeated —though only after they had inflicted terrible losses on us and our Allies—and the bombing of Germany continued. Whether final victory would have come sooner had our forces been differently allocated at an earlier date is likely to continue to be a subject of

[1] See pp. 351–352.
[2] See Chapter III.

dispute. For what it is worth this writer's view is that in the early spring of 1943 we had a very narrow escape from defeat in the Atlantic; and that, had we suffered such a defeat, history would have judged that the main cause had been the lack of two more squadrons of very long range aircraft for convoy escort duties.

While these difficult controversies were being thrashed out around a table in London, early in April Coastal Command carried out another series of intensive patrols for a week in the Bay of Biscay. As the First Sea Lord said to Air Marshal Slessor, 'I feel that enough has been written about the poor old Bay offensive, and that what we want to do is to collect the necessary aircraft . . . and get on with the job'. The results were similar to those achieved in March—U.376 was sunk by a Wellington, and another U-boat was badly damaged. At the end of April a series of night attacks, which defeated the German warning receivers, caused Dönitz to commit perhaps his biggest mistake of the war. His faith in the German counter-measures to our radar was destroyed, and he reversed the previous policy by ordering all U-boats to dive by night and to surface by day for long enough to charge their batteries. The immediate result was a decrease in night sightings by our aircraft, and a corresponding rise in day sightings. During the first week in May three outward-bound U-boats (U.332, 109 and 663) were sunk in day attacks, and three more were damaged. On the 15th U.463, an outward-bound supply U-boat, was destroyed by a Halifax of No. 58 squadron—the first of the valuable 'milch cows' to be sunk. The increased losses in day attacks, combined with the anti-aircraft success of U.333 already mentioned, resulted in Dönitz ordering his crews 'to stay on the surface and fight it out with the aircraft', not only on the Bay transit routes but around our convoys. Increased A.A. armaments were to be fitted, and special A.A. U-boats were sent to patrol the Bay, seeking encounters with our aircraft. At the same time he ordered the U-boats to return home in groups of from three to six, so that they could support each other more effectively. On the last day of May U.440 and U.563, which had stayed on the surface in accordance with this new policy, were both sunk. Thus was the stage set for the period of high accomplishment by Coastal Command on the Biscay transit routes.

In April six U-boats and a 'milch cow' arrived in the waters off Freetown, 'the old battle-ground' where the enemy had so often found easy targets in earlier phases.[1] Five independents were quickly sunk and then, on the 30th of April convoy TS.37 (Takoradi-Sierra Leone), of eighteen ships escorted by a corvette and three trawlers, was attacked when approaching Freetown. The Senior Officer of

---

[1] See Vol. I, pp. 351–353, 463 and 470.

the escort had picked up U-boat transmissions, but did not break wireless silence to tell the shore authorities. Instead a message was sent through a patrolling Hudson. The aircraft merely included the message in its normal report, with the result that it did not reach the Headquarters of the Flag Officer, West Africa, until after the convoy was attacked that evening. Three destroyers were at once sent out to reinforce the escort, but they did not arrive until after a second attack had taken place early on the 1st of May. Seven merchantmen of 43,255 tons were lost that night to the attacks of only one enemy—U.515. These heavy sinkings were described by Mr Churchill as 'deplorable', and the Admiralty had again to point out how we were always liable to suffer from a sudden re-appearance of U-boats in an area which had for some time been free from them. Actually, since these convoys were started in September 1941, 743 ships had sailed in them and only eight had been sunk. To indicate the size of our commitments off West Africa at the time, a large WS convoy with troops for the invasion of Sicily was passing through, a floating dock was being towed from Gibraltar to Freetown, an OS convoy of twenty-one ships was bound for the same base, and one of twenty ships was sailing from Freetown to Takoradi. Escorts had to be provided for all of these and it was, said the Admiralty, impossible to give them all as strong protection as we should have liked. The enemy kept an average of four U-boats off Freetown until the end of May, but they did not repeat the success scored against TS.37.

To return now to the northern convoy routes, the month of April started with only one large group of U-boats actually at sea in the favourite waters north-east of Cape Race, and ready for operations; but a stream of new or refitted boats amounting almost to a flood was coming out from Germany by the northern route, or leaving the Biscay bases. No less than ninety-eight sailed during the month. The first attempt made by the enemy's new concentration was against HX.233 in the middle of April. The convoy had been routed along a southerly course passing some 400 miles north of the Azores, and the attack on it was not at all a success. The escort received a timely reinforcement in the shape of the *Offa's* ubiquitous support group, only one ship was lost, and U.175 was sunk. The next Halifax convoy was sent by the northern route; both it and the corresponding outward convoys ONS.3 and 4 were shadowed and attacked[1], but their losses were slight and the air and surface escorts accounted for U.189 and U.191. For the month of April our losses fell to fifty-six ships of 327,943 tons sunk by U-boats—little more than half the March losses—and only sixty-four ships of under 350,000 tons from all

[1] The numbering of the ONS series was restarted in March 1943 at ONS.1. This was the first of the series to be sailed to Halifax instead of New York (see p. 204 fn (2) above). It left Britain on 15th March.

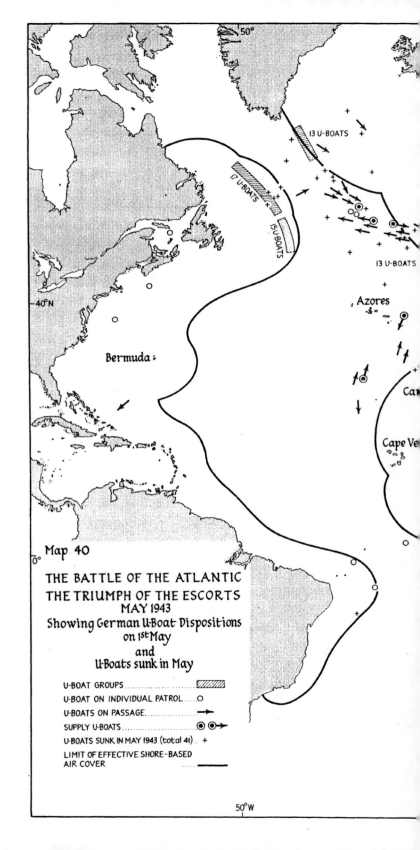

50°

13 U-BOATS

17 U-BOATS

15 U-BOATS

13 U-BOATS

Azores

40°N

Bermuda

Can

Cape Ve

0°

Map 40

THE BATTLE OF THE ATLANTIC
THE TRIUMPH OF THE ESCORTS
MAY 1943
Showing German U-Boat Dispositions
on 1st May
and
U-Boats sunk in May

U-BOAT GROUPS .... ▨
U-BOAT ON INDIVIDUAL PATROL ..... ○
U-BOATS ON PASSAGE .... →
SUPPLY U-BOATS .... ◉ ◉→
U-BOATS SUNK IN MAY 1943 (total 41) .. +
LIMIT OF EFFECTIVE SHORE-BASED
AIR COVER
                                    ....

50°W

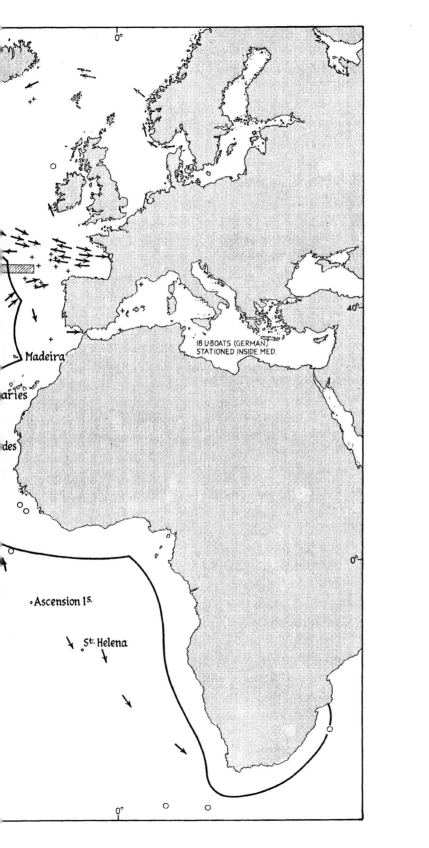

Madeira

aries

des

18 U-BOATS (GERMAN)
STATIONED INSIDE MED.

40°

0°

Ascension I⁵.

St. Helena

0°

0°

causes. There had been no less than five support groups working in the Atlantic during the month, two of them with their own escort carrier; and the number of V.L.R. aircraft had risen to over thirty. 'This', said the Admiralty, 'shows what our counter measures can achieve against the enemy's most strenuous efforts'. There had, moreover, been what the Naval Staff described as 'a considerable slaughter' of U-boats during the last week of the month, and they listed five successes to our surface and air escorts—all of which, and two more, have since been confirmed as accurate. Indeed the accuracy of our contemporary assessments of losses inflicted is not the least creditable aspect of this, as of earlier phases.[1]

In spite of the losses he had recently suffered, on the 1st of May the enemy had about sixty U-boats, organised in four groups ready to seek battle. The disposition of these groups, waiting on the limits of the 'Greenland air gap', are shown on Map 40 (opp.), as are the positions of all other U-boats which were at sea at this critical juncture. The same map shows how the 'air gap' had narrowed since the early days, and also how air cover had been extended in the coastal waters of the central and south Atlantic.[2]

On the 29th of April the enemy made contact with ONS.5, which was taking the northerly route, in stormy weather some 500 miles east of Cape Farewell. At first his pursuit accomplished little. The convoy was escorted by an experienced group led by the destroyer *Duncan* (Commander P. W. Gretton), and consisting of two destroyers, one frigate, four corvettes and two rescue trawlers.

But the watchers on shore saw the seriousness of the threat now developing, and on the 29th of April the 3rd Escort Group of five destroyers led by the *Offa* was ordered from St. John's to meet and reinforce the ocean escort. In very bad weather—a full gale and low visibility, which had forced the convoy virtually to heave to, the support group had great difficulty finding it. Not until 8 p.m. on the 2nd of May was contact made. Meanwhile the enemy had managed to place no less than thirty U-boats, only eight miles apart, right across the convoy's track; and eleven more were lying in wait further ahead. Gale succeeded to gale, and the convoy became much scattered; heavy seas and the presence of icebergs and pack ice made it impossible to fuel the escorts. On the 3rd of May the *Duncan* had to make for St. John's, and command of the escort devolved on the frigate *Tay* (Lieutenant-Commander R. E. Sherwood, R.N.R.). Next day, the 4th, two of the *Offa's* group also had to seek harbour to replenish their tanks, but the Commander-in-Chief, Western Approaches, ordered the 1st Escort Group (Commander G. N.

---

[1] See Vol. I, pp. 23 and 134 regarding the work of the Admiralty's U-boat Assessment Committee.
[2] Compare Vol. I, Map 38.

Brewer), consisting of the sloop *Pelican*, three frigates and an ex-American cutter, out from St. John's to reinforce the escort. Air cover by Royal Canadian Air Force flying boats was available on this day. Two of them attacked U-boats approaching the convoy, and one sank U.630. The real battle was joined after dark on the 4th, by which time the weather had moderated and thirty ships of the convoy had been collected together. Commander Brewer's support group did not join until the 6th; it will be told shortly how the junction took place at a most fortunate moment. Meanwhile the convoy was sore beset. Only the *Tay*, four corvettes and the two remaining destroyers of the *Offa's* groups (the *Offa* and *Oribi*) were with it at the time. Attack and counter-attack followed each other rapidly and fiercely, and five merchantmen (one a straggler) went down that night. At daylight on the 5th there were twenty-six ships left, but luckily it was possible to start refuelling the escorts. Four more ships were sunk in daylight attacks, but the corvette *Pink*, which had been rounding up stragglers and had managed to collect some half dozen into a small convoy under her charge, sank U.192. That evening a V.L.R. aircraft from Iceland, at the limit of its endurance, was with the convoy for a short time.

On the night of the 5th-6th 'about twenty-four attacks took place from every direction except ahead' and, as the Senior Officer of the escort reported, 'the battle continued without a stop until 4.20 a.m. [on the 6th]. One can well understand that 'the situation was confused'. But the little ships hit back hard, and triumphantly. No more of the convoy were lost, and a heavy toll was exacted from the attackers. The first success was scored by the corvette *Loosestrife*, which chased and sank U.638. Then, in the small hours of the morning of the 6th, the destroyer *Vidette* attacked with her 'Hedge-hog' and sank U.125; a short while later the *Oribi* got a contact, and U.531 'slid out of the fog' close at hand. She was promptly rammed and sunk. Finally at about 4 a.m. the sloop *Pelican* ran down a radar echo, made several depth charge attacks and destroyed U.438. The *Pelican* and her group had, as already mentioned, just joined from St. John's, and had replaced the last two ships of the 3rd Escort Group—the *Offa* and *Oribi*. The western local escort also met the convoy that morning, the 6th of May, and no more incidents occurred. Twelve ships were lost from the convoy, but, apart from the successes achieved by the surface escorts, and the sinking of U.630 by the R.C.A.F., a Coastal Command Flying Fortress had sunk U.710 early on in the convoy's passage. The total cost of the operation to the enemy was therefore seven U-boats. The Western Approaches and North-West Atlantic Commands and the escort groups concerned had good grounds for satisfaction over these events, and Admiral Horton paid warm tribute to the latter in his report to the Admiralty on the adventurous passage of convoy ONS.5. Surface escorts alone had inflicted grave losses on an exceptionally strong concentration of attackers.

The enemy attributed our success, with some reason, to the efficiency of our radar, and to the fact that his search receivers could not give warning of the transmissions from our ten-centimetre sets; but he also became aware, and apprehensive, of the new weapons, like the 'Hedgehog', now in use against him, and of the vastly heavier and more deadly depth charge patterns being fired. He also learnt that the new, large and more complicated boats (Type IX) were more vulnerable than the smaller and older ones (Type VII)[1], and decided to transfer the former to the safer waters in the south.

In spite of his losses, and his apprehensions, the enemy at once reformed the survivors to renew the battle. HX.237 and SC.129, whose routes lay much further south, were next located. Three ships were sunk from the former, but a like number of U-boats was destroyed by the air and surface escorts. Carrier-borne aircraft, this time from the *Biter*, again did good work in defending this convoy; while shore-based aircraft sank one U-boat and shared another with the surface ships. It was indeed a combined operation by all arms and services. The enemies sent against the slow convoy did no better than those which had been so severely handled while attacking the faster one. They were repeatedly driven off by the surface escorts; and they lost two of their number, while many others were seriously damaged, all for a return of only two ships sunk. The *Biter* was diverted from HX.237 to the slower convoy (SC.129) when the latter was threatened, and again showed the great value of the continuously available carrier aircraft.

Two complete enemy failures followed rapidly in the wake of the slight successes achieved by him in these last operations. Convoy SC.130, of thirty-eight ships, sailed from Halifax on the 11th of May. On the 14th B7 Escort Group[2], led by the *Duncan* (Commander P. W. Gretton), which we last encountered stoutly defending ONS.5, sailed from St. John's. Early next morning they met the convoy in thick fog east of Newfoundland, and took over responsibility from the western local escort. In course of transferring papers to and from the Commodore's ship, the Escort Commander passed the word that, as he was getting married very soon after the convoy was due to arrive, it was most important that, throughout the long eastward journey the convoy should maintain, or if possible improve on, its rated speed. The Commodore promised his full co-operation, and it is pleasant to record that, although four groups of U-boats were concentrated to attack the convoy between the 15th and 20th,

---

[1] See Appendix K regarding particulars of U-boats.
[2] 'A' groups were American, 'B' groups British and 'C' groups Canadian.

and the air and surface escorts were heavily engaged with them, no ships were lost. The convoy made excellent progress, and the Escort Commander steamed into Londonderry in ample time to keep his appointment. Moreover by way of wedding present to the leader of this splendid group, to whose 'outstanding ability' Admiral Horton paid warm tribute, five U-boats were sunk during the convoy's passage. U.954 and U.258 were destroyed by Liberators of No. 120 Squadron of Coastal Command, U.209 by the *Jed* and *Sennen* of the 1st Escort Group, which had joined to reinforce the threatened convoy, a Hudson of No. 269 Squadron accounted for U.273, and the Senior Officer's *Duncan* herself had a hand in disposing of U.381. This fine achievement was largely due to the almost continuous presence of air cover during the time when the convoy was being threatened. The second enemy failure was against HX.239. This time it was the carrier-borne aircraft of U.S.S. *Bogue* and H.M.S. *Archer* which did the damage. The latter's success was obtained with the new rocket projectiles, which had just been fitted to three of her aircraft, only two months after the first suggestion that they should be tried for anti-submarine purposes had been mooted.

Thus did the enemy fail, and fail most expensively, in a whole series of convoy battles; and it is perfectly plain today that it was the sea and air escorts of the convoys which achieved this decisive victory. 'We know now', wrote Admiral Horton to a brother flag officer shortly after these events, 'what strength and composition of forces is necessary to deal with the U-boat menace against convoys'.[1] But the immense debt owed to the Commander-in-Chief, Western Approaches, himself must also be recorded, for without his intimate knowledge of submarine warfare, and his great determination and drive, the victory could not possibly have been won. As his principal air colleague, Air Marshal Sir John Slessor, stated after the war, 'no one . . . played a more critical part in the Battle of the Atlantic than Admiral Horton.'[2] At the end of May 1943 the Naval Staff noted with a relief that can still be felt today 'the sudden cessation of U-boat activity which occurred on or about the 23rd of May'; and remarked that SC.130, which arrived at its destination on the 25th, 'was the last convoy to be seriously menaced'.

The great contribution of the support groups and of the air escorts in these decisive weeks is shown in tabular form at the end of this chapter. Throughout the whole of the present phase only two ships were sunk in convoy in the Atlantic while an air anti-submarine escort was present; and not one of the ships lost from the convoys shown in Table 32 (pp. 380-382) fell victim to a U-boat while her convoy was receiving air protection.

---

[1] Rear-Admiral W. S. Chalmers *Max Horton and the Western Approaches*, p. 300.
[2] Lecture at the Royal United Service Institution, 1947.

By the 22nd of May, when the Germans made up their minds that they must accept defeat and withdraw the survivors from the field of battle, they had already lost thirty-three U-boats; and the toll taken during the whole month was forty-one.[1] Dönitz declared that the withdrawal was only temporary 'to avoid unnecessary losses in a period when our weapons are shown to be at a disadvantage' and that 'the battle in the north Atlantic—the decisive area—will be resumed'; and it is true that six months later he did renew the campaign on the convoy routes. But, as will be told in our final volume, the battle never again reached the same pitch of intensity, nor hung so delicately in the balance, as during the spring of 1943. It is therefore fair to claim that the victory here recounted marked one of the decisive stages of the war; for the enemy then made his greatest effort against our Atlantic life-line—and he failed. After forty-five months of unceasing battle, of a more exacting and arduous nature than posterity may easily realise, our convoy escorts and aircraft had won the triumph they had so richly merited.

As we shall now take leave of the Battle of the Atlantic so far as this volume is concerned, it will be appropriate to summarise the world-wide results of the onslaught by Axis U-boats against our shipping from January 1942 to May 1943. These are set out in the next table. It will be seen that losses of independently-sailed ships were very high during the campaign in American waters (January-June 1942), and that sinkings of U-boats, especially by convoy escorts, were then low. From February to May 1943, during the second campaign on the convoy routes, independently-sailed losses were comparatively small. Losses of convoyed ships were high until the victories of May 1943 were won, but then declined sharply. Sinkings of U-boats on the other hand were then very heavy, especially those accomplished by the sea and air escorts. The figures given below show more emphatically than many words of description how it was the convoy system which reduced our losses, and also brought us the victory over the U-boats.

---

[1] See Map 40 (opp. p. 373). Though full particulars of the sinking of U-boats are given in Appendix J it may be worth recording here the various forces which destroyed the fifty-six lost to the Germans during the decisive months of April and May 1943, and their employment. They were as follows:

Surface Escort Vessels	16
Surface Escort Vessels and Carrier air escorts (shared) .	2
Surface Escort Vessels and Shore-based air escorts (shared)	4
Shore-based air escorts	10
Shore-based aircraft (air support)	3
Shore-based air patrols (Bay of Biscay and northern transit area)	9
Other Shore-based air patrols	3
Carrier air escorts	2
Submarine Patrols	2
Other causes—Mine (1), Accident (2), Unknown (2) .	5
TOTAL	56

Table 31. Allied Shipping Losses in Convoy and Independently Sailed, and U-boats Sunk

1st January 1942–31st May 1943

(All Theatres)

Month	Allied ships sunk in convoy		Allied independently sailed ships sunk		Axis U-boats sunk by sea and air convoy escorts and support	Axis U-boats sunk by all other means	Remarks
	By U-boats only	By all enemies	By U-boats only	By all enemies			
1942							
Jan.	3	9	48	60	4	5	⎫ The
Feb.	9	16	67	78	2	0	⎪ U-boat
March	0	8	88	98	5	4	⎪ Campaign
April	4	11	69	104	1	3	⎬ on the
May	13	24	111	119	1	5	⎪ east
June	20	29	121	135	1	5	⎪ coast of
July	24	44	70	81	8	7	⎭ America
Aug.	50	60	51	56	9	8	
Sept.	29	39	58	62	6	7	
Oct.	29	33	54	56	9	8	
Nov.	39	46	70	75	9	8	
Dec.	19	25	33	38	6	7	
							⎫ The second
1943							⎪ U-boat
Jan.	15	18	14	19	5	6	⎪ campaign
Feb.	34	38	16	18	17	6	⎬ on the
March	72	77	23	25	6	10	⎪ Atlantic
April	25	29	22	24	9	8	⎪ convoy
May	26	31	19	19	28	19	⎭ routes
TOTALS	411	537	934	1067	126	116	

NOTE: During the same period 108 allied ships which were stragglers from convoy were sunk by U-boats and 114 by all enemies.

It remains to mention one other very important fact concerning this phase of the Battle of the Atlantic. We are not here directly concerned with the parallel struggle of the Allied shipyards to build more and still more merchant ships, and to build them faster than the enemy was sinking them. For the technical problems involved in that stupendous accomplishment, and the success ultimately accomplished, chiefly by our American Allies, the reader must refer to the appropriate volumes of the Civil Histories.[1] Although our losses of ships in convoy had never, since the beginning of the war, fallen below our gains of merchant shipping from new construction and other sources, our total losses had so far always exceeded our gains.[2] It was, however, just after the end of the present phase—to

[1] See '*British War Production*' by M. M. Postan (H.M.S.O. 1952) and *Merchant Shipping and the Demands of War*' by C. B. A. Behrens (H.M.S.O. and Longmans, 1955).

[2] See Map 41 (p. 379).

be precise in July 1943—that the rising curve of Allied merchant ship construction overtook and crossed the more slowly rising curve of sinkings by the enemy; and never again did the former fall below the latter. Had this victory of production not been won, the sacrifices of the escorting ships and aircraft, and of the merchant seaman, were all bound to have been made in vain. As long as the enemy was sinking more ships than we were building, the final victory would remain in the balance—as the Germans very well realised. Hence their determined effort to achieve a decisive success in the Battle of the Atlantic in the first half of 1943. The men who manned the escorts and the merchant ships—and flew in the far-ranging aircraft, will be the first to acknowledge the contribution of the shipyards to the defeat of that purpose. The appropriate curves of new construction and losses, covering the whole war, are shown below.

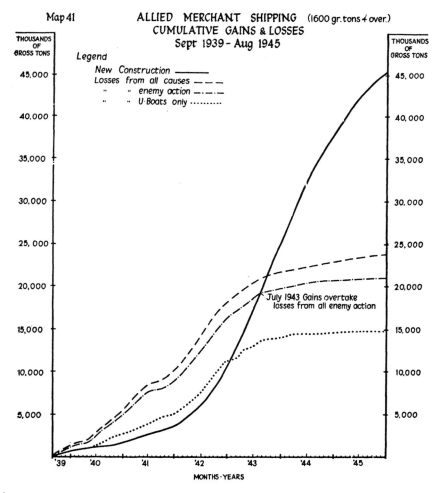

Map 41   ALLIED MERCHANT SHIPPING (1600 gr. tons + over.)
CUMULATIVE GAINS & LOSSES
Sept 1939 - Aug 1945

Legend

New Construction ———
Losses from all causes — — —
   "   "   enemy action —·—·—
   "   "   U-Boats only ··········

July 1943 Gains overtake losses from all enemy action

MONTHS·YEARS

Table 32. *The Work of the Escort and Support Groups, and of Air Escorts and Supports on the North Atlantic Convoy Routes, 14th April–31st May, 1943*

Convoy and Number of Ships	Ports of Departure-Arrival	Dates of Departure-Arrival	Escort and Senior Officer's Ship	Support Group and Senior Officer's Ship	Whence Sent	Period With Convoy	Ships of Convoy Lost and Tonnage	U-Boats Sunk During Convoy Passage and Remarks
HX.233 54 ships	New York-Liverpool, etc.	6/4/43-21/4/43	A3 Group U.S.S. *Spencer*	3rd Escort Group H.M.S. *Offa*	Londonderry	6.40 a.m. 17/4 to 3.45 p.m. 18/4	One (7,134)	U.175 by U.S.S. *Spencer* 17/4/43.
SC.126 38 ships	Halifax-Liverpool, etc.	8/4/43-23/4/43	B5 Group H.M.S. *Havelock*	3rd Escort Group H.M.S. *Offa*	HX.233	8.55 a.m. 19/4 to 8.15 a.m. 20/4	Nil	
HX.234 43 ships	New York-Liverpool, etc.	12/4/43-28/4/43	B4 Group H.M.S. *Highlander*	4th Escort Group H.M.S. *Faulknor*	Greenock	8.0 a.m. 25/4 to 8.0 p.m. 25/4	One in convoy (10,218) One straggler (7,176)	U.189 (by Liberator of 120 Sqdn. R.A.F.) 23/4/43.
ONS.4 32 ships	Liverpool-Halifax	13/4/43-5/5/43	B2 Group H.M.S. *Hesperus*	5th Escort Group H.M.S. *Biter* 1st Escort Group H.M.S. *Pelican*	Hvalfiord SC.127	9.0 a.m. 23/4 to 11.30 a.m. 26/4 9.0 p.m. 26/4 to 10.30 a.m. 28/4	Nil	U.191 (by H.M.S. *Hesperus*) 23/4/43. U.203 (by H.M.S. *Pathfinder* and aircraft from H.M.S. *Biter*) 25/4/43.
SC.127 55 ships	Halifax-Liverpool, etc.	16/4/43-3/5/43	C1 Group H.M.S. *Itchen*	1st Escort Group H.M.S. *Pelican* 4th Escort Group H.M.S. *Faulknor*	Londonderry HX.234	7.32 a.m. 24/4 to 9.30 a.m. 25/4 9.40 a.m. 27/4 to 4.30 a.m. 30/4	Nil	
HX.235 36 ships	New York-Liverpool, etc.	18/4/43-3/5/43	C4 Group H.M.S. *Churchill*	U.S.S. *Bogue*	Argentia	2.0 p.m. 25/4 to 8.0 a.m. 28/4	Nil by enemy One by collision (5,248)	U.174 (by U.S. aircraft off Nova Scotia) 27/4/43. [Note.—It is uncertain which convoy this aircraft was escorting at the time of its success.]
ONS.5 42 ships	Liverpool-Halifax	21/4/43-12/5/43	B7 Group H.M.S. *Duncan*	3rd Escort Group H.M.S. *Offa* 1st Escort Group H.M.S. *Pelican*	St. John's St. John's	8.30 p.m. 2/5 to 8.09 a.m. 6/5 5.50 a.m. 6/5 to 10.30 p.m. 8/5	11 in Convoy (52,587) 2 stragglers (9,372)	U.710 (by Fortress of 206 Sqdn. R.A.F.) 24/4/43. U.630 (by Canso of No. 5 Sqdn. R.C.A.F.) 4/5/43*. U.192 (by H.M.S. *Pink*) 5/5/43. U.531 (by H.M.S. *Oribi*) 6/5/43. U.638 (by H.M.S. *Loosestrife*) 6/5/43. U.125 (by H.M.S. *Vidette*) 6/5/43. U.438 (by H.M.S. *Pelican*) 6/5/43. *A "Canso" was an R.C.A.F. Catalina.
HX.236 46 ships	New York-N.W., etc.	24/4/43-9/5/43	B1 Group H.M.S. *Hurricane*	2nd Escort Group H.M.S. *Starling*	Londonderry	6.30 a.m. 3/5 to 6.0 p.m. 5/5	Nil	U.465 (by Liberator of 86 Sqdn.) 4/5/43.
SL.128	Freetown-N.W.,	29/4/43-14/5/43	27th Escort Group	2nd Escort Group	HX.236	8.05 p.m. 7/5 to	One (9,892)	Note.—This South Atlantic

Convoy	Route	Dates	Close Escort Group	Support Escort Group	Port	Period	Ships sunk by enemy	U-boats sunk
SC.129, 26 ships	Halifax-Liverpool, etc.	2/5/43-20/5/43	B2 Group H.M.S. *Hesperus*	5th Escort Group H.M.S. *Biter*	SC.129	2 p.m. 14/5 to 11.30 a.m. 16/5	Two (7,627)	U.456 (by H.M.S. *Lagan*, H.M.C.S. *Drumheller* and Sunderland of 423 Sqdn. R.C.A.F.) 13/5/43. U.186 (by H.M.S. *Hesperus*) 12/5/43. U.266 (by Liberator of 86 Sqdn. R.A.F.) 14/5/43.
ON.182, 56 ships	Liverpool-New York	6/5/43-22/5/43	C5 Group H.M.C.S. *Ottawa*	4th Escort Group H.M.S. *Archer*	ONS.6	1 p.m. 12/5 to 7.45 p.m. 14/5	Nil	Nil
HX.238, 45 ships	New York-Liverpool, etc.	7/5/43-22/5/43	C3 Group H.M.C.S. *Skeena*	Nil	—	—	Nil	Nil
O¹S.7, 40 ships	Liverpool-Halifax	7/5/43-25/5/43	B5 Group H.M.S. *Swale*	3rd Escort Group H.M.S. *Offa*	St. John's	2.40 a.m. 18/5 to 11.0 a.m. 19/5	One (5,196)	U.657 (by U.S. aircraft) 14/5/43. U.640 (by H.M.S. *Swale*) 17/5/43.
ON.183, 32 ships	Liverpool-New York	10/5/43-25/5/43	B4 Group H.M.S. *Highlander*	Nil	—	—	Nil	
SC.130, 38 ships	Halifax-Liverpool, etc.	11/5/43-26/5/43	B7 Group H.M.S. *Duncan*	1st Escort Group H.M.S. *Wear*	St. John's	7.25 p.m. 19/5 to 11 a.m. 22/5	Nil	U.273 (by Hudson of 269 Sqdn. R.A.F.) 19/5/43. U.954 (by Liberator of 120 Sqdn. R.A.F.) 19/5/43. U.381 (by H.M.Ss *Duncan* and *Snowflake*) 19/5/43. U.209 (by H.M.Ss *Jed* and *Sennen*) 19/5/43. U.258 (by Liberator of 120 Sqdn. R.A.F.) 20/5/43.
ON.184, 39 ships	Liverpool-New York	15/5/43-1/6/43	C1 Group H.M.S. *Itchin*	6th Escort Group U.S.S. *Bogue*	Iceland	8 a.m. 19/5 to 10.30 a.m. 25/5	Nil	U.569 (by aircraft from U.S.S. *Bogue*) 22/5/43.
HX.239, 42 ships	New York-Liverpool, etc.	13/5/43-27/5/43	B3 Group H.M.S. *Keppel*	4th Escort Group H.M.S. *Archer*	Argentia	8 a.m. 21/5 to 1 p.m. 25/5	Nil	U.752 (by aircraft from H.M.S. *Archer*) 23/5/43.
SC.131, 31 ships	New York-Liverpool, etc.	18/5/43-31/5/43	B6 Group H.M.S. *Viscount*	3rd Escort Group H.M.S. *Offa* / 40th Escort Group H.M.S. *Lulworth*	St. John's / Londonderry	3 p.m. 23/5 to 5.30 a.m. 28/5 / Noon 27/5 to 5.30 a.m. 28/5	Nil	Nil
ONS.8, 52 ships	Liverpool-Halifax	18/5/43-1/6/43	C4 Group H.M.S. *Churchill*	2nd Escort Group H.M.S. *Starling*	Iceland	5.55 p.m. 22/5 to 11.30 p.m. 25/5	Nil	Nil
HX.240, 56 ships	New York-Liverpool, etc.	19/5/43-4/6/43	C5 Group H.M.C.S. *Ottawa*	2nd Escort Group H.M.S. *Starling*	ONS.8	9.50 a.m. 27/5 to 10.30 p.m. 30/5	Nil	U.304 (by Liberator of 120 Sqdn. R.A.F.) 28/5/43.

TOTAL OF SHIPS SAILED IN CONVOY:

6th April-19th May, 1943

912

TOTAL OF SHIPS SUNK BY ENEMY

(1) In Convoy .. 17 (86,565 tons)
(2) Stragglers .. 6 (37,937 tons)

TOTAL .. 23 (124,502 tons)

TOTAL OF U-BOATS SUNK BY CONVOY SURFACE AND AIR ESCORTS AND SUPPORTS:

27

CHAPTER XV

COASTAL WARFARE

1st January–31st May, 1943

> 'It will comfort you to know that my role in this war has been of the greatest importance. Our patrols far out over the North Sea have helped to keep the trade routes clear for our convoys and supply ships'.
>
> From a letter by Flying Officer V. A. W. Rosewarne, R.A.F., to his Mother, originally published in the 'Times' of 18th June 1940 as *An Airman's letter to his Mother*.[1]

THROUGHOUT the war the winter months aggravated the difficulties and perils of the east coast convoys; nor were January and February 1943 any exception to that rule. The frequent North Sea gales always produce seas of a peculiarly short and vicious variety in among the shoals and sandbanks with which the coastal waters are studded. In peacetime the traffic either takes shelter from the gales in one or other of the many adjacent harbours or rides them out in solitary, but comparatively safe, discomfort. In war time neither solution could be applied, because of the navigational risks involved in handling forty or fifty ships in close proximity to each other, because of the very real danger of allowing any vessel to wander from the 'straight and narrow way' of the swept channel and because of the enemy's invariable attention to stragglers. Only the destroyers and corvettes of the Nore Command and the Rosyth Escort Force, which week after week and month after month shepherded these unwieldy convoys, in which some of the masters were as unamenable to convoy discipline as their rusty, salt-caked, smoky coasters were incapable of co-ordinated manoeuvres, fully understood and will remember the peculiar problems which the east coast convoys involved. Fortunately the British sailor's gift of humour rose above all the difficulties and dangers; and it may be that the ironic banter often sent over the senior officer's loud hailer to a particularly stubborn straggler, and the delighted reception accorded to

---

[1] Flying Officer Rosewarne was a Bomber Command pilot, but was employed on Coastal Command duties, flying Wellingtons, at the time of his death. He was reported missing on 30th May 1940, but his body was subsequently washed ashore near Ostend and buried in Furnes cemetery. His letter to his Mother was found among his papers by his Commanding Officer.

the inevitably abusive retort from the coaster's bridge, did more than
the most carefully framed convoy orders and the most courteously
conducted convoy conferences to keep these little ships sailing. Perhaps some extracts from one Senior Officer's report may be preserved to typify the spirit in which these convoys were conducted.

Convoy FN.944[1] (of twenty ships) from Southend to Methil in the
Firth of Forth sailed on Sunday the 14th of February 1943, escorted
by the destroyers *Valorous* (Lieutenant-Commander W. W. Fitzroy)
and *Walpole*, both veterans of the 1914-18 war, the corvette *Kittiwake*
and a trawler. After sailing 'an exchange of compliments with the
Commodore ensued, during which the current problems were discussed in order of merit (Navigation, E-boats, Air Attack, Stragglers,
Convoy Speed, Arrival at the Tyne, and Smoke). The close proximity
of B2 buoy ended the conversation . . . Communication was soon
established with the fighters which proved to be clipped-wing
Spitfires with United States markings. The temptation to carry on a
"trans-Atlantic" conversation was mastered with difficulty . . .
Balloons were ordered to be flown at 1,000 feet, for the sky had
cleared. We wished the Sunk Head Fort 'Good afternoon' and
received a cheerful response. Soon the magnetic sweepers close ahead
of us turned back. At 1.0 p.m. . . . the convoy was formed into two
columns, its length being thus reduced to two miles. At this juncture
a ship three miles astern was taken to be a straggler until she replied,
rather happily, that her troubles were nearly over, for she was bound
for Harwich . . . After a cruise round the convoy we were able to
report to the Commodore that all ships were closed up, and their
armaments properly manned . . . At 4.0 p.m. the Commodore
took over guide again, and we gave our fleet a dog watch serenade
and a semaphore exercise . . . The weather prophets still held to
their westerly gale, but it was not until the convoy reached Hais-
borough Light that it became evident . . . *Monday morning, 15th
February*. Two ships bound for Iceland joined the convoy. Heavy
seas were now encountered . . . So far as the eye could see there
was a white sheet of foam on the water, and the Yorkshire coast
looked bleak and forbidding . . . We spent the dog watches rounding up the stragglers and making other ships close up. At 5.0 p.m. the
convoy extended over seven and a half miles. Our average speed
along the Northumbrian coast was four knots. *Tuesday, 16th February*.
Off the Farne Islands we cheered the Commodore by relating the
exploits of Grace Darling . . . The convoy reached Methil at
7.30 p.m.'

That convoy suffered no attacks by the enemy. Although the
decline of the German air effort, combined with the far greater
effectiveness of our fighter and anti-aircraft defences, now gave most

[1] See p. 255 footnote [1].

Famous Escort Group leaders, 1942–43.

Top. H.M.S. *Duncan* (Commander P. W. Gretton), B7. Group. (See pp. 373–6).

Bottom. H.M.S. *Starling* (Captain F. J. Walker), 2nd Escort Group. (See pp. 201–367).

An East Coast
Convoy, May 1943.
(Note A.A. balloons
flying).

A U-boat forced to
the surface, but not
sunk, by Whitley V.
of No. 58 Squadron in
the Bay of Biscay,
16th May 1942.

A U-boat on the
surface and
abandoning ship after
attack by an escort
vessel. (Note empty
shell cases in the fore-
ground and survivors
in the water).

east coast convoys the enjoyment of comparatively quiet hours of daylight, their nights were still frequently disturbed by German E-boats. At the start of the New Year these were very active off the east coast, in minelaying on the convoy route and in making torpedo attacks. Often both were combined. Our escorts were, however, so watchful that casualties to the merchantmen were comparatively rare. In the whole of this phase E-boats only succeeded in sinking two ships (6,580 tons); but, in spite of the shore radar stations' greatly improved tracking and reporting, our escorts and patrols still found them elusive targets. Although there were many engagements with them, few E-boats were sunk. Indeed, comparison of our own records with those of the Germans shows how often both sides were wrong in thinking that they had destroyed an enemy; and we now know that it was the destroyer escorts of the convoys which the German E-boats chiefly feared. Thus on the night of the 17th-18th of February a group of these enemies was detected by shore radar near the convoy channel and reported to the destroyers on patrol. The German boats, which were actually engaged on a minelaying sortie, were caught by the destroyers *Garth* and *Montrose* off Yarmouth and one of their number was destroyed. On the 28th-29th March a strong enemy force of seven boats tried to attack the south-bound convoy FS.1074 off Smith's Knoll, but the escort drove off some whilst others were pursued by the motor gunboats. The latter were led by Lieutenant D. G. Bradford, R.N.R., one of the most forceful and successful leaders of our coastal craft. Having led his group of two motor gunboats (Nos. 33 and 321) to attack five enemies, and damaged one of them, he proceeded to carry the ancient principle of close engagement to its logical conclusion by ramming another. His report states that 'the captain of the E-boat had been clearly visible on the bridge immediately before ramming, and appeared somewhat agitated; however he was calmed down by machine gun fire and became resigned to the situation'. The enemy in question (the motor torpedo-boat S.29) was later scuttled by the Germans, after they had rescued her survivors.

There were now Coastal Force bases at Great Yarmouth, Lowestoft and Felixstowe (commissioned as H.M.S. *Midge*, *Mantis* and *Beehive* respectively). In February 1943 Captain H. T. Armstrong was appointed as Captain, Coastal Forces, for the whole Nore Command; and he did a great deal to improve training and tactics. Until a high standard was achieved in these matters success could not be expected in the confused and fast-moving night actions which were typical of coastal craft operations. Many sweeps and attacks on shipping off the Dutch coast were made at this time, but successes were not common and we suffered several losses on these forays. March was, however, a good month for our motor torpedo-boats, with which No. 16 Group's aircraft sometimes co-operated by flare-dropping, and in four actions they succeeded in sinking four ships totalling 9,273 tons, and damaging several others. These successes were by no means accomplished without loss to the attackers; for the German minesweeper and trawler escorts were heavily armed and very alert while on the dangerous sections of their routes. In April the Nore Command Coastal Forces lost their most successful exponent of this type of warfare, when Lieutenant-Commander R. P. Hitchens, R.N.V.R., was killed in action leading his M.G.B. Flotilla to attack a German convoy. But attacks with guns and torpedoes, alternated sometimes by minelaying operations, continued throughout this phase, whenever a suitable target was reported; and there can be little doubt that the inshore convoy route leading to the Dutch ports was thereby made more dangerous to the enemy.

Though the enemy's air minelaying was now far less intensive than in the previous year, his aircraft still came over in small numbers; they and the E-boat minelayers already mentioned prevented any reduction of our minesweeping effort. Many of the trawlers and drifters, which had served us so well since the beginning, were now being replaced by the new motor-minesweepers; the latter were designed specially for the purpose of inshore sweeping, and were better equipped and much handier. But it should not be forgotten that for nearly four years it had been the converted fishing vessels, mostly manned by Reservists and by men of the R.N. Patrol Service, which had kept the channels swept and our vital east coast harbours open. The Humber minesweepers alone had, by the middle of March 1943, accounted for 1,000 enemy mines, and several of its trawlers had impressive personal scores, such as the 181 swept by the trawler *Rolls Royce*, the 165 by the *Ben Meidie* and the 140 by the *Fitzgerald*. On the 2nd of June the Nore Command minesweepers detonated their 3,000th mine.

But the emphasis in coastal warfare was now shifting. Although the channels still had to be swept and the convoys escorted, our various forces were now far more active in the enemy's coastal waters than his were in our own. And, as harbingers of an even more important swing of the pendulum, Combined Operations bases and training establishments were now springing up all round our coasts; new and strange types of vessels were appearing, and officers of all three services joined new staffs, the fruits of whose labours were soon to be gathered from the great overseas expeditions now being planned. By the end of this phase it was plainly apparent that in coastal warfare the balance, if temporarily only steady, would soon move heavily in our favour.

To turn to the air, bombing attacks on our coastal shipping had become quite rare occurrences, though fighter-bombers working from

French airfields still caused us some embarrassment by surprise attacks at dusk in the Channel. They were difficult to counter, because our radar plots rarely gave sufficient warning of these fast, low-flying targets to allow our fighters to get to them. But the attacks were neither frequent enough nor heavy enough to cause us appreciable damage. In fact at this time the great majority of the merchantmen lost to air attacks were sunk in the Mediterranean.[1] The extent to which the enemy's offensive against our coastal shipping, which a year previously had been causing us appreciable losses[2], had now collapsed is shown in the next table.

Table 33. German Air Attacks on Allied Shipping and Royal Air Force Sorties in Defence of Shipping
(Home Theatre only)
January–May 1943

Month 1943	Estimated German Day and Night Aircraft Sorties for		Allied Shipping Sunk by Direct Attacks (Day and Night)		Royal Air Force Sorties in Defence of Shipping (Day and Night)	Royal Air Force Losses
	(1) Direct Attack	(2) Mine-laying	No.	Tonnage		
January	403	95	Nil		1,418	2
February	348	98	Nil		1,636	2
March	640	52	Nil		1,612	2
April	553	70	Nil		796	2
May	518	58	Nil		293	1
TOTAL	2,462	373	Nil		5,755	9

Coastal Command continued to fly many sorties off Norway and off the north German and Dutch coasts, to attack shipping; but the successes achieved were still small. Thus in January 461 sorties led to fifty-eight attacks, but only two ships of 5,168 tons were sunk. The winter did a kindness to the enemy by never freezing the Kattegat, the Belts or the Kiel Canal. Because he could continue to use those passages, he could avoid sending ships up and down the west coast of Denmark, where they would have been far more exposed to attack.

February brought an interesting encounter in the Channel. On the 10th a heavily guarded ship was detected off Gravelines steering west. It was actually the *Togo* (Raider K), outward-bound.[3] She was bombarded, though without effect, by the Dover batteries that evening, and then attacked by Whirlwind bombers. Having been

---

[1] See Chapter XIX.
[2] See Table 13 (p. 166).
[3] See Appendix M.

considerably damaged by one of their bombs, she put into Boulogne. Heavy bombers were then turned on to the port, but she escaped further damage, and was ordered to return to Germany. On the 14th she left Boulogne and was again fired on by the shore batteries; but she reached Dunkirk safely. On the 26th she was hit by another bomb; but she managed to get to sea again, and to evade an attack by the Dover M.T.Bs. On the 2nd of March she reached Kiel. Yet another disguised raider thus passes out of our story. Of the nine German armed merchant raiders which reached the oceans only one was now still at sea—the *Michel* in the Far East; and she had done us very little damage recently.[1] None the less it was not, from our point of view, satisfactory that the *Togo* should survive so many forms of attack close to our shores. It showed that we still did not possess the right aircraft to stop enemy traffic through the Channel. For day attacks, or for use on clear nights, the Whirlwinds and 'Hurribombers' were the best types; for dark nights and for minelaying Coastal Command needed a comparatively slow aircraft like the naval Albacore torpedo-bomber. These latter were also the most suitable types to use against enemy E-boats on their night forays against our coastal convoys, and since the summer of 1942 the Admiralty had lent the Royal Air Force Commands several naval squadrons equipped with these types. Now, however, the expansion of the Fleet Air Arm, and the urgent needs of the Mediterranean and Indian Ocean for carrier-borne aircraft, prevented such loans being continued. In spite of appeals from the Air Ministry, at the end of April the Admiralty named the 1st of June as the date when the squadrons must be returned to naval service. This would leave no suitable aircraft to deal with E-boats by night in home waters, so a compromise was finally found whereby one squadron was re-equipped partly with Albacores transferred by the Admiralty. Its aircraft would be flown by the R.A.F. and operated by Fighter Command. Once again British capacity for compromise produced a sensible, if not a wholly satisfactory, solution.

In the early spring the problem of Germany's merchant shipping became for a time rather less acute, and that in spite of the increasing momentum of our varied onslaught on it. The Reich Commissioner Kaufmann, who had been put in charge of every aspect of its use[2], had contributed a good deal to this, particularly by eliminating wasteful requisitioning of ships by the fighting services; but the mildness of the winter, already mentioned, had also played a part. We, on the other hand, were just about to restore to front line service the Beaufighter Strike Wing, which had taken a severe knock in November 1942 when it had been used on an operation rather prematurely,

---

[1] See pp. 267–268.
[2] See p. 259.

before all the intricate problems of co-ordination and training had been adequately studied.[1] In particular it was now realised that very strong single-seater fighter escort was essential to the safety of the attacking aircraft, and that training had to reach a high pitch of efficiency before a squadron could justifiably be thrown into battle. In this manner Fighter Command came to share with Coastal Command responsibility for the operations of the Strike Wing of the latter's No. 16 Group. The minimum force which it was considered economical to employ was eight torpedo-Beaufighters ('Torbeaus'), sixteen escort-Beaufighters and two squadrons of single-seater fighters. Rehearsals were carried out in April, and then the Strike Wing was ready for the fray. Unhappily the heavy demands for these types of aircraft from the Mediterranean station deferred for another nine months the achievement of the desired strength of ten Beaufighter squadrons in Coastal Command. None the less the re-entry of the Strike Wing into service is of historical importance, because it led to the definition of each Royal Air Force Command's responsibilities for making the anti-shipping campaign a success. Under what was described as a 'tripartite pact' the Commanders-in-Chief, Coastal, Bomber and Fighter Commands, each issued complementary directives. That issued to Coastal Command over the signature of Air Marshal Sir John Slessor opened with words which merit preservation for posterity, namely 'The Royal Air Force shares with the Royal Navy the responsibility for sea communications within range of shore-based aircraft'. Looking back today on the losses and tribulations suffered during the first three and a half years of war, one cannot but wonder how many of them could have been avoided had such a simple truth been accepted by both services in 1939. The revised instructions to the Royal Air Force Commands covered every aspect of the anti-shipping campaign—preliminary reconnaissance, final reporting, escort and attack. On the 18th of April, ten days after they had been issued, the Strike Wing of No. 16 Group, stationed at North Coates in Lincolnshire, carried out its first operation. The strength employed was nine torpedo, six bomber and six cannon Beaufighters covered by three squadrons of No. 12 Group's fighters. The target was a convoy of nine merchant ships with six escorts sighted off the Dutch coast. The German warships were smothered by the cannon and machine-gun fire of the fighters, and the largest ship of the convoy, of nearly 5,000 tons was sunk. Not one of our aircraft was lost.

A fortnight later a second attack was carried out in rather similar circumstances, and with about the same strength. It took place off the Texel, and the enemy convoy had a very powerful escort which, the

---

[1] See p. 259.

Germans having taken a leaf out of our own book, was flying balloons. None the less three of the six ships in the convoy (totalling 9,566 tons) were sunk for the cost of one Beaufighter. On the 17th of May the Strike Wing, escorted by nearly three score Spitfires, went into action once more against a convoy of similar composition to the last one. Again the attack went well, and three merchantmen (4,237 tons in all) were sunk. In the last operation of the phase these successes were, however, not repeated. Bad weather and imprecise last-minute reconnaissance led to loss of surprise, and so to failure. Plainly the price of success still remained careful planning, faultless co-ordination and thorough training. None the less enough had been learnt by the end of May to indicate that a bright future was in store for the Strike Wing and its similarly organised successors; and the approaching introduction of rocket projectiles made the auguries still brighter.

One favourable result of the increasing successes of our varied offensive off the Dutch coast was a big reduction of enemy mercantile traffic in and out of Rotterdam. That port was much the best entry for the Swedish iron ore needed by the Ruhr industries, and also the best outlet for German coal and coke which the Swedes demanded in return. But now the Swedes showed increasing unwillingness to allow their ships to go to Rotterdam, and the Germans therefore had to divert much traffic to Emden. This put additional strain on their inland transport system, and was an altogether uneconomic proposition. But the Germans had to accept it, or lose the services of much Swedish shipping.

While No. 16 Group was thus profiting from past experience and turning it to good effect off the Dutch coast, No. 18 Group's Hampdens and Beaufighters were constantly sweeping the Norwegian coast for enemy shipping. In addition the Group had also to divert its main effort several times to fleet reconnaissance work, in order to locate, and if possible attack the enemy's heavy warships whenever they showed themselves. Thus the movement of the *Scharnhorst* from the Baltic to Norway in March, and that of the *Nürnberg* south to Germany in May[1], called for many reconnaissance flights and the despatch of striking forces. Though no success was achieved against these important ships, No. 18 Group's aircraft, which were on occasions able to use a technique similar to that of the Strike Wing, sank three merchantmen (17,398 tons in all) in April, and another of nearly 6,000 tons in the following month. The Hampdens of Nos. 455 and 489 Squadrons and Beaufighters of Nos. 235 and 404 were the mainstay of No. 18 Group's effort, and it was their work, combined with the good results obtained by No. 16 Group's Strike Wing, which

---

[1] See pp. 400 and 402.

caused the sharp increase in enemy ships sunk during the last two months of this phase, as is shown in the next table.

At this time No. 19 Group of Coastal Command was mainly employed trying to intercept blockade-runners in the Bay of Biscay, and searching for the iron ore ships which were still running from Bilbao to French ports. The Germans attached a good deal of importance to this traffic, particularly now that the Swedish Government was reluctant to charter its merchantmen to Germany to carry ore from Swedish mines, and felt sufficiently strong to drive harder bargains regarding payment and return shipments of coal and coke from the Ruhr. In the spring the ore traffic from Spain reached 70,000 tons a month, a figure which we could not tolerate. But generally we were only able to use aircraft on transit flights to Gibraltar to seek the iron ore ships, and they were rarely successful. It was mainly diplomatic and economic pressure on Spain which caused a reduction of the enemy's imports from Bayonne to 22,000 tons in June.

So much for Coastal Command's offensive against enemy seaborne traffic in this phase. The three Fighter Command Groups stationed in southern England (Nos. 10, 11 and 12) shared the responsibility for anti-shipping operations, suited to their types of aircraft, between the Dutch coast in the east and the Channel approaches in the west. In addition they frequently co-operated with our Coastal Force craft on their offensive sweeps. It was natural that successes by fighter aircraft against ships should generally be confined to small craft and auxiliaries, and in April and May some half dozen of these were sunk.

The main feature of this period of coastal warfare thus was the growing realisation of the inter-dependence of all the various arms and services employed. The Strike Wing, the Nore and Dover M.T.B. and M.G.B. flotillas, the daylight and night bombing of enemy ports, the reconnaissance flights by Coastal Command, and the fighter cover overhead were all complementary. They had the same object, to stop the enemy's coastal traffic. Each gave something to the others, and received in return a contribution essential to its own success. A motor gunboat by sinking a 'flak' ship in the North Sea might save a night bomber bound to attack Germany. The latter's bombs might delay a convoy and destroy part of its escort, and so make the Strike Wing's work easier. The searching eyes of the reconnaissance aircraft might bring the M.T.Bs a favourable opportunity, but protection by the fighters was essential to the safe return of the latter. Only by complete co-operation and full understanding of each other's problems could success be achieved, and that desirable end was just beginning to be attained in the coastal offensive. The results achieved by the Royal Air Force in direct attacks on enemy ships at sea in this phase are shown overleaf.

Table 34. The Air Offensive against Enemy Shipping by Direct Attacks at Sea

(All Royal Air Force Commands—Home Theatre only)

January–May 1943

Month 1943	Aircraft Sorties	Attacks Made	Enemy Vessels Sunk		Enemy Vessels Damaged		Aircraft Losses
			No.	Tonnage	No.	Tonnage	
January .	836	63	2	5,168	Nil		11
February .	658	45	Nil		Nil		10
March .	696	50	1	90	Nil		8
April .	1,362	215	12	37,506	3	9,221	29
May .	1,599	199	7	11,772	Nil		32
TOTAL .	5,151	572	22	54,536	3	9,221	90

To turn to the other methods of carrying the offensive into the enemy's coastal waters, the Home Fleet's submarines were generally few in number, because the demands of the Mediterranean station were so heavy, and work on the North African supply routes was of such critical importance. Those that remained, generally about half a dozen, were most often disposed off the Norwegian coast or near the Faeroes, on the U-boat's northern transit route. They thus had few opportunities of attacking the inshore traffic. The Norwegian-manned 30th Motor Torpedo-boat Flotilla, however, made frequent incursions into the Leads, and its boats often spent several consecutive nights lying up in enemy waters to await suitable targets. On the night of the 23rd-24th of January four M.T.Bs landed a party of Commandos in the fiords of Bergen to attack various shore targets, including a pyrites mine. No. 18 Group's aircraft co-ordinated their attacks with the Commando raiders, and Admiral Tovey commented that 'the whole operation was as creditable as it was enjoyable to the Norwegians who carried it out'. In the same month a party of these intrepid Allies left in a whaler to cut out an enemy convoy near Lister Light, and sail it to Britain. They did not succeed in that bold purpose, but the party remained in Norway, and at the end of February they did seize several small ships and fishing craft, which were sailed to Scottish ports. It can well be imagined how infuriating such pin-pricks must have been to the enemy, especially as most of the Norwegian raiders got back safely to their temporary homeland. In mid-March the Norwegian-manned M.T.Bs scored a success by sinking two ships in the Leads. Though small in themselves, such efforts all helped to add to the enemy's embarrassment, and his difficulties in making his coastal shipping routes secure.

At the start of this phase Coastal Command's minelaying effort depended entirely on two squadrons of naval Swordfish lent by the

Admiralty. By April they had been transferred overseas, and thereafter the whole air minelaying campaign devolved on Bomber Command. In the first three months of the year 3,575 mines were laid, mostly off the north German and Dutch coasts. Then the fitting of the new ten-centimetre radar in our bombers enabled them to attack unseen shore targets, so minelaying was only carried out on nights which were unsuitable for bombing Germany, or by aircrews not yet fully trained. It thus came to pass that, although our stocks of mines were still rising, the rate of laying them remained about stationary.

None the less it was now fully realised that air minelaying was causing the enemy a good deal of annoyance and heavy shipping losses, and in March a new operational order was issued to Bomber Command to the effect that on specially selected nights a really heavy minelaying effort was to be made in certain waters. This coincided with the introduction by the Admiralty, which was responsible for the design and production of all mines, of a combined acoustic and magnetic firing mechanism. To achieve surprise and the greatest possible effect it was desirable that the first lays of these new mines should be large ones, as had been the case in September 1942 with the first British acoustic mines[1]—a need which the enemy had often failed to observe with his own new developments.[2] This Admiralty request fitted in well with Bomber Command's new plans, and on the night of the 27th-28th of April 459 mines were laid in the Bay of Biscay and off the Dutch and north German coasts. A number of the new mines were mixed in with those of older patterns. On the following night an even bigger effort was made, and 568 mines were laid in many different waters, mostly off the enemy's Baltic ports; but we lost twenty-three of the 226 aircraft which took part. The short nights then caused a cessation of distant minelaying sorties, but the work continued on a small scale in the nearer waters, right up to the end of this phase.

Two-thirds of the enemy's losses from mines were suffered in the Baltic, and it is likely that the two big operations already referred to, combined with the introduction of the new type of mine, contributed a good deal to these results. The biggest prize which fell to Bomber Command's minelayers was the liner *Gneisenau* (18,160 tons), which was used to carry troops from Germany to the Russian front. She was sunk in the Baltic on the 2nd of May; but many merchantmen, minesweepers and auxiliary war vessels also fell into the bag. Only against U-boats entering and leaving the Biscay ports were successes small, doubtless because they were always specially swept in and out of harbour. U.526, sunk on the 14th of April off Lorient, was the

[1] See p. 263.
[2] See Vol. I, p. 327.

only victim in this phase. Mines were also laid in the Baltic waters where U-boats were known to do their trials and training, but none was sunk there until later in the year. In fact throughout the war the contribution of our mines to the defeat of the U-boat was insignificant compared with the losses inflicted by convoy escorts, and by air patrols on the enemy's transit routes.[1] It was in the disruption of his coastal traffic that the air minelaying campaign yielded really substantial results. The next two tables give statistics covering the present phase, and it will be seen that air minelaying still remained very much more profitable, both in losses inflicted on the enemy and in the fewer aircraft losses suffered by ourselves, than direct attacks on shipping.

Table 35.   The R.A.F.'s Air Minelaying Campaign
(Home Theatre only)
January–May 1943

Month 1943	Aircraft Sorties	Mines Laid	Enemy Vessels Sunk		Enemy Vessels Damaged		Aircraft Losses
			No.	Tonnage	No.	Tonnage	
January .	608	1,296	13	5,634	Nil		20
February .	545	1,130	15	17,550	Nil		17
March .	534	1,176	12	4,102	4	8,309	24
April . .	673	1,809	16	20,824	2	2,745	33
May . .	363	1,148	18	29,595	4	7,671	8
TOTALS .	2,723	6,559	74	77,705	10	18,725	102

---

[1] See Appendix J.

Table 36. Comparative results obtained by the Royal Air Force from Minelaying and from Direct Attacks on Enemy Shipping at sea.
January 1942–June 1943

Three-month period	(1) AIR MINELAYING							(2) DIRECT ATTACK AT SEA						
	Aircraft sorties	Mines laid	Enemy Vessels sunk		Enemy Vessels damaged		Aircraft losses	Aircraft sorties	Attacks made	Enemy Vessels sunk		Enemy Vessels damaged		Aircraft losses
			No.	Tonnage	No.	Tonnage				No.	Tonnage	No.	Tonnage	
1942														
Jan.-March	685	722	15	22,535	2	62,600*	31	3,070	289	8	3,597	2	11,131	94
April-June .	1,316	2,746	47	59,129	8	22,305	38	2,630	531	16	34,778	12	39,145	87
July-Sept. .	1,329	2,960	64	62,459	13	34,533	52	2,312	480	11	12,616	1	8,998	39
Oct.-Dec. .	1,577	3,283	61	53,482	9	14,787	53	1,854	295	7	10,037	6	22,878	39
1943														
Jan.-March	1,687	3,602	40	27,286	4	8,309	61	2,190	158	3	5,258	Nil	Nil	29
April-June .	1,462	4,131	48	60,522	7	15,385	48	4,411	636	23	56,163	3	9,221	81
TOTALS .	8,056	17,444	275	285,413	43	157,919	283	16,467	2,389	68	122,449	24	91,373	369

* The German battle cruisers *Scharnhorst* and *Gneisenau* during their escape up-Channel.

CHAPTER XVI

HOME WATERS AND THE ARCTIC

1st January–31st May, 1943

'Our escorts all over the world are so
attenuated that losses out of all proportion
are falling on the British Mercantile Marine'.
Mr. Churchill to Mr. Eden, 9th
January 1943.[1]

IT will be remembered that the landings in North Africa in the
autumn of 1942 caused the temporary suspension of the Arctic
convoys, greatly to the disgust of our Russian allies. Then, just at
the turn of the year, convoys JW.51A and B were fought through
with outstanding success.[2] It made no difference to the Russian
authorities whether other pressing needs, such as the supply of Malta
or the combined operations in the Mediterranean, claimed for a time
first call on our resources; they seem not to have cared whether recent
convoys had suffered terrible losses or had survived the most menacing dangers; such considerations as the perpetual daylight of the
summer months seemed to trouble them not a whit. Their stubborn
pressure for convoys to be run, cost what they might, continued
relentlessly and monotonously. Most of this pressure fell, as was
natural, on Mr Churchill; for the American President was able to
take a more detached view of the problems involved and the risks
entailed. The Prime Minister fully understood the urgency of
Russian needs, and was prepared to do all he could to meet them;
but he was not prepared to sacrifice Malta, to jeopardise Allied
strategy in the west or to press the Admiralty and the Commander-
in-Chief, Home Fleet, beyond a certain point. He has left a full
record of the way the Russians treated him in this matter, and little
need be added here.[3] Early in 1943 his patience was exhausted, and
on the 9th of January he told the Foreign Secretary that 'Monsieur
Maisky is not telling the truth when he says I promised Stalin convoys of thirty ships in January and February. The only promise I have

---

[1] Churchill, Vol. IV, p. 825.
[2] See pp. 291–299.
[3] See Churchill, Vol. IV, pp. 239–243, 505, 518, 825.

made is contained in my telegram of December 29th.[1] . . . Maisky should be told that I am getting to the end of my tether with these repeated Russian naggings, and that it is not the slightest use trying to knock me about any more'. None the less the next east-bound convoy (JW.52) sailed from Loch Ewe less than a week after the arrival of the preceding west-bound one (RA.51). January was the last month during which lack of daylight would probably defeat the enemy's air reconnaissance. Moreover from February until mid-summer ice conditions would force us to use a more southerly route, passing within 250 miles of the enemy's air bases for four days of the passage, and even closer to the surface ships in Altenfiord. These two factors meant that after the end of January any convoys run would have to be escorted as strongly as had been PQ.18.[2] If, therefore, a large number of cargoes were to reach north Russia early in 1943, there were cogent arguments in favour of doing all that we could quickly.

The strength of the Home Fleet was, at the moment, reasonably satisfactory, except that it possessed no aircraft carrier. In addition to the three new battleships *King George V*, *Anson* and *Howe*, the *Malaya* was working up after a refit; and there were four 8-inch and five 6-inch cruisers, and about a score of destroyers. Of the enemy's ships, the *Tirpitz* and *Lützow*, the *Hipper* (which had been damaged in the fighting on New Year's Eve[3]), the *Nürnberg* and *Köln*, about eight destroyers and some twenty U-boats were based on Norway; the *Scharnhorst* and *Prinz Eugen*, the light cruisers *Emden* and *Leipzig* and eleven destroyers were in the Baltic; and we believed, incorrectly, that the *Graf Zeppelin* was approaching completion. German air striking forces in Norway had been greatly reduced, but their reconnaissance was still efficient. On the 11th of January the *Scharnhorst* and *Prinz Eugen* were sighted off the Skaw steering north-west.[4] Admiral Tovey had for some time expected that these two ships would be sent to reinforce the squadron in north Norway, or to break out into the Atlantic. No. 18 Group of Coastal Command flew strong reconnaissances, six submarines were sent to patrol off the Norwegian coast, and a destroyer flotilla, supported by two cruisers, was ordered to sweep the waters south of Stadlandet. The enemy, however, reversed course soon after he had been sighted; our reconnaissance aircraft lost touch, and the striking forces which had

---

[1] In the telegram referred to here Mr Churchill told Stalin 'The December PQ convoy has prospered so far beyond all expectation. I have now arranged to send a full convoy of thirty or more ships through in January, though whether they will go in one portion or two is not yet settled by the Admiralty'. In the event only fourteen ships sailed in the January convoy (JW.52) but twenty-eight were sent in February (JW.53). See below pp. 399–400.

[2] See pp. 280–285.

[3] See pp. 292–298.

[4] See Map 37 (opp. p. 363).

been sent out failed to find him. Meanwhile the heavy ships of the Home Fleet in Hvalfiord had made ready to deal with an Atlantic break-out; but none of these precautions were actually necessary.

A fortnight later the German warships repeated the attempt to pass to north Norway. Though they were again sighted off the Skaw, the very bad weather 'robbed [our aircraft] of their prey', and they again reached home safely. Admiral Tovey and Air Marshal Joubert now discussed ways and means of improving our air shadowing tactics; but in truth it was the weather rather than any fault in the conduct of the searches which had defeated Coastal Command.

Early in February the *Hipper* and *Köln* returned to the Baltic, leaving only the *Tirpitz*, *Lützow* and *Nürnberg* in the north. When the enemy announced that Dönitz had succeeded to Raeder, Admiral Tovey expected greater enterprise to be shown in attacks on our convoys in the Barents Sea and that 'a chance for us to accept fleet action under conditions of exceptional favour might occur', or that the enemy 'might venture all on a desperate break-out' into the Atlantic. He and the Admiralty reviewed the steps needed to cope with either eventuality. They were to bear fruit at the end of the year, though not until after Admiral Tovey had relinquished command of the Home Fleet.

To retrace our steps for a short distance, convoy JW.52, originally of fourteen ships, enjoyed unusually good weather and made a fast passage. One merchantman had to be sent back, but the remainder arrived at Kola Inlet on the 27th of January. Enemy air attacks were on a small scale, and the escort drove off the U-boats by energetic counter-action based largely on direction-finding wireless reception. The cruiser covering force (the *Kent*, *Glasgow* and *Bermuda*) went right through with the convoy, and Admiral Fraser (Second-in-Command, Home Fleet) in the *Anson* provided distant cover from a position south-west of Bear Island. Only two days' rest were allowed to the escorts, and then they sailed again with the eleven ships which were all that were ready to join the homeward-bound convoy RA.52. One ship was sunk by a U-boat on 'the nineteenth consecutive day for the majority of the escort in these wintry northern waters'. The rest of the convoy arrived at Loch Ewe on the 8th of February.

The next east-bound convoy (J.W.53), for which only twenty-eight of the thirty ships detailed for it were ready, sailed a week later. The initial escorts were relieved off Iceland by the *Scylla* (Captain I. A. P. Macintyre), the escort carrier *Dasher* and fifteen destroyers. It was essential to protect this convoy on the full 'summer scale' because, in the Barents Sea, the hours of daylight were now increasing rapidly. Admiral Burnett, in the *Belfast*, with the *Sheffield* and *Cumberland* provided the cruiser cover, while the heavy ships of the fleet carried out their usual watchful rôle of distant cover.

Exceptionally severe gales beset the convoy. The *Dasher* and *Sheffield*
were both damaged and had to return, as did several merchantmen.
The main convoy was badly scattered and delayed, but by the 20th
twenty-two ships were rounded up by the escorts. Thereafter they
made good progress. Though the convoy was sighted and shadowed
by enemy aircraft, bombing attacks were light, and the escorts again
kept U-boats at a distance. All twenty-two ships reached Russian
ports safely.

The corresponding homeward convoy (RA.53) of thirty ships was
less fortunate—chiefly because another heavy gale caused the
merchantmen to scatter; and that, as so often before, gave the U-
boats their chance. Three ships fell victim to them, and one foundered
in the gale. On the 8th of March our reconnaissance aircraft found
that the *Scharnhorst* had left Gdynia. Admiral Fraser in the *Anson*
moved to Hvalfiord. The fleet carriers *Indomitable* and *Furious*, which
were in the Clyde, came to short notice and the usual air and surface-
ship 'break-out' patrols were restarted in the Denmark Strait and
the Iceland-Faeroes passage. Cruisers were sent out from Seidisfiord
to meet the approaching convoy RA.53.

On the 11th the *Tirpitz* was sighted leaving Trondheim, and our
aircraft soon found that she, the *Scharnhorst* and the *Lützow* were all in
Altenfiord. Dönitz had by this time pursuaded Hitler to revoke his
'irrevocable decision' to pay off the big ships[1], and thus we were
faced with the most powerful concentration yet assembled in the far
north. To provide additional safety to our Atlantic shipping the
American Task Force 22, which normally included a battleship and
a fleet carrier and had recently been covering the convoys from
America to North Africa, now reassembled in Casco Bay (near Portland in the Gulf of Maine) and was placed prospectively under
Admiral Tovey's control if a break-out into the Atlantic should take
place. 'The return of this force at the time of the enemy concentration
in Norway', wrote the Commander-in-Chief, 'was most welcome'.

Although the Atlantic routes were thus well covered from Scapa,
Iceland and the American coast, the Arctic route could not be
similarly safeguarded. With the hours of daylight now greatly
lengthened and so powerful an enemy squadron in Altenfiord,
Admiral Tovey considered the risks involved in sailing further convoys to Russia unjustified. Even such strong escorts as had been
provided in the previous summer could not guard against a surface
ship threat on this scale.[2] If the convoys must continue, the battle
fleet would therefore have to be sent into the Barents Sea—a risk
which the Commander-in-Chief had always been unwilling to
accept. The attitude of the Russians themselves was, at this time,

[1] See pp. 299 and 353–354.
[2] See pp. 280–282.

Convoy JW.53 passing through pack ice on passage to North Russia, February 1943.
(See pp. 399–400).

Clearing ice from the forecastle of H.M.S. *Scylla* while escorting convoy JW.53,
February 1943.

Destroyers *Matchless*, *Musketeer* and *Mahratta* in rough seas in the Arctic.

Merchantmen of Convoy JW.53 arrive North Russia, February 1943. H.M.S. *Norfolk* and two destroyers of escort shown. (See pp. 399–400).

hardly calculated to improve our willingness to accept great risks with our fleet on their behalf; for they started a new campaign of obstruction against our officers in North Russia, and lost no opportunity of indulging in the exasperating game of pin-pricking their Allies. Two of the four British wireless stations in the north were closed in February, and permission was refused to land the R.A.F. ground staff, which was essential to the running of summer convoys. Such a policy, which seems to have been dictated from Moscow and was 'apparently repugnant' to the Russian naval Commander-in-Chief in the north, must in any case have made continuation of the convoys difficult. But in the event it was another, and overwhelmingly important, factor which was decisive. For it was in this same month of March 1943 that Dönitz made his supreme effort with the U-boats against our Atlantic convoys, and we were suffering terrible losses there.[1] By postponing the next pair of Russian convoys, about twenty-seven flotilla vessels and an escort carrier could be released from the Home Fleet to reinforce the hard-pressed Atlantic escort groups. The crisis which had arisen in our one absolutely vital theatre was so serious that all other needs had to be sacrificed to meet it. As Mr Churchill told the President, 'the sinkings in the North Atlantic of seventeen ships in two days in convoys HX.229 and SC.122[2] are a final proof that our escorts are everywhere too thin. The strain upon the British Navy is becoming intolerable'. Mr Roosevelt agreed, and at the end of March every possible escort vessel was accordingly transferred from the Home Fleet to the Western Approaches Command. At the same time the final decision was taken to postpone the sailing of the next pair of Arctic convoys. This rapid switch of our flotilla strength was as successful as it was necessary, for it was mainly these splendidly trained and led ships which were formed into the Atlantic 'Support Groups'; and their great contribution to the 'Triumph of the Escorts' in May 1943 has already been recorded.[3]

As no more convoys sailed to the Arctic until November we may summarise the results achieved in this phase. Enemy air and submarine attacks had been much lighter than in the preceding phase, and no losses were caused to the warships involved on either side.

While the Battle of the Atlantic was rising to its climax, and was being fought with unparalleled ferocity, comparative quiet reigned in the northern waters for which the Home Fleet was responsible. The removal of a large part of Admiral Tovey's destroyer strength was bound to cramp the offensive use of the rest of his fleet. Furthermore several cruisers and destroyers were lent to the Commander-

---

[1] See pp. 365–368.
[2] See pp. 365–366 and Map 38 (opp. p. 365).
[3] See pp. 373–377.

in-Chief, Plymouth, in May, to cover convoys crossing the Bay of
Biscay against attack by the German destroyers which had reached
Bordeaux.

Table No. 37. *Russian Convoys, 1st January–31st May, 1943*

Convoy	No. of Ships	Ships Turned Back	Ships Sunk	Ships Arrived	Escort Losses	Enemy Losses
JW.52 . .	14	1	0	13	Nil	2 aircraft
RA.52 .	11	0	1	10	Nil	—
JW.53 . .	28	6	0	22	Nil	—
RA.53 .	30	0	4 (1 by weather)	26	Nil	—
Independents (all Russian)	6	0	2	4	—	—
TOTALS .	83+6 Independents	7	5+2 Independents	71+4 Independents	—	2 aircraft

In the same month substantial transfers of strength took place
between the Home and Mediterranean fleets, with the purpose of
building up our forces on the latter station for the invasion of Sicily.
The new battleships *King George V* and *Howe* went out, and the
Rodney followed the *Malaya* home. To compensate for this weakening
of the Home Fleet the American battleships *South Dakota* and *Alabama*, with five destroyers, under Rear-Admiral O. M. Hustvedt,
U.S.N., came from Argentia to Scapa. On the enemy's side the
Tirpitz, *Scharnhorst* and *Lützow* all remained in the far north, but the
Nürnberg went back to the Baltic early in May. She was several times
sighted between Stadlandet and Stavanger[1], and Coastal Command's torpedo-bombers were sent to attack; they failed, however, to
find her. Two of our motor torpedo-boats attacked the light craft
which were escorting the enemy cruiser, but success eluded them as
well. In our home waters the phase thus ended in a state of suspense.
The powerful enemy squadron in the north remained a serious
challenge, and it was impossible for us to attack it at such a distance
from our home bases. Nor could the long-range bombers and torpedo-
bombers deal with the enemy squadron effectively, unless they could
work from north Russia; and, apart from the climatic and administrative difficulties of doing that, we were unwilling to jeopardise our
still inadequate air striking power by sending a large proportion of it
to so great a distance, except during the passage of the Arctic convoys. Because the few torpedo-bombers available at home might at
any time be needed off southern Norway, or in the northern passage
to the Atlantic, we could not afford to keep them in Russia waiting
for an enemy sortie from Altenfiord. Moreover if they were sent
there heavy losses were likely to be incurred on the ground, for the

---

[1] See Map 37 (opp. p. 363).

Russian bases were still ill-defended. All Admiral Tovey could do was to keep his heavy ships disposed at Scapa and at Hvalfiord, so as to cover the Atlantic passages, while he awaited the return of his flotilla strength and the resumption of the Russian convoys. The latter was bound to lead to further heavy demands on his fleet, and to reintroduce the possibility of another major clash with the German surface ships. But neither was to come to pass within the period of Admiral Tovey's command, for on the 8th of May he struck his flag and was succeeded by his second-in-command, Admiral Sir Bruce Fraser.

For two and a half years Admiral Tovey had commanded the fleet to whose officers and men he now paid warm tribute for their 'devotion to duty . . .and their cheerful patience in bleak surroundings'. He also recorded his 'appreciation of the whole-hearted co-operation received from Coastal and Fighter Commands [of the Royal Air Force]', and his admiration for the gallant perseverance of the aircrews'. The action for which Admiral Tovey will, of course, be chiefly remembered is the chase and sinking of the *Bismarck* in May 1941.[1] It happened early in his period of command—nearly two years before his relief. Nothing of equal dramatic interest took place during the succeeding two years; yet month after month his ships had fought the Russian convoys through, had provided reinforcements for the Malta convoys and sometimes for still more distant operations, had covered the vital Atlantic passages, and had never relaxed the watch on the enemy's major warships. It was those 'far distant ships' of the Home Fleet which made much else possible. Without them the Atlantic convoys could not have gone steadily on, to and fro, winter and summer; nor could the Middle East troop convoys have been sent safely off on the first stretch of their long journeys, nor the coastal convoys sailed along the routes which girdled the British Isles. The Home Fleet's strength helped to launch the first strategic offensive in Africa, and it contributed greatly to the offensive harrying of the enemy's coastal shipping. All these, and many other equally important duties had been faithfully and unremittingly carried out throughout Admiral Tovey's long period in command; his fleet knew him and trusted him to lead them to victory whenever the chance should arise. In his dealings with the Admiralty, and even with the Prime Minister, Admiral Tovey had been outspoken if he felt that unacceptable demands were being made; and his forthright opinions had not always been welcomed in London. None the less his courage and his utter integrity inspired confidence throughout the fleet, which he turned over to his former second-in-command in splendid fighting order. His next appointment was that of Commander-in-Chief, The Nore.

[1] See Vol. I, Chapter XIX.

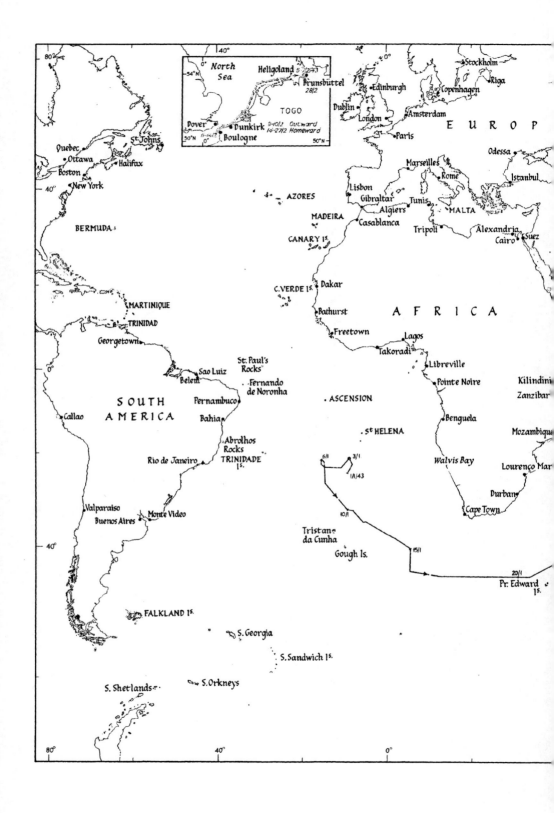

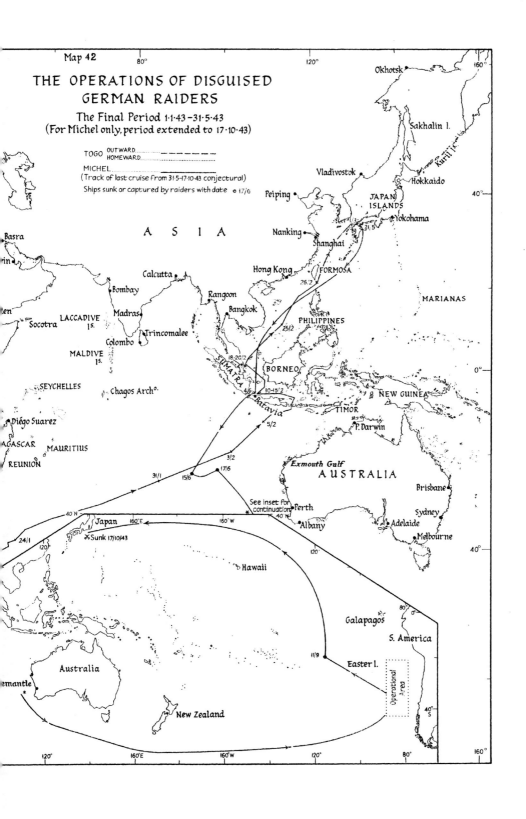

Map 42

THE OPERATIONS OF DISGUISED
GERMAN RAIDERS
The Final Period 1·1·43 – 31·5·43
(For Michel only, period extended to 17·10·43)

TOGO OUTWARD.......... — — — — —
HOMEWARD..........
MICHEL.................. ——————————
(Track of last cruise from 31·5–17·10·43 conjectural)
Ships sunk or captured by raiders with date   ○ 17/6

CHAPTER XVII

OCEAN WARFARE
1st January–31st May, 1943

> 'Much if not most of the Navy's work goes on unseen'.
>
> Mr. Churchill. At a conference of Ministers, 20th April 1943.

AT the beginning of 1943 ocean warfare in the sense in which it has so far been treated in these volumes, namely the *guerre de course* by enemy surface warships and disguised raiders, had almost become a thing of the past. No German or Italian warships had broken out into the Atlantic since May 1941, and the powerful foray by the Japanese into the Bay of Bengal in April 1942 was the only occasion on which they adopted commerce raiding on a big scale.[1] Only two disguised raiders appeared in this phase, and the defeat of the *Togo's* intended break-out down the English Channel in February has already been described.[2] The other German raider was the *Michel* (Raider H). It was told in an earlier chapter how, late in December 1942, she returned from the Indian Ocean to her favourite hunting ground in the Atlantic south of St. Helena, and that while there her captain received instructions to go to Japan instead of returning to western France.[3] On the 3rd of January she found one more victim in the Atlantic, the British ship *Empire March*, after which she again rounded the Cape of Good Hope and steamed right across the Indian Ocean to Java.[4] She then spent a few days in Batavia and Singapore before sailing up the China Sea to Japan. On the 2nd of March she arrived at Kobe. We will return to her final cruise later.

But if ocean raiding of the type which we had experienced from the beginning had by this time been defeated, in another sense the whole maritime war was now ocean warfare; for the U-boats were ranging far and wide in their endeavour to find lightly protected targets, and had in fact taken over the work of the earlier surface raiders in the more distant waters. To illustrate what this meant to Britain and her Allies we may remind the reader that in October

---

[1] See p. 28.
[2] See pp. 387–388.
[3] See p. 268.
[4] See Map 42.

1940 we were giving anti-submarine escort to our Atlantic convoys for only the first three or four hundred miles of their journeys.[1] Now not only were all the north and central Atlantic mercantile and military convoys escorted right through to their destinations, but anti-submarine escorts had also to be found for the remote focal areas such as the Cape of Good Hope, the Caribbean, off West Africa and Ceylon, and as far away as Australia.[2] The effort which the newer, long-range U-boats forced us to deploy was far greater than had been needed to deal with the ocean raiders. We could never have enough escorts everywhere, so it was natural that a sudden appearance by U-boats in distant waters would still sometimes bring them substantial, if short-lived, success. When the air and surface escorts arrived, or were reinforced, things quickly became too hot for them and they moved elsewhere. Their excursions into distant seas regularly followed this pattern in 1943.

At the beginning of the year there were actually few U-boats in remote waters. Four were working in the Caribbean, two were off the coast of Brazil and one was cruising between Freetown and Natal in Brazil. In January a group of four large boats accompanied by a U-tanker left for the Cape of Good Hope. On Hitler's orders one of them, U.180, had embarked at Kiel the Indian nationalist leader Chandra Bose, who had reached Germany from Russia. The U-boat was also to carry a special cargo of constructional drawings and war material for the Japanese. She sailed on the 9th of February, and passed round the north of the British Isles into the Atlantic. After fuelling from another U-boat in mid-ocean she rounded the Cape of Good Hope on the 12th-13th of April, and met a Japanese submarine to the south of Madagascar on the 23rd. Cargoes were exchanged with some difficulty, owing to heavy seas, but by the 29th U.180 started her homeward journey with, among other items, two tons of gold aboard. She arrived at Bordeaux on the 3rd of July. Chandra Bose and his adjutant were landed safely in southern India, with the object of stirring up trouble for those who were trying to defend that country.

On reaching their operational area off the Cape the U-boats found that conditions had completely changed since the first group had achieved its big successes there late in 1942.[3] Nearly all shipping was now convoyed through the focus, and air escorts were regularly present. From the Cape the U-boats worked up the east coast of Africa as far as Durban and Lourenço Marques, and it was off the former port that, early in March, U.160 sank four ships totalling 25,852 tons from a convoy. Though this success to the enemy was an

---

[1] See Vol. I, Map 9.
[2] See p. 415 regarding Japanese submarines off eastern Australia at this time.
[3] See pp. 269-271.

isolated one it caused the Prime Minister to be 'shocked at the renewed disaster off the Cape'. 'We simply cannot afford losses of this kind on this route' he minuted to the First Lord and First Sea Lord.[1] The Admiralty replied at length, stating the policy for convoying shipping off South Africa, the surface and air escorts available and the reinforcements expected, and pointed out that, out of the vast volume of shipping passing through the focus, we had only lost seven ships since convoy was introduced. 'Nowhere', said the First Lord, 'either in the North Atlantic, the Mediterranean, off Freetown or the Cape are we sufficiently strong to be able to guarantee the safety of every convoy'. Mr Churchill replied that he was 'sure the Admiralty, as ever, are doing their best'.[2] The total successes of the U-boats in South African waters amounted to fifteen ships of 76,948 tons in February and March 1943.

Apart from operations in the North Atlantic, which Dönitz considered the only theatre where a decision could be obtained, the most substantial successes were achieved to the south of the Azores. It was there that U.514, returning from the Caribbean, sighted the tanker convoy TM.1 bound for Gibraltar from Trinidad on the 3rd of January. Five days later twelve U-boats had assembled, and between them they sank seven tankers.[3] The group then refuelled from a 'milch cow' and continued to work in the same waters. They were still being aided by the enemy's ability to decypher certain Allied convoy signals. Towards the end of February the chance sighting of a convoy of empty tankers bound for Curaçao led to a long pursuit in which three of the convoy and one U-boat were sunk.

In March the U-boats made a sudden return to the Caribbean, where they hoped to find that their recent neglect of those waters had led to a reduction of the American defences. Their hope was not fulfilled, but in an encounter with a convoy off French Guiana they sank two ships and damaged four others.

At the end of the month a few U-boats were sent to probe the defences off the east coast of North America. Their reception was not at all to their liking, for the surface escorts were now numerous and better trained, and the convoys had continuous air cover. Two U-boats were sunk by aircraft for a very small return to the enemy.

In April, before the Germans knew that the last group of U-boats sent to South Africa had not accomplished very satisfactory results, six more large boats were on their way to those same waters. They arrived in late April and early May, and worked in a similar fashion to their predecessors along the off-shore shipping routes from Walvis Bay in West Africa to Lourenço Marques or the Mozambique

---

[1] Churchill, Vol. IV, p. 832.
[2] Churchill, Vol. IV, p. 834.
[3] See p. 356.

Channel in the east.[1] Again they sought unescorted or lightly escorted targets, of which decreasing numbers were to be found. Their accomplishments were about the same as those of the previous group. Fourteen ships of 86,151 tons were sunk in those waters in April and May. Most of the group continued to work off the south and east coasts of Africa until August, when they started to withdraw eastwards to replenish at Penang. Sinkings in June and July were 67,000 and 89,000 tons respectively—almost all of them independents.

It was mentioned earlier that in August 1942 the Germans started a second blockade running campaign, which aimed to bring 140,000 tons of dry cargo and 70,000 tons of 'edible oils' back from the Far East, and to send to Japan certain cargoes of specially valuable machinery and warlike stores.[2] This traffic continued until May 1943, when it died down; it was not renewed until the following autumn. The adventures of the blockade runners up to the end of 1942 have already been recounted.[3] Here we will take up the story of those which had not yet reached European waters, or had not yet sailed outward-bound at the start of the New Year.

Home Fleet cruisers were sent to patrol off the Azores in February, when several homeward-bound ships were expected to pass through the narrowest part of the Atlantic; but they had no luck until the 26th, when an American Liberator flying more than 800 miles from its base sighted a suspicious looking tanker, which she reported and then shadowed. The cruiser *Sussex*, on patrol about 190 miles away, intercepted the Liberator's signals and closed her position. That evening she caught and sank the tanker *Hohenfriedburg*, an ex-Norwegian prize.[4] The cruiser did not stop to pick up survivors for fear of U-boats in the vicinity. That her action was justified is shown by our present knowledge that three of them were escorting the tanker at the time, and that one actually fired a salvo of torpedoes at the *Sussex*. As a result of this success it was decided to put all operations against blockade runners under the Commander-in-Chief, Plymouth. One cruiser was always to be kept at that base, and in March several Home Fleet destroyers arrived to give the patrolling cruisers anti-submarine escort. The revival of the use of the great naval base at Plymouth for ocean operations in the South-West Approaches to these islands is to be remarked. Since July 1940, when all our Atlantic convoys were routed north of Ireland[5], Plymouth had been generally used only by Coastal Forces and Channel convoys, and as a base for special operations such as the raid on St.

---

[1] See Map 42 (opp. p. 405).
[2] See p. 273.
[3] See pp. 273–276.
[4] Originally named *Herborg*. See p. 178 regarding her capture.
[5] See Vol. I, p. 349.

Nazaire.[1] Now that operation 'Torch' had succeeded, and our command of the air over the Channel had so greatly improved, Plymouth resumed something of its old importance, even though our Atlantic convoys were not yet able to approach these islands by the shortest and traditional route south of Ireland.

The successes achieved by our intercepting forces early in the year led the Admiralty to expect the enemy to change his methods, and to send out several blockade runners simultaneously from the Biscay ports, on the chance that some of them would get through. This expectation was strengthened by the arrival of four of his large 'Narvik' class destroyers at Bordeaux early in March. It seemed certain that their purpose was to escort outward-bound blockade runners, and possibly to meet those which were homeward-bound as well. In addition they might be used to attack our convoys running to and from Gibraltar, which therefore still had to be strongly escorted. The Admiralty's deductions were correct, except that the Germans used U-boats rather than surface ships to meet the inward-bound blockade runners. The U-boat command strongly disliked the diversion of their forces from offensive operations to the passive rôle of providing escorts, but the German Naval Staff had its way, and the practice became common at this time.

On our side the Commanders-in-Chief, Home Fleet, Plymouth and Coastal Command were all concerned in the efforts to catch the blockade runners. As soon as there were indications of activity, Coastal Command started to watch the Gironde ports, and warned all its aircraft flying on Bay patrols to look out for suspicious ships. On the 17th of March the cruiser *Newfoundland* and two destroyers were sent to Plymouth, all naval and air forces were brought to the alert, and systematic air searches were flown for several days. We now know that three blockade runners sailed outward-bound at the end of March. One (the Italian ship *Himalaya*) was sighted by an aircraft and forced to turn back, another (the *Osorno*) was sighted but got through, while the third (the *Portland*) was not sighted at all. The *Osorno* reached Japan, but the *Portland* was sunk in the Atlantic by the French cruiser *Georges Leygues* on the 13th of April.

At the time when these outward movements were taking place our intelligence indicated that certain inward-bound ships were approaching. Wide air searches were organised, British and American submarines were sent on patrol in the Bay, and the escorts of convoys running to and from Gibraltar were warned to be on the lookout. But it was a German U-boat which caused the first casualty. The *Doggerbank* was an ex-British prize, the *Speybank*. She was unexpectedly sighted by U.43 off the Canaries on the 3rd of March, a

---

[1] See pp. 168–173.

long way from where she should have been. The U-boat mis-identified her and sank her. The incident is of interest to show how the enemy, for all that he had very few merchantmen at sea, found it difficult to keep constant track of their positions. It will be re-membered that we were constantly plagued by similar difficulties of identification, when our warships sighted suspicious vessels.[1] A week after the sinking of the *Doggerbank*, American warships caught the *Kota Nopan*, an ex-Dutch prize, south of the equator[2]; but the Italian ship *Pietro Orseolo*, though torpedoed by an American sub-marine off the Gironde on the 1st of April, succeeded in making harbour with most of her cargo intact.

Our intelligence next suggested that the enemy might try once again to get his ships home by the Denmark Strait or the Iceland-Faeroes passage[3], even though he had not sent blockade runners north-about since 1939. Admiral Tovey accordingly sent cruisers to patrol those routes, and air co-operation was arranged with the Iceland Air Force. These measures were quickly rewarded when on the 30th of March the cruiser *Glasgow* caught the *Regensburg* off the north of Iceland. The surface patrols in the northern passages were maintained for a few weeks longer, but indications that U-boats were moving that way then made their withdrawal advisable. Actually the enemy sent no more ships by the northern route.

April saw a second attempt to break out by the *Himalaya*, but she was again sighted, damaged by bombs and put back for the second time. Next on the 9th of that month, German destroyers were seen to have left Bordeaux and air searches were begun. The minelayer *Adventure*, which was homeward-bound from the Mediterranean, intercepted the *Irene* (ex *Silvaplana*) from Japan next evening off Finisterre.

The enemy's second blockade running effort now ended. In the sum its results were far less satisfactory to him than the previous campaign between April 1941 and May 1942. Of the fifteen ships which sailed homeward four were recalled to Japan and seven were sunk. Three-quarters of their total cargoes (122,900 tons) were lost. Of seventeen outward-bound ships, three were recalled or turned back, and four were sunk. Less than 25,000 tons of cargo were delivered to Japan.[4] On our side the intelligence which gave warning of the enemy movements had been excellent, but it had not been found at all easy to catch the ships. Air searches were invaluable to

---

[1] See Vol. I, p. 549.

[2] See Vol. I, pp. 381 and 547 regarding the capture of the *Speybank* and *Kota Nopan* respectively.

[3] See Map 37 (opp. p. 363).

[4] To compare with the results obtained in the 1941–42 campaign see pp. 182–183 and Appendix N.

locate them, but the Commander-in-Chief, Coastal Command, disliked using his precious long-range aircraft for such purposes at a time when they were badly needed to escort our convoys far out in the Atlantic. Casualties were very probable if they flew near to the Spanish coast, or if they made low attacks on ships furnished with powerful anti-aircraft armaments. But the Cabinet and Chiefs of Staff attached importance to stopping these leaks in the blockade, and whenever intelligence indicated the departure or approach of enemy ships the Admiralty continued to demand wide air searches. Nor were our patrolling submarines more successful than our aircraft in sinking the blockade runners. To illustrate the difficulty our aircraft experienced in identifying a suspicious ship with certainty, one blockade runner was sighted and photographed in the Bay; but when she hoisted the Red Ensign the aircraft forebore to attack. It was indeed soon found that air searches were indispensable to locate, and often to shadow the ships; but that interception by surface warships working in close co-operation with the aircraft was the only sure way of bringing the blockade runners finally to book.

Although we here have considered only the efforts made to deal with the blockade runners at the European end of their journeys, in fact world-wide steps were taken to track them. For example the cruisers of the South Atlantic Command repeatedly swept the southern Indian Ocean looking for the *Dresden*, which was believed to have left Saigon late in 1942. But she got through to Bordeaux safely. Indeed there is no doubt that we had to devote a big effort to preventing these comparatively few cargoes from reaching the enemy, nor that he exhibited considerable ingenuity in getting even a proportion of them through the oceans which we and our Allies were controlling ever more tightly.

In May, at about the time when the last of the blockade runners of the 1942-43 wave was approaching France, the last German disguised raider, the *Michel*, sailed from Japan. Although her cruise takes us beyond the period covered by this volume, we will follow her now to the end of her career. For her last cruise the *Michel* was commanded by the former captain of the *Thor*, whose ship was blown up in Yokohama in November 1942.[1] She replenished in Batavia and then passed into the Indian Ocean, where she sank two ships.[2] Because her Captain could find few targets there he next moved right across the Pacific. On the 11th of September the *Michel* sank a large Norwegian tanker, the *India*, off Easter Island. That was her last victim. In mid-October she reported herself to Berlin when about three days steaming from Yokohama. On the 17th of October she was sunk to the south of that port by the American submarine

[1] See p. 267.
[2] See Map 42 (opp. p. 405).

Tarpon. A Japanese escort which should have met the raider failed to do so, but the *Michel's* captain certainly took few precautions for his ship's safety when passing through waters in which he must have known that Allied submarines might be encountered.

Thus disappeared the last of the long line of German disguised raiders. Her active career had been a long one, lasting from the 20th of March 1942 to the 17th of October 1943, during which she covered thousands of miles of ocean. In all she sank seventeen ships of 121,994 tons; but most of her successes were obtained under her first captain in the South Atlantic.[1]

We may here summarise the results of the enemy's *guerre de course.* During the period covered by this volume the only merchantmen sunk by German surface warships were in our Russian convoys; and even there it was the U-boats and aircraft which did by far the greatest damage. In the broad oceans from the 1st of January 1942 until the sinking of the *Michel,* German disguised raiders sank thirty-one ships of 207,437 tons.[2] Japanese auxiliary cruisers added a further four ships of 29,033 tons. Although raiders caused us a good deal of trouble and anxiety, the total number of their victims forms but a tiny proportion of the vast allied military and mercantile traffic which traversed the oceans in that period. They never approached the U-boat, nor even air attacks and minelaying, in the losses they caused and the difficulties they produced. None the less the cost to the enemy of fitting out and operating such ships cannot have been heavy. As long as their expectation of life was reasonable, and a fair number of unescorted ships could be found, he was probably right in considering that they yielded a sufficient return to justify themselves. But by the middle of 1943 neither condition held good, and it is not surprising that the disguised raider now disappears from the scene.

---

[1] See pp. 267–268.

[2] The individual accomplishments of disguised raiders are given in Appendix M.

CHAPTER XVIII

THE PACIFIC AND INDIAN OCEANS
1st January–31st May, 1943

> 'Attack, not defence, was the road to sea
> power in his [i.e. Suffren's] eyes; and sea
> power meant control of the issues on land,
> at least in regions distant from Europe'.
> A. T. Mahan. *The Influence of Sea
> Power on History*, p. 425.

W E must now return briefly to the struggle in the East, which
we left at the turn of the year. Compared with the many
hard-fought sea and air battles which had punctuated the
preceding phase, the first half of 1943 was relatively quiet. The
dangerous Japanese thrusts against Midway, against Port Moresby
and against the islands which formed the reinforcement links from
America to Australia and New Zealand, had all been parried, though
at a heavy cost in Allied ships and aircraft. It was natural that a
period of recuperation should now be needed, to prepare for the
next offensives.

At the Casablanca Conference various decisions affecting the war
against Japan had been taken. That with which we here are principally concerned was the decision to mount twin offensives from
New Guinea and the Solomons, with the object of breaking through
the powerful enemy defences based on New Britain, New Ireland
and the other islands of the Bismarck Archipelago, which barred the
approaches to the Philippines from the south-east.[1] This defensive
position was aptly called the 'Bismarck barrier' by the Americans. The
key to it lay in Rabaul, with its fine harbour and several adjacent
airfields.

The South and South-West Pacific commands, of Admiral Halsey
and General MacArthur respectively, were both concerned in the
prosecution of this object. In March their naval forces were renamed
the 3rd and 7th Fleets, and each of them included an 'Amphibious
Force' trained and organised to undertake the new offensive.[2] That
of the 7th Fleet was building up at Brisbane under Rear-Admiral

---

[1] See Map 2 (opp. p. 9).

[2] The American fleets in the Pacific were given odd numbers, namely the 3rd (South),
5th (Central) and 7th (South-West) Pacific Fleets. Those in the Atlantic and in European
waters were given even numbers.

D. E. Barbey, while Halsey's amphibious flotillas remained under
Rear-Admiral R. K. Turner, who had already gained great experience of that type of work in the Guadalcanal landings.[1] His bases
were at Noumea in New Caledonia and Espiritu Santo in the New
Hebrides.

Not only was Brisbane the base of the 7th Fleet's Amphibious
Force, but a growing flotilla of American submarines was now working from there. During the present phase its strength reached
twenty boats. Another flotilla was at Fremantle in Western
Australia, with an advanced base in Exmouth Gulf.[2] Their hunting
ground was mainly in the approaches to the Dutch East Indies.
Yet more American submarines were reaching out from Pearl Harbour to the coast of the Japanese mainland, and their individual
performances had greatly improved since the early months. The
total Japanese merchant shipping losses in this phase was 152 ships
of 666,472 tons, of which 105 ships of 479,918 tons were sunk by
submarines. The rate of loss was far more than Japan could sustain.
For the first time her Government became alarmed at the decline of
her mercantile tonnage; yet it was not until the autumn of 1943
that, except in forward areas, an attempt was made to work an
ocean convoy system. By then it was too late. By contrast to the
heavy blows struck at Japan's sea communications, her own submarines caused us few losses. The Japanese Navy still clung to the
idea that the functions of its submarine arm were to make reconnaissances for the main fleet and to ambush the other side's major
warships. It is interesting to remark that we held to very similar
ideas regarding the functions of our submarines for the first eighteen
months of the war, and had been markedly reluctant to free them
for attack on merchant shipping, even after the enemy had adopted
unrestricted submarine warfare.[3] Though Japanese submarines had
scored some outstanding successes in the preceding phases, notably
by sinking the *Yorktown* and *Wasp* and damaging the *Saratoga* and
North Carolina, they were now doing us little harm; and twelve of their
number were sunk within the South and South-West Pacific Commands between the start of the Solomons campaign in August 1942
and the end of the present phase.[4]

The American 3rd and 7th Fleets were, of course, divided into
Task Groups and Task Forces to undertake particular operations, as
each need arose. The naval forces directly under General Mac-
Arthur were however still very slender. Rear-Admiral V. A. C.
Crutchley, V.C., had the cruisers *Australia* and *Hobart* (R.A.N.) and

---

[1] See p. 222.
[2] See Map 42 (opp. p. 405).
[3] See Vol. I, pp. 355 and 438–9.
[4] See Appendix J for details.

the *Phoenix* (U.S.N.) under his command; but that was all there was to supply a 'battle force'.[1] Moreover here as in every other theatre there was a chronic shortage of flotilla vessels, many of which had to be detached at this time to escort convoys up and down the east coast of Australia, where Japanese U-boats had made their presence felt by sinking several Allied ships.

Halsey's 3rd Fleet was a very different affair from his neighbour's 7th Fleet. True he was still weak in fleet carriers, since only the *Saratoga* and *Enterprise* had survived the earlier clashes, and none of the new *Essex* class had yet commissioned for service[2]; but in addition to the *Saratoga*'s and *Enterprise*'s Task Forces he had two others composed of battleships and escort carriers (the latter brought in to mitigate the weakness in large carriers), and two more comprising good modern cruisers and destroyers. These latter forces had been specially formed to work in 'the Slot' north of Guadalcanal, and were commanded by Rear-Admirals W. L. Ainsworth and A. S. Merrill, U.S.N. We shall meet them again later in our story. The ships of the New Zealand Navy (the cruisers *Achilles* and *Leander*, and a number of smaller vessels) were placed under Admiral Halsey, and a number of R.N.Z.A.F. squadrons also came up to join the South Pacific Air Command of Vice-Admiral A. W. Fitch, U.S.N.

It was at the urgent request of the Americans, made at a time when they were in dire straits for fast aircraft carriers, that the British *Victorious* (Captain L. D. Mackintosh) was sent to the Pacific.[3] She reached Pearl Harbour on the 4th of March, and at once started training her ship's company and aircrews in American methods. In April she spent several periods exercising at sea off Pearl Harbour, and on the 8th of May sailed for Nouméa with the battleship *North Carolina* to relieve the *Enterprise*, whose bomb damage had not yet been properly repaired, in Admiral Halsey's 3rd Fleet. The *Saratoga* and *Victorious* exercised together from Nouméa, and Captain Mackintosh soon reported that his ship had found no difficulty in settling down with her new companion; they were perfectly capable of operating each other's aircraft. These two ships remained the only fleet carriers in the South Pacific until the next phase, when the centre of gravity of the war against Japan moved from the south to the central Pacific, and the Americans formed the famous 'Fast Carrier Striking Force'.

It was to be expected that during this period of weakness in air striking power Halsey would remain on the defensive, for there

---

[1] See Vol. I, p. 9 fn (1) for definition of 'battle force'.

[2] The *Essex*, the first of her class of new fleet carriers, commissioned on the 31st of December 1942. Sixteen more were completed before the end of the war. The early ships displaced 27,100 tons and carried about 90 aircraft. Later models displaced 30,800 tons and carried 100 aircraft.

[3] See pp. 230–231.

were no replacements for the last two Allied carriers. But Yamamoto, who again possessed four carriers (*Zuikaku, Zuiho, Junyo* and *Hiyo*), might well have seized the chance to avenge Midway, by provoking another battle with Halsey. As it turned out he chose a totally different strategy, as will be told later, and threw away his temporary advantage. It thus happened that the *Victorious*, to her great disappointment, never got the chance to show her mettle in a great carrier air battle like Coral Sea, Midway, the Eastern Solomons or Santa Cruz[1]; but her presence in a predominantly American fleet at a critical time at least showed that, in spite of its overriding responsibilities in connection with the defeat of Germany, the British Government were anxious to contribute to the Pacific struggle.

The Japanese base at Buna on the north coast of Papua was captured on the 2nd of January, and before the end of that month the Australians and Americans had cleared the Papuan peninsula of enemies. An advance base was then immediately set up at Milne Bay, on the tip of the peninsula, for use by the 7th Fleet's amphibious force.[2] The Japanese, who realised the threat developing towards Rabaul, were meanwhile reinforcing Lae and Salamaua on the north coast of New Guinea and extending their hold on that island to the westward. It will be seen how important to both sides were these hitherto practically unknown tropical harbours, and their adjacent air strips. Possession by one side or the other could, and often did, decide the outcome of the struggle for maritime control over vast areas. It is also in the early months of 1943 that we find in American planning circles the first thoughts regarding development of the 'leap-frogging' strategy, leaving enemy strong points untouched far in the rear of their thrusts. It was to become a marked feature of later phases. Our Allies realised, however, that, as long as a substantial proportion of their strength was devoted to the combined operations in North Africa and the Mediterranean, they must await the completion of new flotillas of landing ships and craft, and the training of many more men, before they could take such bold measures in the Pacific.

In the Solomons, the Japanese decision of the 4th of January to evacuate Guadalcanal did not slow down the tempo of the struggle. More American reinforcements were flung in early in the year without loss, while a diversionary night bombardment of the airfield and installations at Munda in New Georgia was carried out by a cruiser and destroyer task force.[3] It was during the withdrawal from this operation that the cruiser *Achilles* (R.N.Z.N.) was hit by a bomb, and had to be sent back to England to be fitted with a new turret.

---

[1] See pp. 35–36, 38–41, 226 and 228–229, respectively.
[2] See Map 5 (opp. p. 33).
[3] See Map 22 (opp. p. 220).

The need to send ships whose equipment had been damaged in battle half way round the world for repairs was one of the inescapable difficulties of operating British ships in waters where, since the loss of Singapore, we had no major base.

While the Americans' maritime control was thus sufficient to enable reinforcements to be landed safely on Guadalcanal from surface ships, the Japanese were forced to have recourse to supplying their garrison by submarine. In January as many as twenty were employed on such work, and it was one of them, the large boat I.1 of 1,955 tons, which was caught off Guadalcanal on the 29th by the little 600-ton minesweeping trawlers *Kiwi* and *Moa* of the New Zealand Navy. The submarine was fought, rammed, harried and finally driven ashore and destroyed by her diminutive adversaries.

The 'Tokyo Expresses' run down 'the Slot' by Japanese destroyers carrying reinforcements were now few and far between; but Japanese aircraft were still ranging over the approaches to the American bases in the Solomons, and they caused trouble to any ship caught without fighter cover. On the same day that the New Zealand trawlers scored their success, the heavy cruiser *Chicago* was damaged in a dusk torpedo-bomber attack off Rennell Island.[1] Next day, the 30th, Japanese aircraft sank her. She had been the first big American warship to join the hard-pressed Anzac squadron of the early days, and Anzac sailors were very sad to see her go.[2]

The Japanese were successful in disguising and concealing their intention to evacuate Guadalcanal. When, on the 1st of February, numerous destroyers were sighted coming down 'the Slot' it was thought that they must be bringing fresh troops and supplies. In fact they had been sent to embark the first elements of the Japanese garrison, which purpose they accomplished with only slight loss. On the nights of the 4th and 7th two more evacuations were successfully carried out, and by the morning of the 8th the Americans were surprised to find they no longer had any enemies facing them. One must give the Japanese credit for the skill with which they carried out these withdrawals, in waters where the greater degree of maritime control certainly rested with the Allies. Though it was disappointing that a garrison of some 12,000 men should be allowed to slip away to fight another day, the conquest of Guadalcanal was a valuable moral as well as strategic success to the Allies. As to the former, it had shown that well-trained and well-equipped men of all Allied services could fight and beat the Japanese on their own ground; its strategic significance was that the enemy thereby lost the initiative thoughout the whole south Pacific theatre, and the threat to the main Allied bases further south was finally eliminated.

[1] See Map 22 (opp. p. 220).
[2] See p. 7.

Though they had accepted defeat on Guadalcanal, the Japanese had no intention of abandoning the whole Solomons chain. In the vital matter of airfields, they were favourably placed to continue the struggle, for there were four near Rabaul, and five more had recently been constructed on various islands reaching down the Solomons as far as New Georgia. Their central strategic position, buttressed by the defences of the Bismarck archipelago, was plainly a powerful one; and the reinforcement routes from the Marshall Islands and from the Japanese homeland, though long, were reasonably adequate. Lastly they had some 200 aircraft in the theatre, and Yamamoto, though short of aircraft carriers and destroyers, still possessed a powerful fleet in the background. Though there were about 300 American aircraft of all types available in the Solomons theatre, they still only had Guadalcanal to serve as a forward base; and the Allies were, as has already been mentioned, weak in carrier air striking power. The Japanese belief that they could successfully defend the Bismarck barrier was certainly reasonable. What they could hardly have known was that the new types of American aircraft now coming into service were greatly superior to their own, and that American pilots were far better trained than formerly. It was the combination of stronger numbers and superior quality in the air which was to prove decisive. But the Japanese, like Hitler, made the mistake of frittering away much of their strength by trying to hold on everywhere; and their intention to do so was soon revealed by the construction of airfields at Munda in New Georgia and at Vila on Kolombangara Island only about 170 miles north-west of Guadalcanal.[1] These soon became favourite targets for bombing by the Americans and for bombardment by their cruisers and destroyers; but a coral air strip is easily repaired, and the damage done was never proportionate to the enormous quantities of explosive expended in such operations.

On the 29th of March the American Chiefs of Staff issued a new directive ordering MacArthur to clear eastern New Guinea and the Solomons of enemies, and to attack New Britain. Admiral Halsey was to work under the South-West Pacific Commander's strategic direction. Assaults on New Georgia and the Trobriand Islands off Papua were originally planned for mid-May, but had to be postponed several times. They did not finally take place until the next phase. Meanwhile on the 20th of February a force of 9,000 men was embarked to assault the small Russell Islands, just north of Guadalcanal.[2] On landing they encountered no opposition, and the operation was distinguished chiefly for the defeat by gunfire of a heavy night torpedo-bomber attack on the convoy on its way north on the

---

[1] See Map 22 (opp. p. 220).
[2] See Map 28 (opp. p. 293).

17th. It was one of the first occasions on which the new 'radio proximity' fuze was used against enemy aircraft, and it immediately proved its value.

It is worth making a brief digression into the technical field to give the story of this new development. British scientists and technicians had been working on the proximity anti-aircraft fuze since the early days of the war, and by 1940 they had achieved considerable progress. It was, however, far from being ready for production when the threat of invasion and the tense conditions of the war in the west made it very difficult for us to give the development the high priority it deserved. As with the results of our research into short-wave radar, the whole of the data and knowledge we had acquired regarding proximity fuzes was therefore given to the Americans. They devoted immense energy and effort to the problem of its design and production, and by early 1943 the fuzes were streaming off their production lines. To explain it briefly, the fuze consisted of a miniature radar set, powered by its own batteries, carried in the nose of each anti-aircraft shell. The signals sent out by this set were reflected off a solid object such as an aircraft, and when the interval between despatch of an outward signal and receipt of a reflected signal became very short (i.e. when the shell was passing close to the aircraft), the fuze detonated the shell. The principle was a fairly simple one, but the design was a remarkable achievement, and the mass production of so delicate and intricate a mechanism was one of the many miracles accomplished by American factories. The fuze was much superior to the previously used clockwork time fuzes, each of which had to be specially set before firing. We benefited later from this technical accomplishment, because large allocations of the fuzes were made to assist us to defeat the V-1 flying bomb, and it quickly proved itself the ideal counter to this new weapon. Furthermore British warships received fuzes specially made in America at a priority second only to meeting the U.S. Navy's own requirements. Britain and the Royal Navy owe a deep debt to the American Navy Department and to the Office of Scientific Research and Development for the speed and generosity with which our pressing needs for proximity fuzes were met.

In combined operations the need to plan so that the attackers will have a substantial local superiority over the defenders is undeniable. The degree of numerical superiority required has been variously assessed, from as low as two to one to as high as four to one. It is certain that no rigid rules can be laid down, for the success of each assault depends on a great many factors besides the numbers of fighting men who face each other at 'H hour'. Thus in the invasion of

the Admiralty Islands in 1944 the Japanese defenders greatly outnumbered the Allied attackers; yet the latter finally, if narrowly,
prevailed. On the other hand in the assault on Munda in 1943 and
on Tarawa in 1944 the attackers held a three to one superiority, and
it was barely sufficient. While we may accept that he would be a rash
Commander of an assault from the sea who did not try to achieve
numerical superiority over the defenders, the great strength deployed
by the Americans against the Russell Islands, and the quantity of
their shipping locked up in Pacific bases without any very apparent
effort to ensure that it was profitably employed, provide an opportunity to review the conflicts of strategy and of material allocations
which developed at this time. Enough has been written in this
volume to indicate the anxieties of the British Government at the
start of the fourth year of the war, and how serious was our situation
at that time. Shipping losses had been very high in 1942, and in no
small measure had they been due to the Americans' slowness in organising the defences on their eastern seaboard.[1] We had suffered
crushing defeats in the Far East, and were barely holding on in the
Indian Ocean. Imports had fallen drastically, and rationing was
tighter than ever before. In the autumn the heavy commitments of
Operation 'Torch' had to be met; and they were. While Britain,
though no less stubbornly determined to see the matter through to
victory than she had been in 1940, was thus very hard-pressed on
the oceans, and had been sorely battered in her cities and in every
theatre where her forces were engaged, it could not escape her
leaders' attention that great quantities of supplies were being sent
to Pacific bases, and that shipping was being used by our Allies in a
manner which to our austerity-bound island seemed extravagant.
In the relevant volume of the British Civil Histories the responsibility for this state of affairs has been placed mainly on the American
Chiefs of Staff, and on the lack of any civilian control over the
natural rapacity of all fighting services for ships[2]; and the present
writer's experiences in the Pacific certainly tend to support the view
that shipping was often used there in a very uneconomical manner.
At the same time, and in fairness to our Ally, it should be mentioned
that, because of the vast distances in that theatre, needs had to be
anticipated months in advance, and regardless of the fact that they
might have completely altered before the ships and landing craft,
the men and the stores, had reached their destinations. Furthermore
big combined operations had to be mounted from island bases where
there had originally been nothing whatsoever of military value.
Everything had to be hauled there from the west coast of America, or

---

[1] See pp. 93–102.
[2] See C. B. A. Behrens *Merchant Shipping and the Demands of War*, Chapters XII and
XX (H.M.S.O. and Longmans, Green & Co., 1955).

from Australia and New Zealand. Conditions in the Pacific thus differed considerably from those which prevailed in Africa and Europe. When in 1942 the time came to take the offensive against the Japanese, heavy losses of landing craft and of equipment, of which other theatres also stood in urgent need, were inevitable; for the assaults often had to be made over reefs and through heavy surf, and ships had generally to lie in exposed anchorages. Salvage and repair work were therefore both hazardous and difficult. As the momentum of the American offensive gathered, more and more ships, landing craft and stores were needed; and it is incontrovertible that in several critical instances the Americans found themselves short of small craft, or of essential equipment. Moreover in attempting to put the matter into fair perspective it is right to mention that the economical use of shipping was not aided by the dilatory work and repeated strikes by dockers in Antipodean ports. These, to the shame of the British race, often forced American combat troops to load their own ships, which was hardly the best preliminary to entering some of the most arduous fighting of the whole war. Finally, and in spite of the fact that certain authoritative American post-war publications have admitted that in some respects their supply organisation for the Pacific was unduly lavish[1], it should be recorded that every British ship that served in the theatre was allowed to draw freely on the U.S. Navy's stores, and to make the fullest use of its highly efficient maintenance and repair staff; and when the British Pacific Fleet arrived to take part in the final operations against Japan the Americans went far beyond the letter of their undertaking to assist with the supply and servicing of our ships.[2]

It is of course impossible to prove that, had shipping been more economically employed in the Pacific, the Allied victory would have come sooner; but it is certain that the apparently wasteful use of tonnage in that theatre caused grave concern in British circles at the time. At Casablanca it was decided that an offensive would be started in 1943 to drive the Japanese out of Burma. This major undertaking required not only great strengthening of our forces in India, which could only be done by sea, but a numerous and well-trained flotilla to work on the long and intricate Burma coast. At the Quebec Conference in August 1943 the British representatives made

---

[1] See for example *Air Campaigns in the Pacific War* (United States Strategic Bombing Survey, Military Analysis Division, July 1947) p. 62 para. 2.

[2] As an example of the U.S. Navy's efficiency and generosity in this respect it may be mentioned that, when the author's ship berthed for a short time in Pearl Harbour in May 1943, Admiral Nimitz at once boarded her, welcomed her officers and men, and placed the whole facilities of that great base at their disposal. By working night and day in continuous shifts for a week the Navy Yard put right virtually all her defects and deficiencies; and she sailed again for the Solomons theatre well equipped for action, and excellently supplied with stores.

it plain that the Burma offensive could not be undertaken that year. We were at full stretch to meet the requirements of the invasion of Sicily, to prepare for the subsequent advance up Italy and for the invasion of northern Europe. Ships and landing craft, and especially the latter, were the controlling factor in the launching of every one of these combined operations. Moreover our American Allies often urged us to launch offensives (such as the much-discussed 1942 cross-Channel operation 'Sledgehammer') earlier than we believed possible[1]; and one reason why we were unable to do so was that many of the vessels needed were, so we felt, tied up in the Pacific and not being used to the best advantage.

Just after the Americans had used the amphibious steam hammer already mentioned to pulverise the small coral nut of the Russell Islands, the Japanese embarked somewhat similar strength (6,900 men) at Rabaul to reinforce their garrison at Lae.[2] The expedition, of eight transports and a like number of destroyers, sailed on the 28th of February, unaware that very strong air forces had been sent to the Allied bases in Papua. Over 200 bombers and about 130 fighters were available, and the former were supplied with a five-second-delay bomb fuse which enabled a new technique of very low attack, aptly called 'skip bombing', to be employed. The Japanese convoy was sighted on the afternoon of the 1st of March. During the next two days it was completely destroyed, and only four destroyers of the escort escaped. Over 3,000 Japanese soldiers were lost. This Battle of the Bismarck Sea was a substantial victory, and it was won entirely by the U.S. Army Air Force and the Royal Australian Air Force. It is pleasant to record that the latter employed the Beaufighters which, for all our acute needs for them at home and in the Mediterranean[3], had been sent out to Australia on the British Government's orders.

Meanwhile in the southern Solomons the enemy's reinforcement of New Georgia and his extension of the air bases at Munda and Vila had attracted American attention once again, and the two cruiser-destroyer task forces of Rear-Admirals Ainsworth and Merrill mentioned earlier came into play. On the night of the 6th-7th of March the latter took his ships into Kula Gulf, sank two Japanese destroyers which he fortuitously encountered, and then carried out a heavy bombardment of Vila.[4] The bombardment was spectacular, but its moral results were probably greater than the material damage

---

[1] See Churchill, Vol. IV, Chapter XXV.
[2] See Map 5 (opp. p. 33).
[3] See pp. 258–260 and pp. 390–391.
[4] See Map 22 (opp. p. 220).

it inflicted. To make the approaches to Vila still more hazardous the Americans laid several minefields at this time. Japanese sweeping technique was poor, and two of their destroyers fell victims to mines in May. The bombing and bombardment of the New Georgia bases and the laying of mines off their entrances continued to the end of this phase; but in April the Japanese attempts to reinforce their garrison at Vila were on the whole successful.

Late in March Yamamoto himself arrived at Rabaul to direct a new offensive against the Allied bases in the southern Solomons and Papua. Over 150 aircraft from Nagumo's four fleet carriers came ashore to the airfields of New Britain and the northern Solomons, to reinforce the substantial numbers already there. In all Yamamoto assembled over 300 torpedo-bombers, dive-bombers and fighters. This concentration did not escape the notice of Allied reconnaissance planes, and the Americans prepared to meet the expected onslaught.

On the 7th of April nearly fourscore dive-bombers covered by more than a hundred fighters, most of which came from the Japanese aircraft carriers, attacked the anchorages off Guadalcanal and Tulagi. The fighters from Henderson Field went up to meet them, and fought fierce battles with the Japanese fighters. Although many of the dive-bombers got through untouched, they only sank a tanker, a destroyer, and the trawler *Moa* (R.N.Z.N.) for the loss of twenty-one Japanese aircraft. It was a poor result from the enemy's point of view. Indeed the use of his fleet's main striking power to attack a heavily defended base, and moreover one in which no major warships were stationed, was a bad strategical error on Yamamoto's part. He would have done far better to preserve these irreplaceable aircrews against the day of another major clash with the Allied carriers, which might have affected the whole course of the war. Five days later he repeated the mistake by attacking Port Moresby in similar strength. Not a ship was sunk. Lastly, on the 14th, it was the turn of Milne Bay. Good warning enabled the harbour to be cleared of most of the shipping. Two merchant ships, one of them British and the other Dutch, were sunk by dive-bombers; but that was all. Then the Japanese carrier planes, whose claims of damage inflicted bore no relation to the truth, were sent back to their ships. Yamamoto believed the attacks had restored the balance in his favour; but no Commander-in-Chief was ever more mistaken. The whole offensive had made very little difference to Allied strength, and none to Allied intentions. Indeed this operation now seems to have been a good example of the misuse of air power; and it made no difference at all to the defence of the Bismarck barrier.

Four days after the final air attack on Milne Bay Yamamoto and many of his staff embarked in two bombers at Rabaul to visit an air base in the south of Bougainville Island. They had a powerful

fighter escort; but American intelligence had discovered the programme for the visit, and a strong force of fighters was sent up from
Guadalcanal. Both bombers were destroyed, and most of the
passengers were killed. It cannot be doubted that the elimination of
Yamamoto, who held a position in the Japanese Navy comparable
to that of no other Admiral since Togo, was a severe blow to that
service's morale. He was succeeded by Admiral Koga.

While the struggle in the steaming, foetid heat of the Solomon
Islands and New Guinea was thus developing favourably for the
Allies, and forces were poised for the assaults on New Georgia and
Rabaul, far away in the foggy and rock-bound Aleutian Islands
events had also taken a favourable turn. When the Japanese landed
on Kiska and Attu in June 1942, they had no thought of striking at
Alaska or anywhere else on the American Continent.[1] Their purpose
merely was to deny to the Americans the use of the Aleutian chain as
stepping stones to northern Japan. In fact our Allies never considered
striking in that direction, chiefly because they were well aware that
the weather conditions in those high latitudes made it quite impossible to mount a large-scale combined operation there. None the
less they regarded enemy occupation of two of the islands as a matter
not to be tolerated, for political rather than military reasons; but their
pre-occupation in the south Pacific prevented anything much being
done about it in 1942, except to keep watch on the Japanese garrisons. On the 26th of March 1943 a small American force of cruisers
and destroyers encountered a superior Japanese expedition bound for
Kiska. In the battle that followed neither side lost any ships, but the
Japanese transports were turned back.[2] The encounter made the
Japanese realise that to reinforce their garrisons by transports was
too risky, and thenceforth they employed only destroyers and submarines. They thus still further reduced the number of those
valuable vessels which they could employ on profitable operations.
In May the Americans recaptured Attu, and prepared for a full
scale attack on the main garrison on Kiska. Late in July, however,
the Japanese removed their troops unbeknown to the Americans;
and when the latter attacked the place in the following month they
found that the birds had flown some time previously. It is true that
the Combined Chiefs of Staff had, at Casablanca, agreed on the
intention 'to make the Aleutians as secure as may be'. But it none the
less now seems that possession by the enemy of some of those remote
islands was not doing the Americans any military harm; and that to
let the enemy waste his resources by occupying them was more
profitable to the Allied cause than to expend our own in recovering
them. Their ultimate fate would be settled when command of the

---

[1] See p. 42 and Map 1 (opp. p. 5).
[2] See Morison Vol. VII, p. 23, et seq. regarding the Battle of the Komandorski Islands.

Pacific was decided, and meanwhile they might well have been left to 'wither on the vine'.

In the Indian Ocean this phase was distinguished only by the further running down of Admiral Somerville's fleet, to a point at which any offensive operations were out of the question. His last aircraft carrier, the *Illustrious*, was brought home in January for refit and modernisation, preparatory to her further employment in the Mediterranean. The *Valiant* soon followed her, and in April the *Warspite*, the cruiser *Mauritius* and several destroyers were taken away as well. The few ships left were barely adequate to meet the command's escort commitments. This major redistribution of our forces was dictated by the need to prepare for the invasion of Europe, and was made possible by the absorption of the Japanese in the South Pacific and by the losses they had suffered at the hands of the United States Navy. Frustrating though it was to those who had been trying to build up sufficient strength in the Indian Ocean to take the offensive, the soundness of the moves cannot be questioned. There was no longer any real likelihood of a repetition of the Japanese raids of April 1942, and the first assaults on Hitler's European fortress simply had to succeed. The sacrifices of the Eastern Fleet at least contributed substantially to the latter purpose, as will be told in our final volume.

Meanwhile the development of the Indian Ocean bases, and especially those at Colombo and Trincomalee, was proceeding steadily. Because the danger in the Indian Ocean was now less pressing, it had been decided that Addu Atoll should only be used as an occasional fuelling base. Somerville warmly welcomed this decision, since an enormous amount of work was needed to make it a satisfactory fleet base; and even if the work were undertaken the bad climate and the total lack of amenities would still be severe handicaps. 'As a boy', wrote Admiral Somerville to the First Sea Lord, 'I always had a hankering after coral atolls; anyone can have the things now so far as I am concerned'. But with the steady improvement of the bases at Colombo and Trincomalee, and the construction of more airfields in Ceylon and southern India, it was plain that, when the time came once more to build up our strength in those waters, the offensive possibilities would be such as Somerville had never so far been granted. Until that time came the Eastern Fleet could only continue to keep the sea routes open, ensuring that the rising tide of supplies and equipment reached the Middle East, India and Ceylon in safety.

CHAPTER XIX

THE AFRICAN CAMPAIGNS
1st January–31st May, 1943

'Sink, burn and destroy.
Let nothing pass'.
Admiral Cunningham to the ships
on patrol in the Sicilian Channel,
8th May 1943.

IN the preceding phase the maritime problems involved in trans-
porting overseas the great armies for the invasion of North Africa,
and in landing them on time at their various points of assault, had
been the overriding requirement of Allied strategy. Now that the
initial assaults and the hazardous period of the first building-up were
things of the past, and the armies were fighting their way forward
towards their goal of driving the Axis out of Africa, priorities had
completely changed. The needs of the land forces now took first
place, and the maritime services' duty was to see that they were
adequately supplied and reinforced, that their seaward flanks were
guarded, and that the use of the sea to succour his own troops was
denied the enemy. All the naval and maritime air forces in the eastern
and western Mediterranean toiled unceasingly throughout the first
five months of 1943 to satisfy these needs. It was hard and generally
unspectacular work; but to fulfil it was a traditional function of the
Navy, and all arms working on or below the surface of the sea, or
in the air above it, threw themselves wholeheartedly into their new,
if subordinate, rôle.

This phase was not many days old when, on the 14th of January,
the Casablanca Conference opened. Of the many subjects there
discussed by the Combined Chiefs of Staff we are here principally
concerned with the decision that, after the Axis had been driven out
of Africa, the next Allied objective was to be Sicily.[1] This required
early revision of the Mediterranean naval command areas. It was
certain that Admiral Cunningham, to whose 'profound contribution
. . . to the Allied cause in North Africa'[2] warm tribute was paid at
Casablanca, would remain in supreme command of the maritime

---

[1] See Churchill, Vol. IV, Chapter XXXVIII for a full account of the Casablanca
Conference.
[2] Churchill *op. cit.* p. 613.

side of the next Allied assault. It was therefore logical that his authority should be extended to include the bases from which the expedition would be launched, and all the waters across which it would pass. Accordingly on the 20th of February Cunningham relinquished his title of Naval Commander, Expeditionary Force, and resumed his former, and perhaps more famous position as Commander-in-Chief, Mediterranean. His jurisdiction now extended not only over the whole of the western basin, but over the greater part of the former North Atlantic Command. Admiral Harwood became Commander-in-Chief, Levant instead of Mediterranean, and the boundary between Cunningham's and Harwood's commands was shifted further east. It now ran from the Tunis-Tripoli frontier to 35° North 16° East, and thence to Cape Spartivento on the 'toe' of Italy.[1] Admiral Cunningham thus became responsible for the whole Tunisian coast, in whose ports part of the expedition against Sicily was to be prepared and trained, for the key position of Malta and for the waters around Sicily itself. All the naval forces based on Malta, including the famous 10th Submarine Flotilla and the hard-hitting surface striking forces, came under him once more; and he was also given powers to arrange the distribution of naval forces between the Levant and Mediterranean commands to suit his requirements. It was a happy augury for the next combined offensive that the great naval Commander, who had led his fleet so brilliantly in these waters in the early days, should command the Allied fleets which were soon to regain complete control over them. A minor change in naval organisation was made at the same time on the west African coast where, subject to Cunningham's general authority, a French command was established between Sierra Leone and the frontier of French Guinea.

These digressions have, however, taken us ahead of the hard fighting still in progress early in 1943, and it is to the beginning of the year and the two commands as they were then organised that we must return.

In the western Mediterranean the fast troop convoys (KMF) were arriving at Algiers about every three weeks, and one or two slower supply convoys (KMS) generally came in a few days after the fast ships. The reinforcing troops were quickly sent forward to the more advanced bases such as Bone by Landing Ships Infantry (L.S.Is), which ran a constant ferry service for the purpose. The three Landing Ships Tank (L.S.Ts) which were all that Admiral Cunningham possessed of this invaluable class, were used to carry American tanks and guns forward from Oran to Philippeville, while smaller landing craft plied between Bone and the little ports near to the front line

---

[1] See Map 31 (opp. p. 313). On 1st June 1943 the boundary between the Mediterranean and Levant command areas was moved still further east, from 16° to 20° East.

with urgent supplies of petrol and ammunition. Commodore G. N. Oliver, who had latterly been in charge of all the flotilla vessels working with the 'Torch' convoys, was appointed Senior Naval Officer, Inshore Squadron, to serve the First Army in the same way as the similarly named squadron in the Eastern Mediterranean had for so long served the Eighth Army. His headquarters were initially at Bone, and his orders were to move forward as the army advanced. Bases for the landing craft had meanwhile been established at Bougie and Djidjelli.[1]

The enemy's reaction to the constant flow of ships along the north African seaboard was to attack the convoys with aircraft and U-boats, and to bomb the ports which they were using. Neither Algiers nor Bougie suffered very heavily from air bombardment, but in the more forward base of Bone a good deal of damage was done. Being the chief terminal of the troop ferry service already mentioned, it was a very busy port; and several casualties occurred among the crowded shipping using it. The Italians generally kept about a dozen submarines on patrol in the western Mediterranean; but they did us little harm and, as in earlier phases, suffered heavy losses themselves. In the first five months of 1943 eight Italian submarines were sunk inside the Mediterranean by all our varied counter-measures.[2] The German U-boats proved, as before, to be far more dangerous enemies. Some of the losses which they caused us will be mentioned later in this chapter. Here it will be convenient to summarise their fortunes. At the start of this phase there were twenty-three German U-boats inside the Mediterranean. Several attempts were made to reinforce them, but our air and sea patrols had now made the passage of the Straits much more dangerous. One got through in January, two in April and three more in May; but several were sunk on passage, or damaged and forced to turn back. Furthermore the losses we inflicted steadily outstripped the reinforcements. Seven German U-boats were sunk in the Mediterranean in the first three months of the year, and three more in May[3]—the month which marked the great victories of our escorts and patrols in the Atlantic.[4] At the end of this phase there were eighteen left in the Mediterranean, but thereafter their strength declined still more rapidly. Between June and September six were sunk, and no more reinforcements arrived. By the autumn of 1943 their numbers were down to twelve. The defeat of the U-boats in the Mediterranean thus took place slightly later than the decisive victory gained over them on the Atlantic convoy routes.

---

[1] See Map 31 (opp. p. 313).
[2] See Appendix J for details.
[3] See Appendix J for details.
[4] See pp. 372–377.

Among the losses we suffered at this time, the cruiser *Ajax* was severely damaged by air attack in Bone on New Year's Day 1943. She was replaced by the *Penelope*, which had repaired in America the damage suffered earlier in Malta[1], and had now returned to the station on which she had served many years with distinction. On the 1st of February the fast minelayer *Welshman* was torpedoed and sunk on passage from Malta to Alexandria by U.617. She was a valuable ship, and had done good service for Malta at its time of crisis.[2] Next month, on the 13th, the liner *Empress of Canada* (21,517 tons) was sunk by U-boat off Sierra Leone, and the *Windsor Castle* (19,141 tons) in convoy KMF.11 was sunk by aircraft torpedo inside the Straits on the 23rd. But, considering the density of traffic passing Gibraltar and flowing thence to the east, the losses were astonishingly small; and our salvage organisation was now so efficient that a large proportion of torpedoed ships—in March eight out of twelve—reached harbour. During the two months following the initial landings in Africa (8th November 1942 to 8th January 1943) the whole 'Torch' area received 437,200 Allied fighting men and 42,420 vehicles. By the beginning of February four-and-a-half million tons of shipping had entered ports inside the Mediterranean, and our total losses were only 229,500 tons. Only one 'Torch' convoy was seriously mauled by the enemy, and that was the tanker convoy TM.1 which fell foul of a pack of U-boats off the Azores, and lost seven of its nine ships.[3] Rarely if ever in history can maritime power have been so successfully exploited to prosecute an offensive on such a scale at such great distances from the armies' home bases.

To turn now to our counter-offensive against the Axis supply lines, the New Year saw a great intensification of the blockade by our aircraft, submarines, surface forces and coastal craft. The Royal Air Force now had in Malta a big offensive force composed of Wellington torpedo-bombers, Beauforts and Beaufighters, eight squadrons in all. These were additional to the five squadrons of day and night fighters.[4] There were also three squadrons (Nos. 821, 828 and 830) of naval Swordfish and Albacores, which did very good work—particularly in night torpedo attacks on enemy convoys. A fourth naval squadron (No. 826) soon moved to Bone to work under the Coastal Air Force command. On the 8th of January the Chiefs of Staff stressed to the Supreme Commander the need to devote powerful shore-based air forces to the disruption of the enemy's sea borne supplies. Of our surface forces, the 15th Cruiser Squadron (the *Cleopatra*, *Orion* and *Euryalus*) and about four destroyers (Force K)

---

[1] See pp. 57–58.

[2] See pp. 75 and 340.

[3] See p. 407.

[4] The offensive force consisted of Nos. 39, 40, 46, 69, 89, 104, 227 and 272 Squadrons of the R.A.F. The fighter Squadrons were Nos. 23, 126, 185, 229 and 249.

worked from Malta, while the 12th Cruiser Squadron (the *Aurora*, *Penelope*, *Dido* and *Sirius*) and another four destroyers (Force Q) were generally stationed at Bone. In addition to the cruiser and destroyer striking forces, the Coastal Force flotillas of motor torpedo-boats and motor gunboats were also gaining strength. They too worked from Malta and from Bone, and often went right into the entrances to the enemy's supply ports to find their targets. While all these ships worked close up to the front, in the background, to ensure that the main Italian fleet made no attempt to interfere with our convoys, lay Force H, which now consisted of the *Nelson*, *Rodney*, *Formidable* and about a dozen destroyers. Though a close watch was kept on all the Italian bases, their fleet never showed signs of serious activity. It was seriously handicapped by shortage of fuel. In January Force H came to Algiers for a time, after covering the approach of the troop convoy KMF.6. For the rest of the month Admiral Syfret's ships stayed in Oran, chiefly to impress the local population by the sight of such a powerful Allied fleet. At the end of the month Admiral Syfret fell ill, and Vice-Admiral Sir Harold Burrough, who had gained much experience in previous operations in these waters, temporarily relieved him in command of Force H.

Of our own Mediterranean submarine flotillas, the 1st was still working from Beirut, the 8th had moved from Gibraltar to Algiers, and the 10th flotilla, now commanded by Captain G. C. Philips, was still based on Malta. As with our air forces, the Chiefs of Staff now stressed the need to allocate the greatest possible submarine strength to the Mediterranean. Early in the year the Admiralty told the Prime Minister that there were thirty-two operational boats, —about two-thirds of our total strength—in the three flotillas. As the year advanced reinforcements were received, but they generally only balanced the losses suffered. Included in the new arrivals were several boats manned by Greek, Dutch, Free French and Polish crews. The great contribution of the submarines to cutting the Axis supply lines to Africa has been emphasised earlier in our story.[1] It was continued unremittingly throughout the present phase, but in these shallow and narrow waters it was inevitable that a heavy price would be paid by the submarine service. Between January and May 1943 we lost seven boats in the Mediterranean. Among them was the *Turbulent*, commanded by Commander J. W. Linton who had held submarine commands since the beginning of the war and was one of the Royal Navy's most successful exponents of that type of warfare. Only a man of exceptional strength of character could have stood the strain of patrol after patrol, especially in the dangerously confined waters of the central Mediterranean. He was to have taken the *Turbulent* home to refit after this, his ninth patrol in command of her.

[1] See Vol. I, pp. 425, 438–9, 524–6 and pp. 75 and 342 of this volume.

He sailed from Algiers on the 24th of February. We now know that he unsuccessfully attacked an Italian ship off Bastia in Corsica on the 11th of March, and that his ship was sunk by counter-attacking Italian anti-submarine vessels. He was awarded the Victoria Cross for his many successful patrols in the *Turbulent*, but the award was not gazetted until after his death.[1]

Table 38. Enemy Merchant Shipping Losses, 1st January–31st May 1943

(1) Italian (includes losses outside the Mediterranean)

Number of ships : Tonnage

Month	By Surface Ship	By Submarine	By Air Attack (See Note 2)	By Mine	By Other Cause	TOTAL (See Note 3)
Jan.	9 : 5,825	16 : 19,246	13 : 27,223	1 : 5,186	33 :42,651	72 :100,131
Feb.		18 : 42,636	26 : 32,223	4 : 7,668	12 : 808	60 : 83,335
March		15 : 21,976	36 : 41,845	3 : 2,218	10 :13,847	64 : 79,886
April	5 : 939	17 : 35,530	55 : 52,668	3 : 1,641	24 : 6,268	104 : 97,046
May	1 : 3,566	12 : 12,469	101 : 58,482	—	30 :20,548	144 : 95,065
TOTAL	15 :10,330	78 :131,857	231 :212,441	11 :16,713	109 :84,122	444 :455,463

(2) German and German-Controlled (Mediterranean only)

Month	By Surface Ship	By Submarine	By Air Attack	By Mine	By Other Cause	TOTAL
TOTAL (See Note 1)	2 : 2,173	11 : 29,546	28 : 57,700	6 : 10,442	15 : 11,206	62 : 111,067

NOTES: (1) The considerable increase in German and German-controlled shipping losses compared with earlier phases is attributable to the acquisition by the Germans of a substantial tonnage of shipping after the occupation of 'Unoccupied' France in November 1942.

(2) The great increase in shipping sunk or destroyed by air attack is attributable to the much heavier effort devoted to shipping in enemy ports. Of the total tonnage sunk by air attack in this phase 41 ships of 111,088 tons were sunk at sea, and 218 ships of 159,053 tons in port.

(3) Of the 506 ships sunk in this phase, 170 were of more than 500 tons and 336 of less than 500 tons.

Having considered the many-sided offensive launched against the enemy's supply traffic early in 1943 we may analyse the losses which he suffered throughout the whole of this phase. It will be seen from the table above that in these five months the Axis powers lost over

---

[1] The other six British submarines sunk in the Mediterranean in this phase were:
P.311 Presumed mined about 2nd January.
Tigris Probably mined west of Sicilian Channel in March.
Thunderbolt Sunk by Italian corvette *Cicogna* off Sicily, 13th March.
Regent Probably mined southern Adriatic, April.
Splendid Sunk by German (ex Greek) destroyer *Hermes* off Capri, 21st April.
Sahib Sunk by Italian corvette *Gabbiano* off north Sicily, 24th April.

The destruction of U.660 by the corvettes *Lotus* and *Starwort* in the Mediterranean, 12th November 1942 (See p. 337).

(*Above*) H.M.S. *Marne* showing stern blown off by a U-boat's torpedo, 12th November 1942. (See p. 334).

(*Left*) The stern of H.M.S. *Marne* looking forward, showing damage caused by torpedo.

The damage caused to H.M.S. *Delhi* by a bomb hit, Algiers Bay, 20th November 1942.

The Hunt-class destroyer
Avon Vale, showing damage caused
by air torpedo off Bougie,
29th January 1943.

five hundred ships of more than half a million tons in the Mediterranean. True, many of them were small (336 were of less than five hundred tons), but they were none the less valuable for inshore supply purposes. Air attacks accounted for more than half of this total, but a great proportion of the ships sunk by that means was destroyed in enemy ports. It is certain that the combined result achieved by all arms was the severance of the Afrika Korp's sea communications, and that this contributed greatly to the collapse in Africa shortly to be recounted.

In the eastern Mediterranean the phase opened with loaded convoys running to Malta, Tobruk and Benghazi, and also between Port Said and Alexandria. Though they still had to be heavily escorted, the Malta and Benghazi convoys now ran in both directions with almost monotonous regularity. U-boats were still working off the African Coast, but the losses they caused were not serious; and the air threat to our supply traffic had declined almost to insignificance. The Malta-based cruisers and destroyers met the convoys to the east of the island to reinforce the escorts. Royal Air Force Beaufighters watched overhead, and dealt decisively with any attackers which might approach, while anti-submarine Beauforts swept ahead of the ships. It was a Beaufort which on the 14th of January sighted and attacked the Italian submarine *Narvalo* ahead of convoy ME.15.[1] Two destroyers of the escort finished her off, and once again effective air-sea co-operation was shown to be deadly to the U-boats.

The Red Sea was still a part of Admiral Harwood's command, but it was now unusual for him to experience any anxiety regarding our control over the very important routes running up and down it. The appearance of Japanese submarines in the Indian Ocean[2] and the sinking of a few ships off Aden caused him to send the *Teviot Bank* to lay a defensive minefield in the straits of Bab-el-Mandeb early in the New Year. But the Japanese never attempted seriously to interfere with our heavy traffic through that vital corridor. In January the 9th Australian Division had to be sent back to their own country, and four 'monster' liners (the *Queen Mary*, *Aquitania*, *Ile de France* and *Nieuw Amsterdam*) arrived at Red Sea ports to embark them. The cruiser *Devonshire* and an armed merchant cruiser went with the troopships as ocean escorts, while Mediterranean destroyers were sent south to escort the troopships clear of the narrow waters where submarines might be lurking. In the event this large movement took place without any untoward incidents.

On the 15th of January the Eighth Army, which had been held up in front of strong enemy positions east of Tripoli, attacked again and with complete success. Eight days later Tripoli was captured, and

---

[1] ME Convoys ran from Malta to the east, MW to Malta from the east.

[2] See p. 271.

the westward advance continued rapidly.[1] On the 29th our troops crossed the frontier into Tunisia for the first time. For this offensive the Navy had poured supplies in through Benghazi, and had also employed a mobile party to carry urgently needed stores right on to the beaches behind the front line. This small party moved west as the army advanced, and its services won a warm tribute from the Eighth Army Commander.

As soon as the attack on land started, the Malta destroyers and motor torpedo-boats intensified their nightly sweeps in the Sicilian channel, to frustrate enemy attempts to run reinforcements across. The *Nubian* and *Kelvin* sank one supply ship on the night of the 15th-16th, and the *Pakenkam* and *Javelin* another the following night. At the same time the submarine *Thunderbolt* was sent with two 'chariots'[2] to destroy the blockships with which the enemy was preparing to obstruct the port of Tripoli; but the operation was unsuccessful.[3] Meanwhile Wellingtons from Malta bombed the port heavily, while naval Albacores and R.A.F. Beauforts mined the approaches, and motor torpedo-boats went in 'to interfere with demolitions and blocking'. On the night of the 19th-20th the Malta destroyers swept along the coast of Tripolitania and sank a torpedo-boat and ten small ships. The Albacores were out again at the same time and added two supply ships to the score. This combined sea and air offensive effectively cut the enemy's supply line at a critical juncture.

To stop a determined enemy from destroying and obstructing a port which one wishes to use oneself as soon as possible after its capture is bound to be difficult. In the case of Tripoli none of the various measures adopted produced much result. In spite of all we could do the enemy managed to destroy the port facilities very thoroughly, and to block the entrance completely with six merchant-men, a sheer-legs[4], a rock crusher and many barges filled with concrete. To give the enemy his due it was, in Admiral Harwood's words, 'the successful delaying actions [fought on land which] gave him time to carry out most effective and thorough demolitions of the harbour and port'. The problems facing the Navy were, therefore two—to clear the harbour and to get supplies in through it as quickly as possible. The naval parties, under the commander of the Inshore Squadron (Captain C. Wauchope), moved in hard on the heels of the Army. Mine clearance, diving operations and blowing

---

[1] See Map 31 (opp. p. 313).

[2] See pp. 342–343.

[3] For an account of this attack and of the subsequent escape of one of the 'chariot' crews see Warren and Benson *Above us the Waves*. (Harrap, 1953) pp. 94–103.

[4] Sheer-legs. 'A hoisting apparatus of two or more poles attached at or near the top and separated at the bottom for masting ships or putting in engines, etc, used in dockyards or on sheer-hulk . . . ' (Concise Oxford Dictionary).

up of the blockships started at once. The first supply convoy, composed of landing craft, had left Benghazi two days before Tripoli fell, and the first merchant ship convoy sailed simultaneously from Alexandria. By the 25th a small passage had been cleared to enable landing craft to enter; next day the first proper convoy arrived, but had to anchor outside. On the 26th a beginning was made by getting 370 tons of cargo discharged, and thereafter matters improved rapidly. Then a violent storm caused damage among the landing craft, and delayed clearance and salvage work. The same storm struck Benghazi and damaged the moles so badly that it was 'reduced to a fair weather port'. None the less by the 29th the gap in the blockships in Tripoli was wide enough for L.C.Ts to enter, and 1,000 tons of cargo were discharged next day. The first supply ship entered on the 2nd of February, in spite of having only six inches of water beneath her as she passed through the gap in the blockships, and a foot or so clearance on either side. On the same day the port received its first enemy air raid. In spite of all difficulties the rate of discharge improved so rapidly that on the 14th 2,700 tons were unloaded. 'By accepting risks', wrote Admiral Harwood, 'we were able to meet the Eighth Army's requirements'. Meanwhile regular convoys (XT-TX) had started to run between Alexandria and Tripoli. The U-boats at once tried to attack them, but with unhappy results to themselves. U.205 was sunk by the destroyer and air escorts of convoy TX.1 on the 17th of February, and U.562 suffered a similar fate two days later when she tried to approach XT.3. In addition to the U-boats enemy aircraft, chiefly Ju.88s, also sometimes attacked the Malta and Tripoli convoys, but they rarely accomplished much result. MW.22 and XT.4 had two ships damaged by them at the beginning of March.

Early in February General Alexander (the Commander-in-Chief, Middle East) and the Prime Minister both visited Tripoli, and saw for themselves its condition and the difficulties involved in clearing and reopening the port. Mr Churchill sent his congratulations on the large amount of stores landed on the 14th.

The story of the blocking and reopening of Tripoli has been told in some detail, because complaints were made by the Eighth Army Commander about the way the Navy tackled the job. These reached Cairo while the Prime Minister was there. At about the same time Mr Casey, the Minister of State, gave it as his view that the Navy's representation on the Commanders-in-Chief, Middle East, Committee was not as strong as that of the other services. On his return to London Mr Churchill took the matter up with the First Sea Lord, who decided that Admiral Harwood should be relieved. In his letter to the Commander-in-Chief Admiral Pound said that 'the arrangements for the clearance of Tripoli harbour are largely responsible for this'. It cannot be doubted that the failure of the attack on Tobruk in September 1942 had aroused questioning anxieties in London[1], nor that by the following February Admiral Harwood was in bad health. On the particular issue of the measures taken to reopen Tripoli harbour, an impartial examination of the facts at this distance of time does appear to indicate that at Naval Headquarters, where the urgency of the matter to the Army must have been realised, the capabilities of the salvage ships allocated to the task were not studied sufficiently thoroughly, nor far enough in advance. Equally it appears that, as we had several days' warning that the enemy was taking exceptional steps to block the harbour, more could have been done to send adequate quantities of explosives forward quickly. Finally there is no doubt that, when clearance operations were started, a technical mistake was made by using too heavy charges in an attempt completely to disintegrate the blockships, rather than smaller charges to eat away the obstructions gradually. But it must be remembered that we had not previously encountered concrete-filled blockships on anything like the scale used by the Germans at Tripoli. The First Sea Lord summed the matter up in a letter to Admiral Cunningham in which he said 'The actual work of the salvage party at Tripoli was very good and they were commended, but the staff arrangements left too much to chance, which was quite unacceptable when one takes into consideration what the clearing of Tripoli meant to the Army'.

Although it is right to admit, therefore, that certain mistakes were made on the naval side of the clearance work, it none the less seems doubtful whether in the sum they caused appreciable delay to the unloading of the Army's supplies. The harbour quays had been so thoroughly wrecked that no berths were ready until some weeks after the first merchantman entered. Though it is true that once the ships could enter the harbour lighterage was less delayed by sea and swell, it would in any case have been necessary to use lighters. Furthermore, whatever may have gone wrong at Tripoli, the accomplishments of the Inshore Squadron throughout the campaign remain most impressive. Between the start of the Army's advance in November 1942 and the capture of Tripoli on the 23rd of January 1943, the squadron's little ships landed 157,070 tons of supplies in the various ports used, or over the beaches. In February alone 115,137 tons were put ashore at Tripoli, Buerat and Benghazi. That the Army's next advance was not in fact held up by any failure of supply by sea appears to be indicated by the fact that in April General Montgomery signalled his appreciation of the Navy's efforts to the Commander-in-Chief, Levant, in these terms—'Without the safe conduct of tanks, petrol and other munitions of war to

---

[1] See pp. 309–310.

Tobruk, Benghazi and Tripoli, the Eighth Army would have been unable to launch the offensive'; and in his own account of these events, after describing the state of the port on our entry, General Montgomery writes 'All our energies were concentrated on getting it [the port] working again, and indeed this was achieved with remarkable speed and reflected very great credit on the Royal Navy and Army Staff and units concerned'.[1] Finally Mr Churchill has left it on record that the efforts to keep the Eighth Army supplied were 'crowned by the rapid opening up of Tripoli'.[2]

The change in the Levant Command did not actually take place until the 27th of March, by which time Admiral Harwood's health had broken down. He was temporarily succeeded by Admiral Sir Ralph Leatham, who had been in command at Malta during most of 1942, and on the 5th of June Admiral Sir John Cunningham took over permanently.

After the capture of Tripoli the policy for supplying the Eighth Army was reviewed by the Commanders-in-Chief. It was decided to continue to land stores at Benghazi up to its full capacity of about 2,000 tons a day, to work up the small port of Buerat to take as much as it could, and to restore the capacity of Tripoli so that it could handle 4,000 tons daily. The last was an ambitious proposal, and it threw very heavy escort commitments on the Navy. For example on the 6th of February a convoy of seven ships for Tripoli (XT.2) and five for Malta (MW.20) sailed from Alexandria escorted by twelve destroyers. The *Euryalus* and two more destroyers came east from Malta to meet the convoy, all of which arrived safely. Admiral Harwood next reorganised the thirty-five escort vessels available to him into four groups. Two would look after the Alexandria-Tripoli convoys, which would run on a twenty-two day cycle, one group would run on a shuttle service to and fro between Tobruk and Benghazi, while the fourth group would be responsible for Levant convoys and those sailing between Port Said and Alexandria.

We had not been in possession of Tripoli for long before the Luftwaffe turned its attention to the port. But the weight of its attacks could not be compared with those which Malta had suffered a year earlier. By day our fighter defences held the upper hand, and the arrival of barrage balloons, the installation of smoke producing apparatus, and the deployment of a big concentration of anti-aircraft guns soon made dusk or night attacks difficult and hazardous. On the 19th of March enemy aircraft used a new weapon, a circling torpedo. It was a promising development for use against a harbour crowded with shipping, since the longer the torpedoes

---

[1] Field Marshal Viscount Montgomery *El Alamein to the River Sangro*. (Hutchinson and Co.) p. 37.
[2] Churchill, Vol. IV, p. 644.

circled the more likely they were to hit something. On this occasion thirteen were dropped and two merchantmen were sunk. The same weapons were used later against Algiers, but there no appreciable success was obtained. We had by that time learnt that small arms fire was an effective way of sinking them, or blowing them up prematurely.

In March Admiral Harwood reported that 'the discharge figures for Tripoli [had] met the Eighth Army's requirements'. Three large supply convoys and one troop convoy were sailed direct from Alexandria, and only one ship from all of them was lost. On the 27th of March over 5,000 tons were unloaded in the port, and by the end of April the daily average exceeded that figure. The original aim of 4,000 tons daily had been easily surpassed. Tripoli remained the principal supply port for the Eighth Army right to the end of the campaign. Malta was now also receiving its needs almost unhindered. In March 40,000 tons of cargo were unloaded there.

On the 20th of March the Eighth Army launched its new attack against the powerful defences known as the Mareth Line. Nine days later they were in our hands, and our troops occupied the port of Gabes. Once again the mobile naval parties moved right up to the front to land urgent supplies over beaches or through the small ports.

While the Eighth Army was preparing for its next drive forward Allied plans for the offensive against Sicily were being prepared. They included movements designed to mislead the enemy into expecting attack either against Crete and the Aegean Islands as stepping stones to Greece, or against Sardinia. To further this design troops were moved from Beirut into Cyprus on a considerable scale. Over 4,000 were taken there in January, mainly by the fast minelayer *Welshman*. In addition Marauders and Beaufighters of No. 201 Naval Co-operation Group of the R.A.F. started to attack enemy bases in the Aegean from Egypt, while submarines of the 1st Flotilla patrolled and attacked supply vessels in those same waters, and also moved up the Adriatic as far as Split.

In Admiral Sir Andrew Cunningham's command the month of March saw a great intensification of the offensive against the enemy's sea communications. The Royal Air Force and Fleet Air Arm squadrons made daily sweeps from Malta, the surface forces from that same base or from Bone were out on most nights, while the submarines 'continued to drain the supply lines to the Axis forces in Tunisia', and the Coastal Force craft swept along the diminishing coastline held by the enemy. Lastly mines were laid by the *Abdiel* on the enemy's routes between Sicily and Tunis, while the submarine *Rorqual*, motor-launches and British and American M.T.Bs infested the approaches to his African supply ports. Continuous operations in such confined waters were bound to lead to losses. Those suffered by our submarines have already been mentioned[1], but new arrivals, including three French and two Polish boats, kept the 1st and 10th Flotillas at full strength. As we now had plentiful surface and air forces to look after the dangerous shallow waters off Tunis, the submarines were no longer sent into them. Instead they patrolled west and north of Sicily and off the ports of the Italian mainland. In addition to our submarine losses, the destroyer *Lightning* of Force Q was sunk by E-boats during a sweep in the Sicilian Channel on the night of the 12th-13th. She was at once replaced by the Polish *Blyskawica*, one of the destroyers which had escaped to Britain in 1939, when the Germans invaded Poland, and had since rendered splendid service in many operations.[2]

Meanwhile in the west the troop and supply convoys continued to arrive steadily from Britain and the U.S.A., and the reinforcements were at once ferried forward to the advanced bases. Force H, now commanded by Vice-Admiral A. U. Willis, generally covered the big convoys inside the Mediterranean, but was ordered to Gibraltar early in March because there were indications that the German capital ships now concentrated in north Norway might be intending a foray into the Atlantic.[3] On the 14th the Admiralty reported that a large warship had passed through the Kattegat north-bound a week earlier, and ordered Force H to remain at Gibraltar. The reader will remember that the *Scharnhorst*, after two unsuccessful attempts in January, succeeded at this time in joining the other major German warships in north Norway.[4] Even at a time when the climax of victory in north Africa was plainly approaching the Admiralty kept a watchful eye open, to detect any threat against the vital North Atlantic routes. But in this case it was the Russian convoys that the enemy intended to attack; and the Home Fleet was ready to look after them. As to the security of our own African bases, Bone was still the chief target of the Axis bombers, but they did no serious damage in March. Oran was attacked by Italian 'limpeteers' on the 23rd-24th, while Algiers twice experienced the circling torpedoes already used against Tripoli. The limpet attack failed completely, and the circling torpedoes only damaged one ship.

On the 10th of April the Eighth Army occupied Sfax, and the Inshore Squadron at once moved in.[5] The harbour was blocked, and a good deal of damage had been done to the quays; but three berths were available next day, and by the 13th a channel sixty feet

---

[1] See p. 432 and fn (1).
[2] See Vol. I, p. 69.
[3] See p. 398.
[4] See p. 400.
[5] See Map 31 (opp. p. 313).

wide and eighteen deep had been cleared. The first convoy from Tripoli arrived on the 14th, and four days later over 1,500 tons of cargo was unloaded. By the end of April 20,000 tons had been discharged there. Sfax was the sixth major port to be cleared and reopened by the Navy during the Eighth Army's advance. Meanwhile Sousse had also been captured. There little damage had been done, and shipping could be berthed at once. The mobile beach party took over the port, mines were swept, and on the 22nd of April the first motor torpedo-boats arrived from Malta to use it as their forward base during the final operations. Measures were also put in hand at once to develop both Sfax and Sousse as landing craft bases for the invasion of Sicily, and to improve their port facilities to receive the large number of ships needed for the next offensive.

As the climax approached, our strangle-hold on the Sicilian Channel was tightened. Almost every night the destroyers and M.T.Bs from Malta or Bone were out seeking targets. Their only complaint was that too few could by this time be found. In spite of Italian opposition Hitler insisted that the endeavour to run supplies and reinforcements to Tunisia by sea should be continued to the end. In April out of twenty-six Axis ships which sailed on that route fifteen were sunk and four were damaged, most of them by air attacks; but 27,000 tons of supplies and 2,500 troops reached Africa. By the beginning of May our blockade was almost complete. In that month eight supply ships and fifteen small craft carrying some 7,000 tons were sunk and only 2,163 tons of cargo were safely landed. The enemy tried to compensate for his loss of maritime control by using supply- and troop-carrying aircraft on a large scale, but they too suffered heavy losses. None the less he managed to fly in 18,000 men and 5,000 tons of supplies during April, but at a cost of 117 transport aircraft. When day trips became too dangerous flights were made by night, but by the end of the month the rate of supply by air was also falling drastically.

In April, as in March, our light forces working against the Axis supply traffic did not escape unscathed. In the early hours of the 16th the destroyers *Pakenham* and *Paladin* from Malta encountered two Italian destroyers off Pantelleria. One enemy, the *Cigno*, was sunk, but the *Pakenham* received an unlucky hit in the engine room. She was taken in tow by her consort, but after enemy aircraft had attacked them Admiral Bonham-Carter, who was now in command in Malta, ordered the damaged ship to be sunk. The *Pakenham* was however soon avenged. On the 4th of May three of her flotilla from Malta (the *Nubian*, *Paladin* and *Petard*) found and sank a large merchantman bound for Tunis with munitions, and also the Italian destroyer *Perseo* which was escorting her.

At the end of April there was a significant event at the other extremity of the Levant command. The Combined Operations Headquarters ships *Bulolo* and *Largs* and a number of large landing ships arrived at Aden on the 30th. They were the advance section of the new Overseas Assault Force for the invasion of Sicily. Rear-Admiral T. H. Troubridge hoisted his flag in the *Bulolo* and Rear-Admiral R. R. McGrigor his in the *Largs*. Rear-Admiral Sir Philip Vian later hoisted his flag at home in a third Headquarters ship, the *Hilary*.

As April drew to a close the situation on land moved steadily in our favour. The First Army attacked on the 22nd from the west, but met stubborn resistance. The Eighth Army was also held up near Enfidaville. General Alexander therefore switched powerful forces from the Eighth to the First Army, and on the 6th of May the culminating blows were struck towards Tunis and Bizerta from the west. Both were entered by Allied troops on the 7th, and next day the naval Commander-in-Chief made the executive signal for the operation 'Retribution', the destruction of all Axis forces which might attempt to escape by sea. Admiral Cunningham has stated that he made the signal which heads this chapter in no spirit of vengefulness[1]; nor would anyone who knew him ever suspect that he could have been actuated by such motives. Yet he and his fleet could but remember our experiences off Dunkirk's beaches, Grecian harbours and Cretan cliffs. Such memories justified the expectation that an enemy who was still possessed of a great fleet, a substantial merchant navy and powerful air forces would not abandon his trapped armies to their fate. Not only would such timidity have been unthinkable in our own Services, had the rôles been reversed, but it was realised that the Tunisian ports were much nearer to his home bases than Greece or Crete had been to Alexandria. A determined and resourceful enemy could reasonably expect to get at least some of his soldiers home; and since the war was obviously far from ended, to allow his north African armies to get away and fight against us once again on European battlefields would have been an act of folly. Hence the need to 'let nothing pass'.

The coastal and Malta convoys had been temporarily stopped to release their escorts to the blockading flotillas, and Cunningham had under his control eighteen destroyers of all classes to patrol in the Sicilian Channel, west of Marittimo and off the north African coast each side of Cape Bon.[2] Inshore of the destroyers cruised the coastal flotillas, while Allied aircraft swept the skies. The only casualties on our side came from attacks by friendly aircraft, and after three such incidents Admiral Cunningham ordered the destroyers to paint their upper works an unmistakable British red. Two enemy merchant vessels were caught off Skerki Bank and sunk in the early hours of

---

[1] Viscount Cunningham of Hyndhope. *A Sailor's Odyssey* pp. 529–530.

[2] See Map 31 (opp. p. 313).

the 9th, and a number of small craft were also destroyed. About 800 prisoners were captured at sea, but the attempt at evacuation had been very half-hearted. The German account tells us that 'only a few hundred men succeeded in reaching Sicily by adventurous means'. On the 13th resistance ceased on land, and hordes of enemy troops marched or drove themselves into the Allied prisoner-of-war cages. On conclusion of the campaign King George VI signalled that 'the debt of Dunkirk [was] repaid', and Admiral Cunningham gave warm tribute to his light forces.

Meanwhile immediately after the capture of Bizerta the naval parties arrived. Commodore Oliver, the senior officer, Inshore Squadron, actually entered rather prematurely in an M.T.B., which was heavily fired on and suffered casualties. He was compelled to submit to the indignity of arriving instead by road. The enemy had sunk about fourteen vessels at the seaward entrance to the Bizerta Canal, and the naval dockyard at Ferryville had been badly damaged. None the less on the 10th, three days before the surrender of the Axis armies, Bizerta was ready to receive the first L.C.T. convoy from Bone. Four days later over 1,000 tons were discharged there. The clearance of Bizerta was carried out as a combined British-American operation. In spite of the poverty of their resources, the constructor officer on Admiral Cunningham's staff (Captain I. E. King) and American salvage experts rapidly blasted a channel through the obstructions.

It was at Bizerta that the senior officers of the two hard-worked Inshore Squadrons, Commodore G. N. Oliver from the west and Captain C. Wauchope from the east, finally met and knew that their tasks were completed. They had travelled far, to and fro along the African coast, and they and their predecessors had opened many ports, and carried in through them thousands of tons of supplies. Rarely had the work of their little ships caught the limelight, but all who fought on land to drive the Axis out of Africa knew how greatly they were indebted to the Inshore Squadrons. The Senior Officers' appointments now lapsed, and they and their men turned to other duties. On the 20th of March Rear-Admiral (Admiral, retired) Sir Gerald Dickens hoisted his flag in command of the ports of Bizerta and Tunis.

It now remained for our maritime services to carry out two essential operations. The first was to sweep the Sicilian Channel clear of the innumerable mines which had obstructed it for the last three years. Convoy escorts were reduced in order to release as many mine-sweepers as possible. The 12th, 13th and 14th Minesweeping Flotillas from Malta, two groups of minesweeping trawlers, motor-launches and motor-minesweepers all took a hand. By the 15th of May a channel two miles wide and 200 miles long had been swept from the

Galita Channel to Sousse, and thence on to Tripoli.[1] Nearly 200 moored mines were cut. That day Cunningham signalled that 'the passage through the Mediterranean was clear', and that convoys from Gibraltar to Alexandria could be started at once. The Admiralty sent its congratulations. The Navy thereupon took up the second of the two new duties mentioned—that of escorting these ships safely through the waters which had for so long been closed to our shipping.

The first convoy consisted of four fast merchant ships. Escorted by the A.A. cruiser *Carlisle* and four destroyers they reached Tripoli on the 22nd. Four more merchantmen joined up there, and the Malta destroyers strengthened the escort for the second part of the journey. All ships arrived safely at Alexandria on the 26th. It was the first through-Mediterranean convoy to run since operation 'Tiger' in May 1941.[2] After this special convoy a regular series (called GTX and TXG) was started between Gibraltar and Alexandria. The saving of shipping achieved by the reopening of the Mediterranean was enormous. Before operation 'Torch' was launched the Naval Staff estimated that it would bring us at least a fifty per cent saving of shipping bound for the Middle East, and about a twenty per cent saving of ships sailing to and from India. In addition more than half of the eighty-five ships permanently employed on the WS convoy route could, so they expected, be released. At the end of 1942 the prospective gain was assessed at about a million tons of shipping; and a further half million tons in French ports had come into our use. On the other hand we lost over a quarter of a million tons of shipping during the North African campaign; delays and postponements of Atlantic convoys had deprived Britain of a million tons of imports, and the enemy gained to his use some 875,000 tons seized in the Mediterranean ports of metropolitan France. Although therefore in terms of statistics the saving of tonnage to the Allies was not very much greater than the losses suffered and the gains received by the enemy, in terms of strategy the advantages to our cause were immense. Quite apart from merchant shipping, our warships and maritime aircraft could now be more economically employed, and more advantageously disposed. To give but one example, flotilla vessels were now released to strengthen local Mediterranean convoys and, still more important, to work with the newly-forming combined assault forces.

With the fall of Tunis and Bizerta the supply ports to the west, such as Bougie and Bone, were much reduced in importance, as was Benghazi to the east. Bone had played a big part in keeping the First Army supplied, and Benghazi and Tripoli had done the same for the Eighth Army. Now supplies and reinforcements could be

---

[1] See Map 31 (opp. p. 313).
[2] See Vol. I, p. 437.

carried direct to the ports on the Tunisian 'hump', and a vast amount of transhipment and ferry work was saved.

While the sweeping of the Sicilian channel was in progress the small island of Galita was 'liberated' by coastal craft from Bone. The senior officer of the flotilla reported that 'the ceremony was interrupted by the need to salvage firstly the delegates' hats, which they kept throwing into the air and the wind blew into the sea, and secondly the Mayor, who fell overboard'. Though the people of that small island were among the first to give a tumultuous welcome to those who freed them from the Axis yoke, all over Europe oppressed peoples were now awaiting the day when they too could release their pent-up feelings; and the success of operation 'Torch' had made it plain that, even though a long and painful road still had to be traversed, that day would come to them as well. Other islands off the North African coast were occupied soon afterwards and, as the next step towards Sicily, the fortified island of Pantelleria was now blockaded, and bombarded from the sea and air. On the 11th of June it surrendered. Another development was that the French Admiral Godfroy at last ended his long period of vacillation. On the 17th of May the Commander-in-Chief, Levant, received a letter from him expressing the desire 'to join the French Navy in North Africa'. Docking of his ships was at once started at Alexandria, and the Mediterranean Fleet was rid of another tiresome responsibility.

Meanwhile far away in the west landing ships and craft, built in American yards, were crossing the Atlantic by way of Bermuda, generally in UGS convoys. The crews of British warships repairing damage in America were extensively used to man the Tank Landing Ships (L.S.Ts) and Infantry Landing Craft (L.C.Is), and the former carried across the invaluable Tank Landing Craft (L.C.Ts) as deck cargo. The L.C.Is came over in flotillas under their own power, small though they were to undertake the Atlantic crossing. Other ships earmarked for the next combined operations, and many thousands of the fresh troops who were to take part in it, had already sailed from Britain to Egypt in WS convoys. At home, at the head of the Red Sea, and at the new landing craft bases recently established inside the Mediterranean at Bizerta, Sousse and Sfax, the ships and vessels were training and exercising under the watchful eyes of Admiral Sir Bertram Ramsay and of three of our most brilliant young Flag Officers—Rear-Admirals Vian, Troubridge and McGrigor. It was plain that, at long last, after nearly four years of war, we were to reap the benefits of 'the patient pursuit of a maritime strategy'[1], and that throughout the Middle East theatre the balance had come central. The phase ended with the skies aglow with hope on the European horizon.

---

[1] See Vol. I, p. 2.

Appendices

APPENDIX A

The Board of Admiralty
January 1942–May 1943

Date of Appointment

First Lord: Rt. Hon. Albert V. Alexander   12.5.40

First Sea Lord and Chief of Naval Staff:
Admiral of the Fleet Sir A. Dudley P. R. Pound   12.6.39

Deputy First Sea Lord:
Admiral Sir Charles E. Kennedy-Purvis   29.7.42

Second Sea Lord and Chief of Naval Personnel:
Vice-Admiral Sir William J. Whitworth   1.6.41

Third Sea Lord and Controller:
Vice-Admiral Sir Bruce A. Fraser   1.3.39
Vice-Admiral Sir W. Frederick Wake-Walker   22.5.42

Fourth Sea Lord and Chief of Supplies and Transport:
Vice-Admiral Sir John H. D. Cunningham   1.4.41
Rear-Admiral F. H. Pegram   8.5.43

Fifth Sea Lord and Chief of Naval Air Services:
Rear-Admiral A. L. St. G. Lyster   14.4.41
(In abeyance from July 1942)

Chief of Naval Air Services:
Admiral Sir Frederick C. Dreyer (Ret'd)   11.7.42
(Not a member of the Board)

Fifth Sea Lord and Chief of Naval Air Equipment:
Rear-Admiral D. W. Boyd   14.1.43

Vice-Chief of Naval Staff:
Vice-Admiral Sir Henry R. Moore   21.10.41

Assistant Chief of Naval Staff (Trade):
Vice-Admiral E. L. S. King   21.10.41
Rear-Admiral J. H. Edelsten   7.12.42

[In February 1943 title was changed from 'Trade' to 'U-boat Warfare and Trade']

Assistant Chief of Naval Staff (Weapons):
Rear-Admiral R. R. McGrigor   9.9.41
Rear-Admiral W. R. Patterson   8.3.43

Assistant Chief of Naval Staff (Foreign):
Rear-Admiral Sir Henry H. Harwood   2.12.40
(Membership of the Board ceased when
appointment was relinquished 8.4.42)

		Date of Appointment
Assistant Chief of Naval Staff (Home):		
	Rear-Admiral A. J. Power	27.5.40
	(Membership of the Board ceased when appointment was relinquished 28.5.42)	
Parliamentary and Financial Secretary:		
	Sir Victor Warrender	4.4.40
(Parliamentary Secretary only, as Lord Bruntisfield) from		9.2.42
Financial Secretary:		
	Rt. Hon. G. H. Hall	9.2.42
Civil Lord:	Captain A. U. M. Hudson	15.7.39
	Captain R. A. Pilkington	5.3.42
Controller of Merchant Shipbuilding and Repairs:		
	Sir James Lithgow	1.2.40
Permanent Secretary:		
	Sir Henry Vaughan Markham	5.12.40

Assistant Chiefs of Naval Staff, not members of the Board:

Foreign:	Rear-Admiral H. B. Rawlings	8.4.42
	Rear-Admiral R. M. Servaes	22.2.43
Home:	Rear-Admiral E. J. P. Brind	28.5.42
Air:	Rear-Admiral R. H. Portal	1.1.43

APPENDIX B

Summary of Principal Warships

built for the Royal Navy under the 1942 and 1943 Naval Building Programmes including Supplementary Programmes

NOTE: Only Ships which were actually completed and accepted are shown in this table.

1942 PROGRAMME		1943 PROGRAMME	
Fleet Carrier	*Eagle* (Completed post-war).		—
Light Fleet Carriers	*Glory, Ocean, Colossus, Venerable, Vengeance. Theseus, Triumph, Warrior, Magnificent, Terrible, Majestic* (all completed post-war). *Perseus, Pioneer* (aircraft repair ships: completed post-war).	Light Fleet Carriers	*Albion, Bulwark, Centaur, Hermes.* (All completed post-war).
Escort Carriers	*Nairana, Campania, Vindex, Pretoria Castle**	Escort Carriers	*Ameer, Atheling, Begum, Trumpeter, Emperor, Slinger, Empress, Khedive, Nabob, Shah, Patroller, Speaker, Ranee, Premier, Queen, Ruler, Rajah, Arbiter, Smiter, Trouncer, Puncher, Reaper* (All built in U.S.A. under Lend-Lease)
Cruisers	—	Cruisers	—
Flotilla Leaders and Destroyers	BATTLE Class—16 CHEQUERS Class—25	Flotilla Leaders and Destroyers	WEAPON Class—3 BATTLE Class—9
Submarines	'T' Class—5 'S' Class—13 'U' Class—13 'A' Class—4	Submarines	'S' Class—4 'A' Class—12
Frigates	LOCH Class—5 RIVER Class—11 CASTLE Class—10 CAPTAIN Class—14‡ COLONY Class—21‡	Frigates	CASTLE Class—17 LOCH and BAY Class—25
Corvettes	FLOWER Class—4	Corvettes	—
Minesweepers	ALGERINE Class—10 Motor Mine-sweepers—85	Minesweepers	ALGERINE Class—24 (19 built in Canada) Motor Mine-sweepers—36 (24 built in Canada)
Trawlers	ISLES Class—38 MILITARY Class—3	Trawlers	ISLES Class—20 MILITARY Class—3 FISH Class—4

* Converted from Merchant Ship.
‡ Built in U.S.A. under Lend-Lease.

APPENDIX C

Coastal Command of the Royal Air Force

Establishment and Expansion 1939–1943

Role	1st Sept., 1939		1st Jan., 1940		1st July, 1940		1st Jan., 1941		1st July, 1941		1st Jan., 1942		1st July, 1942		1st Jan., 1943		1st July, 1943	
	Squad-rons	Air-craft	Squad-rons	Air-craft	Squad-rons	Air-craft	Squad-rons	Air-craft	Squad-rons	Air-craft	Squad-rons	Air-craft	Squad-rons	Air-craft	Squad-rons	Air-craft	Squad-rons	Air-craft
General Reconnaissance																		
Very Long Range									1	9	1	9	1	16	3	52	7	105
Long Range	1	9	3	72	5	105	9	174	13	242	15	300	1	12	5	66	3	45
Medium Range	9	200	8½	182	8	162	7	138	4	82	1	18	19	370	13	278	9	186
Short Range																		
Flying Boats	5	40	6	48	7	46	7½	60	10	81	9	76	10	91	11	111	10	120
Torpedo/Bombers and Torpedo/Fighters	1	16	2	34	4	84	3	60	4	80	5	100	5	100	5	100	5	100
Fighter and Fighter/Strike					4½	93	6	132	8	182	6½	130	6	120	5	100	5½	108
Special Duty																	2	29
Total Squadrons	16		19½		28½		32½		40		37½		42		42		41½	
Total Aircraft		265		336		490		564		676		633		709		707		693

NOTES:—1. Squadrons operating from Gibraltar or temporarily detached to the Mediterranean Air Command are included throughout.
2. Aircraft on loan from Bomber Command are included throughout.
3. All Hudsons are classified as Medium Range.
4. The column headed "aircraft" includes both Initial Equipment and Immediate Reserve.
5. Squadrons shown are those *established*, and were not necessarily all operational, or up to full strength.

APPENDIX D

The Fleet Air Arm of the Royal Navy

Composition and Expansion 1939–1945

(Numbers of Aircraft on the Strength of Front Line Units)

Role	1939 Sept.	1940 April	1940 Sept.	1941 April	1941 Sept.	1942 April	1942 Sept.	1943 April	1943 Sept.	1944 April	1944 Sept.	1945 April	1945 Sept.	Type
Fighter / Fighter/Dive bomber / Fighter/Reconnaissance	36	59	78	130	129	175	252	257	339	513	645	826	739	Skua, Roc, Sea Gladiator, Fulmar, Sea Hurricane, Wildcat (Martlet in R.N.), Seafire, Hellcat, Corsair, Firefly
Torpedo/Bomber / Torpedo/Reconnaissance	140	149	169	184	198	196	209	255	349	479	549	500	205	Swordfish, Albacore Avenger and Barracuda
Reconnaissance	56	56	63	60	60	75	85	66	19	1	2	10	15	Walrus, Seafox, Kingfisher Sea Otter
TOTAL	232	264	310	374	387	446	546	578	707	993	1,196	1,336	959	
British aircraft	232	264	310	362	346	416	453	470	409	554	623	599	483	
American aircraft	—	—	—	12	41	30	93	108	298	439	573	737	476	Wildcat, Hellcat, Corsair, Avenger and Kingfisher

NOTE: The dependence of the Fleet Air Arm on U.S. naval aircraft is strikingly shown in the above figures. It will be observed that at the peak of its strength in April 1945 there was a majority of American aircraft in front line units. In general, these aircraft, which were the product of continuous development between the two wars, were found to be superior in performance and robustness to their British counterparts.

APPENDIX E

North Atlantic Troopship Movements ('Operational Convoys')

January 1942–December 1943

Month	OUTWARD		HOMEWARD	
	Number of Convoys	Allied fighting men carried (all services)	Number of Convoys	Allied fighting men carried (all services)
January 1942 .	1	2,752	3	9,156
February 1942 .	3	4,554	2	9,322
March 1942 . .	2	6,359	3	14,059
April 1942 . .	2	4,017	2	17,961
May 1942 . .	2	2,776	4	28,533
June 1942 . .	2	3,280	3	13,454
July 1942 . .	2	4,554	2	6,052
August 1942 .	3	2,396	6	14,951
September 1942 .	3	2,954	4	52,228
October 1942 .	2	7,206	2	14,864
November 1942 .	1	5,260	4	23,568
December 1942 .	3	12,650	3	22,575
TOTAL 1942 .	**26**	**58,758**	**38**	**226,723**
January 1943 .	3	9,576	8	27,041
February 1943 .	2	7,646	1	3,974
March 1943 . .	3	7,994	3	25,616
April 1943 . .	4	11,433	1	4,532
May 1943 . .	3	7,069	7	54,345
June 1943 . .	5	7,252	5	42,794
July 1943 . .	6	13,365	7	78,198
August 1943 .	8	11,052	5	43,051
September 1943 .	5	13,392	5	75,646
October 1943 .	4	12,032	8	175,224
November 1943 .	1	13,546	9	82,474
December 1943 .	1	12,463	7	68,336
TOTAL 1943 .	**45**	**126,820**	**66**	**681,231**

NOTES: (1) Convoys seldom exceeded four ships and were normally less than that number.
(2) Each 'monster liner' sailed as a single-ship convoy.
(3) The largest liners used frequently in North Atlantic troopship 'operational convoys' during 1942 and 1943 were:

Name	G.R.T.	Number of Crossings (both directions)	Approximate Maximum Troop Carrying Capacity
Queen Elizabeth	83,700	23	15,000
Queen Mary	81,200	32	15,000
Aquitania	44,800	13	8,000
Mauretania	35,700	10	7,600
Pasteur (French)	29,300	14	4,500
Empress of Scotland	26,000	10	4,200
Andes	25,700	11	4,200

Principal Allied Convoys during 1942 and 1943

Type	Code Letters	Route	Date of Starting	Remarks
Indian Ocean	AB	Aden–Bombay	Nov. '42	
East African Coastal	AKD	Aden–Kilindini–Durban	Sept. '43	Replaced all previous southward East African coastal convoys.
Military	AS	U.S.A.–Freetown	March '42	
Military	AT	U.S.A.–U.K.	Jan. '42	Monster Liners
Military	BA	Bombay–Red Sea Ports	May '41	
Military	BT	Sydney (N.S.W.)–U.S.A.	Jan. '42	
East African Coastal	CD	Cape Town–Durban	Nov. '42	Ceased Sept. '43.
U.K. Coastal	CE	St. Helen's (Isle of Wight)–Southend	Sept. '40	
Ocean Homeward	CF	Cape Town–West Africa–U.K.	May '41	
N.W. African Coastal	CG	Casablanca–Gibraltar	Jan. '43	Originally FT.
Military	CM	The Cape, Durban or Kilindini–Red Sea Ports	June '40	
Military	CT	U.K.–North America	Aug. '41	
Ocean Homeward	CU	Caribbean–U.K.	Feb. '43	Tankers
U.K. Coastal	CW	Southend–St. Helen's (Isle of Wight)	Sept. '40	
Indian Ocean	CX	Colombo–Maldives and Chagos	April '43	
East African Coastal	DC	Durban–Cape Town	Dec. '42	Ceased Sept. '43.
East African Coastal	DKA	Durban–Kilindini–Aden	Sept. '43	Replaced all previous northward East African coastal convoys.
U.K. Coastal	EN	Methil–Loch Ewe	Aug. '40	Originally to Clyde.
North African Coastal	ET	North African Ports–Gibraltar	Nov. '42	
U.K. Coastal	FN	Southend–Methil	Sept. '39	
U.K. Coastal	FS	Methil–Southend	Sept. '39	
Central Atlantic	FT	Freetown (Sierra Leone)–Trinidad	July '43	
Caribbean	GAT	Guantanamo–Trinidad	Aug. '42	Originally WAT July '42.

Type	Code Letters	Route	Date of Starting	Remarks
N.W. African Coastal	GC	Gibraltar–Casablanca	Nov. '42	Originally TF
Caribbean	GK	Guantanamo–Key West	Sept. '42	
Military	GM	Gibraltar–Malta	July '41	
U.S.A. Coastal	GN	Guantanamo–New York	Aug. '42	
Mediterranean	GTX	Gibraltar–Tripoli–Egypt	May '43	
Primarily Military	GU	North Africa–U.S.A.	Nov. '42	
Ocean Homeward	HG	Gibraltar–U.K.	Sept. '39	Ended Sept. '42. Thereafter homeward bound ships from Gibraltar were included in MK convoys.
Ocean Homeward	HX	Halifax–U.K.	Sept. '39	Started from New York Sept. '42.
South American Coastal	JT	Rio de Janeiro–Trinidad	July '43	Originally BT Nov. '42.
Arctic to N. Russia	JW	Loch Ewe–North Russia	Dec. '42	Originally PQ q.v.
Caribbean	KG	Key West–Guantanamo	Sept. '42	
Military 'Torch'	KMF	U.K.–North Africa	Oct. '42	Eventually extended to Egypt.
Ocean Homeward	KMS	U.K.–North Africa	Oct. '42	Primarily military. From April '43 left in company with OS convoys (and with OG convoys from July '43) and sailed with them as far as Gibraltar area
U.S.A. Coastal	KN	Key West–New York	May '42	
Special 'Torch'	KX	U.K.–North Africa	Oct. '42	
Local Mediterranean	LE	Port Said or Alexandria–Famagusta–Haifa or Beirut	July '41	
From Malta Eastbound	ME	Malta–Alexandria	July '40	Interrupted when Malta was besieged. Resumed Nov. '42.
Military	MG	Malta–Gibraltar	Dec. '40	
Military ex 'Torch'	MKF	North Africa–U.K.	Nov. '42	Primarily military. From April '43, MKS and SL convoys sailed from the Gibraltar area in company.
Ocean Homeward	MKS	North Africa–U.K.	Nov. '42	

Type	Code Letters	Route	Date of Starting	Remarks
To Malta West-bound	MW	Alexandria–Malta	July '40	Interrupted when Malta was besieged. Resumed Nov. '42.
Military	NA	North America–U.K.	Jan. '42	
Pacific Ocean	NE	New Zealand–Panama		
U.S.A. Coastal	NG	New York–Guantanamo	Aug. '42	
U.S.A. Coastal	NK	New York–Key West	Aug. '42	
Ocean Outward	OG	U.K.–Gibraltar	Oct. '39	Stopped temporarily Aug. '42. Resumed in May '43. From July '43 sailed in company with KMS as far as Gibraltar area. Ceased in Oct. '43.
Ocean Outward	ON	U.K.–North America	July '41	Replaced former OB convoys.
Ocean Outward	OS	U.K.–West Africa	July '41	Stopped temporarily Sept. '42. Resumed in Feb. '43. From April '43 sailed in company with KMS convoys as far as Gibraltar area.
U.S.A. Coastal and Central Atlantic	OT	New York–Caribbean –N.W. Africa	Feb. '43	Fast tankers for 'Torch'.
Arctic to N. Russia	PQ	Iceland–North Russia	Sept. '41	Replaced by JW q.v.
U.K. Coastal	PW	Portsmouth–Bristol Channel	July '41	
Arctic from N. Russia	QP	N. Russia–Iceland and U.K.	Sept. '41	Replaced by RA q.v.
Arctic from N. Russia	RA	North Russia–Loch Ewe	Dec. '42	Originally QP q.v.
West African	RS	Gibraltar–Sierra Leone	Feb. '43	
Ocean Homeward	SC	Halifax–U.K.	Aug. '40	From Sept. '42 to Mar. '43 left from New York.
Ocean Homeward	SL	Sierra Leone–U.K.	Sept. '39	Stopped temporarily in Oct. '42. Resumed Mar. '43. From May '43 SL and MKS convoys sailed home in company from the Gibraltar area.
West African	SR	Sierra Leone–Gibraltar	Feb. '43	

Type	Code Letters	Route	Date of Starting	Remarks
West African Coastal	ST	Sierra Leone–Takoradi	Dec. '41	
Military	SW	Suez–Durban or Cape		Returning WS convoys q.v.
Military	TA	U.K.–U.S.A.	Mar. '42	Monster liners.
Caribbean	TAG	Trinidad–Guantanamo	Aug. '42	Originally TAW July '42.
Military	TB	U.S.A.–Sydney (Australia)	Jan. '42	
Mediterranean Coastal	TE	Gibraltar–North African Ports	Nov. '42	
Central Atlantic	TF	Trinidad–Sierra Leone	Nov. '42	
South Atlantic	TJ	Trinidad–Rio de Janeiro	July '43	Originally TB Oct. '42.
Central Atlantic	TM	Trinidad–Gibraltar	Jan. '43	Special tanker convoys.
Central Atlantic	TO	N.W. Africa–Caribbean–New York	'42	Fast tankers from 'Torch'
West African Coastal	TS	Takoradi–Sierra Leone	Aug. '42	Originally LS April '42.
U.S. Military	TU	U.K.–U.S.A.	Sept. '43	
Mediterranean Local	TX	Tripoli (Libya)–Alexandria	Feb. '43	
Ocean Outward	UC	U.K.–Caribbean	Feb. '43	Special tanker convoys.
Military 'Torch'	UG	U.S.A.–North Africa	Oct. '42	
Indian Ocean	US	Australia-Middle East	Jan. '40	
U.S. Military	UT	U.S.A.–U.K.	Aug. '43	U.S. troopers.
U.K. Coastal	WN	Loch Ewe–Methil	July '40	Originally from Clyde.
Military	WS	U.K.–Middle East (via Cape of Good Hope)	June '40	'Winston's Specials' ended Aug. '43.
U.K. Coastal	WP	Bristol Channel–Portsmouth	July '41	
Indian Ocean	XC	Chagos and Maldives–Colombo	May '43	
Special ex 'Torch'	XK	Gibraltar–U.K.	Oct. '42	
Mediterranean Local	XT	Alexandria–Tripoli (Libya)	Jan. '43	
Mediterranean	XTG	Alexandria–Tripoli (Libya)–Gibraltar	June '43	

NOTE: In certain cases the speeds of different convoys between the same ports were not uniform and to distinguish them a letter was added as follows:

Suffix 'F' indicated 'Fast'
Suffix 'M' indicated 'Medium'
Suffix 'S' indicated 'Slow'

APPENDIX G

British Escort Vessel Strength and Dispositions

1st January, 1942, 1st August, 1942
and 1st January, 1943

1. WESTERN APPROACHES

A. Londonderry

Date	Organisation	General Function	STRENGTH			
			Destroyers	Sloops	Corvettes	Others
1/1/42	3 'Special Escort Groups'	Arctic Convoys, Atlantic Troop Convoys etc.	12	—	—	—
	3 Groups (Destroyers and Corvettes)	North Atlantic Convoys	9	—	15	—
	5 Groups (Sloops and Cutters)	South Atlantic Convoys	2	16	—	10 Cutters
	Unallocated	Miscellaneous	1	—	3	—
		TOTAL	24	16	18	10
1/8/42	1 'Special Escort Group'	Arctic Convoys, Atlantic Troop Convoys etc.	7	—	—	—
	1 'Special Escort Division'		7	—	3	—
	3 Groups (Destroyers and Corvettes)	North Atlantic Convoys	8	—	16	—
	6 Groups (Sloops and Cutters)	South Atlantic Convoys	2	19	4	8 Cutters
	Unallocated	Miscellaneous	—	—	1	—
		TOTAL	24	19	24	8

457

APPENDIX G

WESTERN APPROACHES (*Contd.*)

A. Londonderry (*Contd.*)

Date	Organisation	General Function	STRENGTH			
			Destroyers	Sloops	Corvettes	Others
1/1/43	2 'Special Escort Groups'	Arctic Convoys, Atlantic Troop Convoys etc.	6	—	4	—
	1 'Special Escort Division'		4	—	—	—
	3 Groups (Destroyers and Corvettes)	North Atlantic Convoys	8	—	18	—
	7 Groups (Sloops and Cutters)	South Atlantic Convoys	2	11	25	7 Cutters
	Unallocated	Miscellaneous	—	3	—	—
		TOTAL	20	14	47	7

B. Liverpool

Date	Organisation	General Function	STRENGTH			
			Destroyers	Sloops	Corvettes	Others
1/1/42	3 'Special Escort Groups'	Arctic Convoys, Atlantic Troop Convoys etc.	13	—	—	—
	3 Groups (Destroyers and Corvettes)	North Atlantic Convoys	8	—	15	—
	1 Group (Sloops and Corvettes)	South Atlantic Convoys	—	2	17	—
	Unallocated	Miscellaneous	1	—	4	—
		TOTAL	22	2	36	—
1/8/42	1 'Special Escort Division'	Arctic Convoys, Atlantic Troop Convoys etc.	7	—	4	—
	3 Groups (Destroyers and Corvettes)	North Atlantic Convoys	9	—	17	—
	2 Groups (Sloops and Corvettes)	South Atlantic Convoys	—	4	12	—
	Unallocated	Miscellaneous	2	—	—	—
		TOTAL	18	4	33	—

WESTERN APPROACHES (*Contd.*)

B. Liverpool (*Contd.*)

Date	Organisation	General Function	STRENGTH Destroyers	Sloops	Corvettes	Others
1/1/43	1 'Special Escort Division'	} Arctic Convoys, Atlantic Troop Convoys etc.	12	—	—	—
	1 'Special Escort Group'		—	—	4	—
	3 Groups (Destroyers and Corvettes)	North Atlantic Convoys	9	—	18	—
	1 Group (Sloops and Corvettes)	South Atlantic Convoys	—	2	9	—
	Unallocated	Miscellaneous	4	—	—	—
		TOTAL	25	2	31	—

C. Greenock

Date	Organisation	General Function	STRENGTH Destroyers	Sloops	Corvettes	Others
1/1/42	5 'Special Escort Groups'	Arctic, Atlantic Troop Convoys etc.	16	—	—	—
	2 Groups (Destroyers and Corvettes)	North Atlantic Convoys	6	—	10	—
	Unallocated	Miscellaneous	2	—	3	—
		TOTAL	24	—	13	—
1/8/42	1 'Special Escort Division'	Arctic, Atlantic Troop Convoys etc.	9	—	4	—
	1 Group (Destroyers and Corvettes)	North Atlantic Convoys	3	—	6	—
		TOTAL	12	—	10	—

WESTERN APPROACHES (*Contd.*)

C. Greenock (*Contd.*)

Date	Organisation	General Function	STRENGTH			
			Destroyers	Sloops	Corvettes	Others
1/1/43	1 'Special Escort Division'	Arctic, Atlantic Troop Convoys etc.	7	—	—	—
	1 Group (Destroyers and Corvettes)	North Atlantic Convoys	3	—	3	—
	2 Groups (Corvettes)	Miscellaneous	—	—	8	—
		TOTAL	10	—	11	—

D. Irish Sea Escort Force (*Belfast & Milford Haven*)

Date	Organisation	General Function	STRENGTH			
			Destroyers	Sloops	Corvettes	Others
1/1/42	A.A. Escorts	Local Irish Sea Convoys	—	—	3	4 A.A. Ships / 3 Misc.
1/8/42	3 A.A. Groups	Ditto	—	—	—	6 A.A. Ships / 3 Misc.
1/1/43	A.A. Groups	Ditto	—	—	—	3 A.A. Ships / 3 Misc.

2. ROSYTH

Date	Destroyers	Sloops	Corvettes	Others	TOTAL
1/1/42	20	5	—	—	25
1/8/42	21	2	—	1 A.A. Ship	24
1/1/43	22	—	—	1 A.A. Ship	23

3. NORE

Date	Destroyers	Sloops	Corvettes	Others	TOTAL
1/1/42	21	—	7	—	28
1/8/42	23	—	7	—	30
1/1/43	24	—	7	—	31

4. PORTSMOUTH

Date	Destroyers	Sloops	Corvettes	Others	TOTAL
1/1/42	4	—	—	—	4
1/8/42	7	—	—	—	7
1/1/43	4	—	—	—	4

5. PLYMOUTH

Date	Destroyers	Sloops	Corvettes	Others	Total
1/1/42	6	—	—	—	6
1/8/42	5	—	—	—	5
1/1/43	9	—	—	—	9

Note: Rosyth and Nore ships escorted East Coast Convoys, Portsmouth and Plymouth Ships Channel Convoys.

6. NORTH ATLANTIC (Gibraltar)

Date	Organisation	General Function	Strength			
			Destroyers	Sloops	Corvettes	Others
1/1/42	1 Destroyer Flotilla	Local Convoys	3	—	6	—
	1 Escort Group (Lent from Liverpool)		—	2	9	—
	A/S Trawlers		—	—	—	8
	Total		3	2	15	8
1/8/42	2 Destroyer Flotillas	Local Convoys	7	—	6	—
	A/S Trawlers		—	—	—	9
	Total		7	—	6	9
1/1/43	(1) *Gibraltar Escort Force:*					
	1 Destroyer Flotilla	Local and 'Torch' Convoys	5	—	—	—
	4 Escort Groups		4	9	7	—
	A/S Trawlers		—	—	—	12
	(2) *Western Mediterranean Escort Force* (under A.N.C.X.F. at Algiers)					
	2 Destroyer Flotillas	'Torch' Convoys	14	—	—	—
	4 Escort Divisions		—	—	16	—
	Total		23	9	23	12

7. SOUTH ATLANTIC (Freetown)

Date	Organisation	General Function	STRENGTH			
			Destroyers	Sloops	Corvettes	Others
1/1/42	1 Destroyer Flotilla	⎫ South Atlantic Convoys	8	—	—	—
	Freetown Escort Force	⎭	—	5	24	—
	Ocean Escorts	WS and Ocean Convoys	—	—	—	12 A.M.Cs
	3 Groups A/S Trawlers	Local Escorts	—	—	—	16 A/S Trawlers etc.
		TOTAL	8	5	24	28
1/8/42	1 Destroyer Flotilla	⎫ South Atlantic Convoys	7	—	—	—
	Freetown Escort Force	⎭	—	3	20	—
	Ocean Escorts	WS and Ocean Convoys	—	—	—	7 A.M.Cs
	3 Groups A/S Trawlers	Local Escorts	—	—	—	16 A/S Trawlers etc.
		TOTAL	7	3	20	23
1/1/43	Freetown Escort Force	South Atlantic Convoys	—	—	—	12 A/S Trawlers etc.
	Ocean Escorts	WS and Ocean Convoys	—	—	—	6 A.M.Cs
	West African Command Escorts	Local Escorts	—	4	15	7 A/S Trawlers
		TOTAL	—	4	15	25

8. WESTERN ATLANTIC

(Royal Navy and Royal Canadian Navy Only)

Date	Organisation	General Function	STRENGTH			
			Destroyers	Sloops	Corvettes	Others
1/1/42	R.C.N. (or lent R.N.)	Western Local Escorts	2	—	17	—
	Newfoundland Escort Force (R.C.N. or lent R.N.)	Mid-Ocean Escorts	14	—	43	—
		TOTAL	16	—	60	—

8. WESTERN ATLANTIC (*Contd.*)

Date	Organisation	General Function	STRENGTH			
			Destroyers	Sloops	Corvettes	Others
1/8/42	R.C.N. (or lent R.N.)	Western Local Escorts	18	—	29	—
	Tanker Escort Force (R.C.N.)	Special Tanker Convoys	—	—	4	—
	Gulf Escort Force (R.C.N.)	Gulf of Mexico Convoys	—	—	—	5 Mine-sweepers
	Newfoundland Escort Force (R.C.N. or lent R.N.)	Mid-Ocean Escorts	11	—	41	—
	Lent to U.S. Navy	U.S. Coastal Convoys	—	—	—	19 A/S Trawlers
		TOTAL	29	—	74	24
1/1/43	Bermuda	Local Escorts	—	2	1	—
	Atlantic Coast Command, St. John's (R.C.N. or lent R.N.)	Western Local Escorts	18	—	20	—
	Under U.S.N. Eastern Sea Frontier Command (R.C.N.)	New York Convoys	—	—	6	—
	Halifax Force (R.C.N.)	St. Lawrence River Convoys	—	—	4	—
	Newfoundland Command (R.C.N. or lent R.N.)	Mid-Ocean Escort Force	12	—	29	14 A/S Trawlers
		TOTAL	30	2	60	14

APPENDIX H

Operation 'Torch'

Composition of Allied Naval Forces taking part in the operation

FORCE 'H'	2 Battleships (*Duke of York, Rodney*(1)) 1 Battle cruiser (*Renown*) 3 Fleet carriers (*Victorious, Formidable, Furious*(1)) 3 Cruisers (*Bermuda*(2), *Argonaut, Sirius*) 17 Destroyers(1)
AZORES COVERING FORCE	2 Cruisers (*Norfolk, Cumberland*) 3 Destroyers
FUELLING FORCE	2 Tankers 1 Corvette 4 A/S trawlers
EASTERN NAVAL TASK FORCE (Algiers)	1 Headquarters ship (*Bulolo*) 3 Cruisers (*Sheffield, Scylla, Charybdis*) 1 Carrier (*Argus*) 1 Auxiliary carrier (*Avenger*) 3 A.A. ships (*Palomares, Pozarica, Tynwald*) 1 Monitor (*Roberts*) 13 Destroyers 3 Submarines 3 Sloops 7 Minesweepers 6 Corvettes 2 Landing Ships Infantry (Large) 2 Landing Ships Gantry 8 A/S trawlers 8 Motor launches

ALGIERS INSHORE LANDING GROUPS—partly formed from Eastern Naval Task Force

Western Landing group	*Centre Landing group*	*Eastern Landing group*
3 Landing Ships Infantry (Large) 1 A.A. Ship 1 Landing Ship Gantry 4 Mechanical Transport Ships 2 Sloops 2 Corvettes 3 Trawlers 3 Motor launches	1 Headquarters ship (*Bulolo*) 1 A.A. Ship 7 Landing Ships Infantry (Large) 9 Mechanical Transport Ships 1 Landing Ship Gantry 4 Destroyers 1 Sloop(4) 2 Corvettes(4) 3 Minesweepers 3 A/S trawlers 3 Motor launches	4 Combat loaders (U.S.)(3) 1 Landing Ship Infantry 1 A.A. Ship 3 Mechanical Transport Ships 2 Destroyers 1 Sloop 2 Corvettes 4 Minesweepers 2 A/S trawlers 2 Motor launches

NOTES: (1) *Rodney, Furious* and three destroyers were detached to support Centre Naval Task Force.
(2) *Bermuda* was detached to support the Eastern Naval Task Force.
(3) One combat loader was torpedoed on the 7th November and towed into Algiers later.
(4) One sloop and two corvettes shown here are also shown under the Eastern Landing group, to which they proceeded.

CENTRE NAVAL TASK FORCE (Oran)	1 Headquarters ship (*Largs*) 2 Auxiliary carriers (*Biter, Dasher*) 2 Cruisers (*Jamaica, Aurora*) 2 A.A. ships (*Alynbank, Delhi*) 13 Destroyers 2 Submarines 2 Sloops 8 Minesweepers 6 Corvettes 2 Cutters 1 Landing Ship Infantry (Large) 2 Landing Ships Infantry (Medium) 3 Landing Ships Infantry (Small) 3 Landing Ships Tank 1 Landing Ship Gantry 8 A/S trawlers 10 Motor launches

ORAN INSHORE LANDING GROUPS—partly formed from Centre Naval Task Force

Western Landing group	*Centre Landing group*	*Eastern Landing group*
1 Landing Ship Infantry (Large) 2 Landing Ships Infantry (Medium) 1 Landing Ship Tank 4 Mechanical Transport Ships 1 Cruiser (*Aurora*) 1 Destroyer 2 Corvettes 1 A/S trawler 1 Motor launch	3 Landing Ships Infantry (Large) 2 Mechanical Transport Ships 2 Destroyers 4 A/S trawlers 5 Motor launches	6 Landing Ships Infantry (Large) 3 Landing Ships Infantry (Small) 2 Landing Ships Tank 1 Landing Ship Gantry 1 Cable Ship 15 Mechanical Transport Ships 6 Merchant vessels 1 Cruiser (*Jamaica*) 1 A.A. Ship (*Delhi*) 3 Destroyers 5 Corvettes 2 Cutters 1 Sloop 8 Minesweepers 3 A/S trawlers 4 Motor launches

GIBRALTAR ESCORT FORCE	2 Destroyers 4 Corvettes 13 A/S trawlers
GIBRALTAR MISCELLANEOUS FORCE	1 Submarine Depot Ship (*Maidstone*) 7 Submarines 5 Auxiliary minesweeping trawlers 1 Controlled minelayer 3 Salvage vessels 4 Tugs 18 Tankers 23 Merchant vessels 25 Motor launches 32 Motor minesweepers 6 Landing craft tanks
WARSHIPS NOT INCLUDED IN FORCES ORGANISED FOR 'TORCH', BUT WHICH WERE AVAILABLE FOR VARIOUS SERVICES AFTER THE OPERATION HAD BEEN LAUNCHED	3 Destroyers 10 Sloops 5 Cutters 2 Minesweepers 8 Corvettes 4 Trawlers 1 Coastal craft depot ship 1 Army port repair ship

2G

Composition of United States Naval Forces

COVERING GROUP

1 Battleship (*Massachusetts*)
2 Cruisers (*Wichita, Tuscaloosa*)
4 Destroyers
1 Oiler

NORTHERN ATTACK GROUP
(Port Lyautey)

1 Battleship (*Texas*)
1 Cruiser (*Savannah*)
2 Auxiliary carriers (*Sangamon, Chenango*)
1 Seaplane tender
9 Destroyers
1 Submarine (*Shad*)
6 Transports
3 Merchant vessels
2 Minesweepers
1 Oiler

CENTRE ATTACK GROUP
(Casablanca)

3 Cruisers (*Augusta, Brooklyn, Cleveland*)
1 Carrier (*Ranger*)
1 Auxiliary carrier (*Suwanee*)
15 Destroyers
2 Submarines
12 Transports
3 Merchant vessels
2 Minelayers
4 Minesweepers
1 Oiler

SOUTHERN ATTACK GROUP
(Safi)

1 Battleship (*New York*)
1 Cruiser (*Philadelphia*)
1 Auxiliary carrier (*Santee*)
10 Destroyers
1 Submarine (*Barb*)
5 Transports
1 Merchant vessel
1 Minelayer
2 Minesweepers
2 Oilers
1 Tug

APPENDIX J

German, Italian and Japanese U-boats sunk

1st January, 1942–31st May, 1943

Table I. German U-boats

Number	Date	Name and task of killer	Area
U.577	9 Jan. '42	Aircraft of 230 Squadron—air patrol	Eastern Mediterranean
U.374	12 Jan. '42	*Unbeaten*—S/M Patrol	Eastern Mediterranean
U.93	15 Jan. '42	*Hesperus*—sea escort	North Atlantic
U.581	2 Feb. '42	*Westcott*—sea escort	North Atlantic
U.82	6 Feb. '42	*Rochester* and *Tamarisk*—sea escort	North Atlantic
U.656	1 Mar. '42	Aircraft of U.S. Squadron 82—air escort	Off Newfoundland
U.133	14 Mar. '42	Mine	Aegean
U.503	15 Mar. '42	Aircraft of U.S. Squadron 82—air escort	South East of Newfoundland
U.655	24 Mar. '42	*Sharpshooter*—sea escort	Arctic
U.587	27 Mar. '42	*Leamington, Grove, Aldenham* and *Volunteer*—sea escort	North Atlantic
U.585	29 Mar. '42	*Fury*—sea escort	Arctic
U.702	? Apr. '42	Unknown	North Sea
U.85	14 Apr. '42	*U.S.S. Roper*—on passage	East coast of U.S.A.
U.252	14 Apr. '42	*Stork* and *Vetch*—sea escort	North Atlantic
U.573	1 May '42	Aircraft of 233 Squadron—air patrol	Western Mediterranean
U.74	2 May '42	*Wishart, Wrestler* and aircraft of 202 Squadron—air/sea patrol	Western Mediterranean
U.352	9 May '42	U.S. Coastguard *Icarus*—sea patrol	East coast of U.S.A
U.568	28 May '42	*Eridge, Hero* and *Hurworth*—sea escort	Eastern Mediterranean
U.652	2 June '42	Aircraft of 815 (F.A.A.) and 203 squadrons—air patrol	Eastern Mediterranean
U.157	13 June '42	U.S. Coastguard *Thetis*—sea patrol	Off Cuba
U.158	30 June '42	Aircraft of U.S. Squadron 74—air escort	Bermuda area
U.215	3 July '42	*Le Tiger*—sea escort	East coast of U.S.A.
U.502	5 July '42	Aircraft of 172 Squadron—Bay air patrol	Bay of Biscay
U.153	6 July '42 or 13 July '42	Aircraft of U.S. Squadron 59—air patrol or *U.S.S. Lansdowne*—sea patrol	Caribbean Sea
U.701	7 July '42	Aircraft of U.S. Squadron 396—air patrol	East coast of U.S.A.
U.136	11 July '42	*Spey, Pelican* and *Léopard* (French)—sea escort	North Atlantic
U.576	15 July '42	Aircraft of U.S. Squadron 9 and U.S. M/V *Unicoi*—air/sea escort	East coast of U.S.A.
U.751	17 July '42	Aircraft of Squadrons 502 and 61—Bay air patrol	Bay of Biscay
U.90	24 July '42	*St. Croix* (R.C.N.)—sea escort	North Atlantic
U.213	31 July '42	*Erne, Rochester* and *Sandwich*—sea escort	North Atlantic

Table I. German U-boats (Contd.)

Number	Date	Name and task of killer	Area
U.588	31 July '42	*Wetaskiwin* (R.C.N.) and *Skeena* (R.C.N.)—sea escort	North Atlantic
U.754	31 July '42	Aircraft of R.C.A.F. Squadron 113 —air patrol	Off Nova Scotia
U.166	1 Aug. '42	Aircraft of U.S. Squadron 212— air escort	Gulf of Mexico
U.335	3 Aug. '42	*Saracen*—S/M patrol	Shetlands
U.372	4 Aug. '42	*Sikh, Zulu, Croome, Tetcott* and aircraft of 203 Squadron—air/sea patrol	Eastern Mediterranean
U.612	6 Aug. '42	Accident	Baltic
U.210	6 Aug. '42	*Assiniboine* (R.C.N.)—sea escort	North Atlantic
U.379	8 Aug. '42	*Dianthus*—sea escort	North Atlantic
U.578	10 Aug. '42	Aircraft of Czechoslovak Squadron 311—Bay air patrol	Bay of Biscay
U.464	20 Aug. '42	Aircraft of U.S. Squadron 73—air escort	Iceland
U.654	22 Aug. '42	Aircraft of U.S. Squadron 45—air patrol	Caribbean Sea
U.94	28 Aug. '42	*Oakville* (R.C.N.) and aircraft of U.S. Squadron 92—air/sea escort	West Indies
U.756	1 Sept. '42	Aircraft of U.S. Squadron 73—air escort	North Atlantic
U.222	2 Sept. '42	Accident, collision	Baltic
U.705	3 Sept. '42	Aircraft of 77 Squadron—Bay air patrol	Bay of Biscay
U.162	3 Sept. '42	*Vimy, Pathfinder* and *Quentin*—sea escort	West Indies
U.446	9 Sept. '42	Mine	Off Danzig
U.88	12 Sept. '42	*Faulknor*—sea escort	Arctic
U.589	14 Sept. '42	*Onslow* and aircraft from *Avenger* (825 Squadron)—carrier sea/air escort	Arctic
U.261	15 Sept. '42	Aircraft of 58 Squadron—air patrol	South of Faroes
U.457	16 Sept. '42	*Impulsive*—sea escort	Arctic
U.253	23 Sept. '42	Aircraft of 210 Squadron—air escort	Arctic
U.165	27 Sept. '42	Mine	Bay of Biscay
U.512	2 Oct. '42	Aircraft of U.S. Squadron 99—air patrol	French Guiana
U.582	5 Oct. '42	Aircraft of 269 Squadron—air escort	South of Iceland
U.179	8 Oct. '42	*Active*—sea escort	Off Cape Town
U.171	9 Oct. '42	Mine	Bay of Biscay
U.597	12 Oct. '42	Aircraft of 120 Squadron—air escort	North Atlantic
U.661	15 Oct. '42	Aircraft of 120 Squadron—air escort	North Atlantic
U.619	15 Oct. '42	*Viscount*—sea escort	North Atlantic
U.353	16 Oct. '42	*Fame*—sea escort	North Atlantic
U.216	20 Oct. '42	Aircraft of 224 Squadron—Bay air patrol	Bay of Biscay
U.412	22 Oct. '42	Aircraft of 179 Squadron—air patrol	N.E. of Faroes
U.599	24 Oct. '42	Aircraft of 224 Squadron—air escort	North Atlantic
U.627	27 Oct. '42	Aircraft of 206 Squadron—air escort	North Atlantic
U.520	30 Oct. '42	Aircraft of R.C.A.F. Squadron 10 —air escort	North Atlantic
U.559	30 Oct. '42	*Pakenham, Petard, Hero, Dulverton, Hurworth* and aircraft of 47 Squadron—air/sea patrol	Eastern Mediterranean
U.658	30 Oct. '42	Aircraft of R.C.A.F. Squadron 145 —air escort	N.W. of Newfoundland
U.116	? Oct. '42	Unknown	Atlantic
U.132	5 Nov. '42	Aircraft of 120 Squadron—air escort	North Atlantic
U.408	5 Nov. '42	Aircraft of U.S. Squadron 84—air escort	North of Iceland
U.272	12 Nov. '24	Accident, collision	Baltic

Table I. German U-boats (Contd.)

Number	Date	Name and Task of Killer	Area
U.660	12 Nov. '42	*Lotus* and *Starwort*—sea escort	Western Mediterranean
U.605	13 Nov. '42	*Lotus* and *Poppy*—sea escort	Off Algiers
U.595	14 Nov. '42	Aircraft of 500 Squadron—air patrol	Western Mediterranean
U.259	15 Nov. '42	Aircraft of 500 Squadron—air patrol	Off Algiers
U.411	15 Nov. '42	*Wrestler*—sea escort	West of Gibraltar
U.173	16 Nov. '42	*U.S.S. Woolsey, Swanson* and *Quick*—sea escort	North Atlantic
U.331	17 Nov. '42	Aircraft of 500 Squadron and aircraft from *Formidable* (820 Squadron)—air patrol	Western Mediterranean
U.98	19 Nov. '42	Aircraft of 608 Squadron—air patrol	Western approaches to the Mediterranean
U.184	20 Nov. '42	*Potentilla* (Norwegian)—sea escort	North Atlantic
U.517	21 Nov. '42	Aircraft from *Victorious* (817 Squadron)—carrier air escort	North Atlantic
U.254	8 Dec. '42	Aircraft of 120 Squadron—air escort	North Atlantic
U.611	10 Dec. '42	Aircraft of U.S. Squadron 84—air escort	North Atlantic
U.626	15 Dec. '42	U.S. coastguard *Ingham*—sea escort	North Atlantic
U.357	26 Dec. '42	*Hesperus* and *Vanessa*—sea escort	North Atlantic
U.356	27 Dec. '42	*St. Laurent, Chilliwack, Battleford* and *Napanee* (all R.C.N.)—sea escort	North Atlantic
U.164	6 Jan. '43	Aircraft of U.S. Squadron 83—air escort	Off Brazil
U.224	13 Jan. '43	*Ville de Quebec* (R.C.N.)—sea escort	Western Mediterranean
U.507	13 Jan. '43	Aircraft of U.S. Squadron 83—air escort	Off Brazil
U.337	16 Jan. '43	Aircraft of 206 Squadron—air escort	North Atlantic
U.301	21 Jan. '43	*Sahib*—S/M patrol	West of Corsica
U.553	? Jan. '43	Unknown	North Atlantic
U.265	3 Feb. '43	Aircraft of 220 Squadron—air escort	North Atlantic
U.187	4 Feb. '43	*Vimy* and *Beverley*—sea escort	North Atlantic
U.609	7 Feb. '43	*Lobelia* (French)—sea escort	North Atlantic
U.624	7 Feb. '43	Aircraft of 220 Squadron—air escort	North Atlantic
U.519	10 Feb. '43	Aircraft of U.S. Squadron 2—Bay air patrol	Bay of Biscay
U.442	12 Feb. '43	Aircraft of 48 Squadron—air escort	Western approaches to the Mediterranean
U.620	14 Feb. '43	Aircraft of 202 Squadron—air escort	Off Portugal
U.529	15 Feb. '43	Aircraft of 120 Squadron—air escort	North Atlantic
U.201	17 Feb. '43	*Fame*—sea escort	North Atlantic
U.69	17 Feb. '43	*Viscount*—sea escort	North Atlantic
U.205	17 Feb. '43	*Paladin* and aircraft of S.A.A.F. Squadron 15—air/sea escort	N.W. of Derna
U.562	19 Feb. '43	*Isis, Hursley* and aircraft of 38 squadron—air/sea escort	N.E. of Benghazi
U.268	19 Feb. '43	Aircraft of 172 Squadron—Bay air patrol	Bay of Biscay
U.623	21 Feb. '43	Aircraft of 120 Squadron—air escort	North Atlantic
U.225	21 Feb. '43	U.S. coastguard *Spencer*—sea escort	North Atlantic
U.606	22 Feb. '43	U.S. coastguard *Campbell* and *Burza* (Polish)—sea escort	North Atlantic
U.443	23 Feb. '43	*Bicester, Lamerton* and *Wheatland*—sea patrol	Off Algiers
U.522	23 Feb. '43	*Totland*—sea escort	North Atlantic
U.649	24 Feb. '43	Accident, collision	Baltic
U.83	4 Mar. '43	Aircraft of 500 Squadron—air patrol	Western Mediterranean
U.87	4 Mar. '43	*Shediac* and *St. Croix* (R.C.N.)—sea escort	North Atlantic

Table I. German U-boats (Contd.)

Number	Date	Name and task of killer	Area
U.633	7 Mar. '43	Aircraft of 220 Squadron—air support	South of Iceland
U.156	8 Mar. '43	Aircraft of U.S. Squadron 53—air patrol	East of Barbados
U.444	11 Mar. '43	*Harvester* and *Aconit* (French)—sea escort	North Atlantic
U.432	11 Mar. '43	*Aconit* (French)—sea escort	North Atlantic
U.130	12 Mar. '43	*U.S.S. Champlin*—sea escort	North Atlantic
U.5	19 Mar. '43	Accident, marine casualty	Baltic
U.384	20 Mar. '43	Aircraft of 201 Squadron—air escort	North Atlantic
U.665	22 Mar. '43	Aircraft of 172 Squadron—Bay air patrol	Bay of Biscay
U.524	22 Mar. '43	Aircraft of U.S. Squadron 1—air patrol	Canary Islands
U.469	25 Mar. '43	Aircraft of 206 Squadron—air patrol	South of Iceland
U.169	27 Mar. '43	Aircraft of 206 Squadron—air patrol	North Atlantic
U.77	28 Mar. '43	Aircraft of 233 and 48 Squadrons—patrol	Western Mediterranean
U.163	? Mar. '43	Unknown	Bay of Biscay
U.124	2 Apr. '43	*Stonecrop* and *Black Swan*—sea escort	North Atlantic
U.167	5 Apr. '43	Aircraft of 233 Squadron—air patrol	Canary Islands
U.635	6 Apr. '43	*Tay*—sea escort	North Atlantic
U.632	6 Apr. '43	Aircraft of 86 Squadron—air escort	North Atlantic
U.644	7 Apr. '43	*Tuna*—S/M patrol	Arctic
U.376	10 Apr. '43	Aircraft of 172 Squadron—Bay air patrol	Bay of Biscay
U.526	14 Apr. '43	Mine	Bay of Biscay
U.175	17 Apr. '43	U.S. coastguard *Spencer*—sea escort	North Atlantic
U.602	23 Apr. '43	Unknown	Off Algiers
U.189	23 Apr. '43	Aircraft of 120 Squadron—air escort	North Atlantic
U.191	23 Apr. '43	*Hesperus*—sea escort	North Atlantic
U.710	24 Apr. '43	Aircraft of 206 Squadron—air escort	North Atlantic
U.203	25 Apr. '43	Aircraft from *Biter* (811 Squadron) and *Pathfinder*—carrier air/sea escort	North Atlantic
U.174	27 Apr. '43	Aircraft of U.S. Squadron 125—air escort	Off Nova Scotia
U.227	30 Apr. '43	Aircraft of R.A.A.F. Squadron 455 —air patrol	North of Faroes
U.332	2 May '43	Aircraft of R.A.A.F. Squadron 461 —Bay air patrol	Bay of Biscay
U.659	3 May '43	Accident, collision	North Atlantic
U.439	3 May '43	Accident, collision	North Atlantic
U.630	4 May '43	Aircraft of R.C.A.F. Squadron 5—air escort	North Atlantic
U.465	4 May '43	Aircraft of 86 Squadron—air escort	North Atlantic
U.192	5 May '43	*Pink*—sea escort	North Atlantic
U.638	5 May '43	*Loosestrife*—sea escort	North Atlantic
U.125	6 May '43	*Vidette*—sea escort	North Atlantic
U.531	6 May '43	*Oribi*—sea escort	North Atlantic
U.438	6 May '43	*Pelican*—sea escort	North Atlantic
U.447	7 May '43	Aircraft of 233 Squadron—air patrol	Western approaches to the Mediterranean
U.109	7 May '43	Aircraft of R.A.A.F. Squadron 10 —Bay air patrol	Bay of Biscay
U.663	7 May '43	Aircraft of 58 Squadron—Bay air patrol	Bay of Biscay
U.528	11 May '43	*Fleetwood* and aircraft of 58 Squadron—air/sea escort	North Atlantic

Table I. German U-boats (Contd.)

Number	Date	Name and task of killer	Area
U.186	12 May '43	*Hesperus*—sea escort	North Atlantic
U.89	12 May '43	Aircraft from *Biter* (811 Squadron) and *Broadway* and *Lagan*—carrier air/sea escort	North Atlantic
U.456	13 May '43	*Lagan*, *Drumheller* (R.C.N.) and aircraft of R.C.A.F. Squadron 423—air/sea escort	North Atlantic
U.266	14 May '43	Aircraft of 86 Squadron—air escort	North Atlantic
U.657	14 May '43	Aircraft of U.S. Squadron 84—air escort	North Atlantic
U.753	15 May '43	Unknown	North Atlantic
U.176	15 May '43	Aircraft from U.S. Squadron 62 and Cuban SC-13—air/sea escort	Off Florida
U.463	15 May '43	Aircraft of 58 Squadron—Bay air patrol	Bay of Biscay
U.182	16 May '43	*U.S.S. Mackenzie*—sea escort	North Atlantic
U.128	17 May '43	*U.S.S. Moffett* and *Jouett* and aircraft of U.S. Squadron 74—air/sea escort	Off Brazil
U.640	17 May '43	*Swale*—sea escort	North Atlantic
U.646	17 May '43	Aircraft of 269 Squadron—air patrol	South of Iceland
U.954	19 May '43	Aircraft of 120 Squadron—air escort	North Atlantic
U.209	19 May '43	*Jed* and *Sennen*—sea escort	North Atlantic
U.273	19 May '43	Aircraft of 269 Squadron—air escort	South of Iceland
U.381	19 May '43	*Duncan* and *Snowflake*—sea escort	North Atlantic
U.258	20 May '43	Aircraft of 120 Squadron—air escort	North Atlantic
U.303	21 May '43	*Sickle*—S/M patrol	Off Toulon
U.569	22 May '43	Aircraft from *U.S.S. Bogue*—carrier air escort	North Atlantic
U.752	23 May '43	Aircraft from *Archer* (819 Squadron) —carrier air patrol	North Atlantic
U.414	25 May '43	*Vetch*—sea escort	Western Mediterranean
U.467	25 May '43	Aircraft of U.S. Squadron 84—air escort	North Atlantic
U.436	26 May '43	*Test* and *Hyderabad*—sea escort	North Atlantic
U.304	28 May '43	Aircraft of 120 Squadron—air escort	North Atlantic
U.755	28 May '43	Aircraft of 608 Squadron—air patrol	Western Mediterranean
U.563	31 May '43	Aircraft of 58 and 228 Squadrons and of R.A.A.F. Squadron 10—Bay air patrol	Bay of Biscay
U.440	31 May '43	Aircraft of 201 Squadron—Bay air patrol	Bay of Biscay

Table II. Italian U-boats sunk 1st January, 1942–31st May, 1943

Name	Date	Name and task of killer	Area
Ammiraglio St. Bon	5 Jan. '42	*Upholder*—S/M patrol	Off Sicily
Medusa	30 Jan. '42	*Thorn*—S/M patrol	Adriatic
Ammiraglio Millo	14 Mar. '42	*Ultimatum*—S/M patrol	Off Sicily
Guglielmotti	17 Mar. '42	*Unbeaten*—S/M patrol	Off Sicily
Tricheco	18 Mar. '42	*Upholder*—S/M patrol	Adriatic
Veniero	7 June '42	Aircraft of 202 Squadron air patrol	Balearic Islands
Zaffiro	9 June '42	Aircraft of 240 Squadron—air patrol	Balearic Islands
Perla	9 July '42	*Hyacinth*—on passage. (Captured)	Off Beirut
Ondina	11 July '42	*Protea* (S.A.N.F.), *Southern Maid* (S.A.N.F.) and aircraft of 700 Squadron (F.A.A.)—air/sea patrol	Off Beirut
Pietro Calvi	14 July '42	*Lulworth*—sea escort	South of Azores
Scire	10 Aug. '42	*Islay*—sea patrol	Off Haifa
Cobalto	12 Aug. '42	*Ithuriel* and *Pathfinder*—sea escort	Off Bizerta
Dagabur	12 Aug. '42	*Wolverine*—sea escort	Off Algiers
Morosini	? Aug. '42	Unknown	Bay of Biscay
Alabastro	14 Sept. '42	Aircraft of 202 Squadron—air patrol	Off Algiers
Antonio Sciesa	7 Nov. '42	Aircraft of a U.S. Squadron—bombing	Tobruk
Granito	9 Nov. '42	*Saracen*—S/M patrol	Off N.W. Sicily
Emo	10 Nov. '42	*Lord Nuffield*—sea escort	Off Algiers
Dessie	28 Nov. '42	*Quiberon* (R.A.N.) and *Quentin*—sea patrol	North of Bone
Porfido	6 Dec. '42	*Tigris*—S/M patrol	South of Sardinia
Corallo	13 Dec. '42	*Enchantress*—sea escort	Off Bougie
Uarsciek	15 Dec. '42	*Petard* and *Queen Olga* (Greek)—on passage	South of Malta
Narvalo	14 Jan. '43	*Pakenham*, *Hursley* and aircraft—air/sea patrol	S.E. of Malta
Tritone	19 Jan. '43	*Port Arthur* (R.C.N.)—sea escort	Off Bougie
Santorre Santarosa	20 Jan. '43	*M.T.B.260*—sea patrol	Off Tripoli
Avorio	8 Feb. '43	*Regina* (R.C.N.)—sea escort	Off Philippeville
Malachite	9 Feb. '43	*Dolfijn* (Dutch S/M)—S/M patrol	South of Sardinia
Asteria	17 Feb. '43	*Wheatland* and *Easton*—sea patrol	Off Bougie
Delfino	23 Mar. '43	Accident, collision	Off Taranto
Archimede	15 Apr. '43	Aircraft of U.S. Squadron 83—air patrol	South Atlantic
Mocenigo	13 May '43	Aircraft of U.S. Squadrons—air raid	Cagliari
Enrico Tazzoli	16 May '43	Aircraft of a British Squadron (Possible)—air patrol	Bay of Biscay
Gorgo	21 May '43	Unknown	Mediterranean
Leonardo da Vinci	23 May '43	*Active* and *Ness*	N.E. of Azores

Table III. Japanese U-boats sunk, 7th December, 1941–31st May, 1943

Number	Date	Name and task of killer	Area
I-170	10 Dec. '41	Aircraft from *U.S.S. Enterprise*	North of Hawaii
RO-66	17 Dec. '41	Accident, marine casualty	Off Wake Island
RO-60	29 Dec. '41	Accident, grounding	Marshall Islands
I-160	17 Jan. '42	*Jupiter*—sea escort	Off Java
I-124	20 Jan. '42	*U.S.S. Edsall* and *H.M.A.S. Deloraine, Lithgow* and *Katoomba*—sea escort	Off N. Australia
I-173	27 Jan. '42	*U.S.S/M. Gudgeon*—S/M patrol	West of Midway Island
I-23	29 Jan. '42	*U.S.S. Jarvis* and *Long*—sea escort	Off Hawaii
RO-30	26 Apr. '42	*U.S.S/M. Tautog*—S/M patrol	West of Hawaii
I-28	17 May '42	*U.S.S/M. Tautog*—S/M patrol	East of New Guinea
I-164	17 May '42	*U.S.S/M. Triton*—S/M patrol	South of Japan
RO-35	June '42	Accident, marine casualty	Pacific
RO-32	9 July '42	U.S. Coastguard *McLane*, *U.S.S. YP* 251 and aircraft of R.C.A.F.	Off Queen Charlotte Island
I-123	28 Aug. '42	*U.S.S. Gamble*—sea escort	Solomon Islands
RO-33	29 Aug. '42	*Arunta* (R.A.N.)—sea escort	S.E. of New Guinea
RO-61	31 Aug. '42	Aircraft of U.S. Squadron 43 and *U.S.S. Reid*—air/sea patrol	North of Aleutian Islands
RO-65	28 Sept. '42	Aircraft of U.S. Squadron—air raid	Aleutian Islands
I-30	Oct. '42	Mine	Singapore
I-172	10 Nov. '42	*U.S.S. Southard*—on passage	Solomon Islands
I-3	10 Dec. '42	*U.S.S. PT.59*—sea patrol	Solomon Islands
I-15	16 Dec. '42	Aircraft of U.S. Squadron 55—air patrol	Solomon Islands
I-4	20 Dec. '42	*U.S.S/M. Seadragon*—S/M patrol	New Britain
I-22	25 Dec. '42	*U.S.S. PT.122*	Off New Guinea
I-18	2 Jan. '43	*U.S.S/M. Grayback*—S/M patrol	Solomon Islands
I-1	29 Jan. '43	*Kiwi* and *Moa* (R.N.Z.N.)—sea patrol	Solomon Islands
RO-102	11 Feb. '43	Aircraft from *U.S.S. Helena* and *U.S.S. Fletcher*—sea escort	Solomon Islands
RO-34	4 Apr. '43	*U.S.S. O'Bannon*—sea patrol	Solomon Islands
RO-107	28 May '43	*U.S.S. SC.669*—sea patrol	New Hebrides

Table IV. Analysis of sinkings of German, Italian and Japanese U-boats by cause

1st January, 1942–31st May, 1943

Cause	1942			1943 (1st January–31st May)		
	German	Italian	Japanese	German	Italian	Japanese
Surface ships . . .	32½	9	8	29	5	3
Shore-based aircraft . .	35½	3	1	45	2	—
Ship-borne aircraft . .	1	—	—	2	—	—
Ships and shore-based aircraft	5	1	2	6	1	—
Ships and ship-borne aircraft	1	—	—	2	—	1
Shore-based and ship-borne aircraft . . .	1	—	—	—	—	—
Submarines . . .	2	7	5	3	1	1
Bombing raids . . .	—	1	1	—	1	—
Mines laid by shore-based aircraft . . .	3	—	—	1	—	—
Mines laid by ships . .	—	—	1	—	—	—
Other causes . . .	4	—	1	4	1	—
Causes unknown . .	2	1	—	4	1	—
TOTAL	87	22	19	96	12	5

NOTE: 1. In addition three Japanese U-boats were sunk in 1941, two attributed to accident, and one by ship-borne aircraft.
2. One of the German U-boats shown as being sunk by other causes in 1942 was lost in an old Greek minefield in the Aegean.
3. As the date of sinking of one German U-boat in 1942 is doubtful, it has been allotted half to a surface ship and half to shore based aircraft.

APPENDIX K

German U-boat strength
January 1942–May 1943

Date	Operational	Training and Trials	Total	New Boats Commissioned in Previous Quarter
January 1942	91	158	249	69
April 1942	121	164	285	49
July 1942	140	191	331	59
October 1942	196	169	365	61
January 1943	212	181	393	69
April 1943	240	185	425	69
July 1943	207	208	415	71

PRINCIPAL CHARACTERISTICS OF GERMAN U-BOATS TYPE VII C

NOTE: This was the type of U-boat most commonly employed on the convoy routes. A total of 567 were built and commissioned. A further 92 of similar type but with an increased diving depth of 394 feet also became operational.

Displacement:
    Surfaced: 769 tons
    Submerged: 871 tons

Maximum Speeds (laden):
    Surfaced: 17·7 knots
    Submerged: 7·6 knots (for one hour)

Endurance:
    Surfaced: 9700 miles at 10 knots (Diesel-electric)
                    8850 miles at 10 knots (cruising)
                    6500 miles at 12 knots (cruising)
                    3450 miles at 17 knots (maximum sustained)
    Submerged: 130 miles at 2 knots
                    80 miles at 4 knots

Diving depth: 309 feet (In emergency could be considerably exceeded)

Armament:
    torpedo tubes: four bow, one stern
    outfit: 14 torpedoes (maximum)
              12 torpedoes (normal)
    guns: 1-37 mm. A.A.
           2-20 mm. A.A.

Crew: 44

APPENDIX L

The Japanese Navy

Composition and Disposition, 7th December, 1941

ON the 7th of December 1941, the principal units of the Japanese Navy consisted of:

10 Battleships (increased to 11 by the end of the year)
 6 Fleet carriers
 4 Light Fleet carriers
18 Heavy cruisers
18 Light cruisers
113 Destroyers
 63 Submarines

These ships composed the Combined Fleet.

For administrative purposes six fleets and an air fleet were formed as follows:

First fleet:	Battle Fleet
Second fleet:	Scouting Force
Third fleet:	Blockade and Transport Force
Fourth fleet:	Mandates Fleet
Fifth fleet:	Northern Fleet
Sixth fleet:	Submarine Fleet
First Air Fleet:	Carrier Fleet

These fleets were not organized to operate as balanced tactical units. It was necessary to form Task Forces with ships from any or all of the above for operational purposes.

The Japanese Combined Fleet has therefore been shown divided into the principal Task Forces formed in December 1941. This organisation should only be taken as typical, for the composition of Task Forces varied continually as different needs arose.

MAIN BODY (Admiral Yamamoto)

		Tons	Armament (T.T. & torpedo tubes)	Speed in knots
1st Battle Squadron	*Yamato* (commissioned) (16 Dec. 1941)	63,720	9—18·1 in. 12—6·1 in. (later reduced to 6 guns) 12—5·1 in. A.A.	27
	Nagato *Mutsu*	} 38,980	8—16 in. 18—5·5 in. 8—5·1 in. A.A.	25

476

MAIN BODY (Admiral Yamamoto) (*Contd.*)

		Tons	Armament	Speed in knots
2nd Battle Squadron	*Ise* *Hyuga*	} 35,400	12—14 in. 16—5·5 in. 8—5·1 in. A.A. (Rearmed with flight deck and modified armament mid-1942—mid-1943)	25
	Fuso *Yamashiro*	} 33,000	12—14 in. 16—5·5 in. 8—5·1 in. A.A.	23
9th Cruiser Squadron	*Kitakami*	5,640	4—5·5 in. 4—T.T.	36
	Oi	5,700	7—5·5 in. 2—3·1 in. A.A. 8—T.T.	
	8 Destroyers			
Seaplane Carrier	*Chiyoda*	11,190	6—5·1 in. 30 seaplanes	28

STRIKING FORCE (Vice-Admiral Nagumo)

		Tons	Armament	Speed in knots
3rd Battle Squadron (1st Division)	*Hiyei* *Kirishima*	} 32,250	8—14-in. 8—6-in. 12—5·1-in. A.A.	30·5
1st Carrier Squadron	*Akagi* *Kaga*	} 36,600 36,000	10—8-in. 12—5·1 in. A.A. 63–72 aircraft	30
2nd Carrier Squadron	*Soryu* *Hiryu*	} 18,500 18,000	16—5-in. A.A. 63–72 aircraft	33
5th Carrier Squadron	*Shokaku* *Zuikaku*	} 25,675	12—5·1-in. A.A. 63–72 aircraft	34
8th Cruiser Squadron	*Tone* *Chikuma*	} 11,213	8—8-in. 8—5·1-in. A.A. 12—T.T.	35·5
1st Destroyer Flotilla	*Abukuma* (leader)	5,170	7—5·5 in. 3—3-in. 8—T.T.	36
	16 destroyers			

APPENDIX L

SOUTHERN FORCE (Vice-Admiral Kondo)

		Tons	Armament	Speed in knots
3rd Battle Squadron (2nd Division)	*Kongo* *Haruna*	} 32,250	8—14-in. 8—6-in. 12—5·1 in. A.A.	30·5
4th Carrier Squadron	*Ryujo* *Shoho* (not completed until Jan. 1942)	} 8,500 13,000	8—5·1-in. 31 aircraft	31 26
4th Cruiser Squadron	*Atago* *Maya* *Takao* *Chokai*	} 13,400	10—8-in. 8—5·1-in. A.A. 16—T.T.	33
5th Cruiser Squadron	*Haguro* *Myoko* *Nachi*	} 13,000	10—8-in. 8—5·1-in. 16—T.T.	33·5
7th Cruiser Squadron	*Mogami* *Mikuma* *Suzuya* *Kumano*	} 12,500	10—8-in. 8—5·1-in. A.A. 4—3-in. A.A. 12—T.T.	33
16th Cruiser Squadron	*Ashigara*	13,000	} 10—8-in. 8—5·1-in. A.A. 16—T.T.	33·5
	Nagara *Kuma*	} 5,700	7—5·5-in. 3—3·1-in. A.A. 8—T.T.	36
2nd Destroyer Flotilla	*Jintsu* (leader) 16 destroyers	5,850	7—5·5-in. 3—3·1 in. A.A. 8—T.T.	36
3rd Destroyer Flotilla	*Sendai* 14 destroyers	as *Jintsu*		
4th Destroyer Flotilla	*Naka* 16 destroyers	as *Jintsu*		
5th Destroyer Flotilla	*Natori* 8 destroyers	as *Abukuma*		
4th Submarine Flotilla	*Kinu* 8 Submarines	as *Abukuma*		
5th Submarine Flotilla	*Yura* 6 submarines	as *Abukuma*		
6th Submarine Flotilla	*Chogei* (Depot ship) 4 submarines			

SOUTHERN FORCE (Vice-Admiral Kondo) (*Contd.*)

		Tons	Armament	Speed in knots
Seaplane Carriers	*Chitose*	11,190	} 6—5·1-in.	28
	Mizuho	9,000	} 24–30 seaplanes	21
Seaplane Tenders	*Sanyo Maru*	8,360	} 12–18 seaplanes	19
	Sanuki Maru	7,158	} 3—3-in.	19
	Kamikawa Maru	10,500		19

SOUTH SEAS FORCE (Vice-Admiral Inoue)

		Tons	Armament	Speed in knots
Light Cruiser	*Kashima*	6,000	4—5·5-in. 2—5·1-in.	18
6th Cruiser Squadron	*Aoba* *Kinugasa* *Kako* *Furutaka*	} 9,000 } 8,800	6—8-in. 4—4·7-in. A.A. 8—T.T.	33·5
18th Cruiser Squadron	*Tenryu* *Tatsuta*	} 3,300	4—5·5-in. 1—3·1-in. A.A. 6—T.T.	31
6th Destroyer Flotilla	*Yubari* (leader) 12 destroyers	3,500	6—5·5-in. 1—3·1-in. A.A. 4—T.T.	33
7th Submarine Flotilla	16 submarines			

NORTHERN FORCE (Vice-Admiral Hosogaya)

		Tons	Armament	Speed in knots
21st Cruiser Squadron	*Tama* *Kiso*	} 5,700	7—5·5-in. 2—3·1-in. A.A. 8—T.T.	31

SUBMARINE FLEET (Vice-Admiral Shimizu)

		Tons	Armament	Speed in knots
Cruiser	*Katori*	5,800	4—5·5-in. 2—5·1-in. A.A. 4—T.T.	18
1st Submarine Flotilla 12 submarines				
2nd Submarine Flotilla 8 submarines				
3rd Submarine Flotilla 9 submarines				

ATTACHED FORCES (TRAINING)

		Tons	Armament	Speed in knots
3rd Carrier Squadron	*Hosho*	7,470	4—5·5-in. 2—3-in. A.A. 21 aircraft	25
	Zuiho	13,000	8—5·1-in. 31 aircraft	26

Japanese Naval Air Forces

THE established front line strength of the Japanese Naval Air Forces at the beginning of the war was about 1,750 aircraft of which 660 were fighters, 330 shipborne torpedo-bombers and bombers and 240 shore based torpedo-bombers and bombers. There were also about 520 flying boats and float-planes for reconnaissance purposes.

Fleet carriers usually carried from 63 to 72 aircraft each, of which 27 were fighters and the remainder torpedo-bombers and bombers.

The light fleet carriers usually carried from 24 to 30 aircraft each, of which more than half were fighters.

There were two seaplane squadrons working from seaplane carriers and tenders—in all about 70 aircraft.

The shore-based aircraft were organized into the 11th Air Fleet consisting of three air flotillas under the operational control of the Commander-in-Chief Southern Force. The bulk of this Air Fleet was stationed in Formosa and Indo-China on the outbreak of war.

German Armed Merchant Raiders 1942–1943

Performance data and Results Achieved

Name	German Operational Number	British Designation	Armament Excluding Light A.A. Guns	Auxiliary Equipment (Aircraft M.T.B.s Mines)	Duration of Sortie/Sailing Termination Date	Allied Shipping Sunk or Captured		Operating Areas	Type of Engines and Radius of Action	Max: Speed (Knots)	Remarks
						No.	G.R. Tons				
Thor	Schiff 10	Raider E	6-5.9 in. 4 T. tubes	1 aircraft 60 mines	14 Jan.'42 9 Oct.'42	10	56,037	S. Atlantic and Indian Ocean	Turbine 40,000 M at 10 Kts.	18	Lost by fire in Yokohama on 30 Nov.'42
Stier	Schiff 23	Raider J	6-5.9-in. 2 T. tubes	2 aircraft	20 May'42 27 Sept.'42	4	29,406	Central and S. Atlantic	Diesel 60,000 M at 10 Kts.	18	Sunk by American S.S. *Stephen Hopkins* 27 Sept.'42
Michel	Schiff 28	Raider H	6-5.9-in. 1-4.1-in. 4 T. tubes	2 aircraft 1 M.T.B.	20 Mar.'42 1 Mar.'43	14	94,362	S. Atlantic Indian Ocean	Diesel 60,000 M at 10 Kts.	18	Arrived Japan 1 Jan.'43
Michel (2nd cruise)	Schiff 28	Raider H	do.	do-	21 May'43 17 Oct.'43	3	27,632	Indian Ocean and S. Pacific	do.		Sunk by United States S/M *Tarpon* off Japan when returning from sortie.
Komet	Schiff 45	Raider B	6-5.9 in. 4 T. tubes	1 aircraft	—	—	—	—	Diesel 51,000 M at 10 Kts.	19	Sunk in English Channel on 14 Oct.'42 before commencing sortie.
Togo	Schiff 14	Raider K	6-5.9-in. 2 T. tubes	2 aircraft	—	—	—	—	Diesel 60,000 M at 10 Kts.	18	Attacked and damaged by aircraft whilst passing down channel 13 Feb.'43. Returned to Germany.

481

2H

APPENDIX N

Axis Blockade Runners
January 1941–April 1943

Table 1. (A) Far East to Europe
First Blockade Running Period
April 1941–May 1942

Ship	Sailed	Arrived	Date of Loss	Cause of Loss
Ermland	Jan. '41	3 Apl. '41		
Regensburg	Apl. '41	27 June '41		
Elbe	Apl. '41		6 June '41	Aircraft from *Eagle*
Anneliese Essberger	June '41	10 Sept. '41		
Odenwald	July '41		6 Nov. '41	Captured by *U.S.S. Omaha* and *Somers*
Burgenland	Oct. '41	9 Dec. '41		
Elsa Essberger	Nov. '41	12 Jan. '42		
Cortellazo	Nov. '41	27 Jan. '42		
Spreewald	Dec. '41		31 Jan. '42	U.333
Pietro Orseolo	Dec. '41	24 Feb. '42		
Osorno	Jan. '42	19 Mar. '42		
Rio Grande	Feb. '42	10 Apl. '42		
Fusiyama	Feb. '42	26 Apl. '42		
Munsterland	Feb. '42	17 May '42		
Portland	Mar. '42	10 May '42		
Ramses	Turned back to Japan after sailing			

Approximate total cargo carried (in tons)

Type	Despatched (excluding ship turned back)	Delivered	Lost
Edible oils and fats	44,000	32,600	11,400
Rubber . .	44,450	32,650	11,800
Ore . . .	3,650	2,700	950
Miscellaneous .	9,675	7,050	2,625
TOTAL . .	101,775	75,000	26,775

Number of blockade runners sailed		16
„ „ „ „	arrived	12
„ „ „ „	captured or sunk	3
„ „ „ „	turned back	1

Table 1. (B) Far East to Europe
Second Blockade Running Period
August 1942–April 1943

Ship	Sailed	Arrived	Date of Loss	Cause of Loss
Tannenfels	8 Aug. '42	2 Nov. '42		
Kulmerland	26 Aug. '42	7 Nov. '42		
Dresden	8 Sept. '42	3 Nov. '42		
Rhakotis	5 Nov. '42		1 Jan. '43	*Scylla*
Ramses	23 Nov. '42		10 Dec. '42	Scuttled on interception by H.M.A.S. *Adelaide* and Dutch *Heemskerck*
Hohenfriedburg (ex *Herborg*)	19 Dec. '42		26 Feb. '43	*Sussex*
Doggerbank (ex *Speybank*)	15 Jan. '43		3 Mar. '43	U.43
Rossbach	17 Jan. '43	Recalled to Japan		
Karin (ex *Kota Nopan*)	4 Feb. '43		10 Mar. '43	Scuttled on interception by U.S.S. *Savannah* and *Eberle*
Regensburg	6 Feb. '43		30 Mar. '43	*Glasgow*
Weserland	6 Feb. '43	Recalled to Japan		
Pietro Orseolo	16 Feb. '43	1 Apr. '43		
Irene (ex *Silvaplana*)	20 Feb. '43		10 Apr. '43	Scuttled on interception by *Adventure*
Burgenland	18 Mar. '43	Recalled to Japan		
Rio Grande	18 Mar. '43	Recalled to Japan		

Approximate total cargo carried (in tons)

Type	Despatched (excluding ships turned back)	Delivered	Lost
Edible oils and fats	54,500	16,500	38,000
Rubber	43,000	7,600	35,400
Ore	10,600	1,900	8,700
Miscellaneous	14,800	3,600	11,200
TOTAL	122,900	29,600	93,300

Number of blockade runners sailed	15
" " " " arrived	4
" " " " sunk	7
" " " " turned back	4

Table 2. (A) Europe to the Far East
First Blockade Running Period
September 1941–June 1942

Ship	Sailed	Arrived	Date of Loss	Cause of Loss
Rio Grande	17 Sept. '41	6 Dec. '41		
Portland	Oct. '41	Jan. '42		
Doggerbank	21 Jan. '42	19 Aug. '42		
Regensburg	12 Feb. '42	7 July '42		
Tannenfels	7 Mar. '42	12 May '42		
Dresden	16 Apr. '42	23 June '42		

Table 2. (A) Europe to the Far East (Contd.)
Approximate Total Cargo carried (in tons)

Type	Despatched	Delivered	Lost
Engines, engine parts, Commercial goods, Chemical products	32,540	32,540	Nil

Number of blockade runners sailed   6
,,   ,,   ,,   ,,   arrived   6

Table 2. (B) Europe to the Far East
Second Blockade Running Period
September 1942–May 1943

Ship	Sailed	Arrived	Date of Loss	Cause of Loss
Weserland	8 Sept. '42	1 Dec. '42		
Uckermark	9 Sept. '42	24 Nov. '42	30 Nov. '42	Explosion in Yokohama
Brake	27 Sept. '42	23 Dec. '42		
Pietro Orseolo	1 Oct. '42	2 Dec. '42		
Burgenland	9 Oct. '42	12 Jan. '43		
Rio Grande	10 Oct. '42	31 Dec. '43		
Irene	10 Oct. '42	20 Dec. '43		
Anneliese Essberger	5 Nov. '42		21 Nov. '42	Scuttled on interception by U.S.S. Milwaukee
Karin	6 Nov. '42	30 Dec. '42		
Elsa Essberger	7 Nov. '42	Returned to France after being severely damaged by aircraft		
Spichern	9 Nov. '42	Returned to France after being severely damaged by aircraft		
Cortelazzo	29 Nov. '42		1 Dec. '42	Scuttled on interception by Redoubt
Germania	12 Dec. '42		15 Dec. '42	Scuttled on interception by Egret and Tanatside
Alsterufer	29 Mar. '43	19 June '43		
Osorno	29 Mar. '43	4 June '43		
Portland	29 Mar. '43		13 Apl. '43	Sunk by Free French Georges Leygues
Himalaya	29 Mar. '43	Returned to France after repeated aircraft attacks		

Approximate total cargo carried (in tons)

Type	Despatched (excluding ships turned back)	Delivered	Lost
War materials and commercial products . .	33,829	24,447	9,382

Number of blockade runners sailed   17
,,   ,,   ,,   ,,   arrived   10
,,   ,,   ,,   ,,   turned back   3
,,   ,,   ,,   ,,   sunk   4 (excluding Uckermark)

APPENDIX O

Table I. British, Allied and Neutral Merchant Ship Losses and Causes from Enemy Action
January 1942–May 1943

(Tonnage : Ships)

1942

Month	Submarines	Aircraft	Mine	Warship raider	Merchant raider	E-boat	Unknown and other causes	TOTAL
January	327,357 (62)	57,086 (15)	10,079 (11)	3,275 (1)	—	—	22,110 (17)	419,907 (106)
February	476,451 (85)	133,746 (28)	7,242 (2)	—	—	—	62,193 (39)	679,632 (154)
March	537,980 (95)	55,706 (15)	16,862 (5)	16,072 (8)	8,591 (2)	951 (1)	198,002 (147)	834,164 (273)
April	431,664 (74)	82,924 (17)	15,002 (9)	100,001 (20)	31,187 (5)	—	4,079 (7)	674,457 (132)
May	607,247 (125)	59,014 (14)	18,795 (6)	—	19,363 (3)	—	631 (3)	705,050 (151)
June	700,235 (144)	54,769 (11)	19,936 (8)	—	48,474 (7)	—	10,782 (3)	834,196 (173)
July	476,065 (96)	74,313 (18)	8,905 (2)	—	42,166 (6)	12,192 (5)	4,472 (1)	618,113 (128)
August	544,410 (108)	60,532 (6)	—	—	12,946 (2)	37,570 (4)	5,675 (3)	661,133 (123)
September	485,413 (98)	57,526 (12)	—	3,188 (1)	21,200 (3)	—	—	567,327 (114)
October	619,417 (94)	5,683 (1)	5,157 (3)	—	—	7,576 (3)	—	637,833 (101)
November	729,160 (119)	53,868 (6)	992 (1)	7,925 (1)	5,882 (1)	5,371 (4)	4,556 (2)	807,754 (134)
December	330,816 (60)	4,156 (2)	1,618 (4)	—	4,816 (1)	7,496 (6)	—	348,902 (73)
Date not known	—	697 (1)	—	—	—	—	1,532 (1)	2,229 (2)
TOTAL	6,266,215 (1160)	700,020 (146)	104,588 (51)	130,461 (31)	194,625 (30)	71,156 (23)	323,632 (223)	7,790,697 (1664)

1943 (January to May)

Month	Submarines	Aircraft	Mine	Warship raider	Merchant raider	E-boat	Unknown and other causes	TOTAL
January	203,128 (37)	25,503 (5)	18,745 (5)	—	7,040 (1)	—	6,943 (2)	261,359 (50)
February	359,328 (63)	75 (1)	34,153 (7)	—	—	4,858 (1)	4,648 (1)	403,062 (73)
March	627,377 (108)	65,128 (10)	884 (2)	—	—	—	—	693,389 (120)
April	327,943 (56)	3,034 (2)	11,961 (5)	—	—	1,742 (1)	—	344,680 (64)
May	264,852 (50)	20,942 (5)	1,568 (1)	—	—	—	12,066 (2)	299,448 (58)
TOTAL	1,782,628 (314)	114,682 (23)	67,311 (20)	—	7,040 (1)	6,600 (2)	23,657 (5)	2,001,918 (365)

Table II. British, Allied and Neutral Merchant Shipping Losses from Enemy Action, according to Theatres

1942

(Tonnage : Ships)

Month	North Atlantic	United Kingdom	South Atlantic	Mediterranean	Indian Ocean	Pacific	Total
January	276,795 (48)	19,341 (14)	—	6,655 (1)	46,062 (13)	71,054 (30)	419,907 (106)
February	429,891 (73)	11,098 (5)	—	19,245 (4)	38,151 (18)	181,247 (54)	679,632 (54)
March	534,064 (95)	15,147 (8)	13,125 (3)	19,516 (6)	68,539 (65)	183,773 (98)	834,164 (273)
April	391,044 (66)	54,589 (14)	48,177 (8)	12,804 (6)	153,930 (31)	13,913 (7)	674,457 (132)
May	576,350 (120)	59,396 (14)	9,081 (2)	21,215 (6)	22,049 (4)	16,959 (5)	705,050 (151)
June	623,545 (124)	2,655 (5)	26,287 (4)	59,971 (16)	90,322 (18)	31,416 (6)	834,196 (173)
July	486,965 (98)	22,557 (9)	23,972 (3)	5,885 (3)	47,012 (9)	31,722 (6)	618,113 (128)
August	508,426 (96)	—	35,494 (10)	110,423 (13)	5,237 (1)	1,553 (3)	661,133 (123)
September	473,585 (95)	1,892 (1)	57,797 (7)	813 (4)	30,052 (6)	3,188 (1)	567,327 (114)
October	399,715 (62)	12,733 (6)	148,142 (20)	—	63,552 (11)	13,691 (2)	637,833 (101)
November	508,707 (83)	6,363 (5)	58,662 (10)	102,951 (13)	131,071 (23)	—	807,754 (134)
December	262,135 (46)	9,114 (10)	43,496 (8)	5,649 (3)	28,508 (6)	—	348,902 (73)
Date not known						2,229 (2)	2,229 (2)
TOTAL	5,471,222 (1006)	214,885 (91)	464,233 (75)	365,127 (73)	724,485 (205)	550,745 (214)	7,790,697 (1664)

1943 (January to May)

Month	North Atlantic	United Kingdom	South Atlantic	Mediterranean	Indian Ocean	Pacific	Total
January	172,691 (27)	15,819 (4)	16,116 (3)	47,506 (14)	—	9,227 (2)	261,359 (50)
February	288,625 (46)	4,925 (2)	21,656 (4)	52,718 (14)	15,787 (3)	19,351 (4)	403,062 (73)
March	476,349 (82)	884 (2)	61,462 (4)	86,230 (16)	62,303 (10)	6,161 (2)	693,389 (120)
April	235,478 (39)	9,926 (5)	7,129 (1)	13,972 (6)	43,007 (6)	35,168 (7)	344,680 (64)
May	163,507 (34)	1,568 (1)	40,523 (6)	32,300 (6)	28,058 (6)	33,472 (5)	299,428 (58)
TOTAL	1,336,650 (228)	33,122 (14)	146,886 (22)	232,726 (56)	149,155 (25)	103,379 (20)	2,001,918 (365)

APPENDIX P

Full text of letter from Mr Churchill to Mr Hugh Molson, part of which was quoted on page 362

SECRET   10 Downing Street, S.W.1
                                                       3rd April 1943

Dear Molson,

I have been giving careful consideration to your letter of 17 March in consultation with the Admiralty. The whole business was, I expect you realised, somewhat complicated by the fact that there was a debate on anti-U-boat warfare in the Lords on 24 March, which it would have been unwise to anticipate. You will find much useful material in the Speech which Lord Bruntisfield made on that occasion (House of Lords Official Report 24 March, Cols. 894-902).

It may be helpful however if I deal more particularly with the two questions on which you expressed concern in your letter. The first relates to unified command. Let me say at once that both His Majesty's Government and those fighting the day to day battle fully realise the general advantages of unified command. Efforts to achieve the greatest practical advance towards this ideal in the North Atlantic have been continuous and the recent Washington conference was concerned largely with this question.

There comes a point, however, in the development of all large commands where one must consider whether the general advantages of unity will outweigh the practical difficulties of administration as the size of the command and the complexity of the arrangements increase. In the North Atlantic there are very real practical limits which no paper arguments can possibly overcome. In the first place the endurance of escorts, both sea and air, is limited, so that they cannot take a convoy right across the Atlantic. This means that there has to be a change-over point somewhere. This in turn means that there are different sets of escorts operating from bases on different sides of the Atlantic. It would be extremely difficult for a single command to control adequately escorts operating from bases thousands of miles away on the other side of the ocean. This is all the more apparent when one considers that the problem is not simply one of sending out ocean escorts and bringing them back again; in fact, the movements of the ocean convoys and their escorts have to be co-ordinated at either end of the voyage with all the necessarily complex arrangements for coastal convoys on either side, with minesweeping in coastal waters and the approaches to ports, with all manner of other local operations, and with the administration of the ports and bases themselves. When all this is taken into account, it is clear that the best practical

487

arrangement is to have separate commands, working in close co-operation and unison, on either side of the Atlantic. Subject to this limitation, our constant object, which as I have said was greatly furthered by the recent Washington conference, is to achieve the greatest simplicity and the utmost harmony of working. The improved organisation now being set up as a result of that conference will not be regarded as the last word by anybody but will be kept under continuous review in order to improve it still further.

I can assure you that our experience confirms us in our view that this inevitable delimitation of separate spheres of action, with separate centres of control, is the best practical arrangement. There has been no breakdown so far, and recent improvements in organisation should undoubtedly lead to still better protection for the convoys. There is the closest possible contact between the operational authorities concerned and between the bodies responsible for strategic direction. We have a strong naval representation in Washington and the Americans have a strong naval representation over here. Added to this, communications are very highly developed and there is a constant stream of messages to and fro, all designed to ensure that the best possible use is made of the resources available.

Your second point concerns the "committee of busy departmental chiefs and chiefs of Staff". I take it that here you have in mind the Anti-U-Boat Committee. First, let me say that this Committee is not designed to take charge of the operations against the U-Boats. That is necessarily the function of the operational centres of control on either side of the Atlantic to which I have already referred. These centres have a highly experienced staff who spend their whole time on this work. In the Admiralty and the Navy Department there are also many efficient and experienced officers who spend their whole time devising the new tactics and new weapons, improving convoy organisation, speeding up operational organisation and in fact prosecuting the war against U-boats in every conceivable way. It would be quite impossible to do all this through a Committee however constituted. The purpose of the Committee over which I preside is, as I have already indicated, to focus the energies of all the various Departments of State concerned in the large questions which arise out of this unceasing struggle. I understand the reasons which lead many people to feel that in view of the importance of these large questions the members of the Committee should be free to spend their whole time on the Committee's business. But the core of the problem is this. Either the committee can be constituted of persons who are actually responsible for the provision and administration of the various resources which must be brought to bear, or they can only make recommendations which will still have to be carried out by the persons actually responsible for executive action. I do not think it can be questioned that a Committee constituted in accordance with the first alternative will be the one to reach decisions on the most accurate data and to see that those decisions are carried out with the greatest authority, accuracy and speed.

Yours sincerely,

Hugh Molson, Esq., M.P.   WINSTON S. CHURCHILL

Index

INDEX

(The suffix letter 'n' denotes a footnote)

A.A. ships: request for in Russian convoys, 132; in PQ.17, 137, 142, 144
A.B.D.A. area: lack of integrated command, 6; naval forces in, January, 1942, 6; naval command in, 7; command dissolves, 12, 21; Burma included in, 19
A.N.Z.A.C. area: agreed at Washington, 6; naval command in, 7
Abdiel, H.M.S.: minelaying in the Mediterranean, 438
Abel Smith, Captain E. M. C.: commands 5th Escort Group, 367
Achates, H.M.S.: in battle around JW.51B, 294-299; sunk, 297-298
Achilles, H.M.N.Z.S.: in Anzac Squadron, 7; in S. Pacific Command, 415; damaged by bomb and sent to England, 416
Aconit, Free French corvette: sinks U.432, 365
Active, H.M.S.: sinks U.179, 269
Adak: *see* Aleutian Islands
Addu Atoll, Maldives: state of base at, 23; base not known to Japanese, 25; Eastern Fleet returns to, 26, 27; Eastern Fleet withdraws from, 29; development of base, 32-33, 425
Adelaide, H.M.A.S.: in Anzac Squadron, 7
Aden: U-boats appear in Gulf of, 311; a few ships sunk off, 433
Admiral Hipper, German heavy cruiser: ready for sea, 115; moves to Norway, 125; at Trondheim, 135; threat to PQ.17, 138-142; at Narvik, 277; minelaying in the Barents Sea, 280; moves to Altenfiord, 282, 284, 290; in battle around JW.51B, 291-298, 353; in Norway, January, 1943, 398; returns to Baltic, 399
Admiral Scheer, German pocket battleship: ready for sea, 115; moves to Norway, 118, 119; moves to Narvik, 130, 135; plan to intercept PQ.17, 137; threat to PQ.17, 138-142; at Narvik, 277; sortie by, 279; moves to Altenfiord, 282, 284; returns to Germany to refit, 290
Admiralty: attitude towards defence of Ceylon, 22; allots carriers to Eastern Fleet, 23; suggestion for Eastern Fleet to avoid Ceylon, 28; asked to loan carrier to U.S. Fleet, 37; anxiety about Coastal Command strength, 77, 78; 'Battle of the Air' with Air Ministry, 79; assessment of maritime air requirements, 80, 81; aircraft needs to be met in time, 82; 'Coastal Commands' needed on every station, 83; on effect of lost ships and cargoes, 85; problems of Fleet Air Arm expansion, 85; on optimistic results claimed by bombing Germany, 87; discussions with American mission in London, 96; offer to U.S. Navy of anti-submarine trawlers, 97; prepares

Admiralty—*cont.*
review of Atlantic battle for Admiral Stark, 98; policy to give America all knowledge and experience, 98; on increasing effectiveness of Coastal Command, 102; dissatisfied with sinkings of U-boats by aircraft, 112; most powerful cover to be given Russian convoys, 119; Admiral Tovey embarrassed by instructions of, 124; accuracy of intelligence, 124, 125; intervention in passage of PQ.17, 139-146; precautions taken by, against escape of German battle cruisers up-Channel, 150-153; insistence on keeping an air striking force ready to deal with *Tirpitz*, 160; raises mine production, 166; concern at possibility of Atlantic foray by *Tirpitz*, 168; plans for Madagascar expedition, 186; analysis of Dönitz broadcasts on Battle of the Atlantic, 200; wants to co-operate with Coastal Command in Northern Transit area, 206; work of 'operational research' in, 208-209; review of problems in Battle of Atlantic, December, 1942, 217-218; orders diversion operations in the Indian Ocean, 222-223; lack of information on events in the Pacific, 229-231; anxiety over weakness of Eastern Fleet, 236-238; agrees on formation of permanent naval assault forces, 251; plans for interception of *Komet*, 256; joint Admiralty and Air Ministry committee set up to improve tactical and technical efficiency, 258-259; recommends laying of acoustic mines, 263; anxiety over safety of shipping off S. Africa, 269-270; review of Arctic convoys by, 290; insistence on placing all naval responsibility for 'Torch' on A.N.C.X.F., 313; anxiety on French and Spanish reactions to 'Torch', 314; precautions against U-boat attack on 'Torch' convoys, 317; tribute to work of submarines in Mediterranean, 342; press for bombing Biscay U-boat bases, 351; question of Supreme Commander, Atlantic, 361; on unified control of Atlantic, 362; on Atlantic situation, March, 1943, 367, 368; requirements for aircraft, Biscay, 370; withdraws F.A.A. Squadrons on loan to R.A.F., 388; introduction of mines with new firing mechanism, 393; reviews steps taken to deal with enemy heavy ships, 399; appreciation of enemy intentions as regards blockade runners, 409; estimate saving of shipping in re-opening Mediterranean, 443; members of Board of, Appendix A, 447-448
Adventure, H.M.S.: reinforces east coast mine barrier, 255; carries supplies to Gibraltar for Malta, 34; sinks *Irene*, 410

491

S.O. Code No. 63-111-22-4*

Printed in the United Kingdom
by Lightning Source UK Ltd.
118781UK00001B/4-6